DATE DUE			

by JOHN A. DeNOVO

*American Interests
and Policies in
the Middle East*
1900–1939

THE UNIVERSITY OF MINNESOTA PRESS
Minneapolis

PRINTED IN THE UNITED STATES OF AMERICA AT THE
NORTH CENTRAL PUBLISHING COMPANY, ST. PAUL

3

Library of Congress Catalog Card Number: 63-21129

Second printing 1968

PUBLISHED IN GREAT BRITAIN, INDIA, AND PAKISTAN BY THE OXFORD UNIVERSITY PRESS,
LONDON, BOMBAY, AND KARACHI, AND IN CANADA BY THOMAS ALLEN, LTD., TORONTO

TO MY MOTHER
AND THE
MEMORY OF MY FATHER

PREFACE

☆ THE objective of this book is to present as comprehensively as possible in a single volume a description and assessment of American cultural, economic, and diplomatic activities in Turkey, Persia, and the Arab East during the first four decades of the twentieth century. An explanation of how the study developed should reveal the author's goals while giving the reader an idea of what to expect.

In 1947 when embarking on a study of American petroleum diplomacy in the Middle East, I was handicapped by the lack of a comprehensive regional survey of American relations with that area comparable to the excellent monographs on the Latin American policy of the United States (by Samuel F. Bemis) and the Far Eastern policy of the United States (by A. Whitney Griswold). Ten years later when this gap in the literature of American foreign relations still remained, I decided to prepare a study to fill the lacuna, in part at least. As the magnitude of the undertaking became clear, chronological limits had to be set. By selecting the turn of the twentieth century as the point of departure, by which time the United States was already embarked on its erratic journey to world power, the opening chapter could be used to sketch in the character of American interests inherited from the nineteenth-century experience in the Middle East. There were compelling reasons for terminating this volume with the beginning of World War II, not only because 1939 marked the end of an era, but for the practical reason that the kinds of archival and manuscript sources used by historians were not yet available in sufficient quantity to warrant a later terminal date. A second volume covering the years 1939 to 1950 is projected.

As the research progressed, it was evident that American cultural enterprises, which were at the core of the nation's Middle Eastern interests in 1900, continued to predominate throughout the four decades studied. Until oil entered into the relationship after World War I, economic aspiration bulked larger than economic reality; political ambition and strategic concern were virtually absent throughout the entire period. The character of American contacts thus required that this study be shaped into something other than the traditional diplomatic history. Some readers may wish for more exhaustive treatment of the policies of the European powers; area specialists may think that internal developments within the Middle East should have been given more attention. Ideally, they are right. But it must be noted that European archives for the period will apparently not be opened for many years, probably decades; furthermore, even where Middle Eastern sources have been assembled, access to them is impossible or severely limited. Even more pertinent is the fact that I have located within the United States more source material than could be mastered by one man in more than a decade of intensive research.

I must emphasize, therefore, what the title suggests — that this study presents an American view of American interests and policies. Yet the reader will discover that within the limits of available space and sources I have endeavored to place American activities in a setting, noting relevant features of the local environment and of international politics where they affected American interests. Where I have relied heavily on monographs, I have tried to give appropriate credit to the authors of books and dissertations. I am deeply indebted to the authors of a growing monographic literature on the twentieth-century Middle East for helping me to convey some sense of the changing local setting in which Americans operated. Much unpublished material has been used — more for some chapters than for others. Frequently a topic could not be explored at length if any kind of balance was to be maintained, and the most severe condensation has therefore been necessary. The exciting experiences of many missionaries as well as particular episodes of many kinds have had to be omitted.

I must beg the indulgence of specialists in Middle Eastern languages for inconsistencies they may find in the transliterations of Middle Eastern names and terms. Rather than attempt to follow consistently any one system, I have adopted, in general, forms used by the Department of State because these are apt to be easier for Western readers to follow.

I shall be grateful if this book serves as a useful point of departure for more detailed analyses of particular themes. No doubt my judgments will be challenged when others penetrate more deeply and uncover new facets of this large subject, especially as certain European and Middle Eastern sources become more accessible to scholars.

Many organizations and persons have facilitated the writing of this book. An International Relations Fellowship from the Ford Foundation enabled me to spend a year at the Harvard University Center for Middle Eastern Studies and a summer at the School of Advanced International Studies of Johns Hopkins University during 1956 and 1957. The present study was launched during that year with a bibliographical search, resulting in a bibliographical essay presented at a symposium on twentieth-century American diplomacy sponsored by the Department of History at the University of Kansas in August of 1957. A revision of the essay, assessing the literature on American relations with the Middle East, was subsequently published; it is listed in the bibliography at the end of this volume. Grants from the Central Fund for Research of The Pennsylvania State University enabled me to consult archival and manuscript sources in Washington, New York, and Princeton, and to defray typing expenses. A grant from the Social Science Research Council, freeing me from summer teaching in 1959, made it possible to spend several additional weeks in Washington.

My debts to librarians and archivists are heavy. I was made welcome and given efficient assistance at the National Archives, the Library of Congress, Yale University, Harvard University, Princeton University, the Presbyterian Missions Library in New York, the Near East College Association, and the Pattee Library of The Pennsylvania State University. The Socony-Mobil Oil Company kindly permitted me to use two files on Palestine, and Mr. Colby M. Chester, Jr., graciously allowed me to examine a small collection of family papers in his New York office. To Dr. E. Taylor Parks of the State Department, scholar and friend of scholars, I owe a special word of appreciation for arranging access to Department of State archives, and for clearing my notes and manuscript based on files for the restricted period of the 1930s.

Several chapters have been improved, thanks to helpful criticism from Frederick R. Matson, Roger R. Trask, Gordon Henderson, and Edwin M. Wright. John Wells Davidson shared his unsurpassed knowledge of manuscripts for the Woodrow Wilson era. Shortcomings remaining in the study despite their help are solely my responsibility.

To my seminar students, who patiently permitted me to share my findings with them, and to those among them and my thesis advisees who enthusiastically joined in trying to unravel the history of American relations with the Middle East, I express my appreciation for their stimulation. My thanks go also to George Sweet Gibb, recent editor of the *Business History Review,* for permitting me to use the article on the prewar Chester Project as Chapter 3 in this book. For drafting the maps, I am grateful to Dr. Frederick L. Wernstedt of the Department of Geography at The Pennsylvania State University.

An author's wife customarily receives at least a nod in her husband's preface, but that would be quite inadequate to convey the contribution of my wife, Jeanne, to this endeavor. In addition to performing the usual tedious task of criticizing and proofreading drafts, she placed her historical training at my disposal by serving as an efficient research assistant. I am also grateful to Mrs. Ilene Glenn, Mrs. Esther Spicher, Mrs. Helen G. Yarnell, and my daughter, Anne, for their indispensable typing services.

JOHN A. DeNovo

University Park, Pennsylvania
August, 1963

ABBREVIATIONS

Publication data for all titles listed below and for all footnote entries are contained in the Bibliography, pp. 397–410.

ABC, *AR* — American Board of Commissioners for Foreign Missions, *Annual Reports.*

Brown, *100 Years* — Arthur Judson Brown, *One Hundred Years: A History of the Foreign Missionary Work of the Presbyterian Church in the U.S.A., With Some Account of Countries, Peoples and the Policies and Problems of Modern Missions.*

DBFP — E. L. Woodward and Rohan Butler, eds., *Documents on British Foreign Policy, 1919–1939*, First Series, Vol. 4.

Dodge, AR 1939 — [Bayard Dodge], "Annual Report of the President of the American University of Beirut for the Seventy-Third Year, 1938–1939," Beirut, Lebanon, July, 1939 (mimeographed), files of the Near East College Association.

Dodge, AR 1948 — [Bayard Dodge], "The American University of Beirut, International College, and Damascus College, 1910–1949," Annual Report of June, 1948 (mimeographed), files of the Near East College Association.

DS — Department of State Archives, National Archives, Washington, D.C. Appropriate volume, numerical file, or decimal file designations follow DS.

FR — *Papers Relating to the Foreign Relations of the United States.* The title of these annual volumes became *Foreign Relations of the United States: Diplomatic Papers* beginning with the volumes for 1932.

FR: S, S1, or *S2* — Supplementary volumes for World War I.

FR: LP — *The Lansing Papers, 1914–1920.* Two-volume supplement to *Foreign Relations.*

FR 1919: PPC — *The Paris Peace Conference.* Special 13-volume supplement.

FTC, *Cartel* — Federal Trade Commission, Staff Report, *International Petroleum Cartel* (1952).

Grew, *TE* — Joseph C. Grew, *Turbulent Era: A Diplomatic Record of Forty Years, 1904–1945* (2 vols.).

MRW — *The Missionary Review of the World.*

PC, AR — *Annual Reports of the Board of Foreign Missions of the Presbyterian Church in the United States of America.*

Penrose, *AUB* — Stephen B. L. Penrose, Jr., *That They May Have Life: The Story of the American University of Beirut, 1866–1941.*

RDS — *Register of the Department of State.*

Yeselson, *USPDR* — Abraham Yeselson, *United States–Persian Diplomatic Relations, 1883–1921.*

TABLE OF CONTENTS

Maps

*American Interests
and Policies in
the Middle East*

1

THE HERITAGE OF
THE NINETEENTH CENTURY

☆ By the turn of the twentieth century the United States had passed through the early stages of the transition that was to make it a full-fledged world power within another half century. Although the origins of the new Manifest Destiny of the 1890s can be traced back at least to the 1870s, it took the Spanish-American War with its dramatic consequences to give Americans a sense of having turned a corner and entered new paths of empire, and of involvement with the world powers. At first, the new overseas interests and responsibilities were confined largely to the Western Hemisphere (especially the Caribbean) and to the Pacific Ocean. The classic policy of noninvolvement in European quarrels, shaped in the late eighteenth and throughout the nineteenth century, was still too firmly entrenched in tradition to be suddenly discarded. Captain Alfred Thayer Mahan's dicta that the United States dominate in the Caribbean, cooperate with the powers in the Far East, and abstain from political intervention in Europe expressed precepts in accordance with the broad lines of American thought and foreign policy at the opening of the twentieth century.

American Foreign Policy and the Middle East

The Middle East,[1] with Europe, Africa, and most of Asia outside China and Japan, was not considered a proper sphere for American

[1] For purposes of this study, the Middle East consists of the area of contemporary Turkey, Iran, and the Arab World from Egypt's western boundary to the eastern boundary of Iraq, including the entire Arabian Peninsula. This region, or parts of it (usually adding the lower Balkans), was commonly called the Near East before World War I, but the designation "Middle East" has become widely accepted since World War II. For discussion of boundary and terminology issues,

3

political involvement. The United States would protect its citizens and their interests there as elsewhere, but these interests were for the most part cultural, philanthropic, and commercial, illustrating well two major strands in the national heritage Americans carried into their foreign relations — the curious and interesting blend of the practical and the ideal.

In bold contrast were the attitudes and policies of the six European powers (Great Britain, France, Germany, Italy, Austria-Hungary, and Russia) involved in the troublesome Eastern Question. For them the Middle East was of the greatest political concern, most particularly because of its strategic significance as a communications hub at the junction of three continents. Transit through the Turkish Straits to and from the Black Sea and passage through the Suez Canal, which cut thousands of miles from the voyage between Europe and the Far East, helped to give the Middle East a special importance during an era of international commercial and political rivalry in non-European colonial areas. Communications alone, however, do not explain the struggle for position in the Middle East, where the powers competed in the pursuit of nationalistic, religious, and cultural objectives. France, for example, had become the self-appointed guardian of Roman Catholicism in the Ottoman Empire, Russia of Orthodox Christianity.

These significant differences in outlook between the United States and Europe regarding the Middle East were symbolized in the determination of Americans to cut an isthmian canal through Central America while maintaining an attitude of relative indifference to the problems of the Turkish Straits and the Suez Canal.[2] American reliance on these waterways was slight indeed, which accounts for American unconcern in contrast to the feverish interest in the construction and defense of a canal under American control in Panama. A glimpse into American priorities is furnished by President William McKinley's response in 1898 to a suggestion that American naval vessels be sent to

see Roderic H. Davison, "Where Is the Middle East?" *Foreign Affairs*, 38 (July 1960), 665–675; and G. Etzel Pearcy, "The Middle East — An Indefinable Region," *The Department of State Bulletin*, 40 (March 23, 1959), 407–416.

[2] Harry N. Howard, "The United States and the Problem of the Turkish Straits," *Middle East Journal*, 1 (Jan. 1947), 59–62. American ship traffic through the Suez Canal was exceedingly light. Even in the peak year of 1901, it was only .004 per cent of the total. See Lenoir C. Wright, "United States Policy toward Egypt: 1830–1914," unpublished Ph.D. dissertation, Columbia University, 1954, Table 4, p. 218.

Turkish waters to collect damages for destruction of missionary property during the Armenian massacres of 1894–1896. McKinley told William E. Dodge, the businessman-philanthropist who took a deep interest in American colleges and missions in the Middle East, that even though he was inclined to resort to coercive measures, the Cuban situation required him to keep naval forces in American waters.[3] Actually, the president did not wish to use gunboat diplomacy in Turkey and was probably glad when the Cuban situation offered a convenient excuse for avoiding intervention. Oscar Straus, one-time minister to Turkey (1887–1889) and McKinley's choice to head the Constantinople legation, reported that McKinley "lost sleep" over the risks facing him if he followed the importunings of those who argued "that the only way to deal with Turkey was to send warships and rattle the Sultan's windows." The chauvinistic spirit confronting McKinley appears in Theodore Roosevelt's attitude toward Turkey. Just before resigning as assistant secretary of the navy to join the Cuban fighting, Roosevelt wrote, "Spain and Turkey are the two powers I would rather smash than any in the world." McKinley begged Straus in the spring of 1898 to accept the Constantinople legation again, convinced that Straus could ward off the pressure for American warships which might bring on another *Maine* incident. When Straus met McKinley and high officials of the State Department in August for a round of conferences on Turkish matters before departing for Constantinople, he cautioned against yielding to the jingoes who were clamoring for a big naval demonstration against Turkey. He warned McKinley that jealous European powers would not allow the United States "to interfere in that center of European irritation without encountering the strong hostilities of the nations forming the balance of power alliances." Straus noted in his diary that "the President agreed with me entirely and said 'I shall be guided by you, I shall support you . . . no vessels will be sent to Turkey unless you demand them and only then will any be sent.'"[4] McKinley's reluctance to order a naval demonstration in the eastern Mediterranean had been shared by his predecessor, Grover

[3] Penrose, *AUB*, p. 87 n. 4.
[4] Oscar S. Straus, *Under Four Administrations: From Cleveland to Taft*, pp. 124 (first two quotations), 128–129; *The Letters of Theodore Roosevelt*, Elting E. Morison, ed., I, 602; II, 823 (third quotation); Straus Diary, Aug. 11, Aug. 26 (last two quotations), undated [Dec. 1898], pp. 24–25, 32–34, 89–90, Oscar S. Straus MSS, Box 22.

5

Cleveland, who resisted heavy missionary pressure to intervene in 1895–1896.[5]

More than time and distance separated the United States and the Middle East in 1900; they were "worlds apart" in style of life and outlook. While it is possible to overemphasize the difference between East and West, it is nonetheless apparent that the blurred images of the Arab World, Turkey, and Persia held by most Americans were at least matched by the lack of information and by the misinformation prevalent in the Middle East about the United States.

The impressions lodged in the consciousness of most Americans were products of the Sunday school, the *Arabian Nights*, and for some who recalled their text books, a sketchy remembrance of the ancient civilizations of the Tigris-Euphrates and Nile valleys. The Armenian massacres of the middle 1890s, publicized by the missionaries in particular, left their mark on American thinking, not only in the idealizing of the victimized Armenian, but also in the attitude toward his overlord who became known popularly as the "terrible" or the "unspeakable" Turk. The American stereotype of the Arab pigeonholed him as a desert nomad surrounded by shifting sand dunes, camels, and harems, while Persia was a voluptuous land of beautiful women and luxurious gardens.

The prevailing poverty and lack of educational opportunities throughout the Middle East at the turn of the century prevented the ordinary inhabitant from learning much about the outside world. Ignorance of the United States was not confined, however, to the common man, but sometimes extended into higher social and political strata. Samuel G. W. Benjamin, the first American minister to Persia (1883–1885), found that many Persian officials had never heard of the United States before the establishment of the Teheran legation. A later minister, Lloyd C. Griscom (1901–1903), reported a conversation in which the Shah revealed his vagueness as to how one would journey to America. The Shah expressed an interest in visiting America and hunting

[5] At that time, Great Britain put out feelers looking toward a joint British-American policy in the Ottoman Empire, a proposal finally rejected by the United States, but interesting as an early example of British hopes to enlist the active aid of the United States in supporting British objectives during the *rapprochement* following the resolution of the Venezuelan boundary crisis. See Ernest R. May, *Imperial Democracy: The Emergence of America as a Great Power*, pp. 27–29, 53, 59–60; Rosaline DeGregorio Edwards, "Relations between the United States and Turkey, 1893–1897," unpublished Ph.D. dissertation, Fordham University, 1952, pp. 220–245, 247–253; Alfred L. P. Dennis, *Adventures in American Diplomacy, 1896–1906*, p. 450.

with President Theodore Roosevelt, but when he learned from Griscom that he would have to cross the Atlantic Ocean, the Shah declared he would not go because he was prone to seasickness. The notion of visiting President Roosevelt stayed with him, apparently, for on a visit to London, the Shah ordered a caravan prepared and sent a man to the London "bazaar" to find a guide who knew the caravan route to America. He had gone around the Caspian, and around the Mediterranean, so why not around the Atlantic? [6]

America was different things to different men and groups. To the Christian minorities, especially those of the Ottoman Empire, America was the great country which had sent them missionaries, teachers, and physicians. It was also a powerful magnet drawing Armenian, Syrian, and Greek immigrants to share in its bounty, to flee their grinding poverty. For others it offered an escape from military service in the Ottoman armies. Non-Christians also benefited from the medical philanthropy of American missionaries, but it is difficult to ascertain the exact effect of such aid on their impressions of the United States.

Ottoman officialdom, on the other hand, was often deeply suspicious of Americans for their work with the minorities in a polyglot empire torn by internal dissensions. Yet the official relations of the United States and Turkey could hardly be described as unfriendly. Compared with other foreign powers, the United States appeared, and in fact was, politically disinterested. Ottoman and Persian officials considered the United States a possible source of assistance for economic development.[7] To reformers, including nationalists among the Armenians and Arabs, the United States was an ideal and a beacon to guide them toward liberal nationalism.

The images on both sides were products in part of the relatively few Americans — persons and groups — with direct interests in the Middle East. Diplomats, missionaries, educators, businessmen, and others living in the area conveyed their impressions to people at home in many ways. Since few Turks, Arabs, or Persians visited the United States, most Middle Eastern peoples derived their ideas of what Amer-

[6] Yeselson, *USPDR*, p. 63n; Lloyd C. Griscom, *Diplomatically Speaking*, pp. 191–192, 217–218.

[7] Leland J. Gordon, *American Relations with Turkey, 1830–1930: An Economic Interpretation*, p. 224; Edwards, "Relations between the United States and Turkey," pp. 235–236; *FR 1899*, p. 773; Yeselson, *USPDR*, pp. 18, 27, 33, 39–41, 63; Merle Curti and Kendall Birr, *Prelude to Point Four: American Technical Missions Overseas, 1838–1938*, pp. 72–74.

ica was like from resident Americans in their midst. For Syrians and Armenians, letters from the growing number of relatives and former neighbors who had migrated to America portrayed that country in the most glowing hues. Those who returned for visits spun a dazzling romanticized version of the United States to wide-eyed relatives and friends.[8]

American Interest Groups

Missionaries. Of the Americans active in the Middle East during the nineteenth century, those of greatest consequence were the missionaries of several Protestant denominations who penetrated into many parts of the area. When requesting financial and moral support at home, these missionaries held up a mirror, though an imperfect one, through which Americans saw the Middle East. They frequently requested, and usually obtained, diplomatic support from the State Department.[9] The national support of missionaries is an impressive reminder that American isolation did not extend to cultural relations, for an enthusiastic conviction of the superiority of their civilization drove Americans to export features of their ideology and way of life to those they considered less fortunate.

By 1900, American missionaries were operating in five areas: Anatolia and European Turkey, Syria, Persia, Egypt, and the Persian Gulf region. The movement had begun in 1819, during the presidency of James Monroe and the Age of Metternich, when the American Board of Commissioners for Foreign Missions, representing mainly Congregationalists and Presbyterians, despatched the Reverends Pliny Fisk and Levi Parsons to explore mission possibilities in the Levant. The American pioneers found that a few European Christian missionaries had preceded them in parts of the Middle East. Within two decades American Board missionaries had established stations in western Turkey, Syria, and the Lake Urumia region of western Persia. When the Presbyterians withdrew from the American Board in 1870, there was an amicable division of the field with the Presbyterians retaining the Levant and Persian missions, and the predominantly Congregationalist American Board remaining in Anatolia and European Turkey. The United Presbyterian Church began its American mission in Egypt by

[8] Philip K. Hitti, *The Syrians in America*, p. 52; Brown, *100 Years*, pp. 998–999.
[9] Edward Mead Earle, "American Missions in the Near East," *Foreign Affairs*, 7 (April 1929), 398.

sending a single missionary in 1854. During the last decade of the century, the Dutch Reformed Church in America moved into the Persian Gulf field.[10]

Spurred on by the slogan, "the evangelization of the world in this generation," missionary expansion went forward late in the nineteenth century. By 1900 the American Board in European Turkey and Anatolia claimed 21 stations where their 162 missionaries (including wives and physicians) were assisted by more than 900 native helpers. These servants of God must have indeed been busy, for they had more than 2700 boys and girls in their 36 boarding and high schools, nearly 15,000 more in the 398 primary schools, and 22 students in their four theological schools. The Board expended nearly $200,000 for these activities during the year ending August 31, 1900. The Presbyterians extended their efforts from western Persia eastward, from the original station at Urumia (1835) to Teheran (1872), Tabriz (1873), and Hamadan (1880). The Western Persian Mission also established a station at Mosul in 1892. Their 42 missionaries, wives, and physicians supervised 128 out-stations with the assistance of nearly 250 Persian helpers. Their 108 schools (exclusive of Sunday schools) enrolled 2600 students, while three hospitals and ten dispensaries treated some 24,000 patients. For the support of the Persian mission, the Presbyterian Board expended $64,000 in the year 1899–1900. The Board's somewhat smaller Syria mission, fanning out from the mother station at Beirut (1823), consisted of five stations with 38 missionaries. Somewhat fewer schools than in Persia (95) taught twice as many students (5300), but the medical work was not so extensive as in Persia, undoubtedly because of the developing medical school at the nondenominational Syrian Protestant College (the American University of Beirut after 1920). This mission's two hospitals and one dispensary, however, treated more than ten thousand patients during the year. About five per cent ($48,000) of the Board's budget went to support the Syrian mission.[11]

[10] ABC, *AR 1819*, pp. 229–231; *AR 1820*, pp. 277–281; *AR 1870*, pp. xx–xxvii, 41–43; *A Century of Mission Work in Iran (Persia), 1834–1934*, pp. 1–4, 16–17, 24–30; Brown, *100 Years*, pp. 976–977, 979; Centennial Series, *Iran Mission*, pp. 9, 12–13; Alfred DeWitt Mason and Frederick J. Barny, *History of the Arabian Mission*, Chap. 5; Julius Richter, *A History of Protestant Missions in the Near East, passim.*

[11] ABC, *AR 1900*, pp. 44, 67, 147, 148; PC, *AR 1900*, chart opposite p. 285; Centennial Series, *Iran Mission*, pp. 8–9, 13–14; *A Century of Mission Work in Iran*, pp. 5–11, 24–30; Brown, *100 Years*, pp. 492, 987–989. Syria is used here to cover

American Interests in the Middle East

The United Presbyterians in Egypt claimed in 1901 "6,500 communicants, a synod, 4 presbyteries, 220 stations and churches, 50 native preachers, 200 schools, with 14,000 pupils."[12] The small Arabian Mission, only a decade old at the beginning of the twentieth century, represented the dedication of two men — James Cantine and Samuel M. Zwemer — who began work in the Persian Gulf area about 1890 after preliminary language study in Syria. They established a center at Basra near the head of the Persian Gulf, and within a few years expanded into the Bahrein Islands and Muscat. In 1894 the foreign board of the (Dutch) Reformed Church in America took the handful of missionaries of this remote outpost under its wing.[13]

Although the brief statistical breakdown of these five centers of American missionary activity in the Middle East at the beginning of the twentieth century gives some impression of the extent and distribution of their endeavors, it is no substitute for a qualitative analysis of the impact of the dedicated labors of the missionaries. Unfortunately, scholarly research into the missionary movement is still too slight to permit a comprehensive evaluation. To be sure, we have prodigious records penned by the missionaries themselves in the form of reports, memoirs, biographies, and the like, and while they tell us much, they do not give the complete picture of missionary efforts in the total life of the Middle East. It is possible, however, to describe the general nature of the activities, the rationale in which they were conducted, and to make some tentative judgments about their significance.

To leave one's homeland, family, and friends, to settle among sometimes hostile peoples of strange tongues and different ways, to live a life often without physical comforts in forbidding climates and sometimes full of danger — all this required a cause and a great sense of dedication. Even a superficial study of the lives of selected missionaries reveals their conviction of important tasks to be done. They had some-

Greater Syria, which included modern Syria, Lebanon, Palestine, and part of Trans-Jordan.

[12] *MRW*, 14 (Dec. 1901), 956. The early history of the mission in Egypt is treated in Wright, "United States Policy toward Egypt," pp. 162–176, 253–269, 279–281.

[13] Richard H. Sanger, *The Arabian Peninsula*, pp. 190–191; Kenneth S. Latourette, *The Great Century in Northern Africa and Asia A.D. 1800–A.D. 1914*, p. 61; Mason and Barny, *History of the Arabian Mission*, Chaps. 5 and 6; S. M. Zwemer, "Open Doors in Oman, Arabia," *MRW*, 14 (May 1901), 321–326. There were occasional missionaries in the Middle East representing other denominations, among them Seventh-Day Adventists and the Society of Friends.

thing special in their possession — the Christian faith and the Christian way of life — and they felt a compulsion to share it. Implicit in the attitude was a sense of superiority, perhaps, and an even stronger sense of duty that was part of their Puritan heritage. The unenlightened must be brought into the missionaries' own Kingdom of God. Such worthy work, they took for granted, merited financial and moral support from the congregations at home, and from their government they expected the protection to which American citizens abroad were entitled. On occasion, missionaries even claimed the right of protection because of their large financial investments, and some among them spoke of how they paved the way for American commerce.[14]

Originally the missionary boards' primary objective was to convert the Moslems, and though soon disabused of the prospects for any spectacular success, they never lost hope that a new day of conversions would dawn after the proper preparation. The western Turkey mission of the American Board observed in 1900 that

No large spiritual results can be reported, and there is no general spirit of inquiry and not many accessions to the Protestant community. In a word, it is a day of small things, trying faith and zeal, but not one of discouragement. The missionaries feel that this condition of things is a temporary phase, and that the power of the gospel is working in ways, many of which are unseen. The truth of the gospel is faithfully taught and it cannot be questioned that in due season the harvests will appear.[15]

Consequently, the missionaries channeled their efforts into regeneration and revitalization of decadent native Christian sects of the Middle East — Armenian and Greek Christians, Nestorians, and Copts — as the first step toward the evangelization of the Moslem world. These oriental Christians became the backbone of the American missionary clientele. In reaching these Christian minorities, the American Protestants had to compete with the proselytizing efforts of Roman Catholic and Orthodox clergy. As the Syrian mission put it, "Mohammedans, Muscovites and Monks furnish their full quota of opposition." By practicing the Christian principles of service to their fellow men through medical and educational enterprises, the missionaries hoped to overcome resistance both among Moslems and native Christians. Even

[14] Gordon, *American Relations with Turkey*, p. 245; Earle in *Foreign Affairs*, 7:409–411.
[15] ABC, *AR 1900*, p. 46.

these efforts proved discouraging at times, as the Syria Mission explained in its report of 1900: "A man may send his children to our schools and may come to worship with us, but he does not declare himself of us, for that involves facing a combination of opposing influences that are stronger than any dweller in a Christian land can possibly imagine."[16]

Yet evangelism remained the central objective of the missionaries, variously pursued by establishing churches in cities, towns, and villages, by periodically visiting the remoter rural regions, by printing and distributing the Protestant Bible and other Christian literature. But the most important instruments for gaining access to the people were the missionary schools, hospitals, and dispensaries.[17]

Western-style education and medicine introduced to many parts of the Middle East by the missionaries undoubtedly had a tremendous leavening influence. Scattered testimonials from beneficiaries of missionary educations bear witness to the training of a small but significant number of native leaders. The missionaries wanted their students to serve their communities which so desperately needed their knowledge and skills, but many had seen a vision of the outside world which beckoned to greater opportunities elsewhere, especially in the Western Hemisphere. The missionary literature of the early twentieth century is full of laments about the alarming emigration of the flower of Armenian and Syrian youth. As missionary medicine showed what modern science could do toward relieving pain and curing ailments, it became possible to attack the notion that sickness was a visitation from Allah which must be accepted resignedly and without recourse.[18]

The active role of women in missionary life stood in sharp contrast to the position of their sisters in the Moslem Middle East. The mere presence of these unveiled workers, often wives and mothers, who not only entered into the professional and social life of men but also into community endeavor, could only serve to erode old notions about the

[16] *A Century of Mission Work in Iran*, pp. 1–4, 17–23; Brown, *100 Years*, 969–970, 979–980, 998; Wright, "United States Policy toward Egypt," p. 253; quotations from PC, *AR 1900*, pp. 267, 278–279.

[17] Brown, *100 Years*, pp. 492, 496, 502–503, 989–993; Centennial Series, *Syria Mission*, pp. 8–9; *A Century of Mission Work in Iran*, pp. 2–4, 9, 12–13, 43–51, 74–80; Clarence D. Ussher and Grace H. Knapp, *An American Physician in Turkey*, pp. 10, 97–101; Albert H. Lybyer, "America's Missionary Record in Turkey," *Current History*, 19 (Feb. 1924), 807.

[18] Brown, *100 Years*, pp. 998–999; Ussher and Knapp, *American Physician*, pp. 80–83; Henry H. Jessup, *Fifty-Three Years in Syria*, pp. 595, 689, 717.

place of women in society. Though the missionaries were only one of several factors inducing the evolution in status of Middle Eastern women, there is no denying the part they played. Also nebulous, but no less real, was the missionary impact on aspirations for a better standard of living, at least among segments of the populations among whom the Americans lived. The introduction of simple agricultural implements, sewing machines, and other accouterments of Western living could not fail to attract those whose lives were so hard and whose comforts were so few.[19]

From the inception of their efforts in 1819, the American Board and its missionaries understood the indispensability of training in the local languages and customs of the Middle East. Such training was a prerequisite to reaching the people with the gospel message, which also necessitated years of painstaking work in translating the scriptures into vernaculars. George Antonius has described how these efforts contributed to an Arab literary revival, and thereby unwittingly helped lay the intellectual foundations for modern Arab nationalism.[20]

Colleges. The notable performance of American educators in the Middle East has been the source of justifiable pride. By 1900 none of the Presbyterian institutions in Persia or Syria had yet achieved collegiate status in the American sense, but the United Presbyterians had in 1865 established Assiut College in Egypt. The American Board operated several colleges: one for men and women at Scutari, International College (boys) and American Collegiate Institute (girls) at Smyrna, Anatolia College at Marsovan, Central Turkish College (boys) at Aintab, Central Turkish College for Girls at Marash, St. Paul's Institute at Tarsus, and Euphrates College at Harput. Notwithstanding the designation of these institutions as colleges, most of the work was of preparatory and junior college level.[21]

Three independent American colleges — Robert at Constantinople, Constantinople College for Women, and Syrian Protestant College at Beirut — were established during the last half of the nineteenth century, and exerted an influence far beyond their size. They stimulated an

[19] Lybyer in *Current History*, 19:808; James L. Barton, *Daybreak in Turkey*, pp. 233–236; Gordon, *American Relations with Turkey*, pp. 244–246.
[20] Lybyer in *Current History*, 19:804–805; *A Century of Mission Work in Iran*, p. 2; Brown, *100 Years*, pp. 989–993; George Antonius, *The Arab Awakening: The Story of the Arab National Movement*, pp. 41–43, 51–52.
[21] *A Century of Mission Work in Iran*, pp. 5–14, *passim*; Centennial Series, *Syria Mission*, pp. 8–9; ABC, AR 1900, pp. 47–60, *passim*.

elite native leadership which could assist in shaping political, economic, social, and cultural change in the Middle East. Although these colleges had close connections with the missionary movement, had to some extent actually derived their impetus from missionaries, and were infused with Christian motivation, they could not, strictly speaking, be classified as missionary institutions. Robert College and Syrian Protestant College both had independent American charters and boards of trustees, but Constantinople College for Women maintained a tenuous tie with the American Board which President Mary Mills Patrick could not break completely until 1908.[22]

Though still small in 1900, these colleges had at least survived the considerable difficulties attending their establishment and early years, and their influence would grow mightily in the years ahead. Already they were recognized for their achievement in training young people in the Western liberal tradition which stressed training the mind and developing personality and character. These objectives were not part of the fabric of Middle Eastern education with its strong theological orientation and emphasis on rote learning. Western science and technology, which owed so much to the foundations laid in the earlier Middle East, now began to percolate through the American colleges into a region virtually untouched by the Renaissance and the scientific revolution which had so altered Western society.[23]

Robert College opened its doors in 1863 under the presidency of Cyrus Hamlin, a former missionary of the American Board who had received the backing of a New York merchant, Christopher Robert. Hamlin was succeeded by his son-in-law, George Washburn, who served as president from 1878 to 1903. Of the 297 students enrolled in 1899–1900, 74 per cent were Greek and Armenian, 13 per cent Bulgarian. Less than five per cent of the students were Turkish, and the college would not graduate its first Turk until 1903. President Washburn

[22] The second president of Robert wrote in his memoirs: "We did not in any way relax our efforts to make this a Christian college and to develop the Christian character of our students." George Washburn, *Fifty Years in Constantinople and Recollections of Robert College*, p. 283. See also Penrose, *AUB*, pp. 4–5; Brown, *100 Years*, pp. 988–989; Mary Mills Patrick, *A Bosporus Adventure: Istanbul (Constantinople) Woman's College, 1871–1924*, pp. 86–91, 119.

[23] "Our theory of college education is not new. In substance it is as old as Plato and Aristotle. Its chief end is the highest possible development of character. The principal work of the College is disciplinary." Washburn, *Fifty Years*, p. 295. See also George Sarton, *The Incubation of Western Culture in the Middle East, passim*; *A Century of Mission Work in Iran*, pp. 97–98.

wrote that by 1900 the college had reached "the extreme limit to which it was possible for us to go in receiving students. We were overcrowded in the buildings which we had at that time." A new board of trustees had recently been set up which assumed more responsibility than the old one for facing the pressing problems of expansion. Since most of the students did not know English on arriving at Robert, the college found a preparatory department essential. The home training of the students was such that they accepted discipline easily and President Washburn thought them easier to control than American boys. He also observed that intellectually no one nationality proved more able than another.[24]

The reputation of Robert had already spread widely through the Balkans and Middle East during its first forty years because of the character of its students and alumni, and particularly because of its influence in training many young Bulgarian leaders who had helped to build a free Bulgaria. Washburn served them as counselor and used his remarkable influence in Europe to promote their national aspirations.[25]

Syrian Protestant College, founded in 1866 with 16 students, graduated its first class of five in 1870. During the first decade Arabic was the language of instruction, but then the shift was made to English. Under its first president, Daniel Bliss, who served until his son Howard succeeded him in 1903, gradual expansion took place with assistance from wealthy and influential members of the board of trustees, many of them Presbyterian laymen. The medical school established in the 1870s had from the beginning played a significant part in bringing modern medicine to the Middle East. By 1902 there were 600 students in six departments: preparatory, college, medicine, pharmacy, commerce, and biblical archaeology and philology. As with Robert College, most of the students were non-Moslem; there were only 98 Moslems among the 750 students in 1905. The college was proud that most of its graduates remained in the Middle East instead of going abroad to reap benefits from their education. As of 1903 only 9 out of 221 medical

[24] The best sources available for the early history of Robert College are Cyrus Hamlin, *Among the Turks*, Chap. 19, and his *My Life and Times*, Chaps. 13 and 14. See also Washburn, *Fifty Years, passim*, especially pp. 254–255, 264 (for quotation), 266, 289–290, 293–294, 300–301.

[25] Washburn, *Fifty Years*, pp. 287, 298–299; Griscom, *Diplomatically Speaking*, p. 135.

graduates had left the Middle East, only 8 out of 118 pharmacy graduates, and 43 of 237 arts graduates. Of the latter 43, a number were pursuing graduate study abroad.[26]

The beginnings of Constantinople College for Women were even humbler than those of Robert and Syrian Protestant. Opened as a preparatory school for girls with three pupils in 1871, it soon built a campus at Scutari on the Asiatic side of the Bosporus and enjoyed a slow but promising growth. The efforts of its head, Mary Mills Patrick, and others were rewarded when the Massachusetts legislature granted a college charter in 1890. When the cable carrying the news arrived in Constantinople there was great rejoicing: "Enthusiastic students decorated the buildings and covered the blackboards with the words, 'Long live the College!' written in Turkish and many other languages. Classes were discontinued for the day, and in the evening a banquet was given at which eloquent speeches were delivered in Turkish, English, French, Greek, and Armenian."[27] The college reported 146 pupils in 1900.

Business. Commercial relations with the Ottoman Empire antedated the arrival of the first American missionaries. From the late eighteenth century, Smyrna was the entrepôt from which American vessels carried cargoes of Smyrna figs and raisins to the American market. American ships also visited ports on the Arabian peninsula to pick up dates and a few other local products. Although trade with the Middle East remained modest in volume, it did bring a few Americans into contact with the area and acquainted them with its exotic delicacies and with some of its inhabitants and customs. In 1900 American exports to the Ottoman Empire were calculated at slightly over half a million dollars, but imports from Turkey (including licorice root, rugs, fruit, nuts, wool, opium, hides, and skins) were nearly fourteen times that amount. Toward the end of the nineteenth century, Persian-American trade was so small that it was not even listed separately. Negligible American trade with Egypt consisted of such imports as long-staple cotton, hides, gum arabic, senna, and onions; the major American exports were petroleum and petroleum products, especially kerosene, and a small volume of industrial products.[28]

[26] Brown, *100 Years*, p. 989; Penrose, *AUB*, pp. 20–32, 76–82, 88, 130.
[27] Patrick, *Bosporus Adventure*, pp. 31–32, 83, 93–97. See also ABC, *AR 1900*, p. 47.
[28] Gordon, *American Relations with Turkey*, p. 60, Table 7, and Chap. 3 for a discussion of nineteenth-century trade with Turkey. For Persia, see Yeselson,

Other Interests. In addition to the continuing activities of American businessmen, missionaries, and educators in the nineteenth century, there had been lesser contacts of several kinds. American archaeologists had begun to evince an interest in the remains of earlier civilizations, especially those associated with biblical history. Edward Robinson, a biblical scholar, may be considered the precursor of American archaeologists in the Middle East. His careful topographical studies made in Palestine in 1838 are still acclaimed by eminent contemporary archaeologists. In 1900 the founding of the American School for Oriental Studies at Jerusalem inaugurated a new era in American archaeological inquiry in the Bible lands. Mesopotamia had also attracted an American expedition during 1889 and 1890. Americans had begun to show interest in Egyptology, chiefly through their financial support of the British-controlled Egypt Exploration Fund, to which they contributed $126,000 between 1883 and 1902. By 1900 a new generation of American Egyptologists, including James H. Breasted, George Reisner, and A. M. Lythgoe, was about to begin an important period in archaeology. The first major American expedition was undertaken by the University of California in 1899 and financed by Mrs. Phoebe Hearst.[29]

Visits of naval vessels and employment of Americans with special technical skills afforded other occasional contacts between the United States and the Middle East. By the early twentieth century a fair number of affluent Americans had begun to swell the tourist trade to Egypt and the Ottoman Empire, especially to the Bible lands. The changes in oceanic shipping which stimulated tourism also made it possible for growing numbers of Ottoman subjects to leave for the United States. Among those emigrating, most were Armenians and Syrians, but considerable numbers of Greeks and a few Turks also left their ancestral homes.[30]

USPDR, p. 56n. For Egypt, see Wright, "United States Policy toward Egypt," pp. 238–240.

[29] Ephraim A. Speiser, *The United States and the Near East*, p. 222; William F. Albright, *The Archaeology of Palestine*, pp. 25–26; Albright, "Edward Robinson," and "Eli Smith," in *Dictionary of American Biography*, XVI, 40, and XVII, 257–258; John Hay to Lloyd C. Griscom, July 16 and July 19, 1900, DS Instructions, Turkey, Vol. 7; Seton Lloyd, *Foundations in the Dust: A Story of Mesopotamian Exploration*, pp. 176, 198–201; Wright, "United States Policy toward Egypt," pp. 176–181, 269–273.

[30] John A. DeNovo, "American Relations with the Middle East: Some Unfinished Business," in *Issues and Conflicts: Studies in Twentieth Century American Diplomacy*, George L. Anderson, ed., pp. 71, 92 n. 70; Straus, *Under Four Administra-*

Another contact was that between Jews in America and the Jewish colony in Palestine, which included some of American nationality who were drawn there by religion and sentiment. American Jews, especially the wealthy, took a deep philanthropic interest in their co-religionists and contributed generously to their support. At the close of the century, American Jewry suffered from internal dissensions growing out of disputes over the distribution of funds collected in America for the Jewish community in Palestine. As yet, however, the incipient modern Zionist movement did not deeply trouble American Jewry; only eight thousand members had joined the Federation of American Zionists by 1900.[31]

Organization, Policies, and Problems of American Diplomacy in the Middle East

For the protection of American citizens carrying on these varied activities, the State Department had built up a network of treaties and a corps of diplomatic and consular agents in the Middle East. After years of preliminary effort, the United States and the Ottoman Empire in 1830 signed a most-favored-nation treaty granting the United States important capitulatory rights which subsequently resulted in much controversy. The following year Commodore David Porter became chargé d'affaires of the legation and, between 1834 and his death in 1843, minister resident. Over the years several Americans of prominence, including General Lew Wallace, Oscar S. Straus, and President James B. Angell of the University of Michigan, headed the Constantinople legation.[32] A consul-general also functioned in Constantinople,

tions, pp. 150–151, 152; Griscom, *Diplomatically Speaking*, pp. 160–161; Hitti, *Syrians in America*, pp. 54–55, 62; M. Vartan Malcom, *The Armenians in America*, pp. 62–64; Gordon, *American Relations with Turkey*, pp. 303, 311; Charles M. Dickinson (consul-general, Constantinople), "Reminiscences," pp. 50–55, Charles M. Dickinson MSS.

[31] Frank E. Manuel, *The Realities of American-Palestine Relations*, pp. 80–87, 96–100, 113; Straus, *Under Four Administrations*, pp. 156, 158; Cyrus Adler and Aaron M. Margalith, *With Firmness in the Right: American Diplomatic Action Affecting Jews, 1840–1945*, pp. 3–9, 11–18, 42–63; Oscar Handlin, *Adventure in Freedom: Three Hundred Years of Jewish Life in America*, p. 169; Samuel Halperin, *The Political World of American Zionism*, pp. 10–11. For an account of the so-called American Colony in Jerusalem, see Bertha Spafford Vester, *Our Jerusalem: An American Family in the Holy City, 1881–1949*. The communal colony, organized by the author's parents after their departure from Chicago following a theological dispute among Presbyterians, engaged in activities akin to those of an American settlement house.

[32] David Hunter Miller, ed., *Treaties and Other International Acts of the United States*, III, 541–598; Gordon, *American Relations with Turkey*, pp. 8–12, 369–370.

the diplomatic nerve center of the Ottoman Empire; and to serve the scattered American missionary and commercial interests, eight consuls were located at Alexandretta, Beirut, Erzerum, Harput, Jerusalem, Sivas, Smyrna, and Baghdad. A consul-general in Cairo took care of American interests in Egypt where American judges also served on the International Mixed Courts. Although a treaty had been signed with Persia in 1856, a legation was not established until 1883, after some congressman had become alarmed about the exposed position of Presbyterian missionaries in northwestern Persia. In 1900 the American minister to Persia also functioned as consul-general. Other American consuls were located on the Arabian peninsula at the British anchor port of Aden and at Muscat.[33]

The official business of these American diplomats seemed rather tame and routine compared with the maneuvers of their European counterparts representing powers which regarded the Middle East as a major arena in the contest for power and position. From this international competition the United States took pains to remain free. Noninvolvement, then, was the negative side of American policy, while the positive aspect was the traditional one of protecting American citizens and their individual and group interests. These twin objectives added up to a policy only in the loosest sense, in no way comparable with the elaborate aims of Germany, whose Kaiser made a gaudy state visit to Constantinople in 1898 to promote Germany's economic penetration.[34]

Abstention from the intricate power struggle automatically relegated American diplomats and diplomacy to an inferior position at Constantinople and Teheran. Symbolic of this second-class position was the physical appearance of the legation quarters in Constantinople. When the departing secretary of the legation, John Riddle, was introducing his replacement, Lloyd Griscom, to the city in 1898, Riddle pointed out a shabby building with a dentist's sign, which housed the American legation on the second floor, commenting: "That's the Ameri-

[33] *RDS 1900*, pp. 20, 38, 41–42, 60; Jacob C. Hurewitz, *Middle East Dilemmas: The Background of United States Policy*, pp. 58–60; Yeselson, *USPDR*, pp. 3, 7, 20–26. For the treaty of friendship and commerce with Persia, see Miller, *Treaties*, VII, 429–490; and for the treaty of 1833 with Muscat (Oman), *ibid.*, III, 789–810. See also Sanger, *Arabian Peninsula*, pp. 184–191, for a sketch of American contacts with the Arabian peninsula in the nineteenth century.

[34] Straus, *Under Four Administrations*, pp. 136–139; Griscom, *Diplomatically Speaking*, pp. 136–138; Edward Mead Earle, *Turkey, the Great Powers, and the Bagdad Railway: A Study in Imperialism*, pp. 43–45.

can legation. Not very prepossessing is it?" When Griscom, on orders from Washington, broached the subject of elevating the American legation to an embassy, he found the Sultan singularly unresponsive. Perhaps this was partly in deference to the reluctance of his more powerful neighbors, namely Russia and Germany, who considered it "highly important that no precedent should be established for the United States entering into affairs in the Mediterranean." [35]

Americans in the Ottoman Empire frequently deplored the weakness of American diplomacy. Presidents Washburn of Robert College and Bliss at Beirut became "do-it-yourself" diplomats by negotiating directly with Ottoman officials on many matters. Even the usually irenic missionaries on occasion sounded a chauvinistic blast by demanding warships and naval demonstrations to force proper Turkish respect for their interests, but Washington did not always respond adequately, in their view. American missionaries and educators sometimes turned to the British foreign service for assistance, and American diplomats sometimes returned British favors, as when Oscar Straus informally interceded with the Porte on behalf of the reopening of British orphanages. At the official level, British-American cooperation at the turn of the century was quite in harmony with the growing *rapprochement* of the two countries. [36]

Diplomacy in the Middle East had special complexities and frustrations, not just for the United States but for all the Western powers. These difficulties appeared most sharply in the declining Ottoman Empire, where the Sultan used defensive tactics to blunt assertive foreign demands. His elephantine bureaucracy developed abnormally devious and dilatory tactics, geared to a laboriously observed protocol. Since only an expert could find his way through the labyrinth which led to the seat of power, the Sultan himself, the American legation leaned heavily on the dragoman, Alessandro Gargiulo, an emaciated, gray-bearded Italian long in its service. There were also the unique condi-

[35] Griscom, *Diplomatically Speaking*, p. 132; Patrick, *Bosporus Adventure*, p. 19; Straus, *Under Four Administrations*, pp. 134–135; Griscom to Hay, April 26, 1900, DS Despatches, Turkey, Vol. 68. Griscom was not reporting on the embassy question, but his reference to Russian and German attitudes is applicable here.

[36] Washburn, *Fifty Years*, pp. 258–259; Penrose, *AUB*, pp. 85–88; Straus, *Under Four Administrations*, pp. 148–150; Edwards, "Relations between the United States and Turkey," pp. 235–239; Richard Olney to Alexander W. Terrell, Dec. 11, 1896, DS Instructions, Turkey, Vol. 7; Numbers 224, 264, and 266, DS Despatches, Turkey, Vol. 68; *FR 1901*, pp. 521–523.

tions peculiar to a Moslem country. During the holy month of Ramadan, when the faithful fasted from dawn until dusk, Griscom observed, "Being half starved, the Turks were irritable, easily provoked, and crotchety. No one who could avoid it dreamed of attempting to do business with them."[37]

The phobias of Sultan Abdul Hamid II added to the problems of American and other Western diplomats. By the turn of the century he had become acutely sensitive about the safety of his person and the survival of his regime. Foreigners and foreign influences, he was convinced, whipped up disloyalty, especially among the Armenians, the special concern of American missionaries.[38] The Sultan's extreme sensitivity to subversion is reflected in the tight censorship and the ban on importation of such modern communications equipment as telephones and typewriters. The deep suspicion of foreigners and their technological innovations raised many problems for American diplomats. For example, Hall's Safe Company complained to the State Department in the fall of 1900 that Turkish customs regulations required all safes and refrigerators to be ripped open on arrival and the inside walls examined for contraband articles. This must have amused Secretary of State John Hay when he instructed Griscom to obtain relaxation of the regulations. With tongue in cheek, he commented: "As regards fire-proof safes, the requirement seems to be unreasonable, involving as it does, the virtual destruction of the article; and the same consideration holds in almost equal degree as to refrigerators lined with non-conducting substance."[39]

The Sultan's fears of revolution aided from abroad were at the root of another incident about the same time. The Porte requested Griscom to telegraph Washington at once concerning a reported expedition being launched in the United States by Armenians who allegedly

[37] Griscom, *Diplomatically Speaking*, pp. 131, 142–143, 155–157 (quotation, p. 155). Gargiulo's service ended only with his death from pneumonia in 1912. Rockhill Diary, Jan. 20, 1912, William W. Rockhill MSS.

[38] For evidence of the curtailment of the privileges of missionaries by the Sultan and his subordinate officials by the early twentieth century, see Brown, *100 Years*, pp. 971–972, and Gordon, *American Relations with Turkey*, pp. 230–231, 235.

[39] Hay to Griscom, Dec. 20, 1900, DS Instructions, Turkey, Vol. 7. In response to a request from the Library of Congress about Turkish copyright laws, Griscom answered with some exaggeration: "The censorship of all publications is so rigid that the industry of printing and publishing may be said not to exist. The necessity for a law of copyright is therefore small." Griscom to Hay, March 21, 1900, DS Despatches, Turkey, Vol. 68. On censorship of missionary publications, see Brown, *100 Years*, pp. 993–995.

planned to bring a shipload of arms to Cyprus for revolutionary purposes in Asia Minor. Griscom dutifully complied, although to him "the matter appeared to be simply another of many exaggerated rumours which are being constantly brought to the Palace." The State Department agreed to have the Attorney General and local American customs officials set judicial machinery in motion when more specific information was furnished about the alleged expedition, but apparently nothing was uncovered.[40]

These colorful and sometimes amusing incidents must have been a welcome relief to the tedium of prosaic immigration and other routine cases. American diplomats at Constantinople and Teheran, especially the latter, found themselves with a good deal of leisure to spend in hunting, riding, swimming, yachting, shopping, and partying. The pomp and ritual of diplomatic life in the two capitals reflected a combination of oriental ceremonial and Western *fin de siècle* elegance.[41]

As has already been intimated, American diplomats during their working hours seldom dealt with matters of high policy relating to the rivalries of the Eastern Question. Their major tasks were protection of the persons and property interests of American citizens, both native-born and naturalized, under the capitulations, those political, legal, and economic exemptions long claimed by Western countries for their nationals. The United States rested its capitulatory claims on the most-favored-nation clause in the Turkish-American Treaty of 1830, although Ottoman authorities challenged the American interpretation of the crucial article four setting forth legal safeguards for American citizens. Americans also claimed special status under extraterritorial arrangements in Persia and Egypt. Although the West could make a case for extraterritorial rights in the Middle East, too often these arrangements served as a cloak to shield arrogance and wrongdoing. No wonder Turkey and Persia protested.[42]

As of 1900, the outstanding unsettled diplomatic issue with Turkey was the American demand that Turkey pay an indemnity for damages

[40] Griscom to Hay, Oct. 30, 1900, DS Despatches, Turkey, Vol. 69. See also Hay to Griscom, Oct. 5 and Oct. 11, 1900, DS Instructions, Turkey, Vol. 7.

[41] Straus, *Under Four Administrations*, pp. 133–139, 152; Griscom, *Diplomatically Speaking*, pp. 136, 138–139, 149–153, 164–165, 199–201.

[42] Griscom to Hay, Feb. 6, 1900, DS Despatches, Turkey, Vol. 68; Miller, *Treaties*, III, 542–543, 598; Nasim Sousa, *The Capitulatory Régime of Turkey: Its History, Origins, and Nature, passim*, but especially pp. 131–132; *FR 1900*, pp. 909–919; Yeselson, *USPDR*, pp. 51–52; Manuel, *Palestine-American Relations*, pp. 101–103; Wright, "United States Policy toward Egypt," p. 193.

to missionary property in Anatolia during the Armenian troubles of 1894–1895. The patience of the missionaries had worn thin as several years passed without a settlement despite their pressure on the State Department which had, in turn, repeatedly pressed the legation in Constantinople to keep after Ottoman officialdom. On his arrival in 1898, Oscar Straus pursued the case pressed by his predecessors, Ministers Alexander W. Terrell and James B. Angell. Just before Straus's departure in December of 1899, he wrote Secretary Hay of his regret and disappointment at not having been able to conclude matters, but after protracted efforts he had extracted from the Turks a promise to pay, which was more than the European powers with similar claims had accomplished. Thanks to the preparatory work of Straus, Lloyd Griscom was able to obtain the payment of approximately $90,000 in 1901, but it took patience, personal charm, persistence, threats, and an American battleship to achieve results. To save face, the Sultan insisted on disguising the indemnity payment as part of the cost of a cruiser he purchased from the Cramp shipbuilding firm of Philadelphia.[43]

Missionary need for diplomatic assistance was a continuing concern of America's official agents. Miss Elizabeth Barrows, en route to her station at Van, was detained by Turkish authorities at Erzerum because they interpreted the innocent word "committee" in her instructions as signifying her complicity in an Armenian plot against the government. Upon the assassination of the King of Italy, the Palace had alerted Turkish police to prevent foreign anarchists from entering Turkey, and the Reverend W. E. Ellis was arrested and temporarily detained on arrival at Constantinople because he and his companion presented "a rough and travel worn appearance, which differentiated them from the usual run of travellers." Nor was the property of missionaries always secure. When the house of Dr. L. O. Lee, American missionary at Marash, was broken into "for the purpose of carrying off the safe containing the money and valuables of the American mission," the legation requested the Porte to make every effort to discover and prosecute the robbers.[44]

[43] *FR 1899*, pp. 765–775; *FR 1900*, pp. 906–909; *FR 1901*, pp. 514–515; Straus, *Under Four Administrations*, pp. 141–142; Griscom, *Diplomatically Speaking*, pp. 134–135, 161–164, 169–173; unpublished correspondence in DS Instructions, Turkey, Vol. 7, and DS Despatches, Turkey, Vols. 68 and 69.

[44] Hay to Straus, Jan. 9, 1900; Hay to Griscom, April 12, 1900, DS Turkey, Instructions, Vol. 7; Griscom to Hay, Jan. 30, March 23, and Nov. 8, 1900, DS Despatches, Turkey, Vols. 68 and 69. See also Instructions Nos. 201, 203, 206, 224, and

Not all missionary cases dealt with security of persons and property. Missionaries as well as educators also required diplomatic assistance to lift restrictions on their enterprises. The legation worked for several years before securing official irades permitting the replacement of missionary buildings at Harput, destroyed during the Armenian massacres, and construction of an additional building at Robert College. Similar intercession helped secure approval for rebuilding the theological seminary at Marash and for enabling Dr. William S. Dodd to keep his missionary hospital open at Caesarea.[45]

When American officials dealt with rights of native-born Americans, they were on firmer ground than when claiming rights for naturalized Americans of Ottoman origin. Turkey did not recognize the right of expatriation without the Sultan's approving each case. With the mounting pressure of Armenians anxious to come to the United States by the end of the nineteenth century, American officials devoted much time to the routine of securing the required permission and to facilitating the departure of individual Armenians — sometimes the betrothed of a naturalized citizen of the United States. The department even served as intermediary for the transfer of travel funds for the *emigrés*.[46]

When an Ottoman subject obtained the Sultan's permission to emigrate, he was not supposed to return, but if he did he would be regarded as an Ottoman subject. Herein arose a perennially troublesome problem for the United States, which insisted on going far beyond the practice of European nations in claiming full rights for its naturalized citizens who returned to their homelands. Intricate cases arose out of protests by these naturalized Americans against Ottoman taxation, military service, and other requirements.[47]

From the days of the American Revolution the United States had regarded as deserving national support the promotion of the overseas interests of Americans in affairs of the market place. Assistance to

Despatch No. 161. For the drama of the passage from Erzerum to Van, see Ussher and Knapp, *American Physician*, pp. 39–69.

[45] Griscom to Hay, Feb. 17, April 25, 1900, and Nos. 154, 170, 197, 198, two telegrams of April 24, 1900, DS Despatches, Turkey, Vol. 68; Griscom to Hay, June 28 and Aug. 25, 1900, and No. 223, DS Despatches, Turkey, Vol. 69; Instructions Nos. 222, 252, and 287, DS Instructions, Turkey, Vol. 7.

[46] Nearly one-fourth of the instructions and despatches for 1900 deal with immigration cases.

[47] For examples, see Despatches Nos. 147, 150, 155, 165, 185, 189, 191, and 201, DS Despatches, Turkey, Vol. 68; and Nos. 276 and 278 in DS Despatches, Turkey, Vol. 69.

American businessmen in the Middle East in 1900 was consistent with this tradition. Calls were made on the Constantinople legation to obtain the removal of a ban on American pork products, of restrictions on American flour imports, and to end discrimination against American insurance companies. The difficulties for American flour were traced by Straus and Griscom to the bribery of customs officials by local Greek mill owners who opposed the importation of cheaper American flour.[48] On the Turkish side there were protests against American prohibition on importation of Smyrna figs and raisins based, apparently, on sanitary regulations. The Turkish foreign minister complained to Griscom that the American action was having "a most serious effect on the trade and finances of the Smyrna province."[49]

Perhaps because of its peripheral role in the Eastern Question and because of its unwillingness to use some of the tactics of the European powers, the United States was sensitive to Ottoman slights to its national prestige. Late in 1899, Ottoman authorities seized a quantity of licorice belonging to the third dragoman of the American consulate at Smyrna, Avedis S. Avedikian, who had it stored in a building he had rented. Avedikian, a man of local standing, had invested capital in trade promotion with the United States, assuming that he was entitled to consular immunity. When officials seized Avedikian's licorice without notice to Consul Rufus Lane or the dragoman, Lane ordered the consular kavass to remove the Turkish court seals from the sequestered merchandise, whereupon the kavass was arrested. Lane's actions were not above reproach and brought rebukes from Chargé Griscom and from Consul-General Dickinson in Constantinople, who had to make a special trip to Smyrna just to straighten out the matter. American officials deplored the treatment of the dragoman and the kavass, fearing that it would lessen respect of the local populace and authorities for the consulate and its staff, and for the United States and American citizens.[50]

[48] Nos. 198, 210, 225, 242, 248, 311, and Hay to Straus, March undated and April 6, 1900, DS Instructions, Turkey, Vol. 7; Nos. 151, 159, 181, 184, 190, 215B, and Straus to Hay, March 10, 1900; Griscom to Hay, March 29, 1900, DS Despatches, Turkey, Vol. 68; No. 227, *ibid.*, Vol. 69; Straus, *Under Four Administrations*, pp. 147–148. For difficulties of a missionary physician with Turkish customs officials, see Ussher and Knapp, *American Physician*, pp. 4–5.

[49] Griscom to Hay, Sept. 15, 1900, DS Despatches, Turkey, Vol. 69. See also Nos. 257 and 267, *ibid.*

[50] The essential documents are printed in *FR 1900*, pp. 920–934.

Conclusion

By the opening of the twentieth century, then, Americans had built up interests mainly of a religious, philanthropic, and commercial nature in the Middle East. Through its field agents, the State Department supported these enterprises, but it still wished to steer clear of the international politics of the Eastern Question. Although having no strategic stake in the area and no political ambitions, the United States nonetheless insisted that its citizens enjoy any extraterritorial rights accorded citizens of European powers. If the official behavior of the United States deserves to be described as a policy, that policy was the product of the needs of specific American interest groups operating in the Middle East and of traditional attitudes and practices of the United States in its conduct of foreign relations.

During the years before the beginning of World War I, new forces were eroding the foundations of the old order in the Middle East. Dissatisfaction with existing conditions and the cry of reform were to produce revolutions in the Ottoman Empire and in Persia. These revolutions, combined with a quickening of nationalistic feelings in the Middle East, and the increased tempo of European intervention, were to change the local environment in which Americans pursued their interests and require adjustments in American policy.

2

THE UNITED STATES
AND THE MIDDLE EAST,
1900–1914

☆ IN THE MIDDLE EAST of the early twentieth century, critics of traditional ways and existing institutions instigated movements of far-reaching significance for the future of the area and for its relations with the Western world. Demands for reforms from within and for an end to Western intervention in the affairs of the region began to alter the setting in which foreign interests operated. While most Americans active in the area appeared oblivious to the adjustments which would have to be made eventually, a few perceived somewhat dimly the meaning of the changes which were brewing. Policy-makers in Washington, however, secure in the belief that traditional diplomatic approaches were adequate, made no serious long-range effort to anticipate the accommodations dictated by changing local conditions and attitudes.

Reform Ferment in the Middle East

The twin ideals of progress and human perfectibility to which the Western world was so devoted in the decades before World War I, eventually gained currency among some leaders of opinion in the Middle East. Dissatisfaction with the existing order, combined with a growing conviction that men might shape the future, challenged a dominant belief in Islamic society, namely, that the status quo was a reflection of Allah's will. Internal pressures for reform in the Middle East had unique characteristics, to be sure, but these pressures manifested something of the ferment of the contemporary Progressive Movement in the United States and in the challenges to the old order stirring

27

many parts of Europe. These were years of revolutions, or of the instigation of revolutionary movements, which would continue to rock the world in the twentieth century. Not only in Russia, China, and Mexico, but also in Turkey and Persia, old regimes, old institutions, and old ideas were shaken by upheavals which would touch the future interests of Americans in ways little dreamed of at the time.

Accompanying these movements for internal reform were protests against Western imperialism, then vigorously penetrating Asia, Africa, the Pacific Islands, and the Caribbean. Preliminary rumblings of what would later be labeled anti-colonialism could be heard in native opposition to foreign domination. The United States, as a colonial power faced with troublesome problems in ruling over alien peoples in the Caribbean and Pacific, found itself implicated on an unprecedented scale with overseas relations, although these concerns were still confined largely to the Western Hemisphere and the Pacific Ocean. The challenges to statesmanship posed by these problems were added to preoccupation with domestic reforms required by the industrial age. Together they were of such magnitude as to tax fully the American people and their leadership. Americans had little stomach for forays into the turmoils of Europe or the Middle East.

The Nature of American Interests

Yet American interests in the Middle East were undergoing modest expansion in the years 1900 to 1914, although they remained predominantly cultural, philanthropic, and commercial. The official policy of the United States continued to be one of indifference to the political aspects of the Eastern Question, with one significant exception — when President William H. Taft and Secretary of State Philander C. Knox, in pursuance of their program known as "Dollar Diplomacy," supported the Chester Project, a plan for a gigantic railroad and other economic development projects in the Ottoman Empire between 1909 and 1911. When intervention to promote American economic penetration turned into a fiasco, the Department of State hastily retreated to the orthodoxy of nonentanglement. This episode, which developed into a serious brush with European powers solicitous of their positions in the Ottoman Empire, seemed to confirm the wisdom of abstention from international politics in this remote and turbulent part of the world.[1]

[1] See below, Chap. 3, for a full discussion of the prewar Chester Project.

The view that proliferating American interests could somehow be protected by traditional means stemmed from the questionable premise that cultural and economic commitments could be sealed off in separate compartments from the international struggle for position in the Middle East. Yet frequent instances arose when American interest groups required diplomatic protection, and these interests often impinged on and sometimes conflicted with the objectives of the Great Powers.

Missions. Missionaries with their enterprises in Asia Minor, Syria, Persia, Egypt, and the Persian Gulf area were still the dominant American concern. These were years of great optimism among the missionaries, who hopefully interpreted scattered evidence to mean that they were at last breaking through the barriers of Islamic society to reach a wider Moslem audience. The Persian missionaries, for example, took heart from the increasing enrollments in missionary schools, remarking particularly that a few Moslem students were attending, although there were mixed feelings about the meaning of this development. Did it mean that a new day was dawning, looking toward the evangelization of the Middle East? Certainly many missionaries rhapsodized in this vein. In the perspective of another thirty years, a Presbyterian publication could assess the earlier tendency more realistically:

With the beginning of the twentieth century there were movements for reform along many lines, among them movements for educational reform. Dissatisfaction with the methods and curricula of the mosque schools and private native schools was showing itself in many places. Attempts were made here and there to introduce better methods and to enrich the curriculum with science, geography and other up-to-date subjects; but these attempts were frustrated by the ecclesiastics. The people of Persia, baffled in this direction, resorted in much larger numbers to the mission schools, and from this time on the mission schools ceased to be looked upon as schools for the minorities alone. This influx of Moslem pupils in all the mission schools was not for the sake of Christian instruction. The drawing influences were the sciences and the scientific methods and the high moral character of the teaching staffs. Christian instruction was accepted in the curriculum as a matter of necessity rather than of choice.[2]

Expansion went forward in all the mission fields of the Middle East despite irritating obstacles imposed by the protectors of the status quo. The Presbyterians in Persia added a station at Resht in 1902 for opera-

---

[2] *A Century of Mission Work in Iran*, pp. 31–33, 97–98 (quotation).

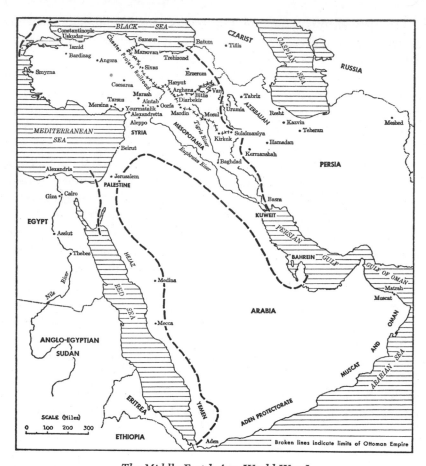

The Middle East before World War I

tions along the Caspian Sea littoral, pushed southward with a new station at Kermanshah in 1905, and six years later made an eastward leap to the Islamic shrine city of Meshed, where a single missionary conducted the work during the early years. These new stations were not the only indication of expanded operations. In 1900 a substation of the Teheran mission was inaugurated at Kazvin, later the transfer point for lend lease supplies brought northward by Americans for transmission to the Russians during World War II. The same year the grade school in Teheran became a high school, and in 1913 achieved the status of a junior college.[3]

[3] *Ibid.*, pp. 5–7, 11–13, 48–49; Brown, *100 Years*, p. 496.

30

Perhaps of equal significance alongside these advances was the growth of American medical activity. Under Presbyterian auspices, Dr. Mary Eddy established the first tuberculosis sanitarium in the Ottoman Empire near Beirut in 1908. By 1914 the American Board operated nine hospitals and ten dispensaries, in which nearly forty thousand patients were treated. At Van, Turkey, Dr. Clarence Ussher of the American Board was among the missionary physicians who saw the crying need for nurses' training and for diffusion of information to help control the terrible epidemics of typhus, cholera, and smallpox which frequently decimated whole areas. Shortly before World War I, he presented a demonstration of the work of his locally trained nurses as well as a public demonstration of techniques for handling epidemics.[4] About the same time, the Arabian Mission of the Dutch Reformed Church in America extended its medical work into the Sheikhdom of Kuweit. Dr. Paul Harrison established a men's hospital which was soon followed by a woman's dispensary conducted by Dr. Eleanor Calverley, the wife of a young missionary accredited to the Arabian Mission after his graduation from Princeton Theological Seminary. The hard struggle of Dr. Calverley to break through the crust of superstition and resistance to a woman doctor bringing "Christian" medicine from the West can best be followed in her own simple but moving autobiographical account. When the Arabian Mission extended its work to Matrah, Oman, in 1910, and Dr. Arthur K. Bennett arrived from Basra in August to take charge of a hospital and dispensary, the American consul at Muscat reported that the doctor spoke fluent Arabic and got along famously with the Sultan at their first meeting. Bennett's successor, Dr. Paul W. Harrison, transferred from Kuweit, also ingratiated himself with the Sultan and the Arab population, partly because he never charged fees for his services.[5]

Many of these American missionaries who worked at the village level with the minorities and Moslems acquired an understanding of Islam which shows more open-mindedness than one might expect from people dedicated to a calling that assumed the superiority of their re-

---

[4] Centennial Series, *Syria Mission*, p. 9; ABC, *AR 1915*, p. 112; Ussher and Knapp, *American Physician*, pp. 89–97, 198–201.
[5] Mason and Barny, *History of the Arabian Mission*, Chaps. 7 and 8; Sanger, *Arabian Peninsula*, p. 167; Zahra Freeth, *Kuweit Was My Home*, pp. 77–78; Paul W. Harrison, *Doctor in Arabia, passim*; Eleanor T. Calverley, *My Arabian Days and Nights, passim*; John A. Ray (consul, Muscat) to Knox, July 29, Aug. 23, Dec. 6, 1910; Jan. 25, 1911, DS 390a.116/14, 15, 16, and 17.

ligious beliefs. At the same time the records show that missionaries could also be narrow-minded and bigoted. Especially when appealing for funds in the United States they exaggerated their denigration of Islam. For example, the American Board made a sweeping indictment of Islam in an appeal of March, 1915, to the Rockefeller Foundation for $1,385,000 to assist its enterprises in Turkey for a two- or three-year period. Speaking of the control over the area exerted for so long by Mohammedan governments, the Board's Prudential Committee wrote: "Surely there is no need of enlarging upon what that means in terms of illiteracy and the absence of sanitary conditions. Islam has, in all history, been the foe of intellectual advance upon the part of the people it governed, and unprogressive in all modern measures for the preservation and promotion of health. A study of the countries here named shows them to be but striking examples of the genius of Mohammedanism in these respects." In their view, the first relief from these bleak conditions had come from the American missionaries: "The lack of advance during the last two thousand years or more in the country, and until the entrance of American missionaries, is notorious. While the improvement made has been marked, it is yet only a beginning compared with the enormous amount yet to be accomplished." The American Board recited in some detail its accomplishments and its qualifications for broadening its good influence in Turkey.[6]

It is not surprising that the missionaries wanted recognition for their considerable accomplishments, for there is no doubt whatsoever of their dedication or that their pride in their efforts was justifiable. But the historian must also call attention to the missionary bias and to the general Christian bias which since the seventh century, and especially since the Crusades, has recognized little but evil in Islam and its society. This prejudice has produced distortion in Western conceptions of the Middle East.

Harassments of many kinds from local officials plagued the missionaries and called for diplomatic intercession. American diplomats in the Ottoman Empire perennially struggled to secure compliance with American treaty rights which had been eroded seriously by administrative fiat in recent years. Missionaries from European nations were also victims of the restrictive policies. After France, in 1901, used a dispute

---

[6] American Board of Commissioners for Foreign Missions to Jerome D. Green, secretary, Rockefeller Foundation, March 2, 1915, DS Inquiry Document No. 838.

over dock rights at Constantinople as a lever to force Turkish concessions for French missionaries, Russia was able to extract comparable pledges for her missionaries. When the Turks refused to extend comparable concessions to American missions and colleges, Minister John G. A. Leishman vigorously protested the discrimination. The Roosevelt administration sent navy vessels on more than one occasion to bolster the minister, and over a period of years the Turks gave in on most of the points at issue. Despite Leishman's best efforts, Turkish interference dogged the missionaries during these years: travel permits were not issued; there were restrictions on Bible sales (removed in 1908 after protests); and Turkish authorities opened their mail.[7]

A notorious outrage against missionaries was the kidnapping of Miss Ellen Stone by Macedonian bandits early in September, 1901. In Macedonia, where feeling ran strong against the Turks, bands of mountaineers sought to embarrass the Ottoman government and further their own political aim of separation from the empire — separation either by setting up an independent state or possibly by union with Bulgaria. Hence there were political overtones in the capture of Miss Stone as well as the objective of securing sizable funds by holding her for ransom. While Washington officials stumbled because they misunderstood the tangled Balkan scene, the Stone case became a *cause célèbre* in American church circles. In the meantime, nearly seventy thousand dollars was raised by public subscription in the United States toward Miss Stone's ransom. Through Dr. William W. Peet of the American Board in Constantinople, this sum was paid over to the brigands in February, 1902, and the abductors then released Miss Stone within two weeks.

The United States government did not press claims against Turkey, partly because of suspicion that the Macedonian Revolutionary Committee planned to use this abduction to further its cause by raising an issue between Turkey and the United States. After studying documents in the case, Professor Alfred Dennis concluded that "the hysterical excitement shown by missionary friends of Miss Stone in America and

[7] Dennis, *Adventures in American Diplomacy*, pp. 457–464; *FR 1901*, pp. 523, 529–530; *FR 1903*, pp. 735–761; *FR 1904*, pp. 818–833. For views of Roosevelt and his advisers, see *Selections from the Correspondence of Theodore Roosevelt and Henry Cabot Lodge, 1884–1918*, II, 49; Morison, ed., *Letters of Theodore Roosevelt*, II, 588, 596; IV, 885, 891; V, 113. See also *FR 1905*, pp. 898–911; *FR 1906*, II, 1396–1398, 1414–1416; *FR 1907*, II, 1067–1069.

the publicity given in the American press were chiefly responsible for the large amount which had to be paid." President George Washburn of Robert College stated that the affair had been "sadly mismanaged" during the early stages and agreed that the publicity given the abduction in American newspapers led the kidnappers to follow closely the accumulation of the ransom fund. Thus, the publicity ruined the good possibility that Miss Stone might have been released within a few days of her capture for a small amount of money.[8]

An even more striking assault against an American missionary was the Labaree murder in March of 1904. The Reverend Benjamin Labaree, a Presbyterian missionary, was attacked by Kurdish tribesmen in northwestern Persia near Mount Ararat, apparently not because of any personal animosity toward him but rather because of a generalized religious fanaticism and race hatred. Under pressure from the missionaries to secure the punishment of the attackers, the American minister, Richmond Pearson, enlisted support from his British colleague, Sir Arthur B. Hardinge, in bearing down on the Persian government. Pearson requested that American warships be sent to the Persian Gulf to strengthen his hand, but Washington officials hedged and thereby weakened the minister's efforts.

The Labaree case appeared finally to be settled when Persian authorities imprisoned the murderer with a pledge to arrest his accomplices (not redeemable when they fled across the border into Turkey), and agreed to pay an indemnity of thirty thousand dollars to Labaree's widow. Unwisely, the State Department kept the case open by insisting that if the murderer's accomplices ever returned to Persia, they must be punished. When Consul William F. Doty at Teheran pressed this point with Persian officials, the Labaree case became mixed up in a futile Persian punitive expedition into Turkey during 1905, leading to a counter-invasion for which Persia blamed the United States.

A scholar of Persian-American relations has called the Labaree murder and its aftermath the first incident of consequence between Persia and the United States. The missionaries tried to dominate American diplomacy in this instance and severely condemned Minister Pearson for his alleged lack of cooperation as compared with the vigorous sup-

[8] Dennis, *Adventures*, pp. 453–456; Washburn, *Fifty Years*, pp. 276–278; *FR 1902*, pp. 502, 997–1023; documents in Charles M. Dickinson MSS, Boxes 1, 3, and 4.

port of their point of view by Consul Doty. Actually, their criticism of Pearson appears to have been motivated largely by their personal distaste for the man and his habits. They were put out because he did not conform to their notions of Sabbath-keeping and temperance. Professor Yeselson has pointed out that the Labaree case highlighted certain fundamental aspects of Persian-American relations at this time, especially "the dangerous position of the missionaries," who were "the continuing dominant feature of the relationship." The "unfortunate inflexibility within the Department" led it "to react automatically along formalized lines without regard for special circumstances. . . . It would appear that the general unimportance of Persia in the overall framework of American diplomacy militated against spending the required time and energy on the problem."[9]

Ottoman officials became increasingly suspicious of the Armenians in their empire as they extended the range and activity of their secret societies and as Armenian nationalism became more outspoken. A second wave of Armenian massacres in 1909 elicited American sympathies for the aspirations of this Christian minority so closely associated with American missionaries.[10]

All through these years a continuing struggle went on to secure adequate recognition of the missionaries' right to conduct their multifarious activities. Ambassador Oscar Straus, on his third mission to Turkey (1909–1910), considered his major task the exemption of American religious, educational, and philanthropic institutions from an onerous Law of Associations under the Young Turk regime following the Revolution of 1908–1909. Straus warned that this law gave "Ottoman authorities, both civil and judicial, the power so to impede the work of these institutions as to prevent them from functioning."[11]

[9] Yeselson, *USPDR*, Chap. 3 (quotations, pp. 83–84); *FR 1904*, pp. 657–677, 835–836; *FR 1905*, pp. 722–734; *FR 1906*, II, 1208–1216; *FR 1907*, II, 941–948; *FR 1908*, pp. 681–682; Morison, *Roosevelt Letters*, V, 698.

[10] *FR 1904*, pp. 836–839; *FR 1906*, II, 1417–1419; *FR 1909*, pp. 557–558; James L. Barton, *Daybreak in Turkey*, pp. 293–297; William E. Strong, *The Story of the American Board: An Account of the First Hundred Years of the American Board of Commissioners for Foreign Missions*, pp. 410–412; *MRW*, 32 (Aug. 1909), 599–608; (Sept. 1909), 709–710; ABC, *AR 1909*, pp. 67–70. Roosevelt's sympathy for the Armenians and his resultant antipathy for the Turks is revealed in Morison, *Roosevelt Letters*, III, 584; IV, 1175; *Correspondence of Roosevelt and Lodge*, II, 197–198.

[11] *FR 1910*, pp. 857–859; Straus, *Under Four Administrations*, pp. 296–298 (quotation, p. 296); Straus Diary, pp. 104–105, Straus MSS.

Colleges. Sharing the optimism of the missionaries, the independent American colleges believed they also had a great role to play in reshaping the Middle East. By 1900, Robert College, Constantinople College for Women (usually called the Women's College), and Syrian Protestant College had passed through their fledgling years, and by 1914 had undergone significant expansion. Robert College in 1903 inaugurated its third president, Caleb Frank Gates, who had behind him two decades of experience in Turkey as an American Board missionary, including eight years as president of Euphrates College at Harput. Indicative of the growth of Robert was the addition of an engineering school in 1912. Young Lynn Scipio, a Purdue graduate, was called from the University of Nebraska to launch the new engineering curriculum and to preside over the school as its dean. After his retirement some thirty years later, he told many interesting anecdotes about his incredible problems during the early years. He had to staff courses, build the shops more through ingenuity than through the use of proper materials and equipment, and see that an unfinished building was completed. He surprised some of his colleagues by overcoming the traditional feeling among students that manual labor was degrading. In his first classes, there was no language to serve as a common denominator, but the symbols of mathematics helped to surmount this obstacle. From the one English-speaking student, who served as translator, his classmates soon learned enough English to facilitate Scipio's conduct of the course.[12]

The Women's College had at its head the energetic Mary Mills Patrick, who in 1908 won her long fight to free the college from its ambiguous ties to the American Board. With the support of several American women who adopted the college as their special interest, a revised charter was obtained from the Commonwealth of Massachusetts and fund-raising brought some gratifying results. For several years efforts to obtain property for a new campus on the European side of the Bosporus were fruitless, but by 1914 the path had been cleared and the college moved to its beautiful new headquarters. Four years earlier a preparatory department had been opened.[13]

The Syrian Protestant College at Beirut made its importance felt in the Middle East even before the war. Its graduates established many

[12] Caleb Frank Gates, *Not to Me Only*, pp. 14–172, *passim*; Lynn A. Scipio, *My Thirty Years in Turkey*, pp. 49–50, 59–65.
[13] Patrick, *Bosporus Adventure*, pp. 106–130, 137–140, 156–159.

modern stores and importation agencies, and organized banks and commercial enterprises throughout the Middle East. The college was now under its second president, Dr. Howard Bliss, who succeeded his father in 1902. The old local board of managers was abolished and the policy-making largely turned over to the faculty and administration which, thanks to better communications, could now keep in closer touch with the board of trustees in the United States. The medical school was flourishing and won a long struggle for recognition by the Ottoman authorities. Before this result was achieved, a delegation of twenty-three prominent Americans called on President Theodore Roosevelt in Washington to beseech his intercession. The president and Secretary Hay were sympathetic to the arguments for strong diplomatic representations to protect American educational, cultural, and philanthropic interests, and called in former Secretary of State John Foster to press American claims in strong instructions to Ambassador John Leishman in Constantinople. Leishman worked diligently and successfully to have medical graduates recognized on the same basis as graduates of French and other medical institutions. Expanded medical facilities, including a women's hospital, were advances of these years, and a dental school was opened in 1910. Most graduates of the college remained in the Middle East; between 1902 and 1910 they formed influential alumni associations, and in 1910 a college magazine, which became a publication of some prestige, now merged with *The Middle East Forum*, an organ of faculty opinion and of Arab nationalism.[14]

Growth did not take place without stress and strain; in 1909, compulsory chapel and Bible class attendance was protested by non-Christian students. A later president, Bayard Dodge, recalled after many years what the college was like when he first joined the faculty in 1913. Most of the students came from missionary schools, a large majority of them village boys from the Christian communities of Mount Lebanon, but also a number of Armenians from Asia Minor who came to study medicine as well as sons of wealthy families of Egypt and Palestine. "Life at Beirut was simple with no night clubs or amusement resorts, other than the coffee houses in the respectable parts of the town, and low down dives in the red light district. There was almost no drinking or gambling

[14] *American University of Beirut: Description of Its Organization and Work,* Autumn, 1934, mimeographed, p. 48; D. Stuart Dodge to G. K. Wilkins, Jan. 24, 1903, and other documents in Archives of American Board of Commissioners for Foreign Missions, ABC: 16.5, Vol. 6; Penrose, *AUB*, pp. 98, 103–116, 128–129.

on the part of the students. The veil and harem system kept the Muslim girls in seclusion . . . In many ways the atmosphere of the country was still medieval." Yet such recently introduced Western pastimes as hiking and swimming were becoming popular at the college, and the annual spring field day brought out high government officials. The college was also trying to start Boy Scouting and summer conferences. Transportation was still primitive and complicated travel for the students. Lebanese students traveled by mule or in old-fashioned carriages; Armenians from the north used animals as far as Aleppo and then took the railroad. Students from Egypt, Palestine, Tripoli, Latakiya, or Greece had a relatively easy journey by ship, but one can imagine the hardship for the few students who came from Iraq and Persia. When an Emir of the Bakhtiari tribe brought his son from Hamadan he avowed "that he would not try to fetch him again for seven years."

Much of the academic work was surprisingly high in quality, although some courses were in the hands of inexperienced American teachers who signed for a three-year term. President Dodge could recall that "in 1913 we had a remarkable feeling of stability and made plans for years ahead with naive confidence."[15]

Business. The optimism of missionaries and educators was matched by the expectations of those who believed in the potential for American business in the Middle East. As Americans surveyed their maturing industrial economy in the prewar years, the possibilities of expanding American commerce and investment abroad attracted much attention, especially during the Taft administration. In the decade before World War I, tobacco rose rapidly to first place (by 1903) in American imports from the Ottoman Empire. While the trade figures show a substantial absolute rise in Ottoman-American trade, the share of Turkey in total imports into the United States rose only from about 1 per cent in 1902 to 1.2 per cent in 1912; Turkey's share of American exports had been about .05 per cent in 1902, but rose to .17 per cent in 1912. By 1913 less than 2 per cent of Turkish imports came from the United States, but 23 per cent of her exports went to the United States.[16]

American investments in the Middle East were small compared with those in the Western Hemisphere and confined largely to the Ottoman

[15] Penrose, *AUB*, pp. 133–143, 147–149; Dodge, AR 1948, pp. 1–5 (all quotations, pp. 3–4).
[16] Gordon, *American Relations with Turkey*, pp. 64–68.

Empire, the most important being in tobacco, licorice, and the marketing of petroleum products and sewing machines. By 1912 the American Tobacco Company was spending $10 million annually in buying and preparing tobacco in Turkey for blending with American leaf into cigarettes, which had become popular. The value of tobacco exported to the United States from Smyrna alone was $2,387,814 in 1913. In 1912 the company had 1750 employees on its payroll in Kevalla, 1000 in Smyrna, 800 in Samsun, and 250 in Ismid.

Among the most interesting commercial activities were the licorice interests of MacAndrews and Forbes with factories at Camden, New Jersey, and offices in New York City. This firm enjoyed a virtual monopoly of the trade between the United States and Turkey in licorice root, which grew wild in many parts of Asiatic Turkey and the Caucasus, where it was considered a pest by the natives. The company rented licorice-bearing fields and hired laborers, who were paid daily according to the quantity collected. In fact, the size of the export depended almost solely on the labor supply available for the collection. The root was dried and baled for shipment from the principal collection stations in Baghdad, Smyrna, Alexandretta, and Batum. In these places the company maintained offices, hydraulic presses, and warehouses. In normal years the company took from forty thousand to fifty thousand tons of licorice root from the Middle East. In 1912, $1,258,299 worth was exported to the United States from all of Turkey, nearly all for MacAndrews and Forbes. The firm's plant in the interior made licorice paste for an extract used in the European trade. After the licorice had been removed, the pulp was compressed into boards. Normally the raw root was shipped to the United States to avoid customs duties on the processed product. The licorice was used chiefly in the manufacture of chewing gum and candy, for sweetening chewing tobacco, and for coloring and sweetening beer.[17]

Before World War I, the Standard Oil Company of New York (Socony) had built up an extensive export market for its products, especially kerosene, in Egypt, the Levant, and Asia Minor. Operating through a subsidiary, the Vacuum Oil Company, Socony established an Egyptian branch about 1898 from which it also served the Levant coast. In 1911 Socony established a distributing agency in Constantinople and

[17] Oscar J. Campbell, "Report on American Interests in Turkey," pp. 22–23, 24–25, DS Inquiry Document No. 84.

completed tanks and warehouses there and at Smyrna. These new facilities helped to increase sales on the Levant coast, where petroleum stoves for heating and cooking had come into vogue, and stimulated the demand for kerosene, previously used chiefly for illumination. Competition from Rumanian and Russian oil had cut into the Egyptian market heavily, but American sales were on the increase in Anatolia and the Levant.[18]

According to its records, the Singer Sewing Machine Company had nearly two hundred agencies or stores in Asiatic Turkey in 1918. In the larger towns there might be several agencies, for example, four in Smyrna. These machines reputedly reached nearly every town and hamlet of importance, penetrating even the remote interior. In Asia Minor alone the company claimed forty agencies and eighty subagencies. Its machines were sold either directly from the United States or from warehouses in Liverpool and Hamburg. Douglas Alexander, president of Singer, claimed he was estimating conservatively that his company did a gross business of one million dollars in Asiatic Turkey during a normal year.

A newer investment enterprise of Americans was participation in the installation of telephone systems in Constantinople by the Western Electric Company of Chicago, in cooperation with British and French firms. There were also small American investments in an American Trade Development Corporation founded at Smyrna in 1912 to develop imports of American-made goods to the Smyrna regions. Before the war this company was importing shoes, oil, leather, stoves, safes, drugs, and proprietary medicines.

During the prewar years sizable quantities of dates continued to arrive in the United States from the port of Muscat, in Oman, where there were an estimated four million trees. The choice hand-selected dates all went to America, particularly those grown in a mountain valley about seventy miles from Muscat. Records from the American consulate at Muscat tell of vessels from Salem and New Bedford leaving Muscat with cargoes of dates as far back as 1843, and the business is known to have existed before that time. The packers of Muscat were without exception agents of New York houses and refused to ship except to their principals. These packers aided in promoting importation

[18] *Ibid.*, pp. 19–21, 36–37; Wright, "United States Policy toward Egypt," pp. 235, 240–242.

of American products by serving as agents for various American firms. Another source of date shipment to the United States was the port of Basra on the Shatt-al-Arab from which three steamers a year customarily sailed for the United States. The total value of dates exported from Turkey to the United States in 1912 was nearly $600,000, rising the following year to more than $700,000.

Before the war nearly all figs imported into the United States came from Smyrna, amounting to about one third of the average annual crop of 25,000 tons. Owing to the competition from the California-grown Calimyrna substitute, some decline set in before the war. Nearly all Sultana raisins coming to the United States were shipped from Smyrna. Although Smyrna shipped raisin exports valued at $96,000 to the United States in 1913, this figure represented only one fifteenth of the district's total raisin exports.[19]

Although American commerce and investment were modest, there were great expectations for a bright future for American trade and capital in the Middle East. The reports of diplomatic and consular officials are filled with references to the possibilities, but at the same time, they were frequently extremely critical of the lack of initiative and the haphazard methods of American firms.[20]

A lively interest in commercial prospects was reflected in the establishment of the American Chamber of Commerce at Constantinople in 1911 and in the organization of steamship lines plying between Turkey and the United States. The American Chamber of Commerce set up branches in the major commercial centers, such as Smyrna, Beirut, Cairo, and Saloniki. The association claimed five hundred members in 1912 and desired to establish branches in the more important American commercial cities. To deal with American trade interests in the area, the chamber sponsored the quarterly *Levant Trade Review*, published in Constantinople beginning August 1, 1911.[21]

American trade with the Middle East was handicapped by dependence on foreign shipping during the latter part of the nineteenth century. In 1899, however, the Barber Steamship Company inaugurated direct service between New York and Turkish ports at rates substan-

[19] Campbell, "American Interests in Turkey," pp. 26, 27–29, 62–63, 64–65.

[20] "By a Diplomatist" [Lewis Einstein], *American Foreign Policy*, Chap. 6; Milo A. Jewett (consul, Trebizond, Turkey) to Philander C. Knox, April 8, 1911, DS 667.1117/—; William W. Rockhill to Knox, March 26, 1912, DS 667.1115/4.

[21] Campbell, "American Interests in Turkey," pp. 4–6.

tially below those of the British "shipping ring," which did not welcome the newcomer. Pressure from the British group eliminated the new company by 1902. During the ensuing decade other competition arose from German, Italian, and Greek companies, which set up direct or transshipment service between the United States and the eastern Mediterranean, although service was irregular. The licorice merchants, MacAndrews and Forbes, formed their own American Levant line in 1912 to carry their cargoes to the United States, but they also accepted general merchandise from other shippers. Their three steamers, of about seven thousand tons each, operated under the British flag, and although the service was irregular, one vessel sailed at least every six weeks from New York for Mediterranean and Black Sea ports. In 1914 the Hamburg-American Line established direct passenger and cargo service between New York and Constantinople, Smyrna, and Odessa. The fast service of this line gave importers in Constantinople their merchandise nineteen days after shipment from New York. Both lines ceased operation during World War I. The Cunard Lines acquired the ships of MacAndrews and Forbes, which were commandeered by the British government, while the Hamburg-American Line was unable to continue these routes during the war.[22]

Immigrants. Improved transportation during the prewar years also facilitated the emigration from the Ottoman Empire of thousands of Armenian, Syrian, and Greek subjects of the Sultan, the trickle becoming a stream following the Armenian troubles of the middle 1890s. Perhaps 16,000 Armenians had come to the United States from Turkey prior to 1899; they were joined by approximately 46,000 more between 1899 and 1914, in which period an estimated 86,000 Syrians entered the United States in addition to those 40,000 to 60,000 who had come before 1899.[23]

For the missionaries, the departure of so many from their native Christian flock was a sore trial. The long-time missionary resident of Syria, Dr. Henry H. Jessup, opined that "Syria is losing its best blood, its enterprising youth," while the American Board reports from the

[22] *Ibid.*, pp. 8–9, 68; Gordon, *American Relations with Turkey*, pp. 119–122; Charles M. Dickinson, "Reminiscences," pp. 50–55, Dickinson MSS.

[23] Malcom, *Armenians in America*, pp. 62–68. To the 46,000 Armenians from Turkey should be added approximately 6000 entering from other countries, notably Russia. Hitti, *Syrians in America*, pp. 62–65.

Anatolian stations and the Presbyterian Board reports from western Persia echoed similar complaints.[24]

Remittances sent home to relatives by those seeking their fortunes in the United States or elsewhere became a significant factor in the economic life of many communities. In the Harput district of Anatolia alone, an estimated $600,000 was received annually by relatives of Armenians who had gone to America. Oscar Campbell, an agent of the Department of Commerce, reported: "These emigrants keep vital the interest in American life and those who return to their native lands to live on the money which they have accumulated, form the nucleus of a very real and growing demand for American articles." No one knows how many immigrants from Turkey eventually returned to their homeland to stay, but the figure may be as high as 14 per cent. The diplomatic documents are full of specific cases growing out of the movement of these Ottoman minorities — passport cases, problems concerned with the protection of naturalized Americans of Ottoman origin returning to the empire, and questions of property, military service, and the like.[25]

Other Interests. American diplomats were also occupied with aiding the archaeological work of Americans in the Middle East. One sign of the cultural maturing of the United States by the early twentieth century was the development of graduate and professional education in a number of universities and the parallel expansion of such facilities as museums. These trends had a bearing in turn on American interests in the Middle East through sponsorship by American institutions of field studies into ancient civilizations. The American School for Oriental Studies in Jerusalem, established in 1900, conducted numerous excavations and served as a training school for archaeologists in Palestine. About 1908 Harvard University began excavations at Samaria. American-sponsored work in Syria, begun in 1899–1900, was continued by Princeton University during 1904 and 1905, with emphasis on standing architectural monuments, mainly of Roman and early Christian date, besides some Nabataean and a few Hellenistic buildings. Early American investigations in Mesopotamia (1889–1900) were not followed up

[24] Quotation from Brown, *100 Years*, pp. 998–999. See also ABC, *AR 1900*, p. 63.
[25] Campbell, "American Interests in Turkey," p. 10; Gordon, *American Relations with Turkey*, p. 311. For specific cases, see *FR 1900*, pp. 939–940; *FR 1901*, pp. 424, 519–521; *FR 1902*, pp. 1023–1025; *FR 1904*, pp. 656–657, 844–848; *FR 1905*, pp. 885–898; *FR 1906*, II, 1410–1412; *FR 1907*, II, 1063–1067; *FR 1908*, pp. 737–745, 757–759; *FR 1909*, pp. 558–562.

until after World War I, but in 1899 the great investigations in Egypt were begun under the auspices of the University of California, with surveys and diggings in southern Egypt both at town sites and in cemeteries. Three years later the expedition commenced the work at Giza, site of the Great Pyramids, which would occupy a generation. Harvard and the Boston Museum of Fine Arts took over the work in 1905 and continued it until the eve of World War II. The Metropolitan Museum of New York entered the Egyptian field in 1906 and contributed through the publication of pictures and inscriptions on many of the tombs at Thebes.

American diplomats found one of their new duties in smoothing the way for expeditions by securing the necessary excavation permits and handling other details. Archæologists saw the need for energetic and sympathetic support from American diplomatic officials, if they were to work with maximum effectiveness. Albert M. Lythgoe, Director of the Egyptian Expedition of the Metropolitan Museum of Art in New York, wrote President Woodrow Wilson from Luxor in 1913 that the new administration of Lord Kitchener threatened "to make certain sides of our work practically impossible." Lythgoe then interceded for the retention of the incumbent diplomatic agent, a young Harvard graduate, Peter Jay, because of his close interest and thorough familiarity with the Metropolitan Museum expedition. If Wilson contemplated a change, Lythgoe hoped he would appoint a man with comparable interest in antiquities. Archaeological work by Americans deserved national support, Lythgoe argued: "In many years of such work which I have had abroad, at first in Greece and then for the past fourteen years here in Egypt — the two countries where diplomatic appointments based on such an interest would seem peculiarly necessary and fitting — it has been only too apparent that rarely has any consideration been given, in the appointments that have been made, to this subject of chief importance in either country." Apparently Wilson did not heed Lythgoe's request, for Jay was soon transferred to Rome. His Cairo replacement was a Rhode Island businessman and politician with no special concern for antiquities.[26]

The antiquities of the Middle East also provided a stimulus for the

[26] Ann Perkins, "American Archaeology in the Near and Middle East," *Background of the Middle East,* Ernest Jackh, ed., pp. 212–216; Straus, *Under Four Administrations,* pp. 283–284; Griscom, *Diplomatically Speaking,* pp. 158–159; Lythgoe to Wilson, March 18, 1913, DS 883.927/ — ; *RDS 1914,* pp. 56, 87.

growing stream of American tourists who, thanks to improved steamship connections, annually visited the area. When Joseph C. Grew recalled his first foreign-service assignment with the consulate in Cairo (1904–1906), he still had "visions of portly females being pulled from in front and pushed from behind up the ledges of the big Pyramid of Cheops." Diplomatic memoirs give brief glimpses of visits from prominent public figures—Vice President and Mrs. Charles W. Fairbanks, Judge and Mrs. Alton B. Parker, Mrs. Grover Cleveland, and Kermit Roosevelt. During the tourist season parties of several hundreds would arrive from the United States. In small but growing numbers, Americans were taking a firsthand look at parts of the Middle East and carrying home their impressions to share with others.[27]

Another occasional contact stemmed from the traditional philanthropic predilections of Americans, who have so often rushed to help foreign peoples in time of disaster. Aside from the continuing efforts of American missionaries, the Italo-Turkish War of 1911–1912 and the later Balkan wars brought the American Red Cross into the field with the benediction of the American government and the active assistance of Ambassador William W. Rockhill.[28]

Nationalism and Revolution

Within the Ottoman Empire, Persia, and Egypt, there was deep dissatisfaction with the existing order among more articulate segments of the population comprising the small middle classes, especially those with a Western orientation—the non-Islamic minorities, military officers, and intellectuals. An autocratic, self-centered Sultan, obsessed with the preservation of his person and regime, presided over a polyglot empire which had been eroded along the edges for a century. His police-state methods, which vainly sought to insulate the empire from Western intellectual currents and technological advances, rankled many of his subjects who wanted to modernize Turkey. Among the Armenians especially, but also among Arabs, Zionist Jews, and Greeks, nationalist aspirations had caught hold and grown under the auspices of secret societies. The ever-present tensions among the welter of non-Islamic

[27] Grew, *TE*, I, 15 (quotation), 22–23; Straus, *Under Four Administrations*, pp. 298–299; Griscom, *Diplomatically Speaking*, pp. 160–161; Charles M. Dickinson, Inspection Report on the Constantinople Consulate, Oct. 24, 1907, Dickinson MSS.
[28] Paul A. Varg, *Open Door Diplomat: The Life of William W. Rockhill*, p. 116; FR 1912, p. xx.

religious groups, who felt the sting of inferior status, could not be overcome even by the *millet* system, which had long permitted a degree of accommodation among conflicting religious groups. The people of the Ottoman Empire were long-suffering victims of an oppressive bureaucracy little interested in their welfare.[29]

Persia suffered from the autocratic rule of the decadent Qajar dynasty, whose shahs had no qualms about mortgaging the country, its resources, and its people to outsiders, to advance their personal comfort and pleasure. Tribal and linguistic diversity would in any event have made centralized rule in Persia difficult, but religious differences and nationalistic aspirations may not have been so troublesome as in the Ottoman Empire. More serious in creating social discontent was the land system, vesting control in the hands of a small oligarchy, which showed little concern for the Persian peasants who worked the land for absentee landlords and had little opportunity in a closed social system. Egypt's masses suffered under grinding poverty and debilitization from disease, to which was added the humiliation of foreign domination — rule by the British since 1882.[30] Persian and Egyptian nationalists from the small middle class seized on foreign domination as the symbol of their inferior status. There was abroad in many parts of the Middle East, at least in urban areas, a ferment of discontent and a yearning for constitutions, representative assemblies, and the right to control the destinies of one's nation without reference to foreign interference.

The accumulating dissatisfaction erupted into revolution first in Persia, where Muzaffar al-Din Shah was forced to set up an assembly (Majlis) in 1906 and to sign a constitution on January 1, 1907, just before he died. The new Russophile Shah, Muhammad Ali, then organized a bloody counterrevolution which merged into a civil war between the Constitutionalists (Nationalists) and the Royalists. Not until the reopening of the Majlis in November, 1909, was the four-year struggle for constitutional government brought to an end.

[29] Ernest E. Ramsaur, Jr., *The Young Turks: Prelude to the Revolution of 1908, passim*; Dankwart A. Rustow, "The Army and the Founding of the Turkish Republic," *World Politics*, 11 (July 1959), 515–516. The Ottomans formalized the *millet* (nation) system allowing non-Moslem communities (Jewish, Greek, Armenian, and Protestant) a large measure of religious, cultural, legal, and quasi-political autonomy.

[30] Ann K. S. Lambton, *Landlord and Peasant in Persia: A Study of Land Tenure and Land Revenue Administration*, pp. 150–181; William S. Haas, *Iran*, pp. 29–39, 137; Percy Sykes, *A History of Persia*, II, Chaps. 80–84 *passim*; H. Wood Jarvis, *Pharaoh to Farouk*, Chap. 30.

One might expect that Americans and their government would applaud the movement as exemplifying the aspirations of 1776, which had long been associated with the reputation of the United States abroad. But from Washington came not the slightest hint of moral support for the revolutionaries. Official interest was shown only when the revolution touched on such traditional concerns as recognition, asylum, nonintervention, or threats to American lives or property. Presbyterian missionaries, however, recoiled from the unbending policy of their government, for their instincts and traditions inclined them to protect the helpless and distressed victims of this civil war. Howard Baskerville, a twenty-one-year-old Princeton graduate who taught at the Presbyterian school in Tabriz, persisted in actively aiding the Constitutionalists even after warnings from the American consul and mission officials. He resigned his teaching post to follow the dictates of his conscience. In April of 1909 he was killed while leading a futile charge on a Royalist barricade. Local Constitutionalists looked on Baskerville as a martyr, but no official tears were shed in Washington.[31]

Professor Yeselson has noted that the neutral attitude of the State Department did not accord with the new dynamism in American foreign policy proclaimed in McKinley's second inaugural and often subsequently by Theodore Roosevelt. Justice for the nearby Cubans in 1898 was one thing; for the distant Persians a decade later another. "It was apparent in the Persian instance, however, that America's more positive role in world affairs in the twentieth century did not include the translation of such pro-democratic sentiments into an official policy of encouragement for revolutionary movements overseas." Idealism aside, the United States was in no position to assist the revolution even if aid or intervention had been considered a desirable policy. Persia was already under the influence of Russia in the north and of Great Britain in the south pursuant to the Anglo-Russian settlement of 1907.[32]

Simultaneously, army officers of the Ottoman Empire, organized into secret societies, were plotting governmental changes in Constantinople. During the Young Turk Revolution of July, 1908, the wily old Sultan

[31] Yeselson, *USPDR*, pp. 86–87; see also Sykes, *History of Persia*, II, Chaps. 82 and 83. The classic account is Edward G. Browne, *The Persian Revolution of 1905–1909*. Fifty years after Baskerville's death a joint United States and Iranian memorial celebration took place in Tabriz (April 1959).

[32] Yeselson, *USPDR*, Chap. 4 (quotation p. 88); *FR 1906*, II, 1216–1218. See also Dexter Perkins, *The Evolution of American Foreign Policy*, p. 55.

saved his throne temporarily by reinstituting the Constitution of 1876. Then came his failure to undo the revolutionary movement in the spring of 1909 and his deposition in favor of Mehmed V. Efforts by the Young Turks in the Committee of Union and Progress to reform Turkey foundered, and the promise of the revolution was soon dissipated. Initially, a great wave of optimism swept over the Americans in Turkey, at early evidences that the old order had indeed passed. Diplomats, missionaries, and others commented in amazement at the camaraderie shown by former religious and racial antagonists. A few Americans familiar with the country expressed reservations about whether daybreak had actually dawned in Turkey. Dr. Clarence Ussher of the Van mission recalled telling a Brooklyn audience in October of 1908 while on home leave that "the slogan of the Young Turk Party was 'Turkey for the Turks'; that its friendship with Christians was a friendship of expediency; within five years there would be a reaction followed by the worst massacre the country had ever known."[33]

President Taft commented in his annual message of December 7, 1909, on "the quick transition of the Government of the Ottoman Empire from one of retrograde tendencies to a constitutional government with a Parliament and with progressive modern policies of reform and public improvement," which he viewed as "one of the important phenomena of our time." In the same message he also applauded the apparent further advance of constitutional government in Persia. "These events," he said, "have turned the eyes of the world upon the Near East." What Taft saw of significance for the United States in these events was the expectation that the new conditions would allow us to "obtain a greater share of the commerce of the Near East." He returned to the same theme in his 1911 annual message when referring to the desire of the new regime in Turkey for closer relations with the United States.[34]

No substantial evidence has yet been forthcoming to indicate that the United States government or its people extended any tangible sym-

[33] Joseph K. Greene, *Leavening the Levant*, pp. 38–44; *FR 1908*, pp. 745–754; *FR 1909*, 562–594; Strong, *Story of the American Board*, pp. 407–408; Barton, *Daybreak in Turkey*, pp. 282–287, 291–300; George E. White, *Adventuring with Anatolia College*, pp. 65–66, 69; Mary Mills Patrick, *Under Five Sultans*, pp. 206–209; Patrick, *Bosporus Adventure*, pp. 134–140; Gates, *Not to Me Only*, p. 189; ABC, *AR 1908*, pp. 52–53; Ussher and Knapp, *American Physician*, p. 165; *MRW*, 31 (Sept. 1908), 641–642; (Oct. 1908), 743–748; (Nov. 1908), 805–806, 844–850; (Dec. 1908), 885–886, 945–946; 32 (Jan. 1909), 32–35; (Feb. 1909), 147; (March 1909), 162–163; (Aug. 1909), 562–563; (Dec. 1909), 948.

[34] *FR 1909*, pp. xiii–xiv; *FR 1911*, p. x.

pathy to Egyptian nationalists protesting the British role in their affairs. In fact, when former President Theodore Roosevelt emerged from the jungles of Africa in 1910 to appear publicly in Cairo, he commended British rule in Egypt as a service to civilization. He took a dim view of Egyptian nationalism, arguing that the Egyptians were far from ready to stand on their own feet.[35]

Of the three most significant nationalist movements (excluding the Macedonian-Bulgarian opposition) challenging the integrity of the Ottoman Empire — Armenian, Zionist, and Arab — American sympathies were most closely bound up in prewar years with the Armenian aspirations because of this Christian minority's close association with American missionaries. American opinion, insofar as there was any, held that the Turks treated the Armenians badly, that the Armenians were the backbone of the Empire and its most progressive element, and that it was appropriate to protest officially against their treatment. But it seems unlikely that the missionaries actively participated in any Armenian plots, even though Turkish officials frequently claimed they did. Rather, their support was indirect in that they educated many Armenians in Western ways and encouraged their pride in their language, religion, and cultural heritage. There is some evidence that Armenian extremists held it against the missionaries that they refrained from overtly and actively supporting the movement for Armenian independence. Extremists may even have instigated attacks on missionaries in order to elicit foreign intervention.[36]

American policy regarding Palestine continued to emphasize the status of resident Jews holding American citizenship. The American immigration law of 1907, however, jeopardized the position of naturalized American Jews in Palestine by requiring them to register, in order to ascertain whether they had resided in the United States long enough to entitle them to American protection. For humanitarian reasons, Consul Thomas R. Wallace managed to delay the registration three years. He knew that if the Jews were denied American protection, they would

[35] Straus, *Under Four Administrations*, pp. 287–291. For an interesting analysis of Roosevelt's utterances in the Sudan, Egypt, and England on British imperialism in Egypt, see David H. Burton, "Theodore Roosevelt and Egyptian Nationalism," *Mid-America*, 41 (April 1959), 88–103. For Roosevelt's views over a period of years, see Morison, *Roosevelt Letters*, III, 105; IV, 138, 773, 775; VI, 1370; VII, 65, 350–351, 402–403, 546; *Correspondence of Roosevelt and Lodge*, II, 198.

[36] Dennis, *Adventures*, pp. 448–450; 457–458; Gordon, *American Relations with Turkey*, p. 224; Earle in *Foreign Affairs*, 7:402–408.

be subjected to prosecution by Ottoman authorities. After the Young Turks came into power, they fought hard against the consular protection of American Jews.

Zionism, a negligible factor within American Jewry in 1900, now began to attract a few more adherents. When Zionists tried to elicit some show of sympathy from the State Department, they encountered a stone wall of negativism explainable probably not so much by anti-Semitism, as Professor Frank Manuel has suggested, but more by the feeling that the political overtones of the Zionist movement would conflict with the American policy of noninvolvement in Turkish affairs. The department knew about but took little notice of the significant growth of the new Zionist agricultural communities in Palestine shortly before the war. It is possible to agree with this much of Manuel's conclusion: "The United States had no strategic plans which involved the Near East and could assume a position of noninterference in the political affairs of Turkey. . . . The Jewish problem in Palestine was extraneous, a nuisance; it had . . . come to implicate the United States in a battle of abstract principles with which no hard national interests were associated."[37]

Even more tenuous were American contacts with the underground Arab nationalist movement of this era. Decades earlier, American missionaries and educators had spurred the revival of classical Arabic literature and thereby helped lay the groundwork for modern Arab nationalism. Nationalist groups groping for a program in the early twentieth century were attracted by the idealized version of the United States as a country which had severed colonial ties with Great Britain and espoused a government based on the natural rights of men. Life, liberty, and the pursuit of happiness, the clarion call of the Declaration of Independence, seemed to have relevance to Arabs as they began to proclaim their aspiration to be masters of their own destiny. America's meaning for them was symbolized in the Statue of Liberty. The Lebanese-American poet, Ameen Rihani, caught the spirit in these verses reputedly memorized by high school students in the Lebanon. Turning to the Statue, he said:

> When will you turn your face toward
> the East, O, Liberty?

[37] Manuel, *American-Palestine Relations*, pp. 88–116 (quotation, p. 116).

Shall the future never see a statue
of freedom near the Pyramids?
Would it be possible for us to behold
your sister over the Mediterranean Sea?[38]

The United States and the Eastern Question

The Great Powers were not indifferent to signs of unrest in the Balkans and the Middle East, for what happened in these areas could seriously affect the balance of power. In contrast, the administration of Theodore Roosevelt took no positive steps during the Balkan crisis of 1908. Three years later, when the Italo-Turkish War broke out and Italy set about acquiring the nominal Ottoman province of Libya, the Taft administration gave some thought to playing the role of mediator. The State Department received many petitions urging that the United States intervene to restore peace. The day the war began, former Ambassador Straus advised Secretary Knox to offer mediation, and subsequent requests were issued by the American Peace Union, the Archaeological Institute of America, the American Board of Commissioners for Foreign Missions, the Massachusetts Peace Society, the Boston Patriotic Association, the W.C.T.U., the League of Peace, the Law and Order Union of New York State, the World Peace Foundation, the Men and Religion Forward Movement, and the New Hampshire Peace Society as well as from a number of private persons. President Taft wrote Knox in December, 1911, of his willingness to discuss American mediation, but the State Department dissuaded and even discouraged a formal Turkish request to mediate. Nearly a year later Taft reopened the possibility of mediation but found the State Department still opposed. Assistant Secretary Huntington Wilson observed that the Near East was so peculiarly a European field that there might be general irritation at the prospect of the United States injecting itself into the situation. Wilson warned that it would be inadvisable to give Europe any excuse for interference in the Western Hemisphere. When the Italians bombarded Beirut in 1912, however, the American college increased its store of good will by serving as a place of refuge.[39]

[38] Nabih A. Faris, "The United States' Image of the Near East As Seen from That Region," p. 9, mimeographed paper delivered at the Princeton University Conference on the United States' Image of the Near East, April 15, 1959.

[39] William C. Askew and J. Fred Rippy, "The United States and Europe's Strife, 1908–1913," *Journal of Politics*, 4 (Feb. 1942), pp. 69–75; William C. Askew,

Hardly had Turkey come to terms with Italy when the Balkan allies resorted to war in seeking to free more of the peninsula from the vestiges of Turkish rule. The State Department, aware of the explosive possibilities in the Balkan situation, instructed Ambassador Rockhill to turn down a Turkish request for American mediation on grounds that the United States had never been involved in the political problems of the area. He was told to stand on the position outlined by the department the previous year when mediation had been advanced and rejected. The administration failed to perceive the relevance of the balance of power in Europe, unlike Theodore Roosevelt during the first Moroccan crisis of 1905–1906 when the United States participated in the Algeciras Conference.[40]

During these Balkan Wars of 1912 and 1913, the United States joined the powers in sending warships to protect Western nationals and their interests. Christians worried about possible Turkish massacres should the Bulgarians march on Constantinople. President Taft's report on these events in his annual message of December 3, 1912, reflected the official attitude of his country:

The United States has happily been involved neither directly nor indirectly with the causes or questions incident to any of these hostilities and has maintained in regard to them an attitude of absolute neutrality and of complete political disinterestedness. In the second war in which the Ottoman Empire has been engaged the loss of life and the consequent distress on both sides have been appalling, and the United States has found occasion, in the interest of humanity, to carry out the charitable desires of the American people, to extend a measure of relief to the sufferers on either side through the impartial medium of the Red Cross. Beyond this the chief care of the Government of the United States has been to make due provision for the protection of its nationals resident in belligerent territory.

He explained that in discharging the latter duties, he had despatched a special-service squadron of two armored cruisers to assist in whatever measures the interested nations might adopt for safeguarding foreign lives and property if events should endanger them. With a large fleet of European warships in the Bosporus, American cruisers were left free

Europe and Italy's Acquisition of Libya, pp. 163–164, 241–242; Varg, *Open Door Diplomat*, pp. 114–116; Penrose, *AUB*, pp. 147–149; FR 1913, pp. 1310–1339.
[40] Ernst Christian Helmreich, *The Diplomacy of the Balkan Wars, 1912–1913*, pp. 200–201; Howard K. Beale, *Theodore Roosevelt and the Rise of America to World Power*, pp. 355–389.

to remain along the Mediterranean coasts "should any unexpected contingency arise affecting the numerous American interests in the neighborhood of Smyrna and Beirut."[41]

The Shuster Mission to Persia

The internal situation in Persia, meanwhile, had stabilized to the point where Persian reformers solicited foreign advisers to straighten out their chaotic and antiquated fiscal arrangements. From their overtures resulted the mission of W. Morgan Shuster in 1911, the first of three similar missions to Persia headed by Americans between 1911 and 1945.[42]

Persian officials had made suggestions to the United States toward securing economic assistance as early as the 1880s, but nothing came of their hopes for attracting American capital to assist in developing their resources. The idea that Americans might come to Persia's rescue was revived during the revolutionary period of the early twentieth century, for only the United States met the fundamental requirement of having no political ambitions in Persia. Persian overtures to Minister Charles W. Russell in 1910 were opposed by Russia as a threat to Russian domination in northern Persia, sanctioned by Great Britain in the 1907 agreement. Baron Roman R. Rosen, Russian ambassador to the United States, emphasized his government's feeling that the United States should respect the predominance of Russia and Great Britain in Persia. Even before Rosen's protests, the department had taken a cool attitude toward Persian requests for American advisers. Then, in September of 1910, American officials saw a chance to trade compliance with Russia for pledges of Russian and British noninterference with American efforts to expand trade and investment in Turkey and the Far East. Nothing would be lost, said Assistant Secretary Wilson, who argued that "our interests in Persia seem about as near nothing as our interest anywhere can be and it is no place for us to waste ammunition, and it would be the veriest folly to irritate any government over a Persian question."[43]

Then quite suddenly, under British coaxing, Russia withdrew her opposition to the appointment of American advisers, and Minister

[41] *FR 1912*, pp. xix–xx; 1341–1354.
[42] Yeselson, *USPDR*, pp. 106–128; Curti and Birr, *Prelude to Point Four*, pp. 74–80; *FR 1911*, pp. 678–686. See also Sykes, *History of Persia*, II, 423–426.
[43] Quoted in Yeselson, *USPDR*, p. 109.

Russell forwarded a formal request from the Persian government. Assistant Secretary Alvey A. Adee shied away from lending American government officials or in any way assuming international responsibility for selecting private persons. He tried to maintain the fiction of American willingness to help Persia by suggesting that London bankers might recommend appropriate experts and the State Department would forward the names. Russell bristled at such a suggestion, pointing out that the Persians did not want advisers proposed by the British. Meanwhile, the Persian minister to the United States had been carrying out instructions by seeking Americans to serve as Treasurer-General and financial assistants. W. Morgan Shuster had learned of the opening and made a formal application to President Taft, which the president forwarded to Secretary Knox with his comments on the importance of well-run governments abroad as an incentive for American investments. Taft was not willing to side-step the issue and thus forced the hand of his State Department.

When the names of Shuster and four assistants were submitted to the Persians, the Majlis approved the selection on February 2, 1911, and consented to three-year contracts for the Americans. The State Department took pains to impress on Shuster and his assistants that they were employees of the Persian government "and in no way represented" the United States government. Shuster, his assistants, and their families arrived at Teheran on May 12, 1911.

Though only thirty-five years old, Shuster already had experience in the Cuban and Philippine customs service (1899–1905), and as Philippine Secretary of Public Instruction (1906–1908). When appointed Treasurer-General of Persia, he was a practicing attorney in Washington. His assistants were also young men ranging in age from thirty to forty-two, three of them with experience in either the Philippine or Cuban customs service, or in both. The American mission started auspiciously with the Persians expecting great accomplishments from the experts. Since there was no organized system of finance, Shuster asked for and obtained from the Majlis a law on June 13, 1911, giving him as Treasurer-General "full and complete powers in the handling of finances." Shuster interpreted literally the Anglo-Russian pledge of 1907 to uphold Persian sovereignty. Russia in particular and Great Britain to a lesser degree found Shuster's new broom unacceptable, fearing a clean sweep would interfere with their special positions. When

Shuster's treasury *gendarmerie* carried out orders from the Persian government to seize properties of the deposed shah's brothers, Russia, which had despatched troops to Azerbaijan in 1909, had intervened and sent additional troops into northern Persia by early November, 1911. At first the Majlis expressed its confidence in the Shuster mission by authorizing the hiring of ten more Americans, but when the British advised Persian authorities not to resist Russian pressure any longer, Persia found further resistance difficult. On November 29, Russia demanded Shuster's dismissal, an ultimatum unanimously rejected by the Majlis. At this point, the deposed cabinet carried out a coup and then accepted Russian demands. Shuster departed on January 11, 1912, leaving behind, in the words of Professor Yeselson "a legacy of unselfish devotion to Persia's interest which made him the idol of patriotic Persians, who, in turn, had demonstrated their courage and willingness to endure sacrifices behind such leadership."[44]

Despite this affront to American prestige, the Department of State adhered to its policy of strict nonintervention. It rejected appeals from the Persian government for support from the United States at the time of the Russian ultimatums. Neither Secretary Knox nor the House of Representatives (which had received an appeal from the Majlis) indicated that a finger would be lifted to help either Shuster or Persia. In the United States there was some public criticism of the abject surrender to the amoral forces of power politics. Petitions to Congress and articles in several periodicals reflected the regret at the do-nothing attitude of Washington. Official support of Shuster and his assistants extended only to responsibility for their safety as American citizens, not to charging Persia with breach of their contracts.

The Shuster episode was the first important nonmissionary incident in Persian-American relations. The vigor and integrity of the young Americans in trying to help Persia modernize its fiscal administration was long remembered by Persian elements sympathetic to reform, and Persians would turn again to American financial advisers. Although American policy remained staunchly noninterventionist, the net result actually seemed to be the enhancement of American prestige in Persia. At the same time, Persia's prestige in the United States was increased, as a weak nation fighting to redeem itself from the forces of imperialism. Shuster contributed further to the favorable image of Persia with his

[44] Quotations from *ibid.*, pp. 113, 114, 115–116.

book published in 1912, *The Strangling of Persia*. Indicative of the tenor of his account is his subtitle: *Story of the European Diplomacy and Oriental Intrigue That Resulted in the Denationalization of Twelve Million Mohammedans, A Personal Narrative.*

Diplomatic Organization and Representation

Although the United States government made no fundamental long-range alterations in its Middle Eastern policies between the turn of the century and 1914, the diplomatic apparatus for looking after American interests in the area was expanded. The legation at Constantinople had finally been elevated to an embassy in 1906, when John G. A. Leishman realized his ambition to become the first American ambassador to the Ottoman Empire. Among his successors were Oscar S. Straus, William W. Rockhill, and Henry Morgenthau, Sr., all men well above the average diplomatic appointee in that era. Within the Empire, Beirut and Smyrna had been elevated to consulates-general by 1914 to supplement the Constantinople consulate-general. While the consulates at Alexandretta and Erzerum had been downgraded (only consular agents were designated there), new posts had been opened by 1914 at Aleppo, Mersina, and Trebizond, and the older stations had been maintained at Baghdad, Harput, Jerusalem, and Sivas. In Persia the American minister functioned also as consul-general at Teheran, and a consular post had been added at Tabriz. The work of the consulate-general in Cairo was now supplemented by a consulate at Alexandria.[45]

As part of a reorganization of the State Department under Secretary Elihu Root toward the close of the Roosevelt administration, several geographical divisions were set up within the department in 1908 and 1909. Not until President Taft and Secretary Knox took over was the Division of Near Eastern Affairs created on December 13, 1909. The first chief of the division, Evan E. Young, outlined the duties of his office in January, 1911, as reading, digesting, and routing all correspondence pertaining to the area; studying the political, economic, and international questions in the various countries; advising with accurate and precise information the assistant secretary of state on matters pertaining to the Near East. Young specifically mentioned the familiarity of the division's officials with Near Eastern conditions

[45] *RDS 1914*, pp. 49, 51–52.

gained by previous service there and by careful study of current literature. Among the duties handled by the division alone or in consultation with the Solicitor, the Bureau of Trade Relations, or with other bureaus and divisions, were the preparatory work in the negotiation or revision of treaties and conventions, and rendering diplomatic assistance to American commercial enterprises that desired to begin or expand operations in those countries.[46] Despite Young's emphasis on economic interests, the protection of American religious, educational, medical, and charitable institutions undoubtedly occupied the energies of the division most heavily.

Conclusion

During these early years of the present century when the Middle East experienced the surge of revolutionary currents within and bristled at interference from without, American policy adhered for the most part to the traditional objective of noninvolvement in the internal and international politics of the area. To the American State Department the Middle East was an extension of Europe, and the traditional isolation from European politics still seemed the best guide for American policy. Yet the old policy often proved inadequate when it precluded the use of means to ensure stronger protection to American interest groups then active in the region.

[46] Graham H. Stuart, *American Diplomatic and Consular Practice*, p. 95; Graham H. Stuart, *The Department of State: A History of Its Organization, Procedure and Personnel*, pp. 216–217; "The Division of Near Eastern Affairs," *The American Foreign Service Journal*, 10 (Jan. 1933), 16–18.

3

DOLLAR DIPLOMACY IN TURKEY:
THE CHESTER PROJECT, 1908–1913

☆ EARLY IN THE TWENTIETH CENTURY, Admiral Colby M. Chester and associates developed a gigantic program for railroad and mining ventures in Asiatic Turkey.[1] They were beguiled by a vision of great commercial and industrial possibilities for Americans in the Ottoman Empire, a mirage similar to that which had already fostered great expectations for American economic enterprise in Latin America and the Far East. In all three instances, the advocates were optimistic about foreign markets for American industrial surpluses.[2]

Had the ambitions of the Chester syndicate materialized, they might well have altered the course of American relations with the Middle East, and even the course of Turkish history. Although fated to be a colossal and embarrassing failure, the project and its relations with the Taft administration offer a revealing chapter in American diplomatic and business history. In assisting the Chester interests the Department of State departed drastically, but only temporarily, from traditional noninvolvement in the international politics of the Eastern Question.

When Admiral Chester began to investigate economic possibilities in the Ottoman Empire, American interests there were still largely humanitarian. Political, military, and strategic concerns on the part of the United States were nonexistent, business investments negligible, and trade during the nineteenth century was modest. Precisely because

[1] This chapter is a slightly altered version of my "A Railroad for Turkey: The Chester Project of 1908–1913," *Business History Review*, 33 (Autumn 1959), 300–329.

[2] "By a Diplomatist" [Lewis Einstein], *American Foreign Policy*, pp. 146–147, 155–156; J. Fred Rippy, *The Caribbean Danger Zone*, p. 135; Charles S. Campbell, Jr., *Special Business Interests and the Open Door Policy*, Chap. 1; Russell H. Bastert, "James G. Blaine and the Origins of the First International American Conference," unpublished Ph.D. dissertation, Yale University, 1952, Chap. 8.

the United States had a humanitarian record uncompromised by any vital political stake or ambition in Turkey, American prestige was high among the Turks, who were receptive to expanding commercial and financial ties with American businessmen.[3]

Dollar Diplomacy and the Eastern Question

Chester's plans took shape at a time when American businessmen were finding sympathy and support in Washington for their foreign enterprises. President Taft and Secretary of State Philander C. Knox were proud to use the resources of government to promote Dollar Diplomacy, an ambiguous concept with invidious connotations, at least for later generations. As Knox expressed it, "Today diplomacy works for trade, and the Foreign Offices of the world are powerful engines for the promotion of commerce of each country. With the expansion of American commerce it became imperative that American exporters should have equally efficient support from their government."[4]

When it came to Turkey, both the policy-makers in Washington and American businessmen exhibited dilettantism. At best, they comprehended only vaguely the nature of Great Power politics in the Ottoman setting. For several decades the Ottoman Empire, already stereotyped as the "sick man of Europe," had languished in the throes of disintegration. As the Empire fell apart, the desire of each of six European Powers (Great Britain, France, Germany, Italy, Austria-Hungary, and Russia) to prevent a competitor from improving its position enabled the Ottoman Empire to survive a little longer by playing off one rival against another.[5] These rivals did not welcome the appearance of the United States.

Not so with the Young Turks who had gained power in the revolution of July, 1908, when they forced the Sultan to institute a parliamentary regime full of bright but unrealized promise for a better Turkey. Among

[3] Gordon, *American Relations with Turkey*, pp. 221–251; Sousa, *The Capitulatory Régime*, Chap. 7.

[4] [Philander C. Knox], Memorandum on the State Department [March, 1909], Philander C. Knox MSS, Vol. VI, p. 949. See also Henry Pringle, *The Life and Times of William Howard Taft, A Biography*, II, 678–699 and *passim*. The dual nature of Dollar Diplomacy is stressed in Julius W. Pratt, *America's Colonial Experiment: How the United States Gained, Governed, and in Part Gave Away a Colonial Empire*, pp. 131–132. See also Rippy, *Caribbean Danger Zone*, pp. 134–136.

[5] Ramsaur, *The Young Turks*, pp. 140–143; Earle, *The Bagdad Railway*, *passim*, especially pp. 3–8, Chaps. 2 and 9.

their plans for modernizing their country, the Young Turks placed economic development high on the list, with proposals for extensive railroad and highway construction, port development, irrigation projects, public utilities, and mineral exploitation. Turkey's appalling lack of native capital and managerial skill required her to look abroad for assistance. While the Turks did not lack bids from Europeans anxious to pour capital into the country, they suspected that the European financial groups intended to advance their interests and their governments at the expense of Turkey. Because the American position was uniquely disinterested, many Turks saw an opportunity to use American capital as a possible counterweight for European political ambitions.[6]

Launching the Project and Eliminating Competition

Admiral Chester's belief that Turkey afforded great opportunities for American entrepreneurs had begun to crystallize as early as 1900 when, as captain of the U.S.S. *Kentucky,* he was sent to press payment of American claims for property damaged during the Armenian massacres. Several years later the Admiral's views were reinforced by the enthusiasm of C. Arthur Moore, Jr., who had visited Turkey in 1906 and returned with a scheme for a railroad from Aleppo to the Mediterranean coast near Alexandretta. Moore persuaded his brother-in-law, Colby M. Chester, Jr., son of the Admiral, to join him, and the two gained the support of their fathers. The elder Moore, a partner in Manning, Maxwell, and Moore, a railroad supply company, possessed the business standing necessary to enlist financial support for the project. At this time, the younger Chester was treasurer of Manning, Maxwell, and Moore. The Admiral's other son, Commander Arthur Chester, was to assist in the preliminary surveys for the contemplated line.[7]

The available records, though leaving some obvious questions unanswered, are sufficient to delineate the origins of the syndicate. In

[6] Milo A. Jewett (consul at Trebizond, Turkey) to the Assistant Secretary of State, April 10 and June 23, 1909, DS 5012/16–18 and 19–20; Lewis Einstein (chargé d'affaires, Constantinople) to Knox, July 15 and July 29, 1909, DS 20784/— and 5012/21. See also Gordon, *American Relations with Turkey,* pp. 252–256, 264; Earle, *Bagdad Railway,* pp. 13, 19.
[7] *FR 1901,* pp. 514–515; *DAB,* XXI, 171; Griscom, *Diplomatically Speaking,* pp. 169–173; Laurence Shaw Mayo, "The Chester Concession under Fire," *Asia,* 23 (July 1923), 521; James M. Laidlaw to Knox, Nov. 24, 1909, DS 5012/31–32. The elder Chester had retired from the Navy as a rear admiral in 1906. Arthur Chester retired in 1905.

the summer of 1908, the Admiral represented the United States in Geneva at the Ninth International Conference of Geographers. With the approval of the State and Navy Departments, he then journeyed to Constantinople for the express purpose of investigating American commercial possibilities in the Ottoman Empire. On this mission he represented not only the Chester and Moore interests, but acted as an agent of the Boston and New York chambers of commerce and the New York State Board of Trade. The Admiral's original contacts were with Sultan Abdul Hamid, but after the revolution of 1908–1909, he had to negotiate with the Young Turk regime.[8]

The original plan for an American-built railroad from Aleppo to the Mediterranean ran into trouble when German interests protested that the line would traverse an area already assigned to their Berlin-to-Baghdad project.[9] Encouraged, however, by the cordial reception the Young Turks had given the Admiral's overtures, the Chester interests in the next few months enlarged their plan into a more ambitious program of railroad building and mineral development.

By the late summer of 1909 the Chester syndicate had applied for concessions to cover lines eastward from Sivas in central Anatolia by way of Harput, Arghana, Diarbekir, Mosul, and Kirkuk to Sulaimaniya near the Persian border. Branch lines were projected from the main line to the Black Sea port of Samsun, to the Mediterranean via Aleppo, and to Van via Bitlis. These lines, comprising at least two thousand kilometers, would have entailed expenditures estimated at more than a hundred million dollars. The projected routes ran through areas reputedly rich in minerals, which the enterprisers intended to exploit along the railroad rights of way. A major attraction for some of the participants lay in the prospects for the sale of railroad construction equipment and rolling stock.[10]

[8] Robert Bacon to Diplomatic Officers of the United States in Europe, April 8, 1908, DS 2793/11A; C. A. Moore (president of Manning, Maxwell, and Moore) to Secretary of State Elihu Root, Oct. 14, 1908; Root to V. H. Metcalf (Secretary of the Navy), Oct. 20, 1908, both DS 16251/–. The business records of the Chester syndicate are in the possession of Mr. Henry Woodhouse of New York City, but he has not made them available to scholars. (Correspondence of the writer with Mr. Woodhouse between 1952 and 1957, and an interview in 1955.)

[9] Einstein to Knox, July 15, 1909, DS 20784/–.

[10] Einstein to Knox, Aug. 27, 1909; Straus to Knox, Sept. 23, 1909; A. Rustem (Ottoman chargé in Washington) to Knox, Dec. 21, 1909, DS 5012/25–26, 29, and 39. During the protracted negotiations with Turkish officials, the exact lines to be included in the Chester Project underwent frequent revision. (Henry Janes — chargé, Constantinople — to Knox, April 1, 1910, DS 867.602 Ot 81/13.) Russia objected to

Actually, the Chester associates were not the first Americans to express interest in railroad lines for Asia Minor. Dr. Bruce Glasgow, representing the Anglo-American firm of J. G. White and Company, had applied earlier (July, 1909) for most of the same lines. Glasgow, furthermore, had filed his claims with the American Embassy in Constantinople and received diplomatic assistance from embassy officials, who reported that the White company was making good progress with the Turks during the summer.

Under these circumstances, the pique of embassy officials with Arthur Chester, Constantinople agent of the Chester interests, is understandable. Previously, the embassy had helped him pursue the more modest Aleppo-Mediterranean railroad scheme and an application for installing a telephone system in Constantinople. But he did not consult with the embassy during the early stages of negotiation for the expanded project. Even when he finally confronted Lewis Einstein, American chargé, with the news that he had applied for many of the same lines the White company was seeking, Chester did not formally file his new claims with the embassy, although Einstein agreed to introduce him to appropriate Turkish officials.[11]

For his part, Arthur Chester believed his plans for American enterprise in Turkey were being obstructed from all sides. Some of his sponsors at home questioned his application for additional lines in Asia Minor. Chester complained also that Glasgow of the White company was spreading information that he was a fraud, that Einstein and the embassy were plotting with Glasgow against him, and that the Turkish press was attacking his proposals unfairly. To his father he wrote: "I hate to think what I will do if I am not backed at home. I have staked my honor on our desire to take this option." He would have to bury himself "on a lonely island away from mankind" if he were not backed. "I absolutely have to carry this through. There is no turning back."[12]

the invasion of her sphere in northern Anatolia by the Sivas-Samsun branch, which the Ottoman government eventually withdrew from the Chester plans. There was extended controversy over the Mediterranean terminal with the syndicate insisting on Suediah, while the Turks held out for Alexandretta or Yourmoutalik on the opposite side of the bay.

[11] Einstein to Knox, July 15, July 29, Aug. 5, and Aug. 27, 1909, DS 20784/—, 5012/21, 20784/1, 5012/25–26.

[12] Arthur Chester to Admiral Colby M. Chester, Aug. 29, 1909, Chester Family MSS.

The competition between two American groups for the same lines embarrassed the State Department, which feared the rivalry might jeopardize the favorable disposition of the Turks toward American capital. Einstein informed his Washington superiors that he tried to support Glasgow, whose success, he believed, would mean a great victory for American enterprise and prestige in the Middle East. When the Chester interests spurned Einstein's urging that they come to an agreement with the White company, the chargé felt he must support both groups diplomatically without partiality, leaving Turkish officials to decide between them.

The upshot of the Chester-Glasgow competition was the virtual elimination of the White company by late summer. The Chesters would accept terms more favorable to Turkey — a broad-gauge instead of a narrow-gauge line, and a land grant of ten kilometers instead of twenty on either side of the railway. But on August 20, the Turkish parliament's Committee on Public Works postponed action to allow additional bidding. The Turks knew how to drive a hard bargain and were maneuvering for the most advantageous terms. Moreover, the granting of the railroad concessions had become a factional issue in Turkish politics.[13]

This was the state of affairs in September, 1909, when Ambassador Oscar S. Straus arrived in Constantinople for his third mission. His despatch summarizing the scramble for concessions indicated that many agents — some American, some not — were claiming to represent American interests in seeking contracts for public utilities from the Turkish government. Many an operator without capital was making a play for big financial returns in Turkey at this time.

Straus pressed the department repeatedly to improve the chaotic system by requiring that all American companies desiring to apply for concessions make their plans known initially in Washington, where the department could ascertain whether they were bona fide American companies, investigate their financial standing, and decide what support they were entitled to from the department's agents in the field. Improved procedures, he thought, might mitigate the disadvantage of American merchants and manufacturers in competing with their European counterparts. The latter sent to Turkey representatives who were usually connected with their firms as managers or part owners. In con-

---

[13] Einstein to Knox, July 15, July 29, Aug. 27, and Sept. 16, 1909; Straus to Knox, Sept. 23, 1909, DS 20784/–, 5012/21, 25–26, 28, and 29.

trast, American concession-seekers and contractors were too often represented by "commercial soldiers of fortune," that is, men not directly connected with the firms they represented, and "who seek concessions or contracts, with some kind of arrangement or understanding with American concerns, which pay a fixed sum or commission to such agents and then endeavor to organize a company to finance the concession and, if successful, arrange to carry on the work required."[14]

Straus may well have made his recommendation on the basis of his early experience with the Chester syndicate. In his view the Admiral was a soldier of fortune, intent on arranging an understanding with several important American concerns for financing the railroad and mining venture if a concession could be obtained from the Ottoman authorities. As for Arthur Chester, Straus complained that he had no conception of the proper limits of official assistance. Arthur's feeling that his various adversaries had hatched a plot against him made it difficult for the embassy to deal with him. Straus's efforts to convince Chester of the desirability of harmonizing his conflicting interest with the White group's were as little heeded as Einstein's had been.[15]

The Ottoman-American Development Company

By the autumn of 1909, the Chester group, after its more attractive terms virtually eliminated the White company, was ready to organize formally and to press for the strongest possible official support from Washington. In November the syndicate organized as the Ottoman-American Development Company, with a New Jersey charter,[16] after which it began in earnest the first of three unsuccessful attempts between 1909 and 1911 to consummate an agreement with the Ottoman government.

[14] Straus to Knox, Sept. 23, and Nov. 25, 1909, DS 5012/29 and 34. Knox evaded Straus's proposal for departmental screening by merely stating that the general policy of the department was to afford opportunities equally to reputable American concerns for submitting proposals to foreign governments. See *FR 1909*, pp. 595–596.

[15] Einstein to Knox, Aug. 5 and Aug. 27, 1909; Straus to Knox, Sept. 23, Sept. 24, and Nov. 4, 1909, DS 20784/1, 5012/25–26, 29, 29, and 30. For further details on Straus's difficulties with concession seekers, see Straus to Knox, Oct. 27, 1909, DS 20784/5–6.

[16] The company reported that its authorized capitalization was $100,000, fully subscribed, with 10 per cent paid in. Laidlaw to Knox, enclosed in Moore to Knox, both Nov. 24, 1909, DS 5012/31–32; Reports for Mr. Carr of the State Department by R. G. Dun and Co. ("The Mercantile Agency"), Dec. 23 and 28, 1909, DS 5012/39.

As the new company sought active support from the Taft administration, it impressed the State Department with evidence of strong financial backing. The principal investors were C. A. Moore, president of Manning, Maxwell, and Moore, Incorporated; E. G. Converse, a director of United States Steel; Admiral Chester; MacArthur Brothers, who were among the country's foremost railroad builders; the Foundation Company, general contractors; and the banking firm of Laidlaw and Company. To impress Turkish officials with the project's sound backing, the Ottoman-American Development Company sent letters of commendation from leading New York financial institutions to field representatives Arthur Chester and his co-worker, James W. Colt, a railroad construction engineer. The company was then ready to make a direct bid for diplomatic support both in Constantinople and with the Turkish embassy in Washington.[17]

Secretary Knox assured company representatives that the administration wished to encourage American enterprise, especially in Turkey, and offered diplomatic aid in bringing the company's field representatives and Turkish officials together. Established policy limitations, however, "would not permit the Ambassador to request the granting of the concession to the company which must rely on its own efforts and merits to obtain this."[18]

Pressure from the Turkish side was added to the importuning of the company for diplomatic support. The Turkish chargé in Washington, Ahmed Rustem, tried to maneuver Secretary Knox into an official endorsement of the Ottoman-American Development Company, arguing that the company's position with the Turkish government would be strengthened if the State Department would state specifically that the composition of the company was "such as to command the thorough confidence of the Imperial Ottoman Government both as regards to the general business standing of this concern and its ability to carry out any contract to which it would put its signature."[19]

Knox parried adroitly, placing the company in a favorable light but without committing his department to underwrite its financial solidity. Instead, he shifted the burden to "substantial bankers and business men in the United States" who had "amply assured" the department

[17] Laidlaw to Knox, Nov. 24, 1909, DS 5012/31–32.
[18] Moore to Knox, Nov. 24, 1909; Knox to Moore, Dec. 8, 1909; Knox to Straus, Dec. 8, 1909, all DS 5012/31–32.
[19] Rustem to Knox, Dec. 20, 1909, DS 5012/39.

that the men making up the Ottoman-American Development Company were "of the highest standing and that any undertakings made by them should inspire your Government's complete confidence." A contract with such a company, Knox emphasized, would have a beneficial effect on all phases of Ottoman-American relations.[20] The informal endorsement of the company's standing was strong, even though it left the department uncommitted.

During the early months of 1910, the representatives of the Chester interests made slow but satisfactory progress in Constantinople and by early March had signed a detailed preliminary agreement with the Minister of Public Works. As evidence of its good faith, the company deposited twenty thousand Turkish pounds in a Constantinople bank.[21] Then followed a delay of nearly three months during which the Grand Vizier, Hakki Pasha, refused to act on the agreement, thereby preventing it from continuing through the prescribed channels — approval by the Council of Ministers and submission to parliament for final confirmation.

During this delay the Department of State showed how far it had moved from the position taken by Secretary Knox the previous autumn when he told company officials that they must rely on their own efforts to obtain the concession, except for routine embassy help. Within a few months the department intervened directly to persuade the Turks to grant the concession, using several favorite objectives of the Young Turk regime as bargaining points: increase in Turkish customs duties from 7 to 11 per cent; purchase of warships in the United States to offset

[20] Knox to Rustem, Dec. 27, 1909, DS 5012/39. The bankers listed by Knox were W. E. Corey, president of the United States Steel Corporation; Messrs. J. P. Morgan & Co.; D. E. Pomeroy, vice president of the Bankers' Trust Company; Thomas Cochran, Jr., vice president of the Astor Trust Company; S. H. Miller, cashier of the Chase National Bank; Paul Morton, formerly Secretary of the Navy and now president of the Equitable Life Assurance Society of the United States; Alvin W. Krech, president of the Equitable Trust Company of New York; F. A. Vanderlip, president of the National City Bank and formerly Assistant Secretary of the Treasury; Gilbert G. Thorne, vice president of the National City Bank; James J. Hill, president of the Great Northern Railway; and others. Before replying to Rustem Bey, the department made some effort to ascertain the financial soundness of the company. See Huntington Wilson to Moore, Dec. 23, 1909; Moore to Wilson, Dec. 23, 1909; M. S. Clayton to Wilson, Dec. 23, 1909; Report for Mr. Carr by R. G. Dun and Co., Dec. 23, 1909, DS 5012/39–41.

[21] Admiral Chester to Huntington Wilson, Jan. 25, 1910; Straus to Knox, March 7, 1910; Laidlaw to Wilson, March 8, 1910; Admiral Chester to Wilson, March 15, 1910; Janes to Knox, March 26 and April 1, 1910, DS 5012/43, 867.602 Ot 81/–, 1, 7, 6, and 13.

additions to the Greek navy; [22] abandonment by the United States of certain capitulatory privileges, most especially the right of forum in cases of Americans accused of criminal acts; and loans to ease Turkey's urgent financial needs. [23]

The Turks were perfectly willing to play this bargaining game by making it appear that they would be more favorably inclined toward American investors if the United States government proved willing to make concessions on these issues, extraneous to the Chester proposition but important to Turkey. Straus did his best to make this instrument of Turkish diplomacy a two-edged sword, but he complained that the State Department would not give enough latitude for maneuver on the issues. The limit to which the department would go was outlined by Assistant Secretary Huntington Wilson, who wrote the Turkish chargé in Washington on March 15, 1910, that the United States would assent to the increase in Turkish customs duties as soon as the Chester concession had been granted. [24] But the capitulations were another matter. The United States played this issue more cautiously by suggesting that it might consider further negotiation on the matter after the granting of the concession. The department was not willing, however, to seek the special congressional authorization required before Turkey could obtain the warship requested in January, 1910. Straus also dangled tempting bait before the Turks in the form of possible future loans from American sources. [25]

[22] Wilson to American embassy, Constantinople, March 12, 1910, DS 867.602 Ot 81/—. Turkey had requested in January, 1910, that the United States sell her a warship to counteract an addition to the Greek navy. This required special authorization from Congress, which the department had been unwilling to seek. Straus to Knox, Jan. 19, 1910; Wilson to the Secretary of the Navy, Jan. 20, 1910; Secretary of the Navy to Wilson, Jan. 20, 1910; Knox to Straus, Feb. 1, 1910, all DS 23186/1 and 2.

[23] Gordon, *American Relations with Turkey*, pp. 190–199; Earle, *Bagdad Railway*, pp. 224–226; Rustem to Knox, Dec. 21, 1909, DS 5012/39; Straus to Knox, May 12, 1910, DS 867.602 Ot 81/15.

[24] Straus to Knox, March 7, 1910; Knox to Rustem, March 15, 1910, DS 867.602 Ot 81/— and 4A. "Favorable action on this concession would be considered by this Government as showing a sincere desire on the part of your Government to further these [commercial] relations. As giving to the United States a reality of actual material interest in Ottoman dominions it would also justify a more advanced position on the part of this Government in furthering various measures by the speedy consummation of which the present enlightened Ottoman Government so naturally and properly sets great store."

[25] Wilson to American embassy, Constantinople, March 20, 1910; Straus to Knox, May 12, 1910, DS 867.602 Ot 81/— and 15.

Defeat of the Concession, 1910

The optimism of the Ottoman-American Development Company throughout March abruptly evaporated in April upon evidence that German interests with the help of their embassy were enlisting formidable opposition to the American project. Up to this time the European powers with vested interests in Turkey had not reacted openly against what they regarded as upstart American interests. The Germans decided not to tolerate a newcomer to the ranks of those interested in the economic exploitation of the Ottoman Empire.[26] It was soon apparent that the influence of the German embassy was behind the procrastinating behavior of Grand Vizier Hakki Pasha in his refusal to place the preliminary agreement before the Council of Ministers.

The Germans charged that Admiral Chester was merely a front for cunning plans of the Standard Oil Trust, which was allegedly angling for control of the oil lands of the Turkish Empire. Whether or not the Germans believed their allegation, the introduction of Standard Oil as a whipping boy was a clever and effective tactic in view of the past and current American attacks on the Rockefeller organization and a suspicious attitude toward the company in Turkish circles.

The German attack worried officials of the Ottoman-American Development Company, who enlisted the assistance of the State Department in an effort to blunt its influence. After company officials hurried to Washington on April 8 with their fears concerning the German-inspired rumors in the Turkish press, an explanation went out to the embassy in Constantinople denying any connection between the Chester interests and Standard Oil, with the instruction: "You will discreetly cause this to be well known."[27]

This German maneuver complicated Ambassador Straus's efforts to induce the reluctant Grand Vizier to press the project. Arthur Chester and James Colt told Straus of their belief that the German embassy

[26] Laidlaw to Wilson, March 8, 1910; Janes to Knox, March 26, 1910, G. B. Ravndal (consul-general, Beirut) to the Assistant Secretary of State, Nov. 23, 1909, DS 867.602 Ot 81/1 and 6, DS 5012/35.

[27] John R. MacArthur to Wilson, April 6, 1910 (letter and telegram); Wilson to MacArthur, April 7, 1910; Wilson to American embassy, Constantinople, April 9, 1910, DS 867.602 Ot 81/9, 8, 9, and 10A. In Washington, Turkish Chargé Rustem's reaction to the rumors led MacArthur and Moore (the trouble shooters for the company on this occasion) to think that official circles in Constantinople might be attaching real importance to the German charges. See MacArthur to Evan Young (chief of the Near Eastern Division), April 9, 1910; Laidlaw to Wilson, April 13, 1910; Wilson to Laidlaw, April 15, 1910, DS 867.602 Ot 81/67 and 12.

strongly opposed the Chester Project because it would compete with the Baghdad railway already under construction. Meanwhile, Hakki Pasha, whose Germanophilia was notorious, found convenient excuses for delay by pleading the priority of imperial problems connected with the Albanian insurrection and the virtual loss of Crete. Straus then tried to force the issue on May 11 by confronting the Grand Vizier with the request for a frank answer as to whether there were political reasons — opposition from Germany or other powers, for instance — which would prevent granting the concession. The Grand Vizier answered in the negative and assured Straus that he would complete his studies in the next ten days; the matter could then be submitted to the Council of Ministers, after which a report would be made to parliament.

Straus told his superiors in Washington that he might be able to make better headway in unblocking the Chester Project and countering German opposition if the department authorized him to give ground on the important but extraneous issues. Even then, Straus had deep misgivings about the prospects for the American promoters. He perceived more clearly than his superiors that the Chester plans collided with the interests of the Great Powers. In his thoughtful analysis of May 12, 1910, he told the department: "The negotiations appear to me hopeful for the American Company; but one can never judge about the ultimate result of any matter of negotiations here, until it is a *fait accompli*. Turkey is so dependent upon the cultivation of good relations with the six great Powers, who practically have in their keeping the political existence of the Empire, that should one or more of these Powers, as for instance Germany or Russia, strongly oppose, this would prove a serious, if not a definite, obstacle to the granting of such a concession. Ordinarily in commercial matters a neutral nation has an advantage, but such is not the case here, where the power to harm counts for much more than good, neutral relations."[28]

It took Washington officials several weeks to comprehend fully that German opposition had thrown obstacles in the path of the American

[28] Straus to Knox, May 12, 1910, DS 867.602 Ot 81/15. The published British, German, and French documents reveal little bearing directly on the Chester Project, but they are instructive on the interests and rivalries of the European Powers in the Near East. See *British Documents on the Origins of the War, 1898–1914*, G. P. Gooch and Harold V. Temperley, eds., V and IX; *Die grosse Politik der europäischen Kabinette, 1871–1914*, Johannes Lepsius and others, eds., XXVII, XXVIII, XXXI, and XXXIII; *Documents diplomatiques français, 1871–1914*, 2d series, 1901–1911, XII and XIII; 3d series, 1911–1914, *passim*.

concession-seekers. A naive notion of Dollar Diplomacy as a commercial concept had not taken into account the realities of international politics. After being alerted by the Ottoman-American Development Company and by Straus, Knox began diplomatic inquiries in the European capitals. Instructions to Berlin on June 3 told Ambassador David Hill "to make a very discreet but strong oral representations [*sic*] to the German Foreign Office on the subject of the German opposition toward our railway enterprise in Turkey." Hill was to refer to cooperation between the United States and Germany in Liberia, China, and Persia. Knox apparently hoped Hill might appeal to the better nature of the *Wilhelmstrasse* by observing that traffic arrangements could be made to conserve both German and American railway interests in Turkey. As if these suggestions were not sufficient indication of Knox's inadequate grasp of the power equation, he also empowered Hill to intimate pointedly that if German cooperation were not forthcoming, the United States might find it necessary to work with other powers in Turkey.[29]

Very shortly Washington had to face the possibility that Germany had already begun to enlist support among the powers against American enterprise. The department asked American representatives in Berlin, Paris, Rome, London, and St. Petersburg to make discreet inquiries as to the validity of rumors that the able German ambassador in Constantinople, Baron Marschall von Bieberstein, was seeking support from his colleagues for the defeat of the American application. The American ambassadors found no tangible evidence of a conspiracy, but the British made it clear they would accept no threat to their primacy in the Persian Gulf area.[30]

That the German Foreign Office had little trouble in dealing with Hill is suggested by the latter's response to Knox's instructions. Hill cabled that the "German Government fully upholds our position regarding [the] open door in Turkey as elsewhere and assert in [a] memo-

[29] Knox to Hill, June 3, 1910, DS 867.602 Ot 81/18.

[30] Knox to American embassy, Berlin, June 11, 1910; Knox to American embassy, Paris, June 11, 1910; Hill to Knox, June 13, 1910; Laidlaw to Knox, June 14, 1910; Bacon to Knox, June 15, 1910; Reid to Knox, June 16, 1910; Leishman to Knox, June 22 and June 26, 1910; Post-Wheeler to Knox, June 29, 1910, DS 867.602 Ot 81/118, 118, 22, 23, 25, 26, 39, 29, and 36. Straus considered Marschall von Bieberstein the ablest ambassador in Constantinople. See Straus, "My Third Mission to Turkey, 1909–1910," p. 10, Oscar S. Straus MSS, Box 11. See also the appraisal in Earle, *The Bagdad Railway*, p. 43.

randum there is no opposition on their part to an American railroad concession in Turkey." Yet Hill was told at the same time that since the American group had taken no steps toward an understanding with German interests, the latter would naturally seek to protect themselves. But the Germans assured Hill that the government "so far" had "not taken part in the affairs." They felt that the two groups might confer "in which case the German Government would willingly exercise its influence on the German interests in favor of an understanding." Obviously, the bland assurances given Hill in Berlin did not square with the rumored actions of Germany's ambassador in Constantinople.[31]

The evidence funneling into Washington during June from Hill, Straus, and the Ottoman-American Development Company pointed clearly to the obstructionist role of the German ambassador. It was reported that Baron Marschall, at a dinner he gave for the Turkish cabinet, had said that the advent of American capital into Turkey would be harmful and that the Americans were interested solely in securing valuable petroleum fields for Standard Oil. The German embassy also resorted to threats and cajolery: Germany might withhold consent to the customs increase if the concession were granted, and there was the attractive suggestion of German support for Turkey in Crete, which had been all but annexed by Greece.[32]

For an interval early in June, it had looked as if the Chester Project would reach parliament before its summer adjournment. Ambassador

[31] By the time Hill sent his despatch he had already been visited unofficially by Arthur von Gwinner, head of the Deutsche Bank of Constantinople, who had indicated on maps where, in his view, the American project invaded rights already held by the Baghdad and Anatolian railway concessions. He too complained that the American plan was not one "for bona fide railroad development but a scheme for controlling certain undeveloped oil fields in order to keep their product out of the market." Hill to Knox, June 13, 1910, DS 867.602 Ot 81/22. A few days later Hill forwarded an article from the *Berliner Lokal-Anzeiger* of June 21, 1910, which used in a sensational way the same arguments von Gwinner had used on Hill. The article, called "American Artful Dodgers," ran in part as follows: "The general public did not know and does not yet know today just what this Mr. Chester, a straw man of the Standard Oil Company and of the financial groups allied with it, was really after." The article then commented that the concession proposed would give the Americans sixteen months in which to lay pre-emptive claims to all minerals in the area which would give them first chance at these resources. The parting sentence reads that "The Turks were on the point of becoming dupes of Rockerfeller's [*sic*] genius, and while they were unsuspecting enough yesterday, today they have something of the feeling of having had a very narrow escape." Translation enclosed in Hill to Knox, June 22, 1910, DS 867.602 Ot 81/34.

[32] Laidlaw to Knox, June 14, 1910; Straus to Knox, June 27, 1910, DS 867.602 Ot 81/23 and 30; Gordon, *American Relations with Turkey*, pp. 260–261.

Straus reported that the papers had successfully passed the Council of State, been approved by the War Department, and returned to the Council. Straus considered the "outlook hopeful" except for the opposition from the German embassy.[33]

Excitement heightened during the latter part of June. Although time was running out because of the approaching adjournment, Straus could do little more to meet stern exhortations from Washington that he exert all his power to see the concession through parliament. He reported on June 21 that the case was *in statu quo*; the Grand Vizier had not yet referred the concession to parliament. Straus also noted that the memorandum from the German government, denying its opposition, was incorrect: "British Ambassador informed me again today that German Ambassador told him he had opposed it before the Grand Vizier. Only yesterday Austrian Ambassador informed me that German Ambassador has opposed the concessions, and stated that as Austrians are interested in the Bagdad Railroad they also oppose it as conflicting with their rights."[34]

The concerted efforts of the company, its Turkish supporters, and the mounting pressure from the State Department were to no avail; parliament adjourned on June 28 without receiving the concession. After this defeat, gloom and disappointment pervaded company quarters, making it doubtful whether the project would be pursued. Although the Grand Vizier promised to take the matter up after adjournment, the company's representative considered this futile, because parliament would not meet for some time and the many amendments suggested by the Ottoman government would mean further delays.[35]

Straus appraised the failure in terms of German opposition and its effect upon the Grand Vizier and the Minister of War. The minister was particularly opposed to the mineral clauses which relieved the company from building the railroad if, after sixteen months of investigation,

[33] Straus to Knox, undated (recd. June 2, 1910) and undated (recd. June 3, 1910), DS 867.602 Ot 81/17 and 18.

[34] Knox to Straus, June 18, 1910; Straus to Knox, undated (recd. June 18, 1910) and undated (recd. June 21, 1910); Laidlaw to Wilson, June 23, 1910, DS 867.602 Ot 81/24, 27, 28, and 43. Laidlaw quoted a despatch from a company agent: "Grand Vizier openly in opposition to Mining feature of our proposition. Will do all in our power and the necessary plans are now being made but result is in doubt."

[35] Straus to Knox, June 27, 1910; Laidlaw to Wilson, June 28, 1910, DS 867.602 Ot 81/30 and 33. The exact scope of the amendments suggested is not clear.. Among other changes the government apparently was proposing the elimination of the Samsun-Sivas line. Alvey A. Adee to Wilson, Nov. 4, 1910, DS 867.602 Ot 81/56.

it turned out that the mineral and oil deposits within the forty-kilometer area were not sufficiently promising. Straus explained that the Germans were in a superior position because they consistently pushed forward their commercial enterprises to advance the political interests of Germany. This was particularly true regarding the Baghdad railroad project on which the German groups had paid out at least 150,000 pounds in bakshish, some of which was believed to have reached the Sultan himself. "It is a great mistake to believe that any of the government concessions or contracts are awarded under an open competition. The openness as well as the competition arc fictions, especially when large contracts or important interests are under consideration." Straus contrasted the German diplomatic support for its commercial enterprises with the inadequate instruments the department had provided him.[36]

Failure of Renewed Efforts, 1910–1911

The Department of State promptly decided to underwrite another attempt to win the Chester concession. Even during the post mortem analyses, influential members of the department, unwilling to give up the project, prodded the company to continue its efforts. Evan Young, chief of the Near Eastern Division, informed Assistant Secretary Francis M. Huntington Wilson that he had telephoned MacArthur (an investor in the company) to send someone to Washington soon "for the purpose of conferring and mapping out a line of action in order that we may exert every pressure as soon as Parliament convenes, looking to the early granting of the concession."[37] Thus the State Department initiated a second attempt to win the Chester concession.

The company's half-hearted and haphazard efforts toward gaining the concession during the autumn and winter months raised doubts among American officials in Constantinople. The earlier enthusiasm of the promoters had turned sour, as their belated surveys indicated that prospects for their ventures were less promising than anticipated. Dissension and lack of cohesion had also infected the company.

[36] Straus to Knox, June 27 and June 29, 1910, DS 867.602 Ot 81/30 and 37.

[37] The department abandoned its suggestion that the company should try to reach an understanding with the complaining German interests. David J. Hill to Knox, June 22, 1910; MacArthur to Knox, July 28, 1910; Evan Young, undated, probably Aug. 2, 1910, DS 867.602 Ot 81/34, 41, and 41. During the summer, talks with Russian diplomatic officials showed that accommodation of American and Russian interests could probably be achieved. See same file, 38, 40, 42, 44, and 45.

From Washington came pressure coaxing the company into a more aggressive course. This tenacious support by the department was surprising in view of the analyses from its agents in the field. Straus, Hoffman Philip, Huntington Wilson, and William W. Rockhill successively sent back pessimistic reports about the possibilities for American commercial enterprise in so notorious an international trouble spot.

Straus drew on his long diplomatic experience in Turkey to observe, as he had in previous despatches, that "In a country such as this, the political and commercial interests of foreign states are very closely allied." He believed this was shown in the activities and attitudes not only of Germany, but in those of Great Britain and France. He told the department categorically that American commercial interests of the magnitude of the Chester concession could not "be successfully advanced and sustained in this Empire without the strong support of our Government." If this were tried he saw no escape from involvement in

the political maze of the "Eastern Question," either on the side of Turkey or on the side of the Triple Alliance. . . . This may not be so apparent in the initial stage as afterwards, when such concession shall have been obtained and the work shall have been begun and thereafter. It must be remembered, judging the future by the past and the subtle diplomatic play of the Powers, that a railway, such as the Ottoman American Company is seeking the right to build, will not only meet with obstruction on the part of such Powers as will regard their commercial interest or spheres of political influence affected, but such a Company will most probably meet with serious hindrances on the part of the Ottoman Government seeking to avoid to live up to its obligations under the express terms of any contract it may enter into. In other words, commercial interests of this magnitude will need the strong arm of the Government all the time, not only to advance them but to protect them from unjust encroachment and from the violation of obligations.[38]

Some years later Straus wrote that he had accepted his third assignment to Turkey because of his long-standing interest in the philanthropic activities of Americans in the Ottoman Empire. He wished to make secure the legal status and rights of these American activities under definite laws in the new Turkish regime, but thought that the commercial policy of the Taft administration would hinder these objec-

[38] Straus to Knox, Aug. 4, 1910, DS 867.602 Ot 81/46. See also Straus, "My Third Mission to Turkey, 1909–1910," pp. 74–75, 98–99, 133–141, Straus MSS, Boxes IV and XI.

tives as well as involve the United States in Near Eastern affairs "for a few American exploiters."[39]

Reservations on narrower grounds as to the wisdom of supporting the Chester concession were expressed by Hoffman Philip, in charge of the embassy after Straus's departure. Philip indicated on October 14, 1910, that Colt, the company's engineer, had recently completed a survey of the territory through which the proposed railway would pass. Arthur Chester, discouraged with the results of the survey, questioned whether the company could attempt the project if it embodied modifications insisted upon, the previous summer, by the Ottoman government. A prevalent opinion in Turkish circles, reported Philip, considered the concession impractical, incapable of financial success, and perhaps designed for speculative purposes. Undismayed by these attitudes, Philip had tried to promote the interests of the company. His private view, however, was that the company should make a much larger deposit in a bank in Turkey to guarantee its good faith and to show that it seriously intended to sink the large amounts of capital required, if it won the concession. (The company had deposited only twenty thousand Turkish pounds in the British bank at Constantinople.) He expressed surprise that the company had committed itself so deeply on the basis of so little specific and practical information. In view of the Colt report, he suggested that the department inquire carefully into the exact plans and attitude of the company.[40]

The department showed Philip's observations to Colby M. Chester, Jr., to enable the company to state its position. Chester assured the department that the company would undertake no project it could not complete, and that "as businessmen we would not undertake anything that was destined to be a failure." He took the position that the company might ask for some changes to compensate for elimination by the Turkish government of profitable features of the original proposal. If the Turks would agree to such changes he could "assure the Department that the road will be built and operated by Americans."[41]

Any reassurance felt by Washington officials must have been quickly

[39] Straus, *Under Four Administrations,* pp. 296–298. See also Straus to Taft, Aug. 27, 1910, Box IV, 1909–1919, and Straus, "My Third Mission to Turkey, 1909–1910," pp. 104–105, Box XI, Straus MSS.

[40] Philip to Knox, Oct. 14, 1910, DS 867.602 Ot 81/53.

[41] C. M. Chester, Jr., secretary, Ottoman-American Development Company to the State Department, Nov. 1, 1910, DS 867.602 Ot 81/55.

dispelled when they received conflicting information from one of their own men, Huntington Wilson, then on a special mission to the Ottoman Empire. Ostensibly as a courtesy gesture to honor the new regime, he had been designated ambassador extraordinary on special mission to Turkey, on September 30, 1910. Wilson testified in his memoirs that he "was also expected to look into the pending Chester Concession" and the possibilities for American trade and expansion. His on-the-spot survey must have been a revealing experience, for the tone of his observations was radically different from what it had been in Washington.

The information Wilson received after his arrival in Turkey increased his "fear that the syndicate may have proposed more than it wishes to perform." There was danger of a fiasco, which would be highly prejudicial to American prestige. He recommended that the department insist upon a definite understanding concerning the company's "line of action and efficient execution of their plans."

Wilson now shared Straus's views on "the weighty questions of policy involved" in efforts to push American commercial enterprise in Turkey. Apparently unconvinced that France and England would welcome the United States as a check to Germany, he also questioned whether it were wise for the United States to have "admitted financial and industrial vested interest" in a country whose internal administration was so chaotic "and which is pressed by such complex outside influences." Recalling his mission years later, he wrote: "the very air was thick with German influence." He believed that Turkey was no natural sphere of influence for the United States in the political sense. To him our heavy interests in the Caribbean and our newly acquired responsibilities in China gave us as much as we could handle; he could not see any useful purpose in courting rebuff in the Near East. He preferred to lay emphasis on the good achieved in Turkey by American educational efforts.[42]

The department followed Wilson's suggestion to press for an under-

[42] F. M. Huntington Wilson, *Memoirs of an Ex-Diplomat*, pp. 223 (first quotation), 227–228 (last quotation, p. 227). Wilson was astonished to find that on the day he arrived in Constantinople, Arthur Chester had departed for Vienna. The company had assured the department that both the admiral and Arthur Chester would be in Constantinople throughout Wilson's visit. Wilson to Knox, Nov. 2, 1910, DS 867.602 Ot 81/56 (all other quotations). After his return to the United States, Straus presented observations almost identical to Wilson's to Secretary Knox on October 25, 1910. Straus, "My Third Mission to Turkey, 1909–1910," pp. 137–138, Straus MSS.

standing with the company. When Colt visited the department on November 4, he again assured officials of the group's complete readiness to carry out the revised concession, except that it might require compensation for the omission of the lucrative Samsun-Sivas line. The department cabled Wilson that it had "entire confidence in the good faith of these assurances."[43]

Wilson spent his several days in Constantinople in a series of whirlwind conferences with Ottoman officials — the Grand Vizier, the ministers of Interior, Public Works, Finance, and War — always stressing the importance his government attached to the concession. The Turkish officials repeatedly told him that three obstacles stood in the way of the concession: its conflict with the rights of the German Baghdad enterprise; its monopolistic mining provisions; and, finally, the American insistence on the right of forum under article four of the 1830 treaty. When the latter issue proved to be the one emphasized by the Grand Vizier before parliament in December, the department gave ground by permitting John R. Carter[44] to inform Ottoman authorities that "this obstacle could be overcome." Knox told Carter, confidentially, that the department was drafting a proposed convention interpreting this right in a way that might satisfy Turkey.[45]

Laborious negotiations continued into 1911 with a Turkish cabinet crisis complicating their progress in February. The Turks shifted the basis for their delay again claiming that it was not yet acceptable to the Germans. The Minister of War told Carter that "nothing would

[43] Adee to Wilson, Nov. 4, 1910, DS 867.602 Ot 81/56. Adee told Wilson that the company was ordering Arthur Chester back to Constantinople, although Chester did not return for more than a month, that is, until a few days after Colt had arrived from the United States.

[44] At the time of Huntington Wilson's special mission to Constantinople, the department did not want the embassy in the hands of a chargé. Carter was transferred from Bucharest to be temporary minister. Adee for Knox to Carter, Oct. 20, 1910, DS 867.602 Ot 81/59A.

[45] Carter to Knox, Dec. 19 and Dec. 20, 1910, DS 867.602 Ot 81/61 and 62. "It is clearly recognized, however, that the granting of the railway concession will bring about such a change in the existing conditions as to render very desirable a more definite and mutual understanding in regard to this matter [interpretation of the 1830 treaty], and when the necessity for such an understanding thus becomes evident this Government will be glad at once to enter into the negotiation of a convention which shall make appropriate concessions in the matter of the right of forum." Knox to Carter, Dec. 22, 1910, DS 867.602 Ot 81/61 (also text quotation).

compensate [the] Ottoman Government for [the] loss of German friendship."[46]

The will of the company to continue its efforts showed signs of breaking before the end of March. The delays and deceits of oriental diplomacy were proving too much for the American promoters, who were preparing to instruct their Turkish representatives to deliver to the Ottoman government an ultimatum that, if the concession was not granted by May 1, the company would withdraw. The department urged that these instructions be withheld until a further report could be requested from the embassy. A despatch already on the way to Washington explained that with so little remaining to be done, the issue should be decided within a few days.[47]

More than a month passed before Carter sent encouraging news that all disputed points had been settled, that the application had gone to the Council of Ministers, and that it would probably reach the parliament in a few days. Another of the periodic ministerial crises then intervened to cause further delay. Carter wrote the department that "It is difficult to explain these dilatory proceedings; and all sorts of suggestions are made to us as to their origin . . . among them . . . 'bakshish.'"[48] On May 14 Carter finally cabled that the Grand Vizier had signed the project and it was now in the hands of parliament for the first time.

At the department, tension and expectation increased during the latter half of May in view of the impending adjournment of parliament. The session was prolonged a few days, however, to consider the railway plan and the budget. The blow fell on June 1, 1911, when parliament voted 77 to 64 to postpone consideration until the next session on grounds that too little time remained to consider it intelligently. Carter

[46] Carter to Knox, Feb. 1 (quotation), Feb. 5 and Feb. 16, 1911, DS 867.602 Ot 81/70, 70, and 75. The Grand Vizier made the absurd claim that negotiations had been going on for only three months; this prompted Carter to retort, more accurately, that they had been started more than two years earlier. Carter to Knox, March 8, 1911, DS 867.602 Ot 81/77.

[47] EEY [Evan Young] to Wilson, March 21, 1911; Wilson to embassy, Constantinople, March 21, 1911, DS 867.602 Ot 81/77A. Carter's optimism was tempered by a closing observation that "in any other country I should say that the negotiations were practically finished, but my brief experience here has taught me that Turkey has very special methods of its own, so that I dare not be too sanguine." Carter to Knox, March 15, 1911, DS 867.602 Ot 81/79.

[48] Carter to Knox, April 22, 1911; Wilson to MacArthur, April 25, 1911; Carter to Knox, April 26, May 6, and May 12, 1911, DS 867.602 Ot 81/82, 84, 86, 87, and 100; Philip to William W. Rockhill, May 8, 1911, William W. Rockhill MSS.

78

was convinced that this was a "preconceived plan to defeat [the] project" on the part of the Grand Vizier.[49] The frustrating and unsuccessful second effort to win the concession had consumed nearly a year.

Dissension within the Company and Withdrawal, 1911

The news that the concession had not been approved "created consternation" in the New York office of the Ottoman-American Development Company, where some participants showed a "strong disposition to give up the whole proposition." Encouragement to continue the fight came from Minister Carter in Constantinople, who now argued that the difficult work had been accomplished in getting the concession before parliament, where there was enough favorable sentiment to augur well for affirmative action during the autumn session. Fortified to reconsider by Carter's optimism, Admiral Chester wrote the department that the full board would soon meet to make the decision. Company officials would be "ready to come to Washington and arrange for the next campaign to be carried on under the American Flag in Turkey."[50]

After Knox and Wilson had seen the Admiral's letter, the Near Eastern Division wrote the Admiral that the department was "much gratified" to learn of the company's plans to continue its efforts, and assured the company of "all possible proper support." The company then announced early in September that it intended to send its authorized representative to Constantinople before the autumn session of parliament.[51]

The extent of the administration's commitment to the Chester Project was revealed in the instructions to the new ambassador to Turkey, William W. Rockhill, veteran diplomat and orientalist, reassigned from St. Petersburg. In the name of President Taft, Knox instructed Rockhill to direct his energies constantly "to the real and commercial rather than the academic interests of the United States in the Near East."[52]

Rockhill soon mastered the previous history of the difficult negotiations for the railway concessions. The chances for approval at the forth-

[49] Carter to Knox, May 14, May 16, May 23, May 26, May 27, June 1, 1911; Wilson to Carter, May 15, 1911; Knox to Carter, May 22, 1911, DS 867.602 Ot 81/89, 91, 93, 94, 96, 99, 89, and 91A.

[50] Carter to Knox, June 1 and June 4, 1911; Admiral Chester to Evan E. Young, June 22, 1911 (quotations), DS 867.602 Ot 81/99, 101, and 104.

[51] Young to Chester, June 27, 1911; Colt to Wilson, Sept. 2, 1911, DS 867.602 Ot 81/104 and 109.

[52] Knox to Rockhill, June 17, 1911; Rockhill Diary, Vol. IV, May 2, 4, Aug. 3, 6, 28, 1911, Rockhill MSS.

coming session appeared reasonably good to him, but he thought the company needed an agent on the spot who should not even overlook "the judicious expenditure of money" as a method of dispelling "the adverse influences." All companies had found such methods needed in Turkey and other Oriental countries.[53]

The bold measures urged by Rockhill came to naught with the development of a new crisis. At issue was a rift within the company, deepened by the outbreak of war between Turkey and Italy in September, 1911, which influenced important elements of the syndicate to withdraw their financial support. The department's first intimation that the company contemplated withdrawing the twenty-thousand-pound deposit (in the British bank at Constantinople for the past two and a half years) came from Colby M. Chester, Jr., on September 28. Chester revealed that certain members of the syndicate thought the war would occupy the full attention of parliament in November, and they were therefore unwilling to continue their share of the cautionary deposit. Consequently, the other members felt obliged to withdraw the entire sum, although there was talk of redepositing the amount when conditions became more promising. The department summarized the syndicate's argument as follows:

they have for almost three years tied up approximately $88,000 pending a result to negotiations which have involved their yielding to the wishes of the Turkish Government on every point, and have resulted in nothing more than the same assurances that were held out to them at the beginning. They do not fear that there is danger of the Turkish Government's giving the concession to other applicants while their claims remain in abeyance. They are convinced, on the other hand, that the withdrawal of the deposit will induce the Turkish Government to reach a definite decision whether or not it desires to grant the concession to the Development Company.[54]

As the debate continued within the syndicate, the internal differences became more pronounced. MacArthur Brothers objected "that this was a very inopportune time to show lack of confidence" but failed to convince their colleagues. Finally, the board of directors informed the department on October 18, 1911, of its final decision to withdraw

[53] Rockhill to Knox, Sept. 18 and Oct. 10, 1911, DS 867.602 Ot 81/111 and 115.
[54] MacMurray to Wilson, "Memorandum of a Conversation with Mr. Chester in regard to the Concession Sought by the Ottoman-American Development Company," Sept. 28, 1911; Adee to Rockhill, Oct. 12, 1911; Knox to Rockhill, Oct. 18, 1911; Rockhill to Knox, Oct. 19, 1911, DS 867.602 Ot 81/110, 113, 117, and 118.

its application and the monetary deposit. The "controlling interests" argued "that conditions have so wholly changed since the concession was first sought that, if obtained, it would probably be burdensome and difficult or impossible to finance, and they are unwilling to proceed further in the matter."[55] While professing a desire to carry out the railroad project, the company asked for changes in the terms of the concession, arguing that it had ceased to be a sound business proposition as then drafted. Otherwise the company was determined to drop the project, but expressed willingness to reopen negotiations on the basis originally suggested by which Turkey would grant either a kilometric guarantee with mining privileges, such as other railway concessions had included, or some other form of subsidy. If the Turks declined to proceed on these terms, the company proposed as an alternative, that the concession contain a twelve-month option for preliminary reconnaissance and study of traffic and resources along the projected routes. If further work seemed warranted, the company would deposit thirty thousand Turkish pounds and proceed with the work, but if unsatisfied after the survey they would surrender to the Turkish government the studies already made.[56]

Concurrent with the effort to modify terms, elements in the syndicate wishing to push ahead made a frantic attempt to obtain sufficient financial backing to replace that withdrawn. Both efforts failed. Pasdermadjian, the friendly deputy from Erzerum, notified Colt on November 7, 1911, that "No modification whatever" was possible in the bill. Interested syndicate members did not at once give up their attempts to raise new capital, but finally concluded it was "hopeless to seek to interest American capital unless the modifications . . . are granted." It would only put the company and the department in an awkward position if the concession were granted on the original terms now unacceptable to the company.[57]

[55] C. W. Fowle to Adee, Oct. 4, 1911; John R. MacArthur to Adee, Oct. 13, 1911 (first quotation); Colt to Knox, Oct. 18, 1911, DS 867.602 Ot 81/114, 116, and 117. For evidence of opinion within the syndicate that the Chesters were poor negotiators and should have been withdrawn earlier, see J. G. A. Leishman (ambassador to Italy) to Knox, personal, Oct. 4, 1911, DS 867.602 Ot 81/119.

[56] Colt to Knox, Oct. 31, 1911; Adee to Rockhill, Nov. 2, 1911, DS 867.602 Ot 81/126 and 121.

[57] Fowle to Adee, Oct. 27, 1911; Adee to Rockhill, Nov. 2, 1911; Knox (by Adee) to Rockhill, Nov. 10, 1911; Rockhill to Knox (from Pasdermadjian for Colt), Nov. 7, 1911; Rockhill to Knox, Nov. 18, 1911; MacArthur to Fowle, Dec. 4, 1911 (second quotation), DS 867.602 Ot 81/120, 121, 124, 124, 131, and 140.

Until the end, the Department of State refused to give official sanction to the withdrawal. The syndicate proposed that the department lend prestige to its withdrawal by allowing it to announce that the action was taken upon the advice, or at least with the concurrence, of the department. After Assistant Secretaries Adee and Wilson counseled Secretary Knox against official endorsement, the company was informed of the department's attitude, and Knox made it clear to Ambassador Rockhill that "this Department, while unable to acquiesce in this decision, is not in a position to avert such action by the company."[58]

Adee in Washington and Rockhill in Constantinople did not concur in the company's belief that the Italo-Turkish War posed an insuperable obstacle to the concession's chances in the autumn of 1911. On the contrary, with a favorable change in cabinet personnel and the diminution of German opposition the prospects seemed quite bright. Although the uncertainty created by the war contributed to its internal difficulties, the root of the company's troubles lay in the unwillingness of the majority interests to accept the concession without major modifications.[59]

Embarrassment on all sides followed the company's withdrawal. The chagrin in the department was matched by the dismay among the Turkish supporters of the concession, for the bill was still scheduled to come up in parliament and its friends were in doubt as to what action the company would take if the bill passed. They believed that "withdrawal of [the] deposit was only a protest against dilatoriness of [the] former administration."[60]

Now that Washington officials had burned their fingers badly, the Taft administration hastened to disengage itself as completely as possible from its untenable position. By the end of the year, the department had reverted to the traditional policy of noninvolvement in the Eastern

[58] MacMurray to Wilson, Sept. 28, 1911; Adee to Knox, Sept. 30 and Oct. 18, 1911; Knox to Rockhill, Oct. 18, 1911; Adee to Rockhill, Oct. 20, 1911, DS 867.602 Ot 81/110, 112, and 117.

[59] Adee to Knox, Sept. 30 and Oct. 18, 1911; Adee to Rockhill, Oct. 12, 1911; Rockhill to Knox, Oct. 26, 1911; Fowle to Adee, Oct. 27, 1911; Colt to Knox, Oct. 31, 1911; MacArthur to Fowle, Dec. 4, 1911, DS 867.602 Ot 81/112, 117, 113, 120, 120, 126, and 140.

[60] Rockhill to Knox, Oct. 26, 1911, DS 867.602 Ot 81/120. Early in November the Erzerum deputy, Pasdermadjian, urged the company to redeposit the cautionary money, and virtually guaranteed acceptance of the project after this was done. Rockhill to Knox (from Pasdermadjian for Colt), Nov. 1, 1911, DS 867.602 Ot 81/121.

Question.[61] Rockhill was instructed "to take necessary steps to obviate further purposeless discussion of [the] present bill in Parliament, and to refrain from all further connection with [the] project" unless terms agreeable to both the Ottoman authorities and the company had been agreed upon.[62]

The department could not complain that Ambassador Rockhill had lacked zeal in trying to implement its policy. He had played the role in spite of his own misgivings that nothing would come of the syndicate. These views he poured out in a personal letter to a friend in the department; he was disgusted, "but in no wise surprised, by the ending of the Ottoman American Development Company's schemes here." This collapse, he believed, would make it difficult for the embassy to work for "any further participation of American financial or industrial enterprise in this country." In Washington, too, the department thought it had been let down awkwardly and that American prestige had suffered in the failure of a project so strongly pressed by American diplomats.[63]

Attempts to Renew the Project, 1912–1914

Admiral Chester did not give up easily. Early in 1912 he approached the State Department again, explaining that the syndicate had been reconstituted and was now stronger financially than before, although he gave no details. This time chastened Washington officials outlined a more cautious policy. Rockhill received instructions that "the Department is disposed neither to assist nor to encourage any effort to revive the project" until the financial strength and seriousness of purpose of

[61] Contemporaneously, the department even discouraged suggestions that the United States offer its services as a mediator during the Italo-Turkish War of 1911 on grounds that the Middle East was a European question; it was argued that the United States should not irritate the European Powers by injecting itself into the situation, and no excuse should be given for European interference in the Western Hemisphere. See above, Chap. 2, p. 51.

[62] Knox to MacArthur, Dec. 7, 1911; Knox to Rockhill, Dec. 8, 1911, DS 867.602 Ot 81/136; Rockhill Diary, Vol. IV, Dec. 12, 1911, Rockhill MSS.

[63] "The Department is very anxious, I know, to extend our relations here; but how the devil are you going to do it if nobody in America, I mean in the business world is willing to give to the extension of our interests in this country either time or trouble or even to pledge to keep good faith with the people here in case something is given them. I trust that you, in your wisdom, will give me full instructions as to how I am to act here because I really don't see what we are to do in the matter of carrying out the wishes of our country." Rockhill to MacMurray, Nov. 6, 1911, Rockhill MSS. See also MacMurray to Clark, Feb. 28, 1912; Wilson to Rockhill, Feb. 29, 1912, DS 867.602 Ot 81/146.

the backers were clear beyond a doubt. Assistant Secretary Adee described the new attitude as one of "benevolent neutrality" until the new syndicate made good on its own.[64]

The suspicions of the department were warranted; the Admiral's assurances that strong new financial backing had been found were apparently premature. Some months later, the Chester interests asked the banking firm of J. P. Morgan & Company to participate in the scheme. Before committing itself, this company sent John R. Carter, formerly of the diplomatic service, to Turkey in June of 1912 to learn the status of the project and the conditions under which the Ottoman government was willing to approve it. His inquiry did not make Carter sanguine about prospects for obtaining the concession, and the Morgan company did not become involved.[65]

Apparently the State Department heard no more from the Chester interests until after the Wilson administration had been installed, when they made another futile attempt to reverse official policy in their favor. On July 1, 1913, Colt wrote Secretary of State William Jennings Bryan that a new company called the Ottoman-American Exploration Company had been formed and its agent sent to Constantinople to negotiate with the Ottoman authorities. The company stated that it hoped to secure the same railroad and mining concession which the defunct company had sought.[66]

Although the new company sought from the department the strongest possible endorsement, the Wilson administration was not disposed to reverse the chary attitude inherited from that of Taft. An intradepartmental memorandum expressed the policy to which the government reverted after three years of active diplomatic intervention to secure extensive economic rights in the Ottoman Empire: "the obtaining of this concession — which, though purporting and purposing to be purely commercial in character, could not be divested of political bear-

[64] MacMurray memorandum, Feb. 29, 1912; MacMurray to Clark, Feb. 28, 1912; Wilson to Rockhill, Feb. 29, 1912 (first quotation), DS 867.602 Ot 81/147, 146, and 146; MacMurray to Rockhill, March 12, 1912 (second quotation), Rockhill MSS.

[65] Colt to Knox, June 7, 1912; Rockhill to Knox, June 22, 1912, DS 867.602 Ot 81/149 and 152.

[66] Colt to William J. Bryan, July 1, 1913; Colt to MacMurray, July 1, 1913, DS 867.602 Ot 81/154 and 153. The principals in the new company were MacArthur Brothers Company, C. M. Chester, Jr., H. C. Keith, and Colt. See Moore to Colt, Nov. 21, 1913; Colt to Moore, Dec. 8, 1913, DS 867.602 Ot 81/156 and 159.

ings — would result in no real and permanent national advantage to this country, but would, on the other hand, entail upon this Government the liability to very serious obligations which might involve us in the international politics of Europe and the Near East, which we have always been solicitous to avoid." Accordingly, the department instructed the Constantinople embassy that the new company could expect only the usual official support given American enterprises abroad both in its negotiations for the concession and in its use if obtained.[67]

The department's policy disappointed the company, which tried to convince the State Department that more positive assistance was imperative if the company was to compete on equal terms with European interests. The prospects for success seemed fairly favorable, the company believed, if the State Department would use for bargaining purposes the desire of the Ottoman authorities to raise Turkish customs duties from 11 per cent to 15 per cent. The powers, including the United State, claimed that their treaties with Turkey entitled them to approve tariff changes.[68]

The department replied in January, 1914, that in authorizing the Constantinople embassy to consent to the increase in customs, the ambassador was instructed to request a pledge from the Turkish government that it would "grant fair consideration to American merchants, manufacturers and contractors who may desire to participate in the commercial and industrial development of Turkey." The company considered the proposed line of attack far short of what was required and argued that a mere hint was not sufficient for the oriental mind unless accompanied by real pressure such as that exerted by the embassies of other nations. Colt suggested that the United States government insist upon a favorable consideration of the desired concession. "Unless something of this kind is done," Colt wrote, "I fear that we may as well consider our matter as dead."[69]

This gratuitous advice on how to run its business exhausted the patience of the State Department and elicited a curt reply from Assist-

[67] MacMurray to John Bassett Moore, July 12, 1913. Moore was in general agreement with this point of view. Moore to MacMurray, July 12, 1913. See also Moore to Philip, July 24, 1913, all DS 867.602 Ot 81/154.

[68] Moore to Colt, July 24, 1913; Colt to Moore, Nov. 15 and Dec. 9, 1913, DS 867.602 Ot 81/154, 156, and 159.

[69] Moore to Colt, Jan. 15, 1914; Colt to Moore, Jan. 24, 1914, DS 867.602 Ot 81/160 and 161.

ant Secretary John Bassett Moore: "I have to advise you that the instructions heretofore given by the Department were sent out after full consideration of all the various aspects of the situation on which this Government was called upon to act, and that the language originally used by the Department in stating the conditions on which consent would be given to an increase of customs duties is thought to cover the ground sufficiently and to be fair to all the various interests concerned." With this letter the Chester Project drops out of the State Department files until 1920, when the Admiral sought to revive it as a method of meeting the oil shortage scare.[70]

Conclusion

This first serious flirtation with the Eastern Question had exposed America's lack of sophistication in the international politics of Asia Minor. Both the American businessmen and the State Department found themselves outmaneuvered. The evidence available casts doubts on the competence of the negotiators, who proposed a grandiose undertaking without adequate surveys and with little appreciation of the international complications certain to accompany their proposed entry into a country already heavily mortgaged to the Great Powers.

In Washington, President Taft and Secretary Knox at first ardently supported the Chester Project, not because of congressional or public pressures, for there were none, but because the administration wished to employ the engines of diplomacy to promote American business activity abroad as part of its policy of Dollar Diplomacy. Ambassador Straus and others in the field judged correctly when they insisted that American commercial penetration of the Ottoman Empire would require a political policy. But the time was not ripe. As yet the ambitious commercial interests were only a negligible group, with no popular ground swell for intervention. The possible commercial advantages did not appear commensurate with the political risks of permanently abandoning the long-standing policy of noninvolvement. The issue was raised, but not faced squarely, as to whether commercial prospects were more important than the humanitarian stakes Americans had built up in the region, and whether the latter would be helped or hindered by

[70] Moore to Colt, Feb. 3, 1914, DS 867.602 Ot 81/161. See below, Chap. 7, for the postwar Chester project.

American political involvement at that particular time. These issues would arise again in changed contexts and with different results. In the meantime the United States reverted to its traditional abstention from the international politics of the Eastern Question, the seed bed for the World War which brought an end to the Ottoman Empire.

4

THE DISRUPTION OF THE
OTTOMAN EMPIRE,
1914–1920

☆ AMID THE GATHERING DIPLOMATIC CRISIS in Europe during the summer of 1914, members of the small American colony in Constantinople assembled at the embassy to celebrate the Fourth of July. Ambassador Henry Morgenthau, Sr., had just left members of the diplomatic corps and Ottoman dignitaries after attending memorial services for the assassinated Austrian archduke, Franz Ferdinand, and his duchess. As Americans watched the fireworks display commemorating the commencement of their independence, some among them had an awareness of the imminence of European war. Americans in the Middle East were, as Dean Lynn A. Scipio of Robert College put it later, at "the beginning of a four-year period of suffering and destruction almost beyond human imagination as we were soon to learn by experience."[1] The war about to break would force difficult adjustments on American interests in the Middle East, and by 1919 would temporarily sweep the United States government more deeply into the whirlpool of the Eastern Question than it had ever dreamed of venturing heretofore.

On the eve of World War I, the Ottoman Empire had been battered by six years of revolution and war. Internal turmoil attending the Young Turk revolution of 1908–1909 had been accompanied by crises in the Balkans and Crete only to be followed by the Italo-Turkish War of 1911–1912, which deprived the Ottoman Empire of its nominal control

[1] Henry Morgenthau, *Ambassador Morgenthau's Story*, pp. 59–60; Scipio, *Thirty Years in Turkey*, p. 93. For a brief summary of the impact of World War I and its aftermath on American interests in Persia and Egypt, see below, Chap. 9, pp. 275–280, and Chap. 10, pp. 366–368.

over Libya. Without respite the two Balkan wars followed with further unfavorable results from the Turkish point of view. By this time, the paramountcy of German influence in Constantinople enabled Germany to manipulate Turkish policy for German ends at the outset of the war. As it turned out, a few leaders among the Young Turks dug the empire's grave through association with Germany and the Central Powers in their lost cause.

Three Stages of Ottoman-American Relations, 1914–1920

During the years of World War I and its immediate aftermath, United States relations with the Ottoman Empire passed through three stages. First, during the period to February, 1917, American policy was governed by the overriding objective of remaining neutral. Within the framework of that aim, the State Department and its field agents pressed vigorously to protect the persons and vested interests of Americans in the Ottoman Empire, objectives which, unlike those of the European Allies, included no strategic stakes. The second stage commenced with the rupture in German-American relations, followed in April of 1917 by formal declarations of war. Turkey broke off diplomatic relations with the United States the same month, but despite sporadic debate in and out of Congress, the United States did not declare war on the Ottoman Empire.

The third stage began with the end of the war, included the Paris Peace Conference of 1919, and extended through the signing of the Treaty of Sèvres between the Allies and Turkey on August 10, 1920. This was the period of greatest American involvement as President Woodrow Wilson found himself inevitably drawn into the monumental questions posed by the defeat of Turkey and the decision to carve up the empire. In addition, the Allies tried desperately to commit the United States to major responsibilities in the settlement and its enforcement. The United States' reversal of its traditional abstention from the politics of the Eastern Question reached a high point before Wilson left Paris in June of 1919; after that, the United States retreated rapidly during the summer and fall to its orthodox policy of noninvolvement. The problem for American policy-makers after the summer of 1919 was how to protect American philanthropic and economic interests in the Middle East without incurring unwanted political responsibilities.

Stage One: Neutrality

American responses to the rapid changes in the Middle Eastern scene between August and December, 1914, set the tone for relations with the Ottoman Empire during the neutrality stage. Although Ambassador Morgenthau was aware of tremendous German influence on key figures of the Committee of Union and Progress in August, 1914, he could not know how completely Enver Pasha, Minister of War, was mortgaging the empire to German ambitions. When Morgenthau conceived the notion of using his influence with Ottoman officials to counsel Turkish neutrality in the burgeoning struggle, Secretary of State William Jennings Bryan instructed the ambassador not to take the initiative in making such a suggestion.[2]

Already it was too late to keep Turkey out of the German camp, for on August 2 the Turks had signed with Germany a secret alliance known only to five men in Ottoman inner circles. Less than a week later, the German cruisers *Goeben* and *Breslau* passed through the Dardanelles under pretext that the Turks had purchased them to replace two ships built for them in Britain, but which the British Admiralty had commandeered. With Admiral Wilhelm Souchon and his German crews pointing the ships' guns on Constantinople, Turkey as a German hostage was compelled to cooperate. When the German officials ordered the Dardanelles closed late in September, the United States added its official protest to those of the Allies, but to no avail.[3]

Although a neutral Turkey served German purposes at first, Turkish belligerency was preferable after the German failures on the Marne. The Germans maneuvered to achieve this objective by despatching the *Goeben* and *Breslau* to raid Russian ships and coastal areas around Odessa late in October. Russia responded with a formal declaration of war on November 4; England and France did likewise the next day.

[2] *FR 1914*, S, pp. 75, 77; Morgenthau, *Morgenthau's Story*, p. 96. On August 8 the Ottoman embassy in Washington had informed Secretary Bryan of Turkey's decision to observe strict neutrality in the European war, and that general mobilization was being ordered as a purely precautionary measure. *FR 1914*, S, pp. 50–51, 61, 134.

[3] *FR 1914*, S, pp. 62–63, 67, 79–80, 113–114; Howard, *Partition of Turkey*, pp. 92–96; Barbara W. Tuchman, *The Guns of August*, Chap. 10; Morgenthau, *Morgenthau's Story*, pp. 105–108. On September 30 the British asked if the United States could prevent the Turkish fleet from acquiring American coal, the only source available to them. The British proposed this as a means of keeping the Turks out of war. See *FR 1914*, S, p. 115. I could not discover the outcome of the request.

With Turkey now in the war, the Sultan called for a *jihad* (holy war) on November 13.[4]

American Reactions, August–December, 1914. During late summer and fall, American communities at Constantinople, Smyrna, and Beirut became greatly agitated. As early as August they urgently requested of American consuls and Ambassador Morgenthau that the navy send warships to deter the Turks from possible measures against Americans and other Christians. Their greatest fear was that a fanatical Moslem population might be incited to wholesale massacres. American commercial interests expressed concern for their property. On August 17, the tobacco and licorice firms asked that warships be sent to Smyrna. American institutions, short of funds owing to the disruption of the usual channels of commercial and banking intercourse, also argued that American ships could relieve them by transporting funds and by carrying food for the needy Jewish community in Jerusalem. The State Department hesitated while it sounded out Great Britain, France, Russia, Germany, and Austria-Hungary as to their attitudes toward the despatch of American naval vessels, but even before the receipt of all replies, the U.S.S. *North Carolina* was ordered to proceed from Falmouth, England, to Turkish waters; shortly, the U.S.S. *Tennessee* received similar orders. Thus, the United States Navy began its considerable but little-known humanitarian work of the war years in the Eastern Mediterranean.[5]

The nervousness of Americans resident in Turkey can be readily appreciated, especially at the announcement in September that the capitulations, hated by the Turks as a badge of inferiority, would be abolished on October 1. Once this shield for Western interests was removed, Westerners had dark forebodings of hideous Turkish prisons as their possible fate under the vagaries of Ottoman justice. The United States, like the Allies, entered vigorous but fruitless protests denying the legality of unilateral abrogation of the capitulations.[6]

As it turned out, the alarm of American residents was not justified by events. Turkish officials repeatedly assured Ambassador Morgenthau

[4] *FR 1914*, S, pp. 126, 127, 129, 132–133, 142–143; Morgenthau, *Morgenthau's Story*, pp. 161–170.

[5] *FR 1914*, S, pp. 62, 66–67, 756–767; ABC, *AR 1914*, p. 75; ABC, *AR 1915*, pp. 76–77.

[6] Morgenthau, *Morgenthau's Story*, pp. 112–117; *FR 1914*, pp. 1090–1094; *FR 1914*, S, p. 767; Scipio, *Thirty Years in Turkey*, p. 99.

that they contemplated no unwarranted interference with American missions, schools, or colleges. On the very day the capitulations were terminated, Enver Pasha accompanied the ambassador on a visit to Robert College where he arranged to have his brother, two sons, and other Turks instructed in special classes. About three weeks later, the Minister of Public Instruction made a similar visit which further reassured American interests and their friends in the United States. However, the attitude of the highest officials in Constantinople was one thing; the behavior of provincial and local functionaries outside the capital was less certain. During the long decline of the empire, subordinate administrators had fallen into the habit of circumventing orders from the Sublime Porte whenever possible. Knowledge of this contingency in Ottoman administration, coupled with delays in communications, left Americans in Smyrna, Beirut, and elsewhere uncomforted by the friendly posture of Enver.[7]

The situation took a turn for the worse late in November. In addition to the concern generated by the *jihad* proclamation, ominous measures against British and French institutions seemed to presage similar moves against American properties. Then, too, fears arose that fanatical Moslems might not be careful to distinguish between Christians of belligerent nations and those of American citizenship. Ambassador Morgenthau weighed the advisability of counseling Americans to depart, but he found the missionaries generally firm in their desire to continue their work.[8]

The storms and uncertainties of the autumn were safely weathered, with no serious breach in official Turkish-American relations, although two incidents might have provoked serious repercussions. The first took place in September when the indiscretion of the Ottoman ambassador to the United States ruffled relations slightly. Ahmed Rustem gave an interview to the Washington *Evening Star* in which he not only criticized hostile American newspaper articles about Turkey, but objected to American policy. He accused the United States of discriminatory behavior in refusing to allow sale of American-built war vessels to Turkey even though vessels had been sold to Turkey's enemy, Greece. Rustem complained to Secretary Bryan as follows:

[7] *FR 1914*, S, pp. 121, 136–140, 767, 768, 775–777; Morgenthau, *Morgenthau's Story*, pp. 117–120, 169.
[8] *FR 1914*, S, pp. 134, 136–143, 157–158, 769–770, 774–779.

For years past, Turkey has been the object of systematic attacks on the part of the press of the United States. These attacks, conceived very frequently in the most outrageous language, spare her in none of her feelings. Her religion, her nationality, her customs, her past, her present are reviled. She is represented as being a sink of iniquity. Excesses which have occurred in her midst and which I, with all other educated Ottomans, deeply deplore but of which there are parallels without the same excuses in the life of other nations constitute an inextinguishable theme of violent denunciation of her.

This attitude of the press has poisoned public opinion in the United States in regard to the Turkish people to such an extent that a member of that race is seldom thought or spoken of in this country otherwise than as the "unspeakable" and when Turkey, defeated and bleeding as the result of the Balkan War, was in need of a kind word, mockery and insult of the most cruel nature were poured upon her by almost every American paper.

The State Department would ordinarily request the recall of an ambassador who made such outspoken comments, but it decided to give Rustem a chance to apologize. He refused the opportunity and announced that he would ask his government to relieve him.[9]

A second incident, which happily left no permanent damage, occurred on November 16 when Turkish shore batteries fired on a launch carrying the commanding officer of the U.S.S. *Tennessee* from his ship into the city of Smyrna. After investigations and diplomatic exchanges, the United States closed the affair with instructions to American officials to heed Turkish orders relating to port entry.[10]

The numerous war-related problems of Americans in Turkey during the early months of the conflict gave a taste of the uncertainties under which they would have to live during the next few years. Their commercial activities virtually ceased with the disruption of essential sea and land transportation routes. But their colleges remained open, and missionaries, despite the closing of some stations, continued to operate throughout the war, both educators and missionaries devoting their energy and resources to relief work.

American Colleges in Wartime. Many difficult problems faced the three independent American colleges. Mobilization depleted the student bodies to some extent, but even this was not the most serious

[9] *FR: LP*, I, 68–75 (quotation, p. 68); Morgenthau, *Morgenthau's Story*, pp. 48–56.
[10] *FR 1914*, S, pp. 771–774, 779–780.

upheaval. College staff members were among those alarmed during the opening months of the war when the attitude of Turkish officials and of the Moslem population was still an unknown. College officials joined in the aforementioned request for American warships, which they hoped would have a tranquilizing effect. As Mary Mills Patrick reflected later, "It was easier to stir up a panic early in the war than it was later on, when we had learned to discount sudden rumors."[11]

Turkish officials, anxious to assert control over foreign schools, issued new regulations appointing the Minister of Education to control and coordinate these schools and requiring that the Turkish language be taught to Ottomans. American colleges deplored another order which forbade religious instruction and attendance at religious exercises for all students except those of Protestant sects. Through the intercession of Ambassador Morgenthau the colleges obtained a delay in applying the new rules until the opening of the next term in September, 1915. During the previous summer, President Howard S. Bliss of the Beirut College journeyed to Constantinople and obtained permission to maintain religious instruction for all Christian students and to make attendance for non-Christians at religious services entirely voluntary.[12] The Turks proved reasonable about the timing and interpretation of the new orders, and American institutions adjusted to them without serious disruption.

It was not long before the colleges settled down to the day-to-day problems of keeping their institutions operating. Of practical and immediate concern was obtaining sufficient food and fuel. Great ingenuity was shown by administrative officials and faculty in getting through these difficult times. Dean Lynn Scipio assisted Robert College in many ways, for example, by constructing a mill to grind wheat into flour for making bread to feed not only Robert faculty and students, but also those of the Women's College and others among the American community in the city. His ingenuity even came to the assistance of the president's wife, for whom he made corset stays of discarded hack saw blades. During these years the physical facilities of the colleges de-

[11] *Under Five Sultans*, p. 274. See also Scipio, *Thirty Years in Turkey*, pp. 95–96; Penrose, *AUB*, pp. 150–151. The enrollment at Robert College for 1913–1914 had been 550. The next year it dropped to 441, with twenty nationalities represented. In 1916 it climbed to about 500. *MRW*, 39 (Sept. 1916), 709.

[12] *FR 1915*, S, pp. 953–955, 958; *FR 1916*, pp. 973–974; Dodge, AR 1948, p. 8; Scipio, *Thirty Years in Turkey*, pp. 100–102; Penrose, *AUB*, pp. 143–144, 152.

teriorated rapidly when little could be done toward making essential repairs.[13]

The faculties of all three institutions were extremely active in relief and medical work during the war years. Despite some initial hostility from the Ottoman governor of the district, the college at Beirut persuaded Constantinople authorities to relax a few regulations. Officials became kindly disposed toward the Beirut college because its medical graduates were the only ones willing to serve in the typhus wards. Non-medical faculty also aided in caring for the wounded, as did faculty members of Robert College in the Constantinople area. Colleges set up relief activity of two sorts: local committees to provide relief in the immediate vicinities of the campuses, and extensive participation in the work of Near East Relief during and after the war.[14]

At times problems seemed so overwhelming that there was serious doubt whether the colleges could remain open, but always the nucleus of dedicated faculty and administrators resolved that the doors should not be closed and that they should conduct, at the very least, a holding operation as a basis for renewed service once the holocaust should end. Personal sacrifices were required of those who kept the colleges open, for they had to do without commodities most Americans considered essential; they were virtually cut off from the United States and even without mail from relatives and friends for long periods of time. A complete sense of mission kept most of them on the job, often working harder than ever before in their lives.[15]

American Missions in Wartime. Difficult as war conditions were for the colleges, they were infinitely more disruptive for American missions.

[13] Penrose, *AUB*, pp. 156–158; Scipio, *Thirty Years in Turkey*, pp. 118–128, 132–141, 144–148, 158; Patrick, *Bosporus Adventure*, pp. 163, 169, 172; Gates, *Not to Me Only*, p. 218; Patrick, *Under Five Sultans*, pp. 267–268, 283, 311–314, 320, 323.

[14] Penrose, *AUB*, pp. 152–155, 158–161; Scipio, *Thirty Years in Turkey*, pp. 96, 181–186; Dodge, *AR* 1948. Writing of the situation in Lebanon, Dodge recalled "that thousands of under-nourished victims succumbed to typhus epidemics during the cold weather, and to widespread malaria in the summer." *Ibid.*, p. 8.

[15] Scipio, *Thirty Years in Turkey*, pp. 118, 122–125, 128–129, 132, 141, 144–153; Patrick, *Bosporus Adventure*, pp. 163–201 *passim*; Penrose, *AUB*, pp. 143–165; *MRW*, 39 (May 1916), 389. Of the 290 girls at Constantinople College for Women in 1915–1916, 63 were Turkish, 102 Armenian, 26 Bulgarian, 62 Greek, Russian, Persian, Italian, Albanian, American, or Jewish. Among the Turkish girls, 14 had their tuition paid by the government; they were to become teachers. One student was the granddaughter of the Grand Vizier. The enrollment for 1916–1917 was about 400. *MRW*, 40 (Jan. 1917), 74.

To be sure, Constantinople and Beirut were the nerve centers for Congregational and Presbyterian activities, but unlike the colleges, whose work was concentrated in the coastal cities, the missions were scattered over hundreds of miles of the interior, many in major combat zones.

When the war began, the American Board alone reported for its Turkey missions 151 American missionaries assisted by 1200 native workers. They presided over nine hospitals; eight colleges, 46 secondary schools, 369 elementary schools (with a total of 25,000 students in all institutions); and 137 organized native churches. By 1916 six missions had been abandoned and only half the board's missionaries were at their regular posts and assisting with local relief. Some of the rest were on furlough, several had died during epidemics, while others carried on relief work in southern Russia or Syria. Just before the United States entered the European war, the American Board reported 24 male missionaries, 16 wives, 51 single women, and 17 children. With the departure of American diplomats, many missionaries followed the urgings of their government to withdraw. At the close of the war, schools and churches with few exceptions had been broken up; the Turkish government occupied most hospitals, equipment and furnishings being scattered or carried off. Only 36 missionaries remained in the field, and possibly only 200 of the former 1200 native workers were alive.[16]

Behind these bare statistics were many stories of heroism. Missionary schools felt the war immediately with decreased enrollments owing to mobilization of teachers and students and impediments to travel. Early in the war the missionaries offered their hospitals within the war zones for the care of wounded and sick Turkish soldiers. On grounds of wartime necessity Turkish authorities seized several hospitals, schools, and other missionary properties, alarming the missionaries and the American government, which obtained pledges that the properties would be restored when conditions permitted. Local officials, however, often took over properties without due notice and without respecting the persons of the missionaries. Frequent charges of outrageous search, inadequate housing, and even of deportation required the constant intercession of American consuls and the ambassador in Constantinople.[17]

[16] ABC, *AR 1916*, pp. 80–82; ABC, *AR 1917*, pp. 70–72; ABC, *AR 1918*, p. 170; *MRW*, 39 (March 1916), 228; (April 1916), 304; 40 (June 1917), 477. Before the end of the war nine stations were temporarily abandoned. They were Van, Diarbekir, Erzerum, Bitlis, Harput, Oorfa, Caesarea, Brusa, and Bagehchejik (Bardizag). ABC, *AR 1918*, pp. 174–175.

[17] ABC, *AR 1914*, pp. 74–75; ABC, *AR 1915*, pp. 79, 81, 87; White, *Anatolia*

The Allied blockade made it impossible for mission boards in the United States to continue shipments to their field workers, resulting in shortages of supplies and foodstuffs. As Mrs. George E. White, wife of the president of Anatolia College at Marsovan, wrote in 1915, "Last winter we found we could do without sugar, without desserts, without many things we were accustomed to." The financial crisis during the opening months of the war was partly relieved by advances from the personal funds of Ambassador Morgenthau and from the Constantinople agent of the Standard Oil Company of New York. Within a few months, however, William W. Peet, treasurer of the American Board, worked out an ingenious system for transferring credits for missionary use. Nevertheless, most missionaries were unable to communicate effectively either with their superiors in Constantinople or with their relatives at home. Mail censorship and restrictions complicated their isolation. For a time they were even unable to correspond in the English language because of an official ban on the use of languages of Turkey's enemies until the ambassador's protests resulted in a firman giving full permission for use of the "American language." "Great is diplomacy!" proclaimed a missionary publication in reporting this minor triumph.[18]

Throughout the war missionary forces doggedly kept up their courage in the conviction that their experience and prestige would be essential for the reconstruction that must come eventually. It was unthinkable to them that they should abandon the work of a century. "There is every evidence that the Lord is working out some mighty plan for that great blood-stained, sin-cursed country. The sacrifices of the last three years can never be in vain. In the Kingdom of Heaven there is no waste."[19]

As the war cut a swath of death, disease, and desolation, the humanitarian instincts of the missionaries impelled them to magnificent efforts to ease the suffering of thousands of wretched people in their midst. Early in the war typhus and smallpox epidemics broke out within

College, p. 81; *MRW*, 39 (Aug. 1916), 624; (Oct. 1916), 786; 42 (Feb. 1919), 149; *FR 1916, S*, pp. 832–836, 838–845.
[18] ABC, *AR 1914*, p. 74; ABC, *AR 1915*, p. 37 (first quotation), 76–79; ABC, *AR 1916*, pp. 79–80; ABC, *AR 1917*, pp. 169–170; *MRW*, 39 (July 1916), 549 (second quotation).
[19] ABC, *AR 1917*, pp. 85–86. For other indications of missionary optimism, see ABC, *AR 1915*, pp. 77–79, 87–89, 93; ABC, *AR 1916*, pp. 104–105, 253; ABC, *AR 1918*, p. 172.

the area of troop movements on the Russian front in eastern Anatolia. From Harput some four hundred deaths daily among soldiers and civilians were reported in December of 1914. Erzerum, Mardin, Van, and Bitlis were all hard hit by typhus. Missionaries, some of them doctors and nurses, journeyed from Sivas to Erzerum to help nurse the sick during the emergency.[20] These trials were only a foretaste of worse to come the following year with the wholesale massacre and deportation of Armenians by Turkish authorities.

Armenian Massacres and Near East Relief. Tensions between the ruling Turks and one of their large non-Turkish minorities, the Armenians, had been accumulating for a generation before they reached a climax in 1915, when wartime leaders in Constantinople decided to rid their land of this dissident minority by invoking a policy approaching genocide. Without attempting to justify Turkish policy, it is important to understand the basis for charges that the Armenians were guilty of traitorous conduct. A significant Armenian faction, the Russian-oriented Dasnak Party, despairing of reform in the Ottoman state, had for some time been demanding an independent Armenian state, to include much of eastern Turkey. By assisting the Russian invasion of Turkey in 1914, the Dasnaks anticipated Russian support for their goal of independence. Hence, they organized several battalions, recruited largely from Turkish Armenians, which were integrated into the Russian forces invading Turkey. Quite understandably, Turkish leaders feared that these Russo-Armenian forces would organize a wholesale uprising among Turkey's Armenians. It did not matter that a substantial part of the Anatolian Armenians pledged their loyalty to the Ottoman state. From the Turkish point of view, they were potentially if not actually guilty of treason.[21]

The first hints of what was happening to the Armenians came to the American Board through veiled inferences in letters from missionaries in eastern Anatolia. Because of severe Turkish censorship to keep events from the outside world, the letters resorted to oblique references to

[20] ABC, *AR 1915*, pp. 79–81.
[21] The welter of polemic on both sides supports the judgment that "the controversy over the disloyal behavior of the Armenians will probably never be resolved." George Lenczowski, *The Middle East in World Affairs*, p. 48. See Sarkis Atamian, *The Armenian Community: The Historical Development of a Social and Ideological Conflict*, pp. 101–117, 185–200; and Ahmed Djemal Pasha, *Memories of a Turkish Statesman, 1913–1919*, Chap. 9. The background for the 1915 events is set forth in Cook, "Armenian Question," pp. 117–121.

Longfellow's story of Evangeline, which seemed, they wrote, "'so applicable to the circumstances under which we live here.'" It was many months before the full scope and severity of the new Turkish policy became known in the United States through reports forwarded to Washington by Ambassador Morgenthau. He reported on April 27, 1915, the arrest of more than one hundred Armenians of the better class "ostensibly to prevent revolutionary propaganda." They were being deported to the interior as part of a concerted movement against all non-Turkish elements.[22]

During the summer, as more information reached him in Constantinople, Morgenthau's despatches took on a more somber and urgent tone. He reported on June 18 that the "persecutions against Armenians [were] increasing in severity." Less than a month later he gave his fullest description to date:

Persecution of Armenians assuming unprecedented proportions. Reports from widely scattered districts indicate systematic attempt to uproot peaceful Armenian populations and through arbitrary arrests, terrible tortures, wholesale expulsions and deportations from one end of the Empire to the other accompanied by frequent instances of rape, pillage, and murder, turning into massacre, to bring destruction and destitution on them. These measures are not in response to popular or fanatical demand, but are purely arbitrary and directed from Constantinople in the name of military necessity, often in districts where no military operations are likely to take place. The Moslem and Armenian populations have been living in harmony, but because Armenian volunteers, many of them Russian subjects, have joined the Russian Army in the Caucasus and because some have been implicated in armed revolutionary movements and others have been helpful to Russians in their invasion of Van district, terrible vengeance is being taken. Most of the sufferers are innocent and have been loyal to Ottoman Government.[23]

The crucial episode inaugurating the anti-Armenian campaign described by Morgenthau had occurred at the Armenian center of Van in the spring of 1915. In the Russian army approaching Van in March were many Russian Armenians. Turkish authorities feared their approach would encourage revolt among the Van Armenians despite pledges of loyalty by the Armenian community. When the Turkish

---

[22] ABC, *AR 1915*, p. 81 (first quotation); *FR 1915*, S, p. 980 (second quotation).

[23] *FR 1915*, S, pp. 982–984. For support of Morgenthau's statement that many Turks protested the treatment of their Armenian neighbors and friends, see James L. Barton, *Story of Near East Relief (1915–1930): An Interpretation*, pp. 36–37.

governor of the province treacherously murdered part of an Armenian delegation calling on him to reaffirm their loyalty, thousands of Van Armenians flocked to the American mission compound where they withstood the siege for a month before Russian troops arrived.

After the arrival of Russian forces on May 18, 1915, American missionaries cared for large numbers of Turkish refugees, who streamed into the compound, bringing the dreaded typhus with them. During the ten-week Russian occupation, Mrs. Clarence Ussher, wife of the missionary doctor, died of typhus, while Dr. Ussher, the Reverend and Mrs. Ernest A. Yarrow, and others were gravely ill. When Russian troops withdrew and Turkish forces were returning, the Armenian remnants and missionary personnel, fearing for their lives, fled on foot toward Tiflis. Starvation and dysentery took their toll during this flight, marked by terror and misery. At the end of the frightful exodus, Mrs. George C. Raynolds, the self-sacrificing wife of one of the medical missionaries, who had broken her leg on the way, died in a Tiflis hospital two days before her husband arrived from furlough in the United States.[24]

The Armenian defense at Van had been reported throughout the empire as an uprising against the government. Exaggerated stories of massacres of Turks by Armenians inflamed Turkish vengeance and provided the government with the excuse for the wholesale massacre and deportation of Anatolian Armenians.

Turkish authorities took swift and decisive action against Armenian men of military age. Many were herded outside their villages and summarily shot. Most of the remaining Armenians — women, children, and older men — were systematically rounded up in village after village by soldiers with bayonets, dispossessed of their property, and without notice sent on foot, marching through the bleak Anatolian plains and mountains toward the Syrian desert. Many from the northeastern provinces escaped through Russian lines into Russia or western Persia; others reached Mesopotamia. Most were driven southward without adequate food or water and without provisions for lodging on the way or at their destinations. Eyewitness accounts of the death march tell of exhausted, diseased, half-starved survivors forced to leave the weaker to die along the roadsides. Statistics on the number massacred or deported are difficult to establish. Probably the majority of the two million Armenians

[24] Ussher and Knapp, *American Physician*, pp. 288–314.

in Turkey (a conservative estimate) perished or suffered intensely. One can only guess at the number of Armenian soldiers and civilians killed outright or the number who died during the death marches. The American Board estimated that by the end of 1915 some three hundred thousand refugees had managed to survive deportation.[25]

Ambassador Morgenthau protested vigorously in the name of humanity and tried to persuade the Turks to end their cruel practices, but he was told that the accounts were fabrications or at least distortions spread by Turkey's enemies. The Armenians had been disloyal, and must be removed for national security. The Turks stood their ground that this was strictly an internal matter in which foreign diplomats had no right to intervene.

On instructions from Washington, throughout 1915 and 1916, Ambassador Morgenthau and Chargé Hoffman Philip continued their protests. Unless the cruelties abated, Morgenthau threatened, the State Department would be forced to accede to public pressure for publication of consular and embassy reports on the atrocities. Efforts to bring German pressure to bear on Turkey were of doubtful efficacy in view of the suspicion that the German government condoned or at least acquiesced in Turkey's designs to eliminate threats to internal security which might weaken her contribution to the war plans of the Central Powers.[26]

Formal American protests were backed at home by public outrage and revulsion. Interested persons and groups memorialized Washington officials on many occasions. The American Board passed a resolution at its New Haven meeting on October 27, 1915, requesting "the President of the United States to do all in his power" to aid the Armenians. The mayors of Cleveland and Philadelphia unsuccessfully sought official endorsement of mass protest meetings. The California synod of the Presbyterian Church, purporting to represent 558 ministers, 1516 elders, and 50,000 communicants in California and Nevada asked President Wilson to continue to use all his "beneficent influence to alleviate the sufferings of the Armenian Christians within the Ottoman Empire."[27]

[25] *Ibid.*, pp. 234–287; Barton, *Near East Relief*, pp. 10–12, 32–34, 39–47, 62; ABC, *AR 1915*, pp. 82–86; *MRW*, 39 (March 1916), 174–180; White, *Anatolia College*, pp. 85–86; *FR 1916, S*, pp. 852–853.

[26] *FR 1915, S*, pp. 979–990; *FR 1916, S*, pp. 846–858; ABC, *AR 1915*, p. 85; ABC, *AR 1916*, pp. 83, 88–90; *MRW*, 38 (Oct. 1915), 723; (Nov. 1915), 805–806; Cook, "Armenian Question," pp. 123–131.

[27] ABC, *AR 1915*, p. 14 (first quotation); Newton D. Baker (mayor of Cleve-

Armenians were not the only group to suffer from Turkish determination to eliminate the minority problem. Zionist Jews, Greeks, and Syrians were visited with arrest, deportation, and sometimes worse during the war. Intercession in their behalf occupied the earnest attention of Morgenthau, Philip, and Abram Elkus, who succeeded Morgenthau as ambassador late in 1916.[28]

As the plight of Ottoman Christians and Jews became known in the United States, Americans rallied behind the relief projects which form an important episode in the history of World War I and American relations with the Middle East. It was inevitable that American educators and missionaries in the Ottoman Empire, whose local efforts to help the sick, hungry, and destitute have already been mentioned, should serve as an important link in carrying out one of the most remarkable examples of American philanthropy.

Ambassador Morgenthau was a key figure in the instigation of these prodigious relief endeavors. He cabled Secretary Lansing on September 3, 1915, as follows: "Minister of War has promised to permit departure of such Armenians to the United States whose emigration I vouch for as *bona fide*. Destruction of [the] Armenian race in Turkey is progressing rapidly. Massacre reported at Angora and Brusa. Will you suggest to Cleveland Dodge, Charles Crane, John R. Mott, Stephen Wise, and others to form committee to raise funds and provide means to save some of the Armenians and assist the poorer ones to emigrate." Within a few days, Cleveland H. Dodge, the businessman-philanthropist, and James L. Barton, secretary of the American Board of Commissioners for Foreign Missions, assembled a number of influential Americans to consider Morgenthau's proposal. At a meeting in Dodge's New York office, September 16, 1915, they decided that since insurmountable obstacles prevented bringing any number of refugees to the United States, they could best help the Armenians by raising funds to be used by Morgenthau for relief. Within two months this committee had become the American Committee for Armenian and Syrian Relief, later (1919) incorporated by Congress as Near East Relief, the name by which it is

land) to Joseph Tumulty, Oct. 15, 1915; Alvey A. Adee to Tumulty, Oct. 20, 1915; Adee to Baker, Oct. 20, 1915; William S. Young to Woodrow Wilson, Oct. 24–25, 1915 (second quotation), Woodrow Wilson MSS, file VI, box 498, folder 2554.

[28] *FR 1915, S*, p. 980; *FR 1916, S*, pp. 851, 852, 927, 930–935, 937; *FR 1917, S 1*, p. 15; Brown, *100 Years*, pp. 1001–1003; Manuel, *American-Palestine Relations*, pp. 144–155; Barton, *Near East Relief*, pp. 71–78; Elkus to Tumulty, March 30, 1917, Wilson MSS, VI, 431, 1323.

usually remembered. At the organization meeting, half the committee's original goal of $100,000 was pledged, a magnificent beginning, but little did the organizers realize that they would raise more than one hundred million dollars in the next fifteen years.[29]

Although Protestant interests dominated Near East Relief, participation by Jewish and Catholic leaders was arranged to broaden the appeal of its campaigns. Funds poured in ranging from pennies gathered in country churches to large donations by the American Red Cross and the Rockefeller Foundation. Cleveland H. Dodge, who had personal and family interests in the colleges and missions of the Ottoman Empire, assumed the costs of administration in the early days so that all funds collected might be applied to food, clothing, medicine, and other essentials. Newspapers gave free space for publicity and articles, while the State Department cooperated fully by giving relief officials access to current files. President Wilson lent his prestige by designating October 21–22, 1916, as the first of several annual relief days for special fund drives. Relief for victims of war in the Near East became a kind of national crusade.[30]

The distribution of relief in the field was supervised by missionaries, diplomats, and others operating from Constantinople, Beirut, Cairo, Jerusalem, Tabriz, and Tiflis. During the war years, relief was devoted to providing essentials to keep alive as many refugees as possible; only later could attention shift to permanent reconstruction work.[31]

By focusing on the need to relieve human suffering, committee officials in the United States hoped to avert conversion of the relief crusade into a vehicle for anti-Turkish and anti-German propaganda. Yet it was inevitable that the public should place much of the onus for

[29] Barton, *Near East Relief*, pp. xi, 4–9, 13–14; *FR 1915*, S, p. 988 (quotation). See also Cleveland H. Dodge to Barton, Sept. 13, 1915; Barton to Dodge, Sept. 14, 1915, American Board Archives, ABC: 16.5, items 128c and 128d; ABC, *AR 1915*, pp. 84–85; *MRW*, 41 (July 1918), 491–492. Reports on amounts collected for various periods appear in *MRW*, 39 (Dec. 1916), 947; 40 (Feb. 1917), 149–150; (May 1917), 384; (June 1917), 473; (Nov. 1917), 808–809; 41 (Jan. 1918), 69; (March 1918), 492.

[30] Barton, *Near East Relief*, pp. 7, 9–10, 14–15, 38–40; *MRW*, 41 (July 1918), 49; Polk to Tumulty, July 14, 1916; C. M. Vickery (executive secretary, Committee on Armenian and Syrian Relief) to Wilson, Nov. 6, 1916, Wilson MSS, VI, 164, 128 and VI, 498, 2554. The latter folder contains other letters of 1916–1919 indicating the close connection of President Wilson with the relief drives. Cook, "Armenian Question," pp. 131–136, also deals with the relief efforts.

[31] ABC, *AR 1916*, p. 84; and on relief administration and distribution, Barton *Near East Relief*, pp. 60–65, 67–69, 72–78.

the plight of Near Eastern Christians directly on the Central Powers. In any case, the relief drives for Armenian, Syrian, and Greek Christians and destitute Jews aroused hostility in the minds of Americans toward the Turks and their abettors, the Germans. The enlargement of the "terrible Turk" image was to have unfortunate repercussions in American foreign policy for more than a decade.[32] It is not surprising that the Turkish people were somewhat unfairly stigmatized, while the Armenians were over-idealized.[33]

Because the Turks resisted a program which might strengthen dissident minorities, organizers of relief frequently required diplomatic assistance. American officials worked hard and long before they could negotiate terms for distributing relief. Transport of relief supplies also required governmental assistance, including the participation of naval vessels. Finally, the Americans had difficulty persuading the Allies to relax their blockade in the eastern Mediterranean to permit passage and landing of relief vessels.[34]

American Diplomats in Wartime Constantinople. During the war years Constantinople was no longer the sleepy embassy post of former days. Ambassador Elkus wrote President Wilson's secretary, Joseph Tumulty, two months after his arrival, that "there is always plenty of work to do. I begin in the morning early and usually finish at ten o'clock at night or later; and it usually lasts seven days in the week." He observed that "the officials here are very difficult to deal with. The policy

[32] Professor Robert L. Daniel has written that "the Armenian-American groups, composed largely of recent immigrants, were too unfamiliar with the English language and American political institutions and too divided in their objectives to formulate a clearly defined program." He points out that "spokesmen for some of these immigrant groups were urged by the relief committee to tone down their more extreme attacks on the Turks lest the Ottoman government stop all relief work and intensify the persecutions." "The Armenian Question and American-Turkish Relations, 1914–1927," *Mississippi Valley Historical Review*, 46 (Sept. 1959), 253–255.

[33] President Wilson apparently felt that the effects on the American public of the Armenian massacre stories had not been wholesome. He discouraged Henry Morgenthau from allowing his account of the Armenian massacres to be made into a movie. He wrote Morgenthau that there had been too many horror movies; they do not "suggest the right attitude of mind or the right national action. There is nothing practical that we can do for the time being in the matter of the Armenian massacres, for example, and the attitude of the country toward Turkey is already fixed. It does not need enhancement." Wilson to Morgenthau, June 14, 1918, Wilson MSS, VI, 229, 234.

[34] *FR 1915*, S, pp. 963, 964, 965–967, 969–974; *FR 1916*, S, pp. 924–940; Barton, *Near East Relief*, p. 74, tells the poignant story of the failure of the U.S.S. *Caesar* to get through with a load of greatly anticipated relief supplies.

104

is always one of procrastination and delay. It is almost impossible to get a decisive reply within a short time to any proposition. Their business is not carried on with any real system or in a business-like way." When he wrote Tumulty a few months later he reported, "I am still very busy; all day long, nights, holidays and sundays [*sic*], with all our interests and nations we represent. We have few pleasures or recreations such as we know in America."[35]

The first priority for Morgenthau and Elkus was protection of the persons and property of American citizens. They had to carry on without the formal protection of the capitulations, which the Turks insisted were "once for all . . . irrevocably abolished." To secure some measure of protection for the Christian and Jewish minorities obviously required enormous energy, as did mediation in behalf of English and French nationals during the spring of 1915 when the Allies menaced the Dardanelles and the Turks threatened to kill hostages if the Allies bombarded unfortified ports or made landings. The diplomats were proud whenever their intervention softened Turkish practices. Though Morgenthau and Elkus both bristled at Turkish policies and practices, they fulfilled the tradition of good diplomats by establishing the closest possible relations with high Turkish officials as a means of protecting American interests and furthering humanitarian objectives. These two men of the Jewish faith won respect and praise from the Christian missionaries whose interests they served so faithfully.[36]

On the whole, American interests were well treated by the Turks; the constant strains already described never reached the point where the United States government seriously entertained severing diplomatic relations before entering the European war.

Stage Two: Diplomatic Relations Ruptured, 1917–1918

As American relations with Turkey's ally, Germany, worsened in 1917, American officials had to re-evaluate relations with the Ottoman Empire. After the United States broke off diplomatic relations with Germany in February, 1917, Secretary Lansing instructed Elkus that the

[35] Elkus to Tumulty, Nov. 18, 1916, and March 30, 1917, Wilson MSS, VI, 431, 1323.

[36] *FR 1914, S*, pp. 136–141; *FR 1915, S*, pp. 958–979; ABC, *AR 1915*, pp. 93–94; *MRW*, 39 (Oct. 1916), 786; Elkus to Tumulty, March 30, 1917, Wilson MSS, VI, 431, 1323. For reiteration of the American position on the capitulations and Turkish rejection of that position, see *FR 1915*, pp. 1301–1306; *FR 1916*, pp. 963–974 (quotation, p. 964).

United States did not want to sever relations with Turkey, although he included instructions just in case. The next day President Wilson wrote his close friend and Princeton classmate, Cleveland H. Dodge: "I have thought more than once of your dear ones in Turkey with a pang of apprehension that was very deep. Fortunately, there is always one of our vessels there, inadequate though it may be, and I hope with all my heart that we can manage things so prudently that there will be no real danger to the lives of our people abroad. Still, I know how very anxious you must be and my heart is with you."[37]

A few days later, Elkus reported that the Turkish foreign office saw no need for a break with the United States. Elkus still considered Turkish-American relations good, and a month later he repeated the foreign office's assurances. Before the end of March, however, as American entry into the war drew near, Elkus and the State Department became more apprehensive. On March 30 Elkus wrote President Wilson: "We are sitting waiting for things to happen next week." The ministers, he continued, were still very friendly and assured him that "they do not want to break with the United States no matter if Germany and Austria go to war with us." The following day Lansing instructed Elkus that although the United States did not wish a break with Turkey, the Germans might force it. When Elkus tried to impress the Grand Vizier with the friendly disposition of the United States a few days later, that official hedged by saying his government had not yet decided what to do in case of war between the United States and Germany.[38]

German pressure won out in the end; the Turks severed diplomatic relations with the United States on April 20, 1917. When the embassy closed, the Swedish legation, assisted by an American missionary, Luther Fowle, represented American interests. Diplomatic and consular officials soon withdrew to be joined later by Ambassador Elkus, who remained behind to recuperate from an attack of typhus. Elkus reported that the Turkish officials extended him the utmost courtesy and consideration.[39]

Not long after the United States entered the war, former Ambassador Morgenthau conceived a plan for a separate peace between Turkey and

---

[37] *FR 1917, S 1*, p. 113; Wilson to Dodge, Feb. 6, 1917, Cleveland H. Dodge MSS. See also Robert L. Daniel, "The Friendship of Woodrow Wilson and Cleveland H. Dodge," *Mid-America*, 43 (July 1961), 182–196.
[38] *FR 1917, S 1*, pp. 134–135, 148–149, 191–192; *FR 1917, S 2*, I, 11; *FR: LP*, I, 787–791; Elkus to Tumulty, March 30, 1917, Wilson MSS.
[39] *FR 1917, S 1*, pp. 598–606.

the Allies. He told Secretary Lansing on May 16, 1917, that he believed "the time was ripe," for he was sure "the Turkish leaders were heartily sick of their German masters." He offered to go to Switzerland to negotiate with former Turkish cabinet members, good friends of his, who would act as intermediaries. Although Lansing doubted the plan could succeed, he wrote President Wilson that "if the chance was one in fifty" he thought it worth a try, for he was unwilling "to leave any stone unturned which will lessen the power of Germany."[40]

Morgenthau's mission was explained publicly as aimed at ameliorating the lot of Palestine Jews. Morgenthau arrived at Gibraltar early in July for conferences with the British Zionist leader, Chaim Weizmann, and a French Zionist, M. Weyl. The State Department had arranged the Gibraltar conference through the British government without knowing that Morgenthau's stated objective served neither the current plans of the British nor those of ardent Zionists in the United States and Great Britain. Louis Brandeis, by this time very influential in Zionist councils, had probably informed Weizmann of the mission's real purpose. Zionists believed their ultimate goal would be hastened by British conquest of Palestine, and the British had decided in June on a Palestine campaign.[41]

Morgenthau and his associate, Professor Felix Frankfurter of the Harvard Law School, were urged by Weizmann and Weyl to abandon the mission. The time was not ripe, they argued, because the Turks had been encouraged by recent British military reverses in the Middle East. Morgenthau succumbed to the pressure, abandoned the mission, and retreated to France, where messages from Washington reached him expressing the surprise and distress of Lansing and Wilson. It appeared that Morgenthau had talked indiscreetly both in New York and at Gibraltar, betraying the real object of his trip and implicating the president and the United States government in this secret diplomacy. Washington was greatly embarrassed by the fiasco.[42]

[40] *FR: LP*, II, 17–19 (quotations, pp. 18–19); William Yale, "Ambassador Henry Morgenthau's Special Mission of 1917," *World Politics*, I (April 1949), 308–320. During his unsuccessful attempt toward a negotiated peace in 1916, President Wilson had acted as intermediary between Turkey and the Allies. There was speculation that Turkey might be ready to consider a separate peace well into 1917. See *FR 1916, S*, pp. 20, 75, 91–92, 97–99, 119, 120; *FR 1917, S 1*, pp. 58–60; *FR 1917, S 2*, I, 16–17.

[41] Yale in *World Politics*, I, 310–318; *FR 1917, S 2*, I, 108–109.

[42] *FR 1917, S 2*, I, 120–122, 129–131, 139, 181–182, 194; Yale in *World Politics*, I, 311–312, 319–320.

Although no overwhelming pressure arose for an American war declaration against Turkey, there were those in and out of Congress who believed Germany's allies should be considered America's enemies. President Wilson was not among them, and his view prevailed. In his annual message of December 4, 1917, Wilson urged Congress to declare war on Austria-Hungary on grounds that it was "an instrument of Germany." He had to admit that by the same logic Turkey and Bulgaria should be included, but there were overriding reasons for exempting them. The same day Senator William H. King, Democrat of Utah, introduced a resolution declaring war on Austria-Hungary, Bulgaria, and Turkey. The following day the president wrote Cleveland H. Dodge that he was "trying to hold the Congress back from following its inclination to include all the allies of Germany in its declaration of a state of war. I hope with all my heart that I can succeed."[43]

Secretary Lansing laid the administration's case before the Senate Foreign Relations Committee on December 6. He wrote Senator William J. Stone, the chairman, that it was obvious that the United States could not engage in any direct military operations against Turkey at that time. In the event of war, there was little to be gained and much to be lost. Missionary and educational property would be destroyed or confiscated, and most likely the Turks would respond to a war declaration with "fresh massacres on the Christians and Jews in the Turkish Empire." How much better it would be for Americans to use this opportunity for continuing their life-saving ministrations through humanitarian relief work.[44]

For several months the issue remained dormant until congressional proponents of war with Turkey revived it in April of 1918. In a meeting with the Senate Foreign Relations Committee on May 2, Secretary Lansing was asked to probe Allied sentiment on the issue. Even though the Allies and the Supreme Council both recommended a declaration of war, Lansing remained unconvinced. He informed Wilson that they failed "to recognize the humanitarian side of the question. . . . Their point of view seems to have been entirely military" in terms of the encouragement it might give the minorities in Turkey. Besides, Lansing noted, the United States had no grievance against the Turkish govern-

[43] *FR 1917*, pp. xi, xii, xiv (first quotation); S. J. Res. 109, *Cong. Record*, 65 Cong., 2 Sess., LVI, part 1, p. 17. (King's resolution was not reported out of the Foreign Relations Committee.) Wilson to Dodge, Dec. 5, 1917, Dodge MSS.

[44] *FR 1917*, S 2, I, 448–454 (quotation, p. 450).

ment comparable with Germany's unrestricted submarine warfare.[45] Again, the administration was able to apply the brakes on those who argued for war.

A few days before the general Armistice on the western front, the Mudros armistice of October 30, 1918, halted the war in the Middle East. Although the United States had not been at war with Turkey, President Wilson was soon drawn into the arrangements for breaking up the Ottoman Empire. This was ironic, for Americans considered the defeat of Germany the central issue of the war. On the battlefields of western Europe, the United States had earned her right to share in the peace negotiations affecting Germany. Not so clear-cut was the basis for American participation in the Turkish settlement.

Stage Three: Peace Conference, 1919–1920

The points of contact between the American public and the Middle East continued to be chiefly the independent colleges, the Protestant missions, and the relief operations. Americans directly connected with these enterprises hoped fervently for stability in western Asia — the educators and missionaries were eager to resume their accustomed tasks, and the relief workers wished to complete their assignment and withdraw. Quite naturally, they expected their government to contribute its prestige to a stabilizing settlement. As early as April 6, 1916, the American Board petitioned Secretary Lansing to have the United States officially represented in the international conference which would eventually settle the future of Turkey.[46] Spokesmen for the Ottoman mi-

[45] *FR: LP*, II, 121–122, 124–126 (quotation, p. 125), 128–129. Senator King introduced a new resolution (S. J. Res. 145) on April 2, 1918. It was identical with the earlier one except for the omission of Austria-Hungary. Senator Frank Brandegee (Republican, Connecticut) introduced S. Res. 229 on April 22 asking that the Foreign Relations Committee give early consideration to and report on King's resolution. *Cong. Record*, 65 Cong., 2 Sess., LVI, part 5, p. 4427; part 6, pp. 5403, 5472–5478. An example of a memorial favoring a war declaration against Turkey is Richard Hurd, Chairman of the Board of Trustees of the American Defense Society to Wilson, April 12, 1918; a cogent detailed argument against war with Turkey was Samuel T. Dutton to Senator James W. Wadsworth, April 24, 1918, copy enclosed in Dutton to Joseph P. Tumulty, April 25, 1918, Wilson MSS, VI, 164, 128.

[46] Edward C. Moore and others to Lansing, April 6, 1919, ABC 16.5, Vol. 6, item 136, American Board Archives. ABC, *AR 1916*, p. 105, declared: "It is expected that when the convention is called to settle future conditions which will govern the administration of all this territory, America will be represented and that American interests in educational, industrial, medical, and missionary institutions will be amply safeguarded for all time to come."

norities — Zionists, Armenians, Arabs, and Greeks — also hoped to enlist official American support for their objectives. Long before the armistice at Mudros, Washington officials were under pressure to shape the postwar Middle East according to the varying designs of numerous interest groups.

Official Preparations and the Power Balance. Although the policymakers were preoccupied with Germany and European questions, they were not wholly ignorant of or uninterested in the course of war and international politics in the Middle East. Even before the Bolsheviks exposed the secret treaties late in 1917, Washington knew that Great Britain, France, Russia, and Italy planned to carve the Ottoman Empire into spheres of influence. When Lord Arthur Balfour gave Colonel Edward M. House a rather hazy explanation of these treaties on April 28, 1917, House expressed disapproval: "It is all bad and I told Balfour so. They are making it a breeding place for future war." President Wilson considered the scheme for grabbing territory quite contrary to American objectives and laid plans to dissociate the United States from the secret treaties and to use his influence to nullify them if possible. As early as December 1, 1917, he cabled House in Paris that "our people and Congress will not fight for any selfish aim on the part of any belligerent . . . least of all for divisions of territory such as have been contemplated in Asia Minor. I think it will be obvious to all that it would be a fatal mistake to cool the ardour of America." [47]

Wilson and House were soon hard at work on Wilson's speech which would lay down the famous Fourteen Points, outlined to Congress in January, 1918. Point 12, dealing specifically with Turkey, was Wilson's way of serving notice on the Allies that the United States would not accept the Allied arrangements for the Ottoman Empire. He declared that "the Turkish portions of the present Ottoman Empire should be assured a secure sovereignty, but the other nationalities which are now

[47] Charles Seymour, ed., *The Intimate Papers of Colonel House*, III, 40–46 (first quotation), 48–51, 61–63; *FR 1917*, S 2, I, 169–170, 331 (second quotation), 490–492, 499–507; Seth Tillman, *Anglo-American Relations at the Paris Peace Conference of 1919*, pp. 9–11. The secret agreements were the Constantinople Agreement of March 18, 1915; the Secret Treaty of London of April 26, 1915; the Anglo-Franco-Russian Agreement of March-April, 1916; the Sykes-Picot Agreement of May 16, 1916; and the St. Jean de Maurienne Agreement of April 17, 1917. See Harold W. V. Temperley, ed., *History of the Peace Conference of Paris*, Chap. 1; Henry H. Cumming, *Franco-British Rivalry in the Post-War Near East*, Chap. 3 and *passim*. Excerpts are printed in Jacob C. Hurewitz, *Diplomacy in the Near and Middle East, A Documentary Record*, II, 7–12, 18–22, 23–25.

under Turkish rule should be assured an undoubted security of life and an absolutely unmolested opportunity of autonomous development, and the Dardanelles should be permanently opened as a free passage to the ships and commerce of all nations under international guarantees."[48]

By the time he prepared the Fourteen Points, Wilson was already relying on reports from the remarkable group known as the Inquiry. This body was organized in the fall of 1917 to assemble and collate data which might be needed by the American delegation when a peace conference assembled. The Inquiry, composed mostly of students of foreign affairs drawn largely from university faculties, functioned as the personal staff of the president under the direction of Colonel House; technically, it was under the Department of State. Wilson and House had carefully considered an early Inquiry report while constructing the Turkish part of the Fourteen Points.[49]

Additional Inquiry studies of the Turkish situation went forward in 1918, notwithstanding difficulties in finding qualified experts to assemble data and interpret Turkish conditions. An Inquiry report of May 10, 1918, confessed that "what is lacking is a real appreciation of the inwardness of internal race and religious questions and their bearing upon international politics." Walter Lippmann, secretary of the Inquiry, wrote Secretary of War Newton D. Baker about the "famine in men" truly expert on such areas as Russia, the Balkans, Turkey, and Africa. "Those are lands intellectually practically unexplored. What we are on the lookout for is genius — sheer, startling genius and nothing else will do because the real application of the President's idea to those countries requires inventiveness and resourcefulness which is scarcer than anything."[50]

Just before the Armistice, Lippmann and his Inquiry colleague, Frank L. Cobb, editor of the New York *World*, prepared an authoritative commentary on the Fourteen Points. A more detailed memorandum of January 21, 1919, supplemented the Lippmann-Cobb memorandum and significantly altered some details. Together these served

[48] Seymour, *House Papers*, III, 322–324, 332; IV, 199 (quotation).

[49] *FR: PPC*, I, 52–53; H. Stephen Helton, comp., "Records of the American Commission to Negotiate Peace," Preliminary Inventories, No. 89, National Archives, p. 1; Ray S. Baker, ed., *Woodrow Wilson and World Settlement: Written from His Unpublished and Personal Material*, I, 108–109; James T. Shotwell, *At the Paris Peace Conference*, Chap. 1; Seymour, *House Papers*, III, 322–324.

[50] *FR: PPC*, I, 86–87 (first quotation), 97–98 (second quotation).

as the basic American program for the Middle East when Wilson departed for the Paris Peace Conference.[51] Wilson had taken his stand on the principle of self-determination which, as he would find out, could not be implemented in full measure because of conflicting national claims. He also pressed as fundamental his conception of a sane new international order with effective international guarantees. Reflecting his confidence in these principles were his proposals for freedom of the Turkish Straits, protection of minorities, and the Open Door for commerce and trade.

Wilson's plan for a Middle Eastern settlement within the framework of a world settlement based on the League ran up against hard political realities during the peace negotiations. Standing in the way were the clashing ambitions of the Allies and the competing national aspirations of Arabs, Zionists, and other groups. The president's troubles arose in part from Great Britain's conflicting commitments to her Allies in the secret treaties, to the Arabs, and to the Zionists. The incompatibility of these several pledges undermined Britain's apparent military and political primacy. At first glance, all seemed to be clear sailing ahead for the British. The war had temporarily eliminated her two chief rivals — Germany and Austria — as factors in the Turkish equation. Furthermore, Russia had forfeited her claims to spoils (Constantinople and northeastern Turkey) promised her in the secret treaties. But Britain's Allies were to prove almost as troublesome as her formal rivals. France, Italy, and Greece all had ambitions in the Middle East which the British did not always find admissible.

Britain's distresses proved to be Wilson's distresses too, if for somewhat different reasons. He was caught in the crossfire of protracted wrangling among the Allies over the division of spoils originally assigned to Russia. The cynical approach signified by the secret treaties was only part of the president's problem as he tried to apply the principle of national self-determination. The British had made commitments to Arab spokesmen in the historic Hussein-McMahon correspondence of 1915–1916. As the price for wartime Arab support, the British had agreed an Arab state should be formed in the Levant after the war. The

[51] Seymour, *House Papers*, IV, 157–158, and 199–200 for the Lippmann-Cobb commentary. See Hurewitz, *Diplomacy*, II, 40–45, for excerpts from the tentative suggestions for President Wilson prepared by the intelligence section of the American Delegation to the Peace Conference (with which the Inquiry was eventually merged).

letters were susceptible to varying interpretations as to precisely what had been promised. Equally vague was another British commitment, that made to the Zionists in the Balfour Declaration of November 2, 1917, pledging British support for a national homeland for the Jews in Palestine.[52] Contemporary evidence indicates considerable difference of opinion among British statesmen, Zionists, and others as to precisely what the British had promised, but many derived implications that there should be free Jewish immigration to Palestine and the right to set up a center of Jewish culture with the possibility that at some future time a Jewish commonwealth might be organized.[53]

These three conflicting commitments of the British — to her Allies, to the Arabs, and to the Zionists — would dog the British for years to come. Wilson had, as we have seen, dissociated the United States completely from the secret treaties. There is no evidence that the United States was ever associated in any way with the promises to the Arabs, although the Arabs looked upon Wilson as their champion because of his espousal of self-determination.[54] The situation was somewhat different with regard to the Balfour Declaration.

American Zionists, by now very influential in the movement, ardently solicited Wilson's endorsement of the Balfour pledge. The president's close adviser, Justice Louis Brandeis, was a prime mover in this effort. Administration councils were divided, however, on the wisdom of the sought-for endorsement, the State Department — especially Secretary Lansing — being strongly opposed to any formal commitment. Putting aside the reservations of his assistants, Wilson eventually gave what

[52] Hurewitz, *Diplomacy*, II, 13–17, 25–26. Balfour's letter to Baron Lionel Walter Rothschild said: "His Majesty's Government view with favour the establishment in Palestine of a national home for the Jewish people, and will use their best endeavours to facilitate the achievement of this object, it being clearly understood that nothing shall be done which may prejudice the civil and religious rights of existing non-Jewish communities in Palestine, or the rights and political status enjoyed by Jews in any other country."

[53] *FR 1917, S 2*, I, 473; William F. Barr, "Woodrow Wilson and the Palestine Question," unpublished seminar paper, The Pennsylvania State University, 1958.

[54] Dr. E. G. Tabet, president, and Ameen Rihani, chairman and acting secretary, the Syria-Mount Lebanon League of Liberation — North American Branch, to Wilson, Aug. 30, 1917; Joseph E. Balesh, chairman, Syria Division, 4th Liberty Loan, to Wilson (with enclosure), Oct. 3, 1918, Wilson MSS, VI, 164, 128. See also Manuel, *American-Palestine Relations*, pp. 187–188. For a revisionist view of the Arab-British relationship during the war and the peace negotiations, see George Kirk, "*The Arab Awakening* Reconsidered," *Middle East Affairs*, 13 (June–July 1962), 166–173.

seemed to be approval of the Balfour Declaration.[55] Wilson thereby made trouble for himself inasmuch as Palestine was an Arab country, and Zionism was inconsistent with self-determination. The only way to justify the pledge to the Jews for a special position in Palestine was by treating it as a warranted exception.

Thus, when Wilson and his entourage departed from New York on the S.S. *George Washington* in December of 1918 to make a peace with Germany, serious Middle Eastern complications awaited the attention of the peacemakers.

Middle East Issues at Paris, January–June, 1919. The major issues touching on a Middle East settlement at the Paris Peace Conference were territorial and administrative. The territorial issues required decisions on whether Turkey would be allowed to continue as an independent entity and, if so, what her boundaries would be. For those areas to be detached from the Ottoman Empire there were questions of boundaries and the implementation of national self-determination. For the entire area decisions had to be made about the role the European Allies could play in a truncated Turkey and in the detached areas. These basic issues became intricately interwoven in the controversy between traditional notions of power politics and the Wilsonian conception of internationalism.

The Council of Ten made its first decisions on these matters late in January. In discussing whether areas to be detached from the Ottoman Empire should be annexed according to provisions of the secret treaties, President Wilson held forth on the nobility of the mandate concept as a replacement for old-fashioned annexation. Instead of serving its own selfish interests, the mandatory would be performing a service to the people under tutelage and to humanity. David Lloyd George had some reservations and Georges Clemenceau was appalled at the idea of mandates. Both seemed to prefer outright annexation as a solution.[56]

Lloyd George finally announced his readiness to accept the mandate principle for all conquests in the Ottoman Empire. The burdens would

[55] Manuel, *American-Palestine Relations*, pp. 117–118, 125–126, 138–140, 164–169, 172–173, 175–177; Alpheus T. Mason, *Brandeis: A Free Man's Life*, pp. 441–464; Selig Adler, "The Palestine Question in the Wilson Era," *Jewish Social Studies*, 10 (Oct. 1948), 303–334; Tillman, *Anglo-American Relations*, pp. 223–225; *FR: LP*, II, 71.

[56] *FR 1919: PPC*, III, 740–743, 747–748, 749–751, 763–771; and for Wilson's remarks to the plenary session of February 14, 1919, *ibid.*, III, 213–215.

be heavy, he opined, and therefore he requested immediate assignment of the mandatories. Wilson vetoed such precipitant action. On January 30, the Council of Ten adopted the draft resolution by which the powers agreed that Armenia, Syria, Mesopotamia, Palestine, and Arabia were to be separated from Turkey and placed under mandates.[57]

At the same meeting of the Council, the question of whether the United States might accept mandates came before the conference formally for the first time. Wilson alluded to suggestions that his country might assume such responsibilities by warning that "the people of America would be most disinclined to do so." He might be able to persuade them to undertake this burden, but he could not on his own authority guarantee that the United States would accept mandates. This was the first of numerous occasions when Wilson entered such a caveat. On grounds that the United States had not been at war with Turkey, he also rejected the suggestion that the United States furnish occupation troops for Constantinople or Mesopotamia.[58] Already emerging at this early date was the British objective of bringing the United States into the Middle East as a replacement for disqualified Russia.

Subject nationalities within the Ottoman Empire had long anticipated the day when they might bring their cases before the peace conference. In February each appeared before the Council of Ten carrying the banner of Wilsonian principles and armed with its cloak of righteousness. Leading the parade was Eleutherios Venizelos to present the Greek case, and following him came various spokesmen for the Arab cause. On February 6 Emir Feisal of Hejaz, accompanied by Colonel T. E. Lawrence, asked for an independent Arab confederation including all Arabic-speaking peoples south of Alexandretta (including Syria), Lebanon to be excepted if she desired, and Palestine to be set aside for future consideration. Feisal parried Wilson's efforts to get him to designate the preferred mandatory; he proclaimed that his principle was Arab unity and his goal freedom. In a speech before a plenary session, another Hejaz representative questioned the whole idea of mandates and asked that secret agreements affecting Arab rights be declared null and void. The previous day, February 13, the respected Howard Bliss, president of Syrian Protestant College at Beirut, pled eloquently before the Council of Ten for a free Syrian nation and urged that a commis-

[57] *FR 1919: PPC*, III, 787–791, 795–796, 805, 807–808, 817.
[58] *FR 1919: PPC*, III, 788.

sion visit Syria to ascertain the preferences of the Syrian people regarding their future.[59]

Important differences within the Arab camp came out when Bliss was followed by a French-inspired delegation of Syrians and Lebanese who wanted the area set aside as a constitutional monarchy under French mandate. Not all Arabs cared to be included within an Arab confederation.[60]

Before the end of February the Council of Ten heard from the Armenians and the Jews. The Armenian plea was for an independent Armenia under Great Power mandate, while the Zionist delegates asked for implementation of the Balfour Declaration with Great Britain as mandatory.[61] Enough fuel for controversy had been furnished by these conflicting views to kindle a roaring blaze the following month when the Allies returned to the Syrian issue.

Wilson was fast discovering that once the United States was actively involved in one international situation, it became a partner with other states in nearly all phases of international life even though America had not, like the others, approached the Turkish settlement as a victor. How could the conflicting nationalist claims be satisfied and the growing estrangement of Great Britain and France in the Middle East be reconciled at the same time? And how could the details be worked out as part of a world settlement within the framework of a new international order?

These questions became more pressing in March during the Anglo-French quarrel over Syria. When Wilson returned to Washington for a month (February 14–March 14), sporadic discussion took place in his absence about the assignment of mandates. On March 6 Lloyd George and Clemenceau sounded out Colonel House about American willingness to take Constantinople and Armenia, areas originally assigned to Russia. House cabled Wilson that he told the Allied representatives he "thought the United States would be willing when the proposal was brought before them."[62] At an important session of the Council of

---

[59] *FR 1919: PPC*, III, 229, 859–866, 868–875, 888–894, 1015–1021. When Lansing raised the issue of a commission on February 18, the question was postponed. *Ibid.*, IV, 56. See also Shotwell, *Paris Peace Conference*, pp. 175–177.

[60] *FR 1919: PPC*, III, 1021, 1024–1038; IV, 2–5; Shotwell, *Paris Peace Conference*, pp. 178–179.

[61] *FR 1919: PPC*, IV, 147–157, 161–170.

[62] Seymour, *House Papers*, IV, 358–359. In his memorandum of the conference, Lloyd George wrote: "He [House] replied that America was not in the least anxious

Four [63] on March 20, shortly after Wilson's return, England and France became snarled in a deadlock over the Syrian mandate question. Wilson, who remained aloof until the discussants had obviously arrived at an impasse, then suggested sending an Allied commission of inquiry to Syria to ascertain the wishes of the inhabitants. Taking his cue from Bliss's suggestion of February 13, Wilson sought to implement his principle of self-determination and probably to expose French greediness at the same time. Although the Council authorized Wilson to frame terms of reference for such a commission, French and British misgivings delayed implementation and eventually altered the original plan. [64]

Wilson was drawn into another intra-Allied controversy when Italian ambitions in Anatolia frightened Lloyd George and Clemenceau. When Wilson vetoed Italian claims to the Adriatic coastlands as contrary to self-determination, Lloyd George suggested that the Italians might be requited by compensation in Anatolia. Wilson also vetoed this proposal as running counter to self-determination. The frustrated Italians then walked out of the Peace Conference on April 24 and prepared to take matters into their own hands. Five days later an Italian warship arrived at Smyrna, followed on May 2 by a battleship and two destroyers. Reports to the Council of Three suggested that the Italians were inciting the Turks against the Greek population of Smyrna. Lloyd George did not intend to stand idly by while the Italians ousted Britain's Greek ally from Smyrna. He proposed on May 6 that the Greeks be permitted to land two or three divisions at Smyrna and won the approval of Wilson and Clemenceau for this fateful operation to be designated an Allied force under Greek command. Under cover of Allied naval forces, including the American battleship *Arizona* and five American destroyers, landings at Smyrna took place on May 14. Wilson's concurrence and participation were apparently the product of his unilateral decision, since the imminence of a decision was not communicated to any of his advisers. [65]

to take these mandates, but that she felt that she could not shirk her share of the burden and he thought America would be prepared to take mandates for Armenia and Constantinople." David Lloyd George, *Memoirs of the Peace Conference*, I, 189.

[63] The Council of Four consisted of Wilson, Lloyd George, Clemenceau, and Orlando. When the Italian delegate was absent, it was called the Council of Three.

[64] *FR 1919: PPC*, V, 1–14; Tillman, *Anglo-American Relations*, pp. 221–223. See the informative article by Harry N. Howard, "An American Experiment in Peacemaking: The King-Crane Commission," *Moslem World*, 32 (April 1942), 122–146.

[65] *FR 1919: PPC*, V, 106–108, 135–136, 149–150, 202–203, 211, 222, 354, 412,

The Allies, having succeeded in implicating Wilson in the Turkish settlement, hoped to assign the United States even more onerous responsibilities. While the Smyrna operation was being arranged, Wilson was under increasing pressure to accept mandates. Lloyd George, especially, persisted in efforts to make America the mandatory power for both Armenia and the Constantinople-Straits area. Britain balked at having the French take over these areas, and the French were equally opposed to British dominance. The United States had no imperial objectives in the Middle East and could be relied on for impartial and just administration. The other interested powers would therefore assent to American mandates since they could not dominate them directly. Best of all, from the British point of view, America's presence would help protect the British lifeline through the Mediterranean by offering a bulwark to the southward spread of Bolshevism. British objectives would be well served without additional strain on imperial resources, and she would blunt the taunt of land-grabbing about which the British had become sensitive.[66]

Despite frequent charges to the contrary, Wilson gave the Allies little reason to expect that the United States would undertake the proffered responsibilities. He reminded the Council of Four of Turkish opposition to partition and of their desire for a single mandatory if they must have one at all. Such a mandate, he warned, might be more than the United States would be willing to accept; in any case, he could not assent until he had definitely ascertained American opinion.[67]

Wilson weakened on May 14, however, to the extent of agreeing to accept the two mandates subject to the assent of the Senate. A week later when Lloyd George again proposed an American mandate for the whole of Anatolia, Wilson expressed pessimism about the chances of persuading the Senate to accept Constantinople and Armenia, let alone all of Anatolia. Some of Wilson's staff in Paris were already beginning to doubt seriously the wisdom of American mandates in Turkey.[68]

422, 484, 501–505, 553–558, 570–571, 577–578, 688–689, 717–723, 733–734; Thomas H. Galbraith, "The Smyrna Disaster of 1922 and Its Effects on Turkish-American Relations," unpublished M.A. thesis, The Pennsylvania State University, 1960, p. 13; William L. Westermann, "The Armenian Problem and the Disruption of Turkey," in *What Really Happened at Paris: The Story of the Peace Conference, 1918–1919*, Edward M. House and Charles Seymour, eds., pp. 194–195.

[66] Lloyd George, *Memoirs*, II, 67–71; Howard, *Partition of Turkey*, p. 233.

[67] *FR 1919: PPC*, V, 482, 583–585.

[68] *FR 1919: PPC*, V, 614, 616, 622, 758–766; Lloyd George, *Memoirs*, II, 815–816; Elizabeth E. Allison, "American Participation in the Turkish Settlement, 1918–

While Lloyd George was renewing his pressure on Wilson to undertake mandates, the Syrian problem again demanded attention. On May 21, two months after the approval of the commission to Syria, Wilson reopened the matter. The French had been unwilling to have the commission proceed, undoubtedly for fear it would find the local population hostile to French supervision. Wilson now told the Council that he had instructed his American appointees, Dr. Henry Churchill King, president of Oberlin College, and Charles R. Crane, the businessman-philanthropist, to go to Syria to await their Allied colleagues. The Allied colleagues never arrived. France refused to participate until British troops had been completely removed from Syria, and French recalcitrance led Lloyd George to withdraw British participation.[69] The inquiry was carried out as an American project.

During May Lloyd George made several proposals and counterproposals relating to the Ottoman settlement, but either the Council or Lloyd George himself rejected each of them. Stalemate had been reached by May 21. Wilson then advised postponement of further discussion of the Turkish settlement for the time being. Again he advised his colleagues of American reluctance to assume responsibilities in Asia Minor, where the United States had no major material interests.[70]

Under the pressure of Wilson's imminent departure for the United States, the Council had to return to the Turkish question late in June. It seemed unreasonable to prolong the technical state of war with the Ottoman Empire pending a reply from the United States as to the role it would be willing to play. As a stopgap, Lloyd George suggested a possible preliminary agreement outlining future Turkish frontiers and enabling the nucleus of a new Turkish state to organize. Under this arrangement, Allied troops would remain in Armenia, Mesopotamia, and Syria until the final settlement. The conference then agreed on June 27 to postpone a Turkish settlement until the United States could ascertain its role.[71]

The following day, with the signing of the German treaty, the first

1920," unpublished M.A. thesis, The Pennsylvania State University, 1953, pp. 53–55.

[69] *FR 1919: PPC*, V, 766, 812; Seymour, *House Papers*, IV, 468; Howard in *Moslem World*, 32:131–132.

[70] *FR 1919: PPC*, V, 765, 770–771; Tillman, *Anglo-American Relations*, pp. 327–331.

[71] *FR 1919: PPC*, VI, 675–676, 711–713, 729–730; Howard, *Partition of Turkey*, pp. 237–238, 240.

stage of the Paris Peace Conference ended and Wilson departed for home. Because the Allies had failed to agree on a successor from among themselves to supervise areas originally assigned Russia, they had turned to the United States, the one impartial power without ambitions to collide with the national interests of the Allies. Wilson and his advisers had given the Allies only faint reason to expect that the American people and Senate would assume unrewarding responsibilities in the Middle East.

Disintegration of Allied Control, 1919. The situation in the Middle East slipped from the control of the Peace Conference during the last half of 1919. Without Wilson, Lloyd George, and Clemenceau negotiating there, Paris was no longer the focal point of decisions. Increasingly, events in the Middle East and in the United States were undermining the assumption of the Allies that they could in their own time dictate a Turkish peace, with the United States undertaking mandates for areas the Allies did not want.

As the peacemakers turned toward completing treaties with Germany's allies, they decided to resolve the easy ones first, leaving the Turkish treaty until last. Conveniently for them, they could justify these priorities by the need to await word from President Wilson as to American intentions. On June 30 the Heads of Delegation[72] confirmed the decision of June 27 to postpone the Turkish treaty until the president ascertained American opinion on mandates. When the Supreme Council heard from Wilson on July 18 that a considerable delay was likely before the American answer could be given, the Allies responded that they would try to maintain order pending the American decision.[73]

The Supreme Council found to its dismay, however, that the Middle East would not stand still while the Allies and the United States marked time. Fluid and rapidly deteriorating conditions faced the peacemakers as the summer and fall wore on. Armenia and the Caucasus demanded immediate attention, for those tragically devastated areas had to be provisioned and policed. Acting on American initiative, the Supreme Council appointed Colonel William N. Haskell to direct relief activities

[72] During the second stage of the Peace Conference, the principal Allied and Associated Powers met as the Council of the Heads of Delegation, although this group continued to be referred to as the Supreme Council.

[73] *FR 1919: PPC*, VII, 193. Lansing was in charge of the American delegation until his departure on July 12. Frank Polk arrived to take his place before the end of July and remained until early December. *Ibid.*, XI, 616–617.

in Armenia and the Caucasus, as the agent of the Allied and Associated Powers.[74]

The Allies could not, however, solve the policing problem. The British remained unshaken in their decision to remove their occupation troops, overriding the urgent pleading of President Wilson. The president regretfully declined requests to send American troops on grounds that he lacked constitutional authority to do so.[75]

Most significant for the future was the movement taking place in Anatolia where the ill-advised Greek occupation of Smyrna permitted by the Allies had enabled a great new leader, Mustafa Kemal, to rally Turkish nationalists to defy the Allies and the weak Sultanate at Constantinople. Farther south, Feisal and his Arab followers chafed under proposed French control in Syria and British moves to implement the Zionist program in Palestine. Serious Anglo-French differences over the French role in Syria continued into the fall.[76]

The Allies faced the sharp decline in their ability to dominate Asia Minor with a kind of helplessness and in the continuing hope that the United States would come to their rescue. Throughout the summer and early fall the British in particular warned American officials of the alarming trend of events. Ambassador John W. Davis reported Lord Curzon's expressing "the fear that if matters were permitted to drift we might find a Turkish movement strong enough to declare war instead of signing a Treaty."[77]

Retreat from the Middle East, 1919–1920. The United States stood at a crossroads during the summer and early fall of 1919 as the Wilson administration tried to prepare the ground for the country to undertake new responsibilities, including mandates in the Middle East, through

[74] *FR 1919: PPC*, VII, 28, 31, 40–41, 43–44; XI, 264; *FR 1919*, II, 826–827.

[75] John Sharp Williams (Senator from Mississippi) to Wilson, Aug. 9, 1919; Wilson to Williams, Aug. 12, 1919, Wilson MSS; Wilson to Cleveland E. Dodge, Aug. 14, 1919, Dodge MSS; *FR 1919: PPC*, VII, 647–649, 839–840; *FR 1919*, II, 828–831, 832–840; Henry Morgenthau, *All in a Life-Time*, pp. 339–340, 342–343; Cook, "Armenian Question," pp. 154, 190–200.

[76] Roderic Davison, "Turkish Diplomacy from Mudros to Lausanne," in *The Diplomats, 1919–1939*, Gordon A. Craig and Felix Gilbert, eds., pp. 172–209; Davis to Polk, Oct. 14, 1919; Polk to Davis, Oct. 19, 1919; Polk to William Phillips, Oct. 20, 1919, Frank L. Polk MSS. An informative study is Peter M. Buzanski's "The Inter-Allied Investigation of the Greek Invasion of Smyrna, 1919," to be published in *The Historian* in 1963.

[77] Davis to Polk, Nov. 11, 1919, Polk MSS. See also *FR 1919*, II, 829–830; Tillman, *Anglo-American Relations*, pp. 369–371.

participation in the League of Nations. Action went forward on two fronts — in the Middle East and at home.

Independently of the Allies, the United States collected information on the wishes and needs of the Armenians and Levant Arabs and tried to assess what mandate duties in Armenia would entail. The first of its two investigating groups, the King-Crane Commission, reported on July 10 the strong anti-French feeling in Syria and a preference there for the United States as mandatory with Great Britain as second choice. In view of Arab resentment, the commission also recommended a considerable scaling down of the Zionist program for Palestine. The commission reiterated these conclusions in its final report of August 28, when it recommended an independent Syrian state under Feisal with a single mandatory to be chosen by the people. So hostile to French and Zionist aspirations were the commission's conclusions that its report was not made public until 1922.[78]

The second American commission, headed by General James G. Harbord, was organized to assemble data essential to understanding what the responsibilities of the United States would be if it accepted an Armenian mandate. During its thirty-day investigation in Armenia and Transcaucasia, the Harbord Commission visited the Armenian vilayets of Turkey (except Van and Bitlis) and interviewed government officials and representatives of educational, religious, and charitable organizations supported by the American people. Harbord's report of October 16 recommended that Armenia and Transcaucasia have the same mandatory as Asia Minor, Constantinople, and Rumelia.[79]

On the home front, President Wilson was trying to use his dwindling personal prestige and the power of his office to convince the nation that it should choose the path of internationalism, including the burdens

[78] *FR 1919: PPC*, XII, 749–750; and pp. 751–836 for the entire report. See also Bristol Diary, reports for June 1, June 22, July 20, 1919, and entries for June 3, 4, 5, 8, July 21, Aug. 6, 1919, Mark L. Bristol MSS, Box 16; and Daniel in *Mississippi Valley Historical Review*, 46:260–261. The report was first published in *Editor and Publisher*, 55 (Dec. 2, 1922) and excerpts in *The New York Times* of Dec. 3, 1922. Comments on the anti-French and anti-Zionist conclusions of the commission are given in Polk to Lansing, Aug. 30, 1919, Polk MSS, and in W. H. Buckler to Ray S. Baker, Oct. 5, 1938, Ray Stannard Baker MSS, Series I, Box 20.

[79] *FR 1919*, II, 826–828; *FR 1919: PPC*, XI, 312, 358, 377–378, 384, 386, 396; Cook, "Armenian Question," pp. 213–219; Morgenthau, *All in a Life-Time*, pp. 336–347; Bristol Diary, reports for Sept. 7 and 21, 1919; entries for Oct. 11, 12, 13, 14, 15, 1919, Bristol MSS. The report with exhibits and appendices is printed in *FR 1919*, II, 841–889.

which went with it. Powerful counterforces were undermining the president's position and reviving the traditional American course of abstention from foreign entanglements.[80] Until the verdict was rendered, the United States could make no binding commitments to accept the mandates.

But the president pushed his frail body too far in his quest for public support during an arduous September barnstorming tour. When his health failed, the internationalists sorely missed his strong hand at the helm. Despairing British leaders thought Wilson's illness removed the last hope that the United States would take a mandate.[81] A few weeks after the president was stricken, the Senate voted on November 19, 1919, to reject the Versailles Treaty with the League of Nations covenant written into it. Nothing could be quite the same after this critical action.

The administration now saw no choice but to retreat as rapidly as possible from tentative European and Middle Eastern commitments. Accepting a mandate to be held under League supervision would be a grotesque anomaly when the United States had rejected League membership. When the president withdrew Frank Polk from Paris on December 9, the United States ceased to have a plenipotentiary at the conference and was represented only by an observer, Hugh Wallace, ambassador to France.[82]

Long before this forced withdrawal from the Middle East, some members of Wilson's official family had contemplated American participation in the Turkish settlement with misgivings. While on the Supreme Council, Frank Polk had consistently advocated abstention from incriminating commitments. Soon after his arrival he told Allied representatives of his belief that the Allies would appropriate all the potentially valuable areas of the Ottoman Empire, leaving Constantinople with no territory of consequence around it "and two barren wastes, Anatolia and Armenia, absolutely not self-supporting, for the United States to nurse." Polk considered the Turkish situation hopeless in view of the disintegration in Turkey and the delays in completing a peace treaty. As he wrote Lansing, the dilemma was that the Allies claimed

[80] Cook, "Armenian Question," pp. 219–225; Daniel in *Mississippi Valley Historical Review*, 46:262; *MRW*, 42 (Sept. 1919), 707.
[81] Davis to Polk, Oct. 14, 1919, Polk MSS.
[82] Polk to Bristol, Dec. 9, 1919, Polk MSS; W. H. Buckler to American Mission, Dec. 9, 1919, William Yale MSS; *FR 1919: PPC*, IX, 547n; XI, 696–697.

inability to make the treaty until they knew American intentions, "and Asia Minor cannot wait until we have made up our minds."[83]

Those who continued to advocate American responsibility in Turkey had almost unanimously concluded that a separate Armenian mandate would not be viable. Economic, military, and strategic considerations dictated that an Armenian mandate must be part of a larger mandate under a single power. No longer was the issue simply one of an American mandate for Armenia; it was a question of American supervision of all Asia Minor and Constantinople. Both the King-Crane and Harbord commissions had so recommended, and this opinion was shared by many knowledgeable Americans, including Admiral Bristol, Henry Morgenthau, James Barton, Cleveland H. Dodge, and others.[84]

Uncertainty as to the American position had not been the sole reason for delay in taking up the Turkish treaty, even though the Allies found it convenient to blame the United States. The Supreme Council had given priority to the other minor treaties and, even more important, Anglo-French differences had blocked negotiations. France, unwilling to concede British domination at Constantinople, was bitter over British efforts to ease the French out of Syria. The British finally turned over military control of Syria to French troops in November, 1919. Other obstacles were smoothed over sufficiently to permit the Allies to take up the Turkish terms early in 1920. Although the decisive meaning of the United States Senate's rejection of the Versailles Treaty could not be ignored, the Allies still urged American participation in the peace settlement. On January 21, 1920, the Supreme Council announced it was resuming negotiations, regardless of America's decision. The United States would be kept informed and its wishes consulted. When the London Conference assembled on February 12, the United States still did not choose to be represented.[85]

After the Allies had progressed far with drafting the Turkish treaty,

[83] Polk to Lansing, July 31, 1919 (quotations); Polk to Davis, Oct. 19, 1919; Polk to William Phillips, Oct. 20, 1919; Polk to Davis, Nov. 15, 1919, Polk MSS.
[84] For fuller examination of these points, see Cook, "Armenian Question," pp. 177–180; and Daniel in *Mississippi Valley Historical Review*, 46:259–261. Bristol's views are expressed in his Diary, reports of June 22, Aug. 17, Nov. 9, 1919, and Jan. 3, 1920, Bristol MSS, Box 16. See also Polk to Lansing, July 31, 1919, Polk MSS.
[85] Polk to Davis, Nov. 15, 1919; Allen W. Dulles to Hughes, July 22, 1922, Polk MSS; *DBFP*, IV, 523–524, 550, and *passim*; *FR 1919: PPC*, VIII, 207–208; X, 1008–1009; XI, 675–676; XIII, 6–7; Howard, *Partition of Turkey*, p. 242; *FR 1920*, I, 1.

they asked on March 8 if the United States reserved the right to protest the Allied resolutions arrived at after difficult negotiations and in spite of American refusal to assist in their formulation. Acting Secretary Polk felt this matter must be laid before President Wilson. On March 10 he wrote the president that if the Senate again turned down the Versailles Treaty in the vote about to be taken, it would then be difficult for the United States to show adequate reasons for signing the Turkish treaty. While the United States could not, to his mind, admit the ambitions of Great Britain, France, Italy, and Greece in the Middle East, it would be difficult to take a strong stand against their claims owing to lack of interest on the part of the American people and the attitude of Congress, which probably obviated any possibility of assuming commitments in the Middle East. "I must admit," he wrote Wilson, "the situation is puzzling but I take the liberty of suggesting that possibly the best course for us to pursue would be to say that we would not be represented at the negotiation of the Treaty, but at the same time, take the opportunity of expressing the views of this Government."[86]

Wilson concurred in Polk's proposal, but before Polk carried out this plan, Jules Jusserand, the French ambassador, communicated on behalf of the Allies the gist of the contemplated solutions. The United States was particularly interested in the proposed clauses providing that concessions granted by the former Turkish government might be revised or canceled upon payment of an indemnity. The State Department emphasized that regardless of whether or not the United States took part in the Turkish settlement, it would insist that the treaty assure protection to American citizens, corporations, and institutions no less favorable than that given nationals of other powers. The United States, in short, insisted on equal opportunity in the development of the Middle East. The department proclaimed America's vital interest in the issues at stake in the treaty because of their bearing on the future peace of the world.[87]

[86] Jules Jusserand to Polk, March 8, 1920; Polk to Wilson, March 10, 1920, Polk MSS.

[87] "While it is true that the United States of America was not at war with Turkey, yet it was at war with the principal allies of that country and contributed to the defeat of those allies and, therefore, to the defeat of the Turkish Government. For this reason, too, it is believed that it is the duty of this Government to make known its views and urge a solution which will be both just and lasting." *FR 1920*, III, 748–753. See also Division of Near Eastern Affairs (LW) to Polk, March 15, 1920; Polk to Wilson, March 16, 1920, Polk MSS.

Before they informed the United States of their agreement in principle with its views on economic equality, the Allies had already met again at San Remo, Italy, to settle the treaty provisions. There they allocated the so-called A mandates, placing Syria and Lebanon under a single mandate assigned to France, while Mesopotamia and Palestine went to Great Britain. The completed treaty was handed the Turkish representatives on May 11, but Turkey did not sign until August 10, 1920, at Sèvres. Among its provisions, the Sèvres Treaty called for an independent Armenia, much larger than the small Armenian state which had been leading a precarious existence in the Caucasus since late in 1918.[88]

Regardless of the apparent reluctance of most Americans to assume political and military responsibilities in Asia Minor and the forced retreat of their government from that area in 1919–1920, powerful and articulate groups at home continued to insist that the United States take up its rightful duties in the Middle East. Often differing among themselves, sometimes on important matters, missionary leaders, relief interests, and pro-Armenian pressure groups refused to abandon the fight, united in their belief that the United States could not abandon the Armenians. Beset by their demands to work for an Armenian mandate, the sick president finally, on May 24, requested Senate authority to accept the mandate. The Senate's answer was an emphatic no, by a vote of 52 to 23.[89]

In April, the Supreme Council had asked President Wilson to render an arbitral award fixing boundaries for a proposed Armenian state. He accepted the charge on May 17 and appointed a commission headed by William L. Westermann, who had been in charge of the Near Eastern section of the American peace delegation. Wilson cabled recommendations to Paris in November, outlining boundaries, but the Allies did not

[88] Office of the Assistant Secretary (HG) to Polk, May 10, 1920; Leland Harrison to Polk, May 11, 1920, Polk MSS; *FR 1919: PPC*, XIII, 7; *FR 1920*, I, 2; Benjamin Gerig, *The Open Door and the Mandate System*, pp. 106–107; Cook, "Armenian Question," p. 267.

[89] Stanley White and others to Wilson, April 10, 1920; Wilson to Cleveland E. Dodge, April 19, 1920; Dodge to Tumulty, May 19, 1920, Wilson MSS; *Cong. Record*, 66 Cong., 2 Sess., LIX, 7433, 7549, 7714, 7875, 8073. See also Daniel in *Mississippi Valley Historical Review*, 46:263–265; Cook, "Armenian Question," pp. 251–261; and Tillman, *Anglo-American Relations*, pp. 371–376. There are many letters and memorials from individuals and groups on the Armenian problem during the Wilson administration in the Wilson MSS, VI, 468, 2554.

attempt to carry out the Sèvres provisions calling for an independent Armenia.[90]

Die-hards continued to press the Armenian cause, but by the end of the Wilson administration the Turkish nationalists and the Soviets had crushed the Armenian republic. The cause of an independent Armenia was lost, but its ghost was to haunt American policy toward Turkey for the next few years.[91]

Conclusion

War and revolution, having rocked the Middle East since 1908, did not end with the signing of the Sèvres Treaty in August of 1920. Turkish nationalists considered its terms infamous, succeeded in preventing its implementation, and eventually forced the Allies to make a new treaty at Lausanne in 1922 and 1923.

During the first half of 1919 the United States government had entered into Middle Eastern politics as never before, but only to turn and retreat. Yet American interests there were too extensive to permit indifference to the actions of the European Powers. Near East Relief was still active; American missions faced a period of reconstruction and adjustment to Turkish, Persian, and Arab nationalism; commercial interests anticipated lucrative developments in the area; and, above all, the United States had become vitally interested in Middle Eastern oil. To protect and foster these interests the government had to devise an effective policy.

[90] *FR 1920*, III, 779–783, 787–804, 807–808; Cook, "Armenian Question," pp. 244–245, 251, 268–273. In his award of boundaries for Armenia, Wilson found a dilemma regarding self-determination. Areas in which Armenians were concentrated afforded Armenia neither access to the seas nor sufficient food resources. Thus, self-determination violated viability. To make Armenia "viable" a great deal of territory occupied by non-Armenians had to be included.

[91] James Barton and others to Wilson, June 18, 1920, Wilson MSS; Dodge to Wilson, Nov. 19, 1918; Morgenthau to Wilson, Nov. 20, 1918; Wilson to Dodge, Dec. 2, 1920, Dodge MSS; Daniel in *Mississippi Valley Historical Review*, 46:262–265; Cook, "Armenian Question," pp. 235–237, 262, 274–287; *MRW*, 42 (Feb. 1919), 148; (July 1919), 511; 43 (Oct. 1920), 923.

5

THE LAUSANNE CONFERENCE
AND ITS AFTERMATH

☆ "At sundown tonight I looked out of my window and saw the new moon, looking remarkably like a Turkish crescent, hanging directly over the tower of the Hotel du Chateau where the Peace Conference is to take place. Was it an omen? We shall learn eventually."[1] Joseph C. Grew made this striking entry in his diary on November 20, 1922, after attending the formal opening of the Lausanne Conference called by Great Britain, France, and Italy to forge a peace settlement with the Turkish nationalists. The State Department appointed Grew, a career diplomat at the time minister to Switzerland, together with Richard Washburn Child and Admiral Mark Bristol, as observers to look after American interests at Lausanne.

The heartland of the Middle East was still in turmoil four years after the Mudros armistice. Initially, the preoccupation of the Allies with the German peace treaty had delayed a Turkish settlement; then the inability of the principal Allied Powers to reconcile promptly their own differences encouraged further improvisation, as the victors tried desperately to cope with the onrushing changes in the area. When reluctant representatives of the Sultan were finally forced to sign the Treaty of Sèvres on August 10, 1920, that treaty was already obsolete. The New Turks were rising from the ashes of the old Ottoman Empire under the gifted leadership of Mustafa Kemal.

The New Turks
The gross miscalculation of the Allies in sponsoring the Greek invasion of Asia Minor in May of 1919 assisted Kemal's rise as the personality galvanizing nascent Turkish nationalism. After landing at the Black

[1] Grew Diary, Nov. 20, 1922, Grew MSS.

Sea port of Samsun on May 19, Kemal rallied Anatolian Turks to move against the Armenians, resist the Greek invaders, oppose the Allied occupation policies, and replace the discredited Sultan at Constantinople, now the creature of the Allies. The program of Turkey for the Turks — independent, sovereign, and free from foreign domination — emerged from the nationalist congresses at Erzerum and Sivas by early autumn and guided the nationalists who soon became the *de facto* government in much of Anatolia.[2]

Kemal and his New Turks overcame seemingly insurmountable obstacles by astutely taking advantage of the distresses of their adversaries. As France and Italy became increasingly disaffected with the British championing of Greek imperial ambitions in Asia Minor, the New Turks profited from this rupture. Before the end of 1921, France and Italy had begun to come to terms with the Anatolian Turks now ruling from Ankara. Kemal's diplomats had also effected accommodation with the Soviets and mended fences with other neighbors.[3]

Relentless purpose, a prudent program, military successes, and astute diplomacy combined to deal the Greeks and their supporters a stunning defeat. Kemal's forces finally drove the Greeks back to Smyrna and then into the sea during the offensive of August-September, 1922.[4] The Allies had no choice but to meet with the victorious New Turks to recast the obsolete Sèvres Treaty. The Allies had made several earlier efforts, notably at the London Conference of February, 1921, to bring about peace on the basis of some modification of the Sèvres terms. But it was not until after the Mudania armistice of October 11, 1922, that Great Britain, France, and Italy invited Turkey, the United States, and other nations to attend a new peace conference at Lausanne.[5]

[2] Davison in *The Diplomats*, pp. 172–209. See also Howard, *Partition of Turkey*, pp. 253–274; Kemal H. Karpat, *Turkey's Politics: The Transition to a Multi-Party System*, pp. 32–40; Count Carlo Sforza, *Diplomatic Europe since the Treaty of Versailles*, pp. 51–66. For Kemal's personal account, see *A Speech Delivered by Ghazi Mustapha Kemal, President of the Turkish Republic, October 1927*, pp. 9–585, *passim*. The National Pact adopted on January 28, 1920, is printed in Hurewitz, *Diplomacy*, II, 74–75.

[3] Davison in *The Diplomats*, pp. 183–185, 189–191, 193–195; Howard, *Partition of Turkey*, pp. 259–264.

[4] Thomas H. Galbraith, "The Smyrna Disaster of 1922 and Its Effects on Turkish-American Relations," unpublished M.A. thesis, The Pennsylvania State University, 1960; Bristol Diary, Sept. 1922, Bristol MSS.

[5] Davison in *The Diplomats*, pp. 188–189, 198–199; Howard, *Partition of Turkey*, pp. 260, 265–266, 270–272; *MRW*, 45 (June 1922), 499; (July 1922), 522–524; *FR 1923*, II, 889.

American Interests and Policies, 1919–1922

While these momentous events were undoing the Allied design for Turkey, the United States was not usually one of the contenders in the political arena. American officials and citizens were interested spectators who occasionally protested the proceedings or offered advice to the participants. President Wilson had wearily bowed to the national will by retreating as rapidly as possible from European politics when Congress refused to support American entry into the League of Nations. American withdrawal imposed the inevitable corollary of nonparticipation in the Turkish settlement, where American stakes were considerably less than Europe's. In American eyes pacification of the Middle East was an Allied problem.

To justify the American withdrawal, it could be argued that American interests were still too insignificant to warrant intrusion into this cockpit of European rivalries and that the participants richly deserved being left to extricate themselves from the bitter consequences of their past follies. Forty years later, it can be maintained that the course of international affairs might have been less troubled if the United States had exerted its power and influence for a disinterested settlement that would have yielded long-run dividends in greater international stability. This much is certain: failure to assume political burdens complicated the State Department's task of protecting American interests in the Middle East. As it turned out, the United States could not remain totally indifferent to the political settlement, if the government were to fulfill its minimum obligations to American nationals in Turkey, and if it wished to maintain the respect of the world.

Contemporary criticism of American withdrawal from the Turkish settlement came from many quarters — diplomats, church leaders, educators, businessmen, and others. One persistent voice was that of Rear Admiral Mark L. Bristol, high commissioner of the United States in Constantinople between 1919 and 1927.[6] Bristol wore two hats in Constantinople, one as commander of American naval forces in the area, the other as a functioning diplomat in the capital of a government the

[6] Lewis Heck was appointed American commissioner in Constantinople on November 30, 1918, and the consulates were reopened early in 1919. Bristol was appointed high commissioner on August 12, 1919. The department took pains to point out that these appointments did not constitute resumption of diplomatic relations with Turkey. Under directives from the Supreme Council, trade with Turkey was resumed on February 17, 1919. *FR 1919*, II, 810–814.

United States did not recognize. He took his diplomatic duties seriously and acquitted himself admirably, thanks to his mastery of detail, his extraordinary gifts for analysis, and his fair-mindedness.

Bristol fearlessly pressed his considered views on the State Department where his diplomatic talents were highly regarded. On October 10, 1921, he alerted Secretary of State Charles Evans Hughes to the complex and rapidly changing Turkish situation: "It is now quite clear," the admiral wrote, "that the Treaty of Sevres, if it is retained at all by the Allies, will be modified in important particulars. Presumably, there will be further negotiations among the Allies to accomplish this." Bristol argued that it was important for the United States to work for elimination of clauses in the Sèvres Treaty detrimental to American interests and to secure the protection of those interests in the revised treaty. The Tripartite Treaty (August 10, 1920) by which the Allies arranged spheres of interest in Asia Minor convinced the admiral that "we cannot rely upon the Allies to protect our interests in the Near East." The State Department, he urged, should get busy at once preparing data and deciding on its attitude toward a Turkish settlement. It would be easier to prevent adoption of discriminatory measures at the time of negotiation than to counteract their effect by subsequent negotiations with the Allies and Turkey.[7]

The admiral supplemented his observations two months later when he wrote Hughes that American Middle Eastern policy was "too hide bound and conservative." The United States should follow a more realistic course "without involving ourselves in any political adventures." First of all a policy must be formulated as a guide, for "since the withdrawal . . . we have had no voice and have shown no real interest in Near East affairs." Since the peace of the world might well be bound up in a peaceful Middle East, the United States should participate in the Turkish settlement at least to the point of ensuring the Open Door. He did not expect the United States to sign a peace treaty with Turkey because we had not been at war with her, but believed that by participation we would prevent inclusion of provisions, especially those of an economic and financial nature, detrimental to American interests.[8]

[7] Bristol to Hughes, Oct. 10, 1921, DS 711.67/21. The Tripartite Treaty is printed in Hurewitz, *Diplomacy*, II, 87–89.
[8] Bristol to Hughes, Dec. 17, 1921, DS 711.67/24. Bristol soon urged that "in any treaty with Turkey we could properly insist, one, that American interests and American nationals be treated on a most favored nation basis; two, that zones of

Bristol was encouraged by the appointment of Allen W. Dulles, a member of his Constantinople staff, as chief of the Division of Near Eastern Affairs early in 1922. Bristol regretted losing Dulles, but felt it would be "a great advantage" to have him in Washington, for Bristol had "continually felt that the Department was not giving enough attention to Near Eastern affairs and that there was a lack of enthusiasm there that was much to be deplored. I cannot imagine a better choice than Mr. Dulles for this post in the Department."[9]

Bristol had formed his point of view while contending with the day to day problems of protecting American economic and humanitarian interests. His relations with American business representatives in Turkey were close, and his views reflected in part a desire to have the American government clear obstructions to commercial expansion. Speaking also for business interests was the American Chamber of Commerce for the Levant, which on February 8, 1922, asked the State Department for greater American participation in Turkish affairs. E. E. Pratt, the secretary and managing director, complained about Allied economic discrimination and asked that the United States participate in the revisions of the Sèvres Treaty on behalf of American interests.[10]

Also directly concerned with the political future of Turkey was the American Board of Commissioners for Foreign Missions, which had operated missions and allied enterprises in Turkey for a century. At the board's annual meeting in October of 1922, delegates drafted a petition to the president and secretary of state calling for American participation in the forthcoming conference. The petition stressed the vast investment of American life, capital, and effort in religious, educational, and charitable institutions amounting, it claimed, to more than a hundred million dollars — a greater sum than all the other eight nations invited to the conference had at stake in similar enterprises. The resolution also mentioned the continuing need for American relief of hundreds of thousands of orphans. The United States, asserted the resolution,

special economic influence should be abolished; three, that an option should be granted the United States to participate in any civil commissions established under the treaty; four, that no modifications of the capitulations should be made without our consent; five, that our educational and missionary institutions should be protected in all rights enjoyed in 1914." Bristol to Hughes, Feb. 11, 1922, DS 711.67119/1.

[9] Bristol Diary, March 4, 1922, Bristol MSS.

[10] Pratt to Hughes, Feb. 8, 1922; Pratt to Dulles, Oct. 18, 1922, DS 711.67119/– and 3.

132

might bring its influence to bear in the direction of stability and "preservation of civilization in the Near East."[11]

The future of the board's missions in Turkey was especially uncertain at the time of this annual meeting. Turkish authorities vacillated, declaring at one time that missionary work must cease and at another that they would welcome both educational and evangelical workers. The board's report on Turkish missions referred to 1922 as "a year of horrors," with untold loss of life and suffering among the remaining Greek and Armenian Christians in Asia Minor. Working against great handicaps and hardships, the board's missionaries had relieved much suffering. The board recognized that the Turks were bent on eliminating the Christian minorities, the main clients of the American Board in the past. There was uneasiness too over the Turks' unilateral termination of the capitulations which had protected the missionary enterprises. The missionaries were uncertain as to what protection the American government might be able to arrange for the board's future activities.[12]

Spokesmen for the Armenians also pled for American participation in the treaty revision, which they ardently hoped would further their virtually lost cause. The importunings of the Armenia-America Society were contained in a letter of February 11, 1922, to President Warren G. Harding.[13] Closely allied to the pressure groups speaking in behalf of Armenians and other eastern Christians were Protestant sects without direct interests in Turkey. Perhaps the most fiery of them was a southern Methodist Episcopal bishop, James Cannon, Jr., who castigated the Turks as "murderous cutthroats" and "bloodthirsty outlaws." Blind to equally barbarous atrocities perpetrated by Armenian and Greek Christians, Cannon frequently pressed his Turcophobic views before his own churchmen and before meetings called to promote relief drives. Not satisfied to criticize official American policy in thundering speeches, he decided to beard the secretary of state in his own office and throw

[11] ABC, *AR 1922*, pp. 18–19. See also *MRW*, 45 (Nov. 1922), 853–855, 863–866; 46 (Jan. 1923), 61; (April 1923), 247–249.

[12] ABC, *AR 1922*, pp. 73–74, 76. See also *MRW*, 45 (April 1922), 335; (May 1922), 341–343; (Aug. 1922), 658–659; 46 (March 1923), 170–172, 182, 227.

[13] Walter George Smith and George R. Montgomery (of the Armenia-America Society) to Harding, Feb. 11, 1922, DS 711.67119/2. For details on the activities of various pro-Armenian groups, their disagreements on objectives and methods, and Congressional interest in the Armenians during 1921 and 1922, see Cook, "Armenian Question," pp. 292–315. For American relief work among Armenians, and arguments favoring American official intervention, see *MRW*, 44 (Aug. 1921), 590–592; 45 (Feb. 1922), 146–147.

all the weight of his position and prestige behind the cause for American intervention in Turkey. His interview with Hughes in the summer of 1922, during which he presented a memorial adopted by his church, is described by Cannon as follows:

I endeavored to impress Secretary Hughes with the urgency of the need for prompt, definite, and effective action owing to the critical conditions existing, especially in Asiatic Turkey, where the Turks were ruthlessly slaughtering Greeks and Armenians, combatants and non-combatants, children and old people. Secretary Hughes read the resolution and called my attention to what he considered to be the extreme language used, asking what was meant by the words "whatever steps may be necessary." I replied that it meant exactly what it said. "But," said Secretary Hughes, "that could mean war." I replied, "Certainly it could, if the Turks thought the United States government was not in earnest in commanding that they cease committing atrocities; but if war is necessary, the resolutions clearly contemplate war."

When Secretary Hughes expressed surprise that war should be even thought of, I replied, "Our government went to war with Spain because of the persecution of the Cubans and the atrocities practiced by General Weyler. We recently entered a war because of what we held to be German atrocities."[14]

The Harding administration would, of course, have no part of the interventionist policy advocated by Bishop Cannon and other firebrands. Not once but several times the nation had spoken its conviction that America had no proper place in the political controversies of Europe and the Middle East. If American economic and humanitarian stakes required governmental support, however, the United States had no choice but to deal with Great Britain, France, Italy, and the nationalistic Turks. To meet these needs and still remain within the noninterventionist constraints imposed by the national will, the administration had improvised a kind of policy. (Bristol had been less than accurate in charging that the department had no Middle Eastern policy between 1919 and 1922.) Taking a leaf from the nation's Far Eastern diplomacy, the Wilson administration had turned to the open-door principle as a theoretical basis for protecting and fostering American missions, schools, and business and philanthropic enterprises.

[14] Virginius Dabney, *Dry Messiah: The Life of Bishop Cannon*, pp. 162–163 (first quotation); Richard L. Watson, Jr., ed., *Bishop Cannon's Own Story: Life As I Have Seen It*, pp. 225–228 (long quotation, p. 226); Scipio, *Thirty Years in Turkey*, p. 179. For Hughes's account, see *FR 1922*, II, 931–932.

The department began to stress the Open Door as the basis of its Middle Eastern policy in 1919 and 1920, during the acrimonious controversy with the British over their discrimination against American oil interests in Palestine and Mesopotamia. Soon the department adapted the Open Door to benefit noneconomic American interests — missionaries, educators, archaeologists, and American citizens in general.

Adhering to the open-door principle, the United States decided to resolve its dilemma by attending the Lausanne peace conference, represented not by plenipotentiaries, but by observers instructed to stay clear of boundary and other political decisions while working for a settlement according equality of treatment to American citizens and their interests.[15]

Pre-Conference Maneuvers

In preparing for the Lausanne Conference, the British task was to build an effective united front with which the Western nations could confront the victorious and determined Turkish nationalists. Considering the rifts in Allied unity, now complicated by growing Anglo-French estrangement over German reparations, this was no easy assignment. During October the Fascist revolutions in Italy compounded the difficulty. While Mussolini was preoccupied with domestic problems, his position at the forthcoming conference was an uncertain quantity. Lord George Nathaniel Curzon, British foreign secretary, thought it worth a try to seek American backing to strengthen the British position, perhaps by muting British interest in favorable territorial terms and emphasizing instead the identity of Anglo-American interests, especially on the issue of Christian minorities.

As early as September 19, 1922, the British embassy in Washington made unofficial soundings to ascertain from Allen Dulles whether the United States would send representatives to the conference. The State Department did not commit itself immediately, but Hughes let it be known at a press conference that the United States approved Allied statements favoring freedom of the Straits and protection of racial and religious minorities. Cheered by Hughes's declaration, Lord Curzon

[15] *FR 1923*, II, 886–888. See below, Chap. 6 (pp. 169–184) and Chap. 10 (p. 338 and *passim*) for fuller discussion of the origins of the oil controversy and the development of the open-door argument in connection with the British and French mandates.

probed cautiously in an interview with Ambassador George Harvey on October 12. Independently, Austen Chamberlain, a leader in the House of Commons, assured Harvey that British statesmen were united in their conviction that the two countries "inevitably and irresistibly approached international problems from the same point of view."[16]

Under continued prodding from Admiral Bristol, Secretary Hughes and his staff were busy formulating the department's conception of American interests in the Middle East. A few hours before receiving the formal invitation to attend the conference, Hughes had outlined subjects of particular American concern in an aide-mémoire which he instructed the ambassadors in Great Britain, France, and Italy to deliver to the respective foreign offices. In summary, the seven-point American program called for maintenance of capitulations to safeguard non-Moslem interests; protection with proper guarantees of philanthropic, educational, and religious institutions; equality of commercial opportunity; indemnities to Americans for arbitrary and illegal Turkish acts; protection of minorities; freedom of the Straits; and reasonable opportunity for archaeological research and study. In separate instructions, Hughes elaborated on these points, spelled out American strategy and tactics, and added some confidential information not to be conveyed to the Allied governments.[17]

Lord Curzon's reaction on learning that the United States would be represented was more cordial than the formal and perfunctory response from the French. He apparently believed that prospects for American support were bright enough for him to risk a serious overture. The occasion was the British effort to take a strong position against the Turks to protest their treatment of the Greek population during and after the Smyrna rout. On November 10 the British ambassador, Sir Auckland Geddes, requested nothing less than American support of an ultimatum to the Turks. On eliciting from Geddes the admission that the ultimatum amounted to a threat of war, Hughes dissented, disavowing American association with British imperial ambitions. There was no evidence that the American people were prepared to go to war on such an issue, Hughes observed. In a subsequent interview three days later, Geddes

[16] *FR 1923*, II, 879–883. See also Hughes's Memorandum of Conference with the British Ambassador, Sept. 25, 1923, Hughes MSS, Box 175.
[17] *FR 1923*, II, 884–889, 892, 897–899.

renewed his request and the two men covered much the same ground in their discussion. Hughes rejected the idea of threatening war without intending to follow through if the bluff was called. The United States preferred to use diplomatic pressure to secure the protection of Christians in Turkey.[18]

The Lausanne Conference,
First Phase: November 20, 1922 to February 4, 1923

The Lausanne Conference on the Middle East, one of the most important international gatherings after World War I, assembled on November 20, 1922. After reaching an impasse two and a half months later, the conference adjourned on February 4. Following an interval of nearly three months, the conference reassembled on April 23 to complete the new treaty with Turkey, which was signed on July 23, 1923.[19]

Organization of the Conference. Lord Curzon made himself stage manager and director of the conference and left no doubt that he intended this to be his show. As chairman of the commission on territorial and military questions, he headed the first and most important of the three commissions set up to conduct conference business. Marquis Camillo Garroni of Italy chaired the second commission, assigned problems of foreigners and minorities, while France's special interest in financial and economic questions was recognized by making M. Camille Barrère chairman of the third commission entrusted with those issues. These three commissions passed specific problems to subcommissions and teams of experts from their staffs, while an editorial commission hammered agreed-on clauses into proper form. By design, plenary sessions were rare. Because debates were secret, newspapermen

---

[18] *FR 1922*, II, 952–958; *FR 1923*, II, 890–893.
[19] For a useful over-all account of the conference, see Howard, *Partition of Turkey*, pp. 277–314. For documents relating to the conference, see *Turkey, No. 1 (1923), Lausanne Conference on Near Eastern Affairs, 1922–1923: Records of Proceedings and Draft Terms; Conférence de Lausanne sur les affaires du Proche-Orient (1922–1923), Recueil des Actes de la Conférence, Première série*, tomes I–II; *FR 1923*, II, 879–1198. Important memoirs based on the diaries of American delegates are Grew, *TE*, I, 475–555; and Richard Washburn Child, *A Diplomat Looks at Europe*, pp. 79–124. For an interpretation of Lord Curzon and his diplomacy more favorable than mine, see Harold Nicolson, *Curzon: The Last Phase, 1919–1925: A Study in Post-War Diplomacy*, pp. 281–350.

received only an official daily communique. Dissatisfied with the thin diet, they eagerly grasped any rumor which could be inflated into good copy.[20]

American Strategy and Tactics. The three American observers — Richard Washburn Child, ambassador to Italy in charge, assisted by Joseph C. Grew, minister to Switzerland and, after November 26, by Rear Admiral Mark L. Bristol, high commissioner in Constantinople — usually sat in at meetings of the three main commissions. Their subordinates participated in subcommission deliberations and reported to their superiors after each session. As chief of delegation, Child conducted most conversations in behalf of the United States, but Grew and Bristol sometimes assisted by undertaking specific interviews. The three held daily conferences to pool information, make suggestions regarding policies and their implementation, receive delegations, and run the chancery.[21]

The primary objective of the United States in sending observers to Lausanne was, as Child stated to the conference, "to protect American interests, idealist or commercial, humane or financial, without discrimination." The instructions to the American observers urged them to be in the thick of things, forfeiting no advantage, losing no just influence, and making no injurious commitments. In the words of Secretary Hughes, "we should maintain the integrity of our position as an independent power which has not been concerned with the rivalries of other nations which have so often made the Near East a theater of war." Consistent with this independent position and with American national ideals, the observers ought "to protect, whenever possible, humanitarian interests regardless of their nationality." They were also to exercise a mediatory influence toward effecting a durable settlement which would bring peace and stability in the Middle East. Mindful from the outset that the United States would have to make its own

[20] Grew, *TE*, I, 503; Child, *Diplomat*, pp. 86–90, 116; *Turkey No. 1*, p. 13; Nicolson, *Curzon*, pp. 290–293.

[21] *Turkey No. 1*, pp. 82, 87–88; Grew, *TE*, I, 484 n. 2, 496, 513–514; Gates, *Not to Me Only*, pp. 287–292; Grew Diary, Nov. 26, Nov. 28, Dec. 1, Dec. 7, 1922, Grew MSS; Bristol Diary, Nov. 16, Nov. 23, 1922, Bristol MSS, Box 21. Other members of the American delegation were F. Lammot Belin (from the Paris embassy), Copley Amory (from the Rome embassy), Harrison C. Dwight (from the Near Eastern Division in Washington), Julian Gillespie and Lewis Heck (both from Constantinople). Child, *Diplomat*, p. 82.

settlement with the Turks, the American delegation wished to maintain the closest possible relations with the Turkish representatives.[22]

To achieve these basic aims, the American observers often had to work outside the formal machinery of the conference, since so much of the real work went on during private discussions in hotel rooms and over cocktails far into the morning hours. Grew wrote his mother that "we are playing a fairly important part in it — more so than appears on the surface. We have influence on the Turks and we are exerting it." [23]

Conference Issues and American Positions. Several issues vital to the inviting powers and Turkey were of little or no concern to the United States. In this category were territorial and military issues discussed by delegates early in the conference. The disposition of Thrace, its boundaries, possible Bulgarian access to the Aegean Sea, and the status of the Aegean islands were significant to the Americans only in relation to keeping the Straits open to all nations for commercial intercourse.[24]

The rival claims of Great Britain and Turkey to Mosul were in a slightly different category, for although the United States did not really care which adversary won Mosul, it did insist from beginning to end that equality of economic opportunity for Americans should be recognized in that area no matter what its disposition.[25]

Financial questions such as the proportion of the Ottoman public debt to be assumed by the succession states were also out of bounds for the United States, although Secretary Hughes instructed his observers about certain conditions under which it might be desirable to have American representation on a reconstructed Ottoman Public Debt

[22] *FR 1923*, II, 888 (second quotation), 962–964 (first and third quotations); Child, *Diplomat*, p. 120; Grew, *TE*, I, 514, 516–517, 521–522, 534–535, 544–546; Grew Diary, Jan. 6, 1923, and Grew to Dulles, Jan. 15, 1923, Grew MSS. See also *Turkey No. 1*, pp. 11, 92–93, 441–443.

[23] Grew to his mother, Dec. 15, 1922, Grew MSS; Grew, *TE*, I, 513, 546, 549; Child, *Diplomat*, pp. 110, 118. For evidences of the American role as mediator, see Child, *Diplomat*, p. 121; Grew, *TE*, I, 535–538, 541; Grew to Dulles, Jan. 8, 1923, Grew Diary, Jan. 1, Feb. 1, Feb. 5, 1923, Grew MSS; *FR 1923*, II, 963; Beerits Memorandum, p. 9, Hughes MSS, Box 172, folder 35.

[24] Howard, *Partition of Turkey*, pp. 281–297.

[25] Child, *Diplomat*, pp. 97, 108, 114–115, 117, 118; Grew, *TE*, I, 522, 523, 526, 529, 533, 537, 540; Grew Diary, Jan. 23, Jan. 25, 1923, Grew MSS; Howard, *Partition of Turkey*, pp. 297–301. For American invocation of the Open Door in connection with Mosul, see Grew, *TE*, I, 500–501, 537, 548–549; Child, *Diplomat*, pp. 91–93; Grew Diary, Jan. 23, 1923, Grew MSS; *FR 1923*, II, 904–908; *Turkey No. 1*, p. 405.

Commission. The status to be given uncompleted prewar concessions attracted the lively interest of the United States, but the real crisis on this issue did not develop until the second phase of the conference.[26] On the foregoing issues of little intrinsic interest to the United States, American observers frequently played a mediatory role in bringing the parties together for private discussions, explaining to one side the position of the other, and searching for possible compromises.

The Straits question was a different matter, for the United States strongly advocated the founding of a regime that would ensure commercial freedom for all nations and favored those terms best calculated to preserve this important waterway from the rivalries of European powers. The United States would have preferred that the Straits settlement rest on a treaty without an international commission, not wishing to participate in the latter.[27]

The issues on which the American delegation fought hardest were of two types — those identified with specific rights of American nationals in Turkey (safeguards for citizens through capitulations; guarantees for educational, philanthropic, and religious institutions; and the Open Door), and those closely identified with certain American ideals and goals, notably, the protection of Christian minorities in Turkey. Except for the Open Door, it was on these points that the Nationalist Turks were most intransigent and that the Allies and the United States found their widest agreement.[28]

Early in the conference, private talks about capitulations with Ismet Pasha, head of the Turkish delegation, and his staff, revealed that Angora would resist most vigorously any attempt to continue the capitulations or anything resembling them under some new name. Even drastically watered-down proposals, such as one for a system akin to the Mixed Courts of Egypt, were rejected out of hand by the Turks.

[26] *FR 1923*, II, 903–904, 908–909, 968, 972–974; Child, *Diplomat*, p. 119; Nicolson, *Curzon*, p. 296 n. 1. Howard, *Partition of Turkey*, pp. 308–310, discusses the Ottoman public debt, reparations, and concessions during the first phase of the conference. See below, p. 148, for the concession issue during the second phase of the conference.

[27] Grew, *TE*, I, 502, 506–510, 510–512, 514–515, 518; Child, *Diplomat*, pp. 98–101, 110–112, 117–118; *FR 1923*, II, 910–911, 912–915, 916–918, 919–920, 929, 929–930, 931, 935–936, 938, 962, 978–982; Grew Diary, Dec. 3, Dec. 9, 1922, Grew MSS; Hughes memorandum of interview with the British ambassador, Dec. 7, 1922, Hughes MSS, Box 175; *Turkey No. 1*, pp. 145–146; Howard, *Partition of Turkey*, pp. 285–297.

[28] *Turkey No. 1*, pp. 185–187, 470, 493–494.

Impasse on this issue helped precipitate the rupture in the conference on February 4, 1923.[29]

The Turks did inform American observers that they would be willing to give guarantees for foreign educational, philanthropic, and religious institutions. But Allied and American efforts in behalf of an Armenian national home ran up against a stone wall. The Turks had made up their minds that the minorities must go, except any persons who agreed to become integrated into the new Turkish state. The United States achieved some success in pressing for the continuation of the Greek Patriarchate in Constantinople with the understanding that the Patriarch would be stripped of all political functions and confined to a strictly religious role. American observers also obtained exemption for the urban Greeks in Constantinople from the population exchange between Greece and Turkey.[30]

The Conference Atmosphere. The conference seemed to have its own fever chart. The American delegation commented often on the day to day fluctuations which made it impossible to tell at any given moment precisely how matters stood. Rumor within the delegations and from without, taken up by the press, produced abrupt changes in mood. There were intermittent blue periods when the conference seemed about to break up, as it finally did early in February. Grew found the pace hectic and almost as fast as that of the Paris conference. Business and social affairs could not be separated since they went on simultaneously with much wining and dining and even a trace of scandal now and then to provide diversionary gossip. In no small measure, the possibilities and limitations of the conference were shaped by personal and group relationships.[31]

Grew obtained the impression that the British were uneasy about

[29] *Turkey No. 1*, pp. 304–307; Grew, *TE*, I, 492–493, 502–503, 523–524, 536, 537–538; Child, *Diplomat*, pp. 113–114; *FR 1923*, II, 923–924, 925–927, 928, 931–933, 941, 953; Grew Diary, Dec. 6, 1922, Grew MSS.

[30] *FR 1923*, II, 901, 906–907, 910, 915–916, 920–924, 930, 934, 939–948, 950; Grew, *TE*, I, 492, 524–525, 530–531, 533–534; Gates, *Not to Me Only*, pp. 264–267, 288–290; *MRW*, 46 (March 1923), 170–172; (April 1923), 247–249; Howard, *Partition of Turkey*, pp. 301–304; Child, *Diplomat*, pp. 83, 97, 103–108, 115–117; Gordon, *American Relations with Turkey*, pp. 33–34; Grew Diary, Nov. 18, Dec. 7, Dec. 22, Dec. 21–31, 1922, Grew MSS.

[31] Grew, *TE*, I, 497, 513, 515–517, 522–523, 528–529, 531, 535–537, 540, 547; Child, *Diplomat*, pp. 97, 112–113; Grew Diary, Nov. 21, Dec. 12, 1922, Jan. 14, Feb. 1, 1923; Grew to William Phillips, Dec. 3, 1922; Grew to Dulles, Jan. 8 and Jan. 15, 1923; Grew MSS.

the lack of Allied solidarity as the conference began. Curzon was angling for American support and probably trying at the same time to wean the American delegation from any affinity it might have with the Turks. Throughout the first phase of the conference, the American delegates were never quite sure that outward British candor could be trusted as a correct representation of British activities behind the scenes. Grew and Lord Curzon became friends, dining together frequently or relaxing with piano music provided by Grew. Although the two men spoke frankly to each other, Grew objected emphatically to Curzon's brow-beating tactics with Ismet and the Turks. So did Child, whose relationship with Curzon was also friendly, if not so close as Grew's. Both Grew and Child believed that Curzon was incapable of dealing effectively with the new Turks. With Ismet, Curzon played the role of a hard schoolmaster or a viceroy of India; he was haughty, sarcastic, tactless. On one occasion, Child commented that the two "had about as much in common as a lion tamer and a grower of azaleas," and observing Curzon's frustrations at another time, he wrote that "he has the mood of a god with influenza." The Americans were sufficiently detached to sense that the old era of Western domination in Turkey was rapidly passing and that the new situation required different tactics.[32]

Anglo-French tension clouded the conference from the start and impeded Allied dealings with the Turks. French delegates also gave lip service to the importance of a united Allied front when talking with American observers early in the conference, but their bitterness toward England was better revealed by their insistence that France would not send more troops to clean up the situation caused by the mistakes of another nation. "What a comedy!" was Child's sardonic comment at the pretensions of Allied unity when their household was in obvious disarray.[33]

Admiral Bristol's relations with the Turks and their high esteem for

[32] Grew Diary, Nov. 19, 1922; Grew to Dulles, Jan. 8, 1923, Grew MSS; Grew, *TE*, I, 491, 493, 525–526, 528–529, 536 (first quotation), 553; Child, *Diplomat*, pp. 91, 94, 95, 98, 102 (second quotation), 108–109, 112; Bristol Diary, Dec. 11, Dec. 13, 1922, Bristol MSS. The present writer does not concur with Sir Harold Nicolson's rather hostile view of Child and his work at the conference. Cf. *Curzon*, pp. 296–297, 320, 334.

[33] Child, *Diplomat*, pp. 88–90 (quotation), 94, 112, 116, 119, 123; Grew, *TE*, I, 490–491, 495–496, 528–530, 532, 539–540, 543–544, 554; Bristol Diary, Dec. 28, 1922, Bristol MSS; Howard, *Partition of Turkey*, p. 300. The Americans got along very well with the Italian delegates, whom they admired for dealing above the table at all times.

his fairness helped establish a generally excellent rapport with Ismet and the Turkish delegation. Grew and Child also came to have tremendous respect for Ismet's basic honesty and for his skillful parrying of Curzon's thrusts. As the conference wore on, the American observers came to look on themselves as big brothers assisting the inexperienced Turks to relax their rigid positions in the interest of redeeming their reputation internationally. For a period during January relations cooled perceptibly because of Turkish pique at the American stand on the minorities question, but before the conference ended the storm had blown over.[34]

Within the American delegation harmony prevailed except for one significant clash of personalities. Child and Grew got along well, as did Bristol and Grew; the difficulty was between Child and Bristol. It fell to Grew to be the peacemaker, and he was indeed the "Gallatin" who smoothed over the temporary difficulties caused by Bristol's feeling that Child showed insufficient respect for his knowledge of Turkey and by Child's suspicions that Bristol's private friendships among the Turks made them more intransigent toward the Allies.[35]

Most cordial relations existed between department officials in Washington and the Lausanne staff, with Secretary Hughes often commending the American observers on their conduct. "They certainly know how to play ball in Washington," Child commented. It was quite a different story with representatives of the American press who, according to Grew and Child, were hostile to the Harding administration. When hard official information was not available, some reporters evidently manufactured stories out of whole cloth, often giving them an unfriendly slant. In contrast, Allied delegations were able to use European journalists as sounding boards and propaganda agents to press a particular national point of view.[36]

Throughout the conference, American delegates were under heavy pressures both from American interest groups and from foreign delega-

[34] Child, *Diplomat*, pp. 96, 101, 106, 112, 114, 121; Grew, *TE*, I, 492–493, 509, 521–522, 534–535, 536–538, 542, 549; Grew Diary, Nov. 21, Dec. 5, 1922, Jan. 1, 1923, Grew MSS. See also *FR 1923*, II, 970–971.

[35] Grew, *TE*, I, 503–504, 539, 554–555; Grew Diary, Dec. 21–31, 1922, Jan. 14, Jan. 15, Jan. 17, Jan. 22, Jan. 28, 1923, Grew MSS; Bristol Diary, Nov. 26, Dec. 5, 1922, Bristol MSS.

[36] Grew, *TE*, I, 495, 501 (quotation), 502, 512, 517, 519; Grew Diary, Dec. 4, Dec. 7, 1922, Grew MSS; Child, *Diplomat*, p. 94; Bristol Diary, Dec. 21, 1922, Bristol MSS.

tions trying to enlist American support. Child wrote on December 12 of having "had various American missionaries and representatives of relief organizations and humanitarian associations on my neck." Pro-Armenian groups in the United States importuned through the State Department, and the specter of the Senate always loomed in the background. From across the Atlantic also came resolutions from Greek Orthodox congregations and memorials from state legislatures. In the name of Wilsonian self-determination, various foreign delegations sought the intercession of the American observers.[37]

Representing the Federal Council of the Protestant Churches of America at Lausanne were Dr. James L. Barton and W. W. Peet of the American Board; George R. Montgomery was there in behalf of the Armenia-America Society. The statements of these three were submitted by the American observers to the subcommission on minorities on December 30, 1922. President Caleb Frank Gates of Robert College attended as Admiral Bristol's personal adviser on education; no one took exception to the wisdom and experience which justified his presence.[38]

Child admitted that the missionary and relief spokesmen included some "good and unselfish souls," but he took a generally cynical view of others, unnamed, who wrapped themselves in humanitarian causes — "men who claim to represent God, but whose credentials appear to me to be forged."[39] The realistic diplomats could see the Turkish side of the minorities question and the futility of Western efforts to impose unacceptable terms on the resisting Turks. Despite misgivings about the Armenian and Greek programs, the American delegates did what they could for the cause, but their inability to do more augured badly for the reception of the Lausanne settlement in the United States.

Early in February the conference reached an impasse when Ismet refused to accept the judicial and economic clauses in the Allied draft treaty. Until the very moment when Curzon and the British delegation

[37] In a facetious passage, Child mentioned "several Armenian committees, three Egyptian delegations . . . the Tyro-Palestinian, the Macedonian, the Assyrean-Chaldean and an Irish delegation!" Child, *Diplomat*, pp. 103 (text quotation), 107 (footnote quotation); Grew, *TE*, I, 497; Grew Diary, Dec. 21–31, 1922, Grew MSS; *FR 1923*, II, 946.

[38] *FR 1923*, II, 940–941, 943–946; Grew Diary, Nov. 19, Dec. 1, Dec. 19, Dec. 21–31, 1922, Grew MSS; Grew, *TE*, I, 524–525; *MRW*, 46 (Jan. 1923), 61; (Feb. 1923), 148–149; (March 1923), 170–172.

[39] Child, *Diplomat*, pp. 103–106 (quotations, pp. 104 and 103).

made a theatrical departure from Lausanne on the Orient Express, the night of February 4, the American observers were trying desperately to save the conference by persuading Ismet to make further concessions. During the next two days Grew took advantage of Ismet's presence at Lausanne to sound him out on what terms the Turks would accept. He was unable to make much progress, for it became clear that Ismet must report to Kemal and the assembly at Angora before the Turkish course would be recharted.[40]

Interim: February to April, 1923

During the excitement and confusion following the February 4 rupture, the Turks were uncertain whether the Allies intended that negotiations should be indefinitely broken off. Both parties soon agreed, however, that the conference had only been interrupted. After his return to Turkey on February 17, Ismet talked of the nearness of peace with the Allies and of his expectation that negotiations would soon be resumed. On February 27 the Turkish National Assembly began more than a week of turbulent discussions concerning a proposed reply to the Allied draft treaty before announcing that the terms did not accord with the principles of the National Pact. The Turks handed their counterproposals, chiefly economic, to the Allied High Commissioners at Constantinople on March 8. During this period Admiral Bristol reported specific cases in which American educational and business interests were having difficulties with the Turks; some Turkish officials, however, were well disposed toward American interests and were being reasonable in attempts to work out solutions to specific pending questions.[41]

About March 19 the three Allied powers met at a London conference to consider the Turkish counterproposals, decide on a course of action, and set a date and place for resumption of the conference. The failure of the Allies to respond to repeated American requests for information about their deliberations alarmed and irritated Washington officials. The department instructed Ambassador Harvey on March 19 to inform the Foreign Office "'that in view of American interest in many of the

[40] Child, *Diplomat*, pp. 122–123; Grew Diary, Jan. 31, Feb. 1, Feb. 5, 1923, Grew MSS; Grew, *TE*, I, 541, 545–546, 550–554; *FR 1923*, II, 961–964.
[41] *FR 1923*, II, 967, 969–970, 974, 975, 1047–1055; Kemal, *Speech*, p. 600; *Current History*, 18 (April 1923), 176; Howard, *Partition of Turkey*, p. 284; Bristol to Hughes, March 13, 1923, DS 711.67/39.

matters which may be discussed in considering the Turkish reply' he would 'appreciate being apprized of the course of discussions at the forthcoming conference.'" The reply was evasive. In Paris Ambassador Herrick was refused a copy of the Allied reply to the Turkish proposals. The Allies continued to snub American requests for a draft of the reply by saying they had agreed the draft would not be made available to the United States until after it had been publicly released. As late as April 4, Allen Dulles wrote that the department's only information about the details of the Allied reply to the Turks was an Associated Press summary based on a text released to the London press two days earlier.

It was small wonder that the State Department deeply suspected the Allies of making secret trades and agreements prejudicial to American interests. At the root of the slight, the department believed, were American protests against the concessions clause in the Allied draft treaty. It appeared that the Allies were planning to neutralize American efforts to exclude any terms which would validate incompleted concessions granted by Ottoman officials. The department had been wary since Child's caveat to Curzon on February 4 indicating American apprehension about the insertion of concessions clauses without prior discussion. On March 31 the department had sent a memorandum to the British Embassy pointing out more specifically the nature of American objections.

It was crystal clear at the State Department that if economic and judicial rights of American nationals in Turkey were to be adequately safeguarded, the United States must be represented when the conference resumed. Grudgingly, the Allies formally notified the United States that the conference would resume on April 23 at Lausanne. Grew had already been alerted that he would head the American delegation, and Dulles had made recommendations to Secretary Hughes on April 4 which formed the basis for detailed instructions sent to Grew on April 19.[42]

The Lausanne Conference, Second Phase: April 23 to July 24, 1923

Organization. Although the conference was resumed with a general belief that the treaty could be completed shortly, it took three months

[42] *FR 1923*, II, 968, 972–986 (quotation, p. 975).

to achieve this result. Ismet's tenacity had proved that Curzon's earlier steamroller tactics must be softened. The conference again divided into three committees with Sir Horace Rumbold, Curzon's replacement, chairing the first committee on territorial and military matters; Maurice Pellé of France the second on unfinished financial articles; and Giulo Cesare Montagna of Italy the third on economic questions. Groups of experts met as subcommittees. For the United States Grew and Frederick Dolbeare, first secretary of the London embassy, sat in the three committees with all their staff present as advisers. The subordinates also met with groups of experts in three subcommittees.[43]

Hughes's Instructions to Grew. Secretary Hughes had instructed Grew that "the status and functions of the American delegation will remain the same as before adjournment." The primary goal was still to protect American nationals and their interests in Turkey while fostering humanitarian ends and the achievement of peace. The United States had a paramount interest in two specific issues: first, judicial safeguards for foreigners; and second, concessions clauses. Grew had positive orders to prevent the Allies from securing provisions which would validate incompleted Allied concessions, a maneuver attempted in the Allied draft of January 31.[44]

Judicial Declaration and Concession Clauses. The American delegation stood with the Allies in their efforts to improve the judicial declaration calling for foreign legal advisers in Turkey. Ismet resisted mightily all suggestions which could be interpreted as infringements on Turkish sovereignty, but by early June agreement was reached when Ismet informed Rumbold that Turkey intended "to engage at least four legal advisers whose conditions of service will be fixed in common accord between the Turkish Government and the Permanent Court of Justice at The Hague."[45]

[43] *FR 1923*, II, 988–989. Other members of the American staff were F. Lammot Belin from Paris; Consul Maynard Barnes from Constantinople; Edgar Turlington, assistant solicitor from the department; and five clerks. Grew, *TE*, I, 556. Rumbold's objections to American participation in some subcommittee deliberations were soon overcome. *Ibid.*, I, 572; *FR 1923*, II, 997–998, 999, 1000.

[44] *FR 1923*, II, 981–986 (quotation, p. 982); Grew, *TE*, I, 571 n. 6. Hughes considered the Straits and minorities questions largely settled and did not anticipate any need for discussion of Allied claims against Turkey. The department had decided that the Turks could not be moved to grant archaeological rights mentioned in the October 30 aide-mémoire. *FR 1923*, II, 960.

[45] *FR 1923*, II, 984, 987, 990, 994–996, 999, 1000–1002, 1003, 1012–1015 (quotation, p. 1015); Grew, *TE*, I, 564–565, 566, 569.

Although the United States had a community of interest with the Allies on the judicial clauses of the treaty, the case was quite the reverse on the concession terms which brought Grew and Ismet together vis-à-vis the Allies. Even as the conference resumed, the air was thick with feeling against the United States because the Turkish National Assembly had on April 10 formally approved the Chester Concession, granting an American syndicate rights to construct railroads and ports, exploit minerals, and sell agricultural equipment. This comprehensive grant brought loud protests from the British, French, and Russians, who claimed that the American grant infringed upon prior rights of their nationals. If the Turks intended to detach the United States from the Allies, they succeeded temporarily, for the Chester Concession hung heavily over the first part of the conference. Grew wrote Dulles on May 14 that "in the beginning we seemed to be up against a solid wall of suspicion on all sides. The Chester concession loomed large and I had the feeling that everybody suspected us of nefarious schemes and motives. You yourself know the attitude of the British before the Conference began." But the situation had cleared when Grew quieted Allied doubts by insisting that the United States government had no direct connection with the granting of the concession. Grew wrote that the "atmosphere of suspicion has now largely been dissipated."[46]

Not until early in June, when the conference began serious work on the concession clauses, did Grew face his hardest fight in carrying out his instructions. The French wanted treaty provisions recognizing alleged French interests, and the British made heroic efforts to validate the uncompleted Turkish Petroleum Company concession. The Allies attempted to hold secret discussions, but Grew found out what was going on behind his back, largely through Ismet. Grew steeled Ismet to stand up for exclusion of the clauses hateful to the United States by arguing that the Allied intentions compromised Turkish sovereignty. At the final session on this subject, from which Grew was excluded, Ismet received "treatment which would make the third degree in a Harlem police station seem like a club dinner." But the Allies capitulated and no mention of the Turkish Petroleum Company was made in the treaty. Agreement to provide for compensation of two French and

[46] Grew Diary, April 23, April 26, June 15, June 16, 1923; Grew to Allen Dulles, May 14 (both quotations), May 22, May 28, June 11, Sept. 28, 1923; Grew to Tom S. Perry, May 14, 1923, Grew MSS; Grew, *TE*, I, 559–562, 565, 566, 578–579. See below, Chap. 7, for the negotiations leading to the Chester Concession of 1923.

British companies was acceptable to the United States. With Ismet's help, Grew had won his point, although Rumbold asserted at the final session that his government still supported the concession and would continue to support it.[47]

American Relations with the Allied and Turkish Delegations. Notwithstanding the wedge the concessions issue drove into Allied-American relations, Grew frequently acted as a go-between during the conference on issues not directly concerning the United States. During a particularly serious crisis, a war scare arising from Turkish insistence on reparations from Greece for damages in Anatolia, Grew assisted in arranging a compromise by which reparations were given up in favor of cession to Turkey of the town of Karagatch.

Grew and Montagna became close during the conference, exchanging information and confidences throughout. Grew referred to him as "the foreign delegate inclined to be most in sympathy with us." Rumbold, however, proved to be cool and aloof to Grew, although the two men had worked together earlier at Cairo and Berlin. Apparently Rumbold had been alienated by what he considered the pro-Turkish attitude of the Americans during the first phase of the conference, a feeling accentuated by the Chester grant. At the same time, the British government professed to want American support even though its chief delegate made close relations difficult.[48]

The Allied Settlement at Lausanne

When the protracted negotiations were completed, signatures were appended to the network of agreements on July 24, 1923.[49] The settlement abolished capitulations in return for a promise of judicial reforms; the Turks accepted terms for protection of minorities and pledged guarantees for philanthropic, educational, and religious institutions of the Allies. They relinquished all claims to non-Turkish territories lost following World War I, but recovered Eastern Thrace to the Maritza River, with Karagatch; Turkey also received the islands of Imbros and

[47] Grew, *TE*, I, 578–584 (quotation, p. 584); *FR 1923*, II, 990–991, 1007–1008, 1009, 1016–1018, 1021–1036, 1038; Grew to his mother, July 30, 1923, Grew MSS.
[48] Grew, *TE*, I, 557–558, 561–563, 565, 566–578; Beerits Memorandum, Hughes MSS; *FR 1923*, II, 989, 1002, 1010–1012, 1089 (quotation); Grew to Frederick R. Dolbeare, Oct. 10, 1923, Grew MSS.
[49] The Lausanne settlement was embodied in "eighteen conventions, agreements, declarations and protocols and by six letters or exchanges of letters." Arnold J. Toynbee and Kenneth P. Kirkwood, *Turkey*, p. 112.

Tenedos, but the rest of the Aegean Islands went to Greece, Italy retained the Dodecanese, and England, Cyprus. Turkey was not required to make reparations. The Straits were demilitarized and opened to ships of all nations in peace time and in wartime when Turkey remained neutral, but if Turkey was at war, enemy ships (but not neutrals) might be excluded. A separate Turkish-Greek agreement provided for compulsory exchange of populations.[50]

Long before the treaty was ready for signatures, Grew could see that Lausanne would be a great victory for the Turks. He wrote his brother on May 30 that "it is the greatest blow to the prestige of the Great Powers that has occurred in history. But when each of the Great Powers suspects each of the others of nefarious schemes (a largely justified suspicion) and when each follows its own selfish interests rather than the common interest, the solid front is broken and defeat is inevitable. That is just what has happened at Lausanne."[51] As Grew began serious talks with the Turks preparatory to drafting a Turco-American treaty, he was well aware of the quality of the man with whom he must negotiate. He had the highest regard for Ismet and for the altered conditions which gave the New Turks strong trump cards.

The Turco-American Treaty of Lausanne

Both the United States and Turkey were anxious to regularize their official relations. As early as November, 1922, Turkish delegates at Lausanne broached the question of a treaty, although they blew hot and cold during the first phase of the conference. When they returned to the subject in April of 1923, the United States reacted favorably and informed Ismet and the Allies on May 1 of its readiness to begin informal negotiations. The United States made it clear that there was no intention of signing a treaty before the Turks had settled with the Allies. While Ismet and Grew carried on informal discussions, exploratory meetings of their experts went forward during May.[52] Many issues

---

[50] The settlement also provided for redistribution of the Ottoman Public Debt, and for conditions of residence, business, and commercial operations in Turkey. Toynbee and Kirkwood, *Turkey*, pp. 112–113, and *passim*. For his comparison of Sèvres and Lausanne terms, see Kemal, *Speech*, pp. 608–620.

[51] Grew to Henry S. Grew, May 30, 1923, Grew MSS; Grew, *TE*, I, 569–571.

[52] Grew, *TE*, I, 492, 534–535, 559–560, 562–565; Grew Diary, Nov. 29, 1922, and Jan. 14, 1923, Grew MSS; *FR 1923*, II, 901, 956, 958–959, 960, 970, 985–986, 987, 989–991, 993–994, 996, 997, 1003, 1020, 1040–1046, 1061–1062, 1064, 1067–1069.

discussed were related to the Allied negotiations in which the United States had been taking an active part, hoping to influence the terms on matters of special concern to the United States. The State Department fully realized that the limits as to guarantees obtainable from the Turks would be determined in large measure by the provisions of the Allied treaty.

Ismet and Grew agreed by early June that a satisfactory basis existed for formal negotiations, and the department cabled Grew full powers to negotiate and sign a treaty with the Turks. The day the Allied treaty was signed, Grew and Ismet reviewed the issues still outstanding between their two countries. Then they settled down to intensive negotiation of many unsettled details. Grew was at a disadvantage in two respects. In the first place, the completed Allied treaty set definite limits on what Grew could expect to obtain from the Turks; the United States simply could not hope for more than the Allies had already achieved. In the second place, the United States had handed the Turks a proposed draft treaty, thus allowing Ismet to take the offensive by countering American proposals.[53]

Ismet proved to be a wiry and difficult adversary. On July 25 Grew cabled Hughes, "I gained hardly anything from Ismet tonight in a dispute lasting nearly four hours. . . . My feeling is that the negotiations will now develop into a test of tenacity, and will hinge upon the claims question." Grew frequently expressed his respect for Ismet; he wrote somewhat excessively to his father-in-law that "Ismet is Napoleonic — the greatest diplomatist in history. He has played every one of us to a standstill. And he has done it fairly and squarely, all growls to the contrary notwithstanding. I have great admiration for him and personal respect. He is a very great man."[54]

The major issues confronting Grew and Ismet pertained to capitulations, naturalization, claims, a judicial regime for Americans, protection

[53] *FR 1923*, II, 1072–1073; Grew, *TE*, I, 590–596; Grew to his mother, Aug. 19, 1923, Grew MSS. The department had sent a tentative draft treaty to Lausanne with Edgar Turlington, of which no copy has been located in the department's files. *FR 1923*, II, 1060 n. 50, 1063, 1065. By June 2 the American delegation had developed two versions of a draft treaty. The department preferred the longer version. *Ibid.*, II, 1076–1080 (short version), 1080–1085 (long version). See also pp. 1085–1087.

[54] *FR 1923*, II, 1120 (first quotation); Grew to Tom S. Perry, Aug. 2, 1923 (last quotation), Grew MSS. See also Grew's statement of August 6 at the treaty signing (Grew, *TE*, I, 601), and Grew to his mother, Aug. 19, 1923, Grew MSS.

of minorities, and status for philanthropic, educational, and religious institutions. By mutual declaration, the capitulations were completely abrogated. In matters of personal status, domestic relations, and inheritance (formerly within jurisdiction of American consular tribunals), American citizens in Turkey were to be subject exclusively to the jurisdiction of American tribunals or authorities sitting outside Turkey. For trials involving rights of American citizens within Turkey no special judicial declaration was obtainable. Instructed to insist upon provisions protecting the rights of minorities in Turkey, Grew was unsuccessful; his argument that the American public would insist on some such protection in the treaty left Ismet unmoved. The claims issue was also a serious stumbling block and became intertwined with the thorny question of naturalization. The Turks were reluctant to accept claims from Americans whom they did not regard as bona fide American citizens at the time the claims were instigated. The upshot was that neither claims nor naturalization clauses appeared in the treaty proper. On commercial matters the United States obtained what amounted essentially to most-favored-nation treatment. The Turks granted American philanthropic, educational, and religious institutions equal status with Turkish institutions of the same kinds, accepting all American institutions recognized as of October 20, 1914, and pledging to give serious consideration to those operating as of July 24, 1923.[55]

After signing the treaty on August 6, Grew wrote Secretary Hughes that the treaty just signed was

far from what I should have wished to have it. It represents a considerably greater number of concessions on our part to meet the Turkish point of view than concessions on their part to meet ours. Among other concessions we have given up the articles on naturalization and claims, we have failed to obtain the desired modifications in the Judicial Declaration and we have failed to obtain any provision whatever with regard to minorities. . . . Whatever may be the fate of this treaty in the Senate and however it may disappoint the American people, I feel, and the feeling is shared by every member of our delegation, after careful study of the situation as it existed and has developed, that more favorable terms could not have been obtained at this time and that it

[55] The course of negotiations can be followed from documents in *FR 1923*, II, 1043–1148, *passim*. For the text of the general treaty signed on August 6, 1923, see *ibid.*, II, 1153–1166; for the extradition treaty, pp. 1167–1171. For the exchange of letters postponing a claims settlement, pp. 1143–1144. See also Grew, *TE*, I, 588–589; 596–600.

is at least open to doubt whether even equally favorable terms could be obtained later.

Grew commended the honesty of the Turkish delegation and indicated his feeling that the Turks had been logical and frank in their methods, that they knew at the start what they wanted and what they were prepared to give.[56]

Grew had no illusions that the treaty would be popular in the United States or win ready approval in the Senate. Only time would show what the treaty was worth, since it was premised on Turkish integrity and achievement. Although Grew had considerable faith in the intentions of the new Turkish leaders to live up to Western standards, he realized fully that the new Turkey was not the old, and, consequently, he had proved far more flexible in adjusting to the new than had some Allied diplomats, most notably the British.[57]

The Fate of the Treaty: American Pressures

Grew and his staff anticipated their treaty would encounter formidable opposition at home from the pro-Armenian and pro-Greek anti-Turkish forces as well as from those Democratic senators who could be expected to criticize the handiwork of a Republican administration.[58] But American officials could hardly have foreseen the tortuous history of the treaty over the next few years until the Senate finally rejected it on January 18, 1927.

When the Turco-American Treaty of Lausanne was signed on August 6, 1923, the United States Senate was in recess and not scheduled to reconvene until December. Yet President Calvin Coolidge did not submit it to the Senate until May 3, 1924 — nine months after signing. The president delayed because of feeling in the State Department that the treaty's prospects would improve if, before submission, supplementary agreements pertaining to claims and naturalization could be worked out. In the hope of blunting potential opposition, the department instructed Bristol to negotiate with the Turks on these issues

[56] *FR 1923*, II, 1148–1150. On August 7 Hughes sent Grew a generous commendation for his work at Lausanne. Grew, *TE*, I, 603 n. 10.

[57] Grew to Allen Dulles, Sept. 12, 1923; Grew to Henry Fletcher, Aug. 15, 1923; Grew to William R. Castle, Jr., Sept. 10, 1923; Grew to Tom S. Perry, Dec. 12, 1923; Grew talk of September 2, 1923, to American consular officers, Grew Diary, Grew MSS.

[58] G. Howland Shaw, memorandum, Aug. 5, 1923; Grew to Hughes, Aug. 24, 1923, DS 711.672/173 and 174; Grew to Henry Fletcher, Aug. 15, 1923, Grew MSS.

during the fall. Before the end of the year he secured an agreement providing that claims should be handled by a mixed commission within six months after ratification of the treaty. The naturalization discussions reached an impasse, and the department regretfully had to shelve the issue for further negotiation.[59]

During this period the department closely watched the behavior of the Kemal regime toward American interests in Turkey, hoping that evidence of conciliatory actions would dissipate some of the anti-Turkish feeling in the United States. Bristol worked assiduously on the day-to-day problems, hoping the Turks would demonstrate their intention to realize the spirit of the new treaty. Contributing to the policy of watchful waiting was the department's desire to see if and how soon the Allied powers would ratify their treaty with the Turks.[60]

Taking advantage of the delay, opponents of ratification in the United States lost no time in organizing their campaign, spearheaded by Vahan Cardashian, an Armenian-American lawyer who passionately devoted himself to the Armenian cause throughout the postwar period. Using the Armenia-America Society as his vehicle, he played on outraged American sentiment for the Armenians. Cardashian persuaded the influential and articulate James W. Gerard, former ambassador to Germany, to help enlist the support of church and civic leaders and congressmen for the fight against ratification. The Cardashian-Gerard forces had powerful allies in Senator William King, Democrat, of Utah, and Senator Claude Swanson of Virginia, ranking Democratic member of the Foreign Relations Committee.[61]

Early in the fall the Gerard Committee, officially known as the

[59] *Cong. Record,* 69 Cong., 1 Sess., p. 6251; *Journal of the Executive Proceedings of the Senate of the United States,* LXII, Part 1, p. 662 (hereafter cited as *SEJ*); Hughes to Bristol, May 6, May 19, 1924, DS 711.672/285a and 286; *FR 1923,* II, 1172–1194, 1196–1198; Hughes to Coolidge, Oct. 25, Dec. 18, 1923; Coolidge to Hughes, Dec. 19, 1923, Calvin Coolidge MSS.

[60] Bristol to Hughes, Dec. 6, 1923; Barton to Hughes, Dec. 17, 1923; Hughes to Barton, Dec. 22, 1923, DS 711.672/226, 238, and 238; Grew to Tom S. Perry, Dec. 20, 1923, Grew MSS; *FR 1923,* II, 1183, 1185; *FR 1924,* II, 730–732.

[61] Grew to Tom S. Perry, Dec. 12, Dec. 20, 1923, Grew MSS; Dulles to Hughes, Nov. 14, 1923; Paul S. Leinbach (Society for Justice in the Near East) to Hughes, Dec. 3, 1923; Barton to Dulles, Feb. 4, 1923; Cardashian to Hughes, Jan. 28, Feb. 7, 1924; Lodge to Hughes, May 20, 1924, DS 711.672/206, 234, 266, 254, 261, and 293; *Cong. Record,* 68 Cong., 1 Sess., pp. 228, 354–355; James W. Gerard, *My First Eighty-Three Years in America: The Memoirs of James W. Gerard,* p. 286, touches very lightly on his pro-Armenian efforts after World War I and ignores his role in the defeat of the Lausanne Treaty.

American Committee for the Independence of Armenia, issued a pamphlet entitled "The Senate Should Reject the Turkish Treaty." On the inside of the title page Gerard had listed the names of more than fifty prominent Americans, many of whom, it turned out, had not been consulted about the use of their names for this propagandistic effort.[62] Gerard wrote Secretary Hughes on November 19 that many opponents of ratification planned to review a memorandum which they expected would have more than a hundred signatures. They proposed to send copies to senators before the opening of Congress. Gerard reported that he had already communicated with a number of senators of both parties "and found them hostile to the Treaty." "I should be unjust," he wrote, "to conceal from you that there will undoubtedly be very great opposition. I have been amazed at the volume and character of the unfavorable comments which I have already received on this Treaty." He claimed that only a few of the missionaries to Turkey favored it, and their narrow self-interest was evident. Since the treaty did not protect the minorities, and because the Turks could not, in his opinion, be trusted to honor their obligations, Gerard suggested that it would "be more dignified to denounce the Treaty of Lausanne, now, rather than permit it to fail of ratification." Gerard wanted the United States to insist that the Turks accept the independence and unity of Armenia before the resumption of official relations would be considered.[63]

While the opposition was coalescing, the State Department pondered what it could do to smooth the way for the treaty in the Senate. Just before the treaty had been signed, G. Howland Shaw, a member of Grew's staff at Lausanne, wrote that

the nature of the reaction of public opinion in the United States towards our treaty will, I should think, depend largely upon how far the Department is willing to go in educating public opinion with respect to the treaty. If nothing whatever is done in this direction, it is obvious that public opinion will gravitate along one or other of the many conventional grooves of dislike and distrust of Turkey and our treaty will in that case be presented to the Senate for ratification with public opinion already set against it.

[62] See DS 711.672/187, 203, 204, 208½, 212, 220, and 237. See also Dulles to Hughes, Feb. 9, 1924, *ibid.*, 262½.

[63] Gerard to Hughes, Nov. 19, 1923, DS 711.672/207. A second Gerard Committee pamphlet, "The Lausanne Treaty and Kemalist Turkey" (Phillips to Bristol, April 4, 1924), was ably refuted in Bristol to Hughes, Aug. 9, 1924, *ibid.*, 277a and 312. See also Barton to Dulles, April 8, 1924, *ibid.*, 289.

He thought that the treaty required explanation and that the people who knew Turkey were in the best position to provide it. On advice from Senator Henry Cabot Lodge, chairman of the Foreign Relations Committee, the department decided not to publish the full text of the agreements, although the gist of the treaty terms had already become public property.[64]

Allen Dulles, chief of the Near Eastern Division, persuaded Hughes in October of 1923 that the department should prepare exhaustive reports on the background events leading up to the treaty and the negotiations. He proposed to deal with these in a noncontroversial and narrative manner in the belief that facts would tend to disarm criticism.[65] Thus the department had decided to proceed on two fronts — first, continued negotiation with Turkey of the outstanding claims and naturalization issues, and second, a program to line up support at home for the treaty.

During the fall and winter, the department assembled detailed statements from Americans in Turkey. From Constantinople, Bristol furnished evidence of the American colony's overwhelming support. Dulles and others corresponded and conferred with Dr. James Barton, foreign secretary of the American Board of Commissioners for Foreign Missions, and with President Caleb Gates of Robert College. The Near East College Association and the United States Chamber of Commerce also joined the movement. Influential leaders of opinion, together with interested groups, assisted the department in its efforts to secure a favorable hearing for the treaty. Dulles cooperated closely with the Foreign Policy Association, which sponsored meetings and publications stressing the desirability of ratification. He also provided the New York and Chicago chapters of the Council on Foreign Relations with names of prominent treaty backers who might be useful as speakers. Through his friend Walter Lippmann, editorial writer for the *New York World*, he arranged favorable publicity for the treaty. Nor were prominent members of the clergy, university presidents, and faculty members overlooked.[66]

[64] G. Howland Shaw to Grew, Aug. 5, 1923; Hughes to Lodge, Aug. 21, 1923; Lodge to Hughes, Aug. 23, 1923; H. G. Dwight to Harrison, Aug. 24, 1923; Grew to Hughes, Aug. 24, 1923; Phillips to American Legation, Berne, Aug. 28, 1923; Dulles to Hughes, March 7, 1924, DS 711.672/173, 176a, 177, 174, 174, 174, and 270.

[65] Dulles to Hughes, Oct. 13, 1923, DS 711.672/229.

[66] The correspondence (too extensive for complete citation) is found in DS

Employing rapier thrusts, Secretary Hughes engaged in public and private rebuttal of the anti-treaty arguments. He minced no words in telling Gerard that he was grossly misinformed in urging a course of action detrimental to American interests in Turkey. On January 23, 1924, in a speech to the New York Council on Foreign Relations, Hughes refuted at length the charges of Senator King that the United States government had betrayed the Armenian cause. Hughes also alerted Senator Lodge to the kind of propaganda emanating from the Gerard-Cardashian camp, warning that the senators should be acquainted with its gross errors in fact and analysis. The department put into the hands of senators, particularly members of the Foreign Relations Committee material explaining the intent and content of the treaty and the reasons why ratification would serve the national interests.[67]

After submitting the treaty to the Senate on May 3, 1924, the department stepped up efforts to bring about favorable action before the summer adjournment. Hughes suggested that he sponsor a dinner, which apparently did not take place, for members of the Foreign Relations Committee at which they might hear Dr. Albert W. Staub of the Near East College Association and possibly other prominent Americans who had been active in Turkey. When the Foreign Relations Committee took up the Turkish treaty on May 16, Democratic opposition was strong. Senator Swanson wanted to postpone consideration until the next session on grounds that Gerard and former Ambassador Henry Morgenthau wished to be heard. Chairman Lodge agreed there was not sufficient time to give deliberate consideration before adjournment. The committee therefore deferred consideration, and when Congress adjourned on June 12 the treaty was still in committee. It had been submitted too late for action during the hectic windup of the session when other matters demanded priority and relations with Turkey did not seem of crucial moment. The senators who cared most were those of the minority — notably King and Swanson — who opposed the treaty, mainly for partisan reasons. There was much uncertainty at the State

711.672/199, 213, 215, 216, 217, 218, 225b, 230½, 239, 242, 243, 258a, 266, 267a, 270, 271, 273, 275, 276, 276a, 277, 279, 281, 282, 286, 288, 289, 290, 294, 304, 305, 306, and 307; Borah MSS, Boxes 543 and 546; Hughes to Coolidge, Dec. 11, 1923, Coolidge MSS; *FR 1923*, II, 1150–1151.

[67] Hughes to Gerard, Nov. 21, 1923; Hughes to Borah, Dec. 5, 1923; Dulles to Hughes, Jan. 26, 1924; Hughes to Lodge, Jan. 26, 1924, DS 711.672/207, 230¾, 252, 252; *FR 1924*, II, 709–715, 721–724; *Cong. Record*, 68 Cong., 1 Sess., pp. 10292–10296.

Department as to what the Senate lineup might be on the treaty and suspicion that the Democrats might try to capitalize on it during the impending campaign of 1924.[68]

Looking toward the reconvening of Congress in December, the department immediately began to renew its efforts to secure ratification. Bristol was asked to furnish a full report on conditions in Turkey, the status of American interests there, and the views of the American colony on how they were faring under the Kemalist regime. The department wanted "the fullest possible information to meet the various attacks which have been made upon the treaty."[69]

By autumn, after the Allies had ratified their treaties, the State Department considered it more urgent to regularize relations with Turkey, who could not be expected indefinitely to accord American interests the same treatment given powers which had resumed relations under new treaties. Bristol, having wrestled tirelessly with Turkish authorities on a number of special school and other issues which could have been cleared up more readily had the treaty been ratified, reasoned "that the Turkish Government with its nationalistic temper will not be affected by the taking of drastic measures," and the department approved his recommendation to "avoid giving offense, and continue [a] policy of patience and plain speaking." Patient and persistent endeavor had indeed seemed to pay dividends: Dr. James Barton remarked to Allen Dulles late in November, about the status of American Board work in Turkey, that his "most optimistic views of the situation as expressed a year ago were more than realized."[70]

While preparing for action on the treaty, the department was careful to avoid adopting any course likely to provoke bitter political discussion of the treaty during the presidential campaign. The Democrats had inserted the following planks in their 1924 platform:

[68] See DS 711.672/285b, 289, 290c, 290½, 291, 293, 295, 296, 297, 316a; Grew Diary, May 21–27, 1924, Grew MSS; *FR 1924*, II, 724; *Proceedings of the Committee on Foreign Relations, United States Senate from the 68th Congress to the 72nd Congress*, pp. 15–16 (hereafter cited as *SFRC*).

[69] Grew to Bristol, July 30, 1924 (quotation); Bristol to Hughes, Oct. 11, Oct. 21, and Nov. 29, 1924; Hughes to Bristol, Nov. 25, 1924, DS 711.672/310a, 318, 319, 321, and 320a.

[70] Dulles memorandum of conversation with James L. Barton, Nov. 21, 1924, DS 711.672/325; Bristol to Hughes, Aug. 11, 1924; Robert M. Scotten (chargé d'affaires, Constantinople) to Hughes, Aug. 16, 1924, DS 711.67/49 and 50; *FR 1924*, II, 733–738 (Bristol quotations, p. 737); ABC, *AR 1924*, p. 66.

"We condemn the Lausanne treaty. It barters legitimate American rights and betrays Armenia, for the Chester oil concessions.

"We favor the protection of American rights in Turkey and the fulfillment of President Wilson's arbitral award respecting Armenia."

Dulles felt that James Gerard, treasurer of the Democratic National Committee, might welcome any chance to inject his pet issue into the closing days of the campaign if Republican spokesmen gave him an excuse. "If it were raised at this particular juncture it might result in certain Democratic Senators committing themselves in opposition to the Treaty and make its consideration in the Senate all the more difficult next December." Bristol concurred, warning that despite his desire for prompt ratification "American interests in Turkey would be more unfavorably effected [*sic*] by an acrimonious discussion of the treaty than by a delay in its submission to the Senate."[71]

Relations with Turkey and the Turkish treaty continued to suffer from low priority in the thinking of most senators as they convened on December 1 for the short session of the sixty-eighth congress. Excluding the holidays, less than three months remained before the expiration of that congress, and in the interval many issues, including the World Court, were pressing for consideration. Recognizing the situation, Secretary Hughes prodded President Coolidge and Senator William E. Borah, who had replaced the deceased Henry Cabot Lodge as chairman of the Foreign Relations Committee. Early in the session, Hughes reminded Borah of the treaty buried in committee. Since May, he pointed out, the Turkish Republic had carried out substantial judicial and administrative reforms, and most of the treaties with European powers had gone into effect. Events of the previous six months had confirmed Hughes's view "that American interests would best be served by prompt ratification." Otherwise, the United States government would be at a serious disadvantage in safeguarding American interests. He warned that the matter was of "real urgency." On December 18, Hughes wrote President Coolidge in the same vein, urging the chief executive to emphasize to senators the importance of early action.[72]

[71] Kirk H. Porter and Donald Bruce Johnson, eds., *National Party Platforms, 1840–1956*, p. 250; Dulles to Hughes, Oct. 20, 1924; Bristol to Hughes, Nov. 29, 1924, DS 711.672/317 and 321.

[72] *FR 1924*, II, 724–725; Hughes to Coolidge, Dec. 18, 1924, Coolidge MSS, file 193A. Coolidge answered tersely on the same day: "I shall bear this in mind." DS 711.672/330.

Borah's response was pessimistic. While admitting that he had not concluded his study and could not express a view, he did profess his desire to dispose of the treaty without delay. His inquiries among committee members had, however, revealed "considerable opposition," and he doubted whether the committee could get to the matter until after the holidays. Meanwhile the department continued to bombard key senators with relevant data and enlisted the support of the Commerce Department, which warned of commercial disabilities, chiefly tariff discrimination, for American shipping and trade unless the treaty were ratified. Late in January President Coolidge invited members of the Foreign Relations Committee to the White House to hear an explanation of the treaty by Richard Washburn Child. After the congressional session passed the half-way point, Hughes again wrote Borah on February 2, 1925, cautioning that time was short, and that without ratification, the United States would have no adequate basis for protecting American interests in Turkey.[73]

In its relations with senators the department leaned heavily on information provided by the American colony in Turkey and its spokesmen in the United States. Admiral Bristol kept the department well supplied with pro-treaty statements from officials of Robert College, Constantinople College for Women, the American Board, representative business men, and the Levant Chamber of Commerce. Representatives of these interests encouraged their principals at home to take positive measures toward favorable Senate action. Testimony that their call was heeded can be found in many letters to and conferences at the State Department, in resolutions to the Foreign Relations Committee, and in personal contacts established with senators, both favorable and hostile to the treaty. On the basis of all this evidence, Hughes could confidently tell Senator Borah that "it is the unanimous opinion of the Americans who have interests in Turkey, whether philanthropic or commercial, that the ratification of the Treaty is of the highest importance."[74]

[73] *FR 1924*, II, 725 (quotation), 727–729; Hughes to Borah, Dec. 18, 1924; Borah to Hughes, Dec. 19, 1924, Borah MSS, Box 546; Dulles memorandum of conversation with officials from the Department of Commerce, Dec. 15, 1924; Dulles memorandum of conversation with J. L. Barton, Jan. 27, 1925; Hughes to Borah, Feb. 2, 1925, DS 711.672/334, 343½, and 343a. See also DS 711.67/51A; and DS 711.672/332a, 337½, 338a, 340a, 347, 347½, 349a, 349b, 349c, 350¾, 350½, 352a, 353a, and 353b.

[74] Hughes to Borah, Feb. 2, 1925, Borah MSS, Box 546. See also Bristol to L. I.

Bending under heavy pressures, the Foreign Relations Committee discussed the treaty during February, finally voting 9 to 1 (Senator Swanson) on February 21 in favor of reporting it to the Senate. The Senate did not consider it during the rush preceding adjournment on March 4, but the new Congress, which convened immediately in special session, had the treaty before it briefly during executive session on March 13. At that time, Senator Borah moved to have it recommitted to committee. Convinced by his canvass that the necessary two-thirds vote was unobtainable, Borah preferred to recommit the treaty with the hope that its prospects might improve before the next session.[75]

Several weeks before this Senate action, Republican senators, aware of formidable Democratic opposition, warned the State Department and private interests pressing for ratification that prospects were dim. The leader of the Democratic opposition, Senator Swanson, told Dulles flatly that the treaty had no real chance of passage since it had been denounced in the Democratic platform of 1924, and Democratic senators could hardly be expected to repudiate their platform. When he asked Dulles "whether it would be best to kill the treaty at this session by an adverse vote or let it go over," Dulles responded that there was a better alternative — "to act favorably on the treaty as promptly as possible." Rumors that Borah's heart was not completely in the treaty fight were beside the point in view of the partisan opposition; nor was Secretary Hughes's willingness to accept reservations sufficient to win Democratic votes.[76] The department had been unduly optimistic.

The next concerted effort to secure favorable action on the Lausanne Treaty followed the pattern established in the abortive efforts of 1923–

Thomas, Dec. 31, 1924; Bristol to Hughes, Jan. 17, 1925, Bristol MSS, Boxes 9 and 11; *FR 1924*, II, 729; and DS 711.672/316, 323, 324, 325, 328, 333, 335½, 336, 337, 337¼, 338, 341, 341½, 342, 343, 343½, 345, 345½, 351, 352, 354, 356, and 357.

[75] The committee considered the treaty on February 11, 18, and 21, 1925. It was then reported to the Senate in executive session on February 23. *SFRC*, pp. 49–50; *SEJ*, LXIII, Part 1, 68 Cong., 2 Sess., p. 412; *SEJ*, LXIV, Part 1, 69 Cong., 1 Sess., p. 29; Dulles memorandum of conversation with Senators McLean and Moses, Feb. 13, 1925; Dulles memorandum of conversation with Senator Swanson, Feb. 18, 1925; Kellogg to Bristol, March 6 and March 14, 1925, DS 711.672/247½, 350¾, 357b, 358b; and Grew Diary, Feb. 18, 1925, Grew MSS.

[76] Dulles memorandum to Hughes and Grew, Jan. 8, 1925; Hughes to Borah, Feb. 11, 1925; Dulles memorandum, Feb. 13, 1925; Dulles memorandum of conversation with Senator Swanson, Feb. 18, 1925; Hughes to Bristol, Feb. 21, 1925; Dulles memorandum of conversation with Senator Borah, Feb. 24, 1925, DS 711.672/337¼, 353c, 347½, 350¼, 350a, and 350½.

1924 and 1924–1925, the arguments pro and con repeating those heard previously. The new cycle began in October of 1925 when Secretary Frank B. Kellogg, who had succeeded Hughes in March, instructed the Constantinople embassy to send new information to underpin the campaign being readied for the winter session of Congress. The next few months saw an increase in departmental correspondence and discussions with pro-treaty persons and groups — Barton, Peet, representatives of Socony, of American tobacco companies, and others — and renewed protests from Gerard, Cardashian, and King among the die-hard opponents as well as from many whose doubts revealed more sincere soul searching. With assistance from spokesmen for American interests in Turkey, the department maintained liaison with Senate leadership from which came gloomy comments about Democratic criticism. Nevertheless, the Senate Committee reported the treaty out for the second time on January 29, 1926, with minor reservations.[77]

Earlier in January, Bristol and the department had been alarmed to hear that new Turkish tariffs would require American goods to pay 60 per cent higher duties than goods from countries which had already concluded treaties. Fortunately, the Turks agreed to negotiate a modus vivendi in the form of an exchange of notes (signed February 20), extending for six months the tariff benefits of the unratified Lausanne commercial convention in exchange for most-favored-nation treatment. When the Senate had not ratified the Lausanne agreements before the expiration of the modus vivendi in August, the Turks generously agreed to extend it for six months.[78]

After the Senate voted on March 24 to remove the secrecy injunction, the treaties and accompanying documents were published. Notwithstanding the reservations, the treaty did not satisfy the majority of

[77] The extensive correspondence is found in DS 711.672/369a, 370, 371, 372, 373, 376, 378, 379, 380, 381, 382, 382½, 383, 384, 385, 386, 388, 389½, 394¼, 394½, 394¾, 395, 395¼, 395, 395¾, 395½, 396, 397¾, 400, 400½, 401, 448, 473, 480; Henry W. Jessup and Gerard to Coolidge, Dec. 29, 1925, and March 2, 1926, Coolidge MSS; Grew Diary, Sept. 15, 1925, Grew MSS; Kellogg to Borah, Nov. 30, 1925; Borah to Kellogg, Dec. 1, 1925, Borah MSS, Box 546; *FR 1926*, II, 974–975; *SFRC*, p. 56; *SEJ*, LXIV, Part 1, p. 568. One reservation, applying to article 3, reserved the rights of each nation in the field of immigration; the other put time limits on commercial and navigation provisions of article 9, paragraph 2, and article 14. See *FR 1926*, II, 975.

[78] *FR 1926*, II, 993–1000; Gordon, *American Relations with Turkey*, p. 22; DS 711.672/390, 394, 397; Kellogg to Borah, Jan. 9, Jan. 20, March 3, June 19, 1926, Borah MSS; Bristol to Kellogg, May 14, 1926, Bristol MSS.

Democratic or even all Republican senators. Borah and other administration senators advised repeatedly that since the necessary two-thirds vote seemed unattainable, continued delay was the prudent course. Patience and faith "that the logic and weight of the arguments . . . will carry it through successfully" were the only reasonable alternatives to defeat, according to Grew. Even the usually optimistic Grew sometimes became discouraged, as when he wrote his father-in-law, "the opposition hasn't a leg to stand on, but as nobody else knows or cares much about the subject, their oratory will probably reduce this country to tears over the Armenians and defeat the Treaty."[79]

Grew was particularly active behind the scenes in attempting to counter a coup of the Gerard-Cardashian forces, who had persuaded 110 Episcopal bishops to address an anti-treaty petition to the Senate. That there were no Episcopal missions in Turkey and that the American Board had placed its full weight behind the treaty were not considered; all important was the moral issue which pitted the forces of righteousness against the persecutors of Christian Armenians. Critics of the bishops' petition suspected it was "merely a gesture to the Eastern Church," with which the Episcopalians were anxious to establish closer relations. As a result of Grew's correspondence with Bishop Charles Slattery, the latter withdrew his name from the petition.[80]

Grew was not alone in his heroic efforts in behalf of ratification. Kellogg presented a spirited case to an Associated Press luncheon in New York on April 20. At the request of Robert College trustees, President Gates spent the spring of 1926 in the United States devoting his "full time to writing and speaking in behalf of the treaty."[81] On April 29 the Senate received a petition from American philanthropic and commercial enterprises in Turkey requesting prompt ratification.[82] Borah

[79] *SEJ*, LXIV, Part 1, p. 1203; *Cong. Record*, 69 Cong., 1 Sess., pp. 6165, 6251–6256; *FR 1926*, II, 974–977; DS 711.672/397½, 398, 399½, 455; Grew to Jasper Y. Brinton, March 5, 1926 (first quotation), Grew to Tom S. Perry, April 5, 1926 (second quotation), Grew MSS.

[80] Grew, *TE*, I, 675–678; *FR 1926*, II, 979–981; DS 711.672/430, 431, 431¼, 433, 440, 455; Grew to Rt. Rev. James E. Freeman, April 9, May 1, 1926; Grew to Bishop William Lawrence, April 17, 1926; Grew to Tom S. Perry, April 23, 1926, Grew MSS. Quotation is from Albert W. Staub to Dulles, April 6, 1926, DS 711.672/431¼.

[81] Gates, *Not to Me Only*, p. 295 (quotation); *FR 1926*, II, 975–976. DS 711.672 contains about eighty letters, despatches, instructions, and memoranda dated between March 11 and June 28, 1926, bearing on the movement for treaty ratification.

[82] *Cong. Record*, 69 Cong., 1 Sess., p. 8407. The signers of the petition represented the American Board, the Y.W.C.A., the American Chamber of Commerce,

grew weary of the delay and asked President Coolidge to exert pressure on the Senate for action before the summer adjournment. Since the treaty would not command sufficient support, the department decided to postpone action until winter. Although no vote was taken at that session, the Senate agreed on July 2 to place the treaty on the executive calendar for consideration immediately after the holidays in January, 1927.[83]

During the summer of 1926 the pro-treaty forces belatedly realized that their previous efforts, however energetic and persistent, had not matched those of their opponents in organization and centralization. Under the leadership of Rayford W. Alley, chairman of the Council on Turkish-American Relations, treaty supporters mobilized forces in the General Committee of American Institutions and Associations in Favor of the Ratification of the Treaty with Turkey.[84] Early in June the Council on Turkish-American Relations had published a thousand copies of "The Treaty with Turkey: Why It Should Be Ratified," a booklet combining statements of spokesmen, with reports and resolutions of educational, philanthropic, and commercial bodies competent to speak authoritatively by reason of long residence, extensive interest, and intimate acquaintance with Turkish conditions. The booklet was distributed to each senator, representative, and to 220 leading newspaper editors, among others. In December the General Committee issued and distributed two thousand copies of a revised and enlarged edition. By this time, the General Committee had organized extensive publicity and set up headquarters at the Raleigh Hotel in Washington for the purpose of exerting direct influence on the Senate before the forthcoming vote.[85]

Standard Commercial Trading Company, Robert College, Standard Oil of New York, Edgar B. Howard Co., Y.M.C.A., Liggett and Myers Tobacco Co., Lorillard Tobacco Co., and Constantinople College for Women. See also DS 711.672/462, 471, 477, and 477¾.

[83] Borah to Coolidge, May 10, 1926, Coolidge MSS, file 193A; *FR 1926*, II, 977–979, 981–985; *Cong. Record*, 69 Cong., 1 Sess., p. 12, 636. See also DS 711.672/459, 460, 464, 474, 481, 483, 488, 489, and 498.

[84] The letterhead of the General Committee listed the following affiliated organizations: The American Board of Commissioners for Foreign Missions, The Chamber of Commerce of the United States, The Council on Turkish-American Relations, The Federated American Chambers of Commerce of the Near East, The National Council of the Congregational Churches, The Near East College Association, the Y.M.C.A., and the Y.W.C.A.

[85] Alley to Department of State, June 7, 1926; Shaw to Alley, June 16 and June 25, 1926; Alley to Shaw, June 19, 1926; Alley, History of the General Committee, April 25, 1927, DS 711.672/482, 482, 505, 505, and 591.

According to schedule, the Senate finally took up the treaty in closed executive sessions. Despite Kellogg's complaint about difficulty in securing firm information on the secret debates, he was able to apprise Bristol that the opposition emphasized the absence of guarantees for the minorities, who had been "betrayed" for the Chester Concession; inadequate protection for educational and missionary enterprises; and the absence of a naturalization treaty. Until the very end, both sides of the controversy issued a stream of petitions and letters. Kellogg had to confess that reports on the strength of the opposition varied from day to day and that a close vote was likely. When the voting took place on January 18 it was close, with 50 for and 34 against — six short of the required two thirds. Only five Democrats voted for the treaty.[86]

Since the State Department was apprehensive that the defeat might incur Turkish reprisals, Kellogg instructed Bristol to explain that the executive branch had fully supported the treaty, as had a majority of the Senate. Editorial comments from American newspapers deploring the Senate action were forwarded for Bristol's use in mollifying the Turks.[87] Signs of remorse from voters against the treaty led the department to discuss the feasibility of resubmission, a course finally rejected. Much to the relief of Bristol and his Washington superiors, the remarkably temperate Turkish reaction improved the possibility of resuming official diplomatic relations and securing consent to another modus vivendi. These ends were accomplished by notes signed on February 17, calling for resumption of diplomatic relations and continuing favorable treatment of American commerce. In this fashion, the department hoped to bridge the interval until more permanent agreements could be arranged and put through the Senate. Despite frequently expressed fears of Turkish reprisals, American interests managed rather well during the awkward interval. This happy turn of events was owing in no small measure to Admiral Bristol's effective diplomacy from 1919 to 1927, and to the appointment of Joseph C. Grew in 1927 as ambassador, a post in which he served well until 1932.[88]

[86] *SEJ*, LXV, Part 1, pp. 244, 260, 265, 272, 287, 311, 319, 325–327, 338–339; *FR 1926*, II, 986–991; *FR 1927*, III, 765, 766, 769; *Cong. Record*, 69 Cong., 2 Sess., pp. 910–911, 1266, 1412, 1468; DS 711.672/519, 532c, 533a, 534, 535, 538, 539a; *Cannon's Own Story*, p. 231; *Literary Digest*, 92 (Jan. 29, 1927), 10–11. Before the final vote, a third reservation was added stating that the treaty would not be ratified until both countries had approved a naturalization agreement.
[87] *FR 1927*, III, 766–770; *Cong. Record*, 69 Cong., 2 Sess., p. 1966.
[88] *FR 1927*, III, 769–800, 803–804; Gordon, *American Relations with Turkey*,

Conclusion

The crescent moon observed by Grew on the eve of the Lausanne Conference had indeed been an augury. The Kemalist regime had succeeded in undoing the punitive Sèvres Treaty and setting the new Turkish Republic on a course of domestic reform which amazed the world. Accommodation of the United States to the new dispensation had been retarded, however, by an inherited distaste for the Turks, a legacy from decades of missionary castigation of the Turks for their mistreatment of the Christian minorities. Those Americans most directly concerned with readjustment to the changed conditions were able to discard the terrible Turk stereotype far more easily than their countrymen whose emotional and uncritical prejudices were aroused by pro-Armenian pressure interests allied with partisan Democratic opposition in the United States Senate. The common sense and temperate wisdom of Admiral Bristol, Joseph Grew, Allen Dulles, and the many others responsible for drafting and promoting a reasonable treaty with Turkey had not been sufficient to bring about a triumph of reason over emotion and partisanship. Within a few years the forces which harangued the American public on the old wrongs of a past era would wane, and the continuing changes wrought by the New Turks would carry sufficient weight to permit the arrangement of a new network of Turkish-American treaties.

pp. 22–23, 211–212; ABC, *AR 1927*, p. 60; Gates, *Not to Me Only*, p. 296; DS 711.672/541, 574, 591. See below, Chap. 8, for extended discussion of Turkish-American relations from the rise of Kemal to the outbreak of World War II.

6

A STAKE IN MIDDLE EASTERN OIL, 1919–1939

☆ THE ARABIAN-AMERICAN OIL COMPANY (a joint enterprise of Standard Oil of California and the Texas Company) began an elaborate celebration on May 1, 1939, at Ras Tanura, the company's new deep-water port on the Persian Gulf, to mark the opening of this terminal and the loading of the first tanker to carry Arabian oil to the channels of international commerce. Some four hundred automobiles had transported more than two thousand guests across the desert from Jiddah, Mecca, and Riyadh. King Ibn Saud had arrived with a considerable entourage — seventeen members of the royal family, four government ministers, and a military escort of four hundred soldiers. During several days of ceremonies the gathering of officials, merchants, friends, attendants, and servants was housed in a camp of 350 tents near the oil town of Dhahran.[1] This colorful celebration, crowning two decades of intensive efforts to gain entry into Middle Eastern oil fields, demonstrated that the United States had acquired an enormous new interest in the Arab World.

This acquisition of a major petroleum stake in the Middle East was accompanied by international commercial and diplomatic competition, for petroleum had become a vital resource during World War I. Its impressive military and industrial role sharpened competition among the Great Powers and encouraged them to scour the globe for promising future reserves. The United States entered the competition at a time when experts were predicting the exhaustion within a few years

[1] George Kheirallah, *Arabia Reborn*, pp. 179–180; Joseph W. Walt, "Saudi Arabia and the Americans: 1928–1951," unpublished Ph.D. dissertation, Northwestern University, 1960, pp. 131–132.

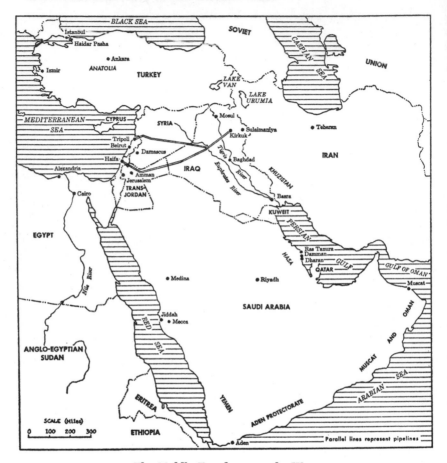

The Middle East between the Wars

of America's bountiful petroleum resources. This was the setting in which American and British interests in the Middle East began to clash at the close of World War I.[2] In their effort to open the door to American development, several large companies came to lean heavily on the State Department for support. An acrimonious controversy broke out between the United States and Great Britain in 1919 and seriously corroded their relations for several years. Blood may have been thicker than water during the war, as devotees of "hands-across-the-seas" sentiments proclaimed, but thinner than oil once the war was over.

[2] See John A. DeNovo, "The Movement for An Aggressive American Oil Policy Abroad, 1918–1920," *American Historical Review*, 61 (July 1956), 854–876.

Origins of the Anglo-American Oil Controversy

In March of 1919 the Standard Oil Company of New York (Socony) laid its troubles with the British in Palestine before the State Department. Explaining the company's interest in the Ottoman Empire, Socony officials pointed out that prior to 1914 they had built up extensive marketing operations, expanding into the production field shortly before the war by acquiring holdings in Palestine, Syria, and Asia Minor. Late in 1913 Socony geologists and mining engineers began work in Palestine. When the war interrupted operations, Socony had obtained full concessionary rights to seven plots in Palestine and had approximately sixty more in either preliminary or intermediate stages of negotiation.[3]

By the time Socony sought to resume its Palestine operations at the close of the war, the area had come under British military occupation. Even before the Armistice, British authorities had shown a suspicious interest in Socony's holdings. Late in the summer of 1918, by intimidating Socony's Jerusalem agent, Ismail H. El Housseini, the British won access to company maps and papers. General Arthur W. Money, British chief administrator of occupied territory, also tried to extract information from Captain William Yale, a former Socony employee in the Levant, engaged in intelligence assignments for the State Department. Yale resisted Money's efforts, told him to pursue his inquiries through proper diplomatic channels, and reported his suspicions of British intentions to Socony officials. It was perfectly clear, he thought, "that by every means possible [the] British will prevent any American Petroleum Company from operating or producing in any territory which they may retain after the war. They did everything possible to find our claims in Palestine and finally when they were unsuccessful, they forced [the agent] to produce all the plans of the vari-

---

[3] *FR 1919*, II, 250–251; William F. Libby (of Socony) to Philander Knox, Sept. 30, 1911; Alvey Adee to William W. Rockhill, Oct. 11, 1911; Rockhill to Knox, March 5, 1912; Libby to the State Department, April 10, 1912; Howard E. Cole (of Socony) to Frank Polk, May 5, 1919; L. I. Thomas (of Socony) to Polk, Sept. 18, 1919, DS 467.11 St /—, —, 3, 7, 31, and 41. Socony was inhibited from completing legal formalities on the 60 preliminary and intermediate claims by an Ottoman decree of late 1914 suspending formalities incident to such concessions during the war. The Ottoman government had assured Socony that the life of all mining permits would be extended for one year after the signing of the peace and that full protection would be accorded certificates of priority until the company could complete their conversion into mining permits. Thomas to Polk, Sept. 18, 1919, DS 467.11 St/41; *FR 1919*, II, 256–257. See also L. Gulmezian (Socony's Constantinople attorney), "Memorandum on Status of Petroleum Mining Permits in Turkey as of April 30, 1919," DS 467.11 St 25/36.

ous claims, which they proceeded to copy." A few weeks later Socony reported that Yale's opinion had been confirmed by other reliable sources.[4]

Such was the background Socony placed before the State Department in March of 1919 to buttress the request for diplomatic assistance. The company argued that British actions endangered American property rights, which could not be protected unless the United States government used its influence to stop British inequities.[5]

Not much alarmed at this information, the State Department approached the British on March 18, 1919, cautiously and politely, merely seeking an explanation of their pressure on Ismail. The British response, which arrived ten weeks later, attempted to gloss over the episode by saying that General Money had simply been conducting a general inquiry to ascertain which of the numerous claims being advanced in Palestine had actually been granted by the Ottoman government. "The action of the British Military authorities was in no way arbitrary nor designed to prejudice the Company's claims."[6]

Washington considered the British response less than frank, particularly in distorting certain facts relating to the military inquiry. In any case, the department's casual attitude of March rapidly gave way to cynicism, and, on the part of a few officials, to more than a touch of Anglophobia. An official on the staff of the foreign trade adviser cautioned his superiors about British aims: "They are leaving no stone unturned to gain control of all oil properties on the surface of the earth, and I am quite certain that if Palestine is to fall under the sphere of British influence the Standard Oil Company will encounter serious difficulties." He recommended that the United States "emphasize to the British authorities that they may expect a scrap if they attempt any freezing out process of American interests in Palestine hereafter."[7]

[4] *FR 1919*, II, 250–251 (quotation, p. 251); Cole to Polk, May 5, 1919; memorandum by Captain William Yale from Constantinople, June 6, 1919, enclosed in Cole to the State Department, July 16, 1919, DS 467.11 St 25/31 and 35. Yale had been one of a party of three sent by Socony to Palestine to investigate oil possibilities during the fall of 1913 and winter of 1914. Yale to the author, Oct. 20, 1947. See also Yale to Lansing, June 30, 1917; Lansing to Yale, Aug. 17, 1917, William Yale MSS.
[5] *FR 1919*, II, 250–252. See also Cole to Polk, May 5, 1919; Cole to the State Department, July 16, 1919, DS 467.11 St 25/31 and 35.
[6] *FR 1919*, II, 252, 254 (quotation).
[7] Office of the Foreign Trade Adviser to Phillips, July 3, 1919, DS 467.11 St 25/34.

The department translated this recommendation into more tactful terms when instructing Ambassador John W. Davis to question diplomatically but pointedly the action of British military officials in Palestine. He was to inquire whether the British had allowed holders of any Ottoman concessions to operate them since the British military occupation. Published British documents suggest that American suspicions were not groundless. Admiral Sir Arthur Calthrope, British high commissioner in Constantinople, warned Lord Curzon in the Foreign Office on June 26, 1919, of the American trade offensive in Asia Minor and commented that the "scramble for concessions has already commenced and we must be ready to support British enterprise."[8]

During the five months Americans waited for a reply to Davis's note,[9] Socony and the department's field representatives sent in further disquieting evidences of British intentions in the Middle East which augured badly for American enterprisers. From Socony's point of view, the most serious evidence of discrimination was the British behavior when three Socony geologists arrived in Palestine in the summer of 1919. Local British military authorities banned them from investigating any claims not actually worked before the war, insisting that they could not relax the ban without orders from London. Despite the opinion of Colonel French, acting chief political officer in Cairo, that Socony held bona fide claims, Lord Curzon flatly refused permission for Socony to work any claims in Palestine. When British officials contended that Socony had not "worked" the seven completed concessions because they had not actually commenced drilling, the company vigorously protested the interpretation as unfair, since they had spent about half a million dollars in geological exploration, built several miles of roads, made considerable expenditure for equipment, and assembled a technical staff. When the war intervened, drilling equipment in transit from the United States was stored in Alexandria. Socony argued that these facts demonstrated good faith and certainly constituted "working" the concession.[10]

Additional indications of British exclusionist intentions came to the

---

[8] *FR 1919*, II, 254. In June the British permitted the Zionist Organization of America to make a confidential oil and mining survey of Palestine. *DBFP*, IV, 277–278, 280, 651 (quotation), 663.

[9] *FR 1919*, II, 261–262.

[10] Thomas to Socony, Aug. 16, 1919; Thomas to Polk, Sept. 18, 1919, DS 467.11 St 25/36 and 41; *DBFP*, IV, 352, 366, 382, 406.

department. A Socony geologist in Jerusalem claimed that British censors in Palestine were taking trade information from his company's mail which Socony's rivals could use profitably. The company's apprehensions were shared by Consul Otis A. Glazebrook in Jerusalem, who wrote that the British "wish to control all economic values in this district." Ambassador Davis even extracted an admission from the British that they had operated oil wells in Mesopotamia temporarily — for military purposes, they said — and that military authorities had been lax enough on one occasion to permit more extended operations by an English oil expert. According to the British explanation, when superior authorities found this out, they compelled him to cease operations and leave the country.[11]

As these reports trickled into Washington, Socony pressed the State Department repeatedly to challenge the British stand on two grounds — the interference with legal American commercial rights, and the importance of foreign oil development to the national interest. Within the department there developed a sympathetic concurrence in the alarm shown by Socony and a feeling that governmental action was needed to protect American interests. Arthur C. Millspaugh of the foreign trade adviser's staff criticized the British effort "to acquire all sources of crude petroleum they can buy or steal outside and inside the United States." He favored supporting American oil companies to the limit "whether . . . monopolistic in tendency or not," and believed that the American point might be gained by taking a strong hand with the British. Concurrently, the oil industry, through the American Petroleum Institute, was exerting pressure on the State Department, and a clamor for governmental action was rising in Congress.[12]

There followed during the autumn an intensive effort by American diplomats working closely with L. I. Thomas of Socony, as he shuttled between Paris and London, to overcome British intransigence. They were unsuccessful, for the British perfected a legal position difficult to assail. Their position in Palestine, said the British, was that of a trustee pending decision as to whether the country would be placed under

[11] Hamson Gary (agent and consul-general, Cairo) to Lansing, Sept. 15, 1919; William Phillips to Glazebrook, Sept. 18, 1919; Cole to Lansing, Oct. 17, 1919, DS 467.11 St 25/44, 36b, and 43; *FR 1919*, II, 257 (quotation).

[12] Millspaugh memorandum to Mr. Lay, Sept. 9, 1919, DS 467.11 St 25/36; Thomas A. O'Donnell (president of API) to Lansing, Sept. 30, 1919, DS 800.6363/89; *Cong. Record*, 66 Cong., 1 Sess., 3303–3310, 3921, 4161–4170, 4282–4283, 5689.

mandate or given independent status. During military occupation, therefore, they would be obliged to prohibit the activities of any explorers, commercial agents, or concessionaires to avoid an embarrassing and confusing flood of applicants. Moreover, the British argued that war conditions still existing in Palestine made geological exploration unsafe.[13]

The American complaint against the British refusal to permit Socony's geologists to examine their Palestine properties was only the first grievance in the emerging controversy over oil. Before the end of 1919 the two governments were also engaged in a dispute over Mesopotamian exploitation, which proved to be longer, more complex, and even more detrimental to Anglo-American relations. Late in August of 1919 when Socony sent two geologists to Baghdad to investigate oil possibilities in Mesopotamia, British authorities refused them permission to look around, although a British geologist had been working there for four months.[14]

British behavior toward possible American oil development in Palestine and Mesopotamia, two areas almost certain to be assigned as mandates to Great Britain, raised serious doubts in Washington about London's conception of the mandate system. The question was whether the British would employ the untried mandate system as a thin veil for old-fashioned protectorates. Such an interpretation being entirely at odds with the American view of mandates as expressed by President Wilson at the Paris Peace Conference, the United States began to shape a position merging its oil grievance with the larger and more fundamental issue of mandate policy. The Senate had not yet acted on the Treaty of Versailles, and there was still good reason to expect that the United States might become a League member.

By October, the State Department was shifting the grounds of its argument. It insisted that the British live up to the mandate principles agreed to earlier, requiring the mandatory to secure for citizens of all League of Nations members (1) equal protection and rights in the acquisition of immovable property, and (2) complete economic, commercial, and industrial equality as well as freedom of transit. Lloyd

[13] *FR 1919*, II, 255–257; Thomas to Polk, Sept. 18, 1919; Cole to Lansing, Sept. 25, 1919; Polk to Davis, Sept. 29, 1919; Thomas to Socony, Sept. 30, 1919, DS 467.11 St 25/41, 46, 40, and 39; *DBFP*, IV, 501–503.

[14] *FR 1919*, II, 259–260; Thomas to Coffin, Oct. 30, 1919; enclosures in Oscar Heizer (consul, Baghdad) to Lansing, Nov. 19, 1919, DS 467.11 St 25/46, and 51.

George, together with the French and Italian representatives, had agreed with President Wilson in the Council of Four that the mandatory should in no case have priority on concessions. The department linked this argument directly to Socony's Palestine claims. It also expected that American firms would have "equal privileges with those of British or other nationalities in Mesopotamia as well as Palestine."[15]

The American arguments did not budge the British from their determination to ban oil operations in occupied territories. Lord Curzon admitted with regret what he called the mistake of having allowed a Shell geologist to work in Mesopotamia early in 1919, but this action had been stopped. Repair of Mesopotamian oil facilities by two Shell men, Curzon excused as essential to military and transportation needs. He disclaimed any intention of discrimination and cited cases of British firms likewise denied permission to enter occupied territories. He proposed to adhere unflinchingly to the principle that the occupying authorities should do nothing to compromise the freedom of future authorities in developing mineral resources.[16]

The State Department wilted in the face of Curzon's argument for a complete nondiscriminatory ban on operations. Ambassador Davis believed that the United States had no legal grounds left for urging reversal of the decision. The venerable second assistant secretary, Alvey A. Adee, concurred and gently informed Socony of the judgment. The department's retreat deeply disappointed Socony officials. Adee's announcement closely followed the Senate's rejection of the League of Nations, which had a demoralizing effect on the personnel conducting American foreign relations. Participation in the Allied deliberations on the Turkish settlement no longer seemed feasible.[17] Rejection of the League also meant that the United States could no longer base its protests against British discrimination on the claim that American adherence to the Covenant guaranteed her citizens freedom from discrimination. The State Department now had to resort to the argument of co-belligerency, claiming equal rights on the basis of American contribution to the over-all Allied victory against the Central Powers.

[15] *FR 1919*, II, 258–260 (quotation, pp. 259–260).
[16] *FR 1919*, II, 260–261; Davis to Lansing, Nov. 24 and Oct. 30, 1919, DS 467.11 St 25/48 and 45; Davis to Polk, Nov. 1, 1919, Frank L. Polk MSS.
[17] Davis to Lansing, Nov. 29, 1919; Thomas to Lansing, Dec. 4, 1919; Adee to Thomas, Dec. 22, 1919, and Jan. 10, 1920, DS 467.11 St 25/48, 49, 48, and DS 800.6363/58; Polk to Bristol, Dec. 9, 1919, Polk MSS; *FR 1919: PPC*, IX, 547.

Washington could not shelve the Socony case indefinitely in view of the accumulating new evidences of British discrimination and the growing irascibility of anti-British feeling in the United States. The department learned that even as the Foreign Office was denying in September that British nationals were receiving special privileges, Shell and Anglo-Persian geologists had been investigating Mesopotamian oil lands.[18] Again in January and February of 1920, Consul Oscar Heizer in Baghdad and Socony geologists presented damaging new evidence of Shell geologists operating in Kurdistan, allegedly as civil employees of the British. That the American charges were not phantasms was supported by the secret message about these Mesopotamian operations in which the Foreign Office told General Sir Edmund Allenby that the intention of the British government was "for the present" to "take all necessary measures to utilise oil products discovered in occupied territory to their own advantage." About the same time Socony questioned the real purpose of a small refinery being built near Baghdad by Anglo-Persian. Lending color to the charge of extensive economic planning in Mesopotamia were reports of preparations by Lancashire cotton experts to supply English mills with Mesopotamian cotton.[19]

All these cases combined with congressional irritation over British oil policies to furnish twin stimuli for another diplomatic protest to the Foreign Office in February, 1920. Ambassador Davis asked for assurance that British or other nationals be treated no more favorably than Americans, either directly or indirectly. He warned that growing adverse criticism of restrictive British policies was seriously injuring Anglo-American relations. Further damage would surely result from exclusion or discrimination in Palestine and Mesopotamia.[20]

After more than a year of close cooperation with Socony, the State

[18] Consul Heizer believed that they had gathered significant information before being stopped on orders from the Foreign Office to the Civil Commissioner after the arrival of Socony agents. Heizer to Lansing, Jan. 10, 1920, DS 467.11 St 25/50.

[19] Bristol to Lansing, Jan. 23, 1920, enclosing copy of Heizer's of Jan. 20; Thomas to Lansing, Jan. 31, 1920; Heizer to Polk, Feb. 17, 1920; Cole to Colby, April 20, 1920, enclosing Sheffield to Thomas of Feb. 25, 1920, DS 467.11 St 25/53, 54, 56, and 59; *BDFP*, IV, 627, 629 (quotation); Bristol to Lansing, Jan. 7, 1920; G. B. Ravndal (consul general, Constantinople) to Colby, April 27, 1920, enclosing Heizer's Jan. 31, DS 800.6363/65 and 134; Bristol to Colby, April 1, 1920, Polk MSS.

[20] *FR 1920*, II, 649–650. Congressional pique at British oil policy took the form of discriminatory clauses in the Mineral Leasing Act signed by President Wilson on February 25, 1920. *Cong. Record*, 66 Cong., 2 Sess., p. 3500; Public Law No. 146, *U.S. Statutes at Large*, Vol. 41, Part 1, pp. 437–451, especially 438.

Department had concluded that the company possessed certain vested rights in Palestine under Turkish law, and that while the British as temporary occupiers could legally enjoin acquisition of further rights, as quasi-trustees they were obligated to protect existing rights. Although without legal grounds to force permission for Socony to explore during military occupation, the department believed it important to impress on the Foreign Office the vital concern of the United States government for protection of American vested rights and maintenance of the Open Door in the mandates.[21] The oil stakes of the Middle East had played a major part in the mounting tension in Anglo-American relations during 1919 and the early part of 1920. This was the situation when the Anglo-French agreement of San Remo, of April 24, 1920, opened a stormy chapter in Anglo-American oil diplomacy.

The Fight for the Open Door in Mesopotamia

Representatives of the Allies gathered at San Remo, Italy, in the spring of 1920 to put the finishing touches on the peace treaty with Turkey, signed later at Sèvres. Great Britain and France took advantage of this meeting to make the San Remo Oil Agreement, the culmination of several years of maneuvering by which France secured a share in the potential oil production of Mesopotamia. In return, France gave permission for a British pipeline to cross French-mandated territory to a Mediterranean terminal and for the construction of port facilities.[22]

These arrangements came as no surprise to the State Department, which had learned nearly six months earlier from Ambassador Davis in London that Anglo-French oil discussions were taking place. As the

[21] *FR 1920*, II, 650–651. Socony finally received British permission to examine its Palestine oil claims in 1922, but the results were not promising and the company gave up all its Palestine claims by 1927. J. E. Schuckburgh (British Colonial Office) to Thomas, March 30, 1922; C. D. Campbell to Cole, June 4, 1927, Socony file 7526. See also DeNovo, "Petroleum and American Diplomacy," Chap. 9, which is based chiefly on DS 867n.6363.

[22] The agreement had other provisions, including some pertaining to oil development in Central and Eastern Europe. The text is printed in *FR 1920*, II, 665–668. The Anglo-French negotiations concerning Mosul and oil can be followed in *DBFP*, IV, 1089–1118; *FR 1919: PPC*, V, 760; Pierre L'Espagnol de la Tramerye, *La lutte mondiale pour le pétrole*, pp. 190–192; Mehdi Hessabi, *Le pétrole en Irak*, pp. 46–48; Edward M. Earle, "The Turkish Petroleum Company: A Study in Oleaginous Diplomacy," *Political Science Quarterly*, 39 (June 1924), 271–272; Cumming, *Franco-British Rivalry*, pp. 59, 62–63, 65; Gerig, *The Open Door and the Mandate System*, p. 143; Temperley, ed., *History of the Peace Conference*, VI, 182–183; Lloyd George, *Memoirs*, II, 673, 710–711.

rumors about the talks continued, officials in Washington reacted uneasily, particularly in view of the secrecy shrouding the negotiations and the inability of American diplomats to obtain officially verified information. By April of 1920, when Ambassador Hugh Wallace in Paris heard from a confidential source that the Anglo-French oil syndicate was about a year old, he concluded that it threatened American interests: "The Anglo-French combination is determined to keep American companies out of the new oil fields of the Near East, and in putting an end to competition between France and England to divide up equally [*sic*] all oil interests in Asia Minor."[23]

Rumors of the accomplishments of the San Remo conference soon filtered into Washington, and within a month of the conference Wallace and Davis had forwarded to Washington copies of the oil agreement, which they had obtained privately and unofficially. Not until late in July, however, did the British acknowledge the failure of efforts to keep the agreement secret, by printing it officially. The terms of the agreement fed the fires of mistrust and reinforced the American view that the British intended to exclude Americans from the exploration for oil in the old Ottoman Empire.[24]

The State Department sharpened its diplomatic weapons for an American offensive, launched with its note of May 12, 1920. Oddly enough, this blast from Washington against the San Remo Oil Agreement could not refer to the agreement directly because it was presumably still secret; the department was not prepared to betray confidential sources through which it had obtained drafts of the agreement. The point of departure for the American note was British acceptance at San Remo of mandates for Mesopotamia and Palestine contingent on the granting of economic rights in Asia Minor to Italy. From this base,

[23] Davis to Lansing, Nov. 6, 1919; Memorandum, Office of the Foreign Trade Adviser (A.C.M. and A.N.Y.) to Messrs. Dwight, Frost, and Merle-Smith, March 3, 1920; Polk to Davis, March 6, 1920; Polk to Wallace, March 6, 1920; Wallace to Colby, April 1, 1920, DS 867.6363/7, 7, 7, 7, and 13; Polk to Davis, March 13, 1920; Davis to Colby, April 28, 1920, DS 841.6363/29A and 45; Wallace to Colby, April 19, 1920, DS 890g.6363 T 84/— (quotation).
[24] Robert Skinner (consul general, London) to Colby, May 1, 1920; Davis to Colby, May 3 and May 7, 1920, DS 841.6363/39, 48, and 43A; Wallace to Colby, May 3, May 3, and May 7, 1920; Davis to Colby, July 26 and July 31, 1920, DS 800.6363/108, 109, 113, 157, and 167. On May 7 Wallace sent a copy and translation of the Draft Agreement obtained from the head of Standard Oil in France who had received it from one of his assistants, a member of the French delegation at San Remo.

the United States built its argument around the denial of equality of opportunity in the mandates, in violation of a cardinal principle for the mandates agreed to at Paris in 1919. "It was on account of and subject to this understanding that the United States felt itself able and willing to agree that the acquisition of certain enemy territory by the victorious powers would be consistent with the best interests of the world." According to the State Department, the British administration of Mesopotamia and Palestine since 1919 had created the impression in the United States that the British were discriminating against Americans, especially petroleum interests, in favor of British private interests "and further that Great Britain had been preparing quietly for exclusive control of the oil resources in this region." In reiterating the principles it expected to be applied in mandates, the United States insisted on its participation in any discussions of concessions already granted because of its vested interests in the area as well as its general interest in the principles involved.[25]

Although the Foreign Office delayed replying, Washington officials were temporarily encouraged during May by a few signs that the British might be moderating their oil policy because of American complaints. The optimism was short-lived in view of new reports from Consul Heizer in Baghdad; from Admiral Bristol in Constantinople; and from W. C. Teagle, president of Standard Oil of New Jersey. Early in June of 1920, Heizer interpreted opinion among the local British officials in the Middle East as favoring exclusive British exploitation of the oil fields on the ground that Great Britain had to bear the expense of administration. The British Civil Commissioner had even declared his opposition to sharing the oil with France. Heizer reported that Socony geologists had been kept waiting in Baghdad for several months, while Shell geologists had just returned from a long expedition to Mosul and Kurdistan allegedly on government business; Anglo-Persian geologists had also been permitted to operate. Teagle cited a recent speech by the British Ambassador in Washington as indicating that the British had no intention of allowing other nationalities to explore for oil in Mesopotamia. From his vantage point in Constantinople, Bristol believed the evidence showed the British were satisfied that they had cornered the Turkish market against American interests.[26]

[25] *FR 1920*, II, 651–655 (quotations, p. 652).
[26] Davis to Colby, May 18, 1920; F. D. Asche (Socony) to Colby, May 28, 1920;

These reports, combined with the British delay in answering the American note of May 12, elicited a second note to the Foreign Office on July 28, in which the department reiterated its interest in effective implementation of the mandates principles. For the first time the San Remo Oil Agreement was mentioned specifically and protested as a violation of the Paris agreements on mandates.[27]

Curzon's prompt answer challenged American premises and opened up new areas of controversy. The British, he insisted, had not assumed the Mesopotamian mandate subject to special arrangements with any other nation. He denied again that British oil policy was discriminatory either in theory or fact. As for the critical point of view developing in the United States, Curzon considered it unwarranted in view of the small British share (only 4½ per cent) of the total oil production of the world, while the United States produced 70 per cent within its own borders and its nationals extracted 12 per cent more from Mexican fields. He pointed to American restrictions on alien exploitation of oil in the public domain as well as the alleged American hampering of British oil prospecting in Costa Rica and Haiti to show that the American record was not without blemish in the application of the open-door policy.

Curzon took advantage of the American failure to join the League by indicating that the Mandate "A" draft referred to in the May 12 note had been abandoned; however, subsequent drafts for Mesopotamia and Palestine had incorporated equal treatment and opportunity for all League members. After the Allies approved these drafts they would be sent to the League Council. The British declared their sympathy with the principles proposed by the United States, but held that the mandate terms could properly be discussed only at the League Council by signatories of the Covenant.

British planning for oil development in Mesopotamia relied on the claim that the Turkish Petroleum Company, dominated by the British government, had obtained a concession from Ottoman authorities in 1914. Curzon now drew attention to these alleged rights by expressing his pleasure that the United States agreed that oil concessions should

Skinner to Colby, June 1, 1920, DS 800.6363/126, 137, and 138; Davis to Colby, May 18, May 21, and May 31, 1920; Millspaugh memorandum, June 3, 1920, DS 841.6363/61, 67, 69, and 70; Heizer to Colby, June 9, 1920; Teagle to Colby, June 10, 1920; Bristol to Colby, June 17, 1920, DS 867.6363/37, 20, and 52.
[27] *FR 1920*, II, 658–659.

be respected. He justified the San Remo Oil Agreement as compensating France for renouncing her long-standing interests in Mosul. Furthermore, the French had given *quid pro quo* in return for the oil benefits — a practice quite in accord, the British observed, with the conditional most-favored-nation interpretation still upheld by the United States.[28]

Curzon's sharp rejoinder kept the State Department busy for three months before a reply was formulated. The day after arrival of the British note, the departmental conference called to begin work on the reply took up the British arguments point by point and then assigned the task of working up particular sections of a proposed answer to various personnel within the department. For several weeks the assembling of data required correspondence with Consul Thomas R. Owens in Baghdad and a careful inquiry into legal aspects of the alleged Turkish Petroleum Company claim.[29]

Action had become imperative by mid-November. Secretary of State Bainbridge Colby explained to President Wilson that the League Assembly was in session and that the British might seek official approval from the League for their course in Mesopotamia. The United States should prevent this, Colby argued, by charging that the British had flagrantly violated the mandate principles in Mesopotamia.[30]

The next day Colby finished a long, peppery note for Ambassador Davis to deliver to Lord Curzon. The major emphasis fell on the American conception of the mandates. Even though the "A" draft discussed at Paris had not been adopted, Great Britain had subscribed to the principles therein and, Colby contended, the United States had been persuaded to agree to the mandate idea specifically because it embodied enlightened principles. The United States did not agree that because it had not joined the League it could be excluded from the benefits of equality of opportunity. There would have been no mandates

[28] *FR 1920*, II, 663–667. As reorganized after World War I, British, Dutch, and French oil companies held 95 per cent of the stock in the TPC; Calouste S. Gulbenkian owned the remaining 5 per cent.

[29] Cole to Colby, July 1, 1920; Adee to Thomas, Sept. 22 and Oct. 9, 1920; Thomas to Colby, Sept. 23, 1920; DS 867.6363/66, 57a, 57a, and 70; Thomas to Colby, July 21, 1920; R. E. Coontz (Acting Secretary of the Navy) to Colby, July 29, 1920; Merle-Smith memorandum, Sept. 9, 1920; DS 890g.6363 T 84/3, 5, and 7; C. A. Jr., memorandum, Aug. 13, 1920; Owens to Colby, Sept. 6, 1920; DS 800.6363/237 and 178; Owens to Colby, Sept. 29, 1920; Office of the Solicitor, Oil Memorandum No. 1 and Oil Memorandum No. 2, both Nov. 18, 1920; DS 890g.6363/8, 24, and 25.

[30] Colby to President Wilson, Nov. 19, 1920, DS 800.6363/288b.

in the Middle East without the military contributions of the United States to the general victory of the Allies. Colby requested, as a right, that the United States see and approve the draft mandates before they were sent to the League Council. Because the mandate system was a new principle on trial, all points, especially the obligations assumed by the mandatory, ought to be discussed frankly and fully. The United States hoped the mandate principle would help to mitigate international strife over raw materials, such as oil.

Moving from the theory of the mandates to the specific issue behind the diplomatic controversy, Colby noted the difficulty in harmonizing the oil division in the San Remo Agreement with the British contention that concessions claims would remain in their prewar status until given equitable consideration upon the establishment of the Arab state. Here Colby touched the Achilles heel of the British. He hoped the British had not taken an *ex parte* and premature decision on the Turkish Petroleum Company claims, inasmuch as American information indicated that the company had not acquired a valid concession. Colby's concluding comments were something less than candid. He strained to make the point that it was not American interest in Middle East oil that dictated the American position as to the true character of a mandate so much as it was concern for the principle of trusteeship.[31]

The British ignored Colby's contention that the United States should approve the draft mandates before they were sent to the League Council. Without consulting the United States, the British government submitted the draft mandates for Mesopotamia and Palestine to the Secretary General of the League on December 6, 1920. In the League Council there was knowledge of the Anglo-American note exchanges regarding Middle East oil and mandates. A League spokesman unofficially asked the United States for a copy of Colby's November 20 note to Curzon, arguing that the contents would assist the Council in deciding on the nature of the draft mandates. The State Department agreed to furnish the Council an official copy of the note to be used unofficially.[32]

Soon the United States found a way to place its grievances against Great Britain directly before the League. A few days before the Council was to meet for discussions of the mandate terms on February 21, 1921,

[31] *FR 1920*, II, 668–673.
[32] *FR 1921*, I, 104–107; Davis to Colby, Dec. 6, 1920; Norman Davis (Acting Secretary of State) to J. W. Davis, Dec. 7, 1920, DS 800.6363/202.

Ambassador Wallace sent Colby information indicating the sincere desire of the Council to bring the drafts into accord with the League Covenant. He saw every reason to believe that the American views would have a sympathetic hearing. But the League could not act formally on the American note of November 20 to Curzon because it had been communicated unofficially. In view of the British refusal to consult the United States on the drafts, Colby took advantage of the opening. He communicated the November 20 note officially and told the League Council that American concurrence was required to validate the mandate drafts. The League Council assured the United States of a chance to express its views before a decision was made on "A" mandates, and invited the United States to participate in its discussions when the final decision was impending. The United States did not take advantage of this invitation.[33]

Transference of the American case directly to the League did not end the exchange of notes. On February 28, 1921, Lord Curzon answered Colby's November note, contending that the Turkish Petroleum Company had acquired rights through a letter from the Turkish Grand Vizier on June 28, 1914. The British cleverly tried to put their Mesopotamian claims in the same category as Socony's Palestine claims. Curzon also hit the United States where it was vulnerable by again calling attention to the failure to follow the open-door principle in regard to the natural resources of the Philippine Islands and in the Caribbean.[34]

Although the note exchange slackened for a few months while the new administration's Secretary of State, Charles Evans Hughes, took over the reins, the British pressed the State Department during the summer and autumn of 1921 for its further views on mandates before the September meetings of the League Council, when they hoped a decision would be reached. The United States restated its conception of the general principles and made specific observations on the form of the mandates proposed. No definite action came out of the September Council meetings, however.[35]

By the autumn of 1921, the problem of economic rights in the mandates had become inextricably intertwined with the specific issue of the validity of the Mesopotamian claim of the Turkish Petroleum Com-

[33] *FR 1921*, I, 88–95; Cumming, *Franco-British Rivalry*, pp. 112–113; Howard, *Partition of Turkey*, p. 325.
[34] *FR 1921*, II, 80–84.
[35] *FR 1921*, I, 96, II, 106–110; Howard, *Partition of Turkey*, pp. 325–326.

pany. George Harvey, the new American ambassador in London, linkec
the two issues in a note of November 17, 1921, to the Foreign Office
The United States disagreed with the British interpretation of the
letter of June 28, 1914, from the Turkish Grand Vizier; the State Department contended that the letter could not be considered "a definite
and binding agreement to lease":

Since both the extent of the participation of the Ministry of Finance in
the operations of the company and the general conditions of the lease
were, according to this communication, to be fixed at a later date by
one of the parties to the alleged agreement, there would seem to be
room for doubt whether, even if war had not intervened, a lease would
actually have been executed. As your Lordship observes with respect
to the letter of June 28, 1914, the Ministry reserved "the right to fix later
on its share in the enterprise as well as the terms of the contract."

If the British continued to assert the claim, the United States asked
again that the matter be settled by suitable arbitration. Harvey also
challenged the British efforts to place the Palestine claims of Socony in
the same category as the TPC claims in Mesopotamia by pointing out
that the American company had complied with all the provisions of the
Turkish mining code before being issued full concessionary rights by
Ottoman authorities.[36]

The British ignored the arbitration suggestion but did make some
concessions to the American demands on mandates before the end of
1921. While disavowing any intention of depriving the United States
of the fruits of victory, the British pointed out that the nations signing
the Versailles Treaty undertook obligations which the United States
had avoided. The British agreed, nevertheless, not to propose or accept
any modifications in mandate terms without previous consultation with
the United States. In any case, they disclaimed any intention of refusing
full equality of opportunity to American companies. As yet, the legal
position of the mandates was still undefined and the Council had not
acted on the mandate drafts. Delay could be expected as long as there
was no genuine peace with Turkey.[37]

[36] *FR 1921*, II, 86–93.
[37] *FR 1921*, II, 110–118. The British had been carrying on without a mandate
in Mesopotamia, which was generally referred to as Iraq after the installation of
an Arab king (Feisal) in August of 1921. The new kingdom remained under
British domination. During 1922 the British gave up the idea of getting League
approval for the draft mandate which had been presented to the Council in December, 1920. British relations with Iraq were regularized, however, by the Anglo-
Iraqi treaty of alliance signed on October 10, 1922. The League Council accepted

During the year and a half following the San Remo Oil Agreement of April 24, 1920, the Anglo-American diplomatic controversy over oil in the Middle Eastern mandates had reached its most acrimonious pitch. The United States built its case around the twin principles of the Open Door and equality of commercial opportunity, firmly established features of American diplomatic theory. The British relied on the sanctity of international contracts, a useful principle if they could prove that the Turks had granted a concession in 1914. Without denying the validity of the principle of economic equality in the mandates, the British weakened American reliance on that principle by coupling with it the corollary of equality of political responsibilities. As the British saw it, the United States had failed to shoulder political obligations in the Turkish settlement which would have entitled it to the economic privileges the State Department demanded. From a practical point of view, the central issue was whether the Turkish Petroleum Company had acquired a valid concession in 1914. In denying the legality of the claim, the State Department had the better case, as was suggested by the British refusal to submit the case to arbitration.

There was a marked and mysterious slackening in the barrage of notes during the early part of 1922. The objectives American diplomacy had been unable to achieve were being pursued by other means. American oil companies had organized to negotiate, if possible, a commercial agreement with the organizations making up the Turkish Petroleum Company. The State Department gave friendly support to the scheme.

The Formation of an American Oil Consortium

The Harding administration worked even more closely with the American oil industry than the Wilson administration in trying to open the door to Middle East oil. Both Secretary of State Hughes and Secretary of Commerce Herbert C. Hoover (a mining engineer by profession) plunged immediately into a reappraisal of the international oil problem. Hoover, who took the initiative in soliciting information and opinions from the industry, found oil men united on one point: they opposed any government policy which might impose restraints on private enter-

a modified form of this treaty on September 27, 1924. Not until then were Anglo-Iraqi relations legally placed on a mandatory basis under League supervision. See Howard, *Partition of Turkey*, pp. 322, 327–328.

prise. R. L. Welch, secretary and counsel for the American Petroleum Institute told the department: "the petroleum industry did not want any legislation along the lines of the bills that have been introduced into Congress, such as the Phelan Bill providing for a Government-controlled oil corporation or the McKellar and Phelan Bills providing for an embargo on the export of oil."[38]

More attractive to the petroleum industry (except for Socony at the outset) was the proposal put forward by Van H. Manning, director of research for the American Petroleum Institute, and others for formation of a syndicate of the principal American companies to operate in Mesopotamia or wherever else a combination of American oil interests might seem desirable. Before endorsing this approach, the State Department sifted various suggestions for a solution of the Anglo-American oil controversy at the diplomatic level. While the study was in progress, encouraging hints came from leaders of the British petroleum industry suggesting their willingness to consider a deal granting American interests a minority interest in the Turkish Petroleum Company.[39]

[38] Office of the Solicitor (E. T.) to Millspaugh, memorandum, Jan. 19, 1921; Millspaugh to Nielsen, March 23, 1921; Office of the Foreign Trade Adviser (by W. F.) to Dearing, March 23, 1921; all DS 811.6363/50. A conference at the Bureau of Mines on April 1, 1921, discussed possible legislative and diplomatic alternatives and was attended by H. F. Bain, director of the Bureau of Mines; J. E. Swigart, petroleum specialist of the Bureau of Mines; W. W. Cumberland, acting foreign trade adviser of the State Department; A. C. Millspaugh; Van H. Manning; and R. L. Welch, secretary and counsel of the American Petroleum Institute. Millspaugh memorandum, April 12, 1921 (quotation), DS 811.6363/46; Director of the Bureau of Foreign and Domestic Commerce, *Annual Report for 1922*, p. 52; Secretary of Commerce, *Tenth Annual Report* [1922], pp. 11, 69–71. For fuller explanation of the Phelan and McKellar proposals, see DeNovo in *American Historical Review*, 61:872–873.

[39] Millspaugh memorandum of conversation with L. I. Thomas, April 14, 1921, DS 890g.6363 T 84/9; Merle-Smith to J. W. Davis, Feb. 7, 1921; J. B. Wright to Hughes, March 23, 1921, both DS 841.6363/121A; Millspaugh memorandum, Dec. 13, 1920, DS 867.6363/74. In May while the State Department was still exploring the possibility of an international oil conference, it called for suggestions from a number of government departments and from leaders of the oil industry. The industry consensus was that American oil could compete successfully in acquiring foreign holdings provided the government could ensure them equality of opportunity. Hughes to Hoover, April 23, 1921; H. P. Fletcher to Secretaries of the Navy, Commerce, Interior, and the Chairman of the U.S. Shipping Board, all April 12, 1921; F. M. Dearing to F. K. Lane (Pan-American Petroleum Company); to J. B. Moore; to A. C. Veatch (Sinclair); to Van H. Manning; to L. I. Thomas (Socony); to Mark L. Requa (Sinclair); to A. C. Bedford (Socony), all April 6, 1921, DS 800.6363/255, 243g, 243h, 243i, 243j, 242a, 243a, 243b, 243c, 243d, 243e, and 243f; Dearing to George S. Davison (Gulf); to E. C. Lufkin (Texas), both April 11, 1921, DS 811.6363/51b.

Secretary Hoover now assumed leadership of the effort to bring American companies together. He wrote the State Department on April 14: "I am in touch with the petroleum industry in the country in an endeavor to organize something specific that we can get behind." When Hoover and Hughes talked over the whole oil problem on April 22, 1921, they worked over details for cooperation with petroleum trade associations and professional groups. Promising private talks about forming a syndicate for foreign operations preceded a Washington petroleum conference called by Hoover for May 16. At this meeting Hoover emphasized how important it was for the American companies to assure the government that, if the door opened in Mesopotamia, they would be prepared to take advantage of the opportunity. Within a week, A. C. Bedford of Socony promised Secretary Hughes that, whenever the door was opened, his company would be ready "to despatch at once an adequate geological party and to take all other usual steps involved in a preliminary examination of supposed oil territory." His company was willing to undertake this activity alone, "or, if the State Department deems best, will make the effort in cooperation with other oil companies, provided only that a reasonable and satisfactory arrangement can be effected among the participating companies." [40]

During the next five months seven large companies succeeded in coming together for projected combined work in Mesopotamia. Writing in behalf of the American Group, W. C. Teagle (president of Jersey Standard) informed the State Department on November 3, 1921, that the seven companies — Standard of New Jersey, Socony, Sinclair, Texas, Gulf, Mexican, and Atlantic — wished to explore prospective areas in Mesopotamia. As soon as they received approval to proceed, they would despatch their geologists and engineers. Teagle concluded that "inasmuch as this subject is one which your department of our government has had under consideration and, as we are advised, has exchanged

[40] Hoover to Fletcher, April 14, 1921; penciled note, unsigned, April 22, 1921, on back of Millspaugh memorandum to Dearing and Fletcher, April 21, 1921, DS 800.6363/272 and 255; Bedford to Hughes, May 21, 1921, DS 890g.6363/28 (last two quotations); Martin Carey (Socony) to Hoover, June 16, 1921, Socony file 7526. Hoover had been president of the American Institute of Mining and Metallurgical Engineers in 1920, and the following year was president of the Federation of American Engineering Societies, which coordinated the work of the foreign policy committees of the AIMME, the Mining and Metallurgical Society of America, and the American Mining Congress. Ralph Arnold to Hughes, April 23, 1921, enclosing memorandum on "Foreign Oil Policy of the United States" adopted at a conference on April 15, 1921, DS 811.6363/69.

communications with the government of Great Britain, we shall appreciate your giving us such information and instructions as may be necessary."[41]

The department answered that it was pleased with the plans of the American Group for Mesopotamian operations, but as yet the British had indicated no decision relative to working the Mesopotamian fields, still adhering to the ban on geological investigation during military occupation. Hughes also referred to the inability of the two governments to reconcile their differences about the Turkish Petroleum Company's claims. As soon as the department received word that the British would allow prospecting, it would promptly notify the companies.[42]

Late in November the American Group hinted to the State Department of their hopes to make effective use of the additional strength from combined action. At a conference in New York on November 21, C. F. Meyer of Socony, Van H. Manning of the American Petroleum Institute, and A. C. Veatch of Sinclair discussed the plans with Arthur C. Millspaugh, foreign trade adviser in the State Department. Meyer announced that Sir John Cadman of Anglo-Persian was coming to the United States and that he might have a plan in mind, since there was some indication that the British were now willing to admit American interests in Mesopotamia. Cadman had recently told Manning that he wanted an amalgamation of American and English private interests in the development of the Middle East fields. Meyer asked what the government's attitude would be if oil interests of the two countries made a private agreement affording Americans twenty-five per cent participation in Mesopotamia, similar to the French share. Millspaugh reminded the conference that the department had taken a firm stand on two points: the demand for equality of commercial opportunity in Mesopotamia, and the falsity of the claim asserted by the Turkish Petroleum Company. Regarding the first requirement, Meyer objected that complete equality of opportunity "would be impracticable, since Japanese, Italian, French, and other nationalities would want to participate." The second requirement could be met, Meyer suggested, if

[41] Teagle to Hughes, Nov. 3, 1921, DS 890g.6363/49. See also Cole to Thomas, Nov. 4, 1921, Socony file 7533. The American Group submitted its letter to Hoover for approval prior to despatching it to the State Department. Millspaugh memorandum to Dearing, Nov. 26, 1921, DS 890g.6363 T 84/24; Hoover to C. F. Meyer, Nov. 4, 1921, Socony file 7533.

[42] *FR 1921*, II, 87–88.

the Turkish Petroleum Company obtained a new concession from Iraq. Millspaugh countered that the department would not dictate to the companies what they should do and would probably approve any equitable arrangements arrived at by the private interests.[43]

Following this conference, the State Department made cautious advances to the British government. American officials saw signs early in 1922 that both British oil executives and their government were making conciliatory gestures. This view was strengthened by Cadman's remarks during his unofficial visit when he told Arthur Millspaugh on January 16, 1922, that the Mesopotamian oil imbroglio was susceptible to Anglo-American cooperation, because American capital and engineering experience were needed to carry out plans for Mesopotamian development. Cadman used the same approach in talks with representatives of the American oil industry.[44]

The Foreign Office stimulated American optimism with indications that it shared Cadman's views on American participation in Mesopotamia. The British government had already given one concrete evidence of willingness to compromise by abandoning its long-standing refusal to allow Socony geologists to explore in Palestine. It was also during these months that the Washington Naval Conference was working out agreements mitigating Anglo-American naval rivalry. Within a short period, a combination of circumstances tended to reduce friction between the two countries.[45]

Fears expressed by some organizers of the American Group early in 1922 that the syndicate might fall apart did not materialize. Instead, the American Group successfully established contact with the Turkish Petroleum Company and carried preliminary negotiations to the point

[43] Millspaugh memorandum, Nov. 26, 1921, "Conversations in New York on November 21, 1921, concerning the Mesopotamian Oil Situation," DS 890g.6363-/76. See also Manning to Hughes, Aug. 10, 1921, DS 800.6363/295.

[44] Millspaugh, memorandum of conversation on January 16, 1922, with Sir John Cadman, Jan. 17, 1922, DS 841.6363/203.

[45] Hughes to Harvey, March 31, 1922, DS 841.6363/209A. See also remarks of Winston Churchill, Minister of Colonies, in the House of Commons on July 11, 1922, reported in Skinner to Hughes, July 13, 1922, DS 890g.6363/127. However, further reports regarding British actions in Mesopotamia tempered the optimism somewhat and led to further protests from Washington, though in a calmer vein. Millspaugh memorandum, Jan. 30, 1922; Hughes to embassy, Great Britain, Jan. 31, 1922; Owens to Hughes, March 4, 1922; Millspaugh memoranda, April 11 and May 9, 1922; Hughes to Hoover, May 2, 1922; Post-Wheeler to Hughes, June 30, 1922, DS 890g.6363/174, 60, 78, 94, 96, 57, and 121; Dearing to Harvey, Jan. 25, 1922; Carr to Skinner, Jan. 25, 1922, DS 841.6363/191A and 191B.

where the Group needed State Department approval before proceeding. In replying with a policy statement, the department reiterated its insistence on the "broad principle of equality of commercial opportunity," and stated that the Mesopotamian oil question furnished "a test of the application of that principle." This meant the department would reject any agreement not in accord with that principle or which repudiated the stand of the United States on the claim of the Turkish Petroleum Company. At the same time, the department did not intend "to make difficulties or to prolong needlessly a diplomatic dispute or so to disregard the practical aspects of the situation as to prevent American enterprise from availing itself of the very opportunities which our diplomatic representations have striven to obtain." The department would raise no objections to private negotiations between American and European companies provided only that any reputable American company wanting to participate was admitted to the negotiations, and that the claim of the Turkish Petroleum Company not be recognized except as the consequence of a fairly conducted arbitration. The American Group soon sent a representative to London to confer with British interests. Ambassador Harvey received instructions to follow discreetly and informally these negotiations without participating in them.[46]

The first few meetings of the London Conference in July, 1922, were devoted wholly to discussions of whether the Turkish Petroleum Company could agree to give full effect to the State Department's open-door requirements for Mesopotamia. The Turkish Petroleum Company finally accepted a draft, known as Exhibit "A," drawn up by Teagle with assistance from Ambassador Harvey, as a method of applying the open-door principle. It provided that the Turkish Petroleum Company would select for its own exploitation, within two years from the date on which the agreement was confirmed, not more than twelve blocks of land, each block not exceeding sixteen square miles. Oil rights for the rest of the concession — totaling about 15,000 square miles — were to be opened for subleasing to any responsible individual, firm, or corporation. The draft outlined in some detail the procedure for granting subleases.

The important issue of the percentage of participation American companies might obtain was still unresolved. Teagle considered as en-

[46] *FR 1922*, II, 337–339 (quotations, p. 337); Thomas to Joblin, June 14, 1922, Socony file 7533.

tirely too low the Turkish Petroleum Company's offer of 12 per cent, and official negotiations were temporarily suspended. Teagle told the department confidentially that he believed 20 per cent could be obtained together with voice in the management of the company equal to that of each of the other partners.

When the American Group inquired whether Exhibit "A" met the State Department requirements for the Open Door, Secretary Hughes responded with an important and frequently cited policy declaration: the department's object was not to set up impractical theoretical barriers which would exclude American interests. Rather, it was to open the door so that American companies might participate if they wished. But, "it rests chiefly with American commercial interests themselves, once the opportunity is offered, to determine the extent and terms of their participation and to decide whether, under existing circumstances, an adequate opportunity is offered." Hughes also commented on certain details of Exhibit "A," but concluded that the proposal conformed to the Open Door — provided that American interests received an equitable share, that all interested American companies were permitted to participate, and that there was no attempt to establish a monopoly in favor of the Turkish Petroleum Company or any other company. Hughes made special note of the self-denying clause by which the partners in the company promised to refrain from exploiting oil in most of the former Ottoman Empire except through the company. American companies could bind themselves in this way if they wished, but the State Department could not be bound by their action and reserved complete freedom to support any American interests in the area concerned. The response from the State Department encouraged the American Group to continue negotiations with the Turkish Petroleum Company later in 1922.[47]

Friendly assistance from the departments of state and commerce had thus helped bring together seven large American oil companies for joint action in Mesopotamia. This American Group began arduous negotiations with the Turkish Petroleum Company for admission of the American interests into that international company. At various stages in the negotiation the American Group consulted freely with the State Department to ascertain if they were keeping within the policy limits defined by the United States government. The American Group wanted

[47] *FR 1922*, II, 339–345 (quotation, p. 343).

190

and needed diplomatic support in their fight to enter the Mesopotamian fields, and proceeded on the reasonable assumption that they stood the best chance of gaining their ultimate objective under the aegis of the Open Door and equality of opportunity.

By the late summer of 1922, the American Group had passed through the first stage of negotiations, but the stumbling block of the percentage to be allowed them still remained. With the convening of the Lausanne Conference to arrange a new Turkish peace treaty in November of 1922, new obstacles would arise.

Oil Complications at Lausanne, 1922–1923

Some of the problems faced by the Lausanne Conference in drafting a new peace treaty with a resurgent Turkey touched on prospective American oil development in the Middle East. Most important were the territorial questions of Mosul and the status of the claims of the Turkish Petroleum Company based on its negotiations with the Ottoman government in 1914.[48]

On the eve of Lausanne, three distinct American interests were trying to establish oil rights in Mesopotamia. One was the American Group of seven large oil companies, which was negotiating with the Turkish Petroleum Company. A second, a syndicate brought together by Admiral Colby M. Chester, was negotiating in Ankara with the Nationalist Turks for railroad and petroleum rights in Mosul even though Turkey's claim to Mosul was disputed. A third and less important American interest represented the heirs of Abdul Hamid, the Turkish sultan who had fallen from power in 1908. These claims rested on the fact that the sultan had reckoned these Mesopotamian oil lands among his personal holdings before the Revolution of 1908. Twenty-two princes and princesses descended from the former sultan agreed in 1918 to turn over their rights to a corporation which would promote and attempt to validate them. Samuel Untermyer, an American attorney, became legal counsel for the corporation which included American interests; he appeared at Lausanne to press their case.[49]

In the face of these three competing interests, the State Department scrupulously avoided giving the impression that it favored one American

[48] See above, Chap. 5, for the American role at the Lausanne Conference.
[49] *FR 1923*, II, 1199; Bristol Diary, Dec. 20 and 21, 1922, Bristol MSS, Box 21; Earle in *Political Science Quarterly*, 39:276; E. H. Davenport and S. R. Cooke, *The Oil Trusts in Anglo-American Relations*, p. 346.

group over another. Fortunately, impartiality was consistent with the theoretical position previously laid down, which maintained the Open Door for any American business interest wanting to operate in the Middle East. Any reputable interest could expect appropriate diplomatic support, but the department would refrain from actual participation in the negotiations or from advising on purely business matters.

The Turkish Nationalists' claim to Mosul guaranteed that Mosul would pose a problem at the conference. The possibility that this oil-bearing area might be awarded to Turkey alarmed the seven American oil companies negotiating with the Turkish Petroleum Company. When Walter Teagle asked the advice of the State Department on whether it might be better to deal with the Nationalist Turks rather than the Turkish Petroleum Company, Secretary Hughes declined to give an opinion, judging this to be a business decision. Even in the event of the rumored political deal whereby Great Britain would let Turkey have Mosul, the United States would oppose any monopolistic concession in the Mosul area. "Any American companies desiring to obtain equal opportunity in territory which might revert to Turkey would receive appropriate support from the Department."[50]

While the British and Turkish delegates were conducting inconclusive exchanges on the Mosul issue at Lausanne, the American Group, after assurances from the Turkish Petroleum Company that no Anglo-Turkish deal was in the making, continued to work for an agreement. By December 12, they had reached a tentative agreement with the British and Dutch partners in the Turkish Petroleum Company. The terms called for admitting the American Group on the basis of a twenty-four per cent participation. Anglo-Persian, the French interests, and the subsidiary of Royal-Dutch Shell would each have the same amount. The remaining four per cent would go to Calouste S. Gulbenkian, an Armenian who had become a naturalized British citizen. He held rights in the prewar Turkish Petroleum Company which Dutch-Shell and Anglo-Persian were forced to consider in any reorganization of that company. Since Anglo-Persian would be reducing its share to make this agreement possible, the other partners would be required to deliver to Anglo-Persian, free of cost, ten per cent of the crude produced from

[50] *FR 1922*, II, 345–347 (quotation); Teagle to Hughes, Oct. 26, 1922; Hughes to Teagle, Nov. 13, 1922; Dulles to Hughes, Nov. 28, 1922, DS 890g.6363 T 84/64, 65A, and 89.

the Turkish Petroleum Company's concession and allow it to be carried through the prospective pipeline at cost. More alarming to the Americans were provisos requiring fundamental changes in State Department policy. The European partners demanded that the department not question the title of the Turkish Petroleum Company, and that the department advise its delegation at Lausanne "to support strongly this arrangement to the exclusion of any other interests American or otherwise."[51]

Secretary Hughes declared these requirements entirely out of the question. The United States government insisted that no attempt be made to develop the claims of the Turkish Petroleum Company until they were confirmed by proper governmental authorities. Hughes emphatically rejected the idea of excluding other American interests: "This Department can never take the position that it will support at any time any arrangement to the exclusion of American interests. The Department's efforts are directed . . . to giving effect to the principle of the Open Door for American interests and not to the support of one American interest as against another or to the conclusion of any particular business arrangements. You will therefore understand that the Department cannot appropriately take the action suggested in your representative's telegram."

Questioning the clarity of this statement, the European partners found it insufficiently concrete and pressed for clarifications in line with their desire to close the door to any Americans except the American Group. Hughes's patience wore thin by the end of December, when he wrote Teagle that in view of his precise exposition of the department's position, he did not see how it could be misunderstood. If the Turkish Petroleum Company's grant was confirmed by Iraq, the department would regard it precisely as it would any other grant. The grant might be contested and it might not be. But if questions did arise regarding the titles of competing American claims, the United States government could not associate itself with one set of claims as against another. In such a case the department would wish to see "a prompt and effective disposition of claims by competent tribunals."

Reinforced by Hughes's backing, the American Group rejected the December proposals from the Turkish Petroleum Company. The next

[51] Teagle to Hughes, Nov. 29 and Dec. 4, 1922, DS 890g.6363 T 84/66 and 59; *FR 1922*, II, 347–348 (quotation).

month the objectionable clauses were eliminated, and the American Group was free to evaluate the terms as a business proposition. Viewing them in this light, the Americans concluded on January 31, 1923, that the offer was impracticable because of the provision that Anglo-Persian be given ten per cent of the oil without cost.[52]

At the suggestion of the Americans, who still believed that acceptable terms could be arranged, the British and Dutch interests sent agents to a New York conference which met between March 25 and April 14. Although the American counterproposals were unacceptable, the conferees made progress by drafting a revised open-door formula. Article one declared that the Turkish Petroleum Company would negotiate a convention with the Iraq government granting and confirming the right to develop petroleum resources in Mosul and Baghdad. This tentative agreement amounted to an admission that the original claim of the Turkish Petroleum Company was invalid.[53]

Paralleling the discussions of the businessmen in London and New York was the second phase of the Lausanne Conference where the Mosul issue and the status of prewar concessions were among the liveliest issues before the delegates. The United States consistently adhered to a position of neutrality in the territorial dispute over Mosul. Great Britain and Turkey finally agreed on June 26 to negotiate directly for a settlement of the frontier line. If they could not reach agreement the case would be sent to the League of Nations Council for a decision.[54]

The second petroleum issue — that of prewar concessions granted by the Ottoman authorities — drew the close attention of the American delegates. The British pressed hard for clauses validating the Turkish Petroleum Company claims. Grew, on the strongest instructions from Washington, fought to have these references eliminated. After a hard struggle, Grew carried his point. The British grudgingly agreed to elimination, but Sir Horace Rumbold, their chief delegate, reasserted

[52] *FR 1922*, II, 348–352 (first quotation, p. 348; second quotation, p. 352); *FR 1923*, II, 242, 1198–1199.
[53] *FR 1923*, II, 243–245. The British and Dutch interests had not been authorized to represent the French interests directly.
[54] Treaty Series No. 16 (1923), *Treaty of Peace with Turkey and Other Instruments* [etc.], p. 15. When direct negotiations failed, the issue went to the League, which awarded Mosul to Iraq in December, 1925. Turkey did not accept the decision until June, 1926. See Howard, *Partition of Turkey*, pp. 301, 336–339; Denna F. Fleming, *The United States and World Organization*, pp. 169–179; Hessabi, *Le pétrole en Irak*, pp. 106–109.

the validity of the concession in his speech at the final sitting. Britain would expect Turkey to honor it in any event.[55]

It is difficult to explain the persistent British intransigence at Lausanne regarding the claims of the Turkish Petroleum Company. As already noted, the company had agreed in April to negotiate a new convention with Iraq. Probably the British government was trying to protect its oil rights in case Mosul eventually went to Turkey. In that event, should Turkey not prove pliable to British requests for a confirmatory or new grant, Britain could fall back on the prewar negotiations of the Turkish Petroleum Company as the basis for her claim to oil rights in Mesopotamia.

At Lausanne, oil did not play the leading role in which a significant part of the world press and public tried to cast it. While the conference succeeded in its major purpose — that of drawing up peace terms with Turkey — it left the oil problem as confused as ever. The Turkish Nationalists had come to the conference claiming the Mosul area. Proceeding as if Mosul were its territory, Turkey had, in April of 1923, granted the momentous Chester Concession which included oil rights along a proposed railroad right-of-way in Mosul. The British protested the grant insofar as it extended to Mosul, which they contended belonged to Iraq. The postponement of a decision on the Mosul question at Lausanne thus left the legal status of the Chester Concession undecided. While the United States refrained from taking sides in the territorial dispute, the State Department held that a railway concession with mineral rights limited in extent along the right-of-way was not in itself monopolistic.

Claiming that Ottoman authorities had in 1914 granted the Turkish Petroleum Company a valid concession in Mosul, the British insisted that the Nationalist Turks must recognize the validity of this claim irrespective of the disposition made of Mosul. On this problem, the United States consistently stood its ground against the legality of the Turkish Petroleum Company's claim, and won its point when this claim was not included among those specifically validated in the treaty.

The United States came to the conference singing the praises of the

---

[55] See above, Chap. 5, pp. 148–149. See also Howard, *Partition of Turkey*, pp. 311–312; Edgar Turlington, "The Settlement of Lausanne," *American Journal of International Law*, 18 (Oct. 1924), 701–702; Philip M. Brown, "From Sèvres to Lausanne," *ibid.*, 18 (Jan. 1924), 114. The text of the signed protocol on concessions appears in Treaty Series No. 16 (1923), *Treaty of Peace with Turkey*, pp. 202–211.

Open Door as the policy on which international economic relations in the Middle East ought to rest. By standing four-square for equality of opportunity, the United States government believed it could best assist its nationals who wanted to participate in the economic development of the Middle East.

During the conference the American Group had continued negotiations with the Turkish Petroleum Company for participation in that consortium. The State Department carefully avoided any show of favoritism toward the American Group, whose aspirations for exploiting Mesopotamian oil conflicted somewhat with those of the Chester Project. For its part, the American Group made strenuous efforts to adjust its prospective arrangements to coincide with the department's open-door policy.

Since the claims of the Abdul Hamid heirs were not taken seriously, and the Chester syndicate collapsed late in 1923, Mesopotamian oil development was left to the American Group so far as American enterprisers were concerned.[56]

Negotiations for Admission to the Turkish Petroleum Company

The discouragements met by the American Group during the first year of negotiations with the Turkish Petroleum Company were mild compared with those attending the tangled proposals, counterproposals, and accompanying *démarches* of the next five years. The problems encountered between 1923 and 1928 were of two major kinds — arranging mutually acceptable business terms, and overcoming obstacles at the governmental level attributable to the development of the consortium idea within a matrix of diplomatic controversy. The American oil executives recognized their need for government support in carrying out their foreign operations, especially since they were dealing with a company closely tied to the British government. The price to be paid was to bring the consortium into harmony with the State Department's interpretation of the Open Door, now the cornerstone of American policy in the Middle East.[57]

[56] Stephen H. Longrigg, *Oil in the Middle East: Its Discovery and Development*, p. 68 n. 2. For the cancellation of the Chester Concession, see below, Chap. 7, pp. 226–227.

[57] Longrigg, *Oil in the Middle East*, pp. 68–69; FTC, *Cartel*, pp. 53–71, 85; Benjamin Shwadran, *The Middle East, Oil and the Great Powers*, pp. 233–249;

Following the course agreed upon in April, 1923, the Turkish Petroleum Company embarked on talks with the Iraq government late in the year. Concurrently, the draft agreement of April, 1923, underwent examination, criticism, and renegotiation. What emerged in November of 1924 was a new draft agreement by which the American Group would eventually take up a 23.75 per cent share in the Turkish Petroleum Company, a share equal to that of each of the other major partners (Anglo-Persian, Royal-Dutch Shell, and the Compagnie Française des Pétroles); Gulbenkian would retain his five per cent interest. Most important were provisions requiring the Turkish Petroleum Company to select twenty-four plots of eight square miles within two years of a new agreement with Iraq. Other areas would be opened to potential sublessees. This agreement was contingent on obtaining a new grant from Iraq by the end of 1925.[58]

The government of Iraq objected to the subleasing terms insisted upon by the Americans to implement the Open Door. Intensely jealous of its new status, Iraq insisted that national dignity required it to have exclusive right to approve sublessees. Just what kind of game the British played behind the scenes in Iraq has been subject to varying interpretations.[59] The British government, it has been charged, made it clear that it would not allow ratification of the new constitution of Iraq until Iraq granted a new concession to the Turkish Petroleum Company. In any case, the British had sufficient command at Baghdad to ensure policies there which would not run counter to the broad objectives of British foreign policy, including petroleum objectives. After a year and a half a new agreement was signed on March 14, 1925, granting rights to the Turkish Petroleum Company and incorporating the ideas for subleasing agreed to between the company and the American Group.[60]

George S. Gibb and Evelyn H. Knowlton, *The Resurgent Years, 1911–1927*, pp. 295–308. See also DeNovo, "Petroleum and American Diplomacy," pp. 317–351.

[58] The ten per cent oil royalty for Anglo-Persian would be confined to the original twenty-four areas which the Turkish Petroleum Company would select under the open-door plan. The self-denying ordinance (obligating the partners to develop oil within the general area of the old Ottoman Empire only through the TPC) would be canceled except for Mosul and Baghdad. *FR 1924*, II, 236–241.

[59] Gibb and Knowlton, *The Resurgent Years*, p. 296. Cf. Shwadran, *The Middle East*, pp. 234, 236. Most instructive on British policy in Iraq and its implementation is Philip W. Ireland, *'Iraq: A Study in Political Development*, especially Chaps. 19–22.

[60] "Law in Connection with the Oil Concession in the Bagdad and Mosul

Three more years were to elapse before the American Group finally joined the Turkish Petroleum Company, a delay owing partly to inability to satisfy the claims of C. S. Gulbenkian. His refusal to accept the plans for making the company merely a producer of crude oil created repeated crises between the fall of 1923 and 1928. Unlike the major partners who had command of refining and marketing apparatus, Gulbenkian had no use for crude oil but was interested in the refining and marketing operations which he expected the Turkish Petroleum Company to undertake. During the difficult negotiations with him, it seemed at times that the major objective of the parties was to "pass the buck" for responsibility in reaching a settlement. Though resenting the implication of the European partners that the Americans were "under obligation to assist them in cleaning their stable," the American Group in 1925 finally had to abandon the position that it was solely up to the Turkish Petroleum Company to come to terms with Gulbenkian.[61]

Another serious stalemate was broken in March of 1927 when the American Group reversed their previous stand by agreeing to take its 23.75 per cent share without prior adoption of a working agreement (insofar as it might conflict with Gulbenkian's interests), but with the collateral understanding that a working agreement be effected as soon as the Gulbenkian problem was resolved. The State Department agreed that the terms, similar to those drafted in November 1924, fulfilled the open-door requirements, but would not comment on the purely business aspects or consent to bind the United States government to any self-denying ordinance the companies might sign.[62]

Early in 1928 the American Group incorporated as the Near East Development Corporation for purposes of taking up its share in the Turkish Petroleum Company. The agreement signed with the Turkish Petroleum Company on July 21, 1928, contained the self-denying ordinance known as the Red Line agreement. By the latter, all "members of the Turkish Petroleum Company bound themselves not to operate, except through the company, within an area bounded on the map by a red line. This area embraced virtually all of the old Turkish Empire,"

Vilayets," Government of Iraq, Ministry of Justice, *Compilation of Laws and Regulations, 1924–1925,* p. 10. The agreement proper is printed in Hurewitz, *Diplomacy,* II, 132–142.

[61] Gibb and Knowlton, *The Resurgent Years,* pp. 297–301 (quotation, p. 299); DeNovo, "Petroleum and American Diplomacy," pp. 339–347.

[62] *FR 1927,* II, 816–817, 822–823.

including the entire Arabian peninsula, Kuweit excepted. The heart of the arrangement was a working agreement providing for delivery of crude to the participants at cost subject only to private understanding that the French company would purchase Gulbenkian's share of crude at market value. An overriding royalty of ten per cent on all crude produced by the company was granted to Anglo-Persian.[63]

The Turkish Petroleum Company changed its name in 1929 to the Iraq Petroleum Company (IPC). Two years earlier, the company had begun drilling operations leading to "the sensational oil-strike at Kirkuk in October 1927," although the transportation problem remained to be solved before Iraq petroleum could enter world commerce. Completion of a pipeline from the Mosul fields to the Mediterranean in 1934 surmounted this obstacle.[64]

The Door Closes in Iraq

Long before the completion of the pipeline, IPC obtained a drastic revision of the concessionary terms of 1925. A major aim was to scrap the much-heralded subleasing system which IPC had never liked and had apparently found useful chiefly as an expedient to satisfy the American State Department that the open-door principle had been honored. IPC claimed the subleasing plan was a bad business proposition; if it were actually implemented, the competitors could take up adjoining holdings from which they might drain oil from IPC holdings.[65]

Since the provisions in the 1925 concession gave IPC almost complete control over the competitive bidding with the right to reject offers or to enter its own higher bids, it is difficult to understand how the State Department could have considered any such arrangement compatible with the open-door principle. Under the restrictions of the subleasing

[63] Gibb and Knowlton, *The Resurgent Years*, p. 306. FTC, *Cartel*, p. 54, indicates that Texas and Sinclair dropped out of the American Group before 1928. The five companies remaining in 1928 were Socony, Jersey Standard, Gulf, Atlantic, and Pan-American (replacing Mexican Petroleum). By 1934 only Jersey Standard and Socony remained.

[64] Gibb and Knowlton, *The Resurgent Years*, pp. 301–305; Longrigg, *Oil in the Middle East*, pp. 69 (quotation), 76–77; Hessabi, *Le pétrole en Irak*, pp. 62–63, 65–66. The first oil reached Tripoli, Lebanon, on July 16, 1934. See James S. Moose, Jr. (chargé d'affaires, Iraq) to Hull, Aug. 21, 1934. On the completion of the pipeline and the formal opening, see C. Van H. Engert (chargé d'affaires, Egypt) to Hull, July 23, 1934; Paul Knabenshue (minister to Iraq) to Hull, Jan. 24, 1935, DS 890g.6363 T 84/572, 569, and 578.

[65] Longrigg, *Oil in the Middle East*, p. 73.

system, it seems unlikely that American companies other than those within IPC could have acquired oil holdings in Iraq. The subleasing system was therefore a deception — a tactical device to be scrapped when it had served to appease the State Department. The general manager of IPC told Alexander P. Sloan, American consul in Baghdad, that the company considered "the 'open door' in oil matters in Iraq to have been 'washed out' when American interests had been allowed to participate in the Iraq Petroleum Company. This statement seemingly gives a clear enough idea of the Company's attitude." Sloan warned that "the actions of the officials of the Iraq Petroleum Company, the actions of the British officials attached to the Iraq Government, and the actions of the Iraqi officials have indicated in the past a disposition on their part to disregard all provisions of the Convention regarding the 'open door' to the Iraq oil fields, and unless these officials change their attitude, any possible American competitors without doubt will experience great difficulty in gaining a foothold in the country." As Gibb and Knowlton have observed, "The Open Door was a shadow and not a reality. Gulbenkian later stated that the impression that the whole world would participate in the exploitation of oil in Iraq was 'eyewash.'"[66]

Behind the scenes, much maneuvering took place before IPC obtained the new concession from the Iraq government in 1931. The new terms abandoned the subleasing system and instead gave the company exclusive rights in an area of approximately 32,000 square miles east of the Tigris River in Mosul and Baghdad vilayets. The company had assurances by this time that there was oil in volume within this area. The new terms also freed the company from its previous obligation to share its pipeline capacity.[67]

[66] Alling memorandum of conversation of Alling and Murray with Harkey M. Macomber of Getty Oil Company, March 4, 1930, DS 890g.6363 Gulf Oil Corp. /4; Alling memorandum of conversation of Alling and Murray with Guy Wellman (general counsel, Standard Oil of New Jersey), April 2, 1930; Alexander P. Sloan (consul, Baghdad) to Stimson, April 28, 1930 (first two quotations) and May 21, 1931, DS 890g.6363 T 84/408, 413, and 480; Gibb and Knowlton, *The Resurgent Years*, p. 297 (last quotation). See also FTC, *Cartel*, pp. 60–61; David H. Finnie, *Desert Enterprise: The Middle East Oil Industry in Its Local Environment*, p. 31.

[67] Sloan to Stimson, May 3, May 7, June 2, 1930; May 12 and June 17, 1931; Alling memorandum, Aug. 22, 1930, DS 890g.6363 T 84/415, 416, 419, 483, 278, and 434; Alling memorandum to W. R. Castle, Jr., June 6, 1931, DS 890g.6363 Wemyss, Lord/73; FR 1930, III, 311 n. 42; FR 1931, II, 604–605; Longrigg, *Oil in the Middle East*, pp. 74–75.

During the protracted negotiations leading to the new concession, companies not affiliated with IPC evinced an interest in Iraq oil development. One was an international group known as the British Oil Development Company (BOD), brought together by Admiral Lord Wester-Wemyss, and including French, German, Italian, and Swiss interests. Another was the company of the American, J. Paul Getty, and because this American company was interested the State Department again thrashed over the meaning of the open-door principle. Wallace Murray, chief of the Near Eastern Division, expressed the view that the new IPC concession was more in keeping with the open-door idea than the old one, provided that the government of Iraq publicly invited competitive bidding for the unassigned area west of the Tigris.[68] After much prodding by the State Department at the British Foreign Office and in Baghdad, the Iraq government went through the form of soliciting bids. Four were submitted, but having decided in advance that BOD should have the concession, Iraq rejected the other bids, claiming they were inferior to BOD's. The manner in which the award was handled froze out any prospective American interests and confronted the department with a *fait accompli* which it had to accept.[69] The department had won a sham battle for a principle when it insisted that Iraq advertise for bids, but in this case the principle did not serve as an effective instrument for securing entry of another American company into the oil fields of the Middle East.

So far as oil development in Iraq was concerned, the open-door policy had quite a hollow ring by the end of the 1930s. BOD sold out to IPC in 1936, and IPC gained still another concession in the Basra region in 1938. This meant that one company, IPC, had a virtual monopoly on the production of oil in Iraq.[70] The Open Door had served

[68] Alling memorandum, March 4, 1930; Stimson to Sloan, May 28, 1930, DS 890g.6363 Getty Oil Co./4 and 7; *FR 1930*, III, 309–311; Murray memorandum, Aug. 25, 1930; Murray to Atherton, Sept. 2, 1930; Murray to Castle, April 10, 1931, DS 890g.6363 T 84/435, 433, and 460; Murray to Stimson, April 21, 1931; Alling memorandum, June 5, 1931, DS 890g.6363 Wemyss, Lord/64 and 73.

[69] Alling memorandum, June 5, 1931; Alling to Castle, June 20, 1931, DS 890g.6363 Wemyss, Lord/73 and 74; Murray to Ward (Legal Section, State Department), July 31, 1931; FXW (Legal Section) to Murray, July 31, 1931; Murray to Herbert Feis (Economic Adviser, State Department), Sept. 18, 1931; F. Livesey (EA) to Feis, Sept. 2 and Oct. 1, 1931; Alling to Murray, Sept. 29, 1931; Murray to Castle, Nov. 18, 1931, all DS 890g.6363/306; Murray memorandum, Aug. 8, 1931; Robert Y. Brown (chargé d'affaires, Iraq) to Stimson, Sept. 8, 1931, DS 890g.6363 T 84/489 and 490.

[70] Knabenshue to Hull, March 28 and Nov. 23, 1933; Moose to Hull, Aug. 26,

its purpose in the 1920s insofar as it contributed to getting American companies into the IPC, but had been of no practical use for placing additional American companies in Iraq. Moreover, it had not forestalled the domination of Iraq oil by a single company. As an idealistic principle serving the objective of affording equal opportunity to nationals of any country, it was of doubtful value. At bottom, the United States government was unable or unwilling to define with precision the meaning of the open-door principle; yet the department's larger objective was clear enough: to keep the Middle Eastern oil fields open to any and all interested American companies. As an instrument toward this goal, the department had relied on a principle beguilingly simple on the surface, but enormously complex and ambiguous when it came to definition and application.

Bahrein, Kuweit, and Saudi Arabia: the 1930s

The American oil industry had forced the door open a crack with the 1928 agreement providing for 23.75 per cent participation in the IPC. During the following decade American oil holdings in the Persian Gulf region underwent a striking expansion. By the end of 1939 Standard Oil of California (Socal) and the Texas Company had exclusive concessions covering the Bahrein Islands and the whole of Saudi Arabia; Gulf Oil was participating in Kuweit with Anglo-Persian on a fifty-fifty basis; and through the Iraq Petroleum Company, American interests were sharing in the oil hunt not only in Iraq but elsewhere on the fringes of the Arabian peninsula. Although the State Department did not play so important a role in the acquisition of these additional concessions as it had between 1919 and 1928, diplomatic assistance was needed in countering British opposition to American entry into Bahrein and Kuweit. No assistance proved necessary in obtaining the Saudi Arabian concessions.

Bahrein. The first new American concession of the pre-World War II decade was on the Bahrein Islands in the Persian Gulf, a few miles off the Arabian coast. Bahrein was one of those strategic Gulf locations the British had brought into a network of protectorates regarded as essen-

1936, DS 890g.6363 Mosul Oil Fields/1, 2, and 3; Knabenshue to Hull, Feb. 16, 1938, DS 890g.6363 T 84/609; Walworth Barbour (chargé d'affaires a.i., Iraq) to Hull, July 30 and Aug. 2, 1938; Knabenshue to Hull, Dec. 2, 1938, and Jan. 16, 1939, DS 890g.6363 Basrah Oil Co., Ltd./1, 2, 3, and 4; Knabenshue to Hull, Aug. 28, 1939, DS 890g.6363/356; Longrigg, *Oil in the Middle East*, pp. 79–83.

tial to the security of British India and its communications approaches. The British had drawn Bahrein into their orbit with treaties in 1880 and 1892. The Sheikh had in 1914 committed himself not to grant any petroleum concession or to exploit his own oil without British consent. These requirements presented no obstacle for the New Zealander, Major Frank Holmes, associated with the Eastern and General Syndicate which in 1925 obtained a prospecting concession from the Sheikh. Before he had established the presence of oil in commercial quantities, Holmes tried unsuccessfully to interest British companies in his option. He then turned to an American company, Gulf Oil, which accepted an option covering Holmes's interests in 1927. Gulf found that its participation in the Iraq Petroleum Company obligated it to offer this option to IPC members, since Bahrein fell within the area defined by the Red Line agreement. When IPC rejected the offer, Gulf obtained Holmes's permission to transfer its option to California Standard, not a participant in IPC. The option terms of December 21, 1928, required Holmes to obtain a renewal of his concession from the Sheikh; it would in turn be transferred to California Standard.[71]

At this juncture the interposition of the British government stood in the way of the transfer of rights to the American company. When the syndicate approached the British Colonial Office for approval of the transfer in October, 1928, the British insisted on clauses requiring that the concessionary company be British registered, that the managing director and a majority of the others be British subjects, and that no rights granted by the Sheikh should be under direct non-British control. These requirements would have precluded direct or indirect American control of the company.[72]

When Socal alerted the State Department to these new evidences of discriminatory British policy in the Middle East, Secretary Frank B. Kellogg took up the case through diplomatic channels. The United States pointed out its extremely liberal policy toward foreign oil concessionaires and asked for "a statement of the British Government's policy respecting the holding and operating by foreigners of petroleum

[71] Walt, "Saudi Arabia and the Americans," pp. 65–66, 71–75; Longrigg, *Oil in the Middle East*, pp. 101–105; Shwadran, *The Middle East*, pp. 370–375; FTC, *Cartel*, pp. 71–74; Finnie, *Desert Enterprise*, pp. 33–35; H. S. Villard memorandum, Oct. 5, 1931, DS 846b.6363/23. Hurewitz, *Diplomacy*, prints many of the British agreements with Persian Gulf rulers, with helpful editorial notes.

[72] Francis B. Loomis (Socal) to Paul T. Culbertson, Feb. 6, 1929, DS 846b.6363/1; *FR 1929*, III, 80–81.

concessions in territories such as Bahrein." The British declared "themselves unable to make any general statement of their policy on this question such as the United States Government desire," preferring, instead, to consider each proposition for foreign petroleum concessions in such territories as Bahrein "on its merits, and in the light of the circumstances obtaining at the time." The British government did accept in principle participation by American interests in the Bahrein concession "subject to their being satisfied as to the conditions on which United States capital will participate, and in particular as to the nationality of the operating company, of its chairman and directors, and of the personnel who will be employed in the Islands." The British government wanted direct discussion of these conditions between the Colonial Office and the Eastern and General Syndicate.[73]

Pressure from the Department of State contributed to an eventual compromise whereby Socal took up the concession through an operating subsidiary incorporated in Canada and whose top management was British. Although the Bahrein Petroleum Company was entirely American-owned, all dealings with the government of Bahrein had to be conducted through the British political agent. Socal organized the Bahrein Petroleum Company (Bapco) in 1930 and immediately began exploration work. After the discovery of oil in 1932, development proceeded rapidly.[74]

Kuweit. The preliminaries to oil development in Kuweit followed a pattern bearing several striking similarities to those in Bahrein. The Sheikhdom of Kuweit, another link in the chain of British control points in the Persian Gulf, had been brought into close treaty relationship in 1899 and 1904. In 1913 the Sheikh committed himself to show the British where any oil might be found in his domains and pledged that only persons appointed by the British government would be granted concessions. An option for a concession covering part of Kuweit, ob-

[73] *FR 1929*, III, 80–82 (quotations); J. Reuben Clark to American embassy, London, March 30, 1929; Atherton to Stimson, April 19 and May 9, 1929, DS 846b.6363/4, 5, and 7.

[74] Walt, "Saudi Arabia and the Americans," pp. 76–80; Finnie, *Desert Enterprise*, p. 35; FTC, *Cartel*, pp. 73–74; Villard memorandum, Oct. 5, 1931; Alling memorandum, March 16, 1933, DS 846b.6363/23 and 35. The Persian government continued to assert its claim to the Bahrein Islands in the 1930s, and protested the Socal operations there. Murray memoranda, May 28 and Dec. 1, 1934; Hugh Millard (London embassy) to Murray, Aug. 1, 1935; Murray to Millard, Aug. 14, 1935; Murray to Welles, Dunn, and Moffat, Jan. 18, 1938, DS 846b.6363/42, 79, 93, 93, and 115; *FR 1934*, II, 890–893.

tained by Major Holmes's Eastern and General Syndicate from the Sheikh in 1925, was transferred to Gulf in November of 1927 after Anglo-Persian had turned it down. Since Kuweit was not within the area defined by the Red Line agreement, Gulf was not obligated to offer the concession to the Iraq Petroleum Company.[75]

Again, the hurdle to be overcome was the hostility of the British government. Invoking the 1913 agreement with the Sheikh, the British would not allow Holmes to grant the concession without a nationality clause requiring the concessionaire to be a British company. Gulf agreed to British or Canadian registry for its operating subsidiary, and let the British know through the State Department that it would accept the Bahrein nationality clauses in this case.[76]

British procrastination in coming to a decision led Gulf to protest through the State Department. Anglo-Persian had by now decided it must acquire any concession granted in Kuweit, apparently to forestall any non-British company from gaining a foothold. The British delayed while allegedly pressing the Sheikh to change his mind about allowing the American company to operate in his domain; meanwhile, Anglo-Persian geologists were finding time to explore the area. Gulf complained that Anglo-Persian had already disqualified itself by turning down the earlier Holmes offer.

After additional diplomatic pressure by the United States, the British agreed on April 9, 1932, to yield on the nationality clause and to allow Eastern and General and others to submit applications for a concession without the requirement of a nationality clause. Further British delay of several months exasperated the United States, but finally the British government forwarded the draft applications of both Gulf and Anglo-Persian to the Sheikh, who received them on January 9, 1933. He rejected them both.

[75] *FR 1932*, II, 20–23; Longrigg, *Oil in the Middle East*, pp. 110–113; Shwadran, *The Middle East*, pp. 384–388; FTC, *Cartel*, pp. 129–134; Finnie, *Desert Enterprise*, pp. 38–40; Zahra Freeth, *Kuweit Was My Home*, pp. 36–39.

[76] Alling, 8-page memorandum of conference with Gulf officials, Nov. 30, 1931, DS 890b.6363 Gulf Oil Corp./2; Finnie, *Desert Enterprise*, p. 38. The Near Eastern Division asked for and received assurances that Gulf was not seeking a monopolistic concession in Kuweit. Wallace Murray wrote Under Secretary William R. Castle, Jr., that "our position in this matter vis-à-vis the British will be greatly weakened if we endeavor to assert the rights of the Corporation in question to a monopolistic concession in Koweit. We obviously could not consistently make such a demand since we have always insisted, in the case of Iraq for example, that all we ask for was equality of economic opportunity." Murray to Castle, Dec. 1, 1931, DS 890b.6363 Gulf Oil Corp./3.

Following the rejection, Gulf and Anglo-Persian buried the hatchet by agreeing to participate jointly in a Kuweit concession to be owned and financed equally by the two companies. Late in 1934 the Kuweit Oil Company, registered under British laws, obtained an exclusive concession to explore for and produce oil in the Sheikhdom of Kuweit. After the discovery of oil in Kuweit in 1938, further exploration proved the existence of large reserves, but the inadequacy of transportation and loading facilities delayed further development until after World War II, when Kuweit eventually rose to be the number one producing area in the Middle East.[77]

Saudi Arabia. The discovery of oil in Bahrein in 1932 stimulated a rush to stake out claims on the Arabian peninsula, most notably in the province of al-Hasa, part of Abdul Aziz ibn Saud's Kingdom of Saudi Arabia. When the ubiquitous Frank Holmes had acquired a concession for al-Hasa in 1923, Ibn Saud was still bound to the British network of protectorates by a treaty of 1915 giving the British power to veto oil concessions in his territories. But in 1927 a new agreement between the British and Ibn Saud specifically abrogated the British veto power. However, Ibn Saud regarded Holmes's rights as lapsed because of non-compliance with terms of the agreement.[78] Thus, al-Hasa was still available when the Bahrein oil discovery in 1932 brightened prospects on the mainland and precipitated international competition for concessions there.

By this stage of Saudi Arabian developments, the American mining engineer, Karl S. Twitchell, had begun to play a major role in the opening of Saudi Arabia to Western business. Twitchell, after experience in Ethiopia, had been drawn to Yemen to undertake survey and development projects sponsored as a philanthropy by industrialist Charles R. Crane of King-Crane Commission fame. Twitchell's work in the Yemen had favorably impressed King Ibn Saud, who asked Twitchell to make

[77] *FR 1932,* II, 1–29; H. L. Dwight, memorandum, March 25, 1932; William R. Castle, Jr., to Atherton, April 1, 1932; Alling memorandum, Oct. 1, 1932; William T. Wallace (Gulf) to Murray, Feb. 8 and Feb. 25, 1933; Alling memorandum to Villard and Murray, Feb. 27, 1933; Stimson to American embassy, London, Feb. 28, 1933; Alling memorandum, March 16, 1933, DS 890b.6363 Gulf Oil Corp./45, 50, 153, 174, 176, 177, 178, and 183; Knabenshue to Hull, Jan. 8, 1935; Murray to Atherton, Jan. 21, 1935, DS 890b.6363 Kuweit Oil Co./1 and 2; FTC, *Cartel,* pp. 131–134.
[78] Longrigg, *Oil in the Middle East,* pp. 106–110; Shwadran, *The Middle East,* pp. 285–300; FTC, *Cartel,* pp. 74, 113–117; Finnie, *Desert Enterprise,* pp. 36–37; Walt, "Saudi Arabia and the Americans," pp. 65–71.

water and mineral surveys in his kingdom during 1931 and 1932. The king then enlisted Twitchell's services to interest American and British capital in mineral development in Saudi Arabia. After many discouragements in the United States and England, Twitchell found that Standard Oil of California wished to apply for an oil concession in Saudi Arabia.[79]

Twitchell returned to Saudi Arabia with a delegation from Socal to pursue the negotiations. Despite lively competition from IPC, the king finally awarded the concession to Socal on May 29, 1933, exciting much speculation about the reasons for his selection of the American company over the British-dominated company. A British version contended that the superior financial terms of Socal were decisive. Another view, prevalent in some American circles, stressed the king's apprehension over possible British domination in his kingdom. David Finnie has offered the reasonable suggestion that British sponsorship of Saud's rivals, the Hashimites, may have influenced the king's decision.[80]

Later in the year, Socal assigned the 360,000-square-mile concession to its subsidiary, the California-Arabian Standard Oil Company. Through a 1936 agreement the Texas Company shared with Socal on a fifty-fifty basis the concessions in Bahrein and Saudi Arabia; Texas, in return, granted Socal a fifty per cent interest in its Far Eastern marketing facilities.[81]

Caltex started exploration work in 1934 with discouraging initial results until 1938 when it brought in the commercially promising Dammam field. In the ensuing international scramble to acquire unassigned

[79] Karl S. Twitchell, *Saudi Arabia: With an Account of the Development of Its Natural Resources*, pp. 139–151; Richard H. Sanger, *The Arabian Peninsula*, pp. 16–17, 20, 243–244; H. S. Villard, memorandum of conversation with Twitchell regarding Saudi Arabia, Nov. 1, 1932, DS 890f.6363/10; Walt, "Saudi Arabia and the Americans," pp. 82–96.

[80] FTC, *Cartel*, p. 114; Twitchell, *Saudi Arabia*, pp. 151–152; Walt, "Saudi Arabia and the Americans," pp. 97–104; Francis B. Loomis (Socal) to Stimson, Oct. 25, 1932; Stimson to Loomis, Oct. 27, 1932; Murray memorandum of conversation with Loomis, Dec. 1 and Dec. 15, 1932; Alling memorandum, May 13, 1938; G.V.A. (Near East Division), memorandum, May 17, 1938, giving an analysis of the 1933 concession, DS 890f.6363 Standard Oil Co./1, 2, 3, 4, 98, and 99; Finnie, *Desert Enterprise*, p. 36; Shwadran, *The Middle East*, p. 290 n. 11; Longrigg, *Oil in the Middle East*, pp. 100–101. For evidence of Ibn Saud's feeling against the Anglo-Persian Oil Company, see Sloan to Stimson, Aug. 6, 1930, DS 890b.6363/31.

[81] FTC, *Cartel*, pp. 114–116; Walt, "Saudi Arabia and the Americans," pp. 105–111, 126–128. The name of the California-Texas Company (Caltex) was changed at the end of 1943 to the Arabian-American Oil Company (Aramco). See Shwadran, *The Middle East*, pp. 320 n. 4, 374.

parts of Saudi Arabia, the Axis powers — Germany, Italy, and Japan — were especially vigorous, but the American bidders won out again. By the supplemental agreement with Saudi Arabia in 1939, the California-Texas combination added some 80,000 square miles to the original concession area.[82]

By the eve of World War II, the pattern of oil ownership and development in the Persian Gulf area had undergone a radical change. British domination had been challenged by American companies. True, the British still had exclusive control of the Iranian fields and dominated the Iraq Petroleum Company operating in Iraq and Qatar with prospecting rights elsewhere. But American companies had acquired nearly a one-fourth holding in IPC, half of the Kuweit concession, and exclusive ownership of the Bahrein and Saudi Arabian grants.[83]

With the acquisition of these new concessions, American policy had to adjust to the growing American stake in the Middle East. By 1939, increasing numbers of Americans were coming to work in the oil regions, the companies were making huge capital outlays to develop the oil holdings, and the Middle East was becoming more closely interlaced with issues of national defense and of America's position in international politics. Although the Saudi Arabian government had been formally recognized by the United States in 1931, the State Department was disinclined to accredit a minister to Jiddah until 1940. Closer ties with Arab rulers were also beginning to have some relevance to American policy on the Palestine issue. King Ibn Saud directed a plea to President Franklin D. Roosevelt on November 29, 1938, soliciting American support for Arab opposition to the Zionist program for Palestine. American

[82] Twitchell, *Saudi Arabia*, pp. 153–154; Murray memorandum, July 5, 1938, DS 890f.6363 Standard Oil Co./102; Paul Knabenshue to Hull, Feb. 17, 1939; Alling memorandum, Jan. 18, 1939; Murray memorandum on "The Struggle for Oil Concessions in Saudi Arabia," to Berle, Messersmith, and Welles, Aug. 2, 1939, DS 890f.6363/20, 105, and 118; Walt, "Saudi Arabia and the Americans," pp. 112–126, 128–130, 134–140. By 1940 Caltex had expended about $29 million on the Bahrein and Saudi Arabian projects. *Ibid.*, pp. 487–488.

[83] Alling memorandum, Dec. 10, 1937, DS 890g.6363 T 84/608. Finnie, in *Desert Enterprise*, pp. 44–45, asks why the British allowed American interests into the Persian Gulf area. He speculates that they may have realized their weakening political and economic power in the area and regarded the United States as "the best of the possible partners" in view of the traditional American policy of deferring to the British politically in this area. For the negotiations of an American oil company in Iran during the late 1930s, see below, Chap. 9, pp. 311, 314–315. On Qatar, see Finnie, *Desert Enterprise*, p. 40; and Alling memorandum, March 16, 1933, DS 890b.6363/450.

oil executives, fearful that the United States was associated with Zionist aspirations in the Arab mind, hoped for an American policy in keeping with Arab sensitivities.[84] As of 1939, however, when Ibn Saud attended the opening of the Ras Tanura terminal of Caltex, relations between Arab rulers in the oil regions and the American companies and government were still cordial.

[84] The issues of recognition and diplomatic representation are discussed below, Chap. 10, pp. 360–365. For the relationship of Arabian oil to the Palestine question, see below, Chap. 10, pp. 344–345.

7

THE POSTWAR CHESTER PROJECT

☆ THE POSTWAR NEED for petroleum in the United States provided a favorable environment for the revival of Admiral Colby M. Chester's ambitious plans for economic development in Asia Minor. Undaunted by the burden of his seventy-six years, the admiral enthusiastically approached the State Department in 1920 with a request for governmental support of what he represented as his legal claims to oil rights in the Middle East. In a letter of May 19, 1920, he summarized the first Chester Project from its origins in 1908 through 1911, emphasizing that the projected railroad construction included mineral rights in a zone measuring twenty kilometers on each side of the right-of-way. Of special note, he explained, was the large tract in the vicinity of Sulaimaniya, not far from the Persian border, "where petroleum was known to exist in large quantities." In his zeal to impress the department, Chester tried to make his claims appear more substantial than the facts justified.[1]

Admiral Chester Seeks Official Support
The elderly admiral followed up his letter with a visit to the State Department on June 9 to talk over his plans. He told officials that several backers of the prewar project, including engineers and capitalists who had held stock in the defunct company, were still interested and were being kept together informally. Apparently Chester regarded his visit as exploratory and rejected an offer by department officials to state their views in writing by replying to his letter of May 19. When the peace

[1] Admiral C. M. Chester to Colby, "Oil lands and American mineral rights in Turkey," May 19, 1920, DS 867.602 Ot 81/162. Chester's account has some factual inaccuracies, and he did not deal with the failure of the renewed efforts to obtain a concession between 1912 and 1914. For the prewar railroad plan of the admiral, see above, Chapter 3.

treaty with Turkey had been concluded and implemented, he proposed to pursue his claims actively.[2]

Chester's feelers looking toward government support did not stop with his letter and visit to the Department of State. In view of his rank, it was natural that the admiral should approach the Navy Department, as he did in a letter to Secretary Josephus Daniels on June 14, 1920, couch- ing his presentation in terms of patriotic motivation: "Knowing the im- portance to American interests and to the U.S. Navy in particular of securing new oil fields for carrying on the industrial development of the country and for its national defence, I deem it my duty to place on record the following facts concerning a just American claim for an oil concession in Asia Minor." He then recounted some details of his prewar negotiations, stressing the German opposition. His "rights" cov- ered, he claimed, about six hundred kilometers of oil-bearing territory in the Mosul region. After commenting on the oil competition between the United States and Great Britain, Chester arrived at his real point — American capitalists could not and would not sink more capital in Middle East ventures "without the strong support of the government."[3]

While the State Department showed only a cautious curiosity, the Navy Department took a bolder view of the Chester possibilities. Any prospect of improving access to foreign oil fields vitally interested nerv- ous naval officials, who were worried by the dismal estimates of Amer- ican petroleum reserves. As early as 1913–1914, Secretary Daniels had unsuccessfully advocated vigorous governmental action to ensure ade- quate oil for naval uses. After the war, the navy had failed to secure appropriations for acquiring foreign oil resources in its own right. As an alternative, the navy had thought of encouraging private companies to acquire such properties abroad, and to give the navy a minority interest in their enterprises in return for a nominal payment. The government's interest would thereby assure the oil companies of a greater degree of diplomatic protection.[4]

[2] *FR 1921,* II, 917–918. C. A. Moore of Manning, Maxwell, and Moore, Incor- porated, of Chicago, prominent in the original Chester Project, was now dead. Be- sides the admiral and his two sons, others of the prewar group said to be financially interested were E. G. Converse, James M. Laidlaw, and James W. Colt.

[3] C. M. Chester to Josephus Daniels, June 14, 1920, enclosed in R. E. Coontz (Acting Secretary of the Navy) to Colby, July 7, 1920, DS/163. Unless otherwise indicated, all references in this chapter to the Department of State archives refer to file 867.602 Ot 81. They will be designated "DS," followed by the enclosure number, as in this note.

[4] John A. DeNovo, "Petroleum and the United States Navy before World War

The Chester plans might serve the navy as an instrument for carrying out such a project. Naval officials recognized, however, that the admiral's aspirations touched on intricate questions of foreign policy and that they needed expert opinion on the validity of the claim. In studying the admiral's case, State Department officials had from the start been skeptical about certain important premises underlying Chester's explanation of his claim. By September, Wesley Frost, acting foreign trade adviser in the State Department, expressed his doubts in a memorandum following a talk with a representative from the Navy Department. Frost believed "that the validity of the Chester concession is regarded as distinctly dubious, and that the [State] Department would probably not be inclined to press immediately for a recognition by England (as mandatory for Mesopotamia) of that portion of the Chester project which involves the building of a branch railway, with petroleum rights, in Mosul." The navy's idea of acquiring direct interest in private oil companies operating abroad to furnish a firm basis for strong diplomatic support presented important legal and policy problems. Such a daring plan, Frost advised, should be discussed by top officials of the Navy and State departments prior to seeking any enabling legislation.[5]

Frost's suspicions appeared warranted by evidence from Constantinople, where the American high commissioner, Rear Admiral Mark L. Bristol, had interested himself in the claims.[6] A member of Bristol's staff, George Wythe, had talked about the project with Arthur T. Chester, the admiral's son, a representative of the United States Shipping Board in Constantinople. The younger Chester had expressed the view that, although the Ottoman-American Development Company had no legal rights, it nonetheless did have a strong moral claim to concessions in

I," *Mississippi Valley Historical Review*, 41 (March 1955), 641–656; DeNovo in *American Historical Review*, 61:864, 873–874.

[5] Frost, memorandum on "Petroleum in the Near East for the United States," Sept. 17, 1920, based on an interview of Sept. 8, 1920, with H. Howe (assistant to the Assistant Secretary of the Navy); Norman H. Davis (Under Secretary of State) to C. M. Chester, Aug. 27, 1920; Davis to Daniels, Sept. 2, 1920, DS/168, 162, and 163.

[6] Bristol had come into possession of German correspondence relating to the 1909–1911 negotiations of the Chester group, found in the archives of the Anatolian Railway Company at Haidar Pasha. See Bristol to Colby, Oct. 18, 1920, DS/166. The State Department requested Bristol to furnish all pertinent documents and information which he could find concerning the Chester Project and its reception by the Turks. N. H. Davis to Bristol, Oct. 25, 1920; Bristol to Colby, Nov. 10, 1920; Merle-Smith to Bristol, Nov. 11, 1920, DS/165A, 167, and 169A.

Asia Minor and Mesopotamia, a claim which Chester believed Great Britain should acknowledge.[7]

Continuing to spin plans for his own oil project, Admiral Chester had developed by the end of November a spectacular scheme for presentation to the Secretaries of State, Navy, and Interior, and to the chairman of the Shipping Board. His proposal called for a government-sponsored expedition to survey his oil claims in the Middle East. According to the plan, the Navy Department would fit out a small squadron of vessels composed of a yacht to act as a tender together with a Shipping Board vessel, manned by a Naval Reserve crew. The naval officer in charge (Admiral Chester, of course) would operate under the orders of the State Department. He would equip the headquarters ship with airplanes, motor vehicles and other matériel for making photographic surveys. Mining experts detailed by the Secretary of the Interior, but under Chester's direction, would conduct field operations. This scheme, Chester believed, would meet the approval of the British, French, and other governments.[8]

The petroleum expert of the State Department, Arthur C. Millspaugh, discussed the Chester plans in detail in a conversation with the admiral on November 29, 1920. After the conference, Millspaugh wrote that "the history of the Chester project and the distinguished character of its leaders imposes upon the Government a peculiar obligation to give it sympathetic consideration." He did not, however, see how the department could support the admiral's survey plans. The project as outlined to him was virtually a government expedition in favor of a single American group, an indefensible undertaking when other American companies were interested in Mesopotamia. "It would signify that the Government had decided to guarantee and to support in a manner that is believed to be unprecedented a private project for obtaining petroleum concessions. It is difficult to see why, if such support were extended to one American group, it should not also be extended to other similar enterprises."

In view of changed international conditions, Millspaugh believed that

[7] George Wythe (trade commissioner, Constantinople) to the Bureau of Foreign and Domestic Commerce, Department of Commerce, Attn. Mr. Hopkins, Aug. 7, 1920, enclosed in C. E. Herring to Wesley Frost, Sept. 9, 1920, DS/165.

[8] Copy of letter from C. M. Chester to the Secretaries of State, Navy, Interior, and the chairman of the Shipping Board, Nov. 20, 1920, enclosed in Millspaugh memorandum, Nov. 30, 1920, DS/171.

the concession would have to be redrafted as three different concessions — one for Turkey, one for Syria, and one for Mesopotamia. In the first place, the State Department had taken the position that there was no authority in the mandated territories at that time which was competent to pass on concessionary claims. Aside from this, the United States was not even in a position to force the British and French to allow American exploration in Mesopotamia, Palestine, and Syria, since these areas were still under military occupation. The issue was complicated further by European claims within the same area in which the Chester Project planned to operate.

Millspaugh hoped that a solution might eventually be reached through diplomatic channels. In working for the admission of American interests to Middle Eastern oil production, he thought that the department must scrupulously avoid favoring any special group. He predicted accurately that American participation would come, if at all, through an international syndicate, and recommended that the department should encourage a strong, representative group of American interests to cooperate for such a project.

For the present, Millspaugh recommended that the Chester group furnish the department with more exact information on its resources, organization, legal counsel, and specific plans. It would be desirable to know if the backers would consider cooperative action with other American companies and possibly with foreign groups.

Chester disagreed fundamentally with Millspaugh's estimates that the issues were primarily diplomatic. The admiral contended that his claims were prior to those of the Turkish Petroleum Company, but this view disregarded the fact that he held no legal claims of any kind. The admiral thought the San Remo Oil Agreement could be ignored as an indication of British intentions, for he had convinced himself of the peculiar notion that the British were anxious for him to exploit Mesopotamian oil.

The conversations of November had not ended on a cordial note. The admiral insisted that the United States government was already committed to the preferential support of his project as a result of its endorsement by Secretary of State Root in 1908. "The Admiral made the statement that if the Department would not support him in the manner suggested he would fight the Department, would enlist the support of other Departments, and would at least win out after March 4."

Considering the admiral's injured attitude and his penchant for giving press interviews, Millspaugh feared that he might criticize the department in an undesirable way.[9]

The department did not hear from the admiral for more than two months. When he called again, on February 8, 1921, seeking official good will for the project, he showed a more conciliatory attitude. Once more the department assured him that it was deeply interested, but pointed out that the military occupation of the mandates and the political instability of the area prevented it from taking any definite action. The admiral replied that he realized the uncertainties of the existing political situation, but he simply wished assurances of the interest and good will of the government. He expected to leave in the near future for Turkey and Mesopotamia to carry on negotiations for securing the concession.[10]

The State Department's reception of the Chester overtures had passed through two phases between May of 1920 and the end of the Wilson administration. At first, while the Chester plans were still amorphous, the department was friendly but guarded. By November department officials were certain that the admiral had no legal rights and that they could not support his grandiose scheme for a survey under government auspices. While unable to give the Chester group exclusive support, the department was quite willing to back him on an equal basis with other American interests after the legal status of the old Turkish Empire finally became defined.

A memorandum prepared by Millspaugh on March 1, 1921, probably to orient the incoming Harding administration, concluded:

The Admiral is now an old man, the Turkish project has become an obsession with him, and he seems to be oblivious to recent changes in the Near East and to the fact that Near Eastern diplomacy centers now in London and Paris rather than in Constantinople. Nevertheless, he has been of great service to American interests in the past and, on account of the strong moral and even quasi-legal claims that he possesses in Turkey and Mesopotamia, it is believed that his project may be of value in countering British claims in that region. It would also seem useful to have in the field an American company with a favorable reputation ready to apply for and receive concessions in Turkey.[11]

[9] The foregoing analysis is based on Millspaugh's memoranda of Nov. 29, 1920 (first two quotations) and Nov. 30, 1920 (last quotation), DS/170 and 171.

[10] *FR 1921*, II, 918.

[11] Millspaugh memorandum, "The Chester Project in Turkey," March 1, 1921, DS/180.

The Chester Interests and the Harding Administration

Soon after the Harding administration took over in Washington, Admiral Chester presented the Navy Department with another bold request. He asked to be appointed naval attaché in Constantinople. This would give his concession efforts a semiofficial standing, which he felt would be of great assistance in dealing with other governments. When the Navy Department sought the advice of the State Department, the latter opposed an appointment intended to give the recipient special status in seeking concessions.[12]

Admiral Chester continued, meanwhile, to hammer away at the State Department with requests that it give his project stronger support of the kind the Roosevelt and Taft administrations had so willingly extended. In interviews and memoranda the admiral expatiated on the merit of his claims, and on their relationship to national defense and American business enterprise.

Secretary Charles Evans Hughes and other department officials, reiterating that he had no legal claims, pointed out to Chester that the department had taken a strong stand against the British-supported monopolistic claims of the Turkish Petroleum Company in Mesopotamia, and Chester's claims appeared to be of much the same questionable status. For this reason, the department could not share his belief that he could privately work out an amicable settlement with the Turkish Petroleum Company. Since neither organization held legal claims, they had no sound basis for negotiations. A sifting of the Chester plans convinced the department that they were vague and not backed by sufficient capital. It could not, therefore, provide the admiral with the requested letters of recommendation.[13]

John R. MacArthur, vice president of Chester's Ottoman-American Exploration Company, visited the State Department on June 10, 1921, to bolster the case. Asked whether his company had approached the Standard Oil Company relative to merging their efforts for a Mesopotamian oil concession, MacArthur said it had not. He admitted that

[12] Chester to the Secretary of the Navy, March 30, 1921, copy enclosed in Chester to Hughes, April 23, 1921; Robbins to Fletcher, memorandum, April 11, 1921, DS/173 and 175; *FR 1921*, II, 919–920.

[13] *FR 1921*, II, 920–924; C. M. Chester to Hughes, April 23, 1921; Millspaugh memoranda, April 27 and July 15, 1921; Robbins, memorandum for the assistant secretary and Mr. Millspaugh, May 10, 1921; Robbins to MacArthur, May 31, 1921; C. M. Chester to Hughes, July 19, 1921; Robbins memorandum, July 25, 1921; DS/173, 173, 179, 176, 177, 179, and 179.

Standard Oil officials had tried to see him, but he had not considered himself free to discuss the matter with them. He implied that if the department had no objections he might get in touch with Standard or some other large oil company about a joint venture.[14] MacArthur's response seems strange in view of Admiral Chester's contacts during April and May with Socony. Socony had shown no interest in the Chester claims, and perhaps MacArthur, who certainly must have known of the admiral's activities, may have been trying to avoid confessing to the department that company's negative reaction.[15]

The Chester associates drop out of the State Department files during the last half of 1921 and do not reappear until February 8, 1922, when the admiral requested an interview to discuss his claims in the light of new developments. He also wished to present his son, Arthur, who would soon return to his post as the representative of the Shipping Board in Constantinople. Arthur would "proceed with negotiations with the Angora Government, at its request, for the consummation of the Chester Project." The department replied coolly that a further interview with the secretary hardly seemed necessary, but that the admiral might take up any new aspects of his claims with officials in the Division of Near Eastern Affairs or the Foreign Trade Adviser's Office.[16] There is no record that Chester followed this suggestion at that time.

Problems of Financing and Reorganization

Between February and June of 1922 the quest for the Chester Concession proceeded along new lines. Several bizarre figures, seeing a chance for profit, became interested. Among them was Henry Woodhouse, known to the State Department as a man of questionable reputation who had recently been writing articles on oil for the Hearst newspapers. Woodhouse, who had met Admiral Chester through their mutual interest in aviation, had in turn influenced a horse-racing promoter, W. E. D.

[14] *FR 1921*, II, 922–924. This was the period when several American oil companies were making plans to combine their efforts to obtain a Mesopotamian oil concession. See above, Chap. 6, pp. 186–188.

[15] The contacts were carried on through the admiral's lawyer son, Colby M. Chester, Jr. See Admiral C. M. Chester to L. I. Thomas (Socony), April 8, 1921; C. M. Chester, Jr., to Thomas, April 30 and May 9, 1921, Socony file 7533. See also Adm. Chester to David T. Day, Aug. 1 and Aug. 16, 1922; Day to Adm. Chester, Aug. 13, 1922; Day to H. C. Folger, Aug. 18, 1922; Thomas memorandum to Pratt, Moyer, Cole, Higgins, Fales, Wilkinson, and Speer, Aug. 25, 1922, Socony file 7526.

[16] *FR 1922*, II, 966–967.

Stokes, to transfer his sporting instincts to the Chester project. The department had evidence that Woodhouse had attempted to persuade Sir John Cadman and the Anglo-Persian Oil Company to take care of the Chester claimants. In these efforts Woodhouse apparently had given the impression that he could then use his influence to stop the acrimonious notes from the State Department to the British Foreign Office and the investigations by congressional committees of British petroleum practices.[17]

The growing parade of names now beginning to appear in the files on the Chester Concession also includes men of more substantial reputation and financial standing. Several such backers became interested in the admiral's railroad and mineral plans through Major K. E. Clayton-Kennedy, a Canadian citizen and a key figure in the project's stormy history. Kennedy seems to fall into a middle category between the "adventurers" and the more reputable businessmen. He, too, had become acquainted with Woodhouse through an interest in aviation and had learned of the Chester plans from him. Although not a man of capital, Clayton-Kennedy had friends willing to provide him with funds while he sought the support of American financial and engineering companies. The department had to be circumspect in dealing with Clayton-Kennedy, however, because he was not an American citizen.[18]

The State Department experienced great difficulty in unraveling the snarled efforts of the Chester associates to form an effective organization in the spring of 1922. By July the situation had temporarily become clearer. A new company, the Ottoman-American Development Company, incorporated in Delaware, had been organized in March to replace the prewar Ottoman-American Exploration Company. The new company was a blend of the old interests with the new. Admiral Chester had insisted that the interests of his family, John MacArthur, Frederick

[17] A. L. P. Dennis to J. Butler Wright, Feb. 11, 1922; Millspaugh to Robbins, Dearing, and Fletcher, Feb. 16, 1922; "Memorandum of Conversation between Major Kennedy and Mr. Millspaugh," March 9, 1922; R. C. Bannerman (special agent, Department of State) to R. S. Sharp (special agent in charge, New York), March 24, 1922, DS/185, 185, 186, and 191; Bristol Diary, Oct. 16, 1922, Bristol MSS, Box 21. The use of the term "Chester Concession" is not strictly correct, particularly after the Chesters lost majority control in 1922. The term is used for the sake of convenience and because contemporaries, including the State Department, used this designation.

[18] Millspaugh memorandum, March 9, 1922; Arthur Chester to A. W. Dulles, April 14, 1922; Max B. Bert to Dulles, April 24, 1922; Dulles to Hurley, May 18, 1922; Bannerman to Sharp, June 1, 1922, DS/186, 190, 188, 198, and 199; *FR 1922*, II, 971–973.

Remington, and other old Chester associates be protected by a forty per cent interest in the new company. Ten per cent was assigned to satisfy the demands of Woodhouse and Stokes, although the active management held an option to buy their shares at any time. The remaining fifty per cent of the stock was held by the active new interests, enlisted largely by Clayton-Kennedy.[19]

The new president and active manager was General George Goethals, the engineer of Panama Canal fame. Among his associates were members of brokerage firms and engineers. The Canadian-British element brought in by Clayton-Kennedy consisted of his personal friend, C. V. Barnard, a Montreal lawyer, and J. W. Clayton, his father-in-law. Other men of capital promised financial support after the granting of the concession.[20]

According to the plans of company officials, Clayton-Kennedy would join Arthur Chester in Turkey where they would negotiate with the Turkish Nationalists for a new concession based on the moral claims of the prewar negotiations. Apparently the promoters thought they could make the grant of a concession by Turkey effective in Mesopotamia and Syria by dating it back to 1909, although Clayton-Kennedy was vague as to how this might be done.

The promoters, in keeping the department informed of their plans at this preliminary stage, asked the State Department to support them. The department "pointed out that in view of the existing political situation this Government cannot be expected to accord full diplomatic support to any rights or concessions granted by unrecognized authorities. On the other hand, it has in each case been stated that the Department has no desire to discourage preliminary investigation by interested concerns, and that this Government will endeavor to secure for American enterprise in Turkey the benefits of most-favored-nations treatment."[21]

Dissension and Complications

Internal dissensions over its management nearly wrecked the company in the autumn of 1922. The first evidence that all was not well between

[19] *FR 1922*, II, 967–975; Bannerman to Sharp, March 24 and June 1, 1922; Bristol to Hughes, May 15, 1922, DS/191, 199, and 195.

[20] *FR 1922*, II, 971–975; Bannerman to Sharp, June 1, 1922, DS/199. The broker-associates were Messrs. Pouch and Potter of Pouch and Company; and Calloway and Fish of Fish and Company. The engineer was Frederick S. Blackall of the Taft Pierce Manufacturing Company.

[21] *FR 1922*, II, 971–975 (quotation, pp. 974–975).

the old Chester associates and the Goethals wing came on September 3, in a letter from Arthur Chester in Constantinople to General Goethals. According to his understanding, Chester complained, he alone was to direct the negotiations in Turkey, but now he learned that Clayton-Kennedy held the power of attorney for the company. In spite of what he regarded as misrepresentation, Chester agreed to assist with the negotiations for the sake of harmony.[22]

Arthur Chester and Clayton-Kennedy arrived in Angora by mid-September to open negotiations for acquisition of railway and mining concessions substantially co-extensive with the Chester Project of 1909. In a short time, they had made preliminary arrangements for a concession. Clayton-Kennedy then returned to Constantinople and sent Goethals a telegram on October 5 briefly describing the terms, which he considered favorable. Turkish officials had agreed to date the concession back to 1909, and the Grand National Assembly was reportedly ready to ratify as soon as the guarantee deposit required by law had been placed in a Constantinople bank. After a two-year period of scientific investigation, the company would have the option of continuing with construction or of giving the results of the surveys to the government. The negotiators had even persuaded the Turks to allow a reduction from $88,000 to $30,000 in the cautionary deposit. Time was of the essence, Clayton-Kennedy pointed out as he begged the company to arrange the deposit at once so that it could maintain its "present unparalleled position with [the] Government."[23]

A few days prior to Clayton-Kennedy's message of October 5, Admiral Chester had intervened with an unauthorized repudiation of Clayton-Kennedy, much to the annoyance of Goethals and the confusion of American diplomats in Turkey who were trying to assist the Chester negotiations. The admiral's telegram of October 2 to Arthur read: "Following sent with approval General Goethals. . . . Major Kennedy has no authority to act on Chester Project. He is proceeding under false pretense and is repudiated by Goethals and all other purported stockholders found." The message indicated that the company would be reorganized on a legal basis with Arthur Chester as its only authorized representative in Turkey.

This repudiation created an explosive situation. On October 7 Admiral

[22] Arthur Chester to Goethals, Sept. 3, 1922, DS/223.
[23] *FR 1922*, II, 976 (quotation), 981–982. See above, Chap. 3, p. 61, for the 1909 project.

Bristol strongly urged the State Department to clear up the question of Clayton-Kennedy's status in the Ottoman-American Development Company. Bristol had seen Clayton-Kennedy's power of attorney, authenticated by the Secretary of State of Delaware, giving him full authority to act for the company. On the basis of this document, Bristol was continuing to support him in spite of Admiral Chester's repudiation.[24]

In a telegram to the State Department on October 14, General Goethals revealed his surprise at learning of Admiral Chester's telegram, sent while Goethals was away from New York. In asserting that he did not repudiate Clayton-Kennedy, Goethals confirmed the Canadian's authorization to act for the company, which the general believed he was doing in good faith. The department then notified Bristol of the Canadian's position and of Goethal's intention to arrange for the required deposit.

Although Secretary Hughes sensed the nature of the disagreement within the company, he felt he could not instruct Bristol definitely regarding the attitude to be taken toward Clayton-Kennedy until harmony was restored and the department could learn who was properly qualified to speak for the company.[25]

The department then set about to study the financial organization of the Ottoman-American Development Company. Goethals confirmed that the company held a Delaware charter and was authorized to issue five thousand shares of stock at no par value. Three of the directors were Americans and the fourth a Canadian. The stock list showed 4347 shares held by American citizens and 623 by British citizens.[26] The Canadian-owned shares had been put in the hands of Americans, but it was not clear whether the Americans followed the orders of the owners in voting on company policy. The Canadians expressed a willingness, however, to pool all their stock and create a voting trust of three American citizens with unrestricted authority to vote the stock. Goethals explained the relationship of the Chester family to the company: "Under the contract with the Chesters a large amount of cash was to be paid in

---

[24] *FR 1922,* II, 976 (quotation), 977. See also Bristol Diary, Aug. 11 and Aug. 18, 1920, Box 20; Oct. 7, 1922, Box 21, Bristol MSS.

[25] *FR 1922,* II, 977–978; Bristol Diary, Nov. 4, 1922, Bristol MSS, Box 21.

[26] The American directors were Goethals, F. S. Blackall, and Kermit Roosevelt. The Canadian director, C. A. Barnard, was Clayton-Kennedy's lawyer-friend from Montreal. Apparently the company had issued only 4970 of the authorized 5000 shares of stock.

installments and I understand negotiations are now under way by which stock holding interests will be substituted for these cash payments, in which case the Chester family would be large holders. The Canadian interests have thus far advanced practically all of the money that has been expended in the venture."[27]

While the company's affairs were in flux, negotiations in the Middle East were running a turbulent course with Turkish suspicion of Clayton-Kennedy at the root of the trouble. When the Canadian applied for permission to return to Angora from Constantinople, the Turks asked the American vice-consul, Robert Imbrie, to vouch for him. Imbrie replied that, since Clayton-Kennedy was not an American citizen, he could neither request that he be allowed to return to Angora, nor could he guarantee him. The Turkish government then informed Imbrie that it had proof that Clayton-Kennedy was an agent of the British government.

When Clayton-Kennedy tried to re-enter Anatolia in November, the authorities arrested him. Arthur Chester returned to Constantinople soon after this and by early December the two were still engaged in trying to clear Clayton-Kennedy of the charge that he was a British spy. The whole episode, fanned by publicity, created an unfavorable impression in Turkey, where it was feared that the Chester Project was a British plot. At a time when negotiations for the concession had nearly been completed, this incident was particularly unfortunate. From Angora Imbrie wrote: "The impression created among Government circles here, and generally in fact, is that there is little back of the Chester proposition. The prolonged negotiations, covering a period of nearly three months, have apparently led to nothing definite. The deposit, an insignificant sum when the magnitude of [the] project is considered, has not been forthcoming."[28]

Modus Vivendi within the Company

Just as these pessimistic reports were coming in to Washington from Turkey, the company officers completed a modus vivendi among the dis-

[27] *FR 1922*, II, 978–979. The earlier agreement by which Barnard was to make payments to Admiral Chester had not been carried out to the admiral's satisfaction; this situation seemed to underlie the admiral's unauthorized repudiation of Clayton-Kennedy.

[28] *FR 1922*, II, 979–983 (quotation, p. 982). Imbrie had advised Arthur Chester from the time he arrived that it was a mistake to associate with Clayton-Kennedy in

sident elements. On December 9, Goethals sent Clayton-Kennedy a telegram reading: "All interests at this end now working harmoniously. Trust that you and Chester will cooperate closely in all matters. Advise if any assistance can be rendered here." With the clarification of the company's business affairs, Goethals asked Secretary Hughes to acquaint American diplomatic officials in Turkey with these facts: Clayton-Kennedy and Arthur Chester were both accredited agents of the company; Americans controlled the Ottoman-American Development Company; the company held all rights to the Chester Project; and the company had made the deposit required to secure the concession.[29]

State Department officials examined the new voting trust agreement executed early in December by Goethals, Barnard, and Admiral Rousseau — the latter apparently acting as a friend of Admiral Chester. This agreement vested control of the company in two American trustees for five years and provided that the concession when obtained should be eventually transferred to a new company in which Barnard would hold 49 per cent of the stock. Convinced that the evidence showed a substantial American interest, Secretary Hughes instructed the high commissioner at Constantinople that he might "give such diplomatic support as may be proper, but of course without participating in [the] negotiations. The Department desires to maintain the principle of the open door and to secure freedom of opportunity to American interests, but it should be borne in mind that the Department plays no favorites and cannot give special support to a single American concern."[30]

The Policy of "No Favorites"

The department's reason for cautioning that it could play no favorites was explained more fully on January 15, 1923, in instructions to Frederic R. Dolbeare, acting high commissioner while Admiral Bristol attended the Lausanne Conference. First, Secretary Hughes explained the situation in terms of policy. Competing American groups, he said, might be

view of the anti-British feeling in Nationalist Turkey. Bristol Diary, Nov. 22, 1922, Bristol MSS, Box 21. In mid-December Turkish authorities permitted Clayton-Kennedy to return to Angora. Dolbeare to Hughes, Jan. 15, 1923, DS/247.

[29] *FR 1922*, II, 980–981, 983 (quotation). If the required deposit had actually been made, Imbrie did not yet know of it on December 7. He did report in February that the company had made the £T50,000 (about $30,000) deposit. Imbrie to Hughes, Feb. 10, 1923, DS/251.

[30] *FR 1922*, II, 981. The department also stated that it had no substantial ground for thinking Clayton-Kennedy was identified with the British secret service.

interested in securing similar rights in the territory of the old Ottoman Empire. The "utmost circumspection" must be observed to avoid giving the erroneous impression that the United States government was more interested in the success of one group than of another. After the acquisition of legal rights from recognized authorities, the American government might "accord more definite support."

Secretary Hughes then illustrated how events of the previous week had required him to apply the policy to a concrete situation. Representatives of three groups of American interests had come to the department to talk over their interests in Asia Minor. These were the group of large American petroleum companies currently negotiating with the Turkish Petroleum Company for a share in the Mesopotamian oil fields, the Ottoman-American Development Company, and the heirs of Abdul Hamid, who had placed their claims in the hands of Samuel Untermyer and other Americans. Hughes explained: "In dealing with these three specific proposals the Department has made it clear that it would accord proper diplomatic support to American citizens and interests but that it played no favorites and could grant no special privileges to any one American company which it would deny to another."[31] By early 1923 these three groups were watching the proceedings at Lausanne where a new Middle Eastern settlement was being shaped to replace the unenforceable Treaty of Sèvres. The outcome there would vitally affect these various efforts.

After the two groups of interests pushing the Chester Project had reconciled their differences late in 1922, Arthur Chester and Clayton-Kennedy returned to Angora. They asked Dolbeare for a statement acknowledging their company's financial stability, but he felt such an endorsement was inappropriate. Secretary Hughes supported Dolbeare's stand.

New obstacles soon obstructed the concession efforts at Angora. Clayton-Kennedy telegraphed Dolbeare from Angora on January 6 that the Turks had broken off negotiations for the Chester Project owing to the attitude of the American observers at Lausanne. Dolbeare reflected on the possible motives for the Turkish action: "The natural inference is that the Turkish Delegation at Lausanne, seeing the stand of the American Delegation on the question of the Minorities and the Armenian Home, believed that anti-American propaganda in the Turkish press,

[31] *FR 1923*, II, 1198–1199.

together with the breaking off of the negotiations concerning the Chester Project, might cause the American Delegation to modify its attitude and to be more favorable to the Turkish point of view."[32]

Turkey Grants the Chester Concession

Uncertainty concerning the character and amount of the financial support as well as the motives of the non-American backers flared up anew in official Turkish circles during the early months of 1923. Vice-Consul Imbrie at Angora shared the view that the Chester group lacked sufficient capital to carry out its imposing schemes. Officials of the State Department were equally skeptical. The British also feared that the concession would interfere with the Turkish Petroleum Company.[33] Yet the Turks resumed negotiations and the National Assembly overwhelmingly approved the granting of the Chester Concession on April 9, 1923, following which the two parties formally signed the agreement on April 29. It cannot be doubted that the Turks were genuinely interested in its ambitious provisions which contemplated railroad, port, mineral, and agricultural development. Imbrie reported that "Every peasant in the country has heard of, and is waiting for the 'American railroads,'" which they seemed to think the United States government would build. But the nationalist government had its motives in approving the concession at a time when the Allies were reassembling at Lausanne to resume efforts to block out acceptable peace terms with the New Turkey. The Turks undoubtedly hoped to drive a wedge into Allied solidarity, to detach the United States from the Allies, and probably expected to obtain American loans to bolster their precarious finances.[34]

The French protested vigorously that the newly granted concession

[32] Dolbeare to Hughes, Jan. 3, Jan. 8, and Jan. 17 (quotation), 1923; Hughes to Dolbeare, Jan. 4, 1923, DS/241, 240, 245, and 241.

[33] Dolbeare to Hughes, Jan. 15, 1923; Imbrie to Hughes, Feb. 10, 1923; Dulles to Harrison, Feb. 12, 1923; Hughes (for C. M. Chester, Jr.) to Bristol (for Arthur Chester), Feb. 3, 1923; Higgins to Sharp, Feb. 21, 1923, enclosed in Bannerman to Dulles, Feb. 23, 1923; Starret (Office of the Economic Adviser) to SKH, ANY, and NE, memorandum, Feb. 28, 1923, DS/247, 251, 250, 248, 256, and 257; *FR 1923*, II, 1209–1210.

[34] *FR 1923*, II, 1202–1203, 1205–1206, 1209–1212, 1248–1249; Imbrie to Hughes, April 11, 1923 (quotation); Bristol to Hughes, April 16, 1923, DS/322 and 263; Eliot G. Mears, ed., *Modern Turkey: A Politico-Economic Interpretation, 1908–1923*, p. 379; John Ise, *The United States Oil Policy*, pp. 476–477. See also above, Chap. 5, p. 148. Clayton-Kennedy handed the State Department photostatic copies of the agreements late in July. See *FR 1923*, II, 1215–1241.

conflicted with prior rights granted to their nationals in Anatolia. The British also made clear their contention that the Angora government could not grant rights in Mesopotamia, because Mesopotamia was not within Turkish jurisdiction. The State Department held, however, that the new Chester Concession was neither monopolistic nor objectionable.[35] It was, in short, in accord with the open-door principle which the United States had been supporting so persistently.

Turkey Cancels the Concession

Renewed dissension in May of 1923 between Clayton-Kennedy and Arthur Chester reflected the struggle between Canadian and American interests for control of the Ottoman-American Development Company. When the incredible internal wrangling prevented the company from making any serious attempt to begin the projects it had agreed to undertake, the enthusiasm of the Turks waned by August. Inability to muster sufficient financial resources also proved to be an insuperable obstacle, although in November the company tried to make a token effort at discharging its commitments under the terms of the concession. Examination of the tangled internal difficulties led the State Department to believe that financial control of the company might have shifted from American hands.[36]

During these continuing crises in the autumn of 1923, Admiral Bristol and his staff urged the State Department to straighten out the chaotic internal affairs of the Ottoman-American Development Company. Bristol agreed with Consul Maynard Barnes, who wrote from Angora: "If the Department considers the controlling factor in the situation to be the protection of American political and economic prestige, and if the Department is able to give material assistance to any American group in a serious effort to carry out the concession, it should give such aid even though it involves a substantial change in the policy which the Department has pursued regarding the Chester concession up to the present time."

Hughes took vigorous exception to these proposals, which exceeded

[35] *FR 1923*, II, 1201–1209, 1212–1215.
[36] Bristol to Hughes, May 1, May 3, May 8, and Nov. 11, 1923; Hughes to Bristol, May 2 and Nov. 17, 1923; Hughes to Goethals, May 7, 1923; Dulles memoranda, May 11, May 15, May 22, and June 8, 1923; Hughes to American Mission, Lausanne, May 12, May 31, and June 11, 1923; Herbert K. Stockton to Dulles, Oct. 5, 1923, DS/293, 297, 310, 428, 294, 430, 305, 330, 320, 331, 345, 310, 329, 345, and 415; *FR 1923*, II, 1241–1251; Mears, *Modern Turkey*, p. 379.

the concept of "appropriate diplomatic support" to which the department had to limit itself. The government had no legal power to interfere in the internal management of an American company, as requested, and would reap trouble if it tried to do so. Hughes could not share the view that the failure of the Chester Concession would injure American prestige in Turkey irretrievably. He believed, on the contrary, that only the Turkish government, which had supported the concession for its own political and financial purposes, would be injured.[37]

The Turkish government became so annoyed with the failure of the Ottoman-American Development Company to begin work that it finally announced on December 18, 1923, the annulment of the Chester Concession. Efforts to reinstate the company failed, and on March 10, 1925, Admiral Bristol commented that there was no reason to think that the Turkish government had changed its view.[38]

Conclusion

For all practical purposes the Chester Concession was dead, although people associated with the syndicate continued to assert its validity for years to come. From the American embassy in Turkey, Sheldon Crosby wrote the State Department on August 16, 1927, that "the final chapter in the famous Chester Concession affair appears about to be written." Crosby reported that the Turkish government had made a demand on the Banca Commerciale Italiana in Constantinople to turn over to the Turkish treasury the fifty thousand Turkish pounds deposited by the Chester group "as an earnest of good faith" when the concession was granted. Clayton-Kennedy objected, claiming that the cautionary deposit could be forfeited only after appropriate judicial proceedings as prescribed in the concession contract. The following year Avni Bey, Turkish Minister of Public Works, brought administrative suit against the company, beginning legal processes which dragged on for more than a decade.[39]

[37] *FR 1923*, II, 1246–1249 (first quotation, p. 1247; second quotation, p. 1248).

[38] *FR 1923*, II, 1251–1252; Dulles to Hughes, Dec. 20, 1923, DS/438.

[39] Crosby to Kellogg, Aug. 16, 1927; Crosby to Kellogg, Nov. 7, 1928; G. Howland Shaw to Hull, Nov. 1, 1933, DS/475, 477, and 482. Shaw reported in 1937 that the case was then before the Turkish Court of Cassation on an appeal from the Banca Commerciale Italiana acting in the name of the Ottoman-American Development Company. Shaw to Hull, July 1, 1937, DS/525. This is the final entry in the Chester file for the 1930s. I have been unable to discover the outcome of this appeal. Admiral Chester died in 1932. Henry Woodhouse tried to salvage some financial gain from the concession during the middle 1930s.

Although the postwar Chester Project had been an even more spectacular failure than the prewar effort initiated by the admiral, there were significant differences. The admiral stressed railroad construction in his earlier plan, whereas he presented his revived project of 1920 as a plan for petroleum development, designed to advance the national security of the United States at a time of concern about future petroleum supplies. In 1920 and after, Washington officials were much more reserved in supporting Chester than the Taft administration had been between 1909 and 1911. The Turkish Grand National Assembly which granted the concession in 1923 acted without the same foreign pressure which had prevented parliamentary approval of a concession before the war. In both cases, however, several European governments protested that the Chester plans infringed on the prior rights of their nationals. Like the Young Turks before them, the Nationalist Turks found the economic development features of the Chester Project very attractive and tempting, but the New Turks also used the granting of the concession as a diplomatic maneuver to wean the United States from the Allies as the second phase of the Lausanne Conference was about to begin.

A common feature of this bizarre enterprise throughout its strange history was the poor business planning, the flimsy financing. Admiral Chester had an idea — a grandiose idea — but he and Arthur seemed to lack the business experience and temperament needed to keep the organization running smoothly. Acting High Commissioner Dolbeare put his finger on the trouble when he wrote Secretary Hughes that "there seems to be a certain visionary and unworkmanlike quality in the way in which the negotiations have been handled."[40] Through the years, the admiral persisted doggedly, apparently hoping that the results might become financially profitable for him, his family, and his friends. But in his desperation to arrange for needed capital, especially in 1922, too many adventurers were permitted to join the enterprise.

Although the State Department spent an enormous amount of time and energy on the Chester Project, Secretary Hughes did not permit the department to become so deeply committed to the businessmen as had Secretary Philander Knox. His circumspection softened the effects of the failure which, contrary to the misgivings of Admiral Bristol, and others, seemed to have no deleterious long-range repercussions on Turkish-American relations.

[40] Dolbeare to Hughes, Jan. 15, 1923, DS/247.

8

THE TURKISH REPUBLIC BEFORE
WORLD WAR II

☆ On July 15, 1939, the Turkish government issued three pairs of postage stamps celebrating the sesquicentennial of the American Constitution. Two stamps carried a map of the United States flanked by portraits of Mustafa Kemal Atatürk[1] and George Washington. Another pair substituted President Ismet Inönü for Atatürk, and President Franklin D. Roosevelt for Washington, while the third set carried a Turkish star and crescent alongside the American flag, surmounted by a large star representing the political freedom of both countries. Reflecting on the significance of this event, the American Board of Commissioners for Foreign Missions concluded that "evidently there is some ground for asserting that Turkey seeks comradeship and coöperation with the great democracy of the West."[2] These commemorative stamps indeed symbol-

[1] The Turkish Grand National Assembly decreed the adoption and use of family names in 1934. It bestowed on Mustafa Kemal the surname Atatürk — first and foremost Turk — and he, in turn, selected names for some of his closest associates. Ismet Pasha thus became Ismet Inönü in remembrance of the site of his victory over the Greeks in 1921. Donald Everett Webster, *The Turkey of Atatürk: Social Process in the Turkish Reformation*, pp. 132–133. The new regime had decreed in 1930 that Turkish place names be employed: Istanbul for Constantinople, Izmir for Smyrna, and Ankara for Angora. Except in quoted passages, the new family names and Turkish place names will usually be used in this chapter.

[2] *The New York Times*, July 30, 1939, X, 8; ABC, AR 1939, pp. 21–22 (quotation). Turkey's action was not unique, for thirteen foreign countries had already responded to the suggestion of Representative Sol Bloom of New York that nations with a constitutional form of government issue postage stamps to celebrate the sesquicentennial of the American Constitution. An error was made in the inscription on the Turkish stamps. In translation, it read, "In Commemoration of the One Hundred and Fiftieth Anniversary of the Independence of the United States of America." J. V. A. MacMurray (ambassador to Turkey) to Cordell Hull, July 21, 1939, DS 867.713/13.

ized the *rapprochement* achieved by Turkey and the United States after World War I.

The Atatürk Revolution

The Turkish-American *rapprochement* was a by-product of the revolution, which was imposed from above by Atatürk, Inönü, and their associates with startling rapidity and dazzling success. When a truncated Turkey, freed from most of its disruptive minorities problems, raised itself by its bootstraps, Americans, like the rest of the world, had to change some of their notions about the Turks. As the new leadership began to achieve its interrelated goals of reform and a respected place for Turkey in the family of nations, the epithet "terrible Turk" became outmoded. World opinion was not transformed overnight, however, and the unfavorable impression of the Turks that had dinned in American ears during the decline and dissolution of the Ottoman Empire still had sufficient strength in 1927 to prevent Senate approval of the Turco-American Treaty of Lausanne, which had been signed in 1923.

Not until after the new Turkey had driven the Greeks from Anatolia and made its peace with the Allies at Lausanne, to a great extent on Turkey's terms, could Atatürk move into the second stage of his revolution dedicated to comprehensive internal reforms. The new leadership expressed its program in six principles — republicanism, nationalism, populism, statism, secularism, and reformism.[3] Only the briefest recapitulation of those reforms most pertinent for understanding Turkish-American relations is possible here.

Basic to the sequent reforms was the proclamation in 1923 that Turkey was a republic in which sovereignty emanated from the people as represented in the Grand National Assembly. Abolition of the Caliphate in 1924 was the first of a series of measures designed to separate church and state. Laws or edicts soon followed, directed against such hallowed Islamic social customs as polygamy and wearing of the fez. The veiling of women was frowned on. The government abolished dervish orders, closed convents, monasteries, and tombs, and in 1928 amended the constitution by deleting the clause declaring that Turkey was an Islamic state. An essential part of the secularization process lay in breaking the hold of Islamic law on the country's legal processes by overhauling the system of justice along Western lines. To promote this goal, the Turkish

[3] Webster, *The Turkey of Atatürk*, pp. 163–172.

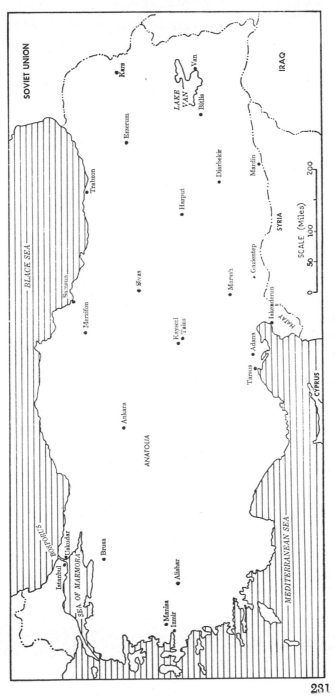

Ataturk's Turkey

SOVIET UNION

IRAQ

Kars

Van

LAKE
VAN

Erzerum

Bitlis

Diarbekir

Mardin

BLACK SEA

Trabzon

Harput

SYRIA

Samsun

Sivas

Marash

Gazientep

SCALE (Miles)

Merzifon

Kayseri
Talas

Iskenderun

HATAY

Tarsus

Adana

Ankara

CYPRUS

ANATOLIA

BOSPORUS

Uskudar

Brusa

Istanbul

Alishar

SEA OF MARMORA

Manisa

Izmir

MEDITERRANEAN SEA

0   50   100   200

231

government opened a new law school at Ankara in 1925 to train young lawyers in Western law; the following year Turkey adopted a civil code patterned after the Swiss, a criminal code modeled after the Italian, and a commercial code adapted from the German system.[4]

Revision of the educational system of the nation attracted close attention from the new regime. Secularization proceeded by stages, beginning with the law of 1924 requiring removal of religious symbols from the interiors of foreign schools. A month later the government abolished all Moslem religious schools and took steps toward establishing a unified school system under the lay Ministry of Public Instruction. Closely related to the aim of accelerating the learning process were alphabet and language reforms begun in 1928 when legislation decreed the use of a new simplified Latin alphabet to replace the Arabic script, which was ill adapted to the Turkish language. In 1931 primary education was reserved to government schools, and in all schools below university level, certain subjects — history, geography, civics, Turkish language, and literature — had to be taught by Turks using Turkish textbooks. The secularization of education went forward despite the handicap of teacher and school shortages. Illiteracy was reduced thanks to the simplified alphabet and the government's mass program of adult education. Foreign schools, including American, though permitted to help meet the pressing needs which the government could not fill at once, had to conform to nationalistic requirements.[5]

The rationale behind the reforms was the creation of a strong Turkey which could hold up its head as the equal of Western nations. Atatürk's exhortation to his people: "Turk — Be Proud, Diligent, Confident,"[6] epitomized the aims of the revolution. Atatürk's ceaseless effort to inculcate a keen sense of national pride was often pressed to the point of fanaticism and xenophobia. At the same time, any socially useful externals of Western civilization were borrowed to promote the larger end — building a cohesive nation-state, economically viable and socially pro-

[4] See *ibid.*, pp. 126–129 and *passim*, an extended account of the Atatürk revolution. An excellent recent appraisal is Bernard Lewis, *The Emergence of Modern Turkey*, especially pp. 250–286. See also Gates, *Not to Me Only*, pp. 305–315; Sydney Nettleton Fisher, *The Middle East: A History*, pp. 390–402.

[5] Webster, *The Turkey of Atatürk*, pp. 110–111, 127, 131–132; Lewis, *Turkey*, pp. 271–274, 426–429. See below, pp. 256–259, 260–263, for the impact of the educational reforms on American schools in Turkey.

[6] For a photograph of the monument in an Ankara park carrying these words, see Webster, *The Turkey of Atatürk*, frontispiece.

gressive. Turkey wanted the modernism of the West, but not for the sake of modernism; Western technology was to be only the handmaiden for the Turkification of nonmaterial culture.[7]

Ardent nationalists were schizophrenic in that their fierce pride in being Turks coexisted with a sense of inferiority because of the prevailing Western view of the Turkish people as an amalgam of central Asian barbarians who had contributed nothing original to civilization while destroying or impairing the cultures with which they came into contact. The Turks had to be convinced of a glorious heritage deeply rooted in the pre-Ottoman past, even if it required taking some liberties with the historical record. As Ambassador Joseph C. Grew expressed it, "the Turkish Revolution has been in search of an ideology." By the middle of 1930, Grew and his staff were reporting to Washington on Atatürk's recent interest in Turkish pre-history "for the evident purpose of enhancing the pride of race of his people and of combatting the 'inferiority complex', which seems to be at the base of much of the almost morbid sensitiveness of the Turks." The Turkish president promoted a grandiose theory which taught that all civilization had its origin in the Turkish "race." He created a Turkish historical society (Türk Tarih Kurumu) in 1931, which was to collect and translate every possible reference to the ancient history of the Turks, and which compiled a four-volume history of the Turks incorporating the Ghazi's theory. Not only were the Turks presented as the ancestors of the peoples who established the great ancient civilizations — Persian, Babylonian, Greek, and Roman — but also the Anglo-Saxon. The latter point rested on such tenuous evidence as the assertion that Kent in England was a contraction of the name of the city of Tashkent.[8] In reporting the work of the history society, the usually sympathetic Grew commented that the organization utilized "with astonishing results philological comparisons in order to establish a connection between the Turks on the one hand and the Hittites and even the British and North American Indians on the other." Lest Americans become too self-righteous, Grew observed that they

---

[7] *Ibid.*, p. 171.

[8] Grew to Henry L. Stimson, March 9, 1932 (first quotation); Jefferson Patterson (chargé d'affaires a.i., Ankara) to Stimson, June 5, 1930 (second quotation); Paul H. Alling (Near Eastern Division) to William R. Castle (Under Secretary of State), July 29, 1932, DS 867.41/6, 1, and 9; Webster, *The Turkey of Atatürk*, pp. 240–243; Lewis, *Turkey*, pp. 352–354. The Grand National Assembly bestowed the title "the Ghazi" on Mustafa Kemal in 1921 after the victory over the Greeks at Sakarya. The title was reserved for eminent Turkish commanders.

might keep in mind their own recent heated controversy over nationalistic American history textbooks which had been openly criticized for lack of impartiality and objectivity.[9]

The Waning of a Stereotype

The American public was not prepared psychologically for the Atatürk revolution when it was in its formative stages. The disparaging attitude toward the Turks harbored by most Americans after World War I was the product of a generation of denigration by missionary forces sincerely trying to justify the importance of their efforts to minister to the downtrodden Christian minorities of the Ottoman Empire. The excessive zeal engendered by the perennial relief drives from 1915 well into the postwar period could not help but direct unfavorable attention on the record of the Ottoman Empire. As for Atatürk, he seemed to most Americans little more than an ambitious upstart, as cruel and ruthless as his Ottoman predecessors and as dedicated to the extermination of Turkey's Christian remnants. The propaganda attending the Greek retreat of 1922 and the burning of Smyrna did nothing to help the cause of the New Turks in the United States. Relief workers and missionaries aiding Turkey's remaining Greek and Armenian population harped on Turkish brutality while ignoring equally reprehensible actions by the favored Christian minorities. In the United States pro-Armenian forces allied with fanatical or ill-informed clergymen, who could not conceive of a regenerated Turkey, impeded the facing of new facts about Turkey.[10]

After the Lausanne settlement the hold of the old stereotypes weakened as Americans re-examined their views of the Turks and Turkey. Diplomats like Admiral Mark L. Bristol and Allen Dulles were among the first to comprehend that Atatürk and Inönü were leaders of a new stripe. Grew came to share this view when he undertook major responsibility for America's Middle Eastern diplomacy at the Lausanne Conference, where he established friendly relations with Ismet Inönü. President Caleb Frank Gates of Robert College was another American

[9] Grew to Stimson, March 9, 1932, DS 867.41/6. Webster makes the same point: "It may not be amiss to remind readers that between 1917 and 1924 a wave of 'one hundred per cent Americanism' and Americanization emphases engulfed the intellectual processes of many citizens of the United States." *The Turkey of Atatürk*, p. 163 n. 2.

[10] Galbraith, "The Smyrna Disaster of 1922," pp. 84–90, 95–98, 103; *MRW*, 45 (Nov. 1922), 853–854; 46 (June 1923), 477–478; (Oct. 1923), 863.

who awakened early to the realization that it would be inappropriate and unproductive in dealing with the New Turks to use the peculiar tactics fashioned to meet the requirements of Ottoman diplomacy.[11]

Missionaries affiliated with the American Board were sharply divided in their reactions toward the New Turks before the completion of the Lausanne settlement. After the conversion of James L. Barton, influential foreign secretary of the board, to the view that cooperation with the new regime required meeting it more than half way, he successfully led his board to endorse a new approach. Clergymen of other American denominations, notably Episcopalians and Methodists, who had no missions in Turkey, severely criticized the Congregational board for its opportunism in coming to terms with the Atatürk regime, maintaining that course to be a compromise with evil. It cannot be denied that Barton's pragmatic approach took into account the consequences of failing to adapt to altered conditions. The American Board stood to lose its properties, the product of a century of effort, and to forfeit any possibility of performing further service in Turkey. Among older missionary hands in Turkey there was much unwillingness to accept the practical realities dictating a change in tactics.[12] Though received with some reluctance, Barton's advice to continue the Turkish missions, making the necessary accommodation to new conditions, prevailed at the board meeting of 1923 at Springfield, Massachusetts.[13] Within the next few years, as deaths and retirements removed some who found it difficult to accept the new dispensation, missionary forces learned by experience that they could perform useful service for the Turks.

Missionaries were among the American interest groups in Turkey which rallied to support the Treaty of Lausanne between 1923 and 1927. These included the American Board, Robert College, Istanbul College for Women, the Near East College Association, the Federated American Chambers of Commerce of the Near East, the Y.M.C.A., the Y.W.C.A., and various firms.[14]

Despite this impressive unanimity and hard work in behalf of treaty ratification, the tide of pro-Armenian sentiment still ran too strongly

[11] Gates, *Not to Me Only*, pp. 288–290. Gates wrote: "I felt that we should get rid of the old mentality which looked upon the Turks as a decadent people from whom concessions must be extorted by force or by strategy, and that we should deal with them in frankness and sincerity."
[12] See above, Chap. 5, pp. 132–134, 155, 156, 160, 162, 163.
[13] For the resolution adopted on October 19, 1923, see ABC, *AR 1923*, pp. 9–10.
[14] See above, Chap. 5, pp. 156–165, *passim*.

against the Turks during the middle 1920s. Later, the marked recession of this tide facilitated a less emotional American approach to the Turks during the decade preceding the outbreak of World War II. The internal reforms of Atatürk began to command world-wide respect and attention, improving Turkey's reputation impressively within a few years. It would be too much to claim that the ebbing tide of Turcophobia swept away all residue of the old stereotypes, for hostile commentary continued in the following decade. But the number of dissenters and the volume of their invective slackened markedly during the 1930s. Admiral Bristol, Ambassador Grew, and their successors could proceed to take up the unfinished business left by the Senate's rejection of the Lausanne settle-ment.

The New Structure of Official Relations

The task of rebuilding the structure of Turkish-American relations went forward slowly as the republic established its program and as public opinion in America responded to the altered situation. Relations had been severed in 1917, not to be resumed formally until 1927, but a month after the Mudros armistice the United States appointed Lewis Heck with the title of commissioner. Early in 1919, when the Supreme Council of the Allies permitted the resumption of trade with Turkey, the United States reopened consulates. On August 12, the United States designated Rear Admiral Mark L. Bristol high commissioner until a peace treaty could be completed and normal diplomatic relations resumed.[15] He served in this anomalous position until 1927, several years after major nations had regularized their relations with the Turkish Republic. The Turks could well have insisted on Bristol's withdrawal during the long delay of the United States Senate in acting on the treaty signed on August 6, 1923, but they showed considerable restraint, recognizing the State Department's difficulties with pro-Armenian and Democratic Party opposition. Turkish dependence on the export trade to the United States and lingering hopes of American economic assistance help to explain Turkish tolerance of the delay. Bristol's success in arranging a commercial modus vivendi in 1926 won favorable treatment for American commerce.[16]

Gravely disappointed by the adverse Senate vote early in 1927, the

[15] *FR 1919*, II, 810–814.
[16] See above, Chap. 5, p. 162.

Coolidge administration decided it could not wait any longer to accredit an ambassador to Turkey, provided Turkish leaders had not been too seriously affronted by the Senate's action. Fortunately the Turks reacted more favorably than the State Department dared hope, and Bristol achieved a personal triumph when he arranged a new modus vivendi of February 17, 1927, opening a new stage in Turkish-American official relations.[17]

The notes exchanged at that time provided for the re-establishment of diplomatic and consular relations on the basis of customary international law and practice; they also preserved the status quo in commercial relations. There were angry outcries from the Turcophobes in the United States (Vahan Cardashian, James G. Gerard, Senators William King and Claude Swanson), charging that the new modus vivendi was a naked attempt to override the will of the Senate.[18] Although the same elements criticized the appointment of Joseph C. Grew as ambassador to Turkey, he departed for Istanbul on an interim appointment and was warmly received by Turkish officials. Several months later the Senate confirmed his nomination. Meanwhile the administration was embarrassed by the delay in the arrival of the Turkish ambassador to the United States, Mouhtar Bey. When Grew convinced Turkish Foreign Minister Tevfik Rusdu Aras that Mouhtar's failure to arrive in Washington before Congress convened in December would furnish anti-Turkish forces ammunition against his own confirmation, Aras ordered Mouhtar to sail at once. He arrived in Washington before Congress assembled. There was some anxiety for his safety on arrival because of pro-Armenian demonstrations and a threat of assassination, but the United States government took extreme precautions to guard the ambassador.[19]

In 1928 the State Department had to consider the feasibility of negotiating a new commercial treaty with Turkey in view of the one-year life of the 1927 modus vivendi. Secretary Frank B. Kellogg believed the

[17] *FR 1927*, III, 765–802; Gates, *Not to Me Only*, p. 296. See also Grew, *TE*, II, 798n; Grew to Kellogg, Nov. 8, 1927 (a telegram and a despatch); Grew to Stimson, April 18, 1929, DS 711.672/600, 599, and 616.
[18] *FR 1927*, III, 794–800. For opposition charges, see Gerard to Coolidge, May 18, 1927, Coolidge MSS, file 193A; Armenian Press Bureau handbill announcing a mass meeting in New York, April 22, 1927; Henry W. Jessup to Coolidge, May 23, 1927, DS 711.672/588 and 595½. For refutations of the opposition arguments, see Kellogg to Senator Swanson, Dec. 14, 1927; Kellogg to Senator Borah, March 31, 1928, DS 711.672/600A and 610A.
[19] Grew, *TE*, I, 703–705; II, 710, 715–716, 719–722, 730–733, 744–745, 747–752.

wounds produced by the Senate's defeat of the Lausanne Treaty were still too fresh to allow the department to risk another rebuff so soon. Talks on a trade treaty were therefore postponed to allow time for anti-Turkish agitation to die down. On May 19, 1928, Grew was able to obtain an extension of the commercial terms until April 10, 1929.[20]

A year later the department instructed Grew to commence informal trade treaty talks. Formal negotiations beginning on September 8 culminated in the signing on October 1, 1929, of the Treaty of Ankara providing for most-favored-nation treatment on tariff duties and other charges. Each nation pledged equal treatment with other countries regarding prohibitions or restrictions on imports and exports. Except for coastwise traffic and other minor exceptions, American vessels in Turkish waters were to receive national treatment, that is, treatment equal to that given Turkish vessels.[21]

Grew's delight at the signing of the treaty was tempered by apprehension about Senate reaction, but the department swung into action with a reminder to Senator William E. Borah, chairman of the Foreign Relations Committee, on February 17, 1930, that the modus vivendi would soon expire, leaving American commerce without protection if the Senate did not act. On the same day, the Senate ratified the treaty without debate.[22] The Treaty of Ankara, a milestone as the first formal agreement between the United States and the Turkish Republic, opened the way for additional treaties to regularize other aspects of Turkish-American relations.

Grew wished to take advantage of overtures from the Turks in 1929 to secure a treaty of establishment and sojourn (residence), but the department held back until late in 1930, preferring to wait until the

[20] Grew, *TE*, II, 798–802; *FR 1928*, II, 950–954. For examples of continuing opposition to the department's Turkish diplomacy, see Cardashian to Borah, March 24, 1928, with a 101-page enclosure entitled, "A Brief in Support of an Application for a Hearing by the Senate upon the Lausanne Treaty," Borah MSS, Box 596.

[21] Grew, *TE*, II, 832–837; *FR 1928*, III, 957–964; *FR 1929*, II, 819–842. Grew obtained a further extension of the commercial modus vivendi to April 10, 1930. A final extension of the commercial modus vivendi was needed to continue its effect until ratifications of the Treaty of Ankara were exchanged on April 22, 1930. See *TE*, II, 798–802, 805–810; *FR 1929*, III, 803–818, 842n.

[22] John Cotton (Under Secretary of State) to Borah, Feb. 17, 1930, Borah MSS, Box 547. The Senate Foreign Relations Committee considered the treaty on January 8 and 30, 1930. *Proceedings of the Committee on Foreign Relations, United States Senate from the 68th to the 72nd Congress*, p. 158. For the vote, see *Senate Executive Journal*, LXIX, Part 1, 71 Cong., 2 Sess., p. 389. See also Grew, *TE*, I, 678–679; II, 842–843.

Senate had acted on the Treaty of Ankara. After a year of negotiation, the Treaty of Establishment and Sojourn was signed on October 28, 1931. It guaranteed the status of Americans resident in Turkey on a most-favored-nation basis. In effect, the obsolete treaty of 1830 was now superseded, and by implication the capitulations were completely ended. The Senate consented to the treaty on May 3, 1932, and exchange of ratifications finally took place in Washington on February 15, 1933.[23]

The diplomats next attacked the unsettled claims issue. The claims had arisen chiefly from Turkish violations of American persons and property between 1914 and 1922. At Lausanne and immediately following, no final solution had been possible, but a note exchange of December 24, 1923, had provided for a mixed-claims commission to meet no later than six months after ratification of the Lausanne Treaty. After the Senate refused to approve the treaty, a new agreement called for a claims commission to meet no later than six months after ratification of treaties of commerce and navigation, and of establishment and residence.[24] Accordingly, the United States reminded the Turks in May of 1933 that the two countries should set up the claims commission. After preliminary discussion about a possible lump-sum payment, the mixed-claims commission held its first meeting in Istanbul on August 15, 1933. It took more than a year to arrive at a settlement, but in October, 1934, it was agreed that the Turkish obligation would be discharged by payment of $1.3 million in thirteen annual installments. Fred K. Nielsen, the claims expert from the Department of State who headed the American delegation, then had to decide on the legitimacy of the many claims filed with the department. He allowed only thirty-three claims totaling about $900,000, the three largest being $261,000 to MacAndrews and Forbes, $192,000 to the American Board of Commissioners for Foreign Missions, and $147,000 to the Socony-Vacuum Oil Company.[25] Since the Nielsen awards aggregated a sum $400,000 short of the liability assumed by Turkey, the department decided to reduce the number of annual payments required, thus winning tremendous appreciation from officials

[23] *FR 1930*, III, 852–872; *FR 1931*, II, 1037–1044; Grew, *TE*, II, 903–906; Roger R. Trask, "The Relations of the United States and Turkey, 1927–1939," unpublished Ph.D. dissertation, The Pennsylvania State University, 1959, pp. 291–299.
[24] See above, Chap. 5, pp. 151–152, 153–154.
[25] *FR 1934*, II, 894–935; Fred K. Nielsen, "General Report," in *American-Turkish Claims Settlement: Under the Agreement of December 24, 1923, and Supplemental Agreements between the United States and Turkey, Opinions and Report*, pp. 4–41. The amounts finally allowed for each claim are listed on pp. 783–784.

of the Turkish Republic. Wallace Murray, chief of the Near Eastern Division, reported that the Turkish ambassador "was obviously deeply stirred on being informed of this offer of the American Government. With tears in his eyes he stated that he was at a loss to give adequate expression to his deep feeling of appreciation of the spirit of uprightness, moral integrity and generosity of our Government. 'This is,' he said, 'incomparably the happiest day of my whole career.'"[26]

An extradition agreement was among the unfinished items on the treaty agenda when Ambassador Grew departed from Turkey in 1932. Talks in 1930 stalemated when the United States refused to accept changes in the 1923 draft desired by the Turks,[27] but two years later the celebrated case of Samuel Insull served to hasten a settlement. Insull, a fugitive from American justice because of his financial machinations uncovered when his utilities empire collapsed, fled to the eastern Mediterranean. After American diplomatic pressure forced Insull to leave Greece, he cruised on a chartered Greek ship, the *Maiotis*, for about two weeks while seeking asylum in a country which would not extradite him. When the ship put in at Istanbul for supplies late in March, 1934, Turkish officials arrested him. Although the United States Senate had approved the extradition treaty of 1923 a few days earlier, the Turkish government had not yet acted. Although there was no extradition agreement actually in effect, a Turkish court decided the fugitive could be extradited under a provision of the Turkish penal code. Insull was turned over to American officials and sent back to Chicago for trial. Under the impetus of this case, the Turkish Grand National Assembly approved the pending extradition treaty; ratifications were exchanged at Ankara on June 18, 1934.[28]

Thus, by 1934, three treaties and a claims settlement formed the new structure of official Turkish-American relations. The perennially troublesome nationality question remained unresolved despite periodic efforts to find a mutually acceptable formula. The central issue was the old con-

---

[26] *FR 1937*, II, 954–958 (quotation, p. 956). For the agreement of 1936 regarding American claims against Turkey for disbursements made while the United States government represented Turkish interests in Washington between 1914 and 1917, see the note and citation in *FR 1936*, III, 529.

[27] *FR 1934*, II, 935–936.

[28] The best account of the relationship of the Insull case to the extradition treaty is in Trask, "United States and Turkey," pp. 315–320. See also *FR 1933*, II, 552–569; *FR 1934*, II, 566–583, 937–939; Francis X. Busch, *Guilty or Not Guilty?*, pp. 133–134.

flict between American acceptance of the right of expatriation and Turkish opposition to this principle. American law required that naturalized Americans be accorded the same protection as native-born citizens, while Turkish regulations proscribed entry of former Turks who had acquired citizenship in another country.[29]

The nationality issue flared up following the Franco-Turkish agreement of 1937 extending the time limit during which Syrians and Lebanese could opt for either Turkish nationality, or for Syrian or Lebanese nationality in accordance with the Lausanne settlement of 1923. Many Americans of Syrian or Lebanese origin wished to opt for the nationality of their native land so that they might inherit property, but American officials cautioned that the exercise of the option would endanger their American citizenship. Assurances from France that these naturalized Americans would be treated as Americans in Syria and Lebanon and, therefore, be accorded inheritance rights, eased this part of the problem. But French assurances could not settle the status of these citizens from the Turkish point of view. Since Turkey would regard these persons as Turkish citizens if they did not elect Syrian or Lebanese citizenship under the option, the State Department again sought a nationality agreement with Turkey to clarify the status of naturalized Americans. In February of 1938 the United States proposed a draft exchange of notes providing that Turkey would renounce the Turkish citizenship of all those coming from areas detached from Turkey by the Lausanne Treaty. The State Department tried to meet Turkish views on two key points: the United States would agree informally to Turkey's right to refuse admission to persons who had given up Turkish nationality, and the United States would agree not to support any claim of a person Turkey regarded as a Turkish citizen at the time of the events giving rise to the claim. For all the protracted discussion between 1938 and 1941, the two nations could not arrive at a meeting of the minds on the nationality problem.[30]

The last agreement arranged during the interwar period, designed to improve the bases for Turkish-American commercial intercourse, was the reciprocal trade agreement of 1939, which superseded the Treaty of Ankara signed in 1929. The Atatürk regime had resorted to extensive regulation of foreign trade and exchange in the 1930s in its effort to build

[29] For a summary of the nationality issue prior to 1937, see Trask, "United States and Turkey," pp. 281–286. See also *FR 1934*, II, 983.
[30] *FR 1937*, II, 923–938; *FR 1938*, II, 1101–1121; *FR 1939*, IV, 849–861; *FR 1940*, III, 1001–1008.

up the Turkish economy. Various regulations, especially those giving preferential terms to German traders, were irritants in the conduct of Turkish-American trade, although Turkish officials tended to interpret rules leniently toward Americans in view of the perennially favorable balance of trade with the United States. The Turks liked the American reciprocal trade agreements program begun in 1934 and suggested that the two countries might arrange such an agreement to replace the Treaty of Ankara. After the United States set in motion its elaborate machinery for study of Turkish-American trade, experts concluded that a treaty was feasible. Many intricate differences had to be ironed out before the agreement was ready for signatures on April 1, 1939. Each nation made tariff reductions on specified products; the Turks finally agreed to forego import restrictions on scheduled items except under limited circumstances; they also agreed to apply equally to all countries restrictions on nonscheduled items. They accepted national treatment for internal taxation. A compromise was arranged on amounts of foreign exchange to be available to American firms. Professor Roger Trask has observed that the press considered the settlement more significant from a political than from an economic point of view because it struck a blow against restrictive trade practices used by totalitarian countries. This view was apparently an illusion, for the treaty did not function so well as hoped, partly because of devices enabling the Germans to increase their trade with Turkey by offering higher prices for Turkish products, thereby improving their exchange position and increasing German exports to Turkey.[31]

When World War II began, however, official Turkish-American relations had been established on a solid treaty basis, reflecting the benefits of the general *rapprochement* achieved in little more than a decade. Several factors made the treaty accommodation possible. On the positive side, each party considered the terms on balance intrinsically advantageous. On the negative side, the agreements reflected the absence of territorial or strategic issues between the two countries. The United States had no territorial ambitions in the eastern Mediterranean, nor did the Turkish Republic threaten the vital interests of the United States. There were few Turks in the United States, and Americans came to

[31] *FR 1934*, II, 940–960; *FR 1935*, I, 1043–1046; *FR 1937*, II, 941–954; *FR 1938*, II, 1052–1101; *FR 1939*, IV, 861–892; *FR 1940*, III, 964–990. The best analysis of the issues and negotiations involved in the reciprocal trade agreement is Trask, "United States and Turkey," pp. 161–177. See also Lewis, *Turkey*, pp. 275–278.

Turkey with irenic intent to pursue philanthropic, cultural, or commercial objectives. Neither nation posed for the other problems central to its foreign policy. Yet both were mindful of advantages accruing from orderly international processes for nations free from aggressive intent and anxious to concentrate on domestic objectives and programs.

The United States and the International Politics of the Turkish Republic

American and Turkish foreign policies during the post-Lausanne era present some interesting similarities and dissimilarities. Geography and tradition allowed the United States a degree of isolation, but Turkey's strategic position at the Straits and as an intercontinental land link did not permit her the luxury of noninvolvement in international politics. However, Atatürk's program calling for forced-draft internal reform did require a climate of international order and stability. As Professor Donald Webster expressed it in 1938, "Isolationism is not a topic for discussion in Turkey. Nor is aggression or expansion!"[32] Turkish and American foreign policy found a common denominator in their mutual interest in a peaceful international system.

Foreign policy was for Atatürk another instrument — a most vital one — for protecting the sovereignty and integrity of his nation from outside intrusion. Turkey's desires for bilateral and multilateral arrangements with her immediate neighbors and for understandings with the greater European powers required her to pay close attention to international politics; this was in sharp contrast to America's proclamation of aloofness from European politics. Although the United States saw no reason to become directly involved in Turkey's international problems, America generally applauded the growing list of treaties between Turkey and her neighbors as evidence of Turkey's growing international responsibility. Turkish friendship with the Soviet Union caused some apprehension in the United States, but the level-headed Turkish leaders, with a keen sense of their own enlightened self-interest, entered into agreements with the Soviets (treaties of friendship in 1921 and 1925, supplemented by a protocol in 1929 and a Soviet loan in 1934). They managed the relationship so well that they protected their northern flank without permitting the virus of Communist ideology to penetrate their people. They did not intend to become mortgaged to Russian imperial-

[32] *The Turkey of Atatürk*, p. 137.

ism and, fortunately for them, the Soviets were at this time preoccupied with their own internal development.[33]

Turkish relations with the recent archenemy, Greece, took a remarkable turn for the better within eight years after the Smyrna evacuation of 1922. Some tension accompanied the population exchanges, but by 1930 prudent leadership on both sides had seized the opportunity to put the past behind them and to solidify their *rapprochement* with a treaty of friendship. By 1934 Turkey had joined Greece, Yugoslavia, and Rumania — all formerly Ottoman domains — in a Balkan Pact pledging mutual respect for each other's territory and consultation on matters of common concern. Turkey participated in a similar entente with her Asian neighbors Iraq, Iran, and Afghanistan, with a pact signed at Sa'dabad in 1937. "Turkey has become the peacemaker of the Near East," proclaimed the American Board. Granting that these two quadrilateral pacts did little to guarantee Turkish security against the growing Italian threat, still they helped establish for Turkey "a solid reputation for reliability, for responsibility in her undertakings, and for devotion to peace."[34]

Turkey's reliance on friendship and nonaggression pacts could not help but win American approval, for the United States was engaged in the pursuit of international stability by way of conciliation, arbitration, and outlawry of war. Secretaries of State Frank B. Kellogg and Henry L. Stimson followed the path laid out earlier by Secretaries Elihu Root, Philander Knox, and William Jennings Bryan by negotiating a series of arbitration and conciliation treaties during the 1920s.[35] In 1928, just as Kellogg was thinking that a conciliation treaty might be a suitable way to inaugurate treaty relations with the Turkish Republic, the Turkish Foreign Minister broached the possibility to Ambassador Grew. Talks carried on between 1928 and 1932 did not lead to a treaty because of Turkey's fear that the United States might sometime try to use the proposed treaty to press the cause of the Armenians. Turkey was not satisfied by American assurances that matters of domestic jurisdiction, to be exempted from the proposed treaty, would certainly include Turkey's

[33] Dankwart A. Rustow, "Foreign Policy of the Turkish Republic," in *Foreign Policy in World Politics*, Roy C. Macridis, ed., pp. 298–299, 301; Lewis, *Turkey*, pp. 278–282; Grew, *TE*, II, 839–842; *FR 1929*, III, 842–845.

[34] Rustow in *Foreign Policy in World Politics*, pp. 299–300 (second quotation); Grew, *TE*, II, 871–872; ABC, *AR 1937*, pp. 7–8 (first quotation).

[35] Robert H. Ferrell, *Peace in Their Time: The Origins of the Kellogg-Briand Pact*, pp. 6, 87, 135, 234, and *passim*.

Armenian citizens. The two nations had been in agreement on broad principles, but Turkish sensitivity over the definition of domestic juris-diction and fear that her sovereignty might be impaired doomed the treaty efforts.[36]

Turkey had also followed with great interest the negotiations leading to the Kellogg-Briand Pact of Paris to outlaw war as an instrument of national policy. Although not invited to be one of the original signatories, Turkey wished to be the first after the United States to ratify the multi-lateral agreement. Ambassador Grew and the Department of State co-operated in speeding word of favorable Senate action, thus enabling Foreign Minister Tevfik Rusdu Aras to leave his sick bed to steer ratifica-tion through the Grand National Assembly.[37]

Time was to prove the superficiality of the disarmament–outlawry-of-war approach to international politics, so attractive in the 1920s, and it is doubtful whether the pragmatic, hard-headed Turks felt that the Kellogg-Briand Pact would go very far toward ensuring their security. Probably the chief attraction of being a signatory was the prestige value in being associated with other nations in so noble an objective as the out-lawry of war. Turkey could also point to her acceptance into the League of Nations in 1932 and her election to the Council two years later as further evidence of her devotion to the cause of international order.

Curiously, although the United States shunned League membership, the League served as a catalyst for easing Turkish-American tension over the narcotics problem. Turkey was one of the world's largest pro-ducers of opium, used in the manufacture of morphine. Because opium cultivation was of considerable economic importance to thousands of Turkish peasants, the government was reluctant to institute controls. Foreign-owned factories in Turkey were the source of much opium which found its way into clandestine international drug traffic. Severe criticism of Turkey in the foreign press for noncooperation in interna-tional controls stung the Turks. Although efforts were being made to bring the international drug traffic under control through the League of Nations, Turkey was not represented at an international conference on the subject until 1930. Turkey also sent representatives to the fourteenth

[36] Grew to Kellogg, July 3, 1928, and Jan. 16, 1929; Murray to Grew, Nov. 12, 1929; Grew to Murray, Dec. 14, 1929, DS 711.6712A/25, 32, 33, and 34; *FR 1928*, III, 940–950.

[37] *FR 1928*, I, 157, 195–196; Grew, *TE*, II, 796–798, 799–800; and 60 enclosures in DS 711.672 Anti-War for the period from April, 1928, through December, 1929.

session of the League's Advisory Commission on Traffic in Opium and Other Dangerous Drugs at Geneva early in 1931. Meanwhile, the United States had protested to Turkey against illicit shipments arriving in American ports. On February 16, 1931, Tevfik Rusdu Aras informed Grew "that largely as a result of our representations concerning the clandestine traffic in narcotics emanating from Turkey the Cabinet had decided immediately to seal up the three factories producing opium derivatives as well as all stocks of the manufactured product now on hand and henceforth to allow no such products to issue from the factories until the manufacturers have submitted documentary proof of destination and Government permits issued." The government was aware of the seriousness of the situation, the Foreign Minister admitted, but it "did not wish to act under fire and had therefore waited until the Commission at Geneva had adjourned and the press campaign against Turkey had abated."[38]

A year later, however, the issue had not been resolved. In a friendly review of the improvement in Turkish-American relations with the acting Foreign Minister just before he left Turkey for reassignment to Tokyo, Grew observed "that there was still one unfortunate element which could exert an adverse effect on these relations; namely, the continued clandestine traffic in narcotics from Turkey to the United States." Under Grew's successor, Ambassador Charles H. Sherrill, the problem was apparently solved. Sherrill took it directly to Atatürk, who prodded the cabinet into adhering to the Hague Convention of 1912 and the Geneva Conventions of 1925 and 1931 for regulating manufacture and sale of narcotics. New legislation also limited and supervised cultivation of drug-producing plants, and established a state monopoly on production and trade in narcotics. Turkey's cooperation elicited much favorable comment in the United States.[39]

Turkey and the United States responded differently to the rising tide of aggression in the middle 1930s. Turkey could not remain indifferent to Mussolini's pronouncement that Italians regarded the Mediterranean as "mare nostrum" and would recreate a Roman Empire. Italian possession of the Dodocanese Islands placed them too near for Turkey's comfort. Turkey's answers were rearmament and pressure for revision of the

[38] Trask, "United States and Turkey," pp. 259–261; Grew, *TE*, II, 883–885 (quotations).
[39] Grew, *TE*, II, 913–914 (quotation); Trask, "United States and Turkey," pp. 261–262; Charles H. Sherrill, *A Year's Embassy to Mustafa Kemal*, pp. 217–223.

Straits regime. The United States responded unsympathetically to Turkish efforts to purchase airplanes and other American products to build up Turkey's military capacity. The State Department demurred on grounds "that, in case of war, this Government could be justly criticized for assisting in the military preparation of one of the parties thereto." Thus, American firms were discouraged from selling products of military significance to Turkey even though Ambassador Robert Skinner recommended giving American traders this opportunity.[40]

These were years of extreme American disillusionment with the bitter fruits of World War I, deepened by preoccupation with monumental domestic problems arising from the Great Depression. Congressional symptoms of American bitterness were the Johnson Debt Default Act, the Nye Senate Munitions Investigation, and the Neutrality Act of 1935. Strong pacifist inclinations were evident in the writings of the "lost generation" and on college campuses. In this climate the United States had no inclination to be a party to Turkish rearmament, preferring to assume a highly moralistic position on the subject of totalitarian aggression.

The Italian threat made the Turks uneasy about their ability to protect their vital interests in the Straits area under the arrangements made at Lausanne in 1923 which provided for an International Control Commission under League of Nations supervision. Although the Turks let their dissatisfaction be known between 1934 and 1936, they bided their time, waiting for an opportune moment, which they felt had arrived in April of 1936. Then they initiated formal negotiations looking toward greater Turkish control over the Straits area. They succeeded in bringing about an international conference at Montreux between June 22 and July 26, resulting in a new convention. It allowed Turkey to rearm the Straits zone and turned over to Turkey the functions of the International Control Commission. The United States had no observers at Montreux, but during and after the conference, the Turks assured the United States that they would fully guarantee American rights under the Montreux Convention. Such assurances made a separate Turkish-American convention unnecessary, although the need for such a bilateral arrangement had been debated in official American circles off and on since 1922.[41]

[40] Rustow in *Foreign Policy in World Politics*, p. 301; *FR 1934*, II, 953–971; *FR 1935*, I, 1046–1051 (quotation, p. 1050); Trask, "United States and Turkey," pp. 138–141.
[41] *FR 1934*, II, 971–990; *FR 1935*, I, 1026–1042; *FR 1936*, III, 503–529; Altemur

The revised Straits agreement achieved at Montreux was a great diplomatic victory for the Turks, not only because of the terms they secured, but also because they had obtained the desired revision by peaceful means. The Turkish reliance on peaceful change stood out in sharp contrast to the methods of revisionist Italy and Germany. Negotiation in good faith commended itself to the Roosevelt administration and increased Washington's esteem for the civilized conduct of foreign relations exemplified by the behavior of Turkish leadership. A decade earlier, although bitterly disappointed over the League of Nations award of Mosul to Iraq in 1925, the Turks had not taken to the battlefield to protest the award.[42]

Shortly before World War II, another situation arose which could have led them to resort to arms, but once again they relied on diplomacy. At issue was the region of Alexandretta, a strategic area with a large Turkish population, which had been incorporated into France's Syrian mandate. France had signed an agreement with the New Turks in 1921 giving Alexandretta a special administration because of its large Turkish population. Turkey did not feel that the electoral regulations permitted Alexandretta Turks adequate voice, and in 1936 they took the issue to the League of Nations Council. The Council granted the sanjak the status of a special political unit by an agreement of January 27, 1937. Not yet satisfied, Turkey shrewdly took advantage of French distresses to bring about recovery of Alexandretta. As part of her price for closer relations with France, Turkey required further recognition of Turkish interests in Alexandretta. France, worried about the German threat, was willing to pay the price by agreeing in 1938 to joint Franco-Turkish administration of the sanjak. After new elections in September registered a Turkish majority, the provincial assembly declared the area to be the autonomous Republic of Hatay. Finally, on September 23, 1939, the French agreed to outright annexation by Turkey in return for the Franco-Turkish Declaration of Mutual Assistance. The United States followed these developments, not with any idea of intervening in the political aspects of the settlement, but only with an eye toward protecting the work of American archaeologists from Princeton University and

Kilic, *Turkey and the World*, pp. 118–122; Trask, "United States and Turkey," pp. 340–344.

[42] Trask, "United States and Turkey," pp. 344–349; Howard in *Middle East Journal*, I, 65–68; Kilic, *Turkey and the World*, pp. 60–61; Rustow in *Foreign Policy in World Politics*, p. 299; Lewis, *Turkey*, p. 250.

the University of Chicago's Oriental Institute in Hatay.[43] Turkish diplomacy had been sharp, but she had not used armed might to press irredentist goals in Hatay. Again, her methods contrasted favorably with those of the totalitarian powers.

American and Turkish foreign policies diverged in their response to the disintegration of international order as Turkey prepared to protect her vital interests against revisionist Italian and German designs, while the United States took a neutral stance. At the same time, the two nations shared the belief that orderly diplomatic processes should govern international change. The United States did not object to Turkey's drawing closer to England and France as threats to their security multiplied. Although the central goals of Turkish and American foreign policy had not converged by 1939, a solid basis of mutual respect had been built up which would facilitate intimate collaboration after World War II when the United States became a full-fledged world power acknowledging vital interests in the Mediterranean and the Middle East.

Turkish-American Diplomacy: Organization and Personnel

At the decision-making nerve center of American foreign policy in Washington, Turkish affairs were under the jurisdiction of the Division of Near Eastern Affairs, established in 1909. After a rather moribund existence under Albert Putney (1913–1920) and lack of continuity under acting or short-term chiefs during the next two years, the division enjoyed a revival under the vigorous leadership of Allen W. Dulles (1922–1926), G. Howland Shaw (1926–1929), and Wallace S. Murray (1929–1942). State Department records suggest that presidents and secretaries of state generally took their cues from the experts in the division, who, in turn, worked harmoniously with the diplomats in the field. The United States was extremely fortunate in four of the five men selected to head the American delegation to Turkey during the interwar years — Admiral Bristol, Joseph C. Grew, Charles H. Sherrill, Robert P. Skinner, and John Van Antwerp MacMurray.

[43] *FR 1936*, III, 483–486; *FR 1938*, II, 1031–1043; *FR 1939*, IV, 832–847; Paul H. Alling, memorandum of telephone conversation with Harold Green (of Socony), July 18, 1939, DS 867.6363/162. For an interpretation favorable to Turkey, see Rustow in *Foreign Policy in World Politics*, p. 302. For a radically different interpretation, see Avedis K. Sanjian, "The Sanjak of Alexandretta (Hatay): Its Impact on Turkish-Syrian Relations (1939–1956)," *Middle East Journal*, 10 (Autumn 1956), 379–382. See also Kilic, *Turkey and the World*, pp. 63–65.

Earlier chapters in this study have shown how large the name of Admiral Mark L. Bristol is written in Turkish-American relations between 1919 and 1927. He saw earlier than most that Americans in Turkey and the United States government would have to face fundamental facts dictated by the change from a corrupt, lethargic, and ineffective government under the Ottoman Empire to the purposeful, progressive, and reforming New Turk regime. His competence and forthright friendliness made a big difference and may even have been decisive during the preliminary stages of the Turkish-American *rapprochement*. Turkish leaders respected and liked him, his Washington superiors trusted and listened to him, and the American colony in Turkey found him a sympathetic advocate of their needs. Surmounting the handicaps put in his way by the energetic but obstructionist anti-Turkish minority in the United States, he achieved some remarkable diplomatic successes, the more notable because he had no previous special training or experience in this field.[44]

Ambassador Grew was able to build on the solid foundation left by Bristol. He was already favorably known to the Turks, particularly to Prime Minister Ismet Inönü through their close association at Lausanne, where Grew's understanding of Turkish aspirations had been warmly appreciated by Ismet. As Under Secretary of State (1924–1927), Grew had been one of the most tireless workers for Senate ratification of the ill-fated Lausanne Treaty.

Grew's talent for winning men's trust opened doors for new treaties and for administrative decisions favorable to American educational, philanthropic, and commercial endeavors in Turkey. His understanding of the temperament of Turkish leaders helped him to attune his methods to the requirements of Turkish nationalism. Indicative of his attitude is a diary entry made soon after his arrival in Istanbul: "I have the greatest admiration for what the Turkish Government has already accomplished, the way it has taken hold of an almost insurmountable problem and already, contrary to many predictions, shown itself potentially capable of solving it. In watching the further development of her destiny, my sympathy will be solidly with Turkey in her larger aims, even if particular measures or decisions call forth my impatience or open wrath." This

[44] Charles Evans Hughes to Bristol, March 28, 1924; Coolidge to Bristol, June 20, 1927, Bristol MSS, Boxes 55 and 12; Gates, *Not to Me Only*, pp. 296, 300; Patrick, *Bosporus Adventure*, p. 205; Ahmed Emin Yalman, *Turkey in My Time*, pp. 78–79.

sympathetic attitude made the ambassador ever alert to the little gestures, which did not go unnoticed by the Turks. For example, at the time of the language reforms in 1928, Grew saw to it that his embassy was the first to use Latin characters on its automobile tags.[45]

In conducting official business with the Turks, Grew's tact produced better results than threats. Grew was convinced "that the two qualities essential to success in dealing with him [the Turk] are first courtesy and second patience, and I would add to these a studious avoidance, in dealing with the higher officials, of any word or gesture reminiscent of the capitulatory regime." Turkish leaders seemed to feel that Grew respected Turkey's sovereignty more scrupulously than did some of his diplomatic colleagues. His method is clearly illustrated in the way he went about protecting American mission schools. When making his representations, Grew was careful to label his remarks as informal rather than formal "and as an appeal rather than as a demand. It helped the Turks to save their face and brings results far more effectively than pugnacity."[46]

Grew's official work was aided by the ready adjustment he and his family made to life in the Turkish Republic, where they were obviously very happy. Little touches in the family's personal behavior helped to establish rapport with the Turks. Daughter Anita's endurance swim from the Black Sea to the Sea of Marmora created a minor sensation. When Anita was married to Robert English in 1932, the ambassador arranged a Turkish civil ceremony as well as a Christian ceremony (presided over by Dr. Gates, president of Robert College), a gesture greatly appreciated by Turkish officials.[47]

The Grews showed genuine regret at leaving Turkey in March of 1932, and their warm feelings for the Turks were reciprocated in a touching leave-taking. Undoubtedly Grew's broad diplomatic experience proved helpful to his work in Turkey, but the secret of his success lay as much in his rare combination of personal traits and energy. These are well illustrated in this diary entry written after four years in Turkey: "Of course I realize, always, that Turkey is a very small spot for the United States on the political map of the world, but my job is to con-

[45] Grew, *TE*, II, 727 (quotation), 748–749, 790, 814. Grew's talent for keen appraisal of the Turkish mentality carried over into his shrewd political analyses of the internal situation in Turkey. See *TE*, II, 859–875, 877–883, 885–888.
[46] Grew, *TE*, II, 805 (second quotation), 814 (first quotation).
[47] Grew, *TE*, II, 899–903, 911–913; Gates, *Not to Me Only*, p. 300.

sider it a large and important spot and to act and think accordingly." [48]

Grew's successor, Charles H. Sherrill, spent less than a year in Turkey.
Previously he had practiced law, engaged in business, and published
a dozen books, many of them dealing with stained-glass tours through
European countries. During President Taft's administration, he served
for two years as American Minister to Argentina. Sherrill used his appointment to Turkey to assemble material for two more books — one
including material on the mosaics of Saint Sophia in Istanbul, the other
a kind of biography of Atatürk based on a series of long interviews with
the Ghazi. Sherrill was not in Turkey long enough to make much of an
imprint on diplomacy, although he did use his personal contacts with
President Atatürk to express American interest in regulation of narcotics
exports from Turkey. American missionaries apparently found Sherrill
acceptable, and he did attempt to build up American exports to Turkey. [49]

Two career men followed Sherrill. In 1933 the Roosevelt administration accredited Robert P. Skinner, a veteran of thirty-six years in the
diplomatic service, who had served since 1926 as minister to Greece and
then to Estonia, Latvia, and Lithuania. While he was in Turkey (1933–
1936), several matters were brought to a successful conclusion. The
claims commission was set up and the extradition treaty was ratified, but
the difficult preparatory work antedated Skinner's tenure. The ambassador interested himself in improving trade relations and unsuccessfully, as indicated earlier, tried to arrange for American firms to sell
planes and arms to Turkey. [50]

John Van Antwerp MacMurray, appointed ambassador in January,
1936, was a career diplomat who had served since 1907 in various assignments in Asia, Eastern Europe, and Washington. Not only had he been
chief of both the Near Eastern and Far Eastern Divisions of the State
Department but accredited as minister to China and to Estonia, Latvia,

[48] Grew, *TE*, II, 913–919. The quotation (p. 899) was an entry in Grew's diary
on August 9, 1931, in connection with the historic nonstop flight from New York to
Istanbul by two Americans, Russell Boardman and John Polando, which Grew believed had beneficial results on Turkish-American friendship. See *TE*, II, 889–899.
[49] *RDS 1933*, p. 253; *Who Was Who in America*, Vol. 1, 1897–1942, p. 1118;
Sherrill, *A Year's Embassy*, pp. 217–233; Sherrill, *Mosaics in Italy, Palestine, Syria,
Turkey and Greece*; Trask, "United States and Turkey," pp. 100–102, 136, 261–262.
Trask indicates that Sherrill was said to be a heavy contributor to the Republican
campaign of 1932 and that his appointment was urged by Republican leaders.
[50] *RDS 1936*, p. 261; Trask, "United States and Turkey," pp. 104, 137–140.

and Lithuania. While in Turkey (1936–1942), he helped arrange the reciprocal trade agreement of 1939 and reported on Turkey's growing *rapprochement* with England and France in the face of the worsening totalitarian threat. In recalling his prewar service in Turkey many years later, he characterized it as "singularly tranquil and uneventful . . . I may be said to have had only a watching brief, in the afterglow of especial friendliness created by Admiral Bristol as High Commissioner and of Grew as our first Ambassador to the new Turkish regime."[51]

Among those on the embassy staff in Istanbul and Ankara who contributed to working out the new friendship, two deserve special mention — Julian Gillespie and G. Howland Shaw. From 1920 until his death in 1939, Gillespie served as trade commissioner and then as commercial attaché at Istanbul, where he became intimately associated with Turkish businessmen and political leaders. The distinguished Turkish journalist, Ahmed Emin Yalman, has written that Gillespie "was a popular and influential figure in Turkey through those years." An ardent Turcophile, Gillespie won many friends among the Turks. His firsthand knowledge and inside view of Turkish affairs were often helpful to the American ambassador. Shaw had served on Admiral Bristol's staff (1921–1926) and at the Lausanne Conference before succeeding Allen Dulles as chief of the Near Eastern Division (1926–1929). In 1930 he returned to Istanbul where, as counselor of the embassy for seven years, his vast knowledge and keen insights underpinned the work of the ambassadors.[52]

During this period, the embassy maintained its headquarters at Istanbul in a building purchased in 1906. A branch was maintained in Ankara, the seat of government, personnel being shifted from time to time as needed. The diplomats reiterated often to the department the inadequacy of embassy facilities and the necessity of establishing the main embassy at Ankara. Finally, property was purchased at Ankara in 1939 for construction of a suitable new embassy building.[53]

American Interests in Turkey between the Wars

The primary purpose of accrediting a diplomatic and consular staff to Turkey and of working out the new treaty structure was to protect

---

[51] *RDS 1942*, p. 195; quotation from MacMurray to Roger R. Trask, Sept. 8, 1958, in Trask, "United States and Turkey," p. 106.
[52] Yalman, *Turkey in My Time*, pp. 126 (quotation), 158–159; Grew, *TE*, II, 833, 851, 859, 860, 890, 893, 896–897, 918; Curti and Birr, *Prelude to Point Four*, p. 183; *Who Was Who in America*, Vol. 1, 1897–1942, p. 456.
[53] Trask, "United States and Turkey," pp. 106–109.

American interests in the new republic. American stakes included the Turkish missions of the Congregationalist American Board; two independent colleges at Istanbul; trade and investment of American businessmen; technical assistance furnished by individual Americans and private organizations; nonmissionary philanthropy; and other cultural enterprises, including archaeological expeditions sponsored by American universities.

Missions. World War I and its aftermath disrupted the work of the American Board in Turkey, particularly in eastern and central Asia Minor where most of the effort had been geared to the large Armenian Christian population. Services of some missionary personnel, displaced from closed stations, had been rechanneled during and after the war into relief work to aid large numbers of destitute refugees.[54] Early in 1922 the American Board carried 137 missionaries on its Turkish roster. Of this number, 110 (about 80 per cent) were actually on duty in the Middle East, 84 carrying on regular missionary tasks, 26 employed by Near East Relief. The remaining 20 per cent were still in the United States or assigned to refugee duty in nearby areas — the Caucasus, Syria, the Aegean Islands, and Greece. The Board still occupied thirteen stations within Turkey, some of them sparsely.[55]

The period of uncertainty extended well into the 1920s, making it difficult for the missionaries to plan with any real assurance for rebuilding a program comparable to that conducted before the war. Political uncertainties dogged them at every step. While Turkey's future was still in flux before the Lausanne settlement, missionary interests looked to the Allies and the United States to write a peace treaty which would protect their vested interests and those of the Christian minorities with whom they had always worked.[56]

The time for decision on the Board's future course was at hand in the fall of 1923 following Lausanne, the issue being whether to continue

[54] *MRW,* 44 (Feb. 1921), 107–115; 45 (Jan. 1922), 35–36, 38; 46 (Jan. 1923), 68; ABC, *AR 1920,* pp. 35–39; ABC, *AR 1922,* pp. 73–74.

[55] The thirteen stations were at Istanbul, Brusa, Izmir, Merzifon (Marsovan), Sivas, Kayseri (Caesarea), Talas, Trabzon (Trebizond), Harput, Tarsus, Adana, Gazientep (Aintab), and Marash. *MRW,* 45 (Feb. 1922), 146–147. As of 1929, old stations at Trabzon, Erzerum, Van, Bitlis, Harput, Diarbekir, and Sivas were vacant. *MRW,* 52 (Aug. 1929), 646.

[56] ABC, *AR 1922,* p. 76; ABC, *AR 1923,* pp. 9–10, 51–55; *MRW,* 43 (May 1920), 321; (July 1920), 583–584; 45 (Nov. 1922), 853; 46 (Jan. 1923), 61, 68; (Feb. 1923), 148–149; (Sept. 1923), 755; (Dec. 1923), 969–971.

large-scale work under drastically altered conditions. Nationalist Turkey had become master of its own house, and the Allies had put their seal of recognition on this fact at Lausanne, having failed to preserve the capitulations. The missionaries' traditional clientele, the Christian minorities, was scattered; if the Board stayed, it would have to shift the burden of its activities to the Moslem Turks, a requirement that was distasteful to some.

Practical considerations triumphed as the American Board elected to remain in Turkey and to make the necessary accommodation to the new nationalism rather than abandon the accumulated effort of a century. The Board's annual report faced the facts:

The effect of the abolition of the Capitulations upon our work has been deep. It has in the first place demanded a complete readjustment in the thinking of those engaged in missionary work in Turkey. They can no longer think of their institutions as being foreign and privileged. These must now be harmonized with the laws of the country and protected by the forces of justice which operate for all the people. Their own lives and property are similarly to be placed on an equality with those of the native people. Nor can the missionaries longer consider themselves privileged advocates of a justice guaranteed from without. They must now be sympathetic supporters of a justice which must be built up from within. It is difficult, if not impossible, for some friends of the Board to make this readjustment in their fundamental attitude toward the position of the American missionaries under Turkish rule.

Victims of their own traditionally hostile estimate of the Turks, the missionaries could not easily escape a past partly of their own making. Nor could their financial and moral backers in the United States throw off at once the product of decades of indoctrination about the wickedness of the Turks.[57] When making the decision to remain, the Board prognosticated accurately that "many things yet remain uncertain. Surprises and disappointment will doubtless follow one another for many years." The years immediately following were indeed trying; missionary activity depended on the sufferance of the Turkish leaders. To make their task more difficult, the missionaries confronted Turkish leadership at its most xenophobic stage. Nationalism was to be the new focus for revitalizing the Turkish people, and nationalism had to play down reli-

[57] ABC, *AR 1923*, pp. 9–10, 51–55 (quotation, p. 52); John Dewey, *Characters and Events: Popular Essays in Social and Political Philosophy*, Joseph Ratner, ed., I, 349–351; *MRW*, 49 (Jan. 1926), 9.

gion and even become a substitute for it.[58] The missionaries were squeezed from two sides at once — by pressures from zealous nationalists (often anticlerical), and by pressures from extreme Moslems who resisted any Christian intrusion.

During these years, Turkish officials placed legalistic impediments in the path of mission hospitals and schools. American doctors were denied licenses unless they had practiced in Turkey before the war; Gazientep (Aintab) hospital was forced to close for a time. Several schools were closed, some permanently, as government officials scanned all foreign schools with a suspicious eye for any practices which might dilute the loyalties of Turkish citizens to the state. Schools remaining open not only had to cease requiring Moslem students to attend Christian worship services but had to accept government-appointed teachers for classes in history, civics, geography, and Turkish language and literature. Eventually, the government selected the textbooks for these subjects.[59]

In imposing these regulations the government was not discriminating against American mission schools alone, for the rules were part of a policy of secularizing all education. Ardent Moslems criticized the government's ban on their schools and insisted that foreign schools not be accorded a privileged position. Placed on the defensive, the government was forced to act in the face of strong feeling against any evidence of proselytizing by mission schools. Perhaps the most notorious case implicated the American Board's school for girls at Brusa, where three women teachers were charged in 1928 with trying to convert three Moslem girls. Moslem feeling in the community was so hostile to the missionaries that the government closed the school and placed the women on trial. The teachers were convicted, but their sentence was very lenient — three days of house arrest and a fine amounting to about one dollar and fifty cents.[60]

[58] ABC, *AR 1923*, p. 55 (quotation); ABC, *AR 1924*, pp. 66–67; *MRW*, 47 (Feb. 1924), 93–94; 48 (May 1925), 347–348.

[59] ABC, *AR 1924*, pp. 67–68; ABC, *AR 1925*, p. 54; ABC, *AR 1926*, p. 79; ABC, *AR 1927*, p. 61; *MRW*, 46 (Dec. 1923), 969–971; 47 (Feb. 1924), 148–149; (March 1924), 224–225; (May 1924), 335–336; (June 1924), 473; (July 1924), 568–569; 48 (Oct. 1925), 818–819; 49 (Jan. 1926), 6–8; (June 1926), 463–464; 52 (Sept. 1929), 727. For a description of the schools operating in 1926, see Frank A. Ross, C. Luther Fry, and Elbridge Sibley, *The Near East and American Philanthropy: A Survey Conducted under the Guidance of the General Committee of the Near East Survey*, pp. 155–160.

[60] Grew, *TE*, II, 755–764, 777, 791–792, 804–805; Scipio, *Thirty Years in Turkey*,

During these transitional years, Admiral Bristol and Ambassador Grew were kept very busy interceding with Turkish authorities in behalf of the missionaries. Frequently they were able to obtain a measure of relief by getting closed schools and hospitals reopened and onerous rules modified.[61]

For their part, the missionaries made a conscientious effort to meet the letter of the law. They took formal religion out of the classroom, but they hoped to demonstrate the virtues of Christianity by stressing Christian ethical and social teachings through friendly personal contacts — "living the life," the missionaries called it. "Not institutions so much as personal relationships are the means; not classroom instruction but personal friendliness is the sure method; not converts to Christianity but those who will follow Jesus' way of life are the fruitage of missionary toil."[62]

Within limits, the government tolerated this "unnamed Christianity," although virulent attacks against the missionaries continued for many years in the nationalist press. An Istanbul newspaper complained in 1926 that "these fanatical Protestants, working like people trying to save valuables from fire, have become inimical to our existence." The new indirect techniques elicited invective from good Moslems and nationalists who found "unnamed Christianity" quite insidious. Teachers might not overtly mention religion, "but by their attitude, their actions, their manner, by the compassion they show to animals, by the help they give to the poor, by loving what is good, by mercy to the unfortunate, they try to show the loftiness of their religion." The critics claimed that innocent Turkish children were taken in by propaganda teaching that all goodness, honesty, and purity stemmed from Christianity. One newspaper warned, "We must awake from our sleep, and we must tell these self-invited guests of ours to desist from this ill-considered ambition of theirs." Furthermore, charged the critics, American schools were "organs of imperialism" whose function was to instill "foreign modes of thought and life" and to engraft American culture on native youth under the guise of character building. They were also guilty of educating the children of the wealthy class. Foreign schools could not develop the kind of citi-

p. 213; *MRW*, 51 (March 1928), 242–243; (Aug. 1928), 674; ABC, *AR 1928*, p. 69; *FR 1928*, III, 964–981; Trask, "United States and Turkey," pp. 221–226.
[61] *MRW*, 47 (March 1924), 224–225; *FR 1927*, III, 804–812.
[62] ABC, *AR 1925*, p. 55. See also ABC, *AR 1924*, pp. 72–73; ABC, *AR 1926*, p. 79; ABC, *AR 1927*, p. 62; *MRW*, 49 (Jan. 1926), pp. 6–8, 68; (June 1926), 463–464.

zens Turkey wanted, and good Turks would not send their children to be hypnotized in these "houses of exploitation." [63]

The nationalistic climate forced the trustees of International College at Izmir to suspend operations. The missionary background of the college and the fact that it had catered almost exclusively to the Christian minorities before the establishment of the republic did not contribute to its popularity in the city which had been the focus of Greek ambitions and the site of the fire and evacuation in 1922. Even though college officials converted their work to training young Turks, nationalist feeling did not welcome this foreign intrusion. When the trustees, deciding that the position of the college was untenable, closed it in 1934, the periodical *Birlik* rejoiced that "the scorpion's nest in Izmir, the American college, is closed." Two years later it relocated in Beirut where it took over preparatory school and agricultural departments for the American University of Beirut.[64]

Yet a new accommodation was slowly worked out between the missionaries and the Turks. By the late 1920s there were signs of a modus vivendi attributable to changes in attitude and behavior on both sides. The missionaries developed a healthy respect for the extraordinary record of the new Turkish leadership. These were not the old Turks of Ottoman days, after all. Moreover, death or retirement removed from missionary ranks many whose memory of former privileges had made adjustment to new conditions most difficult. Concurrently, the Turkish Republic was maturing and gaining confidence. As successful diplomacy improved relations with immediate neighbors and the former Allied Powers, the xenophobic content of Turkish nationalism diminished. The New Turks saw that Western assistance could speed their progress toward modernization. Although they made great strides in establishing government schools, there was still a gap between accomplishments and needs. Missionary education, if properly purged of offensive religious content, could be harmonized with nationalistic objectives. If the government had wished to terminate mission schools entirely, it had a weapon in an order of 1930 requiring heavy taxes on income from dona-

[63] *MRW*, 49 (Jan. 1926), 68–69; (March 1926), 207–208; 51 (June 1928), 467–470; 54 (Sept. 1931), 709; 55 (March 1932), 181–182; 57 (March 1934), 115–116; 58 (Feb. 1935), 89. The direct quotations in the text are from translations of Turkish press articles quoted in several of the foregoing references.
[64] *MRW*, 57 (Sept. 1934), 420; 58 (Feb. 1935), 89 (quotation); Penrose, *AUB*, pp. 261–269.

tions and gifts. When Ambassador Grew pointed out to Prime Minister Inönü that enforcement of this regulation would mean withdrawal of American schools, the authorities interpreted the rules so as to exempt American schools.[65]

The missionary schools made a serious effort to stress "education for life" by enlarging their vocational and technical programs and by emphasizing agriculture, home economics, health, and trades. Turkish authorities responded by sending a number of scholarship students to missionary institutions.[66]

Ironically, just as relations improved, the Great Depression forced the American Board to retrench. Although the percentage of total funds allocated to Turkish missions did not change significantly, the dollar amount had to be shaved annually between 1932 and 1939. Even with the curtailment forced by the Turkish government's restricting primary education to government schools, reduced income forced the American Board to make additional retrenchments.[67]

American consuls reported in 1939 that the Board operated a forty-bed hospital at Gazientep (Aintab) and continued some work at the Adana hospital, although it had been officially closed since 1934. At Talas, an American doctor carried on medical and social work. One unmarried missionary conducted a reading room at Mardin. These together with Tarsus College (a boys' *lycée*), American Collegiate Institute for girls at Goz Tepe (an Izmir suburb), the American Academy for Girls at Scutari, the boys' trade school at Kayseri-Talas, and the publication center in Istanbul were all that remained of the American Board enterprises in Turkey. The missionary force had dwindled to fifty-four.[68]

[65] ABC, *AR 1927*, pp. 60–62; ABC, *AR 1928*, p. 69; ABC, *AR 1929*, p. 189; ABC, *AR 1932*, p. 14; ABC, *AR 1933*, p. 3; Grew, *TE*, II, 811–814, 852–854, 858; *FR 1930*, III, 873–879; *MRW*, 48 (Feb. 1925), 147–148; (Sept. 1925), 663, 727; 49 (Jan. 1926), 10–11; 50 (May 1927), 343–348; 52 (Dec. 1929), 967; 53 (Jan. 1930), 11–12.

[66] ABC, *AR 1926*, p. 79; ABC, *AR 1927*, p. 61; ABC, *AR 1929*, p. 189; *MRW*, 52 (Dec. 1929), 967.

[67] ABC, *AR 1932*, pp. 112, 115; ABC, *AR 1933*, pp. 37–38; ABC, *AR 1934*, pp. 38, 39; ABC, *AR 1935*, p. 43; ABC, *AR 1936*, p. 43; ABC, *AR 1938*, p. 49; ABC, *AR 1939*, p. 63; *MRW*, 55 (March 1932), 181–182; 56 (Dec. 1933), 615; 57 (June 1934), 262; 58 (Feb. 1935), 89. See also Trask, "United States and Turkey," pp. 241–242.

[68] William C. Young (vice-consul, Izmir) to Hull, April 12, 1939; Frederick P. Latimer, Jr. (consul, Istanbul) to Hull, May 15, 1939, DS 811.5031 Near East/305 and 321; ABC, *AR 1939*, pp. 40–41. Thirty-four additional missionaries served in other posts of the Near East Mission of the American Board at Aleppo, Athens, Beirut, Sofia, and Thessaloniki.

The Independent Colleges. Although World War I had less seriously disrupted Robert College and Istanbul College for Women than the missionary enterprises, the colleges were faced with urgent problems of heavy indebtedness and plant deterioration. To coordinate the attack on mutual financial problems, Robert College and the American University of Beirut set up a joint New York office in 1920. Two years later the women's college joined them, and within a few years several other American colleges in the Middle East became associated. Funds raised through the New York office discharged wartime debts and increased endowments during the 1920s. Cooperative fund-raising proved so advantageous that the colleges incorporated the Near East College Association in 1927 to coordinate purchase of supplies, recruitment of staff, and fund drives.[69]

Adjustment to the new Turkish nationalism was the major continuing problem confronting the Istanbul colleges during the interwar period. By the early 1920s, Robert was enrolling nearly 600 students and the Women's College about 500, in each case roughly divided between preparatory and college divisions. Moslem Turks contributed a growing proportion to the student bodies, although the colleges still retained a strong cosmopolitan flavor. The colleges enjoyed a somewhat smoother relationship with the Atatürk regime than did the mission schools, but all were subject to the administrative orders and laws governing foreign schools. This meant, therefore, that the colleges could not teach religion and that Turkish teachers eventually took over the courses in history, civics, geography, Turkish language and literature, and that new textbooks prepared under government auspices had to be used. Robert was required to appoint a Turkish vice president. Adaptation to the government's secularization program and compliance with nationalist objectives were less difficult for the independent colleges without official ties to the mission board; still, the colleges did not escape entirely from criticism in the nationalist press branding them agents of cultural imperialism. There was also the expulsion of Dean Edgar J. Fisher of Robert

[69] Dodge, AR 1939, p. 10; Dodge, AR 1948, pp. 11–15; Hester Donaldson Jenkins, *An Educational Ambassador to the Near East: The Story of Mary Mills Patrick and an American College in the Orient*, p. 261; Scipio, *Thirty Years in Turkey*, pp. 158–159; Penrose, *AUB*, pp. 169, 223, 261; Patrick, *Bosporus Adventure*, pp. 211–212; Frances C. Mattison, ed., *A Survey of American Interests in the Middle East*, p. 91. Some accounts give the incorporation date for the NECA as 1928.

College for furnishing translations of the official Turkish history to an American who wrote a critical review for an American educational periodical. Fisher himself had not written anything hostile, but the Turkish government asked him to leave in 1934 because the reviewer acknowledged his aid in translation.[70]

Government policies other than those designed specifically to secularize education sometimes complicated college administration, as when President Gates of Robert had difficulty obtaining authority for the college to acquire title to properties listed under the names of private persons. Admiral Bristol helped gain permission to effect the change. Through much of the interwar period the colleges, like the missions, were threatened with heavy taxation. As each crisis came to a head, diplomatic intercession persuaded the Turkish government that excessive taxation would drive American educational and philanthropic institutions out of the country, to the great detriment of Turkish-American relations. Concluding that these institutions did the country more good than harm, Turkish officials agreed to interpret the tax laws favorably to the colleges.[71]

The American colleges commended themselves to Turkish officials through their technical programs. Robert's engineering staff had sometimes served the government without fee as consultants by making surveys and submitting estimates and plans for electric lighting, water supply, paving, sewage disposal, and comparable projects. Here too was a source of help for a country eager to train its young people in engineering, scientific agriculture, public health, and other practical fields where trained people were urgently needed. The New Turks were much attracted by the contemporary American educational philosophy that advocated training to meet the everyday problems of modern life. As early as 1925, the government paid the expenses of more than two dozen students enrolled at Robert to study engineering. When trained, these students would be expected to install and maintain public utilities and other modern conveniences. As a token of its willingness to help in pre-

[70] Gates, *Not to Me Only*, pp. 296–297, 301–302, 314; Scipio, *Thirty Years in Turkey*, pp. 213–214, 224–226, 258; MRW, 43 (Dec. 1920), 1074; 45 (Jan. 1922), 65–66; 49 (Dec. 1926), 898; 57 (June 1934), 262; 58 (Feb. 1935), 89. In 1926, when Robert had its largest enrollment (690) up to that time, it claimed twenty-two nationalities among the student body. MRW, 50 (April 1927), 316.

[71] Gates, *Not to Me Only*, p. 300; Trask, "United States and Turkey," pp. 231–237.

paring specialists, the college set up a new agricultural program in 1925.[72]

Trends at Istanbul College for Women reflected to a lesser extent an effort to train Turkish women for professional or technical services so they could contribute to national goals. At both colleges some teachers questioned the trend toward vocationalism, which struck them as inimical to their traditional humanistic orientation and to their strong commitment to character building.[73]

Internally, both colleges encountered administrative problems related to their adjustment to Turkish nationalism. Ambassadors Grew and Sherrill informed the State Department of official hints of displeasure that the colleges had insufficiently adapted to the new Turkish environment. These criticisms came at a time of dual crisis in the early thirties. On the one hand was the problem of transitional leadership. President Gates, in charge at Robert since 1903, seemed unable in his later years to furnish vigorous, forward-looking leadership. Through retirement in 1924, Women's College had lost Mary Mills Patrick, who had completed more than a half century of service in Turkey, thirty-four years of it as president of the college. Her successor, Kathryn Newell Adams, apparently led the college too slowly in the direction desired by Turkish officials, who complained that they wanted more women trained to face Turkey's practical problems.[74]

The issue of leadership came to a head in 1932 when the effects of the Great Depression were beginning to press hard on both colleges. For financial reasons the trustees decided to merge the administrations of the two colleges, and they sought a president who could pilot a course compatible with the nationalistic program. They selected Dr. Paul Monroe, head of Columbia University's Institute of International Education. Monroe was known in the Middle East as the man who had headed an educational survey team sent out by Near East Relief in 1924, and a second mission requested by the government of Iraq in 1932. His surveys

[72] Scipio, *Thirty Years in Turkey*, pp. 207–208, 214, 216–218, 255; *MRW*, 48 (Dec. 1925), 976; 49 (Sept. 1926), 728; 54 (Jan. 1931), 72. The agricultural program was a depression casualty.
[73] Scipio, *Thirty Years in Turkey*, pp. 240, 255; *MRW*, 47 (March 1924), 225; 49 (March 1926), 229; 50 (May 1927), 392–393; 51 (March 1928), 243; 52 (June 1929), 480; Grew to Stimson, June 29, 1931, DS 367.1162/155.
[74] Grew to Stimson, July 28, 1930, DS 367.1164/134; Grew to Stimson, June 29, 1931, DS 367.1162/155; Grew, *TE*, II, 876; Gates, *Not to Me Only*, p. 324; *MRW*, 47 (July 1924), 488; (Sept. 1924), 665; (Dec. 1924), 1007; 50 (Dec. 1927), 885.

had recommended educational programs to serve community needs — health, self-support, economic rehabilitation, and family life. During his administration (1932–1935), Monroe stressed the need for American institutions to "educate for life." Disheartened by the financial plight of the colleges, he felt that the circumstances confined him largely to a holding operation.[75]

More sanguine about the future of the colleges was Monroe's successor, William Livingston Wright, Jr. Long a student of the Middle East, Wright had the benefit of firsthand acquaintance with the area. At the time of his appointment he was a member of the history staff at Princeton University. Having an unusual flair for languages, he became proficient in Turkish within a relatively short time, to the delight of the Turks. His optimism helped to lift the spirits of the staff, which had become demoralized about prospects.[76]

Shortly before World War II, the colleges were performing notable service in training a small number of Turks for leadership. Robert enrolled 554 students — 313 in the academy, 96 in the college of arts and sciences, and 145 in the engineering school. A staff of sixty-three, including thirty-four Americans presided over the college, which claimed local property with a book value of about $1.5 million, and an endowment with a book value of $3.2 million. The Istanbul College for Women's staff of forty-one (sixteen of them Americans) took care of 354 students, with 255 in the preparatory department and 99 in the college. Book value of local investments was $1.25 million and the endowment nearly $2.5 million.[77]

American Business in Turkey. The archives of the Department of State and private papers of American diplomats reveal extravagant expectations for American trade and investments in Turkey after World

[75] Gates, *Not to Me Only*, p. 324; Scipio, *Thirty Years in Turkey*, p. 255; Curti and Birr, *Prelude to Point Four*, pp. 197–198; Sherrill to Stimson, Nov. 1, 1932, DS 367.1164 R 54/83. Scipio has written (pp. 257–258): "Our situation was bad and Doctor Monroe was discouraged from the beginning with good reason. He remarked from time to time that his greatest wish was to keep the college alive while he was there. He saw little hope of making progress, largely because of our financial situation, and he was not alone in his point of view as some of the older members of the staff agreed with him." See also Trask, "United States and Turkey," pp. 244–245.
[76] Scipio, *Thirty Years in Turkey*, pp. 257–258; Gates, *Not to Me Only*, pp. 324–325; *MRW*, 58 (July 1935), 384; Trask, "United States and Turkey," p. 245.
[77] Latimer to Hull, May 15, 1939, DS 811.5031 Near East/321.

War I.[78] In the belief that the mature industrial economy of the United States required foreign markets and capital outlets, various governmental agencies were anxious to build up exports to Turkey. Despite encouragement from both the American and Turkish governments, no striking increases were recorded in the interwar period.[79]

America's imports from Turkey consisted chiefly of agricultural products, of which tobacco was consistently far in the lead. Fruits, nuts, wool, and late in the interwar period, chrome, were also on the list. Turkey's major imports from the United States consisted of automobiles, machinery, parts and accessories, and petroleum products.[80] The trade was more important to Turkey than to the United States in dollar volume, percentage of total foreign trade, and in balance of trade, which was favorable to Turkey and provided her with foreign exchange needed for economic development.[81]

The nature of the products exchanged had a bearing on American investment in Turkey. Branches of American tobacco firms — Liggett and Meyers, American Tobacco, and R. J. Reynolds — had sizable property holdings, especially at Izmir. MacAndrews and Forbes, licorice merchants, had property at Izmir worth $365,000 in 1938. Likewise, American exports of petroleum products required from the leading

[78] The Bristol MSS are a case in point; they contain much evidence of the admiral's efforts to build up American trade in Turkey. The effort of the Bureau of Foreign and Domestic Commerce to promote a market for American tractors in Asia Minor is brought out in Sheldon L. Crosby (chargé d'affaires a.i., Istanbul) to Kellogg, June 30, 1927, DS 667.1115/13. See also B. C. Poole (chargé d'affaires a.i., Istanbul) to Kellogg, Jan. 4, 1928, DS 711.67/63.

[79] Lewis V. Thomas and Richard N. Frye, *The United States and Turkey and Iran*, pp. 147–148; Trask, "United States and Turkey," p. 129.

[80] Trask, "United States and Turkey," pp. 145–150; Mustafa Nebil Kazdal, "Trade Relations between the United States and Turkey, 1919–1944," unpublished Ph.D. dissertation, Indiana University, 1946, p. 110. See Table 9, p. 112, for "Ratio of American Tobacco Imports from Turkey to Total American Imports from Turkey, 1919–1938." See also the elaborate analysis of the reciprocal trade agreement of 1939, including background material on Turkish-American trade between 1923 and 1938 in Department of State, *Press Releases*, 20 (April 8, 1939), 265–287.

[81] Kazdal, "Trade Relations," pp. 110–111, indicates that the percentage of American exports to and imports from Turkey was generally less than one-half of one per cent of the total American imports and exports. The highest figures were between 1919 and 1921 when imports made up .58 per cent of total imports, and exports .39 per cent of total exports. After that "the figures have been insignificant." Between 1919 and 1922, however, Turkish exports to and imports from the United States comprised as high as 60 per cent of total Turkish exports and 34 per cent of Turkish imports. After 1922, Turkish exports to the United States fell below the 1919–1922 level; between 1923 and 1940 exports to the United States usually ranged between 10 and 15 per cent of the total. See also Trask, "United States and Turkey," p. 150.

American firm in Turkey, Socony-Vacuum, an investment of $2.5 million in Istanbul and Izmir by the late 1930s. Various importing agencies and firms, owned and managed by Turkish citizens, handled a variety of imports and exports. For example, the distinguished journalist, Ahmed Emin Yalman, turned to importing for a number of years, specializing in Goodyear products and Dodge automobiles.[82]

State intervention in the Turkish economy raised a number of legal and administrative handicaps to trade and investment. Labor regulations and restrictions on volume of imports by products and countries were rather irritating for American businessmen, but state control of foreign exchange payments earned by foreign companies was the most serious commercial difficulty in the late 1930s.[83]

Some American capital found its way to Turkey for investment in local manufacturing. Most notable, perhaps, was the Ford Motor Company's assembly plant, set up in a tariff-free zone at Istanbul with government permission in 1930. While in operation this plant turned out approximately 4500 assemblies annually, thus stimulating the importation of American components and parts. The Curtiss-Wright Corporation leased a government plant at Kayseri where it assembled planes ordered by the Turkish government. Another sizable investment was that of the Turkish-American Investment Corporation of Delaware, which acquired the match monopoly from the government in 1930 in return for the pledge of a ten-million-dollar loan. Several other negotiations for private investment were undertaken, but proved abortive.[84]

There were, of course, other items of noncommercial nature in the balance of payments picture. The appreciable expenditures for American missions and colleges have been mentioned earlier. Immigrant remittances continued to be of some significance, reaching an estimated one million dollars in 1929, and must have been even larger prior to the exchange of Anatolian Greeks. In 1929 American tourists spent approxi-

[82] Young to Hull, April 12, 1939; Latimer to Hull, May 15, 1939, DS 811.5031 Near East/305 and 321; Yalman, *Turkey in My Time*, pp. 158–159.

[83] Trask, "United States and Turkey," pp. 129–137, 142–145, 182–187. Trask covers such points as conflicting sanitary standards on foodstuffs, port regulations, certificates of origin, infringements of American trademarks by Turkish firms, tariff schedules, exchange controls, and quota and compensation systems. On unsatisfactory trade relations between the two countries, see *FR 1934*, II, 940–960; on the foreign exchange problem, see *FR 1939*, IV, 866–892; *FR 1940*, III, 944–957.

[84] Trask, "United States and Turkey," pp. 190–198; Grew to Stimson, March 6, 1930, DS 867.659 Matches/—. Other documents regarding the match enterprise are located in DS 867.51 Turkish-American Investment Corp.

mately $750,000 in Turkey, and American businessmen and government officials, spending in excess of their official incomes, accounted for another half million in 1929.[85]

The Turkish government's interest in attracting American capital was apparent in the economic mission of a former Minister of Finance, Saradjoglou Shukri Bey, late in 1931. His aim was to raise a large loan in American money markets, to be used for public works and bank credits, and to interest American firms in developing Turkey's cotton industry. Shukri found the American money market so depressed that a loan was not feasible, but he did lay the groundwork for the hiring of American cotton specialists to come to Turkey to improve cultivation of that important crop. He was well pleased with his cordial reception in the United States.[86]

American Technical Assistance. The development of the young Turkish Republic was furthered not only by the work of the missionary schools and medical services, the independent colleges, and by capital investment, but by American technical assistance furnished by private persons or teams at the request of the Turkish government. Americans were called upon to give advice and assistance in many fields: education, cotton culture, mineral prospecting, public health, nursing, communications, and general economic development. Turkey did not, of course, rely exclusively on Americans; advisers also came from the highly developed European countries.

The Atatürk regime assigned high priority to creating a system of public education which would equip the population with the basic skills required for modernization. To give counsel, the government invited experts from England, France, Germany, and the United States. It is not surprising that the American representative was John Dewey, from Teachers College, Columbia University, whose philosophy of educating young people for practical, everyday living had great appeal for the reforming Turks. Dewey's direct influence on education in Turkey is difficult to determine, but subsequent statements by Atatürk and other leaders, expressing approval of the American mode of life and educational methods, suggest the continuing impact of Dewey's thought. Another American educator, one who served in Turkey for several years, was Dr. Beryl Parker, whose work in kindergarten and primary educa-

---

[85] Gordon, *American Relations with Turkey*, p. 63.
[86] Grew, *TE*, II, 907–909; Trask, "United States and Turkey," pp. 187–189.

tion was sponsored by a private association, the American Friends of Turkey.[87]

Concerned with public health, Turkish leaders retained an American engineer and a superintendent of the School of Nursing to work with the Ministry of Public Health. The Rockefeller Foundation also co-operated in public health and medical programs, as did Surgeon William W. King, of the U.S. Public Health Service, who acted as consultant to the Sanitary Commission in 1924.[88]

The New Turks considered it urgent that national resources be de-veloped as a foundation for improving economic conditions. Dr. Stanley P. Clark, of the University of Arizona, worked at Adana for ten years on problems of cotton culture for the Ministry of Agriculture. An observer called him "the most outstanding example of what a technical assistant can accomplish if he has the practical training and instincts, is willing to get into the life of the country, get his hands dirty and has the in-stinct for friendship and understanding of the people with whom he is working."[89]

Several American engineers came to search for minerals. The Ministry of Defense hired two aviation engineering mechanics from the Glenn Martin and Vultee staffs in 1938. Curtiss-Wright also assisted with gov-ernment aerial surveys, planning commercial air routes, and establishing airmail service. The Turkish government requested additional American specialists in hydrography, highway engineering, flood control, police instruction, and military aviation, but was apparently unable to obtain them.[90]

[87] Curti and Birr, *Prelude to Point Four*, p. 198; Scipio, *Thirty Years in Turkey*, p. 214; Jefferson Patterson to Stimson, June 19, 1930, DS 867.61/2; Grew, *TE*, II, 876; Wallace S. Murray, "Turkey Looks to America," Department of State, *Press Releases*, 8 (May 6, 1933), 321; Trask, "United States and Turkey," p. 117. John Dewey, *Characters and Events*, I, 324–351, reprints his interesting articles on con-temporary Turkey published in the *New Republic* in 1924 and 1925. For details on educational progress under the Republic, see Webster, *The Turkey of Atatürk*, pp. 210–239.
[88] Latimer to Hull, May 15, 1939, DS 811.5031 Near East/321; *FR 1924*, II, 743–745. For the work of the Rockefeller Foundation in Turkey, see the organization's annual reports.
[89] Goldthwaite H. Dorr to Merle Curti, Oct. 23, 1951, quoted in Curti and Birr, *Prelude to Point Four*, p. 183.
[90] Trask, "United States and Turkey," pp. 197, 201–203, 207; Latimer to Hull, May 15, 1939, DS 811.5031 Near East/321; Murray in *Press Releases*, 8:321. Among the American advisers listed by Murray were Charles E. Bell, railway adviser; Matthew Van Siclen, formerly of the Bureau of Mines, gold mining exploitation; Sidney Paige, formerly of the Geological Survey, general mining adviser; Robert

The most ambitious undertaking by American experts was a comprehensive economic survey in 1933 and 1934. As early as 1924 the Turkish government had informally sounded out the State Department about hiring an American financial adviser. Allen Dulles, then chief of the Near Eastern Division, did not believe the Turks were prepared psychologically to give an adviser wide power to act, without which, well-qualified economists were reluctant to consider the post.[91] Of a different character was the assignment undertaken a decade later by a team of experts headed by Walker D. Hines, who had managed the federal railway administration during World War I. On the basis of a detailed survey, the team was to draw up a plan for future economic development. When Hines died while engaged in the project, his chief assistant, Goldthwaite Dorr, took over. He called in Professor Edwin W. Kemmerer of Princeton, who had extensive experience in making economic surveys in foreign countries, to help complete the plan and to prepare special reports on money and banking. The experts also reported on railways, resources, and education. Their major report of 1800 pages, "A General Economic Survey of Turkey, 1933–1934," concluded that Turkey's basic need — greater efficiency in production — required improved transportation and communication, "the opening of minds to the new order," improvement of internal security and health, "and the application in the shop and on the farm of better techniques and practical knowledge." The report also pointed out the need for financial stability and a revamped tax structure. The goal, in short, should be improvements in agriculture and transportation — the prerequisites for later large-scale industrial development.[92]

After the report was translated into Turkish and printed, copies were distributed to members of the Grand National Assembly. Unfortunately, the report appeared just as Mussolini proclaimed Italian ambitions in the Mediterranean, and Turkish defense preparations diverted funds which might otherwise have implemented the economic development

H. Vorfield, formerly of the Tariff Commission, reorganization of customs administration; Wallace Clark, formerly of the Shipping Board, reorganization of the government monopolies on tobacco, alcohol, and salt. In 1935 the State Department rejected the Turkish government's request for the assignment of an American army officer to serve as an instructor in the Turkish air force. This request came at the time when the Nye munitions hearings were in progress and American policy ran strongly toward neutrality and noninvolvement. See *FR 1935*, I, 1052–1053.

[91] Memorandum of conversation between Dr. William S. Culbertson, A. W. Dulles, and Richard B. Southgate, Oct. 23, 1924, DS 867.51A/15.

[92] Curti and Birr, *Prelude to Point Four*, pp. 184–185.

program. There is evidence that Turkish officials found the report a guide and inspiration for many years thereafter, but General Brehon B. Somervell, a member of the survey team, wrote in 1951 that "as to how much good the report did, only Allah knows."[93]

The Turks turned to the United States for technical assistance for several reasons. They felt somewhat easier about employing American advisers than European because the United States had historically refrained from political or territorial ambitions in Turkey. The generally good record of American philanthropy and cultural enterprise was also an endorsement. The Turks admired the technical achievements of the United States and the practical attitude Americans exhibited toward material progress. The use of American experts during the interwar period was a prelude to the vast technical and economic assistance programs of the United States government following World War II.

Other Philanthropic and Cultural Contacts. Philanthropic motivation permeated American missionary, educational, and technological assistance which has just been described. Another evidence of the same impulse was the private hospital founded in 1920 at Istanbul. Known as the American Hospital until 1945, when the name was changed to the Admiral Bristol Hospital to honor the memory of the man who had promoted its founding, it admitted Turkish as well as Western patients. Ambassador Grew took a warm interest in the hospital, assisting when it was in crucial financial straits in 1930 by making a radio appeal in the United States for funds. He secured the assistance of John D. Rockefeller, Jr. Early in 1938, $200,000 had been accumulated in a building fund to increase the capacity from forty to sixty beds. Building was in progress in 1939. By that time the only two Americans on the staff — Dr. Lorrin A. Shepard, the medical director, and Dora F. Shank, superintendent of nurses — supervised six Turkish doctors, ten graduate nurses, and five student nurses of the school of nursing connected with the hospital. At that time, the school of nursing had graduated more than one hundred nurses.[94]

A second private hospital at Manisa, near Izmir, was endowed by a Turkish-American, Morris Schinasi, an immigrant who became a well-

[93] Quoted in *ibid.*, p. 186. See also Trask, "United States and Turkey," pp. 203–206.

[94] Patrick, *Bosporus Adventure*, pp. 215–222; Yalman, *Turkey in My Time*, p. 79; Grew, *TE*, II, 856–858; Trask, "United States and Turkey," pp. 255–257; Latimer to Hull, May 15, 1939, DS 811.5031 Near East/321.

to-do tobacco merchant. In his will he provided for the construction and endowment of the International Morris Schinasi Hospital, completed in 1933 at a cost of $200,000. In 1938 the all-Turkish staff of the thirty-bed hospital admitted approximately 500 patients and treated 7000 more in the clinic.[95]

The Y.M.C.A. and Y.W.C.A. operated in Turkey under American auspices, carrying on activities akin to and supplementing missionary and collegiate work. The Ys offered classes in languages, typing, book-keeping, and millinery; sponsored social service projects; and conducted recreational work. Both maintained summer camps on the Sea of Marmora, and the Y.W.C.A. also operated a playground at Merzifon, and at Istanbul a girls' orphanage, a model kindergarten, and a day nursery at the largest cigarette factory in Turkey. These organizations were often the target of nationalists who called them American devices for "peaceful penetration" and accused them of proselytizing. In 1939, when the Istanbul Y.M.C.A. was completing twenty-five years of service and claimed 581 members, the government closed it in compliance with a law of 1938 requiring that all local associations must have their head-quarters in Turkey. Many of its activities were continued by the American School of Languages and Commerce, under the supervision of the Turkish Department of Public Instruction.[96]

When disaster struck in Turkey, Americans were quick to help in alleviating human misery. Near East Relief continued its prodigious efforts, chiefly in behalf of the Armenian and Greek minorities, into the post-World War I years. Its work subsided as the minorities departed, and the organization virtually withdrew from Turkey by 1924. In later years, in times of earthquakes and floods, the American Red Cross rushed in relief supplies and cooperated with the Turkish Red Crescent Society. American relief also helped a considerable number of White Russian refugees located in Istanbul between the wars.[97]

[95] Trask, "United States and Turkey," pp. 257–258; Young to Hull, April 12, 1939, DS 811.5031 Near East/305. The endowment income was administered by the Chemical National Bank of New York City.

[96] Latimer to Hull, May 15, 1939, DS 811.5031 Near East/321; Scipio, *Thirty Years in Turkey*, p. 189; *MRW*, 43 (April 1920), 307; 44 (May 1921), 412; 45 (Aug. 1922), 658; 47 (May 1924), 398; (June 1924), 472; 48 (May 1925), 348; 49 (Jan. 1926), 11, 68–69; (Nov. 1926), 898; 50 (May 1927), 346; 51 (March 1928), 242; 61 (Oct. 1938), 508; Ross, Fry, and Sibley, *The Near East and American Philanthropy*, pp. 160–161; *FR 1940*, III, 990–1001; Mattison, *American Interests in the Middle East*, p. 96.

[97] *MRW*, 43 (Jan. 1920), 72–73; (April 1920), 307–308; 44 (Jan. 1921), 72;

The Turkish Republic before World War II

In their philanthropic activities, Americans had made little effort to bring Turks into a genuine partnership until the American Friends of Turkey was organized in June of 1930. Its founders described it as "a humanitarian organization, having as its purpose the promotion of a better understanding and the development of goodwill between the peoples of Turkey and of the United States." The American Friends of Turkey was an outgrowth of work begun by Asa K. Jennings. As secretary of the International Y.M.C.A. of the United States and Canada, Jennings had played a prominent part in the relief work at the time of the Smyrna disaster in 1922. Assisted by a committee of three Turks and three Americans, Jennings began in 1925 to organize Turkish-American clubs, asserting that "the movement, international, interracial, non-sectarian and non-political, will be based on a program which will seek to develop spirit, mind and body." The clubs were especially active in sponsoring child welfare work.[98]

Jennings' ideas attracted the interest of a number of internationally-minded men brought together in 1930 by William H. Hoover of the vacuum cleaner firm.[99] They designated Jennings executive vice president of the new organization, the American Friends of Turkey. With the cooperation of the Turkish government, Jennings organized a mixed coordinating group of six Turks and three Americans; the Turks established the Society for the Promotion and Support of Good Works to cooperate in setting up playgrounds, libraries, sports clubs, and prenatal, baby, and dental clinics. The organization also supported Dr. Beryl Parker's kindergarten and primary work in Ankara, worked with the Turkish Educational Association on translating and publishing literature in the new alphabet, and set up an American tour for a Turkish debating team. When forced by the Depression to curtail its activities, the American Friends of Turkey maintained a public relations program

(June 1921), 489; (July 1921), 571; 45 (Jan. 1922), 32, 35–36, 38; (Dec. 1922), 997–998; 46 (Jan. 1923), 68; (May 1923), 411–412; 47 (Aug. 1924), 648–649; Trask, "United States and Turkey," pp. 273–277; *FR 1928*, III, 981–988.

[98] "American Friends of Turkey," 23-page pamphlet, dated May 25, 1931, Bristol MSS, Box 96 (first quotation); *MRW*, 48 (Aug. 1925), 644 (second quotation).

[99] Among them were John H. Finley, associate editor of *The New York Times*; Albert W. Staub, director of the Near East College Association; Dr. Stephen P. Duggan of the Institute for International Education; James E. West of the Boy Scouts of America; and Mary Mills Patrick, president-emerita of Istanbul Women's College. Other directors in 1931 were Admiral Bristol, John Dewey, Cleveland Dodge, and Harry Emerson Fosdick.

in the United States, including an elaborate New York celebration of the tenth anniversary of the Turkish Republic in 1933.[100]

The program of the American Friends for bringing Turkish students to study in the United States received hearty endorsement from the Turkish government, which supported a growing number of students at American institutions, training in such fields as cotton cultivation, viticulture, meteorology, education, mathematics, and anthropology. Many of the Turkish students recalled from France and Germany at the start of World War II were brought to the United States to continue their studies. Consul Frederick Latimer at Istanbul reported in November of 1939 that forty-seven students were being sent to the United States by the mineral research division of the Ministry of Economy.[101]

These expanding Turkish-American cultural contacts were part of the process by which American opinion of Turkey underwent rapid transformation. They were potent weapons in dispelling the outmoded image of the Turk as a sharp-featured, paunchy figure garbed in baggy pantaloons and wielding a scimitar. For the future, the transformation was significant because it facilitated the closer political relationship required by shared international dangers at mid-century.

Although American archaeological work in Turkey between the wars was less spectacular than that in Egypt and Iraq, there were several notable projects. Between 1927 and 1932 the Oriental Institute of the University of Chicago excavated Hittite mounds on the central plateau near the Anatolian village of Alishar. In 1932 the University of Cincinnati sponsored work at Troy on the northwest tip of the Anatolian peninsula as a follow-up of the monumental nineteenth-century work of Heinrich Schliemann. Intermittently for fifteen years beginning in 1934, Bryn Mawr College, with the cooperation of other institutions, worked on biblical sites at Tarsus in southern Anatolia. The expeditions undertaken by the Oriental Institute and Princeton University in the Hatay in the late 1930s have already been mentioned. About the same time, Professor Kirsopp Lake supervised a Harvard expedition in the Lake Van region during the summers of 1938 and 1939. Of a different type was the work of the Byzantine Institute of America which sponsored Professor Thomas Whittemore's studies of the Saint Sophia mosaics.

[100] Various letters and pamphlets in Bristol MSS, Box 96; Trask, "United States and Turkey," pp. 115–119.
[101] Trask, "United States and Turkey," pp. 269–270.

The Turks were happy to have all possible scientific evidence of the ancient civilizations of Anatolia to buttress their contention that the Turks had made great contributions to civilization and were not the uncouth barbarians pictured by their detractors. National pride led them to stretch the evidence to support such questionable theories as those which made the ancient Sumerians and Hittites the lineal antecedents of the modern Turks.[102]

Conclusion

A remarkable dual transformation had taken place in Turkey and in Turkish-American relations within two decades. Parallel with the creation of a new Turkish republic which made giant strides toward reshaping the nation, Americans changed their low opinion of Turkey and the Turks. The aims and accomplishments of the Atatürk regime in setting the Turkish nation on new domestic and international courses were commended by knowledgeable Americans.

As the first comprehensive nationalist revolution in the Middle East, the Atatürk program gave the world a preview of the aspirations and problems of other Middle Eastern peoples. The Turkish experiment was, in a sense, a prototype for the Iranians and Arabs, although significant differences obviated a precisely parallel development.[103] The advances made by the Turks were fundamental to the *rapprochement* in Turkish-American relations, because they contributed to the waning of the Terrible Turk stereotype. The generally favorable view of American intentions held by the Turkish leadership also helped to create a favorable climate. So did the heritage of accumulated good will emanating from American cultural and philanthropic endeavors. Both the lack of American political ambitions in Turkey and the absence of fundamental conflicts in national interests prevented friction. Even with these favorable factors the new understanding might not have been achieved without the leadership of Admiral Bristol, Joseph Grew, Ismet Inönü, and Atatürk himself. By establishing rapport with the new leadership between 1919 and 1927, Bristol helped to bridge a difficult transitional period. The mutual personal respect of Grew and Ismet at Lausanne, and the sympathetic attitude of each for the other's point of view, helped

[102] Perkins in *Background of the Middle East*, p. 216; Trask, "United States and Turkey," pp. 263–268; Patterson to Stimson, June 5, 1930, DS 867.41/1; Latimer to Hull, May 15, 1939, DS 811.5031 Near East/321.
[103] See the interesting analysis by Roderic H. Davison, "Middle East Nationalism: Lausanne Thirty Years After," *Middle East Journal*, 7 (Summer 1953), 324–348.

to form a nexus of understanding essential to solving the bilateral problems of the two nations.

When President-Emeritus Gates returned to Ankara in 1938, his old friend, now President Inönü, greeted him in English. Ardent Turk though he was, Inönü's Western orientation was exemplified by his study of the English language, undertaken when he was in his middle fifties.[104] It was appropriate that the portrait of the new president should appear on the commemorative stamps issued by Turkey in 1939. Atatürk's mantle had fallen to the man who was probably the most important Turkish link in the chain of new relationships with the United States.

[104] Gates, *Not to Me Only*, pp. 326–327; Yalman, *Turkey in My Time*, p. 241.

9

IRAN BETWEEN THE WARS

☆ AN UPSURGE OF NATIONALISM dominated the history of Persia during the years between the two world wars. The sovereignty and independence of that ancient country had been gravely compromised during the tragic disruptions accompanying World War I. Although Great Britain was temporarily in the ascendancy at the close of the war, the Soviets were soon able to renew the old Russian competition with Great Britain for power and position in Persia.[1]

The United States was more of a spectator than an actor in the Great Power competition, but American interests in Persia could not escape entirely being identified by Persian nationalists with that complex of Western influences blocking Persian control of Persian destinies. Consequently, as Persia underwent a considerable measure of regeneration under her strong man, Reza Shah, the United States faced continuing adjustments to the new Persian nationalism. These efforts of American missionaries, businessmen, archaeologists, technical advisers, and others — often in collaboration with the State Department — to work out an accommodation to Persian nationalism provide the key to Persian-American relations during the interwar period.

[1] Reza Shah decreed in 1935 that his country should be referred to officially as Iran. Persia and Iran are used interchangeably in this chapter. Especially useful for Persia's foreign relations are George Lenczowski, *Russia and the West in Iran, 1918–1948: A Study of Big-Power Rivalry*, and Nasrollah S. Fatemi, *Diplomatic History of Persia, 1917–1923: Anglo–Russian Power Politics in Iran*. For Persian developments during World War I and between the wars, see Elgin Groseclose, *Introduction to Iran*, pp. 71–76, 119–171; Richard N. Frye, *Iran*, pp. 70–80; Sir Percy Sykes, *A History of Persia*, II, 435–562; Amin Banani, *The Modernization of Iran, 1921–1941*; Joseph M. Upton, *The History of Modern Iran: An Interpretation*, Chaps. 2–5; L. P. Elwell-Sutton, *Modern Iran*, pp. 68–173; William S. Haas, *Iran*, pp. 137–167 and *passim*.

World War I and Its Aftermath

Despite Persia's proclamation of neutrality in 1914, her soil became a battleground for the contending forces. As Russians in the northwest, Turks and Germans in the west, and British in the southwest vied to extend their control, parts of western Persia changed hands several times. The weak Persian government was impotent to protect its citizens, Moslem or Christian. Most Persians were sympathetic to the Germans and Turks, who were fighting Persia's traditional enemies, Russia and Great Britain. In western Persia, however, the Christian minorities concentrated there looked upon the Russians as their protectors.

For the Persian people, Moslem and Christian alike, the war brought severe famine and epidemics of typhus and cholera resulting in thousands of deaths and untold hardship. Particularly hard hit were the Christians of the Urumia region, where Presbyterian missionaries from the United States had long been active. Added to the horrors accompanying the depredations of armies marching over fields and through villages and towns were attacks from neighboring Kurdish tribesmen whose anti-Christian fanaticism was unleashed with full fury during the war years.

The drama of the terrible war years is conveyed in accounts by the Tabriz and Urumia missionaries, whose stations helped care for thousands of desolate refugees, hungry, often half-crazed by the awful sights they had seen, and virtually without hope. The relief problem overtaxed the resources of the missionaries despite heroic assistance from private relief organizations set up in the United States. At Urumia panic spread when Turkish troops forced the Russians, who had occupied the area for several years, to evacuate without warning on January 1, 1915. Some fifteen thousand Christian refugees piled into the Presbyterian mission yards and buildings to escape the plundering Turks and Kurds. Additional thousands, including Armenians from Turkey fleeing ahead of the troops, camped wherever they could in and around Urumia. "Streams of Christians poured into the station compounds for refuge filling all available schoolrooms, cellars, hallways, closets, offices and church. Fiske Seminary was the storm centre. Babies were born and people died outside the kitchen door. A dark closet under the stairs was used for those who had become crazed. The schoolroom was thronged with about 400 people with no room to lie down at night. In the church there were 3,000 . . ." The return of the Russians in May gave the Christians a respite, but they remained in a state of semi-siege as famine conditions worsened in 1916 and 1917.[2]

Some help came directly from the United States through the Presbyterian church and the Persian Relief Committee organized in 1915; before the end of the year it merged with other relief organizations to form the Committee for Armenian and Syrian Relief, which in turn became the famous Near East Relief by congressional incorporation in 1919. These relief efforts added much to the reservoir of good will for the United States. To the American nation, Mar Shimum, patriarch of the Nestorian (Assyrian) church wrote: "'the people left — just a remnant — in the Urumia district of Persia are a monument to the love, sympathy, and philanthropy of America. The direct saviours are the American Presbyterian missionaries and the American consul.'" Relief was not, however, confined to Christians; needy Moslems were sheltered and fed to the limit of the inadequate resources.[3]

Western Persia suffered another wave of incredible human misery in 1917 when Russia withdrew from the war and her forces disintegrated. Turks and Kurds were waiting to repay their debt of bitterness and hatred for harsh treatment received from the Christians. On both sides "every one who had an old score to settle seized his opportunity" in the ensuing confusion. Free-lance Russian officers, with the assistance of Mar Shimum and Agha Petros, a tough Assyrian mountaineer, helped to organize an army of Christian mountaineers. Using abandoned Russian arms, they stood off the Turks and Kurds for several months. This "Assyrian army" received American support through the efforts of Dr. William A. Shedd, a beloved Urumia missionary, who reluctantly accepted a State Department appointment as honorary vice-consul early in 1918. Dr. Shedd's remarkable prestige enabled him to secure a measure of order in the community, but not without incurring criticism from Persians who wanted to liquidate the Christians and from Christians who champed at the restraints Shedd placed on their instincts for vengeance.

[2] Brown, *100 Years*, pp. 515–518 (quotation, p. 517); Mary Lewis Shedd, *The Measure of a Man: The Life of William Ambrose Shedd, Missionary to Persia*, Chaps. 8–12; *MRW*, 38 (April 1915), 267–270; (May 1915), 383–384; (Aug. 1915), 563; Groseclose, *Iran*, pp. 71–73.
[3] Barton, *Near East Relief*, pp. 13, 18, 91–103; Yeselson, *USPDR*, pp. 136–138; *MRW*, 39 (May 1916), 389; (Aug. 1916), 585–588; 40 (Jan. 1917), 5; (April 1917), 309; (May 1917), 384 (quotation); 41 (May 1918), 386–387; (July 1918), 492–495, 550; (Aug. 1918), 626; (Dec. 1918), 948–949.

For several months Urumia was cut off from the outside. Although the Turks were held on the outskirts, they pressed hard on three sides of the city. On July 8, 1918, a daring British officer, Lieutenant Pennington, flew a plane to Urumia to find out what had happened. On the strength of his assurances that British forces would be sent from the south to join Assyrian-Armenian forces, the increasingly hard-pressed Christians panicked and began a headlong flight through the southern pass in the direction of expected British help. Unable to restrain them, Dr. Shedd and his missionary wife accompanied them to provide moral support and leadership. The revered missionary, already exhausted from months of unbearable tension, died of typhus during the flight. Dr. Shedd's heroism and self-sacrifice provide just one vignette among many examples of missionary service in wartime Persia. The missionaries who remained behind at Urumia were captured by the Turks and taken to Tabriz, where they were eventually released.[4] The Urumia affair engendered much suspicion on the part of some Iranian officials who thereafter charged missionaries with being government agents.

During the war Persia had appealed to President Wilson for assistance in maintaining her neutrality and independence, but all she received was sympathy. The fact that the appeal was made to Washington suggested the special position the United States held in Persian thinking as a nation without designs on Persia's territory. The memory of Morgan Shuster's efforts in behalf of Persia was still fresh and contributed to the image of America as perhaps the one powerful and disinterested nation on which Persia might call in her new time of troubles.[5]

Persia looked hopefully toward the peace conference, where she counted on obtaining international guarantees of her independence and sovereignty. Her expectations were greatly increased by President Wilson's espousal of the rights of small nations, hopes that were dashed when the British stood in the way of seating the Persian delegation at the conference. On three occasions President Wilson and others sought a hearing for the Persians, but the British objected that the Persians had been neither belligerent nor subject peoples. These technicalities were only a transparent mask through which British aims were visible. With the temporary elimination of their chief rivals in Persia — Germany and

[4] Shedd, *Measure of a Man*, Chaps. 12–16 (quotation, p. 218); *MRW*, 41 (May 1918), 323–324; 42 (Jan. 1919), 23–25; (Feb. 1919), 148–149; (March 1919), 198; 43 (Nov. 1920), 952–953.
[5] *FR 1914, S*, pp. 129, 130, 149; *FR 1918, S1*, I, 895–914.

Russia — the British sought a virtual protectorate. In this way, imperial interests would be served by securing the British position at the head of the Persian Gulf. The British flank in Mesopotamia would have a buffer, the hold on the Khuzistan oil fields would be firmer, and the approaches to India would be more secure.[6]

Although President Wilson and his advisers took a friendly posture toward Persian requests for recognition, as could be seen in the recommendations put forward by his advisory body, the Inquiry, the compelling fact was that the British had vital strategic interests and important petroleum holdings in Persia while the United States had neither. In this situation there seemed no alternative to deferring to the British. The Persians, recognizing the American friendliness to their aspirations, continued to hope that the United States delegation might challenge British obduracy. But no concrete American support came out of the dinner given by the Persians at Paris in honor of Secretary Lansing and attended by Generals Tasker Bliss and John J. Pershing. The Persians also abandoned a plan to send a delegation to the United States.[7] In the final analysis the Persians received no real encouragement from American officials.

The British capitalized on conditions favorable for solidifying their position by making a treaty with the Persians. The negotiations were carried on in secret between the British and a few pro-British Persian authorities, who signed the treaty on August 19, 1919. When they learned of this treaty, American officials expressed surprise and irritation, both because of the secrecy and because the terms made Persia a virtual British protectorate. The British found it difficult to understand the American reaction since, they claimed, Colonel Edward M. House had been informed that the treaty was being negotiated. Secretary of State Lansing answered that he had learned that House had been casually informed of British plans in a conversation that could hardly be considered official. The American response to the treaty reflected the hold that Wilsonian idealism had on official policy as late as the summer of 1919. During the next two years, however, the unparalleled British position in the Middle East collapsed, and Lord Curzon's dream of British hegemony in the area dissolved. By the end of 1921 the Anglo-Persian Treaty of 1919 had been discarded and Persia, having mended

[6] *FR 1919: PPC*, I, 256–263; IV, 57; V, 153, 498; Yeselson, *USPDR*, p. 159.
[7] Yeselson, *USPDR*, pp. 147–154; *The New York Times*, March 8, 1919, p. 12:7.

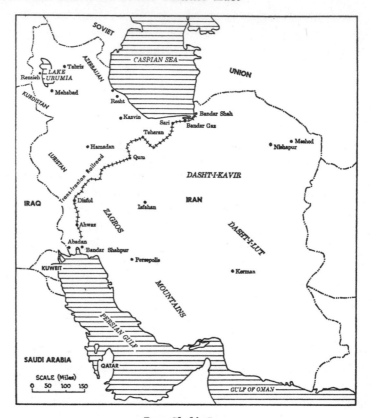

Reza Shah's Iran

her fences with her Soviet neighbor, was closer to true independence than at any time previously during the twentieth century.[8]

Reza Shah: His Goals and Obstacles

Parallel with the decline of British influence, a significant new nationalist movement was gaining strength in Persia. Reza Khan, a commander of the Persian Cossacks, supported a successful coup in February of 1921. Gradually, he emerged as the power behind the new government, first as minister of war, then as prime minister in October, 1923. The Majlis gave him dictatorial powers in February, 1925, deposed the

[8] *FR 1919*, II, 700, 708–711, 714–717; Yeselson, *USPDR*, pp. 149–151, 158–172, 176; John L. Offner, "American-Persian Relations in the Post-War Decade, 1918–1928," unpublished M.A. thesis, The Pennsylvania State University, 1952, p. 17; Banani, *Modernization of Iran*, pp. 13–14, 35–36; Upton, *Modern Iran*, pp. 41–42.

Qajar dynasty in October, and proclaimed Reza Khan the Shah in December. Reza Shah's personal and national goals were ambitious, the more so in view of the formidable obstacles in his path. His first aim was to establish the central government's authority over the provinces, the tribes, and the divisive social groups of Iran. Order and security were prerequisites to a modernization program designed to improve the material lot of Iranians, using Western technology as an instrument. Secularization was a third objective, for the hold of traditional religion appeared to be a major obstacle to desired changes. To promote his objectives, Reza Shah undertook reforms affecting the army, governmental administration, the judiciary, and education. The regime also initiated many measures to promote economic development. Reza Shah's accomplishments during his sixteen-year reign were remarkable considering the disunifying pressures he had to overcome. National disunity, rooted in Iran's geography, diverse population, social organization, and customs, was constantly a brake on change. So was the element of opportunism in the Persian character, which often put personal interest above civic responsibility and national interest. By lending encouragement to divisive forces, foreign influences at work in Persia also contributed to national disunity. These aims and the obstructions which the Shah encountered had a definite effect on American adjustment to his new regime.[9]

The Millspaugh Mission

Faced with an insolvent treasury, Persia's new leadership proposed a program with the dual purpose of obtaining a foreign loan to keep the government alive while working toward the second objective of long-range reform. Both needs might be advanced, they hoped, by hiring foreign experts to undertake fiscal and administrative improvements. It was natural that the Persians should think back to the work W. Morgan Shuster had commenced a decade earlier. In fact, they had never forgotten Shuster's achievements and had made tentative overtures several times, during and shortly after the war, for a new American financial mission to be headed by Shuster or some other American expert.[10]

The Department of State approached such propositions warily until

[9] Banani, *Modernization of Iran*, pp. 45–51 and *passim*; Upton, *Modern Iran*, pp. 16–35, 47–63; Lenczowski, *Russia and the West in Iran*, pp. 70–74.

[10] Curti and Birr, *Prelude to Point Four*, pp. 166–167; Yeselson, *USPDR*, pp. 181–185.

after the failure of the Anglo-Persian Treaty of 1919. Early in 1922 the British government seemed anxious to have an American financial adviser appointed to Persia and pledged full diplomatic support for American efforts to bring about her financial regeneration. Finally, after much maneuvering, the department recommended Arthur C. Millspaugh to head a new financial mission to Persia. Millspaugh, an economist, who had held academic posts before entering government service, had been serving for some time as the department's Economic Adviser. The department insisted that Millspaugh sever his official connection with the United States government and enter upon his new task strictly in the capacity of a private American citizen. This requirement disappointed Persian leaders who had hoped that an official American endorsement of the mission might serve as a further curb on Russian and British ambitions.[11]

The Persian government agreed to five-year contracts for Millspaugh and his staff. Extensive authority was delegated to Millspaugh as Administrator General of Finances, including a virtual veto over all government expenditures. Millspaugh and his staff began their assignments under rather favorable circumstances inasmuch as the Persian officials could see that outside direction was essential to their economic salvation. The impressive accomplishments of the American mission during the next five years included advances in tax collection, control and budgeting of government expenses, revival of commerce and industry, and designation of funds for constructive projects.

The task of the American was not an easy one in a country where administrative inefficiency and chaotic government were deeply ingrained. Undoubtedly Millspaugh was used as a stalking horse by the Persians in their effort to acquire foreign loans. In the long run the obstacles proved more than the Americans could counteract. They encountered jealousy from entrenched bureaucrats and protests from privileged aristocrats not used to paying taxes. Furthermore, Millspaugh and his staff did not always understand Persian customs, or proved unwilling to bow to traditional ways of doing things in Persia. They were accused, as Shuster had been, of being tactless, of not understanding the Persian character and traditions. The honeymoon ended in 1924 with the rise of tensions over the reforms instituted by the Americans and by their methods, but this first serious crisis was weathered, and the

[11] *FR 1921*, II, 633–640; *FR 1927*, III, 523–530.

American mission continued its progressive work until 1927 when a more serious crisis developed. So long as Reza Shah supported Millspaugh's efforts, the opposition could be controlled, but when the Shah felt that Millspaugh was actually encroaching on the powers of the ruler, the days of Millspaugh were numbered. As Reza Shah was said to have put it, "There could be only one shah in Persia." Reza demanded that new contracts for Millspaugh and his staff reduce their authority, but Millspaugh was unwilling to bend, and even though the State Department tried to mediate, the mission broke up before the end of 1927. Parliamentary intrigue, entrenched interests, and the loss of the Shah's support doomed the effort to draw new contracts. Millspaugh had departed in August, and most of his staff by the early part of 1928.

Despite the unfriendliness toward Millspaugh at the time of his departure, openminded Persians appreciated his improvement of the government's taxation and fiscal structure. Moreover, remarkable nonfinancial work had been accomplished in agriculture, municipal administration, transportation, irrigation, and in building up the carpet industry.[12]

In the long run the work of the experts was favorably remembered in Persia, and Millspaugh was asked to return for a second mission between 1943 and 1945.[13] After his departure in 1927, the Shah, apprehensive about the effect on American public opinion toward Persia, went so far as to ask Arthur U. Pope, a specialist in Iranian art and architecture, for help so that Americans might forget the withdrawal of Millspaugh.[14]

Oil in the 1920s

Even before Millspaugh went to Persia, the Persians showed an interest in having American companies undertake development in northern Persia where oil rights were unassigned. They envisaged a package-deal whereby an oil concession would be granted in return for large loans

---

[12] The best analyses of the Millspaugh mission are in Offner, "American-Persian Relations," pp. 25–45; and Curti and Birr, *Prelude to Point Four*, pp. 166–175 (quotation, p. 171). See also Upton, *Modern Iran*, pp. 33, 53; Banani, *Modernization of Iran*, pp. 115–117. For Arthur C. Millspaugh's book-length account, see *The American Task in Persia*. See also *FR 1927*, III, 531–567. Arthur Judson Brown has written that "Dr. Millspaugh brought American engineers who taught the Persians how to build motor roads." He claimed that in 1922 Persia had less than 1000 miles of good roads, while the figure had risen to 14,000 by the middle 1930s. *100 Years*, p. 474.

[13] On the World War II mission, see Arthur C. Millspaugh, *Americans in Persia*.

[14] Curti and Birr, *Prelude to Point Four*, p. 175.

floated by the concessionaires to meet immediate governmental fiscal needs. American oil interests were receptive because of the oil-shortage scare in the United States, which had stimulated hopes of acquiring reserves in the Middle East.[15]

In August of 1920 Standard Oil of New Jersey expressed to the State Department its interest in the northern Persian oil fields, but when the Persian intention of linking an oil concession to a loan became apparent, Standard Oil hesitated. Besides, there was the complication of the Khostaria concession, granted to a subject of Czarist Russia in 1916. The Persian Council of Ministers had declared this grant null and void in 1917, and the Bolsheviks after they came to power denounced all Czarist concessions obtained from Persia. The Anglo-Persian Oil Company had, however, bought the Khostaria concession in 1920, ostensibly in the belief it was still valid. The British government insisted in no uncertain terms that it would back Anglo-Persian claims in northern Persia; it warned the State Department to tell American petroleum companies to stay out of this British province.[16]

The Persian government had, in the meantime, employed Morgan Shuster as its American fiscal agent in the United States to arrange a loan and bids for northern Persian oil concessions. Shuster approached Standard Oil of New Jersey and pressed negotiations to the point where he could tell the Persian government, on November 21, 1921, that the American company would accept a concession. The Majlis quickly empowered the administrative branch of the government to sign a fifty-year concession for five of the northern provinces, but with the requirement that the Majlis must ratify any concession drawn up. The Majlis, furthermore, would have to approve bringing in other capital by the American oil company, and there was a clause stipulating that the concession was nontransferable. Shuster arranged a Standard Oil loan of $10 million on condition the concession became valid.[17]

The granting of this concession was immediately protested vigorously by Great Britain, France, and the Soviet Union, but the State Department defended the legality of the American plan for oil development in northern Persia. Shortly, Standard Oil outmaneuvered the State Department by arranging with Anglo-Persian for the latter's participation in

[15] Yeselson, *USPDR*, Chap. 9; DeNovo in *American Historical Review*, 61: 854–876.

[16] *FR 1920*, III, 347, 351–356; *FR 1921*, II, 640–644.

[17] *FR 1921*, II, 648; *FR 1924*, II, 542; Yeselson, *USPDR*, pp. 212–214.

the enterprise. Jersey Standard's decision to deal with the British was part of a comprehensive effort among British and American oil interests to reconcile their conflicting objectives in the Middle East. Essential to the compromise was the British promise to admit American interests to Mosul and to allow Socony to examine its oil lands in Palestine. In return, Jersey Standard was to admit the legality of the Khostaria concession now held by Anglo-Persian. Jersey Standard had been advised to make its peace with the British company by John Bassett Moore, international lawyer and diplomat. Moore counseled Standard that Anglo-Persian held a monopoly on pipelines through southern Persia, the region through which northern Persian oil would have to be transported to reach marine terminals. The only alternative would be an arrangement with the Soviet Union for transportation through the Soviet Caucasus to the Black Sea outlets. This did not interest Standard because of the instability of the Bolshevik regime and its hostile attitude toward private property and capitalistic enterprise.[18]

Jersey Standard's agreement with Anglo-Persian was the kiss of death for the concession. Moore and Standard officials clearly underestimated the strength of Anglophobia in Persia. The Persians, in no mood to tolerate any extension of British influence in their country, rejected these arrangements in February of 1922.[19]

A second American oil company, Sinclair, had shown an interest in northern Persia as early as July, 1921, and had placed a representative in Teheran by December. He was unable to do much until after the Majlis had turned down the Standard-British proposal the following February. For more than a year Standard and Sinclair jealously competed for the aid and preference of the State Department. For its part, the Persian government was in no hurry, feeling that mistakes had been made earlier in granting concessions and not wanting to compound the errors. In June of 1923 the Majlis broke the deadlock by offering to both companies a new concession incorporating the better terms of the two old ones. Jersey Standard was no longer interested, but Sinclair submitted a similar alternative to the Majlis; after slight differences had been reconciled a new Sinclair concession was signed on December 20, 1923,

[18] *FR 1921*, II, 649–655; Offner, "American-Persian Relations," pp. 57–60. For the contemporary developments in Mesopotamia and Palestine, see above, Chap. 6, pp. 182–183 and 186–188.
[19] *FR 1924*, II, 542–545; Yeselson, *USPDR*, p. 220; Offner, "American-Persian Relations," p. 61.

covering four of the five northern provinces. The concession was to run for fifty years, the government would receive twenty per cent of the profits, and a loan of ten million dollars would be arranged for the Persian government. The Sinclair company had a great advantage in northern Persia because of its friendly relations with the Soviet government; Sinclair's chances of making satisfactory transportation arrangements through Soviet territory were much better than Jersey Standard's.[20]

Shortly after the signing of the Sinclair concession, Ralph H. Soper of Sinclair conferred with the agent of Ulen and Company, an American construction firm, about floating part of the loan (required by the Persian government) in return for earmarking the funds for public works projects to be undertaken by Ulen and Company. By the time Sinclair and Ulen completed their arrangements, Ulen and the Persian government had signed a temporary agreement on April 27, 1924.[21] Before the Majlis could act to ratify either the oil concession or the Ulen concession the Imbrie murder intervened.

Robert W. Imbrie, American vice-consul at Teheran, was murdered on July 18, 1924, when attacked by an irate mob for taking pictures of a religious celebration. In the flurry of excitement following this tragedy, business interests were temporarily overshadowed. Soper, the Sinclair agent, used the Imbrie murder as an excuse for withdrawal from Persia, departing within ten days for Moscow. The real reasons for his exit were not fully revealed at the time. The taint of scandal, the notorious Teapot Dome affair, uncovered by the American Senate in January, 1924, soon implicated Harry Sinclair. Sinclair's arrangements with the Soviet Union for oil transit rested, it has been alleged, on his promise that he could arrange for American recognition of the Soviet Union through his friends, Secretary of the Interior Albert B. Fall and Attorney General Harry Daugherty; charges were also loosed that Sinclair had used bribery in obtaining the Persian concession. With the collapse of the Sinclair-Soviet understanding, Sinclair could not be assured of transportation outlets for northern Persian oil. When the Sinclair Company told the Persian government in 1925 that it could not consider a concession, an oil glut on the American market had made development of Persian fields less attractive.[22]

[20] *FR 1921*, II, 651–652; *FR 1923*, II, 712–736; Offner, "American-Persian Relations," pp. 62–63.

[21] *FR 1924*, II, 545–555, 559–564.

[22] *FR 1924*, II, 547–548, 552 n. 11; Offner, "American-Persian Relations," pp.

Opium Control

Persia's opium problem demanded the attention of Americans whether acting in a private capacity, such as the Millspaugh experts, or officially in behalf of the United States government. Since early in the twentieth century the United States had strongly urged international control of narcotics production and traffic.[23] Persia found it difficult to cooperate wholeheartedly with the Hague Convention of 1912 and with the efforts to restrict trade in narcotics attempted under League of Nations auspices in the 1920s. With a climate favorable to cultivation of the opium poppy, Persia was a big producer, the source of nearly thirty per cent of the world's supply in 1925. Opium production provided a livelihood for thousands of Persian peasants and a significant income for the government. Although it is hard to estimate Persian opium exports because of widespread smuggling, perhaps one-sixth of that nation's exports exclusive of oil was in opium. About nine per cent of the government's annual revenue came from customs receipts on opium shipments in 1925.[24]

Between 1908 and the arrival of the Millspaugh mission in 1922, the Persian government had taken sporadic but generally ineffective measures toward controlling production. The problem was under study by one of Millspaugh's tax experts, Colonel D. W. MacCormack, when pressure built up to have the League of Nations consider international control of narcotics. Sympathetic to the League's efforts, the United States participated in its opium conferences in 1924 and 1925. The United States also followed the British lead in pressing Persia to take measures toward controlling the large smuggling trade in narcotics from the Persian Gulf to the Far East.[25]

Before the League conference met in 1924, Secretary Hughes told the Persian government that the United States hoped very much for Persian

69–72. On the Imbrie murder, see Marjorie M. Whiteman, *Damages in International Law*, I, 136–139, 732–733; and Offner, pp. 36–38, 58–59.

[23] For American cooperation in efforts for international opium control at Shanghai (1909) and the Hague (1911–1914), see references in *FR: General Index 1900–1918*, pp. 315–317; and Charles E. Terry and Mildred Pellens, *The Opium Problem*, pp. 629, 632, 647, 649, 650, 655, 657. Although Persia signed a Hague Convention, she entered a reservation on the important provision to ban exports to countries having prohibitions against opium imports except by licenses. Groseclose, *Iran*, pp. 208–209.

[24] Groseclose, *Iran*, pp. 106–109, 207–210; Offner, "American-Persian Relations," pp. 81–82.

[25] *FR 1924*, I, 89–126; II, 582–591; *FR 1925*, II, 682–690.

participation. Persia assured Hughes that a delegate had been appointed and that he would be assisted by Colonel MacCormack of the Mills-paugh staff, who was familiar with Persia's opium predicament through the exhaustive report he had just completed.

In his report, presented at the conference, MacCormack outlined certain prerequisites to Persia's participation in a control program: a large annual loan to replace lost opium revenues; suspension of debt payments to foreign governments for the time being; and removal of the capitulations so that new industries might be built up behind a high tariff wall. One outcome of the conference was the decision of the League to despatch a commission to study the Persian opium problem in its local setting. An American, Frederick A. Delano, a former member of the Federal Reserve Board, headed the investigating commission and half the commission's expenses was supplied by a private agency, the American Bureau of Social Hygiene.[26]

The sympathetic report of the Delano commission, accepted by the League Assembly in 1925, was considered by Millspaugh a triumph for Persia. Unfortunately, the efforts of Reza Shah's government to restrict production were unsuccessful, and the opium problem still plagued Persia at the close of World War II.[27] Many Persians recognized the humanitarian side of the narcotics problem and accepted in principle the need for strong domestic control, but opium production had become too firmly entrenched in the agricultural and fiscal life of the country. Pressure from the United States in concert with other nations had failed to induce a successful attack on the Persian opium problem in the era of Reza Shah.

Transitional Years, 1927–1928

The year 1927 marks a period of transition in Persian-American relations, in which American interests had to adjust to the demands of an increasingly assertive Persian nationalism. The regime of Reza Shah had become more secure internally, owing in part to the administrative

[26] *FR 1924*, I, 99–101, 121; II, 586–591; Offner, "American-Persian Relations," pp. 85–88; Groseclose, *Iran*, pp. 197–198, 210.

[27] Offner, "American-Persian Relations," pp. 87–88; Terry and Pellens, *Opium Problem*, pp. 720–734, 740; Groseclose, *Iran*, pp. 210–216. See also League of Nations, *Records of the Second Opium Conference*, Geneva, Nov. 17, 1924–Feb. 19, 1925; League of Nations, *Commission on Enquiry into the Production of Opium in Persia*, 5th Commission, Annex 5; League of Nations, *Official Journal*, Special Supplement, No. 54, pp. 120–121.

reforms accomplished with the help of the American financial mission. There was also less danger now of major foreign intervention from the Soviet Union and Great Britain than there had been earlier in the decade. During the year Millspaugh, head of the American technical mission, ended his work amid criticisms; the government issued new orders affecting foreign schools; and the government announced that economic and judicial capitulations would be terminated the following year.

Most significant of the changes was the decision to overhaul the Persian legal system as a preliminary to eliminating all extraterritorial rights of foreigners, an objective long cherished by the new regime. As early as the period of the Paris Peace Conference, the Persians had hoped to present to the assembled victors the case against capitulations. A major goal of the nationalist regime after 1921 had been the abolition of these badges of inferiority, but the time had not quite arrived to pursue the issue all the way. Yet the Persian government claimed that with the abrogation of old Czarist-Persian treaties, especially the Treaty of Turcoman Chai (1828), the main basis for special privileges heretofore granted foreigners had been removed. For the next few years there was some confusion among Western nations as to exactly what extraterritorial rights remained, the United States insisting that its 1856 treaty containing the most-favored-nation clause guaranteed extraterritorial rights to Americans.[28]

Reza Shah did not push the capitulations issue until he felt reasonably certain that he could carry through to his ultimate objective — their complete elimination. He was ready in 1927, when he unfolded a plan for complete revision of the country's legal system by hiring French lawyers to assist Swiss-trained Ali Akbar Davar, the new Minister of Justice (a leading figure in the Shah's "brain trust"), in drafting a code based on French law to replace Moslem and civil codes. When Reza promulgated new legal regulations in April of 1927, he warned that capitulations would soon be abolished. Sooner than foreign diplomats expected, Reza's government formally notified them on May 10, 1927, that one year from that day termination would be effective. During the interval, the Persian government hoped replacement treaties could be negotiated.[29]

[28] Yeselson, *USPDR*, pp. 175–177; *FR 1924*, II, 565–581.
[29] *FR 1927*, III, 567–593; Banani, *Modernization of Iran*, pp. 70–76.

The United States assured the Persian government that it was "prepared to consider in a friendly and sympathetic spirit" the capitulations issue. Little negotiation took place between the capitulatory powers and Persia until early in 1928 when several months of hard bargaining began as Great Britain, the United States, and other powers with lesser interests in Persia sought commitments affording adequate protection for foreign nations. At times the United States seemed to defer to British leadership, but at certain stages Washington pursued a more independent course. Usually, however, the State Department was much interested in the possibilities of a united front of the capitulatory powers. Early in the year Washington supported a ten-point British program calling, among other guarantees, for control of the Persian judicial system by foreign judicial experts, but Persia was adamant against any such compromise. At a later stage, the United States put forward its own six-point proposal for which it sought support from other powers. As the May 10 deadline approached, Washington again sought a united front among Western nations to press Persia for adequate guarantees until the judicial reforms were completed. The British in particular questioned the wisdom of this approach.[30]

The day the old treaties expired, May 10, 1928, Great Britain and France signed new agreements. A few days earlier, the United States and Persia had nearly agreed on a settlement covering diplomatic and consular representation, a Persian declaration of judicial safeguards, and commercial provisions with new tariff schedules. The one stumbling block was the Persian desire for reciprocity in personal status and family provisions. Persia suggested on May 10 that the United States exchange notes without personal status and family law clauses, but with the understanding that these points would be embodied in a subsequent exchange of notes as soon as details could be agreed on.[31] This proposal opened the way to agreement.

The note exchanges were at the time regarded as provisional and perhaps preliminary to more permanent treaty arrangements. The first exchange, defining rights and privileges of nationals, took place on May 14, 1928. An additional exchange on July 11 ironed out the issue of personal status and family law by stating that courts would apply the law of the litigant's home country in these matters.[32]

[30] *FR 1927*, III, 576 (quotation); *FR 1928*, III, 682–745.
[31] *FR 1928*, III, 714–719.
[32] *FR 1928*, III, 719–732, 739–744.

For the missionaries, who had hoped for a recognition of the principle of religious liberty, only half a loaf was obtained through the Persian commitment to recognize the charitable and educational work of the missionaries. The right to conduct evangelistic activities was not specifically included, but missionaries found they could continue this phase of their work if they were willing to risk occasional interference with their public meetings.[33]

In line with the move to end capitulations was the Persian government's assertion of closer supervision over education. To the dismay of American and other foreigners conducting schools in Persia, the Ministry of Education issued new regulations on May 10, 1927. These included stipulations requiring that Koranic law be taught to all pupils, prohibiting teaching any non-Moslem religion to Moslem pupils, and banning dissemination of any propaganda contrary to Islam. The Presbyterians in cooperation with British Anglican missionaries joined in presenting two "deliverances" pointing out the great contributions their educational work had made to the training of young leaders for Persia. After considerable discussion a compromise was arranged whereby the government did not require the schools to teach Koranic law. Permission was given to teach the Bible in the curriculum to non-Moslem students and to use writings of great teachers and prophets in ethics courses for all students. There would be no restrictions on what was taught outside the regular curriculum. Schools would have to conform to the government's education courses, but graduates would enjoy the same privileges and standing as graduates of government schools.[34]

Missionaries and Persian Nationalism

The events of 1927–1928 gave the missionaries their first real taste of what the new Persian nationalism had in store for them, although it would take several years of repeated shocks before they came to understand that their position was nearly untenable in Persia. Their un-

[33] *FR 1928*, III, 720–721; Brown, *100 Years*, 526–527.
[34] Brown, *100 Years*, pp. 527–530; *A Century of Mission Work in Iran*, pp. 39, 99; *MRW*, 51 (April 1928), 332; (Aug. 1928), 674–675; (Nov. 1928), 911; 52 (March 1929), 232; (June 1929), 434; 56 (March 1933), 138. Banani writes: "Governmental policy towards these private schools was consistent with the nationalist-centralist outlook of the Reza Shah regime. The government was not opposed to the operation of these schools . . . but, step by step, they were gradually brought under the full control of the Ministry of Education." *Modernization of Iran*, p. 96. See also pp. 92–101.

quenchable faith in the efficacy of their tasks had enabled them to pick up the pieces after World War I. At the historic Urumia station nothing was left to show for their eighty-year effort except scattered ruins of hospitals, schools, press, and missionary homes; and Bolshevik activity in northwestern Persia during 1920–1921 forced the flight of missionaries and Christian refugees from Tabriz to Hamadan and other cities. As conditions improved, they reoccupied the stations at Tabriz, Meshed, and Resht, and in 1923 re-established Urumia as a regular mission station after the government had permitted Assyrians and refugees to return, reclaim property, and plant fields.[35]

Resumption of traditional activities and a temporarily favorable climate fed the perennial optimism of the missionaries and their spokesmen in the middle 1920s. Every case of conversion was trumpeted hopefully as a triumph and a harbinger of conquests in the offing. Evangelistic activities seemed to meet fewer obstacles than formerly, and marked improvements in travel with the advent of the automobile helped open the more remote rural regions. The missionaries pointed to the growing proportion of Moslem students in missionary schools as another indication that Moslem fanaticism was breaking down. They welcomed the demand for their schools from young Persians interested in Western education as a stepping stone to positions of leadership and status in Persian society. Of the high school at Teheran, Persians were said to have remarked, "The Americans have a factory in Teheran where they manufacture men." A landmark in missionary education was achieved in 1924 when this school for boys was finally granted full collegiate status as Teheran College, and plans were soon progressing for a girls' college at Teheran.[36]

The imperatives of Persian nationalism soon dimmed the missionaries' bright prospects for increased activity and service. The first clap of thunder presaging the stormy weather ahead came in 1926 with

[35] *A Century of Mission Work in Iran*, pp. 4, 36–37; MRW, 44 (Jan. 1921), 17–19; 45 (Feb. 1922), 146; 46 (Jan. 1923), 69–70; (March 1923), 228; 47 (Jan. 1924), 68. Near East Relief assisted in the rehabilitation of Urumia by providing oxen.

[36] Centennial Series, *Iran Mission*, pp. 32–34, 54–56; *A Century of Mission Work in Iran*, pp. 36–38, 104; MRW, 45 (July 1922), 540; (Aug. 1922), 632–635; (Sept. 1922), 713; 46 (Feb. 1923), 149 (quotation); 47 (July 1924), 569; (Nov. 1924), 924–925; 48 (June 1925), 479; 49 (June 1926), 464; (Nov. 1926), 864–866; 50 (Jan. 1927), 19–26; (June 1927), 465–466; (Aug. 1927), 627–628; (Oct. 1927), 777–778; (Nov. 1927), 828–830; 52 (June 1929), 435.

public and governmental objections to overly zealous efforts by a few missionaries whose castigation and denigration of Islam went beyond the bounds of propriety and elicited outraged protests.[37] Then came the difficulties of 1927, already described, when missionary schools were obliged to conform to government regulations bringing them into closer alignment with a national curriculum and procedures.

These early assertions of the new nationalism were followed in the 1930s by a series of edicts and regulations which brought an end to much of the missionary activity in Persia. An order of 1931 forbade foreigners from carrying on propaganda against Islam, a regulation sufficiently vague and inclusive to be used at the whim of the government to block any missionary enterprises deemed undesirable. The order stemmed from concern over the penetration of Communist propaganda.[38]

More serious was the decree of August, 1932, ordering that no Persian subject could attend elementary classes in mission schools. This drastic order closed all foreign schools below the seventh-grade level, but the effects were felt even by the middle schools and by the American college at Teheran through the loss of income to the missionary board, and more significantly, the drying up of a reservoir of properly trained students for the middle and higher schools. In this instance too, the Persian government hinted that the restrictions had become necessary because the Soviets were using elementary schools as vehicles of indoctrination.[39]

A second blow in the same year was a government order restricting the licensing of medical missionaries to doctors who had practiced for five years and who could pass the government examinations, which had been made more difficult. These new rules crippled future missionary

[37] Hoffman Philip (minister to Persia) to Kellogg, March 7, 1926; G. Howland Shaw (Near Eastern Division) to Dr. Robert E. Speer (Board of Foreign Missions, Presbyterian Church in the U.S.A.), April 26, 1926; Joseph C. Grew (Under Secretary of State) to Philip, May 14, 1926 (enclosing copy of answer from Speer to G. H. Shaw of May 5, 1926), all DS 391.1163/—.

[38] *A Century of Mission Work in Iran*, p. 39; William H. Hornibrook (minister to Persia) to Hull, March 1, 1935; Wallace Murray to Secretary Hull and Under Secretary William Phillips, April 11, 1935, DS 391.1163/63 and 65. See also *MRW*, 55 (June 1932), 372; 56 (July 1933), 399; 57 (Oct. 1934), 490; Banani, *Modernization of Iran*, p. 72.

[39] Brown, *100 Years*, pp. 530–531; *A Century of Mission Work in Iran*, pp. 39, 99–100; *MRW*, 56 (March 1933), 138–140. In 1938 this publication reported that in view of the great demand for education, the Ministry of Education asked the Presbyterians to reopen elementary schools at Hamadan and Teheran, but staff shortages made this impossible. *MRW*, 61 (Dec. 1938), 611.

medical expansion because doctors had previously been recruited from among those completing internships.[40]

There had been no time to recover from these restrictive regulations before another cruel blow fell in 1933 with the order to close the historic station at Urumia (now renamed Rezaieh). The government had military and nationalistic reasons for its decision, hoping that religious and racial minorities in western Persia might be brought under closer control of the central government if their sense of separateness could be overcome. Essential to this end was the elimination of schools and religious activities which stressed their historic cultural uniqueness. The Persian government bought all the missionary property at Rezaieh and offered to cooperate in finding new stations elsewhere in the country for the displaced missionaries. The last Presbyterian missionary left the station in July of 1934, one hundred years after the station's founding; most were transferred to other stations, leaving behind at Rezaieh a weak evangelical church.[41]

For each of the foregoing measures the government was able to give a reasonable explanation, and even some missionaries could sympathize with the Persian objective of tighter central control over the centrifugally-inclined minority groups. But the reaction of the missionaries was ambivalent, and it is difficult to be sure whether most of them were prepared to recognize by the middle 1930s that they might expect further curtailment of their work in Persia. There was less uncertainty among American diplomats both in the field and in Washington. They took a pessimistic view, calculating that the Persian government was systematically building legal machinery preliminary to a final blow against foreign missionary enterprises.[42]

It came naturally for the missionaries, accustomed by long tradition to rising above obstacles, to concentrate their gaze on the sunny side of their endeavors. Reflecting this habit are the continuing references in the 1930s to past services and accomplishments and the current and future need in Persia for enlargement of their efforts. As evidence of their successful accommodation to Iranian nationalism, they pointed

[40] *MRW*, 59 (Feb. 1936), 75; Brown, *100 Years*, p. 532.

[41] Brown, *100 Years*, pp. 522–523; *A Century of Mission Work in Iran*, pp. 4–5, 39, 100; *MRW*, 57 (March 1934), 117; (Sept. 1934), 420.

[42] *MRW*, 59 (Feb. 1936), 72–73; Brown, *100 Years*, pp. 530–531; Hornibrook to Hull, May 16, 1934; March 1 and June 21, 1935; Murray memorandum, April 11, 1935; DS 391.1163/59, 63, 68, and 65.

to the growing number of Moslems attending their schools. The year before the closing of Urumia mission, for example, they reported that Fiske Seminary for girls had for the first time enrolled more Moslems than Christians. At the same time, frequent references were made to converts from Islam, to the general decline of Islam in Persia, and to the increasing toleration of evangelical work and the dissemination of Christian literature. As evidence of their effectiveness, they called attention to the number of mission school graduates in government service and teaching. And did not the government's call for assistance in training nurses and its use of missionary educators as consultants by the Ministry of Education prove that the government really valued their services and that measures affecting them adversely had not been taken out of any hostility for missionaries as such? [43]

The general tone of optimism pervading the celebration of the centenary of the Iranian mission perhaps masked any misgivings felt by the missionaries. In their publications and in other ways they celebrated their considerable sacrifices for the benefit of residents of Persia, stressing their educational, medical, and technological contributions and their role in elevating the status of women.[44]

Occasional doubts muted the brave pride. In 1936, Commodore B. Fisher, a Presbyterian missionary at Hamadan, noted the changing attitude in Iran toward the West in these words:

Ten years ago the typical schoolboy oration extolled the glories of the golden age of Cyrus and Darius, lamented the low estate to which the country had fallen and ended with an exhortation to observe the men of the West, learn of them and follow in their footsteps. Patriotism has changed much of this. Today the boys vie with one another in patriotic fervor, praise the language and culture of old Persia (Iran) and point out the weaknesses of Western civilization with its attendant evils, colonial exploitation, the crime wave, the factory system, unemployment and increasing expenditures for armament.

[43] *MRW*, 53 (Feb. 1930), 147; (May 1930), 388; (Nov. 1930), 871–872; 54 (April 1931), 315; (June 1931), 463; 55 (Jan. 1932), 54–55; (Sept. 1932), 471–475; (Dec. 1932), 633; 56 (Feb. 1933), 114; 57 (March 1934), 117; 59 (Feb. 1936), 72; 60 (Feb. 1937), 106; 61 (May 1938), 244.

[44] Brown, *100 Years*, pp. 533–534, 536; *A Century of Mission Work in Iran*, pp. 51–52, 54–62, 64–73, 100, 104; *Iran Mission*, pp. 14–16, 18–19, 22–32. See also Paul Alling memorandum (assistant chief, Near Eastern Division) Oct. 13, 1936, DS 391.1164 Am 3/39; and *MRW*, 55 (April 1932), 252; (Dec. 1932), 634–635; 57 (Jan. 1934), 57; (Dec. 1934), 553–555; 58 (Sept. 1935), 393–396; 59 (Dec. 1936), 613; 61 (Sept. 1938), 419–422.

No wonder that another missionary, Dr. R. E. Hoffman, commenting in 1932 on the growing popularity of Russian, German, and American films, had been ashamed that American films were the worst: "Our films are suggesting to the Persians that American life consists chiefly of cow-punching, rescuing abducted girls, gangster warfare and walking like Charlie Chaplin." American newspapers, he concluded, were too often of the same order: "It is certainly the duty of patriotic Americans to promote as many useful, sane American contacts as possible, if only to counteract the bad advertising of the cheap cinema and sensational newspaper." [45]

For those who would face the facts, there were still fewer than 65,000 Christians in Iran by the middle thirties. Of the entire Protestant flock of some 4000, only about half could be claimed by the Presbyterians. Undoubtedly this numerical weakness accounted in some measure for two parallel movements beginning in the mid-twenties. One was the successful cooperation among Protestant denominations, both American and Anglican, through the All Persia Inter-Mission Conference movement. The other was the encouragement given native Christians to play a larger role in church administration and policy-making. As the Iranian government meted out successive orders curtailing foreign mission activity, it fell to Persian Christians to salvage and perpetuate work formerly carried on by outsiders. During their centennial celebration, the Presbyterians proclaimed the church's "definite policy is to transfer as much of its work as possible to the national church as soon as the church can care for it." In 1934 the Evangelical Church of Iran had been organized with a Persian moderator and officers. The new church comprised 26 organized congregations and 45 groups in North Persia with a total membership of 2272. In 1935 this church was given full autonomy by the General Assembly of the Presbyterian Church in the U.S.A. [46]

The extensive Presbyterian operations were not the only foreign missionary enterprise to feel the brunt of Persian nationalism. The smaller Lutheran Orient Mission, established in 1910 and operating among the Kurds around Saujbulak (Mehabad), was ordered to with-

[45] *MRW*, 55 (Dec. 1932), 633–635 (last two quotations); 59 (Feb. 1936), 71 (first quotation).
[46] *A Century of Mission Work in Iran*, pp. 13–14 (quotation), 39; *MRW*, 49 (March 1926), 229–230; (Nov. 1926), 864–866; 50 (Jan. 1927), 23; 51 (March 1928), 207–211; 52 (June 1929), 439; (Dec. 1929), 967; 58 (June 1935), 312.

draw in 1936. The government's reason for the order was the same used in closing the Presbyterian station at Rezaieh three years earlier — the desire to bring dissident minorities within the orbit of the central government. A property settlement was finally worked out with Iranian authorities.[47]

Unexpectedly, and to the great consternation of the Presbyterian missionaries, the Iranian government announced in mid-August of 1939 that the government would take over all foreign schools in the country before the fall term opened in two weeks. Through diplomatic intercession by American officials, this crippling order was modified to permit the schools to operate under missionary auspices for the current school year while arrangements were being made for liquidating the properties. After long negotiation, the Persian government agreed in 1940 to take over the school properties of the Presbyterian board for $1.2 million, a figure far below the market value of the properties, but perhaps not unreasonable in terms of the original investment.[48] Thus, one hundred and six years after the missionaries came to Persia, their work had been reduced to their hospitals, clinics, and related medical enterprises, and to a curtailed program of evangelism.

The Trans-Iranian Railway

The zealous nationalism of the Reza Shah regime also had its bearing on the first important American industrial operation in Persia, participation in the construction of the celebrated trans-Iranian railroad. Actual American participation was confined to the years 1928–1930, but preliminary discussions dated back to the oil negotiations in 1923 and 1924.[49] Lawrence Bennett of Henry Ulen and Company appeared in Teheran early in 1924. His company planned and built public works, sometimes purchasing bonds for his clients to raise funds for building purposes. Having contacted Ralph Soper of Sinclair, who had just arranged the abortive oil concession signed on December 20, 1923, Bennett proposed that Ulen float $5 million of the proposed $10 million loan provided the government would agree to spend the $5 million on public works to be built by Ulen and Company. Bennett conferred with Reza

[47] See below, p. 313.
[48] *FR 1939*, IV, 525–537; *FR 1940*, III, 693–702; *MRW*, 62 (Dec. 1939), 577–578; PC, *AR 1940*, p. 70.
[49] See above, pp. 285–286.

Khan, then prime minister, who expressed an interest in a railroad project from the Caspian Sea to the Persian Gulf, hopeful that native iron and coal could be used in producing steel for the rails. In the spring of 1924 Sinclair and Ulen nearly completed their deal, but it fell through when Soper departed for Moscow in July. Ulen and the government had, however, signed a preliminary agreement in April, pledging $5 million of the Sinclair loan to the construction of motor roads or railroads. Neither the oil concession nor the Ulen contract was ratified.[50]

The Ulen Company did not lose interest in Iranian projects. A company representative forwarded a railroad concession proposal to Arthur Millspaugh in October of 1925, but the financial czar felt that the time was not ripe. Prospects improved after the Majlis passed, at Millspaugh's behest, a sugar and tea tax, the proceeds of which could be reserved for transportation projects. The Persian government canvassed for an American railway engineer to make a route survey and perhaps direct construction. The State Department tried to help locate a suitable and properly qualified man, but the Persian government was so hesitant about offering an attractive salary that negotiations extended over a year before William B. Poland was hired in September, 1926. Poland and his ten American assistants were known as the American Railway Administration. By this time the government had given up any thought of using Persian steel, deciding instead to give building concessions to foreign companies. The government had chosen a route for Poland to survey, the terminals on the Caspian and Gulf not being those desired by either the Russians or the British, whom the government was in no mood to accommodate.[51]

After evaluating the situation, Poland informed the State Department in November of 1927 that the time was right for Americans to seek the concession. He reported that three different German companies were negotiating for a concession to build between 400 and 500 kilometers of the proposed northern segment between Teheran and the Caspian

[50] *FR 1924*, II, 539, 547–548, 552–557, 561–565.

[51] Philip to Kellogg, Feb. 23, 1925, Feb. 25, 1926, and Jan. 25, 1927; KC memorandum, Sept. 25, 1926, DS 891.77/103, 111, 192, and 176; M. D. Carrel (vice president, Ulen & Co.) to A. W. Dulles (chief, Near Eastern Division), Oct. 26, 1925; Murray memorandum of conversation with Lawrence E. Bennett, Nov. 22, 1926, DS 891.77 Ulen & Co./30 and 35; Philip to Kellogg, Sept. 14 (telegram), Sept. 14 (despatch), Nov. 19, 1926; G. H. Shaw to C. J. Carroll, Nov. 19, 1926; Philip to Kellogg, Dec. 27, 1926, DS 891.77A Poland, W. B./16, 19, 25, 26, 27; Elwell-Sutton, *Modern Iran*, pp. 90–92, 94.

Sea. Poland had suggested to the Persian government that it spend a year building part of the line in order to ascertain unit cost for use in bargaining for construction of the balance of the road. The State Department forwarded this information to Ulen and Company.[52]

Ulen soon sent three representatives under M. D. Carrel's supervision. Following their arrival in Teheran early in 1928, Carrel recommended that Ulen work with the German companies to get a concession, suggesting that each might contract for half the road. Carrel's proposal stemmed from his belief that a joint proposal would deter the Persian government from a natural inclination to play one group off against the other. His method was approved, and the concession was signed on April 26, 1928. This agreement provided for setting up the *Syndicat pour Chemins de Fer en Perse,* consisting of three German organizations and Ulen and Company; Ulen was permitted to bring in French and British companies to assist in the construction of the southern part of the line allotted to the Americans. According to the contract, five trial sections of thirty kilometers each were to be constructed at each end, starting from points already reached by Poland's American Railway Administration. Article 11 protected the government to the disadvantage of the companies, as Ulen would learn to its dismay later. In analyzing the agreement, Wallace Murray, chief of the State Department's Near Eastern Division, commented "that the American-German syndicate appears to be made up either of optimists or philanthropists and that the Persians may congratulate themselves for being in a very favorable position to 'get something for nothing.'" [53] On July 9, 1928, supplementary contracts were signed with Ulen, providing for extension of the railroad from Ahwaz — originally specified as the southern terminus — to Bandar Shahpur on the Persian Gulf.[54]

[52] Kellogg to Philip, Nov. 15, 1927, DS 891.77A Poland, W. B./30; David Williamson (chargé d'affaires a.i., Teheran) to Kellogg, Nov. 17, 1927; G. H. Shaw to C. M. Bounell (Ulen & Co.), Nov. 21, 1927, both DS 891.77 Ulen & Co./38.

[53] Kellogg to Philip, Jan. 4 and Jan. 6, 1928; Philip to Kellogg, Feb. 21, Feb. 25, and May 4, 1928; Murray memorandum to Shaw, June 4, 1928 (quotation), DS 891.77 Ulen & Co./40A, 41, 42, 43, 51, and 51.

[54] Philip to Kellogg, July 11, 1928, DS 891.77 Ulen & Co./54. During the 1928 negotiations with the syndicate, the Persian government had violated its contract with William Poland and his American Railway Administration by refusing him the control entitled by his contract. The State Department told the Persian government that it had treated Poland and his associates outrageously. After finally achieving a satisfactory settlement, Poland departed on November 1, 1928. Philip to Kellogg, Aug. 18, 1927; Aug. 27 and Sept. 15, 1928; Murray to Shaw, Aug. 21, 1928; Castle,

Construction progressed rapidly despite floods and natural incidents, ill-informed official interference, and dilatory payment of advances by the government. The survey was completed in October of 1929, the syndicate giving the government an estimate of $173 million for the entire line, including the trial sections. The Shah inspected the northern section, which was close enough to completion for him to ride from Bandar Gaz to Sari — one hundred and seven kilometers — in December of 1929. The Shah then demanded a comparable excursion on the southern segment of his railroad.[55]

At this time (December, 1929), the southern section was far along toward completion of 250 kilometers from Bandar Shahpur to Dizful except for a few culverts and the Ahwaz bridge. The down trip from Dizful to Bandar Shahpur took place without mishap, the Shah expressing delight and announcing that the rest of the construction work should be given to Ulen. Then on January 10, 1930, began the fateful return trip of the special train after the worst torrential rains in years had undermined fresh roadbed. Special precautions were taken, but about twenty miles north of Bandar Shahpur the Shah's coach, in which he was riding alone, went off the sagging tracks. By the time the train could be brought to a standstill his Majesty was considerably jostled, but he was transferred to another car and the royal train proceeded with the utmost caution. The emergency locomotive following the train soon returned toward Bandar Shahpur, and in a short time the Shah's coach was back on the track and overtaking the special train. To the dismay of Ulen engineers, a few hundred yards from the main train and in full view of the Shah, the unfortunate royal coach again left the rails.

The dejected party finally reached Ahwaz in a deluge of rain only to learn that floods had carried away a kilometer of track north of the city, and that the whole surrounding country was a sea of mud, impassable to autos, so that the Shah had to descend to Ahwaz, where he was marooned for days. The enforced idleness only added to the towering rage of his Majesty who finally insisted on leaving the city on January

"Memorandum of Conversation with the Minister of Persia," Aug. 23, 1928; R. A. Wallace Treat (chargé d'affaires a.i., Teheran) to Kellogg, Oct. 5 and Nov. 1, 1928, DS 891.77A Poland, W. B./29, 46, 47, 41, 40, 49, and 50.

[55] Some data in this and the previous paragraph are taken from a fourteen-page summary of the history of the Ulen project from 1928 to 1931 based on Department of State records. See Jefferson Patterson (Near Eastern Division), "International Consortium Planned," Aug. 5, 1931, DS 891.77 Ulen & Co./192.

25. Arrangements were made for him to proceed up the railroad track by handcar and, where necessary, on foot. The entire unhappy experience erased any good impressions the Shah might have received on the down trip; he was now furious with the Americans and was said to be not at all disposed to give them further construction work. There was hope, however, that once he returned to Teheran his hostility to Ulen might be allayed.[56]

The debacle of the Shah's return trip contributed to making the railroad project a football in the tangled game of Persian politics. The required governmental monetary advances were slower than ever in arriving, and led the company to issue an ultimatum on April 17, 1930, announcing that if advances were not paid by April 28, work would stop on May 1 and the railway would be turned over to the government as it stood on May 15. Payments were not made; work was stopped on May 1 on both sections at a time when some ninety per cent of the original contract had been completed; and on May 15 the government forcibly took over the railroad under conditions which did not allow the foreign companies to make proper inventories.[57]

The original syndicate was soon canceled in view of the Persian government's rescission. Ulen representatives left Teheran on May 17 to meet representatives of the cooperating German firms at Bad Kissingen, where the original syndicate was abandoned. Ulen officials then proceeded to Paris to meet with their colleagues who had been participating in the construction of the southern segment. La Société des Batignolles, assisted by an English firm (Stewart and McDonnell), took over the former Ulen position. Ulen maintained only a material interest in the new arrangement.[58]

Although the State Department had extended routine help and advice to the Ulen Company, it had refrained from intervention in the international intrigue which the company thought partly responsible for its debacle. After hearing the company's version, Wallace Murray wrote that "post-mortems are never very cheerful affairs, but this one was illuminating in some respects." According to the company's vice president, M. D. Carrel, the Soviet embassy had intervened with Persian authorities in behalf of the German consortium. Earlier the Russians

---

[56] *Ibid.*; Williamson to Stimson, Jan. 25, 1930, DS 891.77 Ulen & Co./104.

[57] Patterson memorandum, Aug. 5, 1931, DS 891.77 Ulen & Co./192.

[58] *Ibid.*; M. D. Carrel (vice president, Ulen & Co.) from Lebanon, Indiana, to Murray, June 18, 1930, DS 891.77 Ulen & Co./139.

and Germans had agreed that the German group would keep its work in the north well ahead of American construction in the south, but when the Germans failed to meet Soviet expectations, the Soviets intervened to impede progress in the south. The Soviets were, of course, aware that an efficient railroad in northern Persia would be of inestimable advantage in an invasion of Persia and were interested in impeding, if possible, a southern road advantageous to their traditional rivals, the British. Murray concluded "that the Germans in many respects have played 'dirty ball'" in failing to reciprocate the support given them by their American colleagues. He then cited the cases of Shuster, Millspaugh, and Poland, noting that these Americans made up only a fraction of the French, Belgians, Austrians, Italians, Germans, and Swedes who appeared on the casualty list. The department would do well, he advised, "to bear these victims in mind whenever any rosy picture is painted with regard to the possibilities of rendering American financial or other assistance to Persia." The total picture made "quite an international graveyard of blasted hopes." [59]

The Persian government made a new agreement with the German consortium on July 31, 1930, for completion of the northern section. Subsequently, Danish and Swedish companies were brought into the railroad construction. The entire road from the Caspian Sea to the Persian Gulf was finally opened in 1938, in time to be of crucial importance in supplying the Soviets with Lend-Lease materials during World War II.[60]

[59] Murray memorandum, June 26, 1930, DS 891.77 Ulen & Co./140. More than a year later there were suspicions in the department that "a deeper German motive [for the original collaboration with Americans] may have been that of letting Ulen pull German chestnuts out of the fire and eventually getting the whole railway scheme into German hands." Patterson memorandum, Aug. 5, 1931, DS 891.77 Ulen & Co./192. The rescission by the Persian government required Ulen to pursue its claims for many years. The department felt an obligation to make strong representations in behalf of the rights of the American company. Murray memorandum to William Phillips, Nov. 10, and Nov. 20, 1933; Raymond A. Hare memorandum (Near Eastern Division), Dec. 7, 1935; three bound volumes entitled "Ulen & Company — Persian Claim: References"; DS 891.77 Ulen & Co./260, 267, 328, and 257.

[60] Patterson memorandum, Aug. 5, 1931, DS 891.77 Ulen & Co./192; Elwell-Sutton, *Modern Iran*, p. 93; Haas, *Iran*, pp. 211–215; *MRW*, 61 (Nov. 1938), 548; T. H. Vail Motter, *The Persian Corridor and Aid to Russia*; Joel Sayre, *Persian Gulf Command: Some Marvels on the Road to Kazvin*. The Iranian government made arrangements in 1933 with a Scandinavian syndicate, the "Consortium Kampsax," which then "let out the work in lots to various European companies" — British, Italian, Belgian, Swedish, Swiss, Czech, and others. Supplies came from Soviet Russia, the United States, Australia, Sweden, Belgium, Germany, Japan, and Yugoslavia.

Archaeologists

American archaeologists played an important role in the cultural relations of the United States and Iran during the 1930s when the Oriental Institute of the University of Chicago conducted a major expedition at Persepolis, the capital city of the Achaemenid kings. These excavations grew out of proposals by the illustrious James Henry Breasted, who in 1928 recommended an Iranian expedition as part of a ten-year Oriental Institute program in the Middle East. The Rockefeller Foundation, financial backer of these archaeological enterprises, omitted Breasted's Iranian proposal from the program finally approved.[61]

Two years later the Oriental Institute asked Professor Ernest Herzfeld, the German archaeologist then in Iran, to apply for an option permitting the Oriental Institute to excavate at Persepolis at some later time. Through a misunderstanding, Herzfeld obtained a concession instead of a mere option. Before Secretary of State Henry L. Stimson knew of the misunderstanding, he gave wide publicity to the concession, much to the embarrassment of Breasted, who had no funds with which to undertake the excavations. After strenuous efforts Breasted obtained funds through the generosity of Mrs. William H. Moore, and Professor Herzfeld was put in charge. Iran had recently adopted a new antiquities law which brightened prospects for Western archaeologists interested in Persia.[62]

Major American excavations at Persepolis between 1931 and 1937 unearthed many spectacular finds, including a great terrace containing palaces, audience halls, and public buildings together with a wealth of relief sculpture ornamenting the buildings. Parallel operations uncovered a village nearby — a prehistoric settlement with some beautiful pottery. Meanwhile, the Museum of the University of Pennsylvania was digging at Tepe Hissar on the Iranian plateau between 1931 and 1933.[63]

[61] Raymond Hare memorandum, Dec. 4, 1936, DS 891.927 Persepolis/436. The International Exhibition of Persian Art in London (1931) and numerous exhibitions that followed in various museums and universities of Europe and the United States "were a revelation to people who had never realized the extent and influence of Persia's former civilization." Brown, *100 Years*, p. 468. See also *Iran Mission*, p. 5; and Charles Breasted, *Pioneer to the Past: The Story of James Henry Breasted, Archaeologist*, p. 402.

[62] Charles C. Hart (minister in Persia) to Henry L. Stimson, Dec. 17 and Dec. 26, 1930; Murray, daily report, July 5, 1934; Murray memorandum, Feb. 5, 1936, DS 891.927 Persepolis/44, 44, 84, and 405.

[63] Ann Perkins in *Background of the Middle East*, p. 218; Ernest E. Herzfeld,

Difficulties with Iranian authorities troubled the Persepolis expedition and were serious enough by 1934 to require diplomatic assistance from American officials. Differences over division of the finds, coupled with interference from the Persian government through its commissioner, plagued the archaeologists, who also objected to the permission given foreign correspondents to photograph new finds. The desire of the Oriental Institute to send thirty thousand clay tablets to Chicago for decipherment presented special problems; the task would take years instead of the one year allowed by the Persian government.[64]

The Oriental Institute argued that the Persian government was not living up to the terms of its contract. Consultation with the State Department in Washington elicited some good advice and a pledge of assistance. Wallace S. Murray advised the Oriental Institute to seek a definite understanding with the Persian government, pledging the latter to adhere to its prior agreement on threat of withdrawal by the expedition. Murray cautioned the Institute not to threaten withdrawal unless it was prepared to follow through. In any case, the Institute could count on as much help from the department as would be tendered any reputable American business enterprise abroad. The department also instructed Minister William Hornibrook to make strong representations at the foreign office, supporting the Institute.[65]

When Breasted wrote a letter to Persian officials setting forth the position of the Oriental Institute, the Persian government handed back the letter with the claim that it was "insulting." The Persians did, however, agree to continue negotiations for the transport of the thousands of clay tablets to Chicago.[66]

Wallace Murray's experience in Persia and his understanding of Persian psychology qualified him to advise Breasted wisely during a conference on September 11, 1934. If the Americans would allow for face-saving, he felt they might win terms permitting continuation of

Archaeological History of Iran. For the results of studies conducted in 1934 under the auspices of the Field Museum of Chicago, see Henry Field, *Contributions to the Anthropology of Iran,* pp. 7–12 and *passim.*

[64] Murray memorandum of conversation with Dr. James H. Breasted, May 16, 1934; Murray, daily report, July 5, 1934, DS 891.927 Persepolis/74 and 84.

[65] Murray memorandum, Aug. 6, 1934; Murray, daily reports, July 5 and Aug. 16, 1934, DS 891.927 Persepolis/104, 84, and 115.

[66] Murray, daily report, Sept. 5, 1934, DS 891.927 Persepolis/135. Coping with the Persian government would have been difficult enough even without internal problems among leading personalities making up the expedition. Murray memoranda, May 16 and Aug. 6, 1934, DS 891.927 Persepolis/74 and 104.

the Persepolis expedition on a basis favorable to the Oriental Institute. At the same time, the Americans should make it clear that they could not compromise on fundamentals essential to sound archaeological inquiry. He argued that the advantages to Persia from this work were so great that the Persians would be reluctant to take a stand which would drive the Americans out. The Persians had "reaped benefits from the Institute's work at Persepolis that could not be duplicated by any other organization in the world." The upshot by the end of 1934 was a notable victory for the Oriental Institute, won with the assistance of the State Department.[67] Work went forward until a new crisis threatened in 1936.

The new difficulties, at first financial, were augmented by troubles growing out of the actions of the Persian government. Charles Breasted, son of the archaeologist and business manager for the Oriental Institute, wrote Wallace Murray on January 31, 1936, explaining the financial crisis and soliciting a letter from the department for use in seeking assistance from the Rockefeller Foundation. Murray obliged with a generous letter of commendation, in which he emphasized the enormous cultural and historical significance of the work done at Persepolis. There is no doubt he was expressing his convictions in meting out this praise, but he also had in mind the importance of continuing the enterprise to maintaining American prestige in Persia. The State Department could not, he believed, be disinterested in view of its previous support, and abandonment of the project could have an unfortunate effect on other American interests.[68]

The reduced funds available to the Oriental Institute in 1936 required curtailment not only in Persia but in other parts of the Middle East as well. Various improvisations were suggested in an effort to keep some of the most promising work going despite the financial stringency.[69]

The State Department had learned of further discouragements for the Persepolis excavators from their field director, Erich Schmidt, when he talked with Wallace Murray on December 2, 1936. Schmidt explained

[67] Murray memoranda, Sept. 11, 1934 (quotation) and Feb. 5, 1936; Murray, daily report, Sept. 13, 1934, DS 891.927 Persepolis/151, 405, and 152. See also Elwell-Sutton, *Modern Iran*, p. 152.

[68] Charles Breasted to Murray, Jan. 31, 1936; Murray memorandum, Feb. 5, 1936; Murray to John Wilson (acting director, Oriental Institute), Feb. 7, 1936; Murray to Gordon P. Merriam (second secretary, Teheran), March 2, 1936, DS 891.927 Persepolis/404, 405, 406, and 409.

[69] Paul Alling memorandum, April 20, 1936; Raymond Hare memorandum, Dec. 4, 1936, DS 891.927 Persepolis/412 and 436.

that friction had arisen over the income-tax exactions levied on the excavators by the Persian government and over the division of certain duplicate friezes. He wondered if the department could help again as it had so successfully during the 1934 crisis. Murray could not be reassuring in view of the diplomatic crisis occasioned by the arrest of the Iranian minister to the United States on a speeding charge and subsequent newspaper articles in the American press, which the Shah had considered so offensive that he had withdrawn his minister from Washington. With diplomatic relations nearly severed, all important channels of communication with the Shah had been closed. The situation was radically different from that in 1934 when the State Department had assisted the archaeologists.[70]

Schmidt's initial reaction to Murray's explanation was that he should return to Iran to obtain a division of finds and then withdraw. Before the end of the year, however, there were signs that the Shah's attitude was improving. The Persian government gave tax refunds to the American archaeologists and permitted them to operate their reconnaissance plane more freely. Meanwhile, financial reorganization of the expedition was going forward.[71]

The brighter prospects did not last long. In the spring of 1937 when the Shah was irritated by American press reports which he considered insulting, he made a stormy visit to Persepolis. He complained that the Persepolis project was not progressing rapidly enough and ordered the work speeded up. Instead, the work tapered off, and in the fall of 1939, the Oriental Institute withdrew from Iran about the same time it was curtailing operations in other parts of the Middle East.[72]

The Djalal Incident and Its Effects, 1935–1939

As Reza Shah became increasingly sensitive about his personal prestige and the international reputation of the nation he was trying to reshape, he seized on what ordinarily would have been considered insignificant slights and inflated them into major incidents.[73] What the

[70] Murray memorandum, Dec. 2, 1936, DS 891.927 Persepolis/426.

[71] *Ibid.*; Murray memorandum, Dec. 4, 1936; Hare memorandum, Dec. 4, 1936, DS 891.927 Persepolis/429 and 436.

[72] John A. Wilson to Murray, Dec. 10, 1936; Murray memorandum to Secretary Hull and Under Secretary Sumner Welles, June 2, 1937; Alling memorandum, June 16, 1939; DS 891.927 Persepolis/440, 459, and 464.

[73] Haas, *Iran*, p. 156; Banani, *Modernization of Iran*, pp. 39–40; Upton, *Modern Iran*, p. 60.

Shah chose to consider unpardonable insults served as the basis for a partial break in diplomatic relations with the United States between 1936 and 1939. His behavior during these years weakened the ability of American diplomats to negotiate normally a number of outstanding issues in Iranian-American relations.

The incident triggering the diplomatic breach of the mid-thirties took place on November 27, 1935, when Ghaffar Djalal, Iranian minister to the United States, was arrested in Elkton, Maryland, for speeding. Even though local authorities were not adequately informed about the customs of diplomatic immunity, Djalal was not detained long before proceeding on his motor trip to New York City. Upon his return to Washington, however, he protested to Secretary of State Hull against the actions of the Maryland authorities. Four days later, Hull extended his personal apology together with one from the governor of Maryland. As further balm, Hull informed the minister that the Elkton chief of police and constable had been fined and discharged. Hull could not refrain from delivering a short lecture to Djalal expressing the view that diplomats should obey local laws instead of violating them as Djalal had in this instance by speeding. Hull released the note to the press.[74]

Unhappy with Hull's inference that he was a lawbreaker, Djalal protested to Wallace Murray. After Murray had attempted to smooth over the matter, the department informed William H. Hornibrook, American minister in Teheran, on December 12 that it considered the matter closed. Although it would have been better if the incident had been forgotten, the Iranian press kept it alive with attacks on the way the United States had handled the affair. The Shah's intense displeasure took the form of recalling Djalal, who informed Hull on January 3, 1936, that he had instructions to return to Iran. Although Iran gave no official explanation for the recall at the time, Iranian newspapers asserted that the withdrawal was a protest against the American handling of the speeding incident. On January 14, Hossein Ghods, first secretary of legation, took over as chargé d'affaires.[75]

[74] *FR 1936*, III, 342–344; Department of State, *Press Releases*, 13 (Dec. 7, 1935), pp. 497–498; *The New York Times*, Nov. 28, 29, 30, Dec. 1, 3, 5, 7, 11, 1935; *Time*, 26 (Dec. 9, 1935), 26, 28; *Literary Digest*, 120 (Dec. 7, 1935), 9. Djalal is used here (instead of Jalal) to conform to the transliteration used by the State Department.

[75] *FR 1936*, III, 344–346; *The New York Times*, Jan. 5, 18, 19, 1936.

Iranians continued to protest the treatment of Djalal and suggested that the American attitude was in retaliation against the minister for having circumvented the State Department in 1935 when he resorted to direct pressure on senators for a reservation to the arms convention.[76] Iran also charged the United States with officially sponsoring an anti-Iranian campaign. The department denied both charges.

Further exchanges revealed that Djalal had misinformed his foreign office about details of the Maryland incident. After Hornibrook reviewed the facts again with the Iranian foreign office on January 29, the Iranians decided to drop the matter.[77]

Hardly had the Djalal flurry subsided when a new incident arose to revive the displeasure of Reza Shah. On February 8, 1936, the New York *Daily Mirror* stated that Reza Shah had been a stable boy at the British legation during his boyhood. When the Iranian chargé protested the statement on March 14, he showed Under Secretary William Phillips a message from the Shah threatening to break off diplomatic relations unless the newspaper assertion was retracted. Phillips explained that the reference had appeared in an unimportant publication and that the tradition of freedom of the press in America prevented the department from muzzling newspapers. The following day, a Sunday morning, Wallace Murray called on Ghods to reiterate the explanation of press freedom, but he also carried an olive branch. If the department made an exception by seeking a retraction from a publisher, would Iran consider this a precedent? Ghods assured him it would not. Murray then conferred with Michael J. McDermott, chief of the Division of Current Information, and together they decided to work quietly for a retraction through the Washington representative of William Randolph Hearst, the publisher. The intercession with Hearst resulted in a statement of retraction and regret published in the *Daily Mirror* on March 26. Again officials in the State Department felt they could breathe easily — but not for long.[78]

Two days after the retraction, Ghods informed Hull that all Iranian representatives in the United States were being withdrawn. No official explanation accompanied the foreign office announcement, but Gordon P. Merriam, American chargé in Teheran, learned from an official in

[76] *FR 1936*, III, 347–349. See also *FR 1934*, I, 449–488.
[77] *FR 1936*, II, 349.
[78] *FR 1936*, III, 347, 350–355.

the foreign office that the action was provoked by displeasure at the *Daily Mirror's* retraction because it repeated the substance of the original article. Hull's expression of regret to Teheran and efforts to stay the withdrawal order were unsuccessful, but before Ghods departed, he told Wallace Murray that his government did not want the United States to change the status of the American legation at Teheran.[79]

Immediately, Secretary Hull explored the possibility of healing the breach. He instructed Merriam to ascertain if the Iranian government would welcome a special American envoy sent to bring about restoration of normal relations. The Iranian foreign office approached this overture cautiously with a request for clarification on four points. They asked what rank the proposed envoy would have; they wished to know the wording of any message intended for the Shah; they inquired about the role of the envoy; and they raised questions about what publicity was contemplated for the mission. The Iranian government desired an ambassador extraordinary just to deal with diplomatic relations; furthermore, the sending of the mission should be presented as an American idea.[80] These conditions showed how central the prestige issue was in Iranian thinking. The Iranian government was obviously seeking a propaganda advantage from the appearance that the United States had prostrated itself before the Shah.

Before the United States replied to the Iranian queries and conditions, Hornibrook, who had resigned on March 16, arrived in Washington with information which led Hull to abandon his conciliatory overtures. At a farewell dinner on March 15, the Iranian foreign minister, Bagher Kazemi, suggested to Hornibrook that the United States should limit freedom of the press by amending the constitution. Hull was so exercised when he learned of this suggestion that he abandoned the notion of a special envoy. When Merriam so informed the Iranian foreign office on May 9, he was told that Kazemi must have been misunderstood. In reporting this view to the department, Merriam recommended that the United States accept the explanation. He had, however, taken the liberty of indicating that the department had not been disturbed so much by the impropriety of Kazemi's remarks as by his misunderstanding of American institutions, which boded ill for the pro-

[79] *FR 1936*, III, 356–358; *The New York Times*, March 31, 1936; *Literary Digest*, 121 (April 11, 1936), 14; *Time*, 27 (April 13, 1936), 28, 30.
[80] *FR 1936*, III, 357, 359–360.

posed special mission. Since Kazemi had resided in the United States for some years, Merriam implied that he should be more familiar with American government and institutions than most Iranians.

Secretary Hull rapped Merriam's knuckles by telling him in plain language that the department had not misunderstood Kazemi's remarks at the dinner and by instructing him to refrain from any speculative interpretation of the department's views. Even though Merriam considered the diplomatic impasse with Iran a serious matter, the department did not view it with any particular concern. Uncowed by the sharp instructions from Hull, Merriam told the Secretary on May 17 that he still thought the report of the Hornibrook-Kazemi conversation had been oversimplified and that he believed Hornibrook had, in fact, initiated the conversation about changing the American constitution. It was not until two months later that Hornibrook wrote Merriam his version of the incident, which was the one accepted by the State Department.[81]

Meanwhile, new accounts in the American press continued to irritate the Iranians. They threatened to sever all diplomatic and commercial relations with the United States unless the American press refrained from printing hostile articles. The foreign office told Merriam orally of certain specific newspaper accounts they found offensive, but the department's efforts to get these complaints reduced to writing were unavailing. After a lull of several weeks the Iranian government lodged another protest, this time against an item in the *Brooklyn Eagle* of June 13. As one of the odd facts presented under the heading "Stranger than Fiction," a picture of the Shah was accompanied by the caption that he was not descended from a long line of royalty but had once been a stable boy. Merriam tried to gloss over the Iranian outrage by observing that the self-made man was a popular conception in the United States. The department also tried to soothe the Iranians with assurances that there was no deliberate attempt to attack the Shah and that some of the protested articles should actually have been considered friendly.[82]

[81] *FR 1936*, III, 361–365, 371–373.

[82] *FR 1936*, III, 364–371, 374–375. Note the flippant style of the *Time* article of December 9, 1935 (see note 74). For examples of articles about Iran and the Shah, which were on the whole favorable but may have given offense to Reza Shah, see "Master of Persia: One-Time Robin Hood Becomes Modernizing, Benevolent Dictator," *Literary Digest*, 122 (Dec. 19, 1936), 8–9; John Gunther, "King of Kings: The Shah of Iran — Which Used to Be Persia," *Harper's*, 178 (Dec. 1938), 60–69; Vincent Sheean, "Shah-in-Shah: Reza, Founder of the Pahlavi Dynasty and Heir

An opportunity soon arose for the United States to show its good will toward Iran. A series of natural disasters — floods and earthquakes — in August brought a message of sympathy from President Franklin D. Roosevelt to the Shah, but the message apparently had no visible effect toward easing the ill feeling.[83] As the year wore on, the possibilities of resuming full diplomatic relations were frequently discussed, with no significant results.

Sporadic efforts to normalize relations continued during 1937 and into 1938 without a meeting of the minds. Just after former minister Charles C. Hart had signed an oil concession with the Persian government for operations in North Persia, Chargé Merriam urged Secretary Hull in January of 1937 to appoint a minister to Teheran. The department could not see that such an appointment would eliminate the Shah's extreme sensitivity to foreign criticism. The American legation again became hopeful during the summer when Cornelius Van H. Engert, who had replaced Merriam as chargé, reported an unusually large number of Iranian dignitaries attending the July 4 celebration at the legation. Although Engert thought this might indicate relaxing of tension, no overtures came from the Iranian government until late in the year when the subject of a special mission was reintroduced. Again the department rejected the suggestion.[84]

Engert continued informal talks with Iranian officials and found them anxious to come to some solution, but efforts tapered off with the death of the foreign minister, Enatafollah Samiy, in February, 1938. Engert reported on March 21 that there was little immediate prospect that the Iranian legation in the United States would reopen. When the Iranians again suggested a special American mission (this time a trade delegation) in March, the department stood by its previous position — that the United States was willing to meet the Iranians halfway, but that the initiative should rest with Iran. Then followed four months of relative inactivity before the protracted impasse began to break.[85]

American initiative in August, 1938, started the process of denouement. James S. Moose, now chargé in Teheran, informed the foreign office of the proposed visit to the Middle East by Wallace S. Murray,

to the Glory of Cyrus the Great," *Asia*, 26 (Dec. 1926), 1052–1059 *et seq.*, reprinted in *ibid.*, 37 (March 1937), 175–178.
[83] *FR 1936*, III, 373–374.
[84] *FR 1937*, II, 719–728.
[85] *FR 1938*, II, 726, 729–733.

chief of the Near Eastern Division. During his autumn tour, Murray would be able to visit Teheran, where perhaps the Shah would want to receive him to hear the personal message he would be carrying from President Roosevelt. At first the Iranian government received this proposal warily, feeling that Murray would have no ministerial rank and that his presence might invoke unpleasant memories of difficulties in Iranian-American relations when he had been secretary of the legation between 1922 and 1925. Apparently the latter point was a veiled reference to the Imbrie murder. After Moose reassured the foreign office that Murray would have ministerial rank and reminded the Iranians that Murray's relations with them had always been good, they became more receptive. On August 29, they informed Moose that the Shah would receive Murray.

On his arrival in Teheran early in October, Murray had an hour's interview with Reza Shah and presented President Roosevelt's letter expressing the hope that diplomatic relations could be restored. After the Shah and Murray reviewed old and current issues in Iranian-American relations, the Shah instructed the acting foreign minister, Mohsen Rais, to cooperate with Murray in further discussions. The two men talked over the timing of restoring normal relations and ways of coping with the American press at the time of resumption. Murray departed with a letter from the Shah to President Roosevelt, which he delivered on his return to Washington in November.[86]

Moose reported early in November that the Iranians would soon send a chargé to Washington. On December 28, 1938, Iranian newspapers officially announced the assignment of Ali A. Daftary, then secretary of the legation at Berlin, as chargé in Washington. In the meantime, Engert had returned to his post as chargé in Teheran. Daftary arrived in Washington late in December and soon began conferences with Wallace Murray. The Shah instructed Daftary to present himself to Secretary Hull without fanfare which might bring undue publicity. Hull received him on January 25, 1939, and then held an informal press conference announcing the official restoration of diplomatic relations. A few months later (June 23) the United States appointed Louis G. Dreyfus, Jr., minister to Iran, the first since Hornibrook's resignation in 1936.[87]

The diplomatic breach arising from the Djalal speeding incident and

[86] *FR 1938*, II, 733–743.
[87] *FR 1938*, II, 744–751.

the subsequent press reports in the United States had a mixed effect on specific issues in Iranian-American relations. When the breach began, the missionary activities had already been curtailed because of the requirements of Iranian nationalism. There is only scattered evidence that diplomatic tension further impaired the missionary position. The Reverend William N. Wysham, American missionary at Teheran, was convicted early in 1936 "of distributing literature harmful to the religion of the country." The act had been committed some six years earlier, no charges being filed until 1933, after which the matter had lapsed until November, 1935. Shortly thereafter the Djalal incident occurred, and was possibly a decisive factor — as many speculated — in sentencing Wysham to a month's imprisonment and imposing a heavy fine.[88] The following month, the Iranians demanded the departure of the Lutheran missionaries at Mehabad (formerly Saujbulak) in Azerbaijan within fifteen days on grounds that the missionaries associated with disaffected Kurdish elements in this frontier province at a time when the government was trying to inculcate Iranian nationalism among them. Merriam protested that the missionaries could not dispose of their property in the time allotted. Although he feared a connection between the Djalal incident and the withdrawal order, the Iranians apparently made none, and the mission negotiated a settlement with the government without further direct intervention by the legation.[89] The most serious blow to missionary enterprise, the order of August 1939 expropriating all foreign schools, did not come until after full diplomatic relations had been resumed.[90]

For the archaeologists of the Oriental Institute expedition at Persepolis, the diplomatic breach was of some significance. During their continuing difficulties with Iranian authorities in 1936 they hoped the State Department could again intercede on their behalf as it had two years earlier, but Murray had to explain that the present situation was radically different with avenues of communication to the Shah cut off. But even during the period of diplomatic hiatus the Iranian government had been conciliatory in granting income tax refunds and more freedom in the use of an airplane for archaeological reconnaissance.[91]

[88] Murray memorandum, Feb. 10, 1936, DS 391.1163/89. At the time Murray wrote, the case had been appealed to a higher court.
[89] *FR 1936*, III, 385–391; Engert to Hull, Feb. 7, 1938, DS 391.1163 Lutheran Orient Mission/142; *A Century of Mission Work in Iran*, p. 15.
[90] See above, p. 297.
[91] See above, pp. 305–306.

Nor were commercial relations deflected from their usual patterns during the diplomatic controversy. Imports and exports followed established patterns and fluctuated approximately with the over-all trends in American foreign trade for those years. However, informal discussions looking toward possible negotiation of a trade agreement, initiated in the fall of 1934, were disrupted by the diplomatic rupture. Late in 1937 following the expression of renewed interest by the Iranians, the State Department initiated detailed studies needed for further negotiations. Desultory exchanges took place, but no serious negotiations followed until 1940, and a reciprocal trade agreement was not signed until April 8, 1943.[92]

To express his pique at articles in foreign publications, the Shah ordered his postal officials not to deliver second class (printed) mail originating in the United States. This indiscriminate ban, in effect for more than a year, prevented subscribers from receiving even such innocuous publications as the *American Medical Journal* and *Yachting*, which could hardly have been expected to comment on Iranian politics. Some subscribers circumvented the regulation by having publications remailed from Europe or from other Middle Eastern countries. After persistent inquiries from American postal and diplomatic officials, deliveries were resumed in August of 1937, when subscribers began to receive back copies, including those which Iranian authorities claimed had been destroyed.[93]

The Shah's displeasure with the United States did not prevent him from approving new oil concessions for an American company in northern Iran. The Amiranian Oil Company of New York, a subsidiary of Seaboard Oil Company, sent former minister Charles C. Hart as its representative to Teheran late in 1936. On December 2, Hart began negotiations with the Iranian government for oil and pipeline concessions. A month later (January 3, 1937) two concessions were signed and ratified promptly by the Majlis early in February. The diplomatic tangle

[92] *FR 1934*, II, 884–890; *FR 1935*, I, 909–915; *FR 1938*, II, 757–762; *FR 1940*, III, 663–693; *FR 1941*, III, 366–374; Leland M. Goodrich and Marie J. Carroll, eds., *Documents on American Foreign Relations*, V, July 1942–June 1943, p. 633. The agreement entered into force on June 28, 1944. See *ibid.*, VI, July 1943–June 1944, pp. 329, 691. For correspondence concerning possible discrimination against American trade resulting from the German-Iranian Convention for the regulation of payments (October 30, 1935) and consideration of an Iranian-American clearing agreement, see *FR 1936*, III, 395–400; and *FR 1937*, II, 761–766.

[93] *FR 1936*, III, 375–385; *FR 1937*, II, 728–734.

had no serious effect on these oil negotiations and the legation gave no assistance beyond helping the company explain its completely American status to the Soviets, who were extremely sensitive to exploitation of northern Iranian oil by a foreign company. The Soviets were apparently satisfied at the time that the American company offered no serious threat to their interests. In any case, they were not openly hostile and permitted the company to transport materials to Iran through Russian territory. The Amiranian Company, however, officially relinquished its concessions on June 12, 1938, for a variety of reasons. The economic recession in the United States, death of two company officials, new oil discoveries in Saudi Arabia, and transport and marketing problems and costs all figured in the decision. American fears that the Shah would be furious proved baseless; he accepted the withdrawal calmly with a "so much the better" attitude.[94]

American Interests, 1939

On the eve of World War II, American interests in Iran were not sizable. There were slightly more than two hundred American citizens residing in Iran, more than half of whom were native-born Americans. About twenty American citizens reportedly worked with the Anglo-Iranian Oil Company at Abadan, but the consulate at Teheran did not even have them on the register. Most of the American citizens were connected with the work of the Presbyterian Church in the United States of America in six mission stations at Tabriz, Kermanshah, Hamadan, Resht, Meshed, and Teheran. Each station had a hospital, and seven schools in all were still operating. Total capital invested in missionary properties was estimated at $2,577,000, about two-thirds of it in Teheran. Other small enterprises were the Farman Industrial School and Orphanage of Kermanshah, owned and operated by the former missionary, the Reverend F. M. Stead, with a staff of two Americans and twenty-five students. Virtually inoperative by this time were the Seventh-Day Adventist Mission at Teheran, the Sultanabad mission of the General Council of the Assemblies of God, and the Bahai School for Girls (Tarbiat-ol-Banat).

The archaeological work at Persepolis was being closed down during 1939. Here the Oriental Institute of the University of Chicago had been operating with the cooperation of the University Museum of the University of Pennsylvania, and the Boston Museum of Fine Arts. Professor

[94] *FR 1937*, II, 734–761; *FR 1938*, II, 752–756; III, 719–722.

Arthur U. Pope, of the American Institute for Iranian Art and Architecture, had organized expeditions to Luristan during the spring of 1938 and to Persepolis for six weeks in 1939. At Nishapur, the Metropolitan Museum of Art of New York had conducted some test expeditions. The annual expenditures of these various enterprises was estimated at $80,-000 for 1938–1939.

Although imports from the United States totaled only $5,076,304 for the year ending June 21, 1938, and exports to the United States about $3,370,940, the United States ranked third in Iran's foreign trade. Imports of trucks, tires, tubes, passenger cars, and spare parts ranked first and comprised some 86 per cent of imports from the United States. Iranians also imported American agricultural machinery, lubricating oil, typewriters, sewing and knitting machines. The United States was the best customer for Iranian woolen carpets, the major export. Such exotic products as pistachio nuts, dates, and sausage casing were high on the list of exports to the United States.

American commercial investments were minimal. Four New York City rug firms had about $50,000 invested in Iran, and the Singer Sewing Machine Company had perhaps $60,000 in its fifteen agencies. The missionary investment was far more significant in volume.

Only one American shipping line, the Isthmian Steamship Company, had regular sailings to the Persian Gulf where it operated in conjunction with the German Hansa Line. Twenty-four American ships called annually in the late 1930s.[95]

Conclusion

Notwithstanding her declaration of neutrality, Persia did not escape marching armies of Russian, Turkish, and British Empire troops during World War I. With Russia's withdrawal from the war and Turkey's defeat, the way seemed clear for a British quasi-protectorate in 1919. The Persians, disappointed at not gaining a hearing at the Paris Peace Conference, balked at British domination and refused to ratify the Anglo-Persian Treaty of 1919. Freer from foreign domination by the early 1920s than she had been for a generation, Persia embarked on a program of modernization under the strong leadership of Reza Shah, a program in which Americans took part. At the request of the Persian government,

[95] The data in this and the previous four paragraphs were derived from James S. Moose, Jr. (consul, Teheran) to Hull, April 15, 1939, DS 811.5031 Near East/317.

Arthur C. Millspaugh and his assistants spent several years working on the problems related to fiscal reform. During the 1920s American companies sought participation in oil development and railroad construction, but the only tangible result was the ill-fated work of Ulen and Company on a segment of the Trans-Iranian Railroad. The Shah's displeasure with this company and his generally stiffening attitude toward foreign influences, apparent in the termination of capitulations and restrictions on missionaries, forecast a stormier period for American missionaries, archaeologists, and diplomats as they tried to work out an accommodation with the new Persian nationalism.

Although American interests were not unsympathetic to the Shah's monumental internal problems or unaware of the shadow of his strong Soviet neighbor to the north, relations between the two countries were frequently clouded during the latter years of the Shah's regime as he became more rigid and more sensitive to criticism. Fortunately, time and patience had by 1939 contributed to healing the breach opened in 1935 with the arrest of the Persian minister to the United States.

10

THE ARAB EAST BETWEEN THE WARS

☆ As BAYARD DODGE, president of the American University of Beirut, contemplated the ominous international scene during the fateful summer of 1939, he sensed that the Arab Middle East was at the close of an era. Dodge was representative of a small group of Americans whose careers in education, missionary endeavor, or business had brought them into close contact with the Arab lands. In the report he was preparing for his trustees, he correlated the history of his university with the profound changes in the Eastern Mediterranean where his family before him had devotedly served the university and where he had spent his mature years. His theme was the political and social transformation he had observed during the two decades since the Armistice of 1918.[1] Alterations both in internal structure and in international political relationships had modified considerably the milieu in which American interests carried on their enterprises. To understand the adjustments confronting Americans requires an appreciation of conditioning circumstances in the local environment.

The Changing Middle East

Altered relationships within the Arab World were the product in considerable measure of Western influences slowly eroding traditional society and of resentment toward the West for intrusions into the life of the area. Turning to the West for guide lines, a small local coterie interested in reform believed they found in Western technology and

---

[1] Dodge, AR 1939. In a later report Dodge wrote that "As Alexander of old had flooded the Orient with Hellenism, so Allenby unconsciously flooded the East with modernism." See AR 1948, p. 13.

thought the keys to the advances made by the West in recent centuries while the Middle East had seemed to stand still. Coupled with envy and emulation of the West was resentment at subservience to the colonial powers, a subordination galling to Arab nationalists, who had learned their lessons in modern nationalism from Europe.

Contributing to the ferment in the Middle East during the 1920s and 1930s was the extension of the transportation and communications revolution. As the railroad, automobile, and airplane helped to telescope the time required to traverse vast distances, the resulting mobility of men, products, and ideas acted as a powerful catalyst for change. The automobile cut the time of the trip from Beirut to Baghdad to twenty-four hours. Formerly it had consumed weeks by land and sea or by the tedious caravan route. The advent of commercial aviation provided another alternative to long round-about sea voyages.[2] The communications revolution affected the potency of other instruments of change by enlarging the scope of Western-sponsored schools, colleges, missions, and business enterprises, notably the oil industry. Another new vehicle for bringing to selected metropolitan centers an often twisted version of a different mode of life was the American cinema. Swirling cross-currents were confusing young people in the Middle East. What Khalil Totah, principal of the Friends' School at Ramallah, noted about his students was applicable to Arab youth generally. The student body was "in process of adjusting itself to modern conditions. It is desperately attempting to reconcile Islam, Christianity, Buddhism, Judaism, with Einstein, Edison, jazz, the moving pictures, free love, and bolshevism."[3]

Reflecting the changing conditions and aspirations were alterations in the political superstructure during the interwar years. As yet, there

[2] George Gregg Fuller (vice consul, Teheran) to Hughes, May 1, 1925, DS 890b.797/1; *MRW*, 48 (Dec. 1925), 977; Dodge, AR 1939, p. 4; Dodge, 1948, p. 13; Ruth F. Woodsmall, *Moslem Women Enter a New World*, p. 22. The bus service from Haifa and Damascus to Baghdad established in the 1930s throws an interesting sidelight on desert transportation. The unusual bus, reputedly the largest in the world, was built by the Bender Body Company and Marmon-Herrington Company of the United States. The bus was seventy feet long and eleven feet high, with first and second class compartments, a lavatory, a ninety-gallon water supply, and space for 6100 pounds of freight and baggage. A complete buffet with double plate burner for cooking and a refrigerator holding five hundred pounds of ice ensured ample food and drink for the trip. The crew consisted of a conductor, steward, and three drivers. A telephone connected the driver in the cab with the crew in the passenger coach. The description does not mention the number of passengers that could be accommodated. *MRW*, 57 (March 1934), 150.

[3] Dodge, AR 1939, p. 4; Dodge, AR 1948, p. 13; *MRW*, 53 (June 1930), 464 (quotation).

was no political unity and only an amorphous intellectual foundation existed for building it. When World War I ended, Egypt was still a British protectorate, but Egyptian nationalists, smarting under continuing British overlordship, organized to carry on a steady campaign of resistance. Although the British unilaterally granted nominal inde-

The Arab World between the Wars

pendence in 1922, Egyptians regarded this as insufficient and pressed for more complete British withdrawal from influence in their affairs. To the east, the Allies had dashed dreams of an Arab Confederation by manipulating the mandate system to permit thinly-disguised British protectorates over Palestine, Trans-Jordan, and Iraq, and French protectorates over Syria and Lebanon. Before the era ended, Iraq graduated from the mandate school by achieving nominal independence and entering the League of Nations in 1932, but nationalists kept up their struggle to eliminate continuing British influence. Syrians and Lebanese, who longed to follow the example of Iraq, thought they were well on the road to freedom from foreign overlordship in 1936 until France reversed her course, delaying independence for her mandates. British Palestine was a special case. The Zionist program and Arab resentment of British implementation of the Balfour Declaration made of that troubled land a continuous battleground. To the Arabs, Zionism was a foreign intrusion foisted on them by Western imperialism; to the Zionists, the Arab position would deny them the homeland to which they felt entitled. On the Arabian peninsula and its fringes — in the Persian Gulf sheikhdoms, in the expanding realm of Ibn Saud, in Yemen, and at Aden, where nationalism penetrated more slowly and society remained more traditional — local resentments of foreign domination were slower to develop.

Withal, British hegemony was fairly secure until the middle and later 1930s when Fascist Italy's Mediterranean dreams and then Hitler's thrusts toward southeastern Europe altered the power balance and made Great Britain even more jealous of her control points in Cyprus, Suez, Palestine, Trans-Jordan, Aden, and the Persian Gulf.

American Interests and Policies

Official American policy toward the Arab Middle East was characterized by deference to British political hegemony during the interwar years. Apparent submission to British and French control reflected the particular nature of American stakes, which remained predominantly educational and religious, although an important exception was the expansion of American oil interests during the decade preceding the outbreak of World War II. That official policies of the United States responded sluggishly to the new conditions is attributable to the foreign policy orientation of the American people. These were years characterized by longing to return to "the good old days" when the United States kept out of the politics of Europe and its periphery.

The reputation of America in the Arab World was generally high at the end of World War I because of respect for the good works carried on by Americans in education, medicine, and relief. Unlike the European powers, the United States had remained politically disinterested. The Wilsonian program of self-determination reinforced an idealized image of the United States as a foe of colonialism. True, the United States lost prestige by failing to give positive backing to Arab aspirations after World War I when the American public and Congress dictated a retreat to traditional nonintervention. But a measure of Arab disillusionment was more than counterbalanced by the persistence of the favorable image of the United States at a time when Arab feeling against Britain and France was deepening.

American diplomacy focused, therefore, on protecting "legitimate" American interests — the traditional ones such as missions, schools, relief efforts, business enterprises, and the expanding archaeological ventures of American universities and museums. In terms of official policy, there did not seem to be a really rational approach which weighed the relative merits of philanthropic versus commercial activities. Washington was reluctant, as it had been in the Taft era, to face the question of whether commercial objectives could be achieved in the long run without stronger political policies and possible intervention.

During the early postwar years American diplomacy in the Arab Middle East had to give major attention to building the new structure of official relationships required by changes in political control. Much of the negotiation was therefore carried on with Great Britain and France until local nationalisms successfully reduced colonial domination, when the United States began to deal with independent or quasi-independent Arab nations. Thus America's conception of the mandates system necessarily affected efforts to protect existing and prospective interests.

Syria and Lebanon

The overriding political fact in the Levant between the wars was the Arabs' deep feeling of betrayal by the Allies. Not only had they been denied their goal of an Arab confederation, but over their objections they were saddled with a mandatory power unacceptable to them. From a strictly diplomatic point of view, the big change wrought in Syria and Lebanon by World War I was their transfer from Ottoman overlordship to French tutelage under a League of Nations mandate. The United States henceforth had to conduct its official business in these Levant mandates through the French foreign office. Washington's emphasis was squarely on the rights of the United States and its citizens in Syria and Lebanon and on France's consequent obligations as mandatory. The Wilson administration insisted that the American contribution to the common victory over the Central Powers entitled its citizens to rights and privileges in the mandates equal to those of the mandatories — notwithstanding American nonmembership in the League.[4]

After March 4, 1921, the Harding-Hughes team accepted the Wilson-Colby position and pressed it to the point where the British and French governments agreed by the end of the year that they were prepared to give certain guarantees to Americans, possibly by an exchange of notes. With this groundwork laid, the governments could negotiate a formal agreement delineating American rights in the mandates. Continuation of capitulatory rights was the essential on which the United States insisted. American preference for formal agreements rather than a mere note exchange rested on the legal point that capitulatory rights in the Ottoman Empire derived from treaties and therefore could not be altered or canceled except by treaty.[5]

After the League Council approved the French mandate for Syria and Lebanon on July 24, 1922, protracted negotiations led to a Franco-American Convention regarding Syria and Lebanon signed on April 4, 1924. In the agreement, which set forth the terms of the mandate, the United States consented to the administration of the mandate by France; the United States and its nationals were guaranteed the benefits thereof on the same basis as League members and their nationals. During the life of the mandate, capitulatory rights of foreigners were suspended, but France agreed to establish a judicial system assuring natives and foreigners rights to worship freely, to conduct native schools, to operate religious missions, and guaranteeing freedom from discrimination in trade, taxation, and granting of concessions. Any benefits granted nationals of other governments would be extended to American nationals. Without asking for equivalent treatment for Syrian and Lebanese citizens in the United States, the French agreed to extradite Americans from Syria and Lebanon. They would raise no objections to the establishment of American consuls anywhere in Syria and Lebanon so long as they were American citizens; France would treat them according to inter-

[4] See above, Chap. 6, pp. 173–174, 176, 177–183. See also Green B. Hackworth, *Digest of International Law*, I, 103–108. The French divided Syria and Lebanon into administrative districts, frequently rearranging the divisions in the interest of preventing unity among dissident forces. For the internal and international history of the mandates, see Stephen Hemsley Longrigg, *Syria and Lebanon under French Mandate, passim*; A. H. Hourani, *Syria and Lebanon: A Political Essay*, pp. 163–179; and Nicola A. Ziadeh, *Syria and Lebanon*, pp. 46–61.

[5] Hackworth, *Digest*, I, 108–109; *FR 1921*, I, 925–936; II, 115–118; *FR 1923*, II, 2–3.

national custom and the terms of the Franco-American consular convention of 1853.[6] In this fashion the Convention of 1924 regularized the official relations of the United States with the French mandates in the Levant.

It took some time for Americans in the Levant mandates to adjust to French rule. When Consul Paul Knabenshue reported the Thanksgiving celebration given by the consulate in 1920 for nearly two hundred native-born Americans from the Beirut vicinity, he observed that members of the American colony tended to remain too exclusively to themselves instead of cultivating social intercourse with people of other nationalities, particularly newer arrivals among French officials and their families. Such provincialism was incompatible with Knabenshue's aim of trying to bring closer, more friendly relations between Americans and governing officials and their families. He believed that protection of American interests during the difficult reconstruction period would require the most tactful handling, and that establishing closer and more cordial relations between Americans and French would assist this aim materially.[7]

During the early 1920s, Americans were apprehensive of French discrimination in favor of French cultural and commercial interests to American disadvantage. Missionaries feared repressive measures against Protestant activities. The consular delegate in Damascus told the department of rumored secret French archaeological projects and asked whether the French were using their special position to secure advantage over the archaeologists of other nations, perhaps to appropriate art treasures belonging to Syria. In 1922 the department discussed evidence that American businessmen in Syria and Lebanon would suffer from restrictive concession policies favoring the French. From a representative of Dodge Brothers Motor Company, the Near Eastern Division learned in 1925 of administrative regulations adversely affecting their agent in Beirut. It was rumored that the French were requiring companies engaged in the desert motor transport trade between Syria and Mesopotamia to organize as French companies, to have some French capital invested in them, and to employ French cars and trucks. American

[6] *FR 1921*, I, 99–104, 137–142; *FR 1922*, II, 117–134; *FR 1923*, II, 1–8; *FR 1924*, I, 730–746; Hackworth, *Digest*, I, 110–113. In 1933 the United States successfully invoked article 6 of the 1924 convention providing that the United States must give its approval before any changes in the mandate could affect the 1924 convention. See *FR 1933*, II, 1002–1009.

[7] Knabenshue to Carr, Nov. 30, 1920, DS 890d.46211/–.

interests and their consular representatives were unduly nervous, for in the long run, missionaries learned to live quite successfully with the French regime; the alleged archaeological discrimination turned out to be unfounded; and the French government proved amenable when the State Department protested about discrimination against American business.[8]

Perennial bad feeling between Arabs and French adversely affected Americans, however, especially when tensions broke into open rebellion. Serious outbreaks, beginning as the Druze Rebellion, spread to Damascus and elsewhere, bringing great turbulence and tension in 1925 and 1926. American consular officers entrusted with protecting American nationals and property kept Washington closely informed of conditions. Consul Knabenshue sharply criticized maladroit French colonial policy which, he thought, not only precipitated the rebellion, but also was responsible for its spread. He believed France compounded the hazards by shelling the open city of Damascus without warning. To the State Department he wrote:

France through mal-administration and through following a policy more of colonization than of [a] truly mandatory regime has brought on a revolution in the country which has caused the ruin of at least one hundred thousand of its inhabitants, the destruction of ancient and sacred landmarks, and has endangered the lives, property, and potential interests of foreigners. By further bungling and failure to send adequate military forces to restore public order and security, the dangers to foreigners are increasing.

Only a slight incident might precipitate an uprising in Beirut, where the French had few troops and would have to resort to artillery bombardment. "It is the presence here of American destroyers alone that has given a sense of security to the population." Two destroyers had been despatched at Knabenshue's request in case it became necessary to evacuate Americans. As the consul saw it, "repeated experiences throughout the present upheaval have demonstrated, unfortunately, that we cannot depend upon French assurances."[9]

[8] *MRW*, 43 (March 1920), 235; Charles E. Allen (consular delegate, Damascus) to Hughes, Dec. 27, 1921, DS 890d.927/—; K. C. to A. W. Dulles, memorandum, Sept. 15, 1922, DS 890d.6463/4; Dulles, memorandum of conversation with E. G. Willems, Jan. 5, 1925, DS 890d.7971/3; Henry P. Fletcher to Charles E. Allen, Feb. 23, 1922; Allen to Hughes, March 13 and April 1, 1922, DS 890d.927/—, 1, and 2.

[9] Knabenshue to Kellogg, Nov. 8, 1925, DS 890d.00/27 (quotations). See also Knabenshue's 60-page study called "Political Situation in Syria," in which he advo-

The French resented the presence of American destroyers at Beirut as a reflection on their inability to preserve order. When their embassy in Washington asked Secretary Kellogg to withdraw the ships, Kellogg replied that they would be ordered away "when we thought we could safely do so."[10] By early December, Knabenshue felt the situation had stabilized somewhat. He reported that the departure of the destroyers on December 6 "was interpreted as American confidence in [the] new High Commissioner and in French dispositions to protect coastal regions." Knabenshue thought that henceforth disturbances would be confined to the interior, but he asked to have the destroyers cruise within range of Beirut. The State Department arranged with the Navy to have the ships subject to the consul's call.[11]

During the uprising at Damascus there had been damage to installations of the Socony Vacuum Oil Company, looting of the factory of MacAndrews and Forbes (the licorice firm), and damage to the Singer Sewing Machine warehouse. After thorough study, the Solicitor's Office of the State Department concluded that the United States was entitled to indemnification for American nationals who suffered losses in the insurrection. American private organizations — Near East Relief and the Red Cross — had been asked to rush relief supplies into the stricken mandate. Before long, however, the relief agencies and the department began to have serious reservations about continuing private relief to other than Americans on grounds that the French might shirk their responsibilities by assuming that American relief would do France's job.[12]

cated that the United States approach the British about diplomatic intervention in Syria. He believed American interests would benefit from a consolidated British mandate over Syria, Palestine, and Iraq. Opposite Knabenshue's proposal someone in the department scribbled "No," twice underlined, under which two red exclamation points were added. Knabenshue to Kellogg, Jan. 25, 1926, DS 890d.00/349. The rebellion can be followed in Longrigg, *Syria and Lebanon*, pp. 148–176; *FR 1925*, II, 105–127; *FR 1926*, II, 134–155.

[10] Kellogg, memoranda of conversations with M. Emile Daeschner (French ambassador to the United States), Nov. 14 and Nov. 27 (quotation), 1925, DS 890d.00/260 and 275. The French did not like the presence at Beirut of the American military attaché from Constantinople whom Knabenshue had invited to advise on measures for the protection of American citizens.

[11] Knabenshue to Kellogg, Dec. 11, 1925; Dulles to Grew, Dec. 14, 1925; Dulles to Furlong, Dec. 15, 1925; Grew to Knabenshue, Dec. 14, 1925, all DS 890d.00/302. General Maurice Sarrail was recalled as high commissioner after the shelling of Damascus. The new high commissioner was Henri de Jouvenel.

[12] J. H. Kelley, Jr. (consul, Damascus) to Kellogg, Nov. 2, 1925, DS 890d.00/283; 43-page memorandum by E.L.L., June 28, 1927, DS 890d.01/279½; Dulles memorandum of conversation with Laird W. Archer (director, Foreign Department, Near East Relief), Oct. 31, 1925, DS 890d.48/31; *FR 1925*, II, 113, 114.

Although the French colonial tradition of fostering the French language and culture caused uneasiness at the American University of Beirut, the university solved its internal problems and managed its relations with French authorities so prudently that great growth was possible during the two decades following World War I. Among the problems facing A.U.B. in the early 1920s were a staggering debt, a run-down plant, need for administrative reorganization, and changes in educational policies. The college, begun in 1866 with sixteen students in a rented house, had become a university with twenty-six buildings stretched along a forty-seven-acre campus which skirted the Mediterranean and boasted 3000 graduates scattered throughout the Middle East. The university was on threshold of a transitional era.[13]

Heavy wartime responsibilities had broken the health of President Howard Bliss, contributing to his death from tubercular pneumonia in 1920. Losses by death or illness deprived the Board of Trustees of several of its most stalwart members between 1918 and 1922. Acting-President Edward F. Nickoley, professor of economics, carried on until the university's third president, Bayard Dodge, was inaugurated in 1923. Because of his talent, temperament, and experience, Dodge proved to be a happy choice. Early in his administration several notable changes were effected. A new constitution for the university gave professors and associate professors control of local administration with an executive committee to handle confidential matters of finance and personnel. Appointments were made regardless of nationality, so that Oriental and European professors could be full partners with their American colleagues. Administration was largely delegated to deans and divisional faculties, a budget system was adopted, and a new plan for personnel contracts was enforced.[14]

Inflationary conditions during and after the war forced expenses up at the very time endowment income was dropping, with the result that

[13] Dodge, AR 1948, pp. 11–12; *MRW*, 44 (Jan. 1921), 72; (March 1921), 193–198.
[14] Penrose, *AUB*, pp. 174–177, 199, 201–208; Dodge, AR 1948, pp. 14–15; *MRW*, 50 (Nov. 1927), 867–868. Dodge was the son of Cleveland H. and the nephew of D. Stuart Dodge. After graduation from Princeton in 1909, he studied divinity at Union Theological Seminary. In 1913 he was appointed director of West Hall and executive secretary of the College Y.M.C.A. During the war, he helped in Lebanon relief. Back in the United States during 1918 and 1919 he helped establish the joint college office and assisted in the financial campaign. He returned to Syria in 1920 as director of Near East Relief for Syria and Lebanon. In 1914 he married the daughter of President Howard Bliss.

327

the university had a deficit exceeding $500,000 on July 1, 1920. Nickoley cut operating expenses while fund-raising efforts went forward with the help of trustees and powerful friends of the college. A joint drive in behalf of A.U.B., Robert, and Constantinople College for Women yielded enough to pay off the debt and balance the budget for 1923–1924, but without any provision for expansion. The Fund for Near Eastern Colleges, organized by Albert W. Staub, enlisted the help of more than 3000 A.U.B. alumni and other friends to improve the financial position of participating colleges and the university between 1924 and 1929. The benefits of cooperation led to the establishment in 1928 of the Near East College Association in New York. The association served as a clearing house not only for fund raising, but also for "purchasing equipment, appointing teachers . . . and making the institution known in America." President Dodge wrote in 1939 that "the growth of the past twenty years has been largely due to the work accomplished by the Office in New York."[15]

Expansion at A.U.B. was made possible by the Rockefeller Foundation between 1924 and 1939, which contributed more than $2.5 million. These funds enabled the university to strengthen premedical sciences, the medical school (including health center and nursing program), and the social sciences. President Dodge observed that "the aid of the Rockefeller Foundation should not be stated in terms of money alone, as it also brought a great deal of valuable help and advice from experienced experts in connection with the selection and training of personnel, the development of research, and the formation of the medical library."[16]

Dodge did not exaggerate the intellectual progress made by the university between the wars when he asserted in 1939 that the faculty was stronger, the students better, the standards raised markedly, and more

[15] Dodge, AR 1939, p. 10 (quotations); Dodge, AR 1948, p. 15; Penrose, *AUB*, pp. 199–200, 222–223; *MRW*, 49 (Feb. 1926), 153–154; 50 (May 1927), 393; 53 (April 1930), 315. From the fund drive of 1924 to 1926 to provide $2.5 million for operating expenses at A.U.B., Robert, Istanbul College for Women, American College of Sofia, and International College at Smyrna, A.U.B. derived $950,000. Contributions came from every state in the union, Canada, Alaska, Hawaii, Jamaica, China, Japan, England, France, Germany, Greece, Bulgaria, Turkey, Russia, Egypt, Syria, Palestine, Persia, Iraq, Arabia, Malay States, Sudan, Cyprus, Hauran, Austria, and South America. Staub then organized an endowment campaign for the six colleges (Athens College had been added). By January 1, 1930, $15 million had been raised of which $3 million was added to A.U.B.'s previous endowment of $1,226,000. More than 16,000 people contributed.

[16] Some of the foundation funds went for buildings and endowments. Dodge, AR 1948, p. 16. See also Dodge, AR 1939, pp. 9–10; Penrose, *AUB*, 224–229, 235.

research produced. The medical school in particular reflected the gains, as did the related schools of pharmacy and nursing. The standards of the dental school were made so exacting that few students were willing to undertake the stiff program, and its cost became prohibitive. These factors, coupled with financial stringencies of the Great Depression of the 1930s forced the dental school to close in 1940. Curricular revision extended to other segments of the university — arts and sciences, and the preparatory department. An Institute of Music was added in 1929. The faculty voted to admit women to all classes of the School of Arts and Sciences above the freshman year starting in 1923. International College at Smyrna found the nationalistic climate in Atatürk's Turkey so inhospitable that it sold its properties and became affiliated with the university, taking over preparatory school duties and the farm management course at Beirut in 1936.[17]

Intellectual gains and plant improvements were accompanied by increased enrollments. From the low point of 695 students for 1917, enrollment increased rapidly after the war to 1001 in 1920. Some decline set in during the next two years as local and government schools were organized, but with the opening of the new automobile route over the desert many more students came from Iraq and Persia. After rapid increases through the 1920s there was a temporary setback during the depression, but by 1938–1939 students totaled 1938, slightly more than half in the preparatory department. A notable trend was the growing proportion of students from other Moslem countries. A.U.B. also became the major collegiate institution for war-displaced Armenians.[18]

Quantitative gains would have meant less if not paralleled by the qualitative gains already mentioned. Together they enabled the university to enlarge its influence, not just in Syria and Lebanon, but throughout the Middle East. The university had always stressed character building and civic responsibility. As Professor A. H. Hourani has observed, the American University and the French Université de Saint-Josef illustrate the fundamental difference between the French concept of culture and education and the Anglo-Saxon concept. St. Josef, maintained and largely staffed by Jesuits, Catholic in spirit, and subsidized by

[17] Penrose, *AUB*, pp. 215, 223–258, 261–264; Dodge, AR 1939, p. 8; Dodge, AR 1948, pp. 13, 14, 17, 19–20; *MRW*, 48 (June 1925), 478; (Aug. 1925), 643; 49 (Aug. 1926), 641; 59 (May 1936), 265.

[18] Penrose, *AUB*, pp. 237, 283, 286, 331–335; Dodge, AR 1939, pp. 2, 5–8; Dodge, AR 1948, p. 15.

the French government, concentrated on mastery of French, attachment to France, and distrust of Arab nationalism. Officially nonsectarian and unconnected with Western governments, A.U.B. instructed in Arabic as well as English and French, and unintentionally had become an intellectual center of Arab nationalism. St. Josef was probably the greater center of research and scholarship, although the A.U.B. record in scholarly and scientific work was formidable and increasing; but the tendency had been to exalt character above intellect.[19]

A remarkable evidence of the emphasis on social and civic service was the work undertaken in rural reconstruction and village welfare. In 1930 the university started the Institute of Rural Life jointly with the Near East Foundation. Seventy-five farm boys were given training in agricultural extension work; short institutes were set up to teach modern methods of fruit growing, bee-keeping, poultry husbandry, and seed selection; thirty bulletins were issued in simple Arabic; a rural health center was established; and texts were published for adult education. Aid was given to the Palestine government to train village teachers how to adapt their schools to rural needs. The Village Welfare Service encouraged students to work in villages during summer vacations. As students caught the spirit of the enterprise, volunteers extended the welfare work to Beirut. The emphasis on brotherhood and service was not new for the university, which had been a pillar of support for relief work during and after the war. For the Arab student the attraction of social service was related to nationalism, since a strong, prosperous Arab people depended on forcefully prosecuting the battle against poverty and improving the lot of the less fortunate.[20]

The influence of the university percolated throughout the Levant and surrounding countries. The friendly attitude of upper-class Arabs testified to the increasing respect the university commanded. During the summer of 1924 Professor Anis Khuri conducted a campaign in Iraq. From his Baghdad headquarters he went out to Basra, Kut, Karbala, Mosul, and elsewhere to visit government and private schools where he interviewed classes, teachers, and presidents, and distributed pamphlets about "the great Oriental queen," as A.U.B. was called. King Feisal frequently expressed his approval of the university's work and sent his twelve-year-old son, Crown Prince Ghazi, to the university in 1925.

[19] Hourani, *Syria and Lebanon*, pp. 83–84.
[20] *Ibid.*, pp. 82–83; Penrose, *AUB*, pp. 270–281, 300; Dodge, AR 1939, pp. 11–12; Dodge, AR 1948, p. 19.

By 1927 the governments of Palestine, Iraq, Sudan, and Ethiopia were supporting a number of students at the university.[21]

The best indicator of the university's impact is the role of its graduates and former students. Demands throughout the Midde East for trained men and women far exceeded the supply and taxed the university beyond its capacity. A.U.B. men and women were requested by mandate officials, foreign and local business, and native governments and firms. In 1939 the government of Iraq nccded thirty more graduates for teaching positions than it was possible to supply. Urgent need for doctors, pharmacists, dentists, nurses, chemists, secretaries, and accountants could not be met fully. In 1928 President Dodge reported that 721 graduates were physicians either in government service or private practice, with 151 physicians, pharmacists, dentists, and nurses employed by the governments of Lebanon, Syria, Palestine, Trans-Jordan, Iraq, Egypt, and Sudan. Others wcre in educational, religious, journalistic, or legal work. One graduate headed the Bahai religion in Haifa; two were leading judges in Palestine and Khartoum; another was a leading newspaper editor in Cairo; one served as inspector of education in Iraq. Others were in comparable positions of responsibility. Between the wars, graduates at Jaffa initiated the export of oranges which, with Jewish help, proved to be a principal source of wealth for Palestine. Graduates also contributed to introducing fruit preserving and dairy enterprise in Lebanon, an up-to-date water supply and large cement factory for Damascus, ten cent stores, soda fountains, and talking movies. Some were agents for American auto firms or employees of Shell, Socony-Vacuum, or the Iraq Petroleum Company.[22]

Such was the beacon lighted by American philanthropy which sent its warming rays throughout the Middle East. George Sarton, Harvard's distinguished historian of science, who spent part of 1931–1932 at the university, called it "a nursery of good men and a perpetual fountain of good will."[23]

[21] *MRW*, 48 (Jan. 1925), 67 (quotation); (Dec. 1925), 977; 50 (April 1927), 315–316. Even during the unsettled conditions in the fall of 1939 more than 400 students arrived from Palestine and about half as many from Iraq. Dodge, AR 1948, p. 20.

[22] *American University of Beirut: Description of Its Organization and Work*, Autumn 1934, mimeographed, pp. 48–49; Penrose, *AUB*, pp. 218–221, 288–290; *MRW*, 51 (Oct. 1928), 847; Dodge, AR 1939, p. 5; Dodge, AR 1948, p. 13.

[23] George Sarton, *The Incubation of Western Culture in the Middle East*, p. 42. See also George Sarton, "Second Preface to the Nineteenth Volume of Isis (Beirut)," *Isis*, 19 (July 1933), 326.

That the university was able to fulfill its mission under the mandate despite early fears that the French would raise crippling impediments, was owing in no small measure to the tact of President Dodge. There were difficulties from time to time, but they were surmounted. As a later president wrote, "the administration in Beirut is experienced in the wisdom of reticence." When it was needed, the university had the support of the United States government.[24]

Presbyterian missions in Syria and Lebanon recovered as rapidly as the university from the ravages of World War I. By 1921 the missionaries had in operation every institution functioning in 1914, their best previous year, and church membership was larger than in 1914. Political conditions were unsettled, adjustments had to be made to the French mandate, and much labor had to go into relief for Armenian and other refugees. By 1930, however, the board could state in its annual report that "Our Mission has nothing to complain of as far as government is concerned. There is no actual restriction, and in the few cases where we have applied for permission to extend our education work it has been granted. We are also glad to record the fact that our consular service has always been ready to interpret our position to the French authorities whenever it seemed necessary." A new orientation was apparent in the 1920s as the mission accepted the policy of not trying to persuade faithful members of the ancient Christian churches to leave them. Moslems were less aloof than formerly and, feeling that American missionaries were not politically motivated, some were attracted to their schools. Among the various missionary groups there were many indications of cooperative endeavor and joint projects of an interdenominational and sometimes international character. Americans also welcomed and fostered the larger role played by the native evangelical church.[25]

[24] Staub to Dulles, April 22, 1922; Dulles to Staub, April 22, 1922; Hughes to Knabenshue, May 1, 1922; Knabenshue to Hughes, May 2, 1924; unsigned "Memorandum of Conversation with the Chargé d'Affaires of France," July 30, 1923; J. Butler Wright (Assistant Secretary of State) to Knabenshue, Aug. 11, 1923; Edward M. Broth to Hughes, Sept. 22, 1923; L.H., memorandum, Nov. 15, 1923; Knabenshue to Hughes, March 29, 1924, with enclosure "French Influence in the Levant and French Publicists' Attitude toward American Educational and Missionary Activities in Syria," DS 390d.116/9, 9, 7a, 8, 18, 18, 22, 28, 29; Penrose, *AUB*, pp. ix (quotation), 205–206, 215, 282; *MRW*, 49 (Aug. 1926), 64; Dodge, AR 1948, p. 20; *FR 1931*, II, 267–279; *FR 1936*, III, 460–483, 486–495; *FR 1937*, II, 938. DS 390d.1164 also contains documents on troubles with French authorities in Syria.

[25] *MRW*, 43 (March 1920), 235; 45 (April 1922), 323–324; (Aug. 1922), 657–658; 46 (Sept. 1923), 756; 47 (April 1924), 322; (June 1924), 413–417; 53 (Jan. 1930), 7; 56 (June 1933), 329, 398–399; 58 (June 1935), 311; Centennial Series,

Although devoting themselves mainly to education, missionaries also gave considerable attention to medicine, rural reconstruction and village work, and assistance to orphans. Suffusing the range of activities was a Christian approach emphasizing service to one's fellow man. By cultivating their field in this fashion, the missionaries continued to hope they could someday reap a harvest of conversions to evangelical Christianity.

The Presbyterian Mission operated three major schools for boys. The Gerard Institute at Sidon emphasized vocational training in agriculture and such industrial trades as carpentry and auto mechanics. Boys' schools were also conducted at Tripoli and Aleppo. Many village schools operated by local evangelical churches with some financial and technical aid from the mission spread missionary influence far and wide. Beirut, Sidon, and Tripoli were sites for girls' schools, but the special pride of the mission was the American Junior College for Women at Beirut, opened in 1928 as an outgrowth of the girls' school. The Junior College course included arts and sciences as well as generous attention to home economics and child training. Many girls participated in rural and village work carried on in cooperation with A.U.B. and the Near East Foundation. Some graduates completed the college course at A.U.B., and many went on to obtain further professional training at A.U.B., in Europe, or at American graduate schools. Within a decade the mission spoke with pride of its alumnae who were doing useful work throughout the Middle East as dietitians, doctors, social service workers, or in business offices.[26]

The mission board left medical work in Beirut to the superior facilities of the A.U.B. medical school, but nearby in the Lebanon Mountains it continued to operate the Hamlin Memorial Sanitarium for tubercular patients. At Tripoli, the board's Kennedy Memorial Hospital was the only modern facility of its type. Seeing the great need for medical facilities in the back country of Syria, medical work was organized at Deir-ez-Zore on the Euphrates in the 1920s and soon became a major undertaking of the Presbyterians.[27]

Syria Mission, pp. 9, 11, 12, 13, 16–18; PC, AR 1930, p. 191 (quotation); Brown, *100 Years*, pp. 980, 1003–1004; 1007–1008.

[26] *Syria Mission*, pp. 20–21, 24–26, 30–34; Brown, *100 Years*, pp. 986–987, 1004–1006; *MRW*, 48 (Jan. 1925), 82; 49 (Sept. 1926), 727; 50 (Oct. 1927), 777; 51 (May 1928), 396–397; 53 (March 1930), 228; (Oct. 1930), 790–791; 54 (Feb. 1931), 152–153; 56 (Jan. 1933), 56; (April 1933), 229–230; 57 (Feb. 1934), 104; 58 (Jan. 1935), 43–44; (Feb. 1935), 89.

[27] *MRW*, 46 (Nov. 1923), 956; 47 (Dec. 1924), 1007–1008; 54 (May 1931), 334;

Rounding out the philanthropic efforts of the missionaries were co-operative ventures with the Near East Foundation and A.U.B. in rural reconstruction, village assistance, health projects, and orphan care. The mission press, book store, and reading rooms served as an adjunct to all these enterprises and poured a steady flow of Christian literature into the Middle East. During the celebration of the mission's centenary in 1922, it was estimated that during the hundred years the press had turned out 1,355,795,164 pages in Arabic, Armenian, Turkish, Kurdish, and French. Two new buildings and a modern press acquired that year increased the output for 1923 to 22,782,260 pages.[28]

Although the Presbyterians predominated, several other American denominations operated small missions in Syria and Lebanon. One of them, the Christian and Missionary Alliance, employed rather militant methods which were unacceptable to the French authorities. In 1924 mandate officials banned certain literature prepared by this group on grounds that its disparagement of Islam could lead to breaches of public order. The American consul and State Department concurred in this judgment. Local officials turned down the application of the same group for expansion in 1938, and the State Department again agreed that rejection was justified in the interest of preserving order.[29]

Usually, however, the State Department took the part of the missionaries in their difficulties with the mandate authorities. A case in point was the question of customs immunity for mission supplies. When immunity was withdrawn in 1936, the department negotiated an executive agreement with the French to cover the missionaries together with American educational and philanthropic agencies.[30]

55 (Jan. 1932), 54; Brown, *100 Years*, pp. 995–998, 1004; *Syria Mission*, pp. 35, 38–39, 42–43. The Presbyterians had re-established their work at Aleppo in the early 1920s. See *MRW*, 43 (Jan. 1920), 72; 44 (April 1921), 328; 45 (April 1922), 230; 46 (Feb. 1923), 157; 54 (Feb. 1931), 152–153.

[28] *MRW*, 45 (March 1922), 230–231; (June 1922), 499–500; 46 (June 1923), 477; 47 (Aug. 1924), 648; 53 (Sept. 1930), 714–715; 58 (Jan. 1935), 43; 60 (July–Aug. 1937), 388; *Syria Mission*, pp. 18, 45; Brown, *100 Years*, p. 1005.

[29] Knabenshue to Hughes, May 31, 1924; HML to Dulles, July 7, 1924; Leland Harrison (Assistant Secretary of State) to Knabenshue, Aug. 27, 1924; Harrison to James Hugh Keeley, Jr., Aug. 26, 1924, all DS 390d.116/31; *FR 1938*, II, 1043–1046. Other denominations listed for 1938 were the Seventh-Day Adventists, the Evangelical Church of God, Bible Lands Gospel Mission, and the Christian and Missionary Alliance. James E. Henderson (vice-consul, Beirut) to Hull, July 21, 1939, DS 811.5031 Near East/340. There were also English, Irish, Scottish, French, and Danish Lutheran missions in Syria and Lebanon.

[30] *FR 1931*, II, 267–279; *FR 1936*, III, 460–483; *FR 1937*, II, 938.

American archaeologists in Syria also called on consular officials for assistance and protection. In 1927 Consul Knabenshue obtained a reversal of the French high commissioner's rejection of a research permit.[31] The next year Yale University joined the French Academy in the excavation of Dura-Europas, which extended over ten seasons. Between 1932 and 1939 extensive work around Antioch was sponsored by Princeton University; the Oriental Institute of the University of Chicago dug in the same general vicinity during the 1930s. When negotiations were underway in 1936 toward termination of the mandate regime, the State Department requested France to require Syria and Lebanon to respect the prior rights of American archaeologists to excavate and receive a division of the finds.[32]

The future of the Antioch work and the immediate security of members of the expeditions were endangered by the turbulence of 1938–1939, when Alexandretta (Turkish Hatay) province was first detached from Syria and then annexed to Turkey as part of the price of bringing Turkey into the Anglo-French front against the Axis powers in the Eastern Mediterranean. It is significant that the United States, while following the political aspects of the Alexandretta controversy, confined its official representations to the archaeological projects and other minor American interests.[33]

Americans of Syrian and Lebanese origin also required assistance from the State Department. These naturalized citizens usually maintained close ties with their native land and often had property interests there. Although restrictive United States immigration policies cut sharply the number of new admissions, commercial opportunities in the New

---

[31] The archaeologist was Ephraim A. Speiser, now a respected professor of Semitics at the University of Pennsylvania. Knabenshue to Kellogg, Jan. 28, 1927; Leland Harrison to George A. Barton (secretary of the American Schools of Oriental Research and director of the American School in Baghdad), March 1, 1927; Barton to Harrison, March 5, 1927; Knabenshue to Kellogg, March 7, 1927; Harrison to Barton, March 14, 1927; Barton to Kellogg, March 16, 1927; Harrison to Knabenshue, April 1, 1927; G. H. Shaw (chief, Near Eastern Division) to Barton, April 6, 1927 — DS 890d.927/11, 11, 12, 11, 12, 14, 11, and 14.

[32] Ann Perkins in *Background of the Middle East*, pp. 215–216; *FR 1936*, III, 483–486; C. R. Morey (Department of Art and Architecture, Princeton University) to Shaw, June 24, 1929; Shaw to Morey, June 27, 1929, both DS 890d.927/16. Also participating in the Princeton project, known as the Committee for the Excavation of Antioch and Its Vicinity, were the Baltimore Museum of Art, the Metropolitan Museum of Art, the Louvre of Paris, and the Worcester Art Museum. Henderson to Hull, July 21, 1939, DS 811.5031 Near East/340.

[33] *FR 1938*, II, 1031–1043; *FR 1939*, IV, 832–847.

335

World continued to attract many to less strict South American countries, especially Argentina and Brazil. The sizable flow of immigrant remittances to assist relatives in the homeland fell off sharply during the depression years of the 1930s.[34] Naturalized Americans of Syrian and Lebanese origin confronted a serious dilemma in 1937 as a result of an agreement between France and Turkey allowing Syrians and Lebanese, who had not under provisions of the Lausanne Treaty of 1923 opted for either Turkish on the one hand or Syrian or Lebanese citizenship on the other, to make a choice. Under the new agreement, it appeared at first that if they did not elect Syrian or Lebanese citizenship, they would be considered Turkish citizens which, under Turkish law, would prevent them from inheriting property in Syria or Lebanon. But if they did opt for the citizenship of their native land, they were in serious danger of losing their American citizenship. Their fears were finally put to rest by assurances that France had every intention of recognizing their American nationality "and of assuring to them all rights which may be enjoyed by other citizens of the United States." Although these assurances meant that naturalized Syrians and Lebanese would not have to become citizens of Syria or Lebanon to inherit property or enjoy other rights in their homelands, it was not possible for the United States to settle this issue with the Turkish Republic before the beginning of World War II.[35]

Perennial Syrian and Lebanese pressure for independence was bound to grow stronger after the British loosened their hold on Iraq and Egypt in the agreements of 1932 and 1936. By 1936 it seemed that France might finally bow to the inevitable when she began negotiating treaties of friendship and alliance with Syria and Lebanon preparatory to terminating the mandates and promoting their admission to the League of Nations. The United States protested that under article 6 of the 1924 convention it had the right to be consulted both regarding termination of the mandates and conditions of administration after their cessation. The French government, while rejecting the American contentions about prior consultation, agreed to inform Washington of the general nature of the prospective agreements and to communicate the texts to the United States after ratification. When France seemed to be moving forward

[34] Frederick O. Bird (vice-consul, Beirut) to Hughes, Jan. 6, 1923, DS 890d.56/—; Longrigg, *Syria and Lebanon*, p. 285.
[35] *FR 1937*, II, 923–938 (quotation, p. 936); Hackworth, *Digest*, III, 194–196. Also see above, Chap. 8, pp. 240–241.

with independence plans in 1938, the State Department prepared a draft tripartite treaty (patterned after the one with Great Britain and Iraq of 1930) by which it hoped to protect American rights following the granting of independence. Plans were blown sky high toward the end of the year, however, when France backed away from granting independence to Syria and Lebanon. The Munich agreement and the growing fear of Italy caused French center and rightist groups to become much more solicitous after French imperial interests in the Eastern Mediterranean. In view of altered international conditions and the change in the French political balance, the State Department decided the time was not ripe for pursuing comprehensive tripartite treaty negotiations.[36] Syria and Lebanon had to wait sullenly for several more years before achieving independence.

At the close of the interwar era, the Beirut consulate reported to Washington on American interests in the French mandates. Registered with the consulate were 1405 citizens, 550 of them naturalized, and most of the 855 native-born minor children of naturalized Americans. Imports of about $3 million for 1938 placed the United States fourth as a foreign source, while exports of $1 million ranked the United States fifth. American local business investment was reported at $6.9 million, mostly in oil facilities, but including Singer Sewing Machine, MacAndrews and Forbes, and a number of merchandise-distributing firms. Investments in colleges, schools, missions, hospitals, orphanages, and archaeology totaled $4,474,000.[37]

Statistics notwithstanding, the university at Beirut and the Presbyterian mission enterprises comprised the most significant long-range American stakes. Americans associated with these institutions created the image of the United States as a friend of the Levant Arabs.

Palestine

Between the wars, Palestine was the stage for the opening scene of the tragic struggle between Jews and Arabs. A few American citizens were deeply involved, but officially the United States government was

[36] *FR 1936*, III, 496–502; *FR 1938*, II, 1003–1031.
[37] American Export Lines, Inc., of New York provided regular freight and passenger service between New York and the Eastern Mediterranean with bi-weekly sailings from Beirut. Average transit time was eighteen days. The Isthmian Line called irregularly at Beirut as a stop on the Persian Gulf-India route. Henderson to Hull, July 21, 1939, DS 811.5031 Near East/340.

a bystander except when demanding protection for the persons and property of its citizens. The United States claimed neither strategic interest nor political responsibilities in connection with Palestine's administration.

When World War I ended, Palestine was under British military occupation. At the San Remo Conference on April 24, 1920, the Allies assigned Palestine (including what later became Trans-Jordan) to the British as a mandate under the League of Nations. In approving the amended British mandate for Palestine on July 24, 1922, the League of Nations Council asserted that the mandatory should be responsible for establishment of a national Jewish home in Palestine, assigning to Great Britain full legislative and administrative powers. The mandate provided for facilitating Jewish immigration and for acquisition of Palestinian citizenship for Jews permanently residing there. A Jewish Agency was recognized to advise and cooperate with the British administration. To placate Emir Abdullah, the British provided him with the patrimony known as Trans-Jordan by slicing off part of the Palestine mandate. An agreement of February 20, 1928, between Great Britain and Abdullah recognized Trans-Jordan as an independent government, and the League approved this agreement on September 1, 1928, with the proviso that the mandate was still in force.[38]

Postwar Palestine-American relations thus became a phase of Anglo-American relations, just as they did during the acrid controversy of 1919 and 1920 over British refusal to allow Socony to prospect for oil under the military occupation. American belief that the British were discriminating against American businessmen led the State Department to invoke the open-door policy and to associate it with the general principles governing mandates as agreed upon by the Allied leaders and President Wilson at Paris.[39]

Desire to participate in future Middle Eastern oil development was, then, a major determinant of American policy during the early postwar years, but it was not the sole American concern. A small number of Americans were engaged in missionary, philanthropic, and educational projects in Palestine which the United States sought to protect through continuation of capitulatory rights as ensured by treaty during the Otto-

[38] Hackworth, *Digest*, I, 112–116. For the American attitude concerning the rights of the United States in Trans-Jordan, see *FR 1924*, II, 205, 208–210. See also Manuel, *American-Palestine Relations*, pp. 257, 288, 289–291.

[39] See above, Chap. 6, pp. 169–174. See also *FR 1929*, III, 61–70.

man regime. As specific cases arose where local courts tried American nationals, the State Department protested to the British government and insisted that American consular courts had jurisdiction. Preservation of capitulations was a major consideration of the department in asking the British for modifications in the draft mandate submitted to the League of Nations in December, 1920. Secretary Charles E. Hughes requested that capitulatory rights should be "continued until adequate courts are established," and that provisions should be made "for the revival of capitulatory rights in the event of the termination of the mandate regime."[40]

During the early twenties the State Department persistently stood its ground while negotiating with the British for a formal agreement guaranteeing American rights of equal opportunity, equal protection, and capitulatory rights. These negotiations, carried on parallel to related discussions with France regarding Syria and Lebanon, resulted in the British-American Palestine Convention of December 3, 1924. Ratifications were not exchanged until late in 1925 after the United States was satisfied that British officials would respect the right of American consular courts to dispose of several pending cases involving American nationals. The convention was similar in most respects to the Franco-American Convention of April 4, 1924.[41]

One significant difference in the two conventions reflected the uniqueness of the Palestine situation — the inclusion at British insistence of the preamble of the Palestine mandate with the Balfour Declaration pledging a "national home" for the Jews in Palestine. Although the Zionist movement in the United States was not yet strong, financial support from American Jews contributed significantly to remarkable agricultural, industrial, and cultural advances in Palestine. For example, the purpose of the American Palestine Company, announced at a dinner in New York in March of 1921, was to undertake large-scale industrial development in Palestine. At the dinner nearly $1.5 million of the pro-

[40] *FR 1920*, II, 675–678; *FR 1921*, II, 119–123. The draft mandate of December, 1920, is printed in *FR 1921*, I, 104–105, 110–117. For changes asked by the United States, see *FR 1921*, I, 923–924 (quotations, p. 924); II, 106–108.

[41] *FR 1922*, II, 268–310; *FR 1923*, II, 218–228; *FR 1924*, II, 197–222; *FR 1925*, II, 217–234. See also Manuel, *American-Palestine Relations*, pp. 270–275, 284, 289–290. Unlike the agreement with France, the Palestine convention specifically provided that existing Anglo-American agreements relating to extradition and consular rights should apply to the mandated territory. Prior to signing the convention, the British pledged most-favored-nation treatment for American nationals.

posed $5 million was subscribed. When the Hebrew University opened in Jerusalem in 1925, the Education Committee of the Zionist Organization of America decided to create a development fund of $1 million for the university.[42]

Zionist adherents were less successful in seeking official American backing for a liberal interpretation of the Balfour Declaration, which was an ambiguous blank check whose face value would ultimately depend largely on the vigor of the Zionists in achieving a latitudinarian interpretation. The coolness of the State Department, so apparent during the Wilson era, and its reluctance to commit the United States to any responsibility for implementing the Balfour Declaration continued into the Harding administration and beyond. Officials in the Near Eastern Division were especially displeased at the turn of affairs in Congress in 1922 when Zionist sympathizers passed a joint resolution which endorsed the declaration in principle. The resolution which finally received congressional approval read:

Resolved by the Senate and the House of Representatives of the United States of America in Congress assembled, That the United States of America favors the establishment in Palestine of a national home for the Jewish people, it being clearly understood that nothing shall be done which may prejudice the civil and religious rights of Christian and all other non-Jewish communities in Palestine, and that the holy places and religious buildings and sites in Palestine shall be adequately protected.[43]

Although it is debatable whether the United States incurred any legal obligation through a congressional resolution expressing moral support, this approval compromised the position of the State Department, which nevertheless held fast to the view that the sole official concern of the United States in Palestine was to protect American nationals and their interests and that the Zionist purposes had no part in American interests. Nor did the State Department show any concern when an Arab

[42] *MRW*, 44 (Sept. 1921), 736; 48 (Aug. 1925), 644; Manuel, *American-Palestine Relations*, pp. 276–277, 301–302.
[43] Public Res. 73, *U.S. Statutes at Large*, 67 Cong., Part 1, p. 1012 (quotation); *Cong. Record*, 67 Cong., 2 Sess., pp. 6289, 7937, 9799–9820, 9880, 9881, 10210, 12368, 12587, 12677, 12786, 13186. For accompanying House Report No. 1038, see *House Reports*, 67 Cong., 2 Sess. For S. J. Res. 191, see *Cong. Record*, 67 Cong., 2 Sess., pp. 5376, 6240, 6332. On April 22, 1922, Senator Henry Cabot Lodge presented petitions from 248 citizens of Massachusetts supporting the resolution and a telegram opposing it from the Palestine National League. *Cong. Record*, 67 Cong., 2 Sess., p. 5760. For numerous other pro-Zionist memorials and petitions, see *ibid.*, pp. 4757, 4758, 5844, 7085. See also Manuel, *American-Palestine Relations*, pp. 275–279, 305.

delegation in America appealed to President Harding in 1921 against the "so-called 'Jewish Danger.'"[44]

Notwithstanding the indifference usually encountered at the State Department, American Zionists did not abandon their importunings. Their concern was especially marked during the periodic clashes between Arabs and Jews in the Holy Land, quite understandably in view of the sizable number of Jewish-Americans resident in Palestine and the considerable Jewish-American investment stake. Zionists took advantage of these legitimate occasions for requesting protection of American lives and property to seek official commitments favoring the Zionist program. Such was the case during the disturbances following the Wailing Wall incident of 1929 when several Jewish-Americans were killed. Secretary Henry L. Stimson informed Zionist representatives of the government's intercession with the British for better protection of American interests, but would not be drawn into endorsing Zionism. He told Rabbi Stephen S. Wise that it was "fallacious reasoning" to argue that because several Americans had been killed the United States government "was under some sort of obligation to assist in presenting the Zionist side. . . . Why should the American Government assist in presenting either the Jewish or the Arab side?"[45]

During the latter 1930s a combination of international and domestic circumstances made Palestine a more pressing issue in American foreign policy. Violent Arab uprisings against the Jews in 1936, born of fear that the Jews would take over the country, embarrassed the British government at a time when the dissatisfied Fascist powers were successfully challenging the international status quo. The Fascist threat to British supremacy in the Middle East coincided with massive resistance to the British in Iraq and Egypt during 1936. The turn of events made these strategic areas less dependable fulcra of imperial defense for the long-range future and forced the British to count more than ever on their position in Palestine and Trans-Jordan. Adolf Hitler had by this time stepped up his virulent domestic campaign against the Jews and had begun to exploit the Palestine turmoil to harass the British further. His Italian partner, who had recently swallowed Ethiopia, began to beam propaganda to the Arab World from his transmitter at Bari and thus fed

[44] *MRW*, 44 (Dec. 1921), 907; Manuel, *American-Palestine Relations*, pp. 276–284, 289.
[45] *FR 1929*, III, 46–61 (quotations, p. 59).

Arab resentment against the British and their Zionist clients. Radio Berlin began to broadcast Arabic programs filled with anti-British propaganda in the spring of 1939.[46]

The harried British responded to the 1936 uprising with another official commission, headed by Earl Peel, which in 1937 recommended partition of Palestine into separate Arab and Jewish states. Zionists were not fully satisfied with the proposal; Arabs were generally violently opposed and vented their opposition through new riots. Limited by their rapidly deteriorating position vis-à-vis Hitler, and faced with vigorous protests from several Arab countries, the British bowed to Arab violence by abandoning the partition proposal and finally announced through a White Paper in 1939 drastic curtailment of former policies designed to implement the Balfour Declaration. Zionists cried betrayal.[47]

As the Palestine problem again became a pressing international issue, repercussions were felt in the United States. The Zionist movement gained new adherents and much sympathy from the American public, repelled by Hitler's atrocities. Zionist sympathizers gathered forces to press the Roosevelt administration to abandon its noncommittal attitude. What they wanted was American intervention to force British compliance with a Zionist interpretation of the mandatory's obligation to carry out the Balfour pledge. Petitions from state legislatures and congressmen as well as telegrams from private persons and groups flooded the State Department during the fall of 1938. Paul M. Alling, assistant chief of the Near Eastern Division, noted that about 65,000 telegrams had been received. Western Union had handled about 34,000, a number exceeded only during the controversy over President Roosevelt's proposal to reorganize the Supreme Court. Postal Telegraph's 30,522 telegrams on the Palestine matter exceeded the number received during the Supreme Court fight. On October 14, 1938, an impressive American Jewish

---

[46] For the Arab revolt of 1936 and its collapse, see *FR 1936*, III, 434–444, 446–447, 449, 452. Apparently no American lives were lost, and the State Department was satisfied with British response to its strong representations for adequate protection of American lives and property. See also J. C. Hurewitz, *The Struggle for Palestine*, pp. 21, 25–26, 67–71, 86–90.

[47] Hurewitz, *Struggle for Palestine*, pp. 72–84, 90–93, 98–105; *FR 1936*, III, 445–446, 452–453; *FR 1937*, II, 892, 894–895, 904, 908–914; *FR 1938*, II, 899–901, 929–951, 961, 965–966, 976–978, 989–990. For the reaction following publication of the 1939 White Paper, see *FR 1939*, IV, 774–776, 778–793, 806–807. For the official attitude of the United States, see *FR 1937*, II, 881–922; *FR 1938*, II, 889–1002; *FR 1939*, IV, 694–810, especially pp. 751–757. Secretary Hull gave his version of the Palestine issue from 1936 to 1939 in *The Memoirs of Cordell Hull*, II, 1528–1531.

delegation addressed a memorandum to Secretary Hull outlining the Zionist position and asking the United States government to intervene with the British to prevent unwelcome changes in the mandate. To answer thousands of letters and telegrams on the Palestine question, the State Department issued a press release on October 14, 1938, summarizing the American position on Palestine since 1918.[48]

American Zionists spared no effort to apprise the American public and its representatives of the wretched lot of European Jews whose piteous plight elicited deep humanitarian sympathies. Some counterpressure did build up in behalf of the Arab cause, but it had relatively little impact on the American public and was exerted most strongly through diplomatic channels. The limited effects were attributable in part to the small number of Arabs in the United States and their inability to organize as speedily and effectively as the Zionists. During 1936 Americans of Arab origin finally formed the Arab National League in New York to publicize the Palestinian Arab position. Arab spokesmen could not, however, match the Zionist presentation in emotional appeal.[49]

From the Middle East itself came Arab protests and warnings. American diplomats and consuls in Baghdad, Jerusalem, Cairo, and Beirut informed the State Department of visitations from many Arab delegations expressing apprehension that the intensive Zionist efforts in the United States were blinding Americans and their political leaders to the justice of the Arab position. Did the United States still stand for self-determination, they wondered? More responsible Arabs interceded for continued American neutrality at the very least; less responsible spokesmen threatened retaliation against American interests throughout the Arab World and talked of a boycott against American trade. Faculty members at the American University of Beirut, in daily contact with students from leading families of Syria, Palestine, Lebanon, Iraq, Bahrein, Kuwait, Sudan, Egypt, and Trans-Jordan, reportedly thought that the standing and usefulness of American institutions in the Middle East might suffer appreciably if Great Britain made concessions to the Jews because of pressure from the United States. On November 10, 1938, Minister Paul Knabenshue reported that student riots in Baghdad were mainly directed against the British, but "against the United States in

[48] *FR 1936*, III, 444–448, 450–451, 455–459; *FR 1937*, II, 904, 921–922; *FR 1938*, II, 921–925, 927–929, 952–960, 966; *FR 1939*, IV, 699, 723–725, 748–750, 810.

[49] Hurewitz, *Struggle for Palestine*, pp. 85–86; *FR 1939*, IV, 701–703. See also *MRW*, 58 (Sept. 1935), 437.

part." King Ibn Saud of Saudi Arabia made an eloquent appeal to President Roosevelt in a letter of November 29 criticizing the main points in the Zionist argument and pleading for justice for the Palestinian Arabs on the basis of the principle of self-determination.[50]

Notwithstanding considerable public and congressional support, the Zionists were unable to force a change in official American policy. The State Department resisted repeated urgent entreaties for intervention and reaffirmed the established position that the United States had no responsibility for administration of the Palestine mandate or for implementation of the Balfour Doctrine. Zionists received only a sop in the form of an expression of sympathy for the tragedy of European Jews and admiration for the work Zionists had accomplished in the economic and cultural development of Palestine.[51]

Did the failure of the United States to intervene mean that Arab sympathizers had been decisive in shaping American policy? Although some facts lend color to such an interpretation, present evidence does not convincingly support such a thesis. Consul-General George Wadsworth reported from Jerusalem in October, 1938, that the Christian clergy and missionaries agreed with the Arabs about the threat of "Jewish domination" from continued Jewish immigration. Nearly all members of the Christian religious communities were Arabs, whose views naturally influenced clergy and missionary workers. If the Zionist program was successful, the clergy felt it would be at the expense of Christian privilege and influence in the Holy Land. Wadsworth cautioned, however, that the Christian clergy did not go so far as to support Arab ambitions for independence since "Arab rule of the entire country is regarded, from the Christian point of view, as being almost as much to be avoided as Jewish rule." Yet there is currently no proof that missionary interests were decisive in bringing about reaffirmation of official non-intervention.[52]

What of pressure from American oil interests whose proliferating holdings in Arab lands gave them a stake in friendly official relations between the United States and the Arab World? At least one oil execu-

[50] *FR 1938*, II, 962–974, 979–984 (quotation, p. 984); 989–990, 994–998; *FR 1939*, IV, 694–696, 701–703, 719.

[51] Hurewitz, *Struggle for Palestine*, pp. 76, 95, 105; *FR 1936*, II, 454–459; *FR 1939*, IV, 725–729, 760–765, 768–769. Apparently the State Department overrode some leaning of President Roosevelt's toward intervention. Roosevelt was under pressure from Justice Louis Brandeis. See *FR 1939*, IV, 757–758.

[52] *FR 1938*, II, 971–973 (quotation, p. 971).

tive let the State Department know of his fears that company efforts might be impeded by Arab resentment and possible retaliation against putative pro-Zionism in the United States. Again, documents so far consulted do not indicate that the State Department gave great weight to the apprehension of oil men.[53]

Tradition was the most significant determinant of American policy. The United States was not yet ready to abandon its historic abstinence from Middle Eastern politics. Unwanted international responsibilities could best be avoided in this case by taking a neutral stance. The United States would not declare itself officially for either the Zionists or the Arabs in Palestine. With the crises leading to World War II, there was at least a hint that some State Department officials, mindful of Britain's worsening international position, were reluctant to add to her tribulations by forcing a course which would further alienate the Arab World just when Great Britain was trying to shore up her position in this strategic area to meet growing Fascist inroads.[54]

Some light is cast on the relationship of Jewish-American interests to other American interests in Palestine by a report from the Jerusalem consulate to the State Department in 1939. There were approximately 9100 American nationals in Palestine, comprising about 78 per cent of Americans in the Arab Middle East. The department estimated that of the 9100 some 84 per cent were Jews and 11 per cent Arabs. Of the total, about 6700 were naturalized Americans against whom presumption of expatriation had arisen, although many were believed to be in a position to overcome the presumption. There was the additional factor of large investments by Jewish-Americans in Palestine, estimated at $41 million of the total $49 million invested by Americans.[55]

Non-Jewish American interests consisted of some investment, a very modest volume of trade, four rather small missionary establishments, and miscellaneous educational, relief, and archaeological interests. More than half the nearly $8 million invested in these categories was in busi-

[53] *FR 1937*, II, 893–894; Murray to G. S. Messersmith (Assistant Secretary of State), March 20, 1939, DS 124.90f/6; Murray memorandum on relationship of Ibn Saud's attitude toward American oil companies and United States Palestine policy, July 12, 1937, DS 890f.6363 Standard Oil Co./93.
[54] *FR 1936*, III, 454.
[55] Nearly one-sixth of Jewish-American investment was in some 48 of the 247 agricultural settlements where about 574 American citizens resided. Julian L. Pinkerton (consul, Jerusalem) to Hull, April 12, 1939; Murray to Messersmith, Welles, and Hull, memorandum, May 9, 1939, DS 811.5031 Near East/303 and 318.

ness establishments such as petroleum facilities and import-export firms. Socony-Vacuum had a distributing agency; I.P.C. (23¾ per cent American) had pipeline terminal facilities at Haifa. Imports from the United States in 1937 amounted to $5 million, about 7 per cent of Palestine's total imports, placing the United States in fifth place. Miscellaneous exports to the United States amounted to only about one-tenth of Palestine's total for 1937. More than half of the non-Jewish American investment had been devoted to religious missions, schools, benevolent institutions, and archaeology. The missions were conducted by the General Council of the Assemblies of God, the Southern Baptist Convention, the Church of the Nazarene, and the Christian and Missionary Alliance. The American Society of Friends operated schools for boys and girls at Ramallah, and Americans supported other schools, several under Jewish auspices. The Y.M.C.A. was well housed in million-dollar facilities provided by American philanthropists, and John D. Rockefeller, Jr., had contributed $2 million for the Palestine Antiquities Museum. The American School of Oriental Studies, established in 1900, still served as a focal point for American excavators in the Bible lands. As of 1938 the Oriental Institute of the University of Chicago was still conducting work at Megiddo.[56]

American policy in Palestine between the wars was consistent in emphasizing traditional protection for American citizens and their enterprises on a most-favored-nation basis, with equality of commercial opportunity. Jewish-American stakes in Palestine, larger than all other American interests combined, commanded support from the United States government within its general policy formula. But when Zionists tried to expand the official formula to embrace active sponsorship of maximum Zionist objectives, the State Department resisted. In Palestine, as elsewhere in the Arab World, the United States tended to defer to British dominance. Within half a dozen years, the situation would

[56] Pinkerton to Hull, April 12, 1939, DS 811.5031 Near East/303; *MRW*, 48 (June 1925), 478; 52 (Oct. 1929), 967; 56 (June 1933), 285–286; 57 (Feb. 1934), 104; Breasted, *Pioneer to the Past*, pp. 397, 398, 400; Ann Perkins in *Background of the Middle East*, pp. 213–215. A 1934 report on the total missionary effort in Palestine mentioned twenty-three Protestant missionary organizations plus some "independent forces." There were also some Catholic missions. The whole number of missionaries was 232. In Jerusalem alone there were sixteen missionary societies with 105 missionaries, fifty Protestant schools with 4281 pupils. Only twenty-five Moslem converts were known in all Palestine. *MRW*, 57 (June 1934), 310.

change drastically as the impending genocide of European Jews brought about a reversal of American policy more favorable to the Zionist cause.

Iraq

Although Germany and Great Britain competed for influence in Mesopotamia before World War I, the United States showed little interest either in these prewar maneuvers or in the wartime fighting there. Except for scattered religious and educational work by a small band of missionaries, a little business (chiefly exports of dates and licorice root), and an occasional archaeological venture, Americans had little contact with Mesopotamia, and their government had even less.

When Mesopotamia continued to be a subject of international discussion and negotiation after the war, the United States took a greater interest. Great Britain deemed Mesopotamia vital as a strategic location flanking the indispensable Persian oil fields and guarding the approaches to India. Furthermore, the country was reputedly rich in petroleum, which the British hoped to tap for their growing naval, motor transport, and industrial requirements. It was a foregone conclusion that British diplomats would not permit this strategic plum to slip from their grasp. The form under which control was to be exercised — a League of Nations mandate — was less important than the fact of British influence. Costly local uprisings against the British in 1920 alienated a large element of the British public which pressed for withdrawal. But the prize was too valuable; the British remained, bringing in Feisal, third son of the Sherif of Mecca, to be king in August, 1921. The original British plan for the mandate was altered in favor of a treaty of alliance arranged in 1922 with Iraq (the official name for Mesopotamia). In view of strong national feeling in Iraq, the British decided they could accord that government greater nominal control without seriously jeopardizing British interests. Behind the façade, British officials would still quietly shape Iraq's foreign policy to British requirements. The League of Nations Council accepted a modified form of the treaty as the mandate instrument on September 27, 1924.[57]

[57] Supplementing the treaty were a protocol dated April 30, 1923, and subsidiary agreements dated March 25, 1924. See *FR 1925*, II, 231–238; Hackworth, *Digest*, I, 117. A supplementary treaty signed on January 13, 1926, received the approval of the League Council on March 11, 1926. Useful studies of modern Iraq are Stephen Hemsley Longrigg, '*Iraq, 1900 to 1950: A Political, Social, and Economic History*; Ernest Main, *Iraq: From Mandate to Independence*; Henry A.

Through President Wilson's participation in the Paris Peace Conference the United States had a voice in making the decision that Mesopotamia, as one of the non-Turkish parts of the Ottoman Empire to be detached, should be supervised under the mandate system. Although the United States withdrew late in 1919 from direct responsibility for enforcing the postwar settlement, Washington protested vigorously when it appeared that the British were using their special position in Mesopotamia to favor British oil interests at the expense of American companies. After eight years of diplomatic controversy and business negotiation, American companies joined the international consortium known as the Turkish Petroleum Company (renamed the Iraq Petroleum Company in 1929). Thus, by 1920 oil had become an important new ingredient in American relations with Iraq, although the American role was shadowy and ill-defined owing to British domination of the company's management.[58]

Other American businesses in Iraq also encountered difficulties which contributed to the desire of the State Department to seek treaty assurances for the protection of American interests. Between 1919 and 1922 the occupation authorities placed obstacles in the way of MacAndrews and Forbes, apparently attempting to freeze out this American licorice company in favor of British merchants anxious to take over the business. Inquiries by the American consul brought the retort that the United States had no right to ask for protection of its interests until it recognized the government of King Feisal. A few years later, MacAndrews and Forbes, Hills Brothers (date growers and exporters), and Singer Sewing Machine were caught up in the question of whether they must pay income taxes to the Iraq government, which the United States had still not recognized. This issue arose while the United States was negotiating a treaty with Great Britain and Iraq defining American rights in Iraq. Pending completion of the negotiations, the State Department took the position that collection of taxes from American nationals without the consent of the United States government violated previous American treaty rights. In view of the imminent conclusion of the new treaty, however, the department declared it would not object to American firms

Foster, *The Making of Modern Iraq: A Product of World Forces*; Majid Khadduri, *Independent Iraq, 1932–1958: A Study in Iraqi Politics*; Philip W. Ireland, *'Iraq: A Study in Political Development.*
   [58] See above, Chap. 6, pp. 173–179.

paying income taxes if they believed it desirable "for reasons of business policy."[59]

The negotiations with Great Britain and Iraq referred to by the State Department were the outgrowth of protracted discussions dating back to the League's acceptance in 1924 of the Anglo-Iraq Treaty of alliance as the mandate instrument. Upon learning of the League's action the American government protested the failure of the British government and the League to consult the United States regarding the mandate terms, as had been done in connection with those for Syria, Lebanon, and Palestine. According to the State Department, the Iraq arrangements did not adequately protect American interests in three respects: they did not provide for re-establishment of capitulations on termination of the mandate; they omitted firm assurances respecting equality of commercial opportunity in natural resources exploitation; and they lacked adequate provisions ensuring Americans equal footing with nationals of other powers with respect to economic and other rights. In April of 1925, therefore, the United States invited Great Britain to negotiate a convention similar to the Anglo-American Palestine Convention of 1924, possibly bringing in Iraq as the third signatory.[60]

After several years of negotiation, the Anglo-American-Iraqi Convention was signed on January 9, 1930. By Article 1, the United States for the first time officially recognized the government of Iraq and the British mandate. Hitherto, the American consul, functioning at Baghdad only by sufferance, had been in a difficult position. Both British officials and King Feisal had repeatedly indicated their displeasure at American failure to extend recognition. Other articles conferred on Americans in Iraq all rights to which League members were entitled; guaranteed their vested property rights; and ensured American rights to engage in philanthropic, religious, and educational activities, subject only to local laws for preservation of public order and morality. Article 6 stated that

[59] Thomas R. Owens (consul, Baghdad) to Hughes, March 21, 1922, DS 390g.-115/—; Owens to Hughes, March 21 and July 6, 1922, DS 390g.115 M 11/— and 1. Both Hills and MacAndrews and Forbes supplemented their agricultural export business by acting as agents for American automobiles and miscellaneous products. Consul John Randolph at Baghdad did not see how American companies selling merchandise in Iraq could expect income tax exemption on those sales. Randolph to Kellogg, July 1, 1927, DS 890g.5123/—. See also *FR 1928*, II, 952–953 (quotation, p. 952).

[60] *FR 1925*, II, 230–231, 238; A. W. Dulles, 12-page memorandum, Jan. 17, 1924; Harrison to Hughes, memorandum, Sept. 15, 1924; Turlington memorandum (Solicitor's Office), Feb. 4, 1925, DS 890g.01/83, 123, and 125.

no modification in the mandate would change American rights without the consent of the United States. The final article specified that on termination of Britain's special relations with Iraq, the United States and Iraq would negotiate treaties to govern their future relations.[61]

Later in 1930, Great Britain and Iraq signed a new treaty of alliance looking to the complete freedom, independence, and equality of Iraq, to be operative on Iraq's admission to the League of Nations, which was to occur as soon as the British could persuade the League that Iraq was ready. While Great Britain, Iraq, and the League were completing details prerequisite to terminating the mandate, the United States objected to Britain's neglecting to consult the United States "with respect to the conditions under which Iraq is to be administered upon the cessation of the mandatory relationship." Inasmuch as the League insisted that termination be accompanied by guarantees for the protection of foreigners and their property, the United States accepted the *fait accompli* when Iraq was admitted to the League in 1932, the first of the mandates to emerge from that status.[62]

Once Iraq was technically independent in foreign policy, the Convention of 1930 ceased to be operative, and the United States needed a new set of bilateral arrangements with that country. The United States established a legation at Baghdad, and in 1934 arranged an extradition treaty. After five years of discussion, the two countries signed a treaty of commerce and navigation in 1938. Except for the 23¾ per cent participation in the Iraq Petroleum Company, American investment in Iraq by 1938 totaled only about $850,000. MacAndrews and Forbes still exported licorice root, and Hills Brothers sizable quantities of dates. There were also small exports of wool and skins. Singer imported sewing machines and electric fans. American autos, trucks, tires, batteries, and trailers completed the modest trade exchange.[63]

As World War II approached, the 113 American citizens in Iraq, 93 of them native-born, were occupied chiefly in missionary and related educational endeavors. The best-established missionary work at the close

[61] Randolph to Kellogg, Jan. 20, 1926; G. H. Shaw memorandum, "Iraq Treaty Negotiations," Feb. 4, 1929, DS 890g.01/161 and 208½; *FR 1925*, II, 230–238; *FR 1927*, II, 781–807; *FR 1928*, II, 952–957; *FR 1930*, III, 291–308.

[62] Hackworth, *Digest*, I, 118–122; *FR 1932*, II, 672–685 (quotation, p. 672); Ireland, *'Iraq*, pp. 412–419.

[63] *FR 1934*, II, 781–787; *FR 1936*, III, 401–405; *FR 1937*, II, 767–784; *FR 1938*, II, 763–769; J. C. Satterthwaite (consul, Baghdad) to Hull, April 11, 1939, DS 811.5031 Near East/312.

of World War I was that carried on by the Reformed Church in America (Dutch Reformed) operating from Basra with other stations at Amara and, after 1920, at Baghdad. The area around Mosul, served by the American Board and the Northern Presbyterians in the nineteenth century, had been reassigned to the Church Missionary Society (British), but that organization had been obliged to give up its Mesopotamian work following the ravages of World War I. The vacuum attracted several American denominations sharing a Calvinistic heritage, and they began to consider seriously a possible interdenominational effort in Mesopotamia. Out of their discussions emerged the United Mission in Mesopotamia in 1924, a joint enterprise of the Presbyterian Church in the U.S.A., the Dutch Reformed Church, and the Reformed Church in the United States (German). Their avowed objective was the conversion of Moslems to evangelical Protestantism. Five mission centers were served under the joint sponsorship — Mosul, Dohuk, Hilla, Baghdad, and Kirkuk. They conducted schools for girls at Mosul and Baghdad; a boys' school at Baghdad, opened in 1924, was for a time under United Mission sponsorship, but after 1933 Dr. Calvin K. Staudt of the Dutch Reformed denomination continued it without official support. The Dutch Reformed Church continued some of its enterprises independently of the United Mission, for example, a mission hospital at Amara, and schools for boys and girls at Basra. The only non-Protestant American educational institution was Baghdad College, a junior college established by American Jesuits in 1932.[64]

Calvin Staudt, a leading missionary educator, confided his long-range dreams to Consul John Randolph in 1925. He hoped the foundations being laid in primary education could be extended to secondary schools, which at a later date would serve as feeders for an American University at Baghdad similar to and as successful as that at Beirut. In his report to the State Department, Randolph expressed the optimistic judgment that it was "safe to say that no educational influence in all of Iraq" was so great as that of the American missionaries and the American Univer-

[64] Satterthwaite to Hull, April 11, 1939, DS 811.5031 Near East/312; Mason and Barny, *History of the Arabian Mission*, pp. 187–189, 202–206, 227–228; Brown, *100 Years*, pp. 838–839, 842–846; Longrigg, *'Iraq*, pp. 169, 205; Centennial Series, *United Mission in Mesopotamia*, pp. 7, 10–12, 22–30; MRW, 45 (Sept. 1922), 677–678; 46 (Feb. 1923), 149; (Dec. 1923), 1034; 47 (June 1924), 473; 48 (July 1925), 566; (Nov. 1925), 899; 49 (Nov. 1926), 866–870; 50 (March 1927), 232; (Oct. 1927), 747–748; 51 (Jan. 1928), 86; (April 1928), 332; (May 1928), 406; 53 (Jan. 1930), 22; (May 1930), 326–330; 60 (Oct. 1937), 476; 61 (July 1938), 376.

sity at Beirut. When missionary efforts to open new schools were discouraged by the Iraq government, which objected to their teaching religion, the churchmen decided to fight their battle without asking for help from the consulate. Randolph explained to Washington that

this policy of negotiating directly with the local authorities emanates, I understand, from the headquarters in the United States of the different missions concerned, the missionaries' idea being that their educational work in Iraq may be greatly facilitated if nothing is done to antagonize the local authorities or any of the local people. It is even said that the missionaries would prefer to be delayed rather than to have their request pressed and thereby lose possibly the cordial cooperation of the local authorities.

Randolph had explained to the Prime Minister of Iraq that the insistence on religious instruction really emanated from the financial supporters of the missions in the United States.[65]

The Iraq government apparently held considerable respect for the philosophy and methods of lay education in the United States. In 1932 it commissioned an educational survey led by Dr. Paul Monroe of Teachers College, Columbia University, with assistance from William C. Bagley of Columbia and Edgar Knight of the University of North Carolina. After visiting all types of schools, consulting with agricultural experts and medical men, and studying local traditions bearing on their investigation, the survey team finally recommended local initiative in place of the centralized system in effect. The Monroe survey stressed the need for a new type of agricultural village school which would serve the vast majority of agrarian peoples by convincing them, in a concrete way, that education could improve their lives. Although the Ministry of Education attempted to implement some of the commission's recommendations, namely those advocating village schools, poverty and the weight of tradition prevented carrying them out fully.[66]

Archaeology provided the other major cultural contact of the United

[65] Randolph to Kellogg, Report No. 111, Aug. 1, 1925 (first quotation); Report No. 112, Aug. 1, 1925 (second quotation), DS 390g.1164/— and 1. See also Randolph to Kellogg, Sept. 6, 1929, DS 390g.1164/9. When Iraq was discussing a new nationalistic education law in 1939, the United States protested that the proposed regulations would adversely affect American schools in Iraq. Such a law was, nevertheless, enacted in 1940. The Iraq government gave informal assurances that it would not be inclined to use the law to hamstring American schools. *FR 1939*, IV, 545–554; *FR 1940*, III, 727–747.

[66] Curti and Birr, *Prelude to Point Four*, pp. 198–199; Longrigg, '*Iraq*, pp. 205, 245.

States with Iraq between the wars. American archaeologists joined their European colleagues in digging up the past at numerous rich sites of ancient civilizations. At Ur of the Chaldees, the University Museum of the University of Pennsylvania worked with the British Museum between 1922 and 1934. At Kish, not far from Baghdad, and fourteen miles east of the site of ancient Babylon, the Field Museum of Chicago joined Oxford University between 1923 and 1933 in excavating one of the oldest Sumerian cities. At Khorsabad, near Mosul, the Oriental Institute of the University of Chicago, excavated between 1929 and 1938 at the unfinished capital of the Assyrian Empire and worked with several other institutions at sites on the Diyala River in central Mesopotamia. Sites at Tell Billa and Tepe Gawra near Mosul were examined from 1930 to 1938 by the University Museum and the American School in Baghdad.[67]

Cooperation between American archaeologists and British officials in Iraq appeared to be very cordial and without the strains attending American business operations. In reporting the inauguration of the American School of Oriental Research (A.S.O.R.) at Baghdad in November, 1923, Consul Thomas Owens wrote about the big turnout of the most representative people of Baghdad, observing that "the establishment of the school met the enthusiastic approval of all local people and was not opposed by the British." A.S.O.R. was proceeding with plans for creating an excellent archaeological library, to be housed temporarily at the American consulate until a suitable building could be built on land to be donated by the Iraq government. The library was open to archaeologists of all nationalities. When the rich finds of the 1920s overtaxed the Iraq Museum founded by Gertrude Bell, Americans joined in efforts to finance a new museum. Even after Iraq became independent in 1932, American excavators apparently experienced no nationalistic obstacles so serious as those confronted in Egypt and Iran. Nevertheless, the unearthing by Western archaeologists of the glorious ancient civilizations seated in Mesopotamia paradoxically contributed to nationalistic fervor which hastened the day when Westerners would find it more difficult to carry on their enterprises in the Middle East.[68]

[67] Perkins in *Background of the Middle East*, pp. 216–218; Randolph to Stimson, Aug. 23, 1929, DS 890g.927/29; Longrigg, *'Iraq*, pp. 169–170, 207, 245; Lloyd, *Foundations in the Dust*, pp. 226, 231–234. Other American institutions participating in Mesopotamian archaeology were the Fogg Museum of Harvard University and the Toledo Museum of Art.

[68] Owens to Hughes, Nov. 22, 1923 (quotation), DS 390g.1164 Am 3/—; Ran-

In its main outlines the pattern of American relations with Iraq was not unlike that developed with other parts of the Arab World. Not opposing British primacy except when there was actual or potential discrimination against the commercial or cultural interests of Americans, Washington put no pressure on Great Britain to relinquish its mandate and took no leadership in promoting Iraq's aspirations for full sovereignty. On the contrary, the State Department believed that American interests required the continuation of capitulations or their equivalent. Nor did the United States share Britain's strategic interest in Iraq even when the Germans made heavy inroads there during the late 1930s. At bottom the American relationship with Iraq rested on the activities of private groups — missionaries, archaeologists, and businessmen. Not even the participation of American companies in the new and important oil industry concerned the United States government deeply, once American companies had been admitted to the Iraq Petroleum Company, whose management was essentially British. Most Americans were not yet ready to have their government mix in international politics in Iraq or elsewhere.[69]

The Arabian Peninsula

The vast land mass of the Arabian peninsula from Hejaz on the northwest through Kuweit on the northeast was one of the least-known areas of the world to Americans at the close of World War I. Except for the handful of Dutch Reformed missionaries with the Arabian Mission at the Persian Gulf stations in Bahrein, Muscat, and Kuweit, the United States consul in the British crown colony of Aden was the only American resident in the peninsula.[70]

Among the Great Powers, Great Britain alone had maintained an alert interest in Arabia, which abutted on her communications routes via Suez, the Red Sea, the Indian Ocean, and the Persian Gulf to the oil of Persia, to the empire beyond — India, the dominions of Australia and New Zealand, and to the oriental trade. To guard their interests, Aden provided a strong anchorage from which the British could dominate the

dolph to Stimson, Aug. 23, 1929, DS 890g.927/29; Longrigg, *'Iraq*, p. 245; John Wilson, "Islamic Culture and Archaeology," *Middle East Journal*, 8 (Winter 1954), pp. 1–9.

[69] There was a sharp change in American policy in 1940 after the fall of France. The United States urged the Iraq government to show a more cooperative attitude toward the British government. *FR 1940*, III, 703–727, especially pp. 725–726.

[70] Randolph to Kellogg, March 12, 1926, DS 891.81/—; *RDS 1918*, p. 57.

approaches to the Red Sea; and a network of treaties with the tribal rulers enabled them to protect their flank in the Persian Gulf sheikhdoms and principalities.

Although change came slowly to the Arabian peninsula, where traditions were more impervious to the currents of Westernization than in most other parts of the Arab East, Western influences and connections did make some impact. Witness the contacts of King Hussein, Sherif of Mecca, with the British, leading to the Arab Revolt of World War I, and his ensuing interest in the peacemaking. In the postwar Arab World, Great Britain and France were unable to ignore entirely the claims of Hussein's sons, who were paid off with thrones in Trans-Jordan and Iraq.

The star of the Hashimite ruler of Mecca soon waned, however, as the dynamic figure of Ibn Saud swept from his interior realms in central Arabia to consolidate his rule over the greater share of the peninsula. By 1926 he had control of Nejd, Hejaz, Asir, and the Persian Gulf province of al-Hasa. The ancient kingdom of Yemen bordering the Red Sea escaped his domination; the British held on to Aden and the adjoining protectorate; and several independent sheikhdoms managed to hold out along the Persian Gulf—Kuweit, the Bahrein Islands, Qatar, Trucial Oman, and Muscat.[71]

The story of American relations with the Arabian peninsula between the wars is one of expanding contacts through private individuals, groups, and companies—sporadic during the 1920s, but proliferating during the 1930s. Official contacts were minimal and developed slowly, usually following as a delayed response to actual and potential economic penetration by American interests.

The oldest steady nonofficial American contact with Arabia was through the Persian Gulf missionaries sponsored since the 1890s by the Dutch Reformed Church. From their three centers at Bahrein, Muscat, and Kuweit, less than two dozen missionaries exerted an influence far beyond their numbers. Not that they made many converts, for their score approached zero, but through their medical work they afforded the only association thousands of common folk and their rulers had with Americans. It is perhaps not excessive to say that they helped to prepare a better climate for the American oil men who followed later.

At their oldest station, Bahrein, eight or nine missionaries conducted medical and educational activities. Mason Memorial Hospital usually

[71] H. St. John Philby, *Sa'udi Arabia*, Chap. 10.

kept busy with operations and treatments, and the staff took on the extra load during periodic epidemics of plague, cholera, smallpox, and influenza. In 1927 a new women's hospital was added. Periodic itineration to neighboring villages combined medical service with evangelism. The station also conducted separate elementary schools for boys and girls. Farther south, at Muscat, the remarkable Dr. Sarah Hosman operated a woman's clinic for years before she struck out 140 miles northwestward with a new clinic at Sahan in 1938. The Muscat mission also operated a school, and a book store in the bazaar. The pioneering medical work at nearby Matrah led to the construction of Dykstra Memorial Hospital, dedicated in 1934 by Paul Knabenshue, American minister to Iraq. The Reverend Dr. Dirk Dykstra was forced to be his own architect, contractor, and builder for the hospital. Charles R. Crane, philanthropist and former trustee of Robert College who had served on the King-Crane Commission, unexpectedly came to Dykstra's rescue by donating a complete set of modern plumbing equipment to the hospital, "thereby making it the most livable building in Muscat." The work was similar in Kuweit, where a hospital had been opened in 1914. Within a few years another hospital for women was begun. Here too there were a book shop and a reading room as well as schools for boys and girls. These stouthearted and persistent men and women were without direct contact with an official American, although the consul at Baghdad occasionally toured the Gulf region. For the most part the missionaries enjoyed happy relations with British officials, who sympathetically looked after their interests when they needed help.[72]

From these bases several of the medical missionaries established relations with King Ibn Saud and other princes of the mainland. Ibn Saud first invited Dr. Paul W. Harrison to Riyadh in 1917 to treat the sick; he asked him to return two years later. Between 1921 and 1933 Dr. Louis P. Dame made a series of notable trips through Arabia, treating the ailing king for a week in 1924. Before he returned to his base after this

[72] Randolph to Hughes, March 29, 1924; Randolph to Kellogg, Sept. 16, 1926; Dec. 24, 1927, Feb. 15, 1928, Feb. 2, 1929, and Sept. 9, 1929, DS 390b.1163/—, 1, 2, 5, 6, and 7; Randolph to Kellogg, March 12, 1926, DS 891.81/—; Jay Walker (vice-consul, Cairo) to Hull, April 1, 1939, DS 811.5031 Near East/306; Barny and Mason, *Arabian Mission*, pp. 191–196; Sanger, *Arabian Peninsula*, pp. 192–194 (quotation, p. 194), 196; *MRW*, 43 (Aug. 1920), 675; (Dec. 1920), 1059–1060, 1075; 49 (June 1926), 464; (Aug. 1926), 641–642; 50 (June 1927), 466; (Oct. 1927), 743–746; (Dec. 1927), 951; 51 (June 1928), 513; 52 (March 1929), 232; 53 (July 1930), 544; 54 (July 1931), 546–547; 59 (Jan. 1936), 58; 60 (Oct. 1937), 479–481; 62 (Sept. 1939), 398–399.

tour, Dr. Dame had seen 6552 patients and performed 128 major and 214 minor operations. In 1933 his wife accompanied him to Riyadh, where the king granted her the rare privilege of visiting his harem. On these trips into Arabia, filled with hardships because of difficult travel conditions, even the sturdiest became ill. Still more adventurous was Dr. Harold Storm's five-thousand-mile journey in 1935–1936 from Bahrein across Arabia via Riyadh to the Red Sea. The long voyage around the littoral included many adventures, among them living for three weeks in a native hut where he shared the life of the poorest, plagued by locusts and scorpions. On the leg from Kamaran Island to Hodeidah by sailboat a swordfish thrust sank a boat, forcing a shift to overland travel by camels. Another stage was made by native steamer carrying a cargo of sheep, and that from Mukalla to Dhufar was a thirty-three-day sailing voyage. Back at his base after ten months, Dr. Storm calculated that he had treated 10,406 patients and performed 224 operations.[73]

The missionaries frankly admitted that they regarded their humanitarian medical work as a way of gaining an entree to Moslem hearts. As Dr. Harrison once put it, "No man ever came into a mission hospital who needed his hernia mended one-half so badly as he needed to learn about Jesus Christ." Yet it hard to imagine how the missionaries kept up their enthusiasm year after year in view of their scanty harvest of souls. Although the missionaries might have been happier claiming evangelical progress, their significant contribution was in introducing modern medicine into areas where their doctors could offer a better treatment for anemia than powdered shingle nails.[74]

Ibn Saud's acceptance of medical missionaries did not mean that he was prepared to permit expansion of evangelistic endeavors in his realms. When the Christian and Missionary Alliance sent scouting forays into western Arabia in 1927, the government of Hejaz and Nejd decisively ejected them, vigorously protesting to the American government such use of "the sacred land of Hedjaz" as "a field for the spreading of Christian teaching." Ibn Saud's officials refused to "assume any responsibility

[73] *MRW*, 43 (July 1920), 600; 47 (Nov. 1924), 868; 50 (Nov. 1927), 821–823; 57 (March 1934), 119–121, 149; (Nov. 1934), 517–526; 58 (Dec. 1935), 610; 59 (May 1936), 266; (Sept. 1936), 385; 60 (Jan. 1937), 21–25; 61 (Jan. 1938), 25; (March 1938), 121; Paul W. Harrison, *Doctor in Arabia*, *passim*; Sanger, *Arabian Peninsula*, p. 388; Barny and Mason, *Arabian Mission*, pp. 197–198.

[74] *MRW*, 45 (July 1922), 527–529; 56 (Oct. 1933), 494–495 (quotation, p. 495); 57 (March 1934), 119–121; 60 (Oct. 1937), 479–481; 61 (Sept. 1938), 441; Ameen Rihani, *Around the Coasts of Arabia*, pp. 260–263.

in respect of the fate which might befall venturesome missionaries who enter the country" to preach the Bible and attempt to call the tribes to Christianity.[75]

When the Christian and Missionary Alliance probed for an opening in Yemen, the American consulate at Aden discouraged the plan because of Imam Yahya's well-known hostility to foreigners seeking to penetrate his mountainous retreat. Few private Americans had ever gained entry into Yemen. Early in 1923 the Imam had permitted two geologists to visit the country briefly; about the same time agents of a New York corporation seeking a kerosene monopoly were admitted, although they did not achieve their objective; and the Imam refused an American syndicate a salt concession, claiming he could not allow foreign interests to take over any of his natural resources. American scholars interested in probing the archaeological significance of Yemen and southern Arabia had been frustrated in making the proper contacts. When reporting a German expedition in Yemen, Consul James L. Park remarked in 1928 that he had talked with a Dr. Hough of the Washington National Museum, who said that he and a colleague had long wanted to enter the country of the ancient Sabaens in southern Arabia, but could establish no contact with explorers. The Imam did, however, permit the young archaeologist-anthropologist, Carleton Coon, to visit Yemen in 1933, but barred him from Marib, the site of great ancient dams. Not until the 1950s were American archaeologists able to organize an important expedition to investigate the remains of ancient kingdoms along the old spice route of southern Arabia.[76]

An important successful private contact was made by Charles R. Crane. When Crane was minister to China in the early 1920s, his interest in Yemen had been whetted by stories he heard from Charles Moser, former American consul at Aden. In 1926 Crane established contact with Imam Yahya and visited him at San'a during the winter. When

[75] *FR 1928*, III, 62–68 (quotations, p. 63); Heizer (consul, Jerusalem) to Kellogg, April 10, 1928, DS 390b.1163/4. The board of the Christian and Missionary Alliance claimed that its missionaries had actually been warmly received by the tribes, and only the government had objected to their presence.

[76] Clayton W. Aldridge (vice-consul, Aden) to Kellogg, Feb. 13, 1928, DS 390f.1163 Christian and Missionary Alliance/11; Sanger, *Arabian Peninsula*, p. 245; Longrigg, *Oil in the Middle East*, p. 98; J. L. Park (consul, Aden) to Kellogg, May 9, 1928, DS 890g.927/2; Wendell Phillips, *Qataban and Sheba: Exploring the Ancient Kingdoms on the Biblical Spice Routes of Arabia*; A. Jamme, "Les expéditions archéologiques américaines en Arabie du Sud (1950–1953)," *Oriente Moderno,* 30 (March 1953), 133–157.

Crane suggested that the country contained valuable minerals, the Imam expressed a desire to hire an American engineer to make a survey. The engineer whose services Crane offered as his personal gift was Karl S. Twitchell, "the father of economic development in the peninsula," who had just completed an assignment in Ethiopia. During his six trips to Yemen between 1927 and 1932, Twitchell, accompanied by his unveiled English wife and other assistants, studied Yemen's minerals, surveyed and laid out roads, and helped organize model farms. His most unusual accomplishment was the erection of a steel-truss bridge, the only one on the peninsula, as a gift from Crane.[77]

The Imam's ingrained reserve about contact with Westerners was broken down somewhat by the auspicious friendship with Crane and Twitchell. When Twitchell departed for Aden in 1927, he carried with him the draft of a proposed treaty of friendship and commerce with the United States. But the State Department was not ready for recognition. Under Secretary Joseph Grew informed Vice-Consul James L. Park in Aden that "the unsettled political situation and the resulting uncertainty as to the permanency of the political entities so far established as well as the unimportance of American interests may be mentioned as amongst the more obvious reasons which have led the Department to this position."[78] The United States did not recognize Yemen until 1946.

Far-reaching results followed from Crane's philanthropies and Twitchell's engineering feats when King Ibn Saud invited Crane to visit him at Jiddah in April, 1931. During cordial meetings they discussed the economic possibilities of Saudi Arabia, and Crane offered Twitchell's services for six months. Twitchell soon arrived from the United States to conduct a survey of water resources in Hejaz. Although he had to turn in a discouraging report about water, he did alert the

[77] Twitchell, *Saudi Arabia*, pp. 139–140; Sanger, *Arabian Peninsula*, pp. 16, 243–244 (quotation, p. 244); D. Van der Meulen, *The Wells of Ibn Sa'ud*, pp. 135–137.

[78] *FR 1927*, III, 825–827 (quotation, p. 826). In DS 890b.01/10 is a note indicating that on June 19, 1928, the department issued instructions for personal and unofficial conversations with the Imam on questions of recognition, treaty relations, and promotion of American trade. Recognition would hinge on the security of Yemen's relations with Great Britain and Nejd, and treaty relations would not follow until after formal recognition. The foregoing note is a precis of a document filed under DS 711.90j/5, which could not be located in the archives. In 1918 Imam Yahya had written to Wilson asking for American endorsement of the rights of Imamship in the Yemen and the independence of the Arabs. Wilson took no action. Sanger, *Arabian Peninsula*, pp. 243–244.

king to mineral potentialities in his kingdom. Relying on an ingenious and resourceful combination of modern technology and leads from ancient records, Twitchell uncovered some interesting possibilities for gold exploitation at the ancient mine of Mahad Dahab between Jiddah and Medina, probably the site of one of King Solomon's fabled mines. On the east coast, in al-Hasa province, Twitchell thought it possible that petroleum might be found. Ibn Saud at this time found himself in a precarious fiscal position owing to the sharp decline in pilgrimage revenues. Because Twitchell had won his trust, the king commissioned him to seek commercial exploiters in the United States. Twitchell's efforts to interest American and English mining companies were disheartening until 1934, when he succeeded in making the breakthrough which resulted in the formation of an Anglo-American syndicate, the Saudi Arabian Mining Syndicate (SAM), to work the Mahad Dahab mines. The American Smelting and Refining Company had a 28 per cent share interest ($560,000) by early 1939 in an enterprise which made profits for its organizers and for Saudi Arabia until the veins were virtually exhausted in the 1950s.[79]

Twitchell's overtures to petroleum companies were not immediately successful, but by early 1933 Standard Oil Company of California was ready to negotiate a contract, hoping for results comparable to the promising beginnings in their Bahrein concession. The ensuing progress of American oil operations in Saudi Arabia, detailed in a previous chapter, created a vast new American economic stake in the Arabian peninsula.[80] Diplomatic repercussions were inevitable even before the outbreak of the new world war.

Official Washington had taken little interest in Ibn Saud and his expanding kingdom during the 1920s until the king forced the State Department to face the issue by requesting recognition in 1928. Ten days after receiving the request, Paul Alling, assistant chief of the Near Eastern Division, prepared a long memorandum weighing the pros and

[79] Twitchell, *Saudi Arabia*, pp. 141–144, 146–149, 156–161; Van der Meulen, *Wells of Ibn Sa'ud*, p. 137; Sanger, *Arabian Peninsula*, pp. 16–17, 20, 100–101; Philby, *Sa'udi Arabia*, p. 330; Walker to Hull, April 1, 1939, DS 811.5031 Near East/306; Walt, "Saudi Arabia and the Americans," pp. 82–89, 146–149; *MRW*, 61 (March 1938), 151, noted that twenty to thirty years earlier about 300,000 journeyed on the pilgrimage to the holy cities, but by 1937 the number was down to about 50,000.

[80] Twitchell, *Saudi Arabia*, pp. 144–146, 149–154; Philby, *Sa'udi Arabia*, pp. 330–331; Walt, "Saudi Arabia and the Americans," Chap. 4.

cons of recognition. "It should be frankly stated," he wrote, "that the question of Ibn Saud's formal recognition by the United States is open to discussion. His country is of little commercial importance and one in which the United States has few interests; it is improbable that our relations with the Hejaz will increase to a noticeable extent; and it might be argued that recognition of Ibn Saud would also entail similar recognition of the Imam of Yemen." Turning to the arguments favoring recognition, he noted that the king had established firm control in his domain, was an outstanding figure in one of the world's largest religious movements, and because of his "progressive tendencies," American economic relations might increase. Alling observed that the United States had recognized rulers of less importance — in Afghanistan, Albania, and Oman, for instance. His conclusion was that "on the whole it seems to me that the factors in favor of recognition outweigh the contrary arguments."[81]

Alling's recommendation did not prevail, and the department informed the king's agent that it was "impracticable to reply definitely at the present time." Under prodding from Ibn Saud's legation in Cairo and from H. St. John Philby, the celebrated British explorer who was close to the king, the recognition question was kept before American officials. After the Kingdom of Hejaz and Nejd had signed treaties with Germany, Persia, and Turkey, the department reopened the issue early in 1930, noting that the ultimate decision would hinge mainly on "the character and extent of American commercial interest, actual as well as potential, in the Hejaz." Two other considerations gave the department pause — the feeling that recognition should be extended to Yemen at the same time, and that nothing should be done until the pending convention with Great Britain and Iraq had been ratified. The latter hurdles were withdrawn by February, 1931, when ratification of the treaty with Iraq was imminent and when the department shifted its position on Yemen, deciding that the Imam's relations with neighboring states and the negligible American trade did not warrant recognition. Trade prospects with Ibn Saud's kingdom, however, seemed more promising in the light of information given the department by Ameen Rihani, an Arab-American in friendly contact with the king, and Ralph Ches-

[81] *FR 1930*, III, 281; Alling to Shaw, Oct. 25, 1928, DS 890f.01/11 (quotations).

brough, American Automotive Trade Commissioner for the Near East.[82]

Through Ambassador Charles G. Dawes in London, the United States made overtures to Ibn Saud's representative to ascertain if the king was ready to enter into a treaty of friendship, commerce, and navigation providing for unconditional most-favored-nation treatment. At the same time, the department requested information on the laws governing administration of justice in civil, commercial, criminal, and personal cases involving foreigners. After receiving a favorable response, the United States recognized the government of Hejaz and Nejd in May of 1931, and began negotiations leading to the signing in London on November 7, 1933, of a provisional executive agreement covering consular and diplomatic representation, judicial protection, commerce, and navigation.[83]

Having approached recognition cautiously and finally accorded it with commercial prospects prominently in mind, the department proceeded just as deliberately later in the decade before deciding to accredit a minister to Saudi Arabia, where Socal (joined by the Texas Company in 1936) had begun important oil operations.[84] Although Socal executives had secured the 1933 concession from Ibn Saud without diplomatic assistance, the company soon began to press the State Department for American diplomatic representation.

After receiving requests from the oil interests, the department sent Leland B. Morris, consul-general at Alexandria, to Jiddah in 1936 to investigate the practicability of initiating official representation. Morris advised that American interests were not yet sufficient to warrant establishing official representation, and that the absence of official representation had tended to smooth the company's path. In any case, the oil operations were near the east coast, whereas the diplomatic capital at Jiddah on the west coast was without direct communication with the

[82] *FR 1930*, III, 281–284 (first quotation, p. 282; second quotation, p. 283); *FR 1931*, II, 547–550; Rihani to Alling, Jan. 10, 1931; Murray to Stimson, Jan. 13, Jan. 27, and Feb. 9, 1931; Alling to Rihani, Jan. 14, 1931; Murray to Castle, memorandum (with enclosure of Chesbrough report), Jan. 20, 1931; Murray to Castle, Jan. 22 and Feb. 9, 1931; Murray memorandum of conversation between Stimson and Rihani, Jan. 26, 1931, DS 890f.01/21, 21, 28, 29, 21, 25, 22, 29A, and 27; Walt, "Saudi Arabia and the Americans," pp. 40-51.

[83] *FR 1931*, II, 547–550; *FR 1933*, II, 986–1001; Walt, "Saudi Arabia and the Americans," pp. 51–58.

[84] In 1932 the name of the country was changed officially to the Kingdom of Saudi Arabia. *FR 1933*, II, 986 n. 1.

oil center, which was actually more accessible to the Baghdad legation. Furthermore, Secretary of State Cordell Hull understood that company relations with the Saudi Arabian government had been "of the best" and were unlikely to change. If they did, "the Department would of course not fail to consider what steps it should take to meet the new situation."[85]

The oil interests did not give up. Francis Loomis, a former assistant secretary of state now representing Socal, called at the State Department in January of 1939. He pointed out that American prestige suffered because the United States had no minister at Jiddah. When officials pressed him, Loomis admitted his company had experienced no trouble with the authorities, but he spoke "vaguely of British and German designs in the country against which he feels his company should be protected by the presence of an American Minister." Wallace Murray, chief of the Near Eastern Division, concluded that Loomis's urgent requests for representation were inadmissible "since we obviously could not establish a Legation in Saudi Arabia merely to please the Standard Oil Company of California in contravention of the unbiased recommendations of an experienced Foreign Service officer who has studied the situation on the ground."[86]

A few months later Loomis tried to alarm the State Department with information about Japanese negotiations for an adjacent oil concession in Saudi Arabia aimed at stopping further advances by the American companies. He complained that the Japanese were getting help from their government, diplomatic representation affording them "frequent access to high Arabian officials if they so desire." After calling attention to the inaccuracy of Loomis's implication that Japan had a minister resident in Saudi Arabia, Murray wrote Assistant Secretary George Messersmith that Loomis seemed to believe that one of the tasks of an American minister would be "to prevent the granting of any further oil

[85] Hull was responding to a letter from Nevada Senator Key Pittman, chairman of the Foreign Relations Committee, who had written the secretary that the committee had discussed Persian Gulf matters on several occasions, and that he believed there was a large field for our commerce in that area. Apparently the oil interests had sought Pittman's ear, for he added: "I know that there are some personal interests involved." Pittman to Hull, May 5, 1937; Hull to Pittman, May 12, 1937 (quotation), both DS 124.90b/1.

[86] G. S. Messersmith (Assistant Secretary of State), memorandum, Jan. 24, 1939; Murray memorandum to Welles and Hull, Jan. 27, 1939 (quotations); Messersmith to Murray, March 20, 1939; Murray to Messersmith, March 20, 1939, all DS 124.90f/6.

concessions not already taken up by Americans in that country." Murray thought it unlikely that the department could act in this fashion.[87]

The State Department executed an about-face in policy during the next two months. By May 20 Murray was already re-examining his stand against representation in Saudi Arabia, pointing out that a recent report indicated 273 Americans resided in the country, most of them in the eastern oil region, and that there were strong prospects of large increases in oil production. Perhaps it was time to think of accrediting officials of the Cairo mission to Jiddah so they could take up any urgent matter affecting American interests. Before making a decision, the views of the American ministers in Cairo and Baghdad were solicited. In telegrams of June 21, 1939, both Bert Fish in Cairo and Paul Knabenshue in Baghdad urged accrediting the Cairo officials to Jiddah, but Fish did not believe permanent representation was needed. Conversations with a Socal executive had convinced him that considerations of prestige required this move. Knabenshue gave even heavier stress to the prestige value: it would please Ibn Saud to have an American minister, and it might help counter Arab resentment at alleged American support of the Zionist point of view. Saudi Arabia's oil revenues might also lead to increased opportunities for sales of American products. Before the department received the recommendations of Fish and Knabenshue, another letter from Loomis may have influenced departmental thinking. Loomis called attention to how British contacts were facilitated through their official representation, observing:

It would be of genuine assistance to our American enterprise in Arabia to have the advice and counsel of an American Minister in Jedda, and it would be a source of satisfaction to the King of Arabia. It would assist us in building up the great oil property and region in which we have done, at huge expense, all of the pioneer work in a new field which may mean very much to the people of the United States in the future when their supplies of petroleum begin to fail.[88]

The field recommendations were apparently decisive in shaping the decision to accredit Judge Fish, minister to Egypt, to Saudi Arabia. Fish

[87] Loomis to Hull, April 25, 1939; Loomis to Messersmith, April 25, 1939 (first quotation), DS 124.90f/7 and 8; Messersmith to Murray, April 27 and April 28, 1939; Murray to Messersmith, April 27 (second quotation) and April 29, 1939; Messersmith to Loomis, May 1, 1939, all DS 124.90f/7.

[88] *FR 1939*, IV, 824–827; Loomis to Welles, June 1, 1939 (quotation); Fish to Hull, June 22, 1939; Knabenshue to Hull, June 22, 1939, DS 124.90f/12, 16, and 14.

journeyed to Jiddah at the close of the pilgrimage season and presented his credentials to King Ibn Saud on February 4, 1940. The department did not station a resident official in Jiddah until May 1, 1942, when the Arabic-speaking foreign service officer, James S. Moose, Jr., opened the legation as chargé d'affaires.[89]

Marked but uneven changes in American interests and policies in the Arabian peninsula had taken place during the twenties and thirties. Missionaries of the Dutch Reformed Church still carried on in Bahrein, Oman, and Kuweit, without ever creating any serious continuing diplomatic problems for the State Department. The missionaries preferred to open their own doors without official help from their government. When they did require protection, they customarily turned to the British political agents, who still dominated foreign affairs in the Persian Gulf, and the State Department's acceptance of this relationship signified American recognition of Britain's predominant strategic and political stakes there. Oil and commercial aspirations were the real catalysts speeding up American diplomatic contact with the largest political entity on the peninsula, Saudi Arabia, where in 1938, 273 American residents comprised about sixty per cent of all Americans on the peninsula. In Bahrein, the location of the second heaviest concentration of Americans — 165 or about thirty-six per cent, nearly all connected with oil operations — the United States accepted the leadership of the British political agent. No American residents were reported in Yemen or Qatar, only six in Oman, seven in Kuweit, and eight in Aden Colony and Protectorate. Oman was the only one of these entities with which the United States had a treaty. To celebrate the centenary of the treaty, Paul Knabenshue, minister to Iraq, accompanied by his son and James Moose, secretary of legation, made a ceremonial visit to Oman in 1934. Four years later, the Sultan of Oman returned the courtesy by visiting President Roosevelt in Washington.[90]

By 1939 Washington officials perhaps began to see dimly that American oil holdings in the Persian Gulf region were going to mean greater involvement in the increasingly complex international politics of the Arab World.

[89] *FR 1939*, IV, 827–831; Sanger, *Arabian Peninsula*, pp. 4–5; Walt, "Saudi Arabia and the Americans," Chap. 7.
[90] Donald C. Dunham (vice-consul, Aden) to Hull, March 28, April 4, and May 13, 1939; Walker to Hull, April 1, 1939; Satterthwaite to Hull, April 7, April 8, April 10, and April 13, 1939, DS 811.5031 Near East/297, 298, 323, 306, 311, 309, 310, and 313; Sanger, *Arabian Peninsula*, pp. 192, 194.

Egypt

After serving for two and a half years as American minister to Egypt, former Secretary of Agriculture William M. Jardine wrote the chief of the Near Eastern Division in 1932:

Egypt is a charming post at which to be stationed. The longer I remain here the better I like it. Something new of interest appears on the horizon every day. I don't mean that this is an active post. As I see it there is not much going on here of tremendous consequence to my Government. The facts are, it appears to me to be quite a side-show, but a desirable place to live for a few years and enough going on to keep one's interest in life and politics alive. I recommend it most highly.[91]

From the vantage point of international politics, American relations with the most populous Arab country were far from spectacular; but in the broader context of international relations, Americans, pursuing a variety of enterprises, required sufficient diplomatic assistance to provide a brisk routine for the diplomatic and consular staff.

American interests included an extensive network of United Presbyterian primary and secondary schools both in Upper Egypt (including Assiut College, founded in 1865) and in the delta region around Cairo and Alexandria. Missionaries began another major enterprise in 1920 when they opened the American University of Cairo. Supplementing their schools were hospitals and orphanages; and, of course, the missionaries carried on constant evangelical work through all their agencies. Between the wars Egypt was a mecca for unprecedented numbers of Western archaeologists, including a number from the United States who carried out ambitious expeditions for American museums and universities. The pyramids and other historic sites attracted hundreds of American tourists annually. American businessmen also looked to Egypt more than formerly in their search for markets and investment opportunities, while American experts requested by Egypt to assist with its agricultural and industrial development forged another link in Egyptian-American relations.

Burgeoning Egyptian nationalism conditioned and colored all facets of Egyptian-American relations, as it did Egypt's relations with other Western nations. Egyptian resistance to British domination grew into a formidable movement during and immediately after World War I. Saad Zaghlul, the nationalist leader, and his followers seized on Wil-

[91] Jardine to Murray, Dec. 5, 1932, William M. Jardine MSS.

366

sonian self-determination as a symbol to further their drive for independence from the British, who had formally declared Egypt a protectorate in 1914. President Wilson dashed nationalist hopes for his support at the Paris Peace Conference by ignoring the appeal of the Egyptian nationalist delegation for a hearing and by formally recognizing the British protectorate in April of 1919. An Egyptian delegation sent to Washington during the winter of 1919–1920 to press the appeal for American support was no more successful. Grievously disappointed, the Egyptian nationalists felt that Wilson and the United States had let them down.[92]

The Egyptian situation was in flux between 1919 and 1922 as the British moved cautiously, uncertain of the course they should follow in the face of rising Egyptian feeling against them. American missionaries and their government watched events closely, intent on protecting American interests by maintaining the essentials of the capitulatory regime, especially the Mixed Courts on which the United States had been continually represented.

In 1920 the British proposed reconstitution of the Mixed Courts and transfer to them of jurisdiction exercised by the consular courts. If these changes were made, the British appeared willing to assume full responsibility for the legal protection of foreigners in Egypt. Provided the British would give such guarantees, the missionaries felt they would not be injured, for the British had traditionally been friendly to them. As the British were soon pushed toward granting the Egyptians greater control of their affairs, missionary interests became alarmed. They petitioned the State Department to work for definite, comprehensive, and elaborate formulas covering religious toleration sufficient to furnish an adequate legal basis for defending the rights of religious minorities

[92] George B. Noble, "The Voice of Egypt," *The Nation*, 110 (Jan. 3, 1920), 861–864; U.S. Senate, Foreign Relations Committee Hearings, "Treaty of Peace with Germany," *Senate Doc. 106*, 66 Cong., 1 Sess., pp. 651–678, 1279; G. H. Shaw to Schmavonian, June 19, 1920; H. G. Dwight to Shaw, n.d.; Joseph W. Folk (counsel for the Egyptian delegation to the peace conference) to Shaw, Aug. 31, 1920, DS 883.00/356 and 320. Lord Lloyd, British high commissioner to Egypt (1925–1929), scathingly denounced the role of the United States in misleading the Egyptian nationalists. He attributed Egyptian bitterness and irreconcilability toward the British to "the incursion of America into world politics." See Lord Lloyd, *Egypt since Cromer*, I, 283–284 (quotation), 293–294. For a more penetrating scholarly analysis of the combination of forces entering into Egyptian feeling against the British after World War I, see Nadav Safran, *Egypt in Search of Political Community: An Analysis of the Intellectual and Political Evolution of Egypt, 1804–1952*, especially Chap. 7.

in the future. The department assured the missionaries of its sympathetic consideration and reminded the Foreign Office of the importance of securing firm commitments from Egypt.[93]

Nationalist pressure persuaded the British to proclaim Egypt's nominal independence in 1922. The British embassy informed Secretary of State Hughes that special arrangements guaranteeing British interests in Egypt had been worked out and that the rights of foreign nations and nationals would not be altered by the new dispensation. The special arrangements covered rights and interests which the British permitted no other power to question or discuss, informing all powers that they would "regard as an unfriendly act any attempt at interference in the affairs of Egypt by another Power." Content to regard Egypt as a British bailiwick, the United States recognized the new government in April "subject to the maintenance of the rights of the United States in Egypt, as they have hitherto existed," and soon raised its representation from a diplomatic agency to a legation.[94]

The task of constructing a treaty structure with Egypt proceeded slowly over the next two decades. As first steps, treaties of arbitration and conciliation were signed on August 7, 1929, followed by a provisional agreement signed on May 24, 1930, according unconditional most-favored-nation treatment in customs matters, but efforts to conclude an extradition treaty failed in 1933. The Egyptians maintained pressure to persuade the powers to end the capitulations and by 1936 succeeded in bringing about preliminary negotiations for a conference on the subject. At the Montreux Conference, April 12 to May 8, 1937, Egyptians appreciated American support, which was instrumental in terminating capitulations. The United States then proposed negotiation of a consular convention and an extradition treaty, but no agreements resulted before

[93] J. R. Alexander to American diplomatic agent, Cairo, April 29, 1917 (enclosing copy of a memorandum on "The Promotion and Safeguarding of the Interests of American Missionaries under the Proposed British Protectorate in Egypt"), all enclosed in Charles R. Watson to Albert Putney (chief, Near Eastern Division), Nov. 5, 1917; Watson to Colby, Jan. 22, 1921; Henry P. Fletcher (Under Secretary of State) to Watson, April 1, 1921; Fletcher for Hughes to J. B. Wright, April 5, 1921, DS 383.116/14, 21, 25, and 21; *FR 1920*, II, 216–228; *FR 1921*, I, 903–921; *FR 1922*, II, 106–109. For the extended controversy over the appointment and status of American judges on the Mixed Courts, see *FR 1927*, II, 555–570; *FR 1928*, II, 743–773; *FR 1929*, II, 936–955; *FR 1931*, II, 142–150; *FR 1932*, II, 621–628; *FR 1935*, II, 565–577; *FR 1936*, III, 12–20; Hackworth, *Digest*, II, 512–517. A history by an American judge who served on the courts is Jasper Y. Brinton, *The Mixed Courts of Egypt*.

[94] *FR 1922*, II, 103–106 (first quotation, p. 104; second quotation, p. 105).

the outbreak of the European war in 1939. Preliminary discussions concerning a trade agreement also took place between 1936 and 1939.[95]

Four ministers of widely differing backgrounds and training represented the United States in Egypt between the wars. President Harding selected J. Morton Howell, a Dayton, Ohio, medical doctor without previous diplomatic experience, to serve as diplomatic agent and consul-general in 1921. A few months later, Howell received an appointment as minister when the United States raised its representation to legation level. Howell's appointment was strictly political, resting on his personal friendship with the president, his assistance in the campaign of 1920, and the support of Ohio senators and representatives. Not a happy choice, Howell suffered from an inflated conception of his diplomatic abilities and took a contemptuous view of career men in the service, which made for unusual strain in his relationship with Consul Lester Maynard at Alexandria. Howell's superiors in the department held him responsible for the lack of rapport and adversely criticized the poor caliber of his political reporting.[96]

Howell's malapropos behavior often embarrassed the State Department, and more than once he had to be instructed to mend his ways. On occasion his actions provided Washington with amusement, as when he forwarded copies of the little homilies he enjoyed giving the Egyptians on "Success," "Character," or on aspects of sanitation. A department official perusing a lurid dissertation on house flies as germ carriers, given by Howell to Egyptian school children, asked a colleague: "Do you feel that the Doctor's epic remarks on the quaint habits of the house-fly . . . are deserving of commendation?" The terse reply was, "A closed mouth catches no flies."[97]

[95] *FR 1925*, I, 51–53; *FR 1929*, II, 931–936; *FR 1930*, II, 740–758; *FR 1931*, II, 150–160; *FR 1933*, II, 841–844; *FR 1935*, I, 565–577; *FR 1936*, II, 8–12; III, 28–33; *FR 1937*, II, 615–678; *FR 1938*, II, 705–709; *FR 1939*, IV, 477–506.

[96] Maynard to Hughes, Sept. 5, 1922; Howell to Hughes, Sept. 5, 1922, and attached memorandum by Dulles to Carr, Sept. 25, 1922, DS 883.77/7 and 8; Tuck to Carr, n.d.; Dulles to Wright, Feb. 1, 1924, DS 123 H 836/66 and 83. On Howell's background and appointment, see J. Morton Howell, *Egypt's Past, Present and Future*, pp. 1–6; Breasted, *Pioneer to the Past*, p. 388; *The New York Times*, June 20, 1922, p. 21.

[97] Richard B. Southgate to J. B. Wright, n.d.; Wright to Southgate, May 15, 1925, DS 123 H 836/94. In his remarks to the children on house flies as germ carriers, Howell "told them that nine out of every ten flies seen were born in a manure pile . . . that coming from such sources their bodies and legs teemed with filth; that . . . flies, when feeding constantly regurgitate — vomit — and that particularly when disturbed, they would vomit before leaving whether in the eyes or

Howell's relations with British officials were understandably less than cordial because of his tactless, publicly expressed contempt for British policies, but the minister's Anglophobia endeared him to Egyptian nationalists. He also had a close affinity for leaders of the temperance movement in Egypt, and it was in connection with his antiliquor crusade that he vented some of his most tactless charges against the British. The memory of Minister Howell lingered after his departure, owing to the publication in 1929 of his partly autobiographical volume in which he lambasted the British, who attempted to ban the book from Egypt.[98]

Career diplomats following Howell eased the strains produced by that clumsy appointee, who erroneously regarded himself as a political diplomat in the tradition of Benjamin Franklin and Thomas Jefferson. For several months after his departure, North Winship was in charge at Cairo until another career man, Franklin Mott Gunther, arrived in 1928 to serve less flamboyantly for two years.[99]

Proof that political appointees did not have to be inept is provided by the record of President Herbert Hoover's appointee, William M. Jardine, minister from 1930 to 1933. Jardine's extensive experience with dry-lands farming in the Great Plains region, and the comprehensive knowledge of agrarian problems he gained as Coolidge's Secretary of Agriculture, enabled him to establish good rapport with the Egyptians. Soon after his arrival, Jardine began to write friends at Kansas State College, the U.S. Department of Agriculture, and elsewhere about his avid interest in Egyptian agriculture, mentioning his frequent discussions of farming problems with Egyptians. To the president of Kansas State he wrote: "The Egyptians are very cordial toward me. They seem eager to engage me in agricultural talk, and I am almost winded when I leave the dinner parties and social affairs which I attend." To see Egyptian agriculture at first hand, he made field trips and visits to experimental farms, including those of the American missionary-sponsored Assiut College. Jardine also showed a keen interest in American business enterprises, missionary schools, and archaeological expeditions. He and

on food on the table. Not alone this, but . . . they deposited excreta every five minutes, and . . . in these three different ways . . . carried the most deadly germs." Howell to Kellogg, March 30, 1925, DS 123 H 836/94.

[98] British embassy to the Department of State, June 1, 1927; North Winship (consul, Cairo) to Kellogg, July 26, 1927, DS 883.00/612 and 616; *The New York Times,* July 3, 1927, p. 4; July 7, 1927, p. 6; Sept. 12, 1929, p. 11; Howell, *Egypt's Past,* pp. 247–263.

[99] *DSR 1931,* pp. 159, 257.

members of his family and staff often visited with Dr. Enoch Peterson, director of the University of Michigan archaeological project at Faiyum. Jardine regularly joined with twenty or thirty of his countrymen at the American Luncheon Club in Cairo and held large legation receptions for the American colony. He also became acquainted with leading Egyptian officials, editors, landowners, and businessmen, as well as with his foreign colleagues in the diplomatic corps, and kept in touch with several Egyptians in the civil service, young men who had been students at Kansas State when he was dean of the Agricultural School.[100]

Lack of diplomatic experience seemed no handicap to Jardine in discharging his duties efficiently, although he confessed modestly to Joseph Grew that "it is a long step from being a farmer to being a diplomat." The chief of the Near Eastern Division assured Jardine that the department was well satisfied with his performance, and Jardine commented favorably on the department's treatment of him and his staff. Jardine's correspondence gives the impression that he really would not have minded if the Roosevelt administration had kept him in Egypt longer. But this was not the rule in American politics.[101]

Jardine's successor was Judge Bert Fish, a Florida lawyer and real estate operator, and for several years a criminal court judge. His appointment recognized his services as finance director of the Democratic National Committee during the 1932 presidential campaign.[102] Fish's legal background assisted him in conducting various treaty negotiations and during the important Montreux Conference at which capitulations were abolished. As indicated earlier, he was also called on to inaugurate American diplomatic representation in Saudi Arabia. Of these four diverse ministers — Howell, Gunther, Jardine, and Fish — only Howell's record seems open to serious criticisms because of his defects in personality and temperament.

[100] Jardine to F. D. Farrell, Dec. 3, 1930 (quotation); to Lewis Strauss, Jan. 27, 1932; to Ed Holton, Feb. 9, 1932; to M. S. Mezrah, Feb. 8, 1932; to Dr. Eric Englund, Dec. 1, 1930; numerous exchanges with Enoch Peterson between 1930 and 1932; to H. E. Winlock, July 20, 1931; Jan. 8 and March 17, 1932; Winlock to Jardine, Aug. 22, 1931; Jardine to W. S. Murray, June 5 and Dec. 1, 1931; to Dan C. Green, May 2, 1932; to L. E. Call, Dec. 19, 1932; to Dr. L. C. Melchers, Dec. 3, 1930; to Walter G. Moyle, Dec. 9, 1930; to Thomas W. Butcher, Dec. 8, 1932 — all in Jardine MSS.
[101] Jardine to Grew, Nov. 13, 1930; Murray to Jardine, Feb. 3, May 6, and July 22, 1931; Jan. 7, 1932; Jan. 3 and April 10, 1933; Jardine to Murray, June 5 and Dec. 1, 1931; Dec. 5, 1932; March 23 and July 29, 1933; Jardine MSS; *The New York Times*, Sept. 10, 1933, IV, 3.
[102] *Time*, 35 (Feb. 19, 1940), 35–36.

Inasmuch as the major official responsibility of the diplomats was to protect and promote American interests, it is necessary to survey briefly the character and problems of major American interest groups in Egypt during the 1920s and 1930s. Foremost among them were the United Presbyterian missionaries operating from centers at Cairo, Assiut, and Alexandria.[103] They organized churches and conducted evangelical programs using a variety of means, including a river boat and the Nile Mission Press in Cairo, which produced a flood of Christian literature. They operated hospitals and orphanages at Cairo and Assiut, and were especially concerned with Egypt's alarming incidence of eye disease and blindness, which they tried to alleviate by medical treatment and public health programs. In this work they had to counteract superstitions, such as the belief that a baby must not be washed for forty days after birth. Their most important vehicles for bringing the Christian message to Egypt were schools for boys and girls at various levels from kindergarten through junior college. A dozen or more schools in Alexandria, Cairo, Faiyum, Assiut (Pressley Memorial Institute for Girls), Luxor, and elsewhere enrolled about 19,000 students in 1933.[104]

The respected Assiut College attracted students from every stratum of social life and every section of Egypt, enrolling some 700 in the preparatory department and 350 in the junior college department in 1923. Many of its graduates eventually became doctors, lawyers, judges, edi-

[103] Out of an Egyptian population of 13 million in 1927 there were an estimated 1 million Coptic Christians, 117,000 Roman Catholics and Uniat Christians, and 66,000 Protestants. *MRW*, 58 (Feb. 1935), 88. In addition to the extensive United Presbyterian activity, American consuls reported in 1939 that several other American societies conducted limited operations, among them the Peniel American Mission, the Apostolic Church of God (affiliated with the Assemblies of God of Springfield, Missouri), the Seventh-Day Adventists, and the Pentecostal Faith mission. Robert T. Cowan (vice-consul, Port Said) to Hull, March 30, 1939; Walker to Hull, April 1, 1939; Paul Fletcher (consul, Alexandria) to Hull, April 5, 1939, DS 811.5031 Near East/302, 308, and 316. The missionaries worked closely with the Y.M.C.A. See *MRW*, 46 (March 1923), 225; 48 (April 1925), 331; 51 (Aug. 1928), 672; 55 (Sept. 1932), 506; 60 (Jan. 1937), 55; 62 (May 1939), 267; and Walker to Hull, April 1, 1939, DS 811.5031 Near East/308.

[104] George Brandt (vice-consul, Alexandria) to Hughes, Dec. 29, 1921, DS 883.42/5; *MRW*, 43 (Feb. 1920), 149; (June 1920), 562; (July 1920), 645; 46 (Jan. 1923), 68–69; 47 (Jan. 1924), 25–26; (Feb. 1924), 156; (April 1924), 320; (June 1924), 408, 470; 50 (Oct. 1927), 749–750; 51 (March 1928), 239; (Aug. 1928), 644; 52 (Jan. 1929), 69; (March 1929), 163; (Dec. 1929), 913; 53 (April 1930), 263; (Nov. 1930), 871; 55 (March 1932), 180; 56 (Sept. 1933), 464; 57 (Feb. 1934), 72; 58 (Feb. 1935), 88; (July 1935), 374; 59 (April 1936), 175, 218; (May 1936), 264; (Dec. 1936), 567; 60 (May 1937), 264; (July–Aug. 1937), 388; 61 (April 1938), 204; (July 1938), 375; 62 (Dec. 1939), 552.

tors, teachers, and businessmen, who often praised the college for its service to them and their country. Some were elected to parliament or served their government in other capacities. An agricultural department experimented with vegetables, fruits, cotton, chickens, and especially with dairying in the search for alternatives to Egypt's uneconomic dependence on cotton production.[105]

The lack of a capstone for their educational system long troubled the missionaries, who wanted a university capable of fulfilling a role comparable to the American University of Beirut and Robert College. After years of planning they opened the American University of Cairo in 1920, in a palace once belonging to a pasha. Dr. Charles R. Watson, born in Egypt of missionary parents who had come there in 1861, resigned from the United Presbyterian Board to become the first president, and Robert S. McClenahan resigned from Assiut College to serve as dean. Financial stringency at the start permitted admission of only about 150 applicants, but more than half were Moslems, a remarkable showing when compared with less than fifteen per cent Moslems in other mission schools. As enrollment expanded, many upper-class Egyptians sent their sons to the university. A School of Oriental Studies became part of the university in 1921, and eventually a teacher-training division and an extension department were added. In 1928 the university dedicated its first new building, and three years later the first Egyptian woman obtained a bachelor's degree. In 1934, during the Depression, a third of the American staff had to be released. By 1938 the college department enrolled 204 students, the School of Oriental Studies 95, and the education department 43, while the various lectures offered by the extension division in public health, education, science, and social welfare attracted audiences totaling more than 18,000 in 1937.[106]

Like the other missionary enterprises, the university was caught up in the turbulent politics of Egypt. Egyptian nationalism took on a strong-

[105] *MRW*, 45 (Feb. 1922), 147; 46 (Oct. 1923), 864; 47 (Dec. 1924), 946; 51 (March 1928), 239; (Aug. 1928), 644; 54 (Dec. 1931), 941; 57 (March 1934), 129; 61 (Oct. 1938), 506–507; 62 (May 1939), 267; Howell to Hughes, Feb. 5, 1924, DS 383.1164 P 92/—.

[106] Paul Knabenshue (vice-consul, Cairo) to Lansing, June 30, 1917, DS 383.-116/12; *MRW*, 43 (Nov. 1920), 951; 44 (March 1921), 240; 45 (Feb. 1922), 147; (May 1922), 409; 46 (Sept. 1923), 756; 47 (April 1924), 269–276; 51 (Feb. 1928), 166; (June 1928), 491; 53 (April 1930), 264; 54 (Aug. 1931), 623; 57 (Feb. 1934), 203; 59 (April 1936), 176; Walker to Hull, April 1, 1939, DS 811.5031 Near East/308.

ly Islamic, anti-Western complexion and used missionary activities as a scapegoat for harassing governments regarded as too sympathetic to the West. As early as 1924 a former Moslem student at Cairo attacked the university on grounds that it forced Christianity on its students. Moslem attacks on the university and other missionary endeavors were especially sharp between 1932 and 1934 when a segment of the Wafdist Party assailed foreign interests to embarrass the governments of Sidky Pasha and his successors.[107]

The United Presbyterians, joining other Protestant groups organized in 1919 as the Inter-Mission Council, made a declaration of principles which they hoped would relax Moslem objections to their work. The declaration proclaimed the missionaries' opposition to the use of coercion, bribery, or other unfair methods in proselytizing. They proposed that potential converts appear before administrative authorities, and that no children be baptized without parental consent; they disapproved of any abusive or scornful references to the religious beliefs of others; and they denied resort to subterfuge in their educational and medical work. Finally, they declared their belief in free speech and pledged full cooperation with governmental authorities. To bring about genuine religious toleration in Egypt, the missionaries also called on the American and British governments for diplomatic pressure.[108]

Among missionaries pondering seriously the meaning of Egyptian nationalism for Christian work was the influential president of American University, Dr. Watson, who indulged in an introspective analysis of Western missionary rationale in 1934. Missionary policies, he suggested, had aggravated a sharp reaction in Egypt:

Alas, to this emerging nationalism, how obvious is our Nordic superiority attitude! How manifest our foreign character! How insistent we are upon our foreign ways, our architecture, our organizational forms, our ritual, our hymnology and our theology! How impatient for results, so that instead of planting principles and ideas and allowing them to germinate in the life of a people producing what they may of theological

[107] *MRW*, 47 (Sept. 1924), 748; 55 (Sept. 1932), 505–506; 56 (Sept. 1933), 413–414; (Nov. 1933), 559; 57 (Jan. 1934), 56; (April 1934), 165; (July–Aug. 1934), 375. Despite Islamic feeling against missionary education, the Egyptian government appointed Dr. Watson to a special commission assigned the task of devising a national educational program. *MRW*, 54 (March 1931), 162. For a perceptive analysis of interacting political, economic, and social forces in Egypt between the wars, see Safran, *Egypt in Search of Political Community*, Chap. 12, *passim*.

[108] *MRW*, 43 (Aug. 1920), 734; 57 (April 1934), 165–166; *FR 1930*, II, 759–763; *FR 1936*, III, 20–28.

interpretation, of social outworking, of ecclesiastical organization, we bring in our foreign conceptions.

As a result, the Christian church was regarded as a foreign church. On reading missionary promotional literature and textbooks, non-Christians reacted with resentment: "We thought you were serving us disinterestedly and, lo, we find you nailing our spiritual scalps as trophies upon the walls of your home churches; you glory in the breakdown of our culture and social fabric and time-hallowed traditions." As it turned out, nationalism and Moslem resentment could not be held back. A bill proposing severe curtailment of missionary propaganda in 1938 was enacted into law in revised form two years later.[109]

The anti-Western nationalism in Egypt which plagued the missionaries also posed serious problems for European and American archaeologists engaged in an enormous program of excavation during the interwar years. Among the notable American projects were the Harvard-Boston Museum of Fine Arts expedition at Giza under the direction of George A. Reisner, and the work of the Oriental Institute of the University of Chicago at Luxor and elsewhere under the leadership of the eminent James Henry Breasted and, later, of Harold H. Nelson. New York's Metropolitan Museum of Art was also active during the 1920s, and the University of Michigan's project at Faiyum has already been mentioned in connection with Minister Jardine's visits to the site.[110]

Spectacular finds in Egypt helped to generate an archaeological craze in the United States during the 1920s. As newspapers and magazines sensed the public appetite, "archaeology was editorially rated second only to murder and sex." Much ink was spilled in sensational and superficial explanations of the tragedies visited on several persons associated with the excavation of King Tutankhamen's tomb.[111]

Excitement also ran high in Egypt as archaeologists unearthed treasure on treasure illuminating the country's glorious ancient civilizations. Instead of feeling beholden to Western scientists, nationalists became hostile as the conviction grew that foreign archaeologists were robbing Egypt of her ancient heritage by removing valuable relics to Western museums. Capitalizing on this sentiment, perhaps for his personal ag-

[109] *MRW*, 57 (March 1934), 123–129 (quotations, p. 125); 61 (Oct. 1938), 506; *FR 1940*, III, 491–503.
[110] Perkins in *Background on the Middle East*, p. 213; Walker to Hull, April 1, 1939, DS 811.5031 Near East/308.
[111] Breasted, *Pioneer to the Past*, p. 348.

grandizement, Pierre Lacau, the Frenchman serving as Director of Antiquities, announced that after the 1922–1923 season Egypt would no longer be bound by the 1912 law granting foreign excavators half the finds. The Metropolitan Museum initiated efforts to have Lacau's order rescinded. The trustees of the museum ordered an end to its Egyptian work if the Egyptian government abandoned the principle of equal division. American and British groups joined to put their case before their foreign offices in the hope that diplomatic intercession would secure a modification of the Lacau policy. Although the 1912 regulations were retained for the 1923–1924 season, Egyptian feeling ran high and kept alive the threat of a change.[112]

Tension increased in 1924 when the Egyptian government accused Howard Carter, the English archaeologist excavating for Lord and Lady Carnarvon, of carelessness in his work on the Tutankhamen tomb. Although details of this fascinating case are too complex for exposition here, it must be noted that the incident was a striking illustration of nationalist sensitivity to Western cultural imperialism. An Egyptian newspaper expressed the feeling:

The Government could not humbly submit to Mr. Carter; it is the owner of the Tomb and its contents . . . We hope that this incident will open the eyes of both the Government and the nation to the fact that it is time for Egyptians to study their own antiquities and practise the task of excavation and dealing with discoveries. It is not worthy of a great State and a rising nation to leave this great work to be monopolised by foreigners, while the inhabitants of this country stand by as onlookers in regret at not having the means to do otherwise.[113]

Apparently, calmer heads realized that Egypt was not yet in a position to carry out the important work without the assistance of Western scholars and philanthropists. In any case, after much negotiation an accommodation was arranged in 1926 so that American universities and

---

[112] *FR 1924*, I, 714–723.

[113] Quotation from enclosure in Howell to Hughes, Feb. 23, 1924, DS 883.927/36; Breasted, *Pioneer to the Past*, pp. 348–349, 358–374. Flag-waving nationalism was not confined to the Egyptians as the following "crank" letter received by the State Department indicates:

"Will you respectfully call upon the Egyptian Gov'mt. to assume a more liberal attitude toward Howard Carter and Prof. Breasted in relation to their archaeological work in the present crisis.

"The People of a superior nation like the U. S. of America are getting tired of having their rights trampled on by such a 'sissy like' foreign policy as surrenders the controll [*sic*] of the Pacific to the Japs, leaves the Armenians terrorized and al-

museums could continue the work with reasonable assurance that finds would be divided on an equitable basis.[114]

Unfortunately, irrational nationalistic sensitivities deprived Egypt of a proposed magnificent museum. Professor Breasted had persuaded John D. Rockefeller, Jr., of Egypt's urgent need for such a building to house and display the treasures being unearthed by archaeologists. Rockefeller offered the Egyptian government a gift of $10 million for a museum, a related research building, and further research projects. Although Rockefeller's agents had drawn up the proposal carefully in a genuine effort to respect Egyptian national interests and sensibilities, a strong anti-Western reaction caused the government to reject the generous offer. Pronounced but vaguely defined fears that the proffered gift was a national bribe of some kind killed the project. Egypt lost, but Jerusalem gained an archaeological museum constructed with Rockefeller funds.[115]

Refusal of the Rockefeller gift did not mean that the Egyptians would reject out of hand any type of American assistance. On the contrary, they frequently sought American experts, especially in agriculture, who might assist in the country's development. In contracting for the services of individual Americans there was no taint of large sums of money to arouse suspicion as in the Rockefeller proposal. In 1918 Robert H. Forbes, former director of the Arizona Agricultural Experiment Station, was appointed agronomist to the Sultanieh Agricultural Society where he worked for several years on problems of cotton production and irrigation. At the request of an Egyptian minister, the Department of Agriculture in 1925 tried to put him in touch with a candidate qualified as an economic botanist and another needed for the Botanical and Plant Breeding Section.[116] When a request came through the British ambassa-

lows Mexicans and Haityans to scrimmage till they are worse than brigands or Indians.

"The superior Peoples of this Earth are the Administrators of its International Law." S. W. Craig (of Bowling Green, Mo.) to Hughes, Feb. 14, 1924, DS 883.927/—.

[114] *FR 1926*, II, 58–76; and unpublished documents in DS 883.927.

[115] Breasted, *Pioneer to the Past*, pp. 374–383, 392–400; and DS 883.927.

[116] Hampson Gary (agent and consul-general, Cairo) to Lansing, July 31, 1918; Jardine to Kellogg, Oct. 30, 1925; Kellogg to Jardine, Nov. 16, 1925; Samy Pasha (Egyptian minister) to Kellogg, Nov. 23, 1925, DS 883.61/—, 23, 23, and 24. The correspondence does not indicate whether Americans were appointed to the latter posts.

dor the previous year for an American expert to investigate possibilities for expanding the date industry in the Sudan, the Agriculture Department agreed to make Silas C. Mason, horticulturist in the Bureau of Plant Industry, available for six months. Also in 1925, the Egyptians requested assistance from the State Department in the search for an American engineer to be principal of the Royal College of Engineering at Giza. The following year the department was apparently unsuccessful in locating an American expert in oceanography to head the Egyptian Fisheries Department. An American, Hugh Cooper, did serve with a committee of three foreign experts in 1928 to advise the Egyptian government on the projected heightening of the Aswan Dam. In 1929 the Egyptian government negotiated with Dr. E. C. Westbrook to supervise tobacco cultivation in Egypt.[117]

Bulking larger than the scattered evidences of American technical assistance was the expansion of American business in Egypt between the wars. At Alexandria and Cairo, the nerve centers of these operations, several firms located main offices to supervise branches elsewhere in Egypt or in other parts of the Middle East. Socony-Vacuum, the most active of several American oil companies, had a head office in Cairo to coordinate its business in Egypt, the Sudan, Syria, Palestine, Trans-Jordan, Cyprus, Iraq, Iran, the entire Arabian peninsula, French and British Somaliland, and Italian East Africa. Among their properties were bunkering stations and tank farms at Alexandria and in the Suez Canal zone; storage facilities, a can factory, assembling and filling plants, and a network of filling stations. From Cairo the ubiquitous Singer Sewing Machine Company supervised branches dotting Egypt. General Motors, Ford, and other automobile companies built up a sizable market for American autos and accessories. Among other American firms with Egyptian branches were Kodak, the American Express Company, Remington Typewriter, several motion picture companies, and various importing firms selling American products ranging from ladies' handbags to proprietary medicines and canned goods. By 1938 American business investments probably aggregated $14 million as compared with less

[117] H. A. Chilton to Hughes, Sept. 6, 1924; Hughes to Henry C. Wallace, Sept. 12, 1924; Wallace to Hughes, Sept. 23, 1924; Grew to Sir Esme Howard (British ambassador), Oct. 6, 1924; Grew to Wallace, Oct. 6, 1924, DS 883.6159/—, —, 1, —, and 1. See also DS 883.42/13, 15, 16, 17, 18, and 19; DS 883.628/6 and 7; DS 883.6113/36 and 37; DS 883.61331/1.

than $4 million for the various missionary, philanthropic, and educational properties.[118]

Frequently the businessmen needed diplomatic assistance to counter alleged discriminatory practices of Egyptian or British officials. Willys-Overland and Ford, for example, complained of technical specifications for taxis and buses which they felt were designed to eliminate the use of American vehicles. Socony complained that the Suez Canal Company prohibited transport of tinned petroleum products on ship decks, a regulation which would prevent their competing with European companies possessing Asian supplies and marketing facilities. The State Department protested purported discrimination in favor of a British company in the awarding of irrigation contracts in the Sudan in 1933.[119]

As Americans increased their use of the Suez Canal for international trade and travel, the United States government showed more concern with conditions of transit.[120] Quarantine regulations had a potential bearing on public health in American ports. As early as 1922, Allen Dulles recommended that the United States seek representation on the International Sanitary and Quarantine Board of Egypt. The department learned from a United States Public Health Service official that a ship arriving at New Orleans via Suez in October, 1925, with a case of plague, harbored a large number of infested rats. Another vessel arriving from

[118] Robert T. Cowan (vice-consul, Port Said) to Hull, March 30, 1939; Walker to Hull, April 1, 1939 (two despatches); C. Paul Fletcher (consul, Alexandria) to Hull, April 5, 1939, DS 811.5031 Near East/302, 307, 308, and 316.

[119] George Wadsworth to Hughes, Aug. 6, 1923; Howell to Kellogg, Jan. 10 and July 5, 1927; Winship to Kellogg, Aug. 13, 1927; Alling memorandum, June 21, 1927, and June 26, 1929; R. B. English (of Ford Motor) to Shaw, June 24 and July 29, 1929; W. R. Castle, Jr., to Wadsworth, Aug. 6, 1929; Wadsworth to Stimson, Sept. 20, 1929, DS 883.7971/1, 3, 5, 6, 7, 7, 7, 9, 9, and 10; C. F. Meyer (vice president, Socony) to Hughes, June 12, 1922; Phillips to Coert du Bois (consul, Port Said), June 19, 1922; du Bois to Hughes, June 30, 1922; L. I. Thomas (of Socony) to Hughes, Aug. 11, 1922; H. E. Cole (vice president, Socony) to Hughes, Sept. 14 and Oct. 31, 1922; Dulles memorandum, Sept. 15, 1922, DS 883.812/73, 73, 80, 89, 105, 98, and 105; *FR 1923*, II, 845–848.

[120] Consular reports contain the following figures for American vessels and net tonnage transiting the Suez Canal: 1925, 132 ships, 811,803 tons; 1926, 116 ships, 709,664 tons; 1937, 95 ships, 561,574 tons; 1938, 69 ships, 387,661 tons. The figures for the late 1930s reflected the tightening of international trade. John L. Bouchal (consul, Port Said) to Kellogg, Jan. 25, 1927, DS 883.812/177; Cowan to Hull, March 30, 1939, DS 811.5031 Near East/302.

The consul at Port Said reported that three or more large liners with parties of American tourists ranging from 500 to 800 on round-the-world tours were expected to transit the canal in 1923. Passengers were to disembark at the terminal port at which the vessel first arrived, and proceed to Cairo by rail before returning to the ships at the other terminal. Du Bois to Hughes, Oct. 17, 1922, DS 883.111/24.

the Far East via Alexandria also harbored diseased rats. The problem of board representation dragged on for several years, and although the Egyptian government promised in 1928 to permit the addition of an American member of the board, it rescinded the pledge in 1933. No American member was seated before the international board was abolished in 1939 and its functions transferred to the Egyptian government.[121]

Two features of Egyptian-American relations between the wars stand out in retrospect. First and most obvious were the cultural and economic bases of American interests in Egypt. The nonpolitical character of these interests determined the second major characteristic of Egyptian-American relations — American noninvolvement in the national and international politics of Egypt. Recognizing that Egypt and the Suez Canal were major stakes in the international power balance for Great Britain and other European Powers, the United States deferred to the superior concern of Great Britain. Not yet did American policy-makers see any reason to consider Egypt a vital link in American security. The United States had no desire to identify itself with Egypt's struggle for full independence but preferred to remain aloof, regarding this as an issue to be worked out between Egypt and Great Britain. Fearful for the future of American cultural and economic activities, the United States resisted Egypt's persistent efforts to free itself from the servitude of capitulations, at least until the later 1930s, when it supported Egypt at the Montreux Conference. Although America was of the West and could not escape entirely ardent Egyptian nationalist resentments of colonialist influences, the United States had not stationed troops in Egypt or placed agents in a position to influence policies of the Egyptian government. Disavowing strategic or political stakes, American diplomats considered it their major task to look after the varied missionary, educational, philanthropic, cultural, and business interests and the seven hundred American citizens who were registered at the consulates in 1938.[122]

[121] Dulles memorandum, Dec. 16, 1922; K. C. memoranda, April 13, 1925; March 24, 1926, and Aug. 2, 1926, DS 883.12/10, 18, 24, and 30; *FR 1928*, II, 773–781; Alling to Shaw, April 16, 1929; Alling to Shaw and Murray, May 17, 1929, DS 883.12/46 and 47; *FR 1932*, II, 629–639.

[122] Cowan to Hull, March 30, 1939; Walker to Hull, April 1, 1939 (two despatches); Fletcher to Hull, April 5, 1939, DS 811.5031 Near East/302, 307, 308, and 316.

Conclusion

When President Bayard Dodge of the American University of Beirut prepared his report for the university's trustees during the summer of 1939, he accurately divined that the Middle East was at the close of a twenty-year era. Several thousand Americans who had lived in the Arab East during the two decades had observed the hostile reaction of the Arab World to British and French political domination and had felt the impact of anti-Western tendencies in Arab nationalism. Americans — whether missionaries, educators, archaeologists, or businessmen — found that they were not immune from either traditional Christian-Moslem tensions or the newer political strains accompanying emergent nationalism.

The degree of adjustment made by American interests to the changing environment varied according to the character and aims of the interests, the particular location in which they operated, and the degree to which individuals and groups were able to accommodate their behavior to the local environment. The American University of Beirut prospered because its purposes were generally acceptable to the partly Westernized community it served, and the university's administration and staff emphasized disinterested service while eschewing politics. Without divorcing itself from its Christian origins, the university had managed to become essentially secular and largely escaped Moslem resentment toward missionary-controlled schools and colleges.

American technology, whether represented by automobiles or agricultural experts, was generally welcomed. Even Imam Yahya of Yemen accepted American engineering knowledge, and King Ibn Saud of Saudi Arabia was willing to go several steps further by welcoming missionary medicine and American oil companies. But the king did not want missionaries proselytizing among his Bedouins any more than ardent Moslem nationalists in Egypt favored similar efforts among their co-religionists. Able American archaeologists were well received in most of the Arab World, although nationalist sensitivities in Egypt caused them to be identified with cultural imperialism. Businessmen found markets for their automobiles, accessories, and petroleum products; and other industrial and processed products were attractive to those who could afford them. Occasionally, nationalist-inspired taxes and other regulations presented problems for the businessmen, who also complained about British and French discrimination.

On the official level, the United States government followed a generally conservative course. Nationalist enthusiasts in the Arab mandates and Egypt could take little comfort from Washington's policies, which resisted abridgement of capitulatory privileges through most of the interwar period. The State Department followed a legalistic approach, relying on capitulations to protect American interests and on equality of commercial opportunity coupled with most-favored-nation treatment to smooth the way for expansion of trade and investment. Politically, Britain and France had assumed large responsibilities which they felt would promote their imperial interests. The United States did not share their aims, but neither did it wish to challenge seriously British and French hegemony. Washington followed at a safe distance when it came to recognizing new governments whether in Iraq, Saudi Arabia, or Egypt. Nor did the United States elect to declare for either the Zionist or the Arab position on Palestine.

Yet for all the official conservatism, the position of the United States had changed since 1919. It had accredited ministers to Egypt, Iraq, and Saudi Arabia; it had asked for a place on the International Sanitary Commission for the Suez Canal; and it had particpted in the international conference to revise the capitulatory regime in Egypt. American companies had acquired valuable and exclusive oil concessions in Saudi Arabia and Bahrein, and had joined with Western companies in oil development in Iraq and Kuweit. Notwithstanding its official neutrality on the Palestine question, an influential segment of the American public wanted American policy to adopt a course more favorable to Zionist goals. The missionaries were probably the only major American interest group to suffer some curtailment in parts of the Arab World, but in any case, the growth of American interest in oil and Zionism had relegated the missionaries to a somewhat lower relative position in the hierarchy of American concerns in the Middle East.

American contacts with the Arab World had expanded between the wars, and as of 1939 the United States could count on a considerable reservoir of good will in the Arab East. The groundwork had been laid for an even livelier relationship in subsequent years as America became a full-fledged world power whose security was irrevocably intertwined with the strategically important Arab nations.

11

CONCLUSION

☆ The foregoing survey of American interests and policies in Turkey, Persia, and the Arab East during the first four decades of the twentieth century contradicts the popular assumption that the Middle East was *terra incognita* for the United States before World War II. Without assigning the Middle East a larger role in America's international relations than the record justifies, it is still apparent that the various cultural, educational, and economic enterprises there made up a significant chapter in the extension of American influence into areas where the United States government remained relatively aloof. Although frequently extending benevolent protection to its citizens, the government did so without asserting strategic and political interests of the kind that motivated the European Powers. If the label "imperialism" is at all appropriate for the American relationship, it was chiefly cultural and secondarily economic imperialism, in both cases quite in harmony with traditional national concepts of the American Mission in the world.

The existence of significant cultural and economic ties over many decades conditioned the American approach to the Middle East, complicating readjustments required by the changing imperatives of the national interest in the 1940s and 1950s. If the United States pursued its Middle Eastern policies unsteadily during the middle decades of the century, the reasons may be found partly in the character of the previous relationship.

Although American diplomacy was not often a major factor in the international politics of the Middle East before World War II, American interests underwent a discernible evolution during the four decades surveyed here. Four major factors standing out in this evolution are the alteration in the relative importance of various American groups actively concerned with the area, the changing local environment in the Middle East, the fluctuations in the power balance among the interested foreign powers, and the hesitancy of the United States in facing up to its growing responsibilities as a major world power. Like the history of the Middle East itself, the evolution of American interests and policies over these forty years can be conveniently divided into three periods — the prewar years, the years of war and peacemaking, and the decades between the wars.

The winds of change blowing in from the West had begun to stir in the Middle East by the early twentieth century, carrying with them growing discontent with the status quo and yearnings among middle-class dissidents for liberalizing modifications in the traditional political and social order. Such aspirations coalesced in movements like the Persian Revolution of 1905 to 1909 and the Young Turk Revolution of 1908 and 1909 and were manifest in the surge of national consciousness among Armenians, Arabs, Egyptians, and Zionists. In Egypt and Persia, where foreign influence was strong, preliminary rumblings of anti-colonial feeling sounded, soon to inflame the entire Middle East.

As the tempo of rivalries among the European Powers increased during the prewar years, the Eastern Question engaged the anxious attention of the foreign offices. The delicate power balance was constantly in danger of disruption as the Powers jockeyed for position and sought to further their goals by combinations among themselves. The United States did not consider the competing imperialisms inherent in the Eastern Question relevant to American foreign policy. Because the Middle East was considered an appendage of Europe, the traditional injunction of political noninvolvement applied with even greater force.

Noninvolvement in the politics of the Middle East did not mean that the United States government was uninterested in the cultural and commercial enterprises of American citizens in that part of the world. On the contrary, it was the activities of American missionaries, educators, businessmen, and archaeologists which gave rise to the need for diplomatic and consular representation. In the absence of strategic and political reasons for official intrusion into the Middle East, it followed naturally that the task of American diplomats and consuls was to protect and foster the endeavors of American interest groups.

Missionaries of the Congregational, Presbyterian, United Presbyterian, and Dutch Reformed denominations operating in Turkey, Persia,

Syria, Egypt, and the Persian Gulf area were by all odds still the most important continuing link between the United States and the Middle East early in the century. Frustrated in their goal of evangelizing the Moslem World, but ever hopeful that success lay just over the horizon, these dedicated souls worked chiefly with the Christian minorities. Relying heavily on their schools and medical ministrations as instruments to open the way to the Moslems, these institutions afforded considerable association with the non-Christian population, bringing many Moslems into contact with a different style of life and with benefits of Western technology previously little known to them. The missionaries were thus another of the many Westernizing influences seeping into the Middle East and slowly eroding old thought patterns and traditions. It was to be expected that Moslems who had a stake in the status quo, either political or religious, would regard the Protestant missionaries as an unwanted foreign intrusion. So far as sultans and mullahs were concerned, missionaries stirred up rebellion among the nationalistically inclined minorities.

The independent colleges — Robert and Women's College at Constantinople, and Syrian Protestant at Beirut — were regarded with less suspicion. Although the clientele of the three colleges was predominantly non-Moslem, the steadily increasing number of non-Christians testified to the feeling that college training, even with a strong Christian emphasis, was worth tolerating. The services the colleges rendered by training a small corps of leaders commended them to openminded officials and citizens of the area, for the contributions of graduates in the professions and business spoke well for them.

Much of the work done by missionaries and colleges is entitled to be categorized as philanthropy in the very literal sense. Those Americans who devoted their lives to service far from their native land certainly demonstrated a genuine love for their fellow men, notwithstanding any other motives which might have guided them. Philanthropic impulses also motivated American relief efforts in times of disaster; nor was a high sense of idealism absent from the brief but significant efforts of Morgan Shuster and his young assistants to help modernize the Persian government. The philanthropies of American Jewry for co-religionists in Palestine formed another American link with the Levant before World War I. Appreciation of the rich cultural heritage contributed by the Middle East to Western civilization drew an increasing number of archaeologists and biblical scholars to the region in the early years of the century.

American interests were not exclusively of a cultural and philanthropic nature, however; the affairs of the countinghouse attracted some Americans to trade and investment possibilities in the Middle East, demonstrating once more the curious blend of American idealism and practicality, traits which at the same time have baffled and fascinated students of American character. This dualism, so apparent in twentieth-century American diplomacy, furnishes insights into the nature of American isolationism, which was confined to politics and did not extend to cultural or economic relations. Although the United States government looked benevolently on the idealism of its citizens acting in a private capacity abroad, there was no disposition to become officially involved in the revolutionary and nationalist movements through which reformers were struggling to throw off the shackles of oppressive social and governmental structures in the hope that the common man might achieve his potential and be granted a decent life of reasonable span.

The government of the United States assumed that it could foster and protect American cultural and commercial interests without becoming involved in the politics of the Eastern Question. The premise accorded nicely with the traditional policy of the State Department, and officials in Washington showed no strong disposition to change it except in the case of the Chester railroad and development project. Oscar Straus and others warned that the United States could not hope to sponsor such an ambitious commercial enterprise without becoming embroiled in the international rivalries surrounding the Eastern Question. The failure of the Chester Project embarrassed the State Department and reinforced the conviction that the Eastern Question was not a proper concern of the United States. Afterwards, the Taft administration reverted to the old neutrality by refusing to serve in a mediatory capacity during the Italo-Turkish War and the sequent Balkan Wars. But the mirage of great commercial expectations did not fade. Consular and diplomatic reports continued to stress the possibilities for American business while criticizing businessmen for their lack of imagination and enterprise in breaking into the eastern markets.

By the eve of World War I American interests in the Middle East, encouraged by recent expansion, were optimistic about the future. With the spread of the war into the Middle East in 1914 their hopes were dealt a severe blow, for a somber new era was in the making for that region and for American interests there. The abnormalities of war altered the local environment, making it impossible for Americans to perform their tasks in the accustomed ways. Missionaries, especially those in the interior of Anatolia, in Persia, and in Syria faced unusual problems. Their Armenian clients in Anatolia experienced a cruel fate because of their reputed disloyalty to the Ottoman state. Within zones of military operation, the Turks commandeered school and hospital buildings; Christians in western Persia had to flee for their lives before Turkish armies. When missionary schools and colleges could remain open, they were confronted by erratic enrollments and almost insuperable problems of finance and supply. Almost completely cut off from their American-based trustees, the independent colleges found that feeding students and staff required the utmost ingenuity and courage. With the disruption of shipping and the Allied blockade, American business operations virtually halted.

In keeping with their philanthropic traditions, Americans in the Middle East shifted their efforts to relief work in behalf of the pitiful victims of the war. Missionaries and college staffs provided the leadership for the great national endeavor known popularly as Near East Relief, one of the most notable chapters in the annals of American philanthropy overseas. Doctors from the college at Beirut ministered to Turkish soldiers in the typhus wards; missionaries took the sick and destitute into their compounds and hospitals. Diplomatic activity was also geared to the wartime problems of the missionaries, the colleges, and the relief enterprises. Henry Morgenthau, Sr., Hoffman Philip, Abram Elkus and their staffs became deeply engaged in trying to soften Turkish policy toward the minorities and toward the schools and orphanages of the belligerent Allies, all the while, of course, looking after American interests. These efforts had to be carried on without recourse to capitulatory privileges, which the Turks had unilaterally declared canceled in 1914. Hence, American diplomats had to rely on good will established through close personal relationships with Turkish officials, combined with judicious use of moral pressure and repeated warnings of the outraged reaction in America and the rest of the civilized world to Turkish treatment of the minorities. All this had to be accomplished within the framework of the official American policy of neutrality between 1914 and 1917.

After the United States entered the war against Germany, the Turks, under pressure from their German allies, broke off diplomatic relations in April of 1917. Some Americans advocated a war declaration against Turkey so that all Germany's friends would be enemies of the United States, but those most closely connected with missionary, college, and relief work argued that no useful purpose would be served and much harm would follow from a war declaration. American missions and colleges would have to close down completely and life-saving relief work would be halted. The Turks had all along been cool toward foreign relief for Armenians and Syrians; if at war with the United States, their more ruthless officials would only unleash further vengeance on the Christian minorities. Pursuing this line of argument, President Woodrow Wilson overcame the war advocates in Congress.

The United States had entered the war because of specific grievances against Germany for her submarine warfare. It followed that America's chief concern in the war was to bring about Germany's defeat. As the American president moved to turn the war into a Great Crusade "to make the world safe for democracy," he and the American people were inevitably drawn more deeply into international affairs. Wilson's idealistic pronouncements about the principles which should guide the peacemaking, especially his Fourteen Points, brought the United States to the forefront of postwar planning at Paris. There Wilson found that the problems of international peace and justice were much like a feather pillow; wherever pressure was applied, a bulge appeared somewhere else. Thus it was that the American president was drawn into the problems of the Middle East at the Peace Conference. He faced a cruel dilemma, for after having put his weight behind the principle of self-determination, he now found it necessary to plead eloquently for the mandate system. In view of the positions Wilson had taken, the Allies urgently insisted that the United States share in the responsibilities for policing and administering a Turkish settlement.

The United States had not been a party to the secret agreements by which the Allies planned the disposition of the Ottoman domains if they were victorious. Nor had the United States been privy to British pledges to the Arabs in the Hussein-MacMahon correspondence. But Wilson had been drawn into giving his personal endorsement to the Balfour Declaration, although his State Department opposed any endorsement of the Zionist program, thus rendering debatable just how far the United

States was committed officially to Zionism by sympathetic statements from the president. Though not responsible for the conflicting promises made by the British under stress of their fight for survival, Wilson was nevertheless obliged to share in the task of unraveling the tangled situation.

For a time in 1919 a radical departure from traditional American policy toward the Middle East seemed imminent, especially if the United States should take a mandate for Armenia or a larger portion of the disrupted Ottoman Empire. The decision hinged on whether Wilson's already dwindling prestige at home could carry the people and the Senate along with him in his views about what international responsibilities the United States ought rightfully to shoulder in the interests of international order. Wilson was not without some support from his countrymen, particularly from advocates of justice for the Armenians, but the counterforces were more than he could overcome. The verdict of the Senate on November 19, 1919 (reconfirmed four months later) against American entry into the League of Nations sealed the issue. Nothing could be the same after that action. Little room for choice was left to the sick and defeated president as he reluctantly ordered a hasty official retreat from Middle Eastern responsibilities, despite loud wails from a minority which deplored the "betrayal" of the Armenians and other Christian peoples of the Middle East.

The problem for the State Department was how to protect American cultural and economic interests in the Middle East without assuming correlative political responsibilities. The policy shaped in Washington rested the American case on the argument of co-belligerency, claiming that the United States and its citizens could not be deprived of rights and privileges won as a result of their decisive contributions to the common victory over the Central Powers. Building on this foundation, the State Department used a weapon from the American diplomatic arsenal — the Open Door — by which it claimed equality of treatment for all American interests, whether economic or cultural, comparable to those extended citizens of the European Allies. The American position carried with it emphatic insistence that capitulations or their equivalent be preserved for American interests and that the State Department be consulted and its approval secured in advance of final League of Nations action on mandate drafts.

First applied to a Middle Eastern situation during the diplomatic controversy with Great Britain over the exclusion of American oil companies from Palestine and Mesopotamia in 1919 and 1920, the open-door argument soon proved to be a useful instrument for demanding equal treatment in law and in fact for missionaries, educators, and other non-economic American enterprises.

While on the surface the United States appeared to have reverted to its traditional policy of noninvolvement in the international politics of the Middle East, the facts of international life dictated that the State Department could not effectively protect American cultural and economic interests unless it maintained close watch over the actions of England and France. To do this required that the United States send representatives to the important Lausanne Conference called in 1922 to hammer out a new treaty with the victorious Turkish nationalists after the leadership of Mustafa Kemal had revitalized the Turkish nation. The fiction of political isolation was maintained by designating the American delegates as observers, who stood on the sidelines when such problems as boundaries were under negotiation but who nonetheless played an active role in most conference deliberations. Before the conference was over, the granting of the Chester Concession by the Turkish Republic revealed again how American aspirations in the Middle East could draw the United States into international politics, whether it wished to be involved or not.

The transition from war to peace lasted longer in the Middle East than elsewhere, but even nominal peace failed to impose much internal stability. The power configuration was changing even as local political and social changes were proceeding apace to reshape the Middle East. American interests and their government had to adjust to this altered environment between the two world wars.

At the time of the Armistice in 1918, Great Britain was riding high in the Middle East and appeared to be in a position to arrange a settlement quite in keeping with its imperial interests. British power dominated at Constantinople, Cairo and Suez, in Teheran, and in the Persian Gulf sheikhdoms. British troops occupied Palestine, Syria, and Mesopotamia. The British navy controlled the sea approaches and waterways of the Middle East. This seemingly impregnable position proved illusory as local and international resistance undermined British hegemony within a few years.

The Persians rejected the quasi-protectorate status Great Britain tried to effect through the Anglo-Persian Treaty of 1919; the Bolsheviks and the Nationalist Turks challenged the British in the Caucasus; Atatürk foiled them in Anatolia; Egyptian and Arab nationalists plagued them in Egypt, Palestine, and Iraq. Equally troublesome for the British were the ambitions of their recent allies — France, Italy, and Greece — which collided with British goals. The rift in Allied unity encouraged the resistance of local nationalists to British plans for the Middle East. By their stubborn persistence, the French gained their major objective — special position in Syria and Lebanon — and they were also assigned the confiscated German share in the Turkish Petroleum Company. While Italy was less successful in achieving her ambitions in Asia Minor, and the Greek foray ended in a complete debacle, the British position was weakened in each case by the rivalries of estranged Allies. Only in the Persian Gulf sheikhdoms did the British position seem virtually unimpaired. To be sure, the British could within limits still impose their will in Egypt, Palestine, Trans-Jordan, and Iraq, but even there the tide was slowly running out for them.

From the ruins of the Ottoman Empire, succession states emerged in Syria, Lebanon, Trans-Jordan, Iraq, Palestine, and Saudi Arabia. Mustafa Kemal Atatürk in Turkey and Reza Shah Pahlevi in Persia inaugurated sweeping reform programs, while Egyptian nationalists struggled to emancipate their country from British domination. The Zionist movement made headway slowly at first and then with greater speed under the impetus of Hitler's shameful treatment of European Jews in the middle and late 1930s. Social forces already at work by the turn of the century were given freer reign with improvements in transportation and communication. Women of the Middle East were slowly achieving a new role in society. Other Western influences were brought into the Persian Gulf area as foreign corporations began to develop oil resources.

The overriding problem for American interests in the Middle East and for the United States government was adjustment to the emergent nationalism of Turkey, Iran, and the Arab East. Success varied according to the interest and the location, of course, but some generalizations are possible. Before the end of the interwar period, American missionaries no longer held their former primacy among American interests. In contrast to having made a rapid recovery in Syria after World War I, the missionaries had only painfully picked up the threads of their work in Turkey and Persia by the middle 1920s. In those two countries and in

Egypt fanatical nationalists kept the missionaries under close scrutiny, gradually achieving sufficient influence to limit their privileges and rights. The result was drastic curtailment of evangelical and educational work in Persia and Turkey. In Turkey especially, but also in Syria, Persia, and Egypt, missionaries found their survival dependent on conformity to nationalist regimes bent on borrowing Western technology as a means toward securing a better material life. Insofar as the missionaries turned to vocational education and social service work among the Moslems, their position was somewhat less precarious. Devout Moslems, however, tended to equate "unnamed Christianity" with foreign domination.

The position of the three independent colleges, particularly the American University of Beirut, was more secure because of strenuous efforts to remain as apolitical as possible and to disavow evangelical intentions. Trained native leadership was needed, and these colleges were well equipped to contribute their share.

Near East Relief continued its philanthropic work throughout the twenties, shifting as soon as feasible after the war from outright relief to projects of rehabilitation, particularly for orphans. When disasters such as earthquakes and floods struck, the American Red Cross followed its tradition of tendering assistance. Various foundations, such as the Rockefeller and the Near East Foundation (successor to Near East Relief after 1930), contributed with health and medical programs and technical assistance.

For archaeologists the interwar years became an unprecedented Golden Age, notably in Iraq, Egypt, and Iran. Thanks to the professional competence of its archaeologists and to generous financial support from wealthy citizens, the United States carried a larger responsibility for this important work than ever before.

The great commercial expectations expressed during the early 1920s did not materialize except for the acquisition of an American oil stake, and this turned out to be one of the most potent influences altering American relationships with the Middle East. By 1939, the inroads made by American companies in the Persian Gulf region had broken the earlier British monopoly. After several years of serious Anglo-American tension over Middle Eastern oil, an uneasy accommodation was achieved.

In the political sphere the United States government did not object to Great Britain's primacy in the Arab East, since Washington recognized the paramount British interest in this vital segment of the imperial life line. It therefore seemed quite natural to the State Department that American missionaries in the Persian Gulf region should receive diplomatic assistance from British officials when they needed it; and when an American minister to Egypt, J. Morton Howell, let his Anglophobia become too obvious, the department admonished him. Whatever reservations Washington officials may have had about British and French policies in Egypt and the Arab mandates, they aimed to steer clear of overt criticism. In dealings with the mandatories the United States maintained a legalistic approach, insisting on formal agreements recognizing equal rights and most-favored-nations treatment for Americans. If the United States was not going to contest the political position of England and France in Egypt and the mandates, it followed that official American policy would not identify itself with the nationalist opposition to Britain and France.

Only cautiously did the United States extend its official contacts with the Arab World. The government of Iraq grew impatient waiting for American recognition. Ibn Saud petitioned the State Department repeatedly before his government was recognized, and then he had to wait several more years before a diplomatic representative was accredited to his capital. Yemen did not gain recognition until 1946. Ominous for future American relations with the Arab East was the growing American sympathy for the Zionist cause. Although the State Department tried to hold to a neutral course, the Arab World viewed with misgivings the heavy pro-Zionist pressures on Congress and the president in the late 1930s. By 1939, oil and Zionism were the two most potent factors operating to outmode traditional American noninvolvement in the Arab Middle East.

The United States had not resolved its basic foreign policy dilemma when World War II commenced. It was a large, rich, and powerful industrial nation, most of whose citizens still hoped to preserve their traditional aloofness from the political embroilments of Europe and the Middle East. The price of power was more than Americans were yet willing to pay. They still clung to their traditional view that cultural and economic ties, which they valued highly, might be protected without political involvement. But events had undermined this old assumption, a fact tacitly acknowledged by the State Department when it took its first hesitant steps toward assuming a larger diplomatic role in the Middle East between the wars. Before the United States could enter more fully into the international politics of the area, Americans would have to be convinced that the Middle East was vital to their national security. They had not arrived at that conviction by 1939, but the lightning thrusts of totalitarian might in the early war years shocked them into facing balance-of-power realities. When that time came, the United States was fortunate that its history of disinterested philanthropy and abstention from territorial ambitions had created a generally good reputation.

Viewed in historical perspective, American interests and policies in the Middle East between 1900 and 1939 provide essential background for understanding the problems to be faced later, when the United States had to adjust its policies in the Middle East to the requirements of war and cold war.

Bibliography and Index

BIBLIOGRAPHY

The following listing is confined with very few exceptions to items cited in the footnotes of this study. It therefore omits many books and some sources which provided useful background information.

BIBLIOGRAPHICAL AIDS

DeNovo, John A. "American Relations with the Middle East: Some Unfinished Business," pp. 63–98, in *Issues and Conflicts: Studies in Twentieth Century American Diplomacy*. Edited by George L. Anderson. Lawrence, Kansas: The University of Kansas Press, 1959. In this bibliographical article, the author surveyed the literature in this field as a preliminary to undertaking the writing of the present study. Notes 3, 6, and 7, pp. 83–84, list useful standard bibliographies, most of which will not be repeated in this list.

Division of Communications and Records, Department of State, *Classification of Correspondence*. Washington: Government Printing Office, 4th ed., 1938.

Buck, Elizabeth H., comp. *Materials in the National Archives Relating to the Middle East*. Reference Information Papers, No. 44, May 1955, the National Archives.

UNPRINTED SOURCE MATERIALS

DEPARTMENT OF STATE ARCHIVES, NATIONAL ARCHIVES, WASHINGTON, D.C.*

Despatches, Turkey. Volumes 68 and 69 (1899–1901).
Instructions, Turkey. Volume 7 (1896–1902).

Numerical Files, 1906–1910

2793 Appointment of Admiral C. M. Chester as Delegate to 9th International Conference of Geographers at Geneva and Further Mission to Turkey, 1907–1908.
5012 Railways in the Ottoman Empire.
16251 Chester Railway Project.
20784 American Commercial Opportunities in Turkey.
23186 Turkish Request that United States Sell Them War Vessel, 1910.

Decimal Files, 1910–1939

123 H 836 Personnel File, J. Morton Howell.
124.90b Diplomatic Representation in Saudi Arabia, 1937–1939.

* All files are from Record Group 59 unless otherwise indicated.

American Interests in the Middle East

124.90f Diplomatic Representation in Saudi Arabia, 1937–1939.
367.1162 Schinasi Memorial Hospital, Turkey.
367.1164 American Schools and Colleges in Turkey.
367.1164R Robert College, Constantinople (Istanbul), Turkey.
383.1164 P 92 American Mission Education in Egypt, 1924.
390a.116 Philanthropic Institutions Maintained in Oman by Americans.
390b.1163 American Missions in Arabia.
390d.116 American Missions in Syria.
390f.1163 Christian Missionary Alliance in Hejaz.
390g.115 Protection of American Interests in Mesopotamia.
390g.115 M 11 Protection of American Interests in Mesopotamia, MacAndrews and Forbes.
390g.1164 Schools Maintained in Mesopotamia by Americans.
390g.1164 Am 3 American School of Oriental Research Inaugurated at Baghdad.
391.1163 American Missions in Persia.
391.1163 Lutheran Orient Mission / American Lutheran Missionaries in Persia.
467.11 St 25 Claims of Standard Oil Company of New York in Palestine.
667.1115 Obstacles to American Investment in Turkey.
667.1117 Opportunities for Extension of American Trade in Turkey.
711.67 Treaties between the United States and Turkey.
711.67119 Termination of War between the United States and Turkey.
711.6712A / Arbitration and Conciliation Treaties with Turkey.
711.672 Treaties of Commerce and Navigation (Lausanne) between the United States and Turkey.
711.672 Anti-War / Treaty between the United States and Turkey for Renunciation of War.
800.6363 Petroleum File, General.
811.5031 Near East / Investment of American Capital in Near Eastern Countries.
811.6363 Petroleum, United States.
841.6363 Petroleum, Great Britain.
846b.6363 Petroleum, Bahrein Islands.
867.41 History, Turkey.
867.51 Turkish-American Investment Corp. / Match Monopoly, Turkey.
867.51A Financial Adviser, Turkey.
867.602 Ot 81 Chester Concessions.
867.61 Agriculture, Turkey.
867.6363 Petroleum, Turkey.
867.659 Matches / Manufacture of Matches in Turkey.
867.713 Postal Matters, Turkey.
883.00 Political Conditions in Egypt.
883.111 Regulations Covering Residence, Trade, and Travel in Egypt.
883.12 Public Health in Egypt.
883.42 Education in Egypt.
883.43 American Luncheon Club of Alexandria, Egypt.
883.61 Agriculture, Egypt.
883.6113 Irrigation, Egypt.
883.61321 Cotton, Egypt.
883.61331 Tobacco Cultivation, Egypt.
883.6159 Other Fruits, Egypt.
883.6206 Animal Husbandry Specimens for Collection, Egypt.
883.628 Fisheries, Egypt.
883.6363 Petroleum, Egypt.
883.77 Railways, Egypt.
883.7971 Automobile Laws, Egypt.

883.812 Suez Canal, Egypt.
883.927 Archaeology, Egypt.
890b.01 Hejaz Protest to the United States, 1922.
890b.6363 Petroleum, Kuweit.
890b.6363 Gulf Oil Corp. / Gulf Oil Company in Kuweit.
890b.6363 Kuweit Oil Co. / Kuweit Oil Company in Kuweit.
890b.797 American Automobiles on the Arabian Desert.
890d.00 Political Affairs in Syria.
890d.01 Government, Syria.
890d.46211 Entertainment in Syria by the American Colony.
890d.48 Calamities, Disasters, and Relief, Syria.
890d.56 Emigration, Syria.
890d.6463 Electric Power, Syria.
890d.7971 Automobile Laws, Syria.
890d.927 Archaeology, Syria.
890f.01 Government of Hejaz and Nejd and Dependencies.
890f.6363 Petroleum, Hejaz and Nejd.
890f.6363 Standard Oil Co. / Standard Oil Company of California in Saudi Arabia.
890g.01 Government, Mesopotamia.
890g.5123 Income Tax, Iraq.
890g.6363 Petroleum in Iraq.
890g.6363 Basra Oil Company in Iraq.
890g.6363 Getty Oil Co., George F. / Getty Oil Company in Iraq.
890g.6363 Mosul Oil Fields, Ltd. / Mosul Oil Fields in Iraq.
890g.6363 T 84 Rights of the Turkish (Iraq) Petroleum Company in Mesopotamia.
890g.6363 Wemyss, Lord / BOD in Iraq.
890g.927 Archaeology, Iraq.
891.77 Railways, Persia.
891.77 Ulen & Co. / Railway Construction in Persia by Ulen and Company.
891.77A Poland, W. B. / American Railway Adviser in Persia.
891.811 Rivers, Persia.
891.927 Persepolis / Oriental Institute of the University of Chicago, Expedition to Persepolis.

Records of the American Commission to Negotiate Peace. Record Group 256

Inquiry Document No. 84. Campbell, Oscar James. "Report on American Interests in Turkey."
Inquiry Document No. 838. Letter, American Board of Commissioners for Foreign Missions to Jerome D. Graves, Secretary, the Rockefeller Foundation, March 2, 1915.

PRIVATE COLLECTIONS OF PAPERS *

The American Board of Commissioners for Foreign Missions Archives, Houghton Library, Harvard University; Ray Stannard Baker MSS; William E. Borah MSS; Mark L. Bristol MSS; Colby M. Chester Family MSS, in possession of Colby M. Chester, Jr.; Richard Washburn Child MSS; Calvin Coolidge MSS; Charles M. Dickinson MSS; Cleveland H. Dodge MSS, Firestone Library, Princeton University; Joseph C. Grew MSS, Houghton Library, Harvard University; Charles Evans Hughes MSS; William M. Jardine MSS; Philander C. Knox MSS; Near East College Association Records, New York City; Frank L. Polk MSS, Yale

---

* Unless otherwise indicated, collections are in the Division of Manuscripts, Library of Congress, Washington, D.C.

University Library; William W. Rockhill MSS, Houghton Library, Harvard University; Standard Oil Company of New York Records, Files 7526 and 7533, Socony-Mobil Oil Company, New York City; Oscar S. Straus MSS; William Howard Taft MSS; Woodrow Wilson MSS; William Yale MSS, Yale University Library.

Letter from William Yale to John A. DeNovo, October 20, 1947.

"American University of Beirut: Description of Its Organization and Work," Autumn, 1934. Mimeographed. Harvard University Library.

PRINTED SOURCE MATERIALS
UNITED STATES GOVERNMENT
Congress

Congressional Record: 65 Cong. 2 Sess. Vol. 56; 66 Cong. 1 Sess. Vol. 58; 66 Cong. 2 Sess. Vol. 59; 67 Cong. 2 Sess. Vol. 62; 68 Cong. 1 Sess. Vol. 65; 69 Cong. 1 Sess. Vol. 67; 69 Cong. 2 Sess. Vol. 68.

House Report No. 1038, *House Reports*, 67 Cong. 2 Sess. Washington: Government Printing Office, 1922.

Journal of the Executive Proceedings of the Senate of the United States of America (Washington: Government Printing Office): Vol. 62, part 1, 1959; Vol. 63, part 1, 1959; Vol. 64, 2 parts, 1931; Vol. 65, part 1, 1959; Vol. 69, part 1, 1959.

Proceedings of the Committee on Foreign Relations, United States Senate from the 68th Congress to the 72nd Congress. Washington: Government Printing Office, 1934.

U.S. Senate, Foreign Relations Committee Hearings. "Treaty of Peace with Germany," *Senate Document 106*, 66 Cong., 1 Sess. Washington: Government Printing Office, 1919.

U.S. Senate. Staff Report to the Federal Trade Commission Submitted to the Subcommittee on Monopoly of the Select Committee on Small Business. *The International Petroleum Cartel*. Committee Print No. 6, 82 Cong., 2 Sess.

U.S. Statutes at Large, Vol. 41, 67 Cong. Washington: Government Printing Office, 1921.

Department of Commerce

Director of the Bureau of Foreign and Domestic Commerce, *Annual Report for 1922*. Washington: Government Printing Office, 1922.

Secretary of Commerce, *Tenth Annual Report* [1922]. Washington: Government Printing Office, 1922.

Department of Commerce and Labor

Pepper, Charles M. *Report on Trade Conditions in Asiatic Turkey*. Washington: Government Printing Office, 1907.

Department of State

Nielsen, Fred K. *American-Turkish Claims Settlement: Under the Agreement of December 24, 1923, and Supplemental Agreements between the United States and Turkey, Opinions and Report*. Washington: Government Printing Office, 1937.

Papers Relating to the Foreign Relations of the United States. Beginning in 1932 the title changes to *Foreign Relations of the United States: Diplomatic Papers*. In the list below, the year covered is italicized, followed by the year of publication in parentheses. All were printed at Washington, D.C., by the U.S. Government Printing Office.

  1899 (1901); *1900* (1902); *1901* (1902); *1902* (1903); *1903* (1904); *1904* (1905); *1905* (1906); *1906* 2 vols. (1909); *1907* 2 vols. (1910); *1908* (1912); *1909* (1914).

1910 (1915); *1911* (1918); *1912* (1919); *1913* (1920); *1914* (1922); *1914 Supplement: The World War* (1928); *1915* (1924); *1915 Supplement: The World War* (1928); *1916* (1925); *1916 Supplement: The World War* (1929); *1917* (1926); *1917 Supplement 1: The World War* (1931); *1917 Supplement 2: The World War.* 2 vols. (1932); *1918* (1930); *1918 Supplement 1: The World War.* 2 vols (1933); *1918 Supplement 2: The World War* (1933); *General Index, 1900–1918* (1941); *1919* 2 vols. (1934); *1919: The Paris Peace Conference.* 13 vols. (1942–1947).

1920 3 vols. (1935–1936); *The Lansing Papers, 1914–1920.* 2 vols. (1939–1940); *1921* 2 vols. (1936); *1922* 2 vols. (1938); *1923* 2 vols. (1938); *1924* 2 vols. (1939); *1925* 2 vols. (1940); *1926* 2 vols. (1941); *1927* 3 vols. (1942); *1928* 3 vols. (1942–1943); *1929* 3 vols. (1943–1944).

1930 3 vols. (1945); *1931* 3 vols. (1946); *1932* 5 vols. (1947–1948); *1933* 5 vols. (1949–1952); *1934* 5 vols. (1950–1952); *1935* 4 vols. (1952–1953); *1936* 5 vols. (1953–1954); *1937* 5 vols. (1954); *1938* 5 vols. (1954–1956); *1939* 5 vols. (1955–); *1940* 5 vols. (1955–); *1941* 7 vols. (1959–).

Department of State, *Press Releases.* Vols. 8, 13, and 20. Washington: Government Printing Office, 1933, 1936, and 1939.

Department of State, *Register* for 1900, 1914, 1918, 1931, 1933, 1936, and 1942. Washington: Government Printing Office, 1900, 1914, 1918, 1931, 1933, 1936, and 1942.

FOREIGN GOVERNMENTS AND THE LEAGUE OF NATIONS

France

Ministère des Affaires Etrangères, *Documents diplomatiques français, 1871–1914.* 2nd series, 1901–1911. Paris, 1930–1955. 3d series, 1911–1914. Paris: Imprimerie Nationale, 1929–1936.

Ministère des Affaires Etrangères, *Conférence de Lausanne sur les affaires du Proche-Orient (1922–1923), Recueil des Actes de la Conférence, Première série,* tomes I–II. Paris: Imprimerie Nationale, 1923.

Germany

Lepsius, Johannes, Albrecht Mendelssohn Bartholdy, and Friedrich Thimme (eds.). *Die grosse Politik der europäischen Kabinette, 1871–1914.* 40 vols. Berlin: Deutsche Verlagsgesellschaft für Politik und Geschichte M.B.H., 1922–1927.

Great Britain

Gooch, G. P., and Harold V. Temperley (eds.). *British Documents on the Origins of the War, 1898–1914.* 11 vols. London: His Majesty's Stationery Office, 1922–1938.

Turkey, No. 1 (1923), Lausanne Conference on Near Eastern Affairs, 1922–1923: Records of Proceedings and Draft Terms of Peace. London: Cmd. 1814, 1923.

Treaty Series No. 16 (1923), *Treaty of Peace with Turkey and Other Instruments* [etc.]. London: Cmd. 1929, 1923.

Woodward, E. L., and Rohan Butler (eds.). *Documents on British Foreign Policy, 1919–1939.* First Series, vol. 4. London: Her Majesty's Stationery Office, 1952.

Iraq

Compilation of Laws and Regulations, 1924–1925. Baghdad: Ministry of Justice, 1926.

Compilation of Laws and Regulations, 1931. Baghdad: Ministry of Justice, 1932.

League of Nations

Commission on Enquiry into the Production of Opium in Persia. 5th Commission, Annex 5.

American Interests in the Middle East

Official Journal. Special Supplement No. 54.
Record of the Second Opium Conference. Geneva, Switzerland, Nov. 17, 1924–Feb. 19, 1925.

AUTOBIOGRAPHIES, MEMOIRS, LETTERS, ETC.

Calverley, Eleanor T. *My Arabian Days and Nights.* New York: Thomas Y. Crowell Company, 1958.

Cannon, James Jr. *Bishop Cannon's Own Story: Life As I Have Seen It.* Edited by Richard L. Watson, Jr. Durham: Duke University Press, 1955.

Child, Richard Washburn. *A Diplomat Looks at Europe.* New York: Duffield and Company, 1925.

Dewey, John. *Characters and Events. Popular Essays in Social and Political Philosophy.* Edited by Joseph Ratner. 2 vols. New York: Henry Holt and Company, 1929.

Djemal Pasha, Ahmed. *Memories of a Turkish Statesman, 1913–1919.* New York: George H. Doran Company, 1922.

Freeth, Zahra. *Kuweit Was My Home.* London: Allen and Unwin, 1956.

Gates, Caleb Frank. *Not to Me Only.* Princeton: Princeton University Press, 1940.

Gerard, James W. *My First Eighty-Three Years in America: The Memoirs of James W. Gerard.* New York: Doubleday and Company, 1951.

Greene, Joseph K. *Leavening the Levant.* Boston, New York, and Chicago: The Pilgrim Press, 1916.

Grew, Joseph C. *Turbulent Era: A Diplomatic Record of Forty Years, 1904–1945.* Edited by Walter Johnson. 2 vols. Boston: Houghton Mifflin Company, 1952.

Griscom, Lloyd C. *Diplomatically Speaking.* Boston: Little, Brown and Company, 1940.

Hamlin, Cyrus. *Among the Turks.* New York: Robert Carter and Brothers, 1878.
————. *My Life and Times.* Boston: The Pilgrim Press, 1893.

Harrison, Paul W. *Doctor in Arabia.* New York: The John Day Company, 1940.

Hull, Cordell. *The Memoirs of Cordell Hull.* 2 vols. New York: The Macmillan Company, 1948.

Jessup, Henry Harris. *Fifty-Three Years in Syria.* New York, etc.: Fleming H. Revell Company, 1910.

Kemal Atatürk, Mustafa. *A Speech Delivered by Ghazi Mustapha Kemal, President of the Turkish Republic,* October 1927. Leipzig: K. F. Koehler, Publisher, 1929.

Lloyd George, David. *Memoirs of the Peace Conference.* 2 vols. New Haven: Yale University Press, 1939.

Lodge, Henry Cabot (ed.). *Selections from the Correspondence of Theodore Roosevelt and Henry Cabot Lodge, 1884–1918.* 2 vols. New York and London: Charles Scribner's Sons, 1925.

Morgenthau, Henry. *Ambassador Morgenthau's Story.* New York: Doubleday and Page, 1918.
————. *All in a Life-Time.* Garden City, N.Y.: Doubleday and Page, 1922.

Morison, Elting E. (ed.). *The Letters of Theodore Roosevelt.* 8 vols. Cambridge: Harvard University Press, 1951–1954.

Patrick, Mary Mills. *A Bosporus Adventure: Istanbul (Constantinople) Women's College, 1871–1924.* Stanford: Stanford University Press, 1934.
————. *Under Five Sultans.* New York and London: The Century Company, 1929.

Scipio, Lynn A. *My Thirty Years in Turkey.* Rindge, New Hampshire: Richard R. Smith Publisher, Inc., 1955.

Seymour, Charles (ed.). *The Intimate Papers of Colonel House.* 4 vols. Boston and New York: Houghton Mifflin Company, 1926–1928.

Sherrill, Charles H. *A Year's Embassy to Mustafa Kemal.* New York and London: Charles Scribner's Sons, 1934.

Shotwell, James T. *At the Paris Peace Conference.* New York: The Macmillan Company, 1937.

Straus, Oscar S. *Under Four Administrations: From Cleveland to Taft.* Boston and New York: Houghton Mifflin Company, 1922.

Ussher, Clarence D., and Grace H. Knapp. *An American Physician in Turkey.* Boston: Houghton Mifflin Company, 1917.

Vester, Bertha Spafford. *Our Jerusalem: An American Family in the Holy City, 1881–1949.* Garden City, N.Y.: Doubleday and Company, 1950.

Washburn, George. *Fifty Years in Constantinople and Recollections of Robert College.* Boston: Houghton Mifflin Company, 1909.

White, George E. *Adventuring with Anatolia College.* Grinnell, Iowa: Herald-Register Publishing Company, 1940.

Wilson, F. M. Huntington. *Memoirs of an Ex-Diplomat.* Boston: Bruce Humphries, Inc., 1945.

Yalman, Ahmed Emin. *Turkey in My Time.* Norman: University of Oklahoma Press, 1956.

MISSIONARY BOARD REPORTS

Annual Report of the American Board of Commissioners for Foreign Missions. 1 through 10 [1811–1820]. Boston: Crocker and Brewster, 1834; 60 [1870]. Cambridge: Riverside Press, 1870; 90 [1900]. Boston: Congregational House, 1900; 98–99 [1908–1909]. Boston: Congregational House, 1908–1909; 104–129 [1914–1939]. Boston: Congregational House, 1914–1939.

The Sixty-third Annual Report of the Board of Foreign Missions of the Presbyterian Church in the United States of America [1900]. New York: Presbyterian Building, 1900.

The Ninety-third Annual Report of the Board of Foreign Missions of the Presbyterian Church in the United States of America [1930]. New York: Presbyterian Building, 1930.

The One Hundred and Third Annual Report of the Board of Foreign Missions of the Presbyterian Church in the United States of America [1940]. New York: 156 Fifth Avenue, 1940.

CONTEMPORARY PERIODICALS AND NEWSPAPERS

Current History, 18 (April 1923), 176–177.

"Fish to Jidda," *Time*, 35 (Feb. 19, 1940), 35–36.

"Great Khan in Manacles," *Time*, 26 (Dec. 9, 1935), 26, 28.

Gunther, John. "King of Kings: The Shah of Iran — Which Used to Be Persia," *Harper's*, 178 (Dec. 1938), 60–69.

"Iranian Farewell," *Literary Digest*, 121 (April 11, 1936), 14.

"The King-Crane Report on the Near East: A Suppressed Document of the United States Government," *Editor and Publisher*, 55 (Dec. 2, 1922), Second Section, pp. i–xxviii, lv.

"Master of Persia: One-Time Robin Hood Becomes Modernizing, Benevolent Dictator," *Literary Digest*, 122 (Dec. 19, 1936), 8–9.

The Missionary Review of the World, Volumes 24 (1901), 31–32 (1908–1909), 38–62 (1915–1939).

The New York Times. March 8, 1919; June 20, 1922; Dec. 3, 1922; Jan. 3, July 7, 1927; Sept. 12, 1929; Sept. 10, 1933; Nov. 28, 29, 30, Dec. 1, 3, 5, 7, 11, 1935; Jan. 5, 18, 19, March 31, 1937; Jan. 30, 1939.

Noble, George B. "The Voice of Egypt," *The Nation*, 110 (Jan. 3, 1920), 861–864.

Sarton, George. "Second Preface to the Nineteenth Volume of Isis (Beirut)," *Isis*, 19 (July 1933), 322–329.

Sheean, Vincent. "Shah-in-Shah: Reza, Founder of the Pahlavi Dynasty and Heir

to the Glory of Cyrus the Great," *Asia*, 26 (Dec. 1926), 1052–1059 *et seq.* (reprinted in *ibid.*, 37 (March 1937), 175–178.
"Speeding Diplomat: Persian Envoy Runs Afoul of Constable, Claims Immunity," *Literary Digest*, 120 (Dec. 7, 1935), 9.
"U.S. to Limbo," *Time*, 27 (April 13, 1936), 28, 30.
"Why the Democrats Defeated the Turkish Treaty," *Literary Digest*, 92 (Jan. 29, 1927), 10–11.

COLLECTIONS OF DOCUMENTS

Goodrich, Leland M., and Marie J. Carroll (eds.). *Documents on American Foreign Relations*, V (July 1942–June 1943). Boston: 1944.
Hurewitz, Jacob C. (ed.). *Diplomacy in the Near and Middle East: A Documentary Record*. 2 vols. Princeton: Van Nostrand, 1956.
Miller, David Hunter (ed.). *Treaties and Other International Acts of the United States of America*. 8 vols. Washington: Government Printing Office, 1931–1948.
Porter, Kirk H., and Donald Bruce Johnson (eds.). *National Party Platforms, 1840–1956*. Urbana: University of Illinois Press, 1956.

SECONDARY MATERIALS
BOOKS, THESES, AND PAMPHLETS

Abbott, Freeland Knight. "American Policy in the Middle East: A Study of the Attitudes of the United States toward the Middle East, Especially during the Period 1919–1936." Unpublished Ph.D. dissertation, The Fletcher School of Law and Diplomacy, 1952.
Adler, Cyrus, and Aaron M. Margolith. *With Firmness in the Right: American Diplomatic Action Affecting Jews, 1840–1945*. New York: The American Jewish Committee, 1946.
Albright, William F. *The Archaeology of Palestine*. Penguin Books, revised, 1956.
Allison, Elizabeth. "American Participation in the Turkish Settlement, 1918–1920." Unpublished M.A. thesis, The Pennsylvania State University, 1953.
Antonius, George. *The Arab Awakening: The Story of the Arab National Movement*. Philadelphia: J. B. Lippincott Company, 1939.
Askew, William C. *Europe and Italy's Acquisition of Libya*. Durham: Duke University Press, 1942.
Atamian, Sarkis. *The Armenian Community: The Historical Development of a Social and Ideological Conflict*. New York: Philosophical Library, 1955.
Banani, Amin. *The Modernization of Iran, 1921–1941*. Stanford: Stanford University Press, 1961.
Barton, James L. *Daybreak in Turkey*. Boston: Pilgrim Press, 1908.
———. *Story of Near East Relief (1915–1930): An Interpretation*. New York: The Macmillan Company, 1930.
Bastert, Russell H. "James G. Blaine and the Origins of the First International American Conference." Unpublished Ph.D. dissertation, Yale University, 1952.
Beale, Howard K. *Theodore Roosevelt and the Rise of America to World Power*. Baltimore: Johns Hopkins Press, 1956.
Brinton, Jasper Y. *The Mixed Courts of Egypt*. New Haven: Yale University Press, 1930.
Brown, Arthur Judson. *One Hundred Years: A History of the Foreign Missionary Work of the Presbyterian Church in the U.S.A., With Some Account of Countries, Peoples and the Policies and Problems of Modern Missions*. New York: Fleming H. Revell Company, 1937.
Browne, Edward G. *The Persian Revolution of 1905–1909*. Cambridge, England: The University Press, 1910.

Busch, Francis X. *Guilty or Not Guilty?* Indianapolis and New York: Bobbs-Merrill, 1952.

Campbell, Charles S., Jr. *Special Business Interests and the Open Door Policy.* New Haven: Yale University Press, 1951.

Centennial Series. *Iran Mission.* New York: The Board of Foreign Missions of the Presbyterian Church in the U.S.A., n.d.

————. *Syria Mission.* New York: The Board of Foreign Missions of the Presbyterian Church in the U.S.A., n.d.

————. *United Mission in Mesopotamia.* New York: The Board of Foreign Missions of the Presbyterian Church in the U.S.A., n.d.

A Century of Mission Work in Iran (Persia), 1834–1934. Beirut, n.d.

Cook, Ralph Elliott. "The United States and the Armenian Question, 1884–1924." Unpublished Ph.D. dissertation, Fletcher School of Law and Diplomacy, 1957.

Cumming, Henry H. *Franco-British Rivalry in the Post-War Near East.* New York: Oxford University Press, 1938.

Curti, Merle, and Kendall Birr. *Prelude to Point Four: American Technical Missions Overseas, 1838–1938.* Madison: University of Wisconsin Press, 1954.

Davenport, E. H., and Sidney Russell Cook. *The Oil Trusts and Anglo-American Relations.* London: Macmillan and Company, 1923.

Dennis, Alfred L. P. *Adventures in American Diplomacy, 1896–1906.* New York: E. P. Dutton and Company, 1928.

DeNovo, John A. "Petroleum and American Diplomacy in the Near East, 1908–1928." Unpublished Ph.D. dissertation, Yale University, 1948.

Earle, Edward Mead. *Turkey, the Great Powers, and the Bagdad Railway: A Study in Imperialism.* New York: Macmillan Company, 1923.

Edwards, Rosaline De Gregorio. "Relations between the United States and Turkey, 1893–1897." Unpublished Ph.D. dissertation, Fordham University, 1952.

[Einstein, Louis]. *American Foreign Policy.* By a Diplomatist. Boston and New York: Houghton Mifflin Company, 1909.

Elwell-Sutton, L. P. *Modern Iran.* London: G. Routledge and Sons, Ltd., 1941.

Evans, Laurence. "United States Policy and the Syrian Mandate, 1917–1922: A Study in American Diplomacy." Unpublished Ph.D. dissertation, The School of Advanced International Studies, Johns Hopkins University, 1957.

Fatemi, Nasrollah S. *Diplomatic History of Persia, 1917–1923: Anglo-Russian Power Politics in Iran.* New York: Russell F. Moore Company, 1952.

Ferrell, Robert H. *Peace in Their Time: The Origins of the Kellogg-Briand Pact.* New Haven: Yale University Press, 1952.

Field, Henry. *Contributions to the Anthropology of Iran.* Anthropological Series, Field Museum, Vol. 29, No. 1. Chicago: Field Museum Press, 1939.

Finnie, David H. *Desert Enterprise: The Middle East Oil Industry in Its Local Environment.* Cambridge: Harvard University Press, 1958.

Fisher, Sydney Nettleton. *The Middle East: A History.* New York: Alfred A. Knopf, 1959.

Fleming, Denna F. *The United States and World Organization, 1920–1933.* New York: Columbia University Press, 1938.

Foster, Henry A. *The Making of Modern Iraq: A Product of World Forces.* Norman: University of Oklahoma Press, 1935.

Frye, Richard N. *Iran.* New York: Henry Holt and Company, 1953.

Galbraith, Thomas H. "The Smyrna Disaster of 1922 and Its Effects on Turkish-American Relations." Unpublished M.A. thesis, The Pennsylvania State University, 1960.

Gerig, Benjamin. *The Open Door and the Mandate System.* London: G. Allen and Unwin, Ltd., 1930.

Gibb, George S., and Evelyn H. Knowlton. *The Resurgent Years, 1911–1927.* History of the Standard Oil Company (New Jersey), Business History Foundation, Henrietta Larson, Editorial Director. New York: Harper and Brothers, 1956.

Gordon, Leland J. *American Relations with Turkey, 1830–1930: An Economic Interpretation.* Philadelphia: University of Pennsylvania Press, 1932.

Groseclose, Elgin. *Introduction to Iran.* New York: Oxford University Press, 1947.

Haas, William S. *Iran.* New York: Columbia University Press, 1946.

Hackworth, Green B. *Digest of International Law.* 8 vols. Washington: Government Printing Office, 1940–1944.

Halperin, Samuel. *The Political World of American Zionism.* Detroit: Wayne State University Press, 1961.

Handlin, Oscar. *Adventure in Freedom: Three Hundred Years of Jewish Life in America.* New York: McGraw-Hill, 1954.

Helmreich, Ernst Christian. *The Diplomacy of the Balkan Wars, 1912–1913.* Cambridge: Harvard University Press, 1938.

Herzfeld, Ernest E. *Archaeological History of Iran.* London: Oxford University Press, 1935.

Hessabi, Mehdi. *Le pétrole en Irak.* Paris: Jouve et Cie., 1937.

Hitti, Philip K. *The Syrians in America.* New York: George H. Doran Company, 1924.

Hourani, A. H. *Syria and Lebanon: A Political Essay.* London, New York, and Toronto: Oxford University Press, 1946.

Howard, Harry N. *The Partition of Turkey: A Diplomatic History, 1913–1923.* Norman: University of Oklahoma Press, 1931.

Howell, J. Morton. *Egypt's Past, Present and Future.* Dayton, Ohio: Service Publishing Company, 1929.

Hurewitz, Jacob. *Middle East Dilemmas: The Background of United States Policy.* New York: Harper and Brothers, 1953.

———. *The Struggle for Palestine.* New York: W. W. Norton Company, 1950.

Ireland, Philip W. *'Iraq: A Study in Political Development.* New York: The Macmillan Company, 1938.

Ise, John. *The United States Oil Policy.* New Haven: Yale University Press, 1926.

Jarvis, H. Wood. *Pharaoh to Farouk.* New York: The Macmillan Company, 1955.

Karpat, Kemal H. *Turkey's Politics: The Transition to a Multi-Party System.* Princeton: Princeton University Press, 1959.

Kazdal, Mustafa Nebil. "Trade Relations between the United States and Turkey, 1919–1944." Unpublished Ph.D. dissertation, Indiana University, 1946.

Khadduri, Majid. *Independent Iraq, 1932–1958: A Study in Iraqi Politics.* London and New York: Oxford University Press, 2d ed., 1958.

Kheirallah, George. *Arabia Reborn.* Albuquerque: University of New Mexico Press, 1952.

Kilic, Altemur. *Turkey and the World.* Washington: Public Affairs Press, 1959.

Lambton, Ann K. S. *Landlord and Peasant in Persia: A Study of Land Tenure and Land Revenue Administration.* London and New York: Oxford University Press, 1953.

Latourette, Kenneth S. *A History of the Expansion of Christianity.* 7 vols. New York and London: Harper and Brothers, 1937–1945.

Lenczowski, George. *The Middle East in World Affairs.* Ithaca: Cornell University Press, 1952.

———. *Russia and the West in Iran, 1918–1948: A Study of Big-Power Rivalry.* Ithaca: Cornell University Press, 1949.

L'Espagnol de la Tramerye, Pierre. *La lutte mondiale pour le pétrole.* Paris: Editions de "La Vie Universitaire," 1921.

Lewis, Bernard. *The Emergence of Modern Turkey.* London, New York, and Toronto: Oxford University Press, 1961.

Lloyd, Lord. *Egypt since Cromer.* 2 vols. London: Macmillan and Company Ltd., 1934.

Lloyd, Seton. *Foundations in the Dust: A Story of Mesopotamian Exploration.* Penguin Books, 1955.

Longrigg, Stephen H. *Iraq, 1900–1950: A Political, Social, and Economic History.* London, New York, and Toronto: Oxford University Press, 1953.

——. *Oil in the Middle East: Its Discovery and Development.* London, New York, and Toronto: Oxford University Press, 1954.

——. *Syria and Lebanon under French Mandate.* London, New York, and Toronto: Oxford University Press, 1958.

Main, Ernest. *Iraq from Mandate to Independence.* London: G. Allen and Unwin, Ltd., 1935.

Malcom, M. Vartan. *The Armenians in America.* Boston: The Pilgrim Press, 1919.

Manuel, Frank E. *The Realities of American-Palestine Relations.* Washington: The Public Affairs Press, 1949.

Mason, Alfred D., and Frederick J. Barny. *History of the Arabian Mission.* New York: Board of Foreign Mission of the Reformed Church in America, 1926.

Mattison, Frances C. (ed.). *A Survey of American Interests in the Middle East.* Washington: Middle East Institute, 1953.

May, Ernest R. *Imperial Democracy: The Emergence of America as a Great Power.* New York: Harcourt, Brace and World, Inc., 1961.

Mears, Eliot G. *Modern Turkey: A Politico-Economic Interpretation, 1908–1923.* New York: The Macmillan Company, 1924.

Millspaugh, Arthur C. *The American Task in Persia.* London: T. Werner Laurie, Ltd., 1925.

——. *Americans in Persia.* Washington: The Brookings Institution, 1946.

Morison, Samuel Eliot. *The Maritime History of Massachusetts, 1783–1860.* Boston and New York: Houghton Mifflin Company, 1921.

Motter, T. H. Vail. *The Persian Corridor and Aid to Russia.* Washington: Government Printing Office, 1952.

Offner, John L. "American-Persian Relations in the Post-War Decade, 1918–1928." Unpublished M.A. thesis, The Pennsylvania State University, 1952.

Penrose, Stephen B. L., Jr. *That They May Have Life: The Story of the American University of Beirut, 1866–1941.* New York: The Trustees of the American University of Beirut, 1941.

Perkins, Dexter. *The Evolution of American Foreign Policy.* New York: Oxford University Press, 1948.

Philby, H. St. John. *Sa'udi Arabia.* London: Benn, 1955.

Phillips, Wendell. *Qataban and Sheba: Exploring the Ancient Kingdoms on the Biblical Spice Routes of Arabia.* New York: Harcourt, Brace and Company, 1955.

Pratt, Julius W. *America's Colonial Experiment: How the United States Gained, Governed, and in Part Gave Away a Colonial Empire.* New York: Prentice-Hall, 1950.

Ramsaur, Ernest E., Jr. *The Young Turks: Prelude to the Revolution of 1908.* Princeton: Princeton University Press, 1957.

Richter, Julius. *A History of Protestant Missions in the Near East.* New York, etc.: Fleming H. Revell Company, 1910.

Rihani, Ameen. *Around the Coasts of Arabia.* London: Constable, 1930.

Rippy, J. Fred. *The Caribbean Danger Zone.* New York: G. P. Putnam's Sons, 1940.

Ross, Frank A., C. Luther Frye, and Elbridge Sibley. *The Near East and American Philanthropy: A Survey Conducted under the Guidance of the General Committee of the Near East Survey.* New York: Columbia University Press, 1929.

Safran, Nadav. *Egypt in Search of Political Community: An Analysis of the In-*

tellectual and Political Evolution of Egypt, 1804–1952. Cambridge: Harvard University Press, 1961.

Sanger, Richard H. *The Arabian Peninsula*. Ithaca: Cornell University Press, 1954.

Sarton, George. *The Incubation of Western Culture in the Middle East*. Washington: n.p., 1951.

Sayre, Joel. *Persian Gulf Command: Some Marvels on the Road to Kazvin*. New York: Random House, 1945.

Sforza, Count Carlo. *Diplomatic Europe since the Treaty of Versailles*. New Haven: Yale University Press, 1928.

Sherrill, Charles H. *Mosaics in Italy, Palestine, Syria, Turkey and Greece*. London: John Lane, 1933.

Shwadran, Benjamin. *The Middle East, Oil and the Great Powers*. New York: Frederick A. Praeger, 1955.

Sousa, Nasim. *The Capitulatory Régime of Turkey: Its History, Origins, and Nature*. Baltimore: Johns Hopkins Press, 1933.

Speiser, Ephraim A. *The United States and the Near East*. Cambridge: Harvard University Press, 1947.

Strong, William E. *The Story of the American Board: An Account of the First Hundred Years of the American Board of Commissioners for Foreign Missions*. Boston: The Pilgrim Press, 1910.

Stuart, Graham H. *American Diplomatic and Consular Practice*. New York: D. Appleton-Century-Crofts Company, 2d ed., 1952.

————. *The Department of State: A History of Its Organization, Procedure and Personnel*. New York: The Macmillan Company, 1949.

Sykes, Percy. *A History of Persia*. 2 vols. London: Macmillan and Company, Ltd., 3d ed., 1951.

Temperley, Harold W. V. (ed.). *History of the Peace Conference of Paris*. 6 vols. London: H. Frowde, and Hodder and Stoughton, 1920–1924.

Terry, Charles E., and Mildred Pellens. *The Opium Problem*. New York: Committee on Drug Addiction in Collaboration with the Bureau of Social Hygiene, Inc., 1928.

Thomas, Lewis V., and Richard N. Frye. *The United States and Turkey and Iran*. Cambridge: Harvard University Press, 1951.

Tillman, Seth P. *Anglo-American Relations at the Paris Peace Conference of 1919*. Princeton: Princeton University Press, 1961.

Toynbee, Arnold J., and Kenneth P. Kirkwood. *Turkey*. London: E. Benn, Ltd., 1926.

Trask, Roger R. "The Relations of the United States and Turkey, 1927–1939." Unpublished Ph.D. dissertation, The Pennsylvania State University, 1959.

Tuchman, Barbara W. *The Guns of August*. New York: The Macmillan Company, 1962.

Twitchell, Karl S. *Saudi Arabia: With an Account of the Development of Its Natural Resources*. Princeton: Princeton University Press, 2d ed., 1953.

Upton, Joseph M. *The History of Modern Iran: An Interpretation*. Cambridge: Harvard University Press, 1960.

Van der Meulen, D. *The Wells of Ibn Sa'ud*. London: John Murray, 1957.

Walt, Joseph W. "Saudi Arabia and the Americans: 1928–1951." Ann Arbor, Mich.: University Microfilms, 1960. Ph.D. dissertation, Northwestern University, 1960.

Webster, Donald Everett. *The Turkey of Atatürk: Social Process in the Turkish Reformation*. Philadelphia: The American Academy of Political and Social Science, 1939.

Whiteman, Marjorie M. *Damages in International Law*. 3 vols., Washington: Government Printing Office, 1937–1943.

Woodsmall, Ruth F. *Moslem Women Enter a New World*. New York: Round Table Press, Inc., 1936.

Wright, Lenoir C. "United States Policy toward Egypt: 1830–1914." Unpublished Ph.D. dissertation, Columbia University, 1954.

Yeselson, Abraham. *United States-Persian Diplomatic Relations, 1883–1921.* New Brunswick, N.J.: Rutgers University Press, 1956.

Ziadeh, Nicola A. *Syria and Lebanon.* New York: Frederick A. Praeger, 1957.

BIOGRAPHICAL MATERIALS

Albright, William F. "Edward Robinson," *Dictionary of American Biography.* 22 vols. New York: Charles Scribner's Sons, 1922–1958. XVI, 39–40.

————. "Eli Smith," *Dictionary of American Biography.* XVII, 257–258.

Baker, Ray Stannard (ed.). *Woodrow Wilson and World Settlement: Written from His Unpublished and Personal Material.* 3 vols. Garden City, N.Y.: Doubleday Page and Company, 1922.

Breasted, Charles. *Pioneer to the Past: The Story of James Henry Breasted, Archaeologist.* New York: Charles Scribner's Sons, 1943.

Dabney, Virginius. *Dry Messiah: The Life of Bishop Cannon.* New York: Alfred A. Knopf, 1949.

Jenkins, Hester Donaldson. *An Educational Ambassador to the Near East: The Story of Mary Mills Patrick and an American College in the Orient.* New York and Chicago: Fleming H. Revell Company, 1925.

Mason, Alpheus T. *Brandeis: A Free Man's Life.* New York: The Viking Press, 1946.

Nicolson, Harold. *Curzon: The Last Phase, 1919–1925: A Study in Post-War Diplomacy.* Boston and New York: Harcourt, Brace and Company, 1934.

Pringle, Henry. *The Life and Times of William Howard Taft: A Biography.* 2 vols. New York and Toronto: Farrar and Rinehart, 1939.

Shedd, Mary Lewis. *The Measure of a Man: The Life of William Ambrose Shedd, Missionary to Persia.* New York: George H. Doran, 1922.

Varg, Paul A. *Open Door Diplomat: The Life of W. W. Rockhill.* Urbana: University of Illinois Press, 1952.

Wescott, Allan. "Colby Mitchell Chester," *Dictionary of American Biography.* XXI, 170–171.

Who Was Who in America, vol. 1, 1897–1942. Chicago: The A. N. Marquis Company, 1943.

JOURNAL ARTICLES AND CHAPTERS IN BOOKS

Adler, Selig. "The Palestine Question in the Wilson Era," *Jewish Social Studies,* 10 (Oct. 1948), 303–334.

Askew, William C., and J. Fred Rippy. "The United States and Europe's Strife, 1908–1913," *Journal of Politics,* 4 (Feb. 1942), 68–79.

Brown, Philip M. "From Sèvres to Lausanne," *American Journal of International Law,* 18 (Jan. 1924), 113–116.

Burton, David H. "Theodore Roosevelt and Egyptian Nationalism," *Mid-America,* 41 (April 1959), 88–103.

Buzanski, Peter M. "The Inter-Allied Investigation of the Greek Invasion of Smyrna, 1919," *The Historian* (scheduled for publication in 1963).

Daniel, Robert L. "The Armenian Question and American-Turkish Relations, 1914–1927," *Mississippi Valley Historical Review,* 46 (Sept. 1959), 252–275.

————. "The Friendship of Woodrow Wilson and Cleveland H. Dodge," *Mid-America,* 43 (July 1961), 182–196.

Davison, Roderic H. "Middle East Nationalism: Lausanne Thirty Years After," *Middle East Journal,* 7 (Summer 1953), 324–348.

————. "Turkish Diplomacy from Mudros to Lausanne," in *The Diplomats, 1919–1939.* Edited by Gordon A. Craig and Felix Gilbert. Princeton: Princeton University Press, 1953.

————. "Where Is the Middle East?" *Foreign Affairs,* 38 (July 1960), 665–675.

DeNovo, John A. "The Movement for an Aggressive American Oil Policy Abroad, 1918–1920," *American Historical Review*, 61 (July 1956), 854–876.

——. "Petroleum and the United States Navy before World War I," *Mississippi Valley Historical Review*, 41 (March 1955), 641–656.

——. "A Railroad for Turkey: The Chester Project of 1908–1913," *Business History Review*, 33 (Autumn 1959), 300–329.

"The Division of Near Eastern Affairs," *The American Foreign Service Journal*, 10 (Jan. 1933), 16–18.

Earle, Edward M. "American Missions in the Near East," *Foreign Affairs*, 7 (April 1929), 398–417.

——. "The Turkish Petroleum Company: A Study in Oleaginous Diplomacy," *Political Science Quarterly*, 39 (June 1924), 265–279.

Grew, Joseph C. "The Peace Conference of Lausanne, 1922–1923," *Proceedings of the American Philosophical Society*, 98 (Feb. 1954), 1–10.

Howard, Harry N. "An American Experiment in Peace Making: The King-Crane Commission," *Moslem World*, 32 (April 1942), 122–146.

——. "The United States and the Problem of the Turkish Straits: A Reference Article," *Middle East Journal*, 1 (Jan. 1947), 59–72.

Jamme, A. "Les expéditions archéologiques américaines en Arabie du Sud," *Oriente Moderno*, 30 (March 1953), 133–157.

Kirk, George. "*The Arab Awakening* Reconsidered," *Middle Eastern Affairs*, 13 (June–July, 1962), 162–173.

Lybyer, Albert H. "America's Missionary Record in Turkey," *Current History*, 19 (Feb. 1924), 802–810.

Mayo, Laurence Shaw. "The Chester Concession under Fire," *Asia*, 23 (July 1923), 521–538.

Pearcy, G. Etzel. "The Middle East – An Indefinable Region," *The Department of State Bulletin*, 40 (March 23, 1959), 407–416.

Perkins, Ann. "American Archeology in the Near and Middle East," in *Background of the Middle East*. Edited by Ernest Jackh. Ithaca: Cornell University Press, 1952.

Rustow, Dankwart A. "The Army and the Founding of the Turkish Republic," *World Politics*, 11 (July 1959), 513–552.

——. "Foreign Policy of the Turkish Republic," in *Foreign Policy in World Politics*. Edited by Roy C. Macridis. Englewood Cliffs, N.J.: Prentice Hall, 1958.

Sanjian, Avedis K. "The Sanjak of Alexandretta (Hatay): Its Impact on Turkish-Syrian Relations (1939–1956)," *Middle East Journal*, 10 (Autumn 1956), 379–394.

Turlington, Edgar. "The Settlement of Lausanne," *American Journal of International Law*, 18 (Oct. 1924), 696–706.

Westermann, William L. "The Armenian Problem and the Disruption of Turkey," in *What Really Happened at Paris: The Story of the Peace Conference, 1918–1919*. Edited by Edward M. House and Charles Seymour. New York: Charles Scribner's Sons, 1921.

Wilson, John. "Islamic Culture and Archaeology," *Middle East Journal*, 8 (Winter, 1954), 1–9.

Yale, William. "Ambassador Henry Morgenthau's Special Mission of 1917," *World Politics*, 1 (April 1949), 308–320.

UNPUBLISHED ARTICLES

Barr, William F. "Woodrow Wilson and the Palestine Question, 1917–1921." Seminar paper, The Pennsylvania State University.

Faris, Nabih. "The United States Image of the Near East As Seen from that Region." Paper delivered at the Princeton University Conference on "The United States Image of the Near East," April 15, 1959.

INDEX

Abdul Hamid II: sensitive to subversion, 21–22; opposition to, 45; deposed, 47–48; claims of heirs, 191, 196, 224

Abdullah, Emir: Trans-Jordan created for, 338

Adams, Kathryn Newell: as president of Istanbul College for Women, 262

Adana, Turkey: mission station at, 254n; hospital at, 259; Stanley Clark's work in, 267

Adee, Alvey A.: and Persia's request for economic adviser, 54; against endorsement of Chester withdrawal, 82; proclaims neutrality toward renewed Chester efforts, 84; informs Socony of State Department's retreat, 174

Aden: American consul in, 19, 354, 358; significance to British, 354–355

Admiral Bristol Hospital, 269

Aegean Islands: disposition at Lausanne, 150

Afghanistan: signs pact at Sa'dabad, 244

Agriculture Department: releases Silas Mason to Egypt, 377–378

Ahwaz, Iran: on trans-Iranian railway, 299; Shah marooned at, 300

Aintab, Turkey: site of Central Turkish College, 13. *See also* Gazientep

Allenby, General Sir Edmund, 175, 318n

Aleppo, Syria: U.S. consulate at, 56; site of mission school, 333

Alexander, Douglas, 40

Alexandretta, Turkey: U.S. consulate in, 19; consular agent at, 56; recovered by Turkey, 248, 335. *See also* Hatay

Alexandria, Egypt: U.S. consulate in, 56; Socony equipment stored in, 171; United Presbyterian schools in, 372

Algeciras Conference: T. Roosevelt and, 52

Alishar, Turkey: excavation at, 272

Alley, Rayford W.: supports Turkish treaty, 164

Allies: allow relief ships through blockade, 104; recommend U.S. declaration of war on Turkey, 108; plan for U.S. as mandatory, 120; policing problem of, 120–121; and Sèvres Treaty, 124–127; in disunity at Lausanne, 141–142; at London Conference, 145–146; ratify treaties with Turkey, 158; at San Remo, 176

Alling, Paul M.: appraises Zionist pressure, 342; on pros and cons of recognizing Saudi Arabia, 360–361

All Persia Inter-Mission Conference, 296

Amara, Iraq: Reformed Church station and hospital at, 351

American Academy for Girls, 259

American Board of Commissioners for Foreign Missions: sends first missionaries to Levant, 8; extent of activity by *1900*, 8–9; and infrequent Moslem conversion, 11; operates colleges, 13; trains in local languages and customs, 13; tenuous tie with Istanbul Women's College, 14, 36; medical activity by *1914*, 31; indictment of Islam, 32; laments emigration from Anatolia, 42–43; requests mediation in Italo-Turkish War, 51; extent of Turkish Missions, *1914–1918*, 96 and n; reports mistreatment of Armenians, 98–99, 101; requests U.S. participation in Turkish settlement, 109 and n; asks U.S. participation in revising Sèvres Treaty, 132–133;

instrument of, 108; eliminated from Turkish settlement, 112; tries for oil lands in Saudi Arabia, 207–208; Persia's sympathy for during World War I, 276; competes for influence in Iraq, 347

Getty, J. Paul: bid rejected by Iraq, 201

Ghazi, Crown Prince: attends A.U.B., 330

Ghazi: Atatürk given title of, 233n

Ghods, Hossein: becomes Iranian chargé, 307; informs Hull of withdrawal of Iranian representatives, 308; on U.S. legation at Teheran, 309

Gillespie, Julian: at Lausanne, 138n; contributes to Turkish-American relations, 253

Giza, Egypt: American archaeologists in, 44, 375

Glasgow, Dr. Bruce: J. G. White Company representative in Turkey, 62

Glazebrook, Otis A.: on British economic aims, 172

Goeben: to Constantinople, 90

Goethals, George: heads Ottoman-American Development Company, 219; Arthur Chester complains to, 219–220; confirms Clayton-Kennedy, 221; on company finance, 221–222; on harmony within company, 223; helps execute voting trust agreement, 223

Goz Tepe, Turkey (Izmir suburb): site of American Collegiate Institute, 259

Grand National Assembly: decrees use of family names in Turkey, 229n; grants Chester concession, 225; role of in new Turkey, 230; bestows title of "the Ghazi" on Atatürk, 233n

Great Britain: in Eastern Question, 4; suggests British-American policy in Ottoman Empire, 6n; diplomatic support for U.S. interests, 20, 365; and Persia, 47, 275, 276, 278–280, 289, 290; and Egypt, 49, 320, 368; attitude toward U.S. assistance to Persia, 53–54; attitude toward Chester Project, 70, 195, 225, 226; asks U.S. to bar Turkish fleet from coal, 90n; declares war on Turkey, 90; consulted on sending U.S. ships to Turkey, 91; and Morgenthau plan, 107; plans spheres of influence in Middle East, 110; makes conflicting commitments, 112–113; plans for U.S. in Middle

East, 115, 118; requested as mandatory for Palestine, 116; difficulty with France over Syria, 116–117, 124; and King-Crane Commission, 119; removes troops from Armenia and Caucasus, 121; as mandatory for Palestine, Trans-Jordan and Iraq, 126, 320–321; and Lausanne Conference, 135–137, 141–142, 150; inflexible toward new Turkey, 153; takes interest in Socony's holdings, 169; oil controversy, 169–184 *passim*; and San Remo Oil Agreement, 176, 177; and draft mandates, 179, 180; negotiates over Mosul, 194; ensures foreign policy objectives in Iraq, 197; and oil in Bahrein, 203–204; and oil in Kuweit, 204–205; abrogates veto power over Arabian oil, 206; effect of sponsoring Hashimites, 207; backs Anglo-Persian claims, 284; presses Persia to control smuggling of narcotics, 287; control points in Middle East, 321; Arab feeling against, 322; position in Palestine and Trans-Jordan, 341–342; U.S. policy and international position of, 345, 346; treaty of alliance with Iraq, 347; interest in Arabian peninsula, 354; U.S. defers to in Egypt, 380, 392–393; hegemony jeopardized, 390–391

Great Powers: compete for oil reserves, 167

Greece: American-built ships for, 92; seeks U.S. support at Turkish settlement, 109–110; ambitions in Middle East, 112; Venizelos presents case for, 115; occupation of Smyrna, 121; cedes Karagatch to Turkey, 149; Aegean Islands to, 150

Greeks: in Robert College, 14; emigrate to U.S., 17, 42; nationalist aspirations of, 45; Turkish treatment of during war, 102; Turkish resistance to, 129; driven from Anatolia, 230; defeated at Sakarya, 233n

Greek Orthodox Church: presses U.S. delegates at Lausanne, 144

Greek Patriarchate in Constantinople: U.S. support of at Lausanne, 141

Grew, Anita (daughter of Joseph C.): life in Turkey, 251

Grew, Joseph C.: on tourists to pyramids, 45; at Lausanne, 128, 138, 141,

435

126, 320–321, 391; Socony holdings in, 169; capitulatory rights in, 323; divided into administrative districts, 323n; France considers and refuses independence for, 336–337; U.S. investment and trade in, 337

Syrian Protestant College. *See* American University of Beirut

Tabriz, Iran: Presbyterian mission at, 9, 315; memorial services for Baskerville in, 47n; consulate established at, 56; mission station cares for refugees, 276; captured missionaries taken to, 278; reoccupied as mission station, 292

Taft, William Howard: supports Chester Project, 28; interested in commerce and investment, 38; applauds revolution in Turkey and Persia, 48; willing to mediate Italo-Turkish War, 51; states U.S. policy during Balkan Wars, 52–53; acts on Shuster's application, 54; and Division of Near Eastern Affairs, 56; concept of Dollar Diplomacy, 59

Taft administration: disapproves of Chester withdrawal, 82; reverts to nonintervention (*1911*), 82–83, 386; adopts neutral policy toward Chester efforts (*1912*), 83–84

Talas, Turkey: mission station at, 254n; American doctor at, 259

Tariff: Commerce Department warns of discriminatory, 160; Turks negotiate modus vivendi on, 162

Tashkent: and Turkish race theory, 233

Tarsus, Turkey: site of St. Paul's Institute, 13; mission station at, 254n; Bryn Mawr excavates at, 272

Tarsus College: boys' lycée, 259

Teagle, W. C.: believes Britain to allow no oil exploration in Iraq, 178; informs State Department of American Group's readiness to enter Iraq, 186; on seeking instructions for American Group, 186–187; draws up Exhibit "A," 189; on percentage of participation for American Group, 189–190; seeks advice on dealing with Nationalist Turks or TPC, 192

Teapot Dome: effect of on Sinclair's concession in Iran, 286

Technical assistance: for Turkey, 266–269, 267n–268n; for Egypt, 377–378

Teheran, Iran: legation established at, 6; Presbyterian mission in, 9, 315; leisure for diplomats in, 22; mission schools in, 30; consulate-general at, 56; Presbyterians asked to reopen elementary schools at, 293n

Teheran College: landmark in missionary education, 292

Telephones: installed in Constantinople by Americans, 40; Arthur Chester plans in Turkey, 62

Tell Billa, Iraq: archaeological site of, 353

Tenedos: to Turkey, 149–150

Tennessee, U.S.S.: ordered to Turkish waters, 91; commanding officer fired upon, 93

Tepe Gawra, Iraq: archaeological site of, 353

Tepe Hissar, Iran: Museum of the U. of Pennsylvania excavation at, 303

Terrell, Alexander W.: works for indemnity, 23

Terrible Turk: image of enlarged, 104; epithet outmoded, 230. *See also* Turks

Texas Company: joins Standard Oil of California to form Arabian-American Oil Company, 167; joins American Group, 186; leaves American Group, 199n; concessions in Bahrein and Saudi Arabia, 202; shares Bahrein and Saudi-Arabian concessions with Socal, 207; joins Socal in Saudi Arabia, 362

Thomas, L. I.: works with American diplomats for Socony interests, 172

Tigris-Euphrates valleys: Americans recall ancient civilizations of, 6

Tobacco: imports from Turkey, 38, 39, 264

Tobacco companies: support Turkish treaty, 162

Toledo Museum of Art: and Iraqi archaeology, 353n

Totah, Khalil: on adjusting to modern conditions, 319

Tourism, American: in Middle East, 17; effect of antiquities on, 44–45; expenditures of in Turkey, 265–266; in Egypt, 366, 379n

Trabzon (Trebizond), Turkey: consulate established at, 56; mission station at, 254n

Trade. *See* Business

Trans-Iranian railway: American participation in, 297–302; building of, 300–